Crime Investigation

Crime Investigation
SECOND EDITION

Paul L. Kirk
(deceased)

Edited by
John I. Thornton
University of California, Berkeley

JOHN WILEY & SONS
New York   London   Sydney   Toronto

Copyright © 1953, 1974, by John Wiley & Sons, Inc.

All rights reserved. Published simultaneously in Canada.

No part of this book may be reproduced by any means, nor transmitted, nor translated into a machine language without the written permission of the publisher.

Library of Congress Cataloging in Publication Data:

Kirk, Paul Leland, 1902–1970.
   Crime investigation.

   Includes bibliographies.
   1. Criminal-investigation.   I. Thornton, John I., ed. II. Title.
HV8073.K475 1974   364.12   73-19854
ISBN 0-471-48247-1

Printed in the United States of America

10 9 8 7 6 5 4

Preface

The preparation of this preface would have been the final contribution to this book by Dr. Paul L. Kirk. His death in June 1970 saddened all who knew him as a teacher and friend, and created an acute feeling of loss which has not been dispelled through the passage of time.

At the time of his death, Dr. Kirk was deeply involved in writing a second edition to his classic text, *Crime Investigation*. The manuscript has been completed by former students and colleagues. It should be clearly understood, however, that those of us involved in the editing and rewriting served only to tidy up the work a bit, performing a type of literary janitorial service; the essential character of the text is decidedly that of Dr. Kirk.

Unlike the first edition, the present volume is not intended to serve as a single sourcebook for the laboratory criminalist. The present volume corresponds roughly to Section I of the previous edition, and specific details related to laboratory techniques are not included. The text is written, however, with the interests of both the criminalist and the field investigator in mind.

For reasons of objectivity and efficient operation, the criminal-justice process must utilize physical evidence to a greater extent, and there should be additional emphasis on the laboratory aspects of the investigative process. Judging from the present inadequacy of training facilities for laboratory criminalists, this aspect of the total professional field of criminalistics appears to be the most deficient. While many laboratories have achieved great distinction in training their personnel by means of an "on-the-job" training or apprenticeship system, it is clear that the successes have been the product of outstanding individuals who have demonstrated an intelligent devotion to filling the need. The most pressing current need, however, is the establishment of a system of training that does not require this unusual, and often absent, devotion. In probably no other profession is standardized and effective training so neglected at this time as in the field of criminalistics. When the liberty of an individual may depend in part on physical evidence, it is not unreasonable to ask that the expert witnesses who are called upon to testify, either against the defendant or in his behalf, know what they are doing. While it would be presumptuous to assert that this or any other book will innoculate the expert witness with all the necessary information and expertise he will ever require, it is nevertheless hoped that some up-grading of performance may result from it. There must be at least minimum standards for so responsible a role as that of the expert witness.

While this publication does not cover all of the desirable techniques and possibilities in the examination of physical evidence, it is aimed at presenting certain minimum essentials that should be understood by all investigators, whether they are in the laboratory or in the field. It is believed that the approaches suggested here are reliable; most of them have stood the test of usage over long periods. Naturally, many obsolete techniques must be omitted, and many new ones will have been developed by the time this revision is printed.

As is inevitable in any rapidly developing field, shifts in viewpoint have occurred, both in operational laboratories and in the thinking and philosophy of Dr. Kirk. For the most part, these changes have come about as a result of the considerable expansion of crime laboratory operations throughout the United States, a basic shift in the types of evidence most commonly submitted for examination, and greater experience in recognizing the role of physical evidence in the administration of criminal justice. There has been an increasing trend toward more extensive operation in the drug and narcotics area, as well as in alcohol analysis. In many laboratories these areas alone consume a large fraction of the total laboratory effort.

A revolution has occurred in the technology of the crime laboratory since the original publication of this book. The entire philosophy of the field has undergone considerable development, and at this time there is a very welcome trend toward greater preoccupation with the interpretation of laboratory findings with a view to making the conclusions more objective and less dependent upon subjective evaluations. In short, the field has become more of a science and more of a profession—both very welcome changes. It is sincerely hoped that the pages to follow will reflect these advancements, as well as the large increment of new technical approaches that have become available.

If Dr. Kirk were still living, he would certainly at this point have expressed his appreciation to his students and associates for their many contributions to the book. Much credit for this edition must go to Miss Marjorie Doyle, who edited and rewrote much of the text. There can be no doubt that if it were not for Marjorie, the uncompleted manuscript of the revised edition would be resting, unpublished, in the Bancroft Library of the University of California along with the other papers of Dr. Kirk.

The book is indebted also to Mr. Lowell Bradford for his contribution to

Chapter 29, "Alcohol," and to Mr. Charles Morton for his contribution to Chapter 8, "Photography." It is an inadequate measure of the debt incurred to simply name these individuals, for without their help the book probably would not be.

Dr. Donald Nelson read the entire manuscript with a jeweler's loupe, and made many helpful suggestions and corrections. To him, the book owes gratitude beyond estimation; his careful reading of the rough manuscript has come between the book and disaster on many occasions.

The assistance of Nancy Buchanan, George Sensabaugh, Edward Blake, and Edward Rhodes in the preparation of the manuscript is gratefully acknowledged.

As to my involvement, I have only arranged. Those who arrange must never be confused with those who create.

Berkeley, California *John I. Thornton*

Contents

Introduction   1

The Problem of Identity   9

Equipment for Police Investigation in the Field   18
Equipment for Observation and Record,   19
Equipment for Collection and Preservation of Evidence,   22

The Collection of Physical Evidence   33
The Crime Scene,   35
The Victim,   43
The Suspect,   46
Alternative Procedures,   48

Casts and Replicas   50
Plaster Casts,   50
Detail Casts,   53
Wax Impressions,   55
Thermoplastic Casting,   55
Miscellaneous Casts,   56

Fingerprints   59
Routine Fingerprinting,   62
Latent Prints,   63

Comparison of Prints, 69
Computerization of Prints, 72

Tracks and Trails — 74

Shoeprints, 74
Tire Treads, 80
Comparison Standards, 82
Miscellaneous Tracks, 83
Trails, 83

Photography — 85

Photography and the Police, 85
The Camera, 86
Films, 94
Illumination, 96
Color vs Black-and-White Photographs, 101
Motion Pictures vs Still Photographs, 102
Developing Negatives and Prints, 102
Small-Object Photography, 103
Interpreting Photographs, 104
General Considerations, 105

Preliminary Examination of Microscopic Evidence — 107

Sweepings, 107
Sorting of Microscopic Evidence, 108
Relation to Large Items of Evidence, 110
Value of Microscopic Evidence, 110

Clothing and Cloth — 112

Special Items of Clothing, 114
Cloth as Evidence, 117

Fibers — 124

Collection of Fibers, 125

Fibers in Sweepings, 126
Types of Textile Fibers, 126
Uses and Limitations of Fiber Evidence, 134
Unusual and Nontextile Fibers, 134

Ropes, Cordage, and Packaging Material — 136

Materials of Construction, 137
Rope, 137
Cords and Strings, 138
Packaging Material, 140

Hair — 143

Morphology of Hair, 144
Chemistry of Hair, 151
Physical Properties of Hair, 155
Collection of Questioned Hairs, 157
Preliminary Examination of Hair, 159
Human Hair vs Other Animal Hair, 160
The Future of Human Hair as Evidence, 165

Blood: Physical Investigation — 167

Blood Distribution Patterns, 173
Investigation of Blood in the Field, 177

Blood: General Testing — 182

Tests for the Presence of Blood, 182
Tests for Species Origin of Blood, 190
Washed Bloodstains, 193
Age of Bloodstains, 194

Blood: Individual Factors — 196

Blood Groups, 197
Lectins, 203
Blood Protein Factors, 203

Physiological Fluids Other than Blood — 207
Semen, 207
Urine, 211
Perspiration, 212
Saliva, 212
Serum, 212
Stains of Mixed and Miscellaneous Origin, 213
Typing of Fluids, 213

Cosmetics — 215
Cosmetics as Evidence, 215
Types of Cosmetics, 216
Collection of Cosmetic Evidence, 219
Examination of Evidence, 220

Crystalline Evidence — 222
The Nature and Properties of Crystals, 223
X-Ray Diffraction, 226
Miscellaneous Techniques, 227

Special Chemical Evidence — 229
Investigation, 231
Collection of Evidence, 232
Preliminary Examination, 233
Solubility, 234
Inorganic Substances, 235
Organic Substances, 236
Dyes and Pigments, 237

Paint — 240
The Physical Nature of Paint, 241
The Chemical Nature of Paint, 242
Examination of Paints, 245
Paint Section, 245
Identification of Paint Vehicle, 247

Pigment Composition, 248
Pigment Distribution, 252
Miscellaneous Techniques, 253

Glass 255

Variations in Glass, 257
Strength of Glass, 258
Investigation Involving Glass, 260
Glass Fractures, 261
Glass Identity from Physical Properties, 267
Chemical and Spectrographic Analysis, 270

Soil 273

Soil Formation, 274
Variability of Soil, 275
Collection of Soil Samples, 277
Density Distribution of Soil, 277
Chemical and Spectrographic Analysis, 279

Metals 282

Broken Metal Objects, 282
Metallographic Examination, 285
Restoring Serial Numbers, 286
Metal Failure, 290
Quantitative Analysis, 291
Spectrographic Analysis, 292
Electrophoretic Analysis, 293
Physical Properties, 293
Chemical Properties, 294
Metals in Fires, 296

Plastics and Related Materials 298

The Nature of Plastics, 298
Plastics as Physical Evidence, 299
Examination of Plastics, 300

Miscellaneous Similar Materials, 301
Types of Plastics Commonly Found as Evidence, 302

Vegetable Materials 310

Types of Botanical Evidence, 311

Poisons 322

Types of Poisons, 323
Investigation of Suspected Poisonings, 329
Isolation and Identification of Poisons, 332

Drugs 336

Natural Materials, 338
Synthetic Materials, 342

Alcohol 345

Physiological Aspects of Alcohol Ingestion, 347
Calculation of Alcohol Levels, 350
Investigation, 351

Tool Marks 360

Types of Tool Marks, 360
Investigation of Tool Marks, 370
Comparison of Tool Marks, 371
Investigation of Safe Burglaries, 376

Firearms 379

Types of Firearms, 381
Fundamentals of Firearms Examination, 392

Vehicular Accidents 410

Causes of Vehicular Accidents, 411

Types of Vehicular Accidents, 413
Investigation, 416

Vehicular Impact Evidence — 424

Records, 424
Point of Impact, 427
Energy Dissipation in Accidents, 430
Speed Calculations, 432
Friction Coefficient (Drag Factor), 432
Brakes and Deceleration, 434
Tire Marks, 434
Accidents of Special Types, 439

Physical Evidence from Fires — 443

The Nature of the Action of Fire, 444
Investigation of Fires, 451

Physical Evidence from Explosions — 458

Diffuse Explosions, 458
Concentrated Explosions, 461
Investigation of Explosions, 463
Investigation of Explosive Devices, 466

Documents — 470

Types of Examination, 470
Preliminary Examination, 472
Exemplars, 473
Copies and Photographs, 477
Limitations of the Investigator, 477
Physical and Chemical Examination, 477
Handwriting Identification, 491

Index — 503

Crime Investigation

1
Introduction

All criminal investigation is concerned with *people* and with *things*. Only people commit crimes, but they invariably do so through the medium of things.

A balanced approach to criminal investigation therefore must be dual: it must concern itself both with people and with things—the physical evidence—involved in the crime. The police inspector and the detective-fiction writer share a primary concern with people, but the former must also take cognizance of the physical evidence to achieve a satisfactory performance in a large percentage of the crimes he investigates. Many investigators have failed in some degree to make the most efficient use of this balanced approach to the investigation of crime, often simply because they do not realize the enormous potentialities of physical evidence. The investigator, to realize his maximum goal, must understand (1) what physical evidence is; (2) how to collect and preserve it; (3) how to obtain from it the information it carries; and (4) how to interpret the information so obtained. Accordingly, the purpose of this volume is to aid the conscientious investigator, in the field and in the laboratory, to realize all the advantages that can accrue from a careful collection and intelligent examination of "things."

However careful a criminal may be to avoid being seen or heard, he will inevitably defeat his purpose unless he can also control his every act and movement so as to prevent mutual contamination with his environment, which may serve to identify him. The criminal's every act must be thoroughly reasoned in advance and every contact guarded. Such restraint demands complete mental control. The very fear of detection, which must almost

1

always be present, will make such control next to impossible. Wherever he steps, whatever he touches, whatever he leaves—even unconsciously—will serve as silent evidence against him. Not only his fingerprints and his shoeprints, but also his hair, the fibers from his clothes, the glass he breaks, the tool mark he leaves, the paint he scratches, the blood or semen that he deposits or collects—all these and more bear mute witness against him. This is evidence that does not forget. It is not confused by the excitement of the moment. It is not absent because human witnesses are. *It is factual evidence.* Physical evidence cannot be wrong; it cannot perjure itself; it cannot be wholly absent. Only in its interpretation can there be error. Only human failure to find, study, and understand it can diminish its value. The laboratory must be devoted to this study and understanding if the all-important traces that can speak so eloquently of guilt or innocence are to be heard. To this study must be brought all the resources of science and human understanding if the message is to be clear, complete, and unequivocal. The amount of effort, time, and money being supplied to this end in the administration of criminal justice is increasing, but is still wholly inadequate. Large numbers of criminals still remain free because the physical evidence is not fully understood and utilized, and innocent men may be accused of crimes of which they would be instantly cleared if the physical evidence were allowed to tell its story of what happened and who was present.

It is the duty of the investigating officer to utilize every scrap of physical evidence that can be located. Proper collection and interpretation of physical evidence is fully as important as the interrogation of witnesses or other persons. Formerly, when only animate witnesses could be examined, the proportion of solved crimes was lamentably low. Today, the full utilization of physical evidence can greatly increase this proportion.

Law-enforcement officers probably make more errors in the collecting and subsequent handling of physical evidence than in any other phase of their work.

Fortunately the time has passed when most police officers were likely to act as one particular officer did: Arriving at the scene of a street shooting immediately after it had occurred, he grabbed the abandoned gun from the sidewalk, looked at it, and thrust it in his pocket to deliver to the station. Today, nearly every officer knows the value of the fingerprints that this one effaced, but, hourly, other evidence almost as valuable as fingerprints is discarded by handling it in a way that is exactly analogous to the case cited.

Even the laboratory investigator, who *should* appreciate the value of such evidence more than would any ordinary police officer, frequently destroys it quite casually. He is often confronted with evidence of a type whose examination is unfamiliar to him. His first reaction may be to avoid attempting what to him is impossible. The temptation to destroy the evidence first, so as to avoid embarrassment later, is unfortunately sometimes indulged. If he is really conscientious, he should at least explore the possibility that some other laboratory worker can utilize the evidence.

Another temptation in some cases is to destroy evidence because there is too much of it and it is confused with filth, blood, or some other material that would make difficult its preservation and examination. This is likely to happen in a murder case because the first reaction to a bloody and unsightly scene is to clean it and restore order. In one such murder, most of the debris, which must have contained significant evidence, was burned immediately in a bonfire. In another case, the officer in charge detailed a deputy to scrub the room in which death had occurred. Later investigation indicated that the washed-off blood spots would have had great evidential value. As long as law-enforcement officers devote any part of their attention to cleaning up and therefore destroying evidence that may hold the solution to a crime, they can justly be accused at the very least of incompetence, and at the most of malfeasance. Yet such occurrences are commonplace and are usually accepted as normal human failures.

Today, law-enforcement officers have available better training and more intelligent supervision than has ever before been provided. It remains true that the number who truly appreciate the possibilities—and limitations—of the laboratory in the solution of crime is pathetically small. At the other extreme, there are officers who look upon the laboratory investigator as a miracle-maker. Even the best-managed laboratories often fail to produce the answers desired. This is inevitable in a proportion of cases. The actual number of such cases can, however, be greatly diminished if both field and laboratory investigators understand their mutual problems and cooperate fully.

It can be stated categorically that more laboratory failures are due to inadequate collection of the existing evidence than to the failure of the laboratory to examine evidence properly. A single piece of evidence is rarely sufficient in itself to establish proof of guilt or innocence. Only when the entire story is available can the final, irrevocable proof be produced. To bring to the laboratory a piece of paint and expect it alone to prove that a particular car was involved in a homicide is as futile as offering one piece of a jigsaw puzzle to the expert and expecting him to describe the entire picture. The piece of paint may strengthen an already good case, or it may yield proof of the innocence of a suspect, but the best it can be expected to prove is that a car having that type of paint was the car in question. Inasmuch as there is likely to be a limited but considerable number of cars in a given locality with similar paint, such evidence may be helpful, but when unsupported by other facts it cannot ordinarily be expected to tell the whole story. It is probable that the officer who collected the evidence has overlooked broken glass, cloth impressions, blood, or a wide variety of other useful evidence.

Perhaps the most important function of the police laboratory is to train the police investigators as to what constitutes physical evidence and how it is to be found, collected, preserved, and delivered to the proper laboratory investigator. As soon as the police investigator discovers how helpful a cooperative criminalist may be to him in increasing his efficiency, any distrust or jealousy of the laboratory worker should cease, and a fruitful and mutually profitable liaison will be established. This will result in more effective police work, which will benefit the entire force and the political subdivision it serves. Public relations will improve, police prestige will be increased, and an atmosphere will be created in which confidence and respect, as well as more immediate personal advantages, will accrue to the force. The laboratory investigator and the police officer must always keep in mind that they are not competitive but complementary in their functions. The laboratory cannot produce unless the officer makes it possible, and the officer can solve many more crimes if he utilizes the laboratory to the fullest extent.

The study of physical evidence has a twofold purpose. *First*, and most important, *it is often the decisive factor in determining guilt or innocence.* Thus, the testimony of the scientific expert may be sufficient to determine the final decision of a court. It can do this by supplying the demonstrable facts, thus resolving discrepancies in ordinary testimony, and amplifying the information of the court to a point at which a true and just decision of guilt or innocence may be rendered, unclouded by divergent statements of uncertain or perhaps prejudiced witnesses. *Second, the study of physical evidence can be a material aid in locating the perpetrator of a crime.*

Physical evidence is often very useful to the police investigator before he has a suspect in custody or, in fact, before he even has suspicions of a possible perpetrator. If, for instance, the laboratory can describe the clothes worn by the criminal, give an idea of his stature, age, hair color, or similar information, the officer's search is correspondingly narrowed.

Frequently it is possible to indicate a probable occupation, or to describe a habitat with remarkable accuracy from careful examination of some apparently trifling object found at the scene of the crime. Such facts do not necessarily constitute proof of guilt of any particular person, but they may give a background that is of the greatest value. The use of the laboratory for this purpose is far less frequent than for court testimony; in fact, it is almost universally overlooked by most police departments. Perhaps this is due to the fact that only the most competent and experienced criminalist is completely effective in these more speculative interpretations of evidence. *It must be granted immediately that here the chance of error is much greater than in the more common applications of laboratory examination.* In fairness to the laboratory, it must also be realized that no person's life or liberty depends directly upon this preliminary type of application, as is the case when physical evidence is the basis of court testimony.

Introduction

As an illustration of the possibilities and pitfalls attendant upon deductions from laboratory findings, the following example is illuminating. From examination of a glove left at the scene of a burglary, the following inferences were drawn:

(1) The culprit was a laborer associated with building construction.
(2) His main occupation was pushing a wheelbarrow.
(3) He lived outside the town proper, on a small farm or garden plot.
(4) He was a southern European.
(5) He raised chickens, and kept a cow or horse.

After the culprit was apprehended, all the above inferences were essentially confirmed except for the second: he drove a tractor rather than pushed a wheelbarrow. The observation upon which this deduction rested was that there was a greater amount of wear on the inside surfaces of the fourth and fifth fingers of the glove than on the other three. This could have been caused by thrusting forward on wheelbarrow handles, but it also could be—and was—caused by pulling on sloping tractor levers.

It is not uncommon for a police inspector to feel that the laboratory investigator is invading his territory when the latter desires to collect his own evidence, or when he asks questions not obviously connected with the laboratory examinations. Such an attitude is regrettable. When the laboratory worker wishes to collect his own evidence it demonstrates only that he is not satisfied with the manner in which it has been gathered previously, a fault of the investigating officer rather than overambition on the part of the criminalist. Questions that may not seem relevant to the police officer may actually be vital in serving to direct the emphasis of the laboratory study, or to interpret the results. Thus, when a finding may be interpreted in two different ways, the answer to a single question may completely eliminate one interpretation and point irrevocably to the second.

An item of evidence may have a connection with the crime, or it may be present at the scene from accidental or harmless circumstances that are not connected with the crime. A knowledge of the general situation will usually decide the question and avoid wasting much valuable time in the study of extraneous material. It must be remembered that many laboratory examinations are lengthy and some are expensive. The efficiency of the laboratory usually bears a direct relationship to the willingness of the police officer to keep the laboratory workers informed of all pertinent facts. Complete frankness and confidence between the two types of investigators is most desirable and profitable—and unfortunately not so common as it might be. Only good understanding, by both, of their reciprocal functions can completely eliminate this barrier to the realization of the full benefits of a well-managed crime laboratory.

It is not always understood that the term "physical evidence" embraces (1) any and all objects, living or inanimate, solid, liquid, or gas, and (2) the relationships among all such objects as they pertain to the problem in question, i.e., a crime. A knife, gun, signature, or burglar tool is immediately recognized as constituting physical evidence. Less often is it considered that dust, microscopic fragments of all types, bacteria, even an odor, may be physical evidence, and often the most important of all. In fact, the most useful types of physical evidence are generally microscopic in dimensions, that is, not noticeable by the eye, and therefore most likely to be overlooked both by the criminal and by the investigator. For this reason alone the microscopic evidence persists at the scene of a crime long after all the visible and obvious evidence has been removed. In several instances crimes have been solved by collecting the microscopic evidence and examining it, months or even years after all the other evidence had been removed and found to be indecisive. Naturally there are limitations to the time of collecting microscopic evidence, these being determined by the probability of loss through the natural and habitual activities carried out at the crime scene. Wind may blow it away; housewives may sweep it up; rains may wash it into the soil; or the natural processes of decay and corrosion may consume it. The exercise of judgment as to the possible profit of such delayed action in collecting the evidence is another field in which the expert criminalist is most competent to judge. Where there is even a reasonable probability of finding significant evidence, it should never be neglected, even after the lapse of a long period of time. Here again, close cooperation of the investigating officer and the laboratory will be most effective. The combination of their knowledge and judgment will usually lead to a clear decision as to the desirability of rechecking old microscopic evidence, scenes of crimes, decayed bodies, and the like.

Most published work dealing with physical evidence emphasizes the gross features of such evidence, to the neglect of the microscopic features. Although much can be told of the type of weapon used by examination of the wound, it is the microscopic evidence that can connect the weapon with the perpetrator, or perhaps even with the wound. Likewise, it may be possible to trace a car by means of its tire marks, but it may be much more important to prove that a victim was actually in the car, as can often be done by use of fingerprints, hair, fibers, dusts, and residues. Similarly, the appearance of a poison victim may give a useful clue to the nature of the poison, but it is the final identification of the poison, often by the microscope, that is most critical and necessary.

Even more important to realize is the fact that although the *gross physical evidence is valuable and must receive full attention, it will often be absent; microscopic evidence is present in most cases, and is therefore of much wider availability. If there is a single important lesson to be learned by the investigator, it is the extent to which he may rely on microscopic physical evidence if he is willing to make full use of it.*

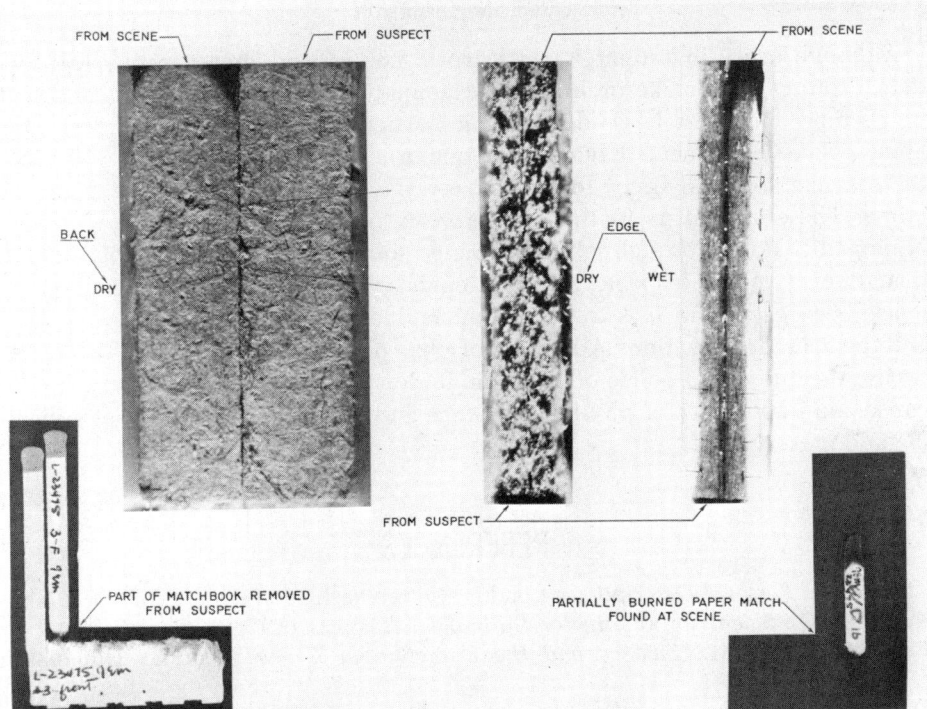

FIGURE 1-1. Common items such as discarded paper matches may be valuable items of physical evidence. A suspect was linked to a crime scene by comparing a burned paper match found at the scene and a matchbook found in his possession. This was done by comparing the appearance of included particles in the cardboard stem of the matches. The adjacent edges of two matches will have many particles in common.

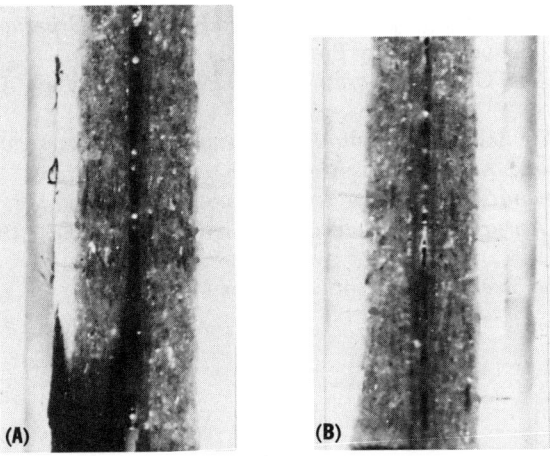

FIGURE 1-2. Enlargement showing the included particles in the upper (A) and lower (B) portions of the adjacent matches. (Courtesy of John E. Murdock.)

Although every investigator can learn to collect and preserve physical evidence, and even to make preliminary examinations of it, the process consumes much time and, in a large department particularly, is not always desirable. Some police departments have trained one or a few men in this field and make them available at all times to accompany the inspectors to the scene of the crime. These specialists in the collection of physical evidence may be fully equipped to do a thorough job, and trained to a degree that would be impractical for every police inspector. This system has worked exceptionally well where it has been used, and it is to be recommended for consideration by any law-enforcement organization. Adoption of this procedure should not, however, excuse the individual police officer from understanding the rudimentary significance and importance of physical evidence and the general methods of collecting and preserving it.

REFERENCES

Allen, A. L.: *Personal Descriptions.* London: Butterworth (1950).
Arthur, R. O.: *Scientific Investigator.* Springfield: Thomas (1970).
Culthbert, C. R. M.: *Science and the Detection of Crime.* London: Hutchinson (1958).
Dienstein, W.: *Technics for the Crime Investigator.* Springfield: Thomas (1969).
Inbau, F. E.: *Scientific Police Investigation.* Philadelphia: Chilton (1972).
Kirk, P. L., and Bradford, L. W.: *The Crime Laboratory, Organization and Operation.* Springfield: Thomas (1965).
Nickolls, L. C.: *The Scientific Investigation of Crime.* London: Butterworth (1956).
O'Hara, C. E.: *Fundamentals of Criminal Investigation,* 2nd ed. Springfield: Thomas (1972).
O'Hara, C. E., and Osterburg, J. W.: *An Introduction to Criminalistics,* 2nd ed. Bloomington: Indiana University Press (1972).
Osterburg, J. W.: *The Crime Laboratory.* Bloomington: Indiana University Press (1968).
Svensson, A., and Wendel, O.: *Techniques of Crime Scene Investigation,* 2nd American ed. New York: American Elsevier (1965).
Thorwald, J.: *Crime and Science.* New York: Harcourt, Brace and World (1966).
Thorwald, J.: *The Century of the Detective.* New York: Harcourt, Brace and World (1964).
Walls, H. J.: *Forensic Science.* New York: Praeger (1968).

2
The Problem of Identity

The central problem of the criminal investigator is the establishment of personal identity—usually of the criminal, sometimes of the victim. The investigator may use direct methods, or he may work indirectly through the identification of physical objects associated with the individual to be identified. The latter type of identification is the main preoccupation of the criminalist.

Because the word "identity" and its derivative "identification" are so widely used and misused in criminal investigation, the concepts and definitions of these terms must be considered here. Philosophically, "identity" refers to unique existence. A thing is identical only with itself, because it is an object with a separate existence, independent of all other objects, no matter how similar. Two objects might be so similar that no test could be devised to tell them apart, but they would never be identical with each other. A situation such as this, in which no test can distinguish between two objects, is only a philosophical abstraction; it is not thinkable in the real world. If it existed, it could be defined as an *identity of properties*; that is, every corresponding measurable property of each of two objects would be found to be the same. Even so it would fall short of the philosophical concept of identity in that one set of properties, *time* and *space,* must be different. With separate existence, two objects could not at the same time occupy the same space. Thus, the philosophical concept has its real counterpart in the physical world.

As a practical matter, the idea that two objects might have a totally identical set of properties is not realistic, and the criminalist will always have to accept the alternate concept that every object in the universe is in some meaningful or measurable manner different from every other object in the universe, regardless of the degree of similarity between them. Different grains of sand from the beach are measurably different, and leaves from the same tree are measurably different. Without this basic concept there would be a very limited theoretical or philosophical background for the establishment of criminalistics as a science or as a discipline.

In the field of criminal investigation, the general use of the word "identification" differs markedly from the classical philosophical concept, since "identity" itself is differently defined. *Identification is the placing of an object in a class or group.* This is the sense in which the word is used in all the natural sciences, and to use it in any other sense in criminalistics is illogical and would tend to label criminalistics as nonscientific. This scientific usage does fly in the face of popular practice, in which a criminal is "identified" from his fingerprint. He is not identified—he is *individualized*. To identify him, the fingerprint would only have to establish that he is a man as opposed to an inanimate object or perhaps that he belongs to some limited group of men. What is proved by his fingerprint is his individual identity, i.e. his *individuality*. The fingerprint not only identifies him, but also proves his individuality as compared with all other members of the species of man.

It is immediately apparent that there is an indefinite number of degrees of identification. An object may be identified as belonging to a large class of similar objects, or it may be identified as belonging to a quite restricted class of more closely similar objects. When the class in which the object can be placed consists of a single unit, that object is not only identified but also *individualized*. Assume that the object appears to be a writing implement. This will classify it in the large group of writing implements, but does not determine whether it is a fountain pen, a pencil, or a ball-point pen. Closer inspection shows it to be a ball-point pen, thus narrowing the class. It is red; it contains blue-black ink; it has a metal rather than a plastic button. Each factor in turn narrows the class in which the object is identified. It is a Parker Jotter, and has a medium ball. Now it is well classified, or identified, but it has not been individualized. Only if it has *some unique feature or property*, such as an initial scratched on it or a peculiar set of scratches or markings, will it be individualized. When such characteristics are lacking, the item can be only identified, not individualized.

Compare this situation with that of the fingerprint. Identification of the latter says only that it is a fingerprint. Further examination of the print shows that it is from a human being, it has a particular type of configuration, e.g., whorl or loop, and so on. Each factor narrows the class to which the print belongs, so that the identification is a progressive process. Finally, when enough factors are categorized, the identification may become an individualization, because the size of the group has been narrowed to that of a single individual.

The foregoing discussion may seem trivial to the practical police investigator, but its importance is readily demonstrated. Consider the space–time property mentioned previously as the only means to distinguish between two objects with otherwise identical properties. This is the very basis of the *alibi*, one of the oldest concepts of concern in the administration of criminal justice. If a person was elsewhere at the time of the commission of the crime, he did not commit the crime, regardless of his similarity to the person who did commit the crime. Confusion between identification and individualization is, unfortunately, the rule in police operation, and even in the criminalistics laboratory at times. An assessment of the degree of discrimination in classifying a piece of evidence is absolutely vital to the administration of criminal justice. It is simple to unwittingly mislead a jury or a judge as to the significance of the evidence presented, partly because of overemphasis on and publicity concerning the value of a procedure or a determination. This has been the case with simple blood grouping, a procedure that is limited and principally of exclusionary value. Misrepresentation has also occurred and is still occurring with respect to many of the more sophisticated instrumental approaches to the examination of physical evidence.

There are at present only a few useful methods for directly individualizing a particular person. Recognition of physiognomy is one such method. It has been greatly refined by the use of anthropometric classification systems for physical features, such as the well-known system of Bertillon. Photography, also promoted by Bertillon, has been indispensable in recording physiognomy for later comparison. Another refinement of direct recognition of physiognomy is the identification of teeth and dental work in bodies not otherwise susceptible to the usual methods of personal individualization. The "portrait parle" system of Bertillon has also been useful in reconstruction of physiognomy. However, the greatest use of physiognomy identification is by the direct eyewitness. A victim identifies his attacker in the police lineup, or a witness describes to the police the perpetrator of a crime. Helpful as this method may be, it is fraught with the greatest dangers, as has been proved repeatedly. It remains an important factor in court trials even when there is excellent reason to doubt the memory and observation of the eyewitness. Under conditions of fear or excitement, a witness is prone to exaggerate the size of the criminal, and to be completely confused as to the details of appearance. Suggestion by others has a strong influence on the eyewitness. Many instances quoted in the criminological literature have established that few eyewitnesses to a crime are capable of providing an accurate or even useful description. At least some of these problems have arisen because the distinction between identification and individualization has not been generally recognized, even by the police.

Friction-ridge individualization (as in fingerprints, palmprints, and to a limited extent bare footprints) has been found to be a highly dependable method because the evidence is physical and therefore not subject to mental impressions, memory lapses, suggestion, or any of the other deficiencies of eyewitness testimony. The almost universal modern use of fingerprints for personal individualization testifies to their reliability and utility. Their chief drawback lies in the fact that most modern criminals are careful not to leave their fingerprints at the scene of the crime, and consequently many police investigators assume that there is no purpose in looking for fingerprints. In jurisdictions where this error has not been made by investigating officers, the number of crimes solved on the basis of fingerprint evidence is quite impressive.

When prints are absent, other methods of identifying the criminal must be called upon. These are for the most part indirect and utilize other physical evidence. The criminalist of the future may well be able to individualize the criminal directly through the hair he has dropped, the blood he has shed, or the semen he has deposited. All these things are unique to the individual, just as his fingerprints are unique to him. However, further research into the means of positive individualization is still needed. At present it is only possible to establish a strong *presumption* of identity using the physical evidence cited.

Indirect individualization of the criminal may be effected through the tool he used, the weapon he fired, the clothes he wore, the writing he made, the soil, glass, paint, and dusts he removed from the crime scene. These are the items most commonly available to the investigator. Here the problem is no longer one of personal identity, nor in the absolute sense even identity of objects, because no two objects can ever be identical. They can and often do have properties that are not distinguishable. If enough of these properties exist, a *comparative identity* is established, and in the ultimate, *identity of source* is established. Thus, the glass in the criminal's pants cuff may not be distinguishable with respect to its fundamental properties from glass broken at the scene. This establishes a comparative identity and indicates a probability of identity of source. If a piece of the glass in the pants cuff can be precisely fitted to the broken glass at the crime scene, an identity of source is established.

The same kind of consideration is applicable to the hair dropped by the criminal at the scene, in comparison with hair from his head. At present, comparative identity is sometimes readily established, but proof of identity of source remains lacking. Likewise, two samples of handwriting, one of which is from a known writer, may be compared to establish comparative identity. Some features of the writing may be so distinctive as to allow a strong opinion of identity of source as well.

One additional type of identity might be defined as *casual identity*, meaning that two results were obtained from the same cause. Thus, two bullets are marked by the same barrel, and the marks can be established as showing causal identity. Two tool marks made by the same tool should show causal identity.

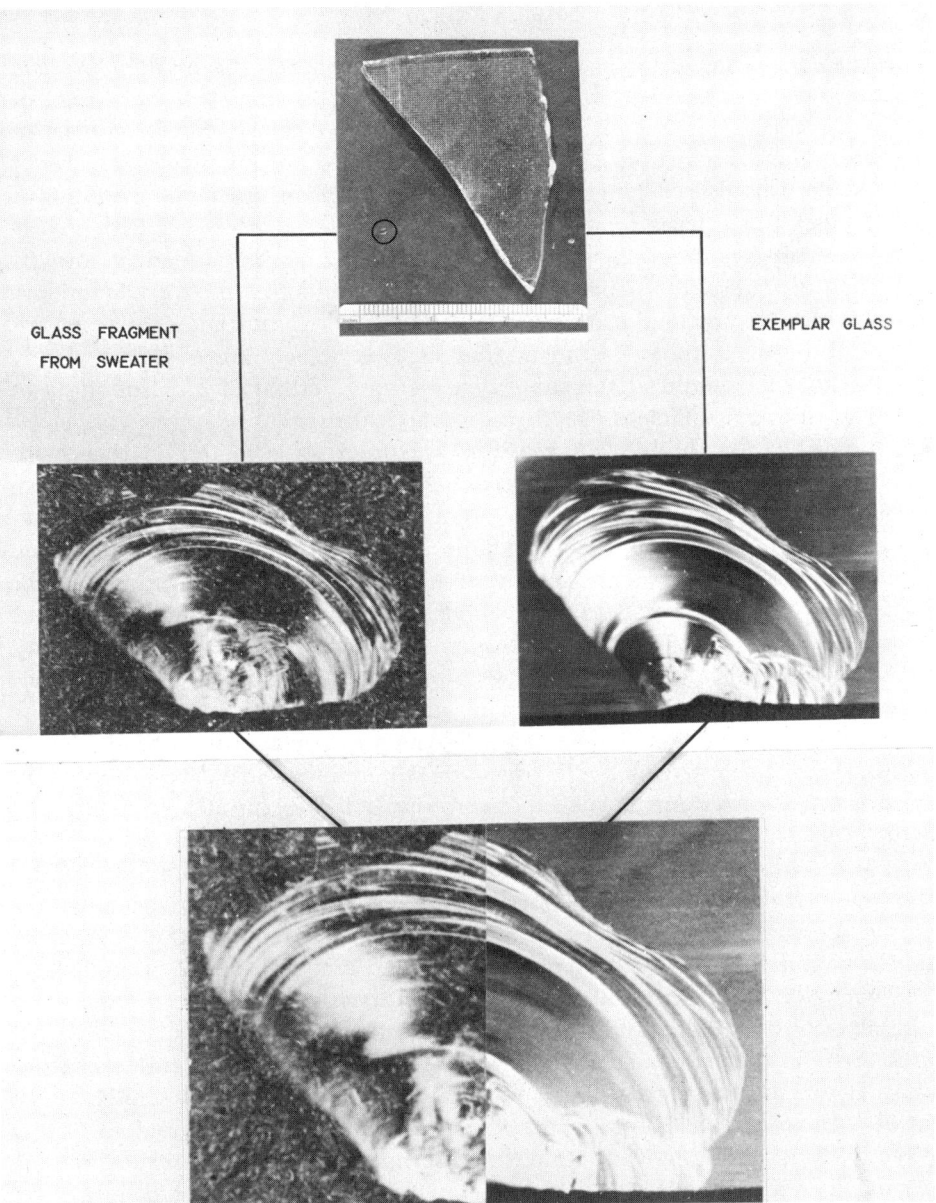

FIGURE 2-1. A suspect was associated with a crime scene by the small fragment of glass found on his sweater. The fragment was found to have originated from the edge of a larger section of glass discovered at the scene. (Courtesy of Dorothy Northey.)

However, in neither instance will absolute identity exist, the marking on one bullet or tool mark being readily distinguished from that on the other bullet or tool mark. In practice, *the above three types of identity are all that will be of concern to the investigator.* Absolute identity of two objects, marks, etc., does not exist and should not be claimed. It is the confusion about the meaning of identity that is the basis for much of the quibbling of attorneys with expert witnesses. Any attorney can state that two objects are not identical and be correct in the absolute sense, even though the identity is overwhelmingly positive from the practical standpoint of origin. The expert witness will be well advised to admit without argument that no two objects are ever completely identical, but he should at the same time be very certain of his ground as to what constitutes a sufficient identity for practical use.

Individualization through fingerprints is a progressive matter in that more and more persons are eliminated by each factor studied. This is true in spite of the fact that there are never two identical fingerprints, even though they are made by the same finger at essentially the same time and under the same conditions. Yet it would be absurd for an attorney to state that a print was not made by a particular finger on the grounds that it was not absolutely identical with another print made by the same finger. But this is exactly the absurdity that is frequently claimed by attorneys in connection with other physical evidence, e.g., handwriting. True, a man's handwriting does not duplicate as accurately as his fingerprints, nor does it remain as constant with time. Nevertheless, the features by which a handwriting is identified are only quantitatively different and less systematic than those from which fingerprint identification is made. This statement must not be interpreted to signify that handwriting identification is as positive as fingerprint identification. It cannot be, for the very reason that it is less constant in its characteristics. However, properly examined handwriting can be identified under reasonably suitable circumstances with a very high degree of certainty, and a causal identity established, even when the variation from an absolute identity is marked.

Similar considerations apply to all identifications, and to all claimed identities. Assume that two pieces of glass show the same density and refractive index. It can then be stated positively that they have the same chemical composition. However, the statement carries two qualifications: (1) the density and refractive index are identical within the experimental limits of observation; and (2) the chemical composition is the same within the limits imposed by (1). It would be impossible to get two pieces of glass with identical composition, molecule for molecule, or with exactly the same number of molecules. Moreover, it would also be impossible to obtain two pieces of glass with the same arrangement of molecules even if they were identical in number and distribution. Here also the statement of identity is a practical, not an absolute one, and merely signifies a very high probability that the two pieces are fragments of the same original glass object.

In the examination and interpretation of physical evidence, the distinction between identification and individualization must always be clearly made, to facilitate the real purpose of the criminalist: to determine *identity of source.* That is, two items of evidence, one known and the other unknown, must be identified as having a common origin. On the witness stand, the criminalist must be willing to admit that absolute identity is impossible to establish. Identity of source, on the other hand, may often be established unequivocally, and no witness who has established it need ever back down in the face of cross-examination.

It is precisely here that the greatest caution must be exercised. The inept or biased witness may readily testify to an identity, or to a type of identity, that does not actually exist. This can come about because of his confusion as to the nature of identity, his inability to evaluate the results of his observations, or because his general technical deficiencies preclude meaningful results. He might claim an identity between two gray rocks because they look alike, even though one is actually granite and the other a variety of sandstone or limestone. He might claim a causal identity between two bullets because they show the same number of lands and grooves, the same caliber, twist and width of lands and grooves, without ever obtaining a match of the fine-line striations. This tendency for the sciolist to decide identities on the basis of inadequate knowledge, experience, and technical facilities is particularly evident in the matter of handwriting identification. Every bank clerk, businessman, and county clerk, as well as the private individual, is frequently called upon to identify handwriting. In no other field of physical-evidence examination do so many people consider themselves competent to decide identities, for the simple reason that they have been doing exactly that to some extent during much of their lives. Yet, handwriting examination is a highly technical matter calling for at least as much experience and knowledge as does any other field of physical-evidence examination.

To sum up: accurate identification must rest on a proper basis of training, experience, technical knowledge and skill, and an understanding of the fundamental nature of identity itself. It should not be attempted without this kind of background, either by the police officer or by the amateur. Highly experienced professional identification men make errors and overlook many significant matters. How much worse the situation would be if every police officer or amateur were to attempt the same identifications, merely because they had an interest in the matter and an opportunity to indulge their desires!

The intelligent police investigator should acquire an understanding of the utility of physical evidence so that he will overlook nothing that will contribute to the final solution of a crime. He should know enough about the technical operations involved so he can cooperate with the criminalist. He may acquire the necessary information and experience on which to base identification work of his own, but he must be certain he actually understands what he is doing, and is not merely following a set of instructions. No author of such instructions can cover all the possibilities, nor include every precaution that would be necessary to meet all conceivable contingencies. It is not even sufficient that the investigator acquire experience. He must also have fundamental knowledge No two cases are identical, and no set of instructions can cover all the variations. In the absence of fundamental knowledge and understanding, a new set of circumstances in a criminal case can nullify any given amount of experience alone. The most experienced witness on the stand can be made to appear foolish by a clever or erudite attorney unless the witness has a broad, basic understanding and thorough knowledge of his field. It is not sufficient that he be correct in his statements if he does not also possess the necessary general background with which to defend himself.

The question of *what constitutes adequate experience* for the expert witness is a critical one in court procedures, and appears to be poorly understood in many quarters. It is quite common for the witness to be interrogated as to the number of years during which he has worked in a field, and the number of cases he has handled, the number of pieces of evidence he has examined, and similar quantitative matters. However, the amount of experience is unimportant beside the question of what has been learned from it. A commuter might well ride the same bus line for years without noting the streets traversed by the bus. The bank clerk may certainly examine signatures in the tens or hundreds of thousands, without ever becoming a handwriting expert.

In a recent case four dealers in different kinds of typewriters were asked whether a sample of typing came from a particular brand of typewriter sold by them. Each of the four had been in business for fifteen to twenty years; each identified the sample as the work of his particular machine. One of them—probably by accident—was right! Long familiarity with the typing of a particular brand of typewriter was not sufficient to impress upon the inexpert observer the minute differences that distinguish the various makes and models of machines. A skillful investigator unfamiliar with the field might be expected to work out the classification scheme in rather short order, even though he had almost no length of experience with typewriters. For reasons such as this, quantitative evaluation of experience is often meaningless.

The average deer hunter may use a rifle for hunting over a period of many years and know virtually nothing of the mechanism of the weapon, of the ballistic properties of its ammunition, or even of the number or pitch of the lands and grooves. In no sense would this hunter be an expert on firearms or even on this particular type of firearm. It is very doubtful whether many courts would exclude this individual if testimony were needed with regard to this particular type of weapon, and if he desired to testify and claimed to be expert because of his long experience.

Qualitative experience, on the other hand, may be very limited and still be entirely sufficient for the matter at hand. The trained and skillful investigator may in the course of one or a few hours master a knowledge of the features necessary to establish an identity with a particular kind of evidence. Short but carefully directed experience, combined with a sound background knowledge of identification work in general, may be more than sufficient to qualify the investigator as an expert in so far as the particular point of the investigation is concerned.

How the court is to distinguish between the careful observer who is versed by his directed and pertinent qualitative experience, and the incompetent witness who claims merely to be familiar with a type of evidence over a long period of years, is a question that is difficult to answer. If, however, the question is raised and considered in every court of law, the answer should eventually be forthcoming. It is certainly not too much to expect of the laboratory investigator that he be completely familiar with all essential points pertinent to the examination of the evidence in question and to the testimony regarding that evidence as it is delivered in court.

REFERENCES

Kirk, P. L., and Kingston, C. R.: "Evidence Evaluation and Problems in General Criminalistics," *J. For. Sci.* 9:434 (1964).

Parker, B.: "Scientific Proof," *Revista Juridica Univ. Puerto Rico* 32:202 (1963).

Wall, P. M.: *Eye-Witness Identification in Criminal Cases.* Springfield: Thomas (1965).

Williams, R. J.: *Biochemical Individuality.* New York: Wiley (1956).

3
Equipment for Police Investigation in the Field

In dealing with physical evidence two types of activity are involved: field investigation and laboratory investigation. Each type of activity calls for different equipment. This chapter is concerned with the equipment useful to the field investigator, whose job is to locate and procure the evidence.

This function may be exercised through the police directly (inspector's bureau), through evidence technicians who are specially trained, or, at times, through other personnel such as patrolmen.

THE PURPOSES

The field investigator will be concerned with the following aspects of investigation as regards physical evidence: (1) Recognition of evidence. This is conditioned only by natural ability, training, and experience. No special equipment is required. (2) The relating of evidence to the sequence and interpretation of the criminal action before the evidence is collected or altered in any manner. This involves both observation and record. (3) Collection and preservation of evidence for later laboratory examination. These three operations are the most critical of all in the solution of a crime through physical evidence and equipment should be chosen with that thought in mind.

EQUIPMENT FOR OBSERVATION AND RECORD

The keeping of accurate records is the most important factor in the routine of a good investigation, and to be effective, records should be kept in more than one way. A notebook and a sketch pad are essential. However, no record is more reliable than a photographic one, so primary emphasis must be placed on the camera. Every field investigator must be familiar with crime-scene photography and must have his camera available for use at all times. Although unusual in practice, it is desirable for the first officer on the scene to be equipped with a 35mm camera and flash, or an Instamatic or similar automatic camera. He may be the *only* one who views the scene before it is disturbed or contaminated. Photographs taken at the earliest practical stage of an investigation, even though they may not be the very best quality, will frequently serve to enhance greatly the value of all later investigation.

Cameras

Individual opinions differ greatly as to the most effective combination of cameras for use at the scene of a crime. In many instances no single camera will fill all needs, although modern cameras are capable of wide modification of performance through the use of interchangeable lenses and other devices.

Despite its general lack of popularity among police photographers, the *35mm camera* has been shown to give excellent results for all but a few crime-scene needs. It is more adaptable than other cameras, and virtually every type of film made is available for it. Most 35mm cameras are true reflex, so there is no reason for photographs being out of focus, as so often happens with more elaborate cameras. With fine-grain film, enlargements to 8 × 10 inches, and even 16 × 20 inches, are quite possible without serious loss of quality. A larger negative is essential for enlargements greater than 16 × 20 inches, a fact which limits the usefulness of the 35mm camera.

A good *press camera* with an $f4.5$ or faster lens is a widely used and highly satisfactory type of camera. It must be equipped with a synchronized flash attachment, preferably a good electronic flash, although flashbulbs are entirely satisfactory. Both wide-angle and telephoto lenses are desirable accessories, especially the former, because in many instances photographs must be taken in cramped surroundings that can be reproduced well with a wide-angle lens. Cut film is preferred to roll film because it comes in more types in the 4 × 5 format, and only exposed sheets need to be processed at one time. A good tripod, although desirable for every camera, however small, is almost essential with the press camera and larger cameras. The increased steadiness allows longer exposures in low-light-level situations.

A *fingerprint camera* is very useful, and is sometimes considered essential, although fingerprints may be photographed with any camera having a proper lens by placing a ruler next to the fingerprint before taking the photograph. This makes possible either enlargement or reduction to exact size in later processing. The need for a fingerprint camera is also diminished by the common practice of dusting the print and lifting it for later photography. When the print is visible without dusting, photograph it before any dust is applied because the powder may obscure some of the detail. The characteristics that make the fingerprint camera useful are (1) it takes the print exact size, (2) it is commonly equipped with an extension of the camera box, which holds it at the exact distance required, and (3) it carries its own illumination. Its usefulness is somewhat restricted to prints on flat surfaces.

The *view camera* has some attractive features. It is bulky, but quite versatile. For some special purposes it is superior, but many of these are laboratory rather than crime-scene functions.

Automatic cameras, which perform some or many of their functions automatically, make it much simpler for the police officer who is not an expert photographer to obtain useful photographs. Probably the most nearly automatic camera, and one that is also inexpensive, is the Instamatic. This type of camera is to be recommended as a constant companion of the officer who, lacking knowledge of expert photography and/or facilities to apply it, has occasion to take pictures at various times in his normal duties.

The *stereoscopic camera* is little used in actual investigation, but it can be quite valuable when a view is best observed in three dimensions. Its critical limitation is that a special viewer must be used to observe the third dimension (depth) in the photographs. Even with its limitation, the stereoscopic camera has received less attention than it deserves.

Miniature cameras, such as the Minox, also deserve mention, not because they produce photographs of high quality, but because they are so convenient for occasional use short of completely photographing a scene. There are many instances in which a quick photograph will keep a record; and the camera that is carried in any pocket can be brought into action immediately. Such a camera is not satisfactory for routine police or investigative work in which photographic prints must be rather large and of high quality.

Polaroid Land cameras have achieved considerable popularity for crime-scene purposes because the photograph may be developed and printed immediately under field conditions. Originally, they were used less by police than by civil investigators because the quality of the prints often left something to be desired. Now, however, Type 55P/N film produces both a positive and a negative of good quality, and is adapted for use in a 4 × 5-inch back, which

FIGURE 3-1. Fingerprint camera. (Courtesy of Sirchie Laboratories, Inc.)

may also be used in the press camera. Both high-speed black-and-white film and color film are available, and the photograph is ready, even in color, in 60 seconds.

Any of the above cameras may be employed for *color photography*, which is becoming increasingly important for police investigation. Many scenes, and items in these scenes, will not be adequately represented on black-and-white film, however skillful the photographer. Blood patterns can be clearly seen in color prints whereas they cannot always be differentiated from grease spots or other stains in black-and-white photographs. Fire scenes are especially difficult to photograph, and sometimes color will yield the desired rendition. Many other special situations require color for proper recording. The police photographer and the evidence collector should have color film available at all times, to be used as the occasion indicates. The 35mm camera is recommended for color photography because of its convenience, its low cost, and the very high quality results it can give. With color-negative film it is not difficult to make enlargements up to 8 × 10 inches with excellent color fidelity.

This brief listing of types of camera equipment, supplemented later in this volume (see Chapter 8), is given only as an introductory guide to the possibilities. Every photographer develops his own preferences and procedures, and will inevitably choose that equipment with which he is best satisfied. It is chiefly important that the photographer possess *skill and experience,* for which there is no substitute, regardless of the actual photographic equipment he elects to use. The investigator who does his own photography should practice photographic techniques until he can obtain the best results his equipment is capable of giving him. In the matter of practice, the 35mm camera is very useful because the film is inexpensive and is quickly loaded into the camera. With 35mm equipment many more photographs may conveniently be taken than will generally be the case with cameras using expensive film in bulky film holders that must be changed. The officer using a 35mm camera is likely to acquire the desirable experience much more rapidly.

ILLUMINATION. The necessity of making photographs under poor lighting conditions requires the use of supplemental lighting facilities. Even in daylight photography added lighting is highly advantageous for filling shadows and for recording on the photograph much more information than would be available without the extra lighting. The police photographer will often carry a variety of large lights and reflectors that can be adjusted to implement the best quality of photography. Such equipment is totally unsuited for use by the regular officer, who needs easily carried facilities such as flash lamps or electronic flash. The latter is to be preferred, and many small but powerful units are available. Both flash lamps and electronic flash are effective only over short distances; when objects in both foreground and background are to be delineated in a photograph, the use of slave illumination is highly desirable. The slave unit is a separate flash or electronic flash equipped with a photoelectric cell. When the flash on the camera is activated, it causes the slave light (or lights) to flash at the same time in the background. It is important not to diminish the exposure when slave supplementary lighting is used, because what results is merely an increased area of illuminated objects, not a greater effective illumination of any of them.

EQUIPMENT FOR COLLECTION AND PRESERVATION OF EVIDENCE

Fingerprint Accessories

Even though the police department may have a special fingerprint technician who is responsible for taking all prints, it is still desirable for the general investigator to be equipped with a minimum amount of good fingerprint powder. There are a number of suitable brands on the market. They are not equally good, nor is any one powder superior for every purpose and under all conditions. Most fingerprint specialists have preferences that have been acquired by experience. The novice, and even the specialist, will find it helpful to obtain all or a number of the available makes and test them under a variety of conditions. Different operators have different methods of using the powders, and the preferences developed will also differ.

Most powders come in gray and black, the gray to be used on dark surfaces, the black on light surfaces. Other colors are available, as are fluorescent powders. Powders differ not only in color and appearance, but in certain physical qualities that prevent them from being uniformly good for all purposes. A powder is retained on a latent print by virtue of a trace of grease that is transferred by the friction ridges of the finger to the surface in question. Other materials that are also transferred, such as moisture and salt, are of little significance, because the moisture evaporates almost immediately and the trace of salt does not hold powder. For that reason, any fingerprint powder must stick tightly to greasy surfaces and not at all to nongreasy surfaces. This differential sticking is what determines the quality of a powder. Some powders "paint," that is, they fill up the intervening spaces between friction-ridge marks. This is a common fault with many commercial powders, and any powder considered for use should be examined for a tendency to paint. Such tests must be conducted on clean surfaces, however.

In addition to the powder itself, the investigator should have some soft camel's hair or fiber glass brushes with which to apply the powder, proper magnifiers, and lifting tape. For the latter, Scotch tape is commonly employed. It is not ideal, because it is not perfectly clear and uniform. Special lifting tapes of better optical and mechanical quality are to be preferred. Magnifiers are of general utility, and are discussed in a separate section in this chapter.

Fingerprints on porous surfaces such as paper, some cloths, and the like, will be of police interest, but are rarely suitable for field development. Fingerprint powders can be used with fresh prints on paper, but older prints rarely respond well. The preferred procedure for such prints is to remove the object bearing prints to the laboratory where more sophisticated procedures can be used.

Vacuum Sweeper

A vacuum sweeper with a special filter attachment is actually one of the most important items in the investigator's equipment—and one that is often omitted. Any type of sweeper that has a hose connection is suitable. Tank and cyclone types are most convenient to transport. As an accessory to the sweeper, a filter attachment is essential. One commercially obtainable type[*] is constructed of

---

[*] Obtainable from the Microchemical Specialties Co., 1825 Eastshore Highway, Berkeley, California 94710.

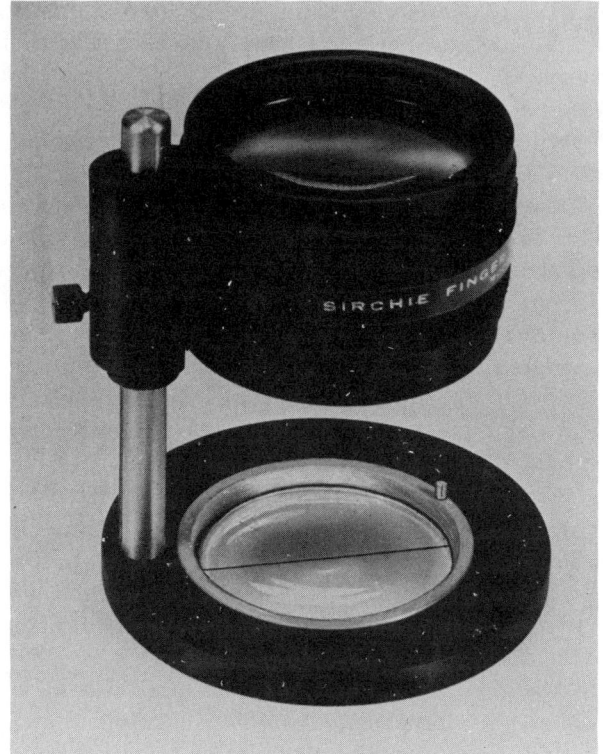

FIGURE 3-2. Fingerprint magnifier. (Courtesy of Sirchie Laboratories, Inc.)

two pieces of clear methacrylate plastic, which join by a bayonet or threaded joint. Mounted in one half-section is a metal screen that gives mechanical support to a 22mm Whatman No. 1 or similar filter paper on which the debris is collected. A fresh filter paper is inserted before each use by opening the filter attachment, laying the paper on the screen, and reassembling the attachment so as to lock the edges of the filter paper. The metal tube on the end carrying the paper is attached to the hose of the vacuum sweeper, and the metal tube on the other end of the hose serves as an intake nozzle. A broad nozzle may be placed on the filter tube, but little is gained because the filter paper restricts the flow of air to a point at which a good vacuum is not obtained with too large an intake.

A clean white-cotton cloth filter may be substituted to advantage, and will allow more rapid air flow, thus speeding the sweeping operation. It is less convenient, however, because of the ready availability of standard circular filter papers that are perfectly clean, have considerable rigidity of their own, and allow reasonably rapid sweeping.

FIGURE 3-3. Vacuum sweeper filter attachment. (Courtesy of Sirchie Laboratories, Inc.)

The bulk of the collected residue should be transferred to a petri dish or a plastic bag by inserting the intake nozzle into the mouth of the bag and tapping the filter with the hand while altering its tilt. The filter attachment should then be opened, leaving the filter paper on the intake half. The paper can be folded with the fingers and pushed down the tube into the dish or bag. With a clean camel's hair brush the remaining debris should be swept from the sides of the filter chamber and pushed down the intake nozzle. When everything has been transferred to the dish or bag, the receptacle is sealed and labeled and the filter reassembled for the next sweeping.

Other vacuum-sweeper filters of various types are available, most of them of narrower design and with some type of tubular filter element. One of the simplest is that of Dr. D. F. Nelson (unpublished, New Zealand Department of Science and Industrial Research, Auckland, N.Z.), who utilizes the "rubber crevice tool" (radiator nozzle) that is supplied with many commercial sweepers. A loose piece of bolting cloth is fitted over the attachment end of the nozzle, which is then attached to the hose. With shop facilities and a little ingenuity, it is possible to construct various useful designs.

Evidence Containers

The field investigator will require a variety of containers for the evidence he collects. These will, as a rule, differ from the containers used while examining the evidence in the laboratory. Plastic bags of the type used for refrigerator storage are available in numerous sizes and have largely replaced the cellophane and paper bags that have been used in the past. It has been observed, however, that hairs and fibers more often adhere electrostatically to the walls of a plastic bag than to those of a cellophane bag. Coin envelopes made of paper are very handy for small objects and for such materials as paint scrapings and other rather small particulate matter. The pages of a small scratch pad can be used to enclose such materials before they are placed in a bag or envelope. For materials that are essentially liquid or semiliquid, it is necessary to have a few glass shell vials. These must be fitted with clean corks, rubber stoppers, or screw caps. They can also be used for many of the items that otherwise could be placed in envelopes or bags. A few large paper bags are convenient for the larger articles of clothing. Even large bags fold conveniently into a small package in the investigator's kit. Wrapping paper is essential. This may usually be obtained from a store near the scene of the crime, and need not always be in the kit. Particularly in outdoor crimes, cardboard cartons are very useful. These also may usually be obtained at or near the scene of the crime.

Containers for collection of organs, tissues, and blood in poisoning cases are a special item for consideration more by the autopsy surgeon than by the ordinary police investigator. Mason jars of various sizes, from one pint to half-gallon, are suitable and readily obtained. Other glass vessels, such as clean mayonnaise jars, may be used when necessary. Metal containers should never be used, and no vessel should be employed if it cannot be tightly closed to prevent the escape of volatile poisonous substances or arson accelerants.

Tools

Certain tools are so often used that they should always be in the possession of the investigator. These include forceps, scalpel or knife, a dissecting needle, and a small pair of scissors. Several pairs of forceps can be profitably carried since they occupy little space, are light, and serve slightly different purposes. A scalpel is useful for scraping surfaces, although a knife may be substituted. A pair of pliers and a saw are handy, the first for cutting wires, and the second for sawing around toolmarks (if for some reason a silicone cast of the mark cannot be made) and for similar uses. Both may ordinarily be obtained at the scene of the crime, if they are not already on hand. A steel measuring tape is a necessity.

The choice of *forceps* merits special consideration. The forceps will commonly be employed for picking up hairs, fibers, and small fragments of a variety of materials. Dissecting forceps, although widely used, are suitable only for grasping tissue and similar soft materials that can be held only by a corrugation. By far the most valuable forceps are those used by jewelers for handling gems and fine watch parts. Even though these forceps are far more expensive than most, several should be available. Cover-slip forceps are likewise useful for special purposes. They have wide, flat jaws and are better adapted than jewelers' forceps to the handling of larger and heavier objects. Inexpensive forceps designed for plucking superfluous facial hair are widely marketed, and are satisfactory despite the disadvantage of being somewhat short. The type having smooth contact surfaces and a pointed tip should be selected. Because such forceps are often rather poorly made, the jaws should be reground and polished so that the tips will be quite pointed and the surfaces will meet truly over the entire area.

Magnifiers

Although a variety of magnifiers are useful, the investigator will often find one or two lenses quite adequate for his purposes. Many investigators use either a reading lens of low power and large field, or a folding single or multiple lens of higher power that is easily carried in the pocket. Both of these selections can be greatly improved upon. For low powers a head loupe, such as is used by the surgeon and the watchmaker, or, more conveniently, a "Magnifocuser" (Edroy Products Co., New York, N.Y. 10016) No. 3 or No. 5, will be found much more useful. The field of view is larger, the instrument is carried on the head, leaving both hands free, and vision is stereoscopic, since both eyes are used. Magnifiers of this type are essential.

Any other magnification required will be higher power, and no single lens can yield good resolution at magnification higher than a few diameters. More useful are doublet or better, triplet lenses having powers from $5\times$ to $20\times$. The best single choice is probably the $10\times$ triplet, and a very useful combination consists of two folding triplet magnifiers of $7\times$ and $20\times$ powers.

For working in dark places, and particularly for examining fingerprints, there are several makes of illuminated magnifiers. Though these are often of low power, they are manufactured in a wide variety of powers, even ranging into the field of the compound microscope. Inasmuch as a combination of powers equipped with an illuminator is very desirable, a single flashlight type with a lens not exceeding $5\times$ will be satisfactory for most purposes. By using a flashlight, any of the other magnifiers mentioned can be substituted, and a flashlight is an essential piece of equipment anyhow.

Pencil-size microscopes that clip into a pocket are available at a reasonably low price. These usually have higher powers than are needed except in very unusual circumstances, such as document examination in the field. If one is available, it is a useful supplement to the field investigator's equipment, but it is far from essential.

Blood-Testing Equipment

There is a real question as to the desirability of having the field investigator perform blood tests at the crime scene. There are times, however, when such tests are necessary, and the facilities for performing them should be available. When possible, bloodstained items should be removed to the laboratory, and it is often possible to remove a bit of a stain from fixed structures rather than to test them in situ.

One test must be done in the field if it is to be done at all: the luminol test, which is used to search for nonvisible traces of blood. It is also convenient to utilize the benzidine test in the field for rapid confirmation of the nature of stains. Other tests may be made, but they are rarely necessary. For the benzidine test, some cotton swabs and a bottle of benzidine reagent that is reasonably fresh and has been checked for activity are used. The swabs are moistened with a little water, rubbed on the questioned stain, and the reagent is applied only to the moist swab. For the luminol test, a freshly prepared reagent must be sprayed on the questioned spot in the dark from a nonmetallic sprayer.

These tests, as well as the phenolphthalin and malachite green tests, have been made available for use in the field by means of a kit that is commercially obtainable.* The advantages of the kit are that the reagents are carried in predetermined quantities in the solid state, and no hydrogen peroxide is required. (The instability of the latter reagent can result in variable sensitivity and unreliability of results.) The kit normally contains all reagents required for the four tests mentioned, packaged in the form of dry, premixed reagents in the proper amounts in capsules, plus solvents. Solvents for the reagents are packaged in small bottles that serve as containers during spraying of the dissolved reagents. Also included in the kit are plastic or glass sprays, a flashlight to facilitate the mixing of the reagents in the dark (essential in the luminol test), filter paper and containers for soaking off blood spots, and other accessory equipment. The kit may also carry special equipment by which very faint blood spots may be removed and concentrated by capillary action in filter paper. The kit is useful in the laboratory, and especially useful for the laboratory investigator who finds it necessary to conduct a field investigation.

Casting Equipment

It is frequently necessary for the field investigator to make casts of markings, in particular those left by burglary tools. Moulage has for a long time been the most satisfactory material, although it is somewhat difficult to use and depends upon a negative cast that is not permanent. With moulage, it is always necessary to make a positive cast immediately after making the negative.

Modern technology has produced a substitute that is better for the purposes

---

* Obtainable from the Microchemical Specialties Co., Berkeley, California.

of the criminalist. This is a room-temperature curing silicone rubber available from the Dow Chemical Company and from retail suppliers. It comes in two containers, one holding the unpolymerized silicone, the other a catalyst necessary to induce polymerization. The two substances are mixed in proportions specified by the manufacturer, applied to the mark in question, and allowed to form a tough, rubbery negative cast that can be freed of overhangs, and will release from virtually all surfaces without difficulty. The field investigator should always have this material on hand, because markings are often located where it is not practical to remove the entire object to the laboratory. Positives may be made from the negative casts with wax, positive moulage (three parts carnauba wax melted with one part of beeswax) or with other material. The detail obtainable with this material is excellent, permitting even microscopic comparison.

Gross casting in which very fine detail is not important, as with shoeprints, tire impressions in mud, etc., is best done with plaster of paris, which should also be always available to the field investigator. A good grade of dental plaster is best, supplemented by some wire mesh or similar stiffening agent to give a less fragile cast.

Ultraviolet Lamp Equipment

A portable ultraviolet lamp is often a necessity at the scene of a crime. It will detect physiological fluids in particular, and it may reveal other types of stain invisible to the eye in ordinary light. A small, convenient type of light is the "Mineralight" (Ultra-Violet Products, 5114 Walnut Grove, San Gabriel, Ca. 91778), obtainable in either a battery-powered portable form or a standard unit for 110V ac. Several ultraviolet bulbs suitable for direct use with 110V ac current are available. One of these with an extension cord is particularly convenient. A proper source of current is essential, and easy portability is highly desirable.

Carrying Cases

Because of the wide variation in the material carried and in its design, there is no universally applicable carrying case. No carrier of reasonable dimensions would accommodate a vacuum sweeper or other large object. These must usually be carried separately. A mechanic's toolcase of rather large dimensions is perhaps as useful as any other readily obtained carrier. Other possibilities will occur to the investigator.

Large Field Outfits

Several large cities and some states have special equipment designed for broader use than the simple items described in this chapter. Ordinarily a truck is equipped for the specific function of collecting evidence, and it may contain all of the desirable items that would be needed in a wide variety of circumstances. It may also be designed to provide emergency facilities for disaster relief; to be capable of operation in rural areas where electricity is unavailable; and to have facilities for communication with whatever agencies are desired, including those at a considerable distance.

It is probable that the most complete unit so far built is that used by the Crime Detection Laboratory of the State of Wisconsin. This unit is designed to serve in almost any possible contingency and under all conditions encountered in the state. No effort will be made to describe the unit completely, but rather to indicate the facilities provided and to underscore some of the problems that must be considered and solved.

Power and Heat. The most important need is for flexible power supply, met by utilizing an air-cooled gasoline motor with generators capable of delivering a continuous 3000W current of 110V, 60-cycle ac, as well as 12V dc for operation of radio equipment, floodlights, etc. Heat is supplied from the 110V source. The truck body is well insulated by glass wool, which is helpful in both hot and cold weather. A small refrigerating unit is provided to cool those items that

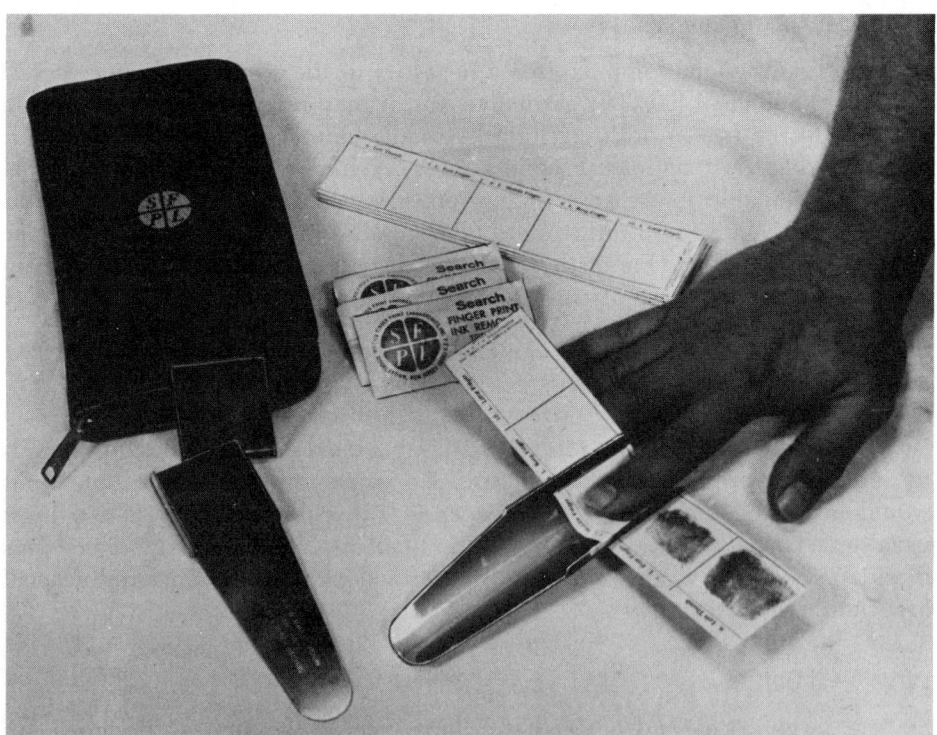

FIGURE 3-4. Post-mortem fingerprint kit. (Courtesy of Sirchie Laboratories, Inc.)

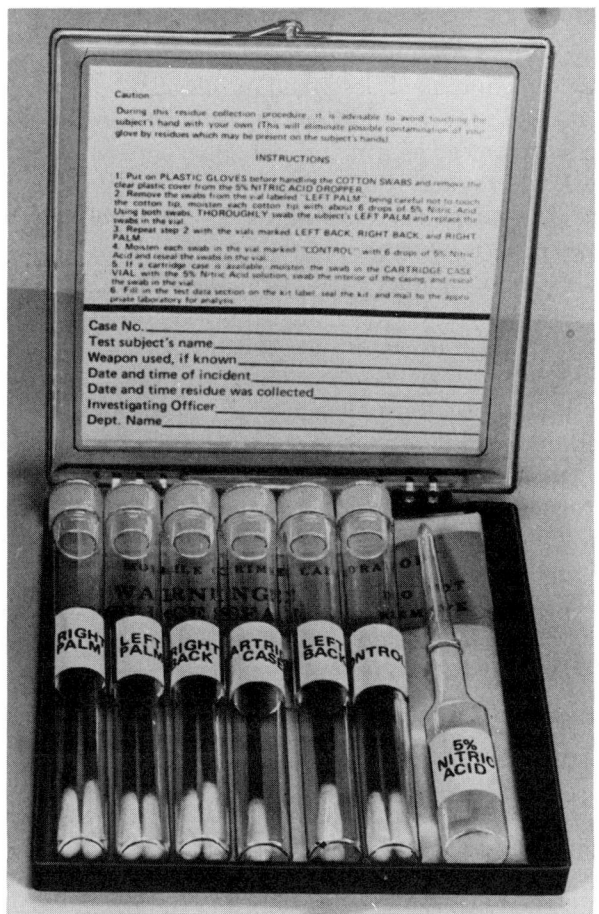

FIGURE 3-5. Swabbing kit for the determination of gunshot residues by neutran activation analysis. (Courtesy of Sirchie Laboratories, Inc.)

require lowered temperature, notably the developing solutions for negatives, which become too warm for use in hot weather.

Communication is provided through transmitting and receiving equipment constituting a part of the unit, as well as "walkie-talkies" by which personnel in the field can communicate with the unit. An electric megaphone is used for projecting the human voice to a distance of one-half mile for the control of crowds and for similar purposes.

Illumination is provided by searchlights and other lighting equipment powered by the electrical supply, and by a variety of battery-operated lanterns. A *portable X-ray outfit,* also powered by the truck's electrical supply, is available for emergency use. A very small *darkroom* is provided for loading of filmholders and for development of negatives in the field. More extensive photographic operations are not considered practical in the field.

Virtually all of the equipment described in this chapter has been incorporated in the Wisconsin field unit. In addition, the unit has been designed to include such emergency equipment as a *metal detector,* a *magnetic lifting device* for recovery of guns, knives, and similar items from under water, improved *dragging equipment,* an *underwater viewing device,* a motor-driven *sifting device,* oxyacetylene *cutting equipment,* and other special items.

The desirability of a complete motorized unit such as this, under certain circumstances, is obvious. Its cost will effectively limit it to the larger law-enforcement agencies. Local conditions vary to such an extent that any such unit must be adapted to serve the particular needs of the locality. In general, a much smaller unit is usually sufficient, particularly for municipal needs. The careful consideration given to the design of this large unit should set a standard useful to the smaller organization in planning its own.

A corollary to the idea of a special evidence-collecting unit is the necessity of specially trained personnel to operate it. The practice of having one or more trained collectors of physical evidence with proper equipment to perform a thorough job is already established in some larger police departments and law-enforcement laboratories. That this practice will be more widely adopted with the passage of time seems both desirable and assured.

REFERENCES

Arther, R. O.: *Scientific Investigator.* Springfield: Thomas (1970).
Collins, R. L.: "Improved Crime Scene Investigations," *J. Crim. Law, Criminol. and Police Sci.* 52:469 (1961).
Cunningham, D. K.: "Police Duties at the Scene of the Crime," *Police* 6:77 (1961).
Friedem, K.: "Possible Ways of Improving Investigation at the Scene of a Crime," *Kriminalistik* 13:109 (1959).
Harris, R. I.: *Outline of Death Investigation.* Springfield: Thomas (1962).
Inbau, F. E.: *Scientific Police Investigation.* Philadelphia: Chilton (1972).
O'Hara, C. E.: *Fundamentals of Criminal Investigation,* 2nd ed. Springfield: Thomas (1972).
O'Hara, C. E., and Osterburg, J. W.: *An Introduction to Criminalistics,* 2nd ed. Bloomington: Indiana University Press (1972).
Smith, H. W.: *Laboratory Aids for the Investigator.* Toronto: The Attorney-General's Laboratory (1964).
Soderman, H., and O'Connell, J.: *Modern Criminal Investigation,* 5th ed. New York: Funk and Wagnalls (1962).
Svensson, A., and Wendel, O.: *Techniques of Crime Scene Investigation,* 2nd American ed. New York: American Elsevier (1965).

4
The Collection of Physical Evidence

Today, as never before, the utilization of physical evidence is critical to the solution of most crimes. No longer may the police depend upon the confession, as they have done to a large extent in the past. The eyewitness has never been dependable, as any experienced investigator or attorney knows quite well. Only physical evidence is infallible, and then only it is properly recognized, studied, and interpreted. The importance of overlooking nothing that will contribute to the final solution of the crime cannot be overestimated. Of the various items capable of contributing to that solution, nothing is more important than microscopic residues. They are the hardest to locate because they cannot be seen, but it is for this very reason that they are available for examination. The criminal seeking to hide his traces will dispose of many macroscopic items, but he will not deliberately destroy evidence he does not notice.

Because both gross and minute types of evidence may be present, both must be collected. It is rarely necessary to instruct the rookie officer that a gun—or a knife or a club—is important evidence. He is already familiar with such items of evidence. He may not be familiar with the hairs, fibers, tiny fragments of glass, paint, wood, metal, etc., which are also important as evidence. He may not know the value of blood distribution, even though he sees it, or the significance of the arrangement of objects at the crime scene and alterations or damage to the normal environment of that scene. Nor may he realize the critical importance of such matters in the final interpretation and reconstruction of the crime.

Essential as it is, the collective of evidence, per se, must always be the *second step* in the investigation. By its nature, collecting disturbs the crime scene and destroys evidence in the form of arrangement of objects within that scene. The first step, interpretation and reconstruction of the scene, will be discussed below, as will the actual collection of evidence. Both steps must be performed by persons familiar with the routine method and the implications that are present. A systematic approach is necessary, and it must be utilized by a person who can observe accurately, record in detail, and collect carefully and completely. This person requires the highest level of training.

THE COLLECTOR. Too often it has been assumed that all police officers are expert in the collecting of evidence. Many officers are gifted in this direction, but to assume that *all* are is a catastrophic mistake. Good evidence collectors tend, like poets, to be born with the ability. They may also be trained, and many detectives acquire the necessary training through long experience. Most large police departments give special training to carefully selected personnel, who may not be detectives but regular patrolmen. Whatever their rank, the task is so important that applicants should be carefully screened. It is of primary importance that the collector have a true appreciation of what physical evidence is, what it means, and what can be done with it in the laboratory. Failure at any of these three points can prevent the officer from being effective in this critically important work.

INTERPRETATION AND RECONSTRUCTION AT THE SCENE. More information is available at the scene of a crime than can be obtained by the examination of evidence removed from the scene. Careful observation at the time of collection will often reveal what happened, something of the sequence of the separate events, and the general nature of the activity. This is most often true with homicides and similar crimes of violence. The most important items to observe are:

(1) Displaced objects, or objects in unusual locations or attitudes.
(2) Distribution, indications of direction, and character of all blood traces, whether they be spots, stains, smears, or pools.
(3) Presence of objects which appear foreign to the environment, e.g., weapons as well as objects, traces, or materials not suitable as weapons but apparently involved with the criminal activity.

After recording the above and any other unusual situations with photographs, drawings, etc., interpretation and reconstruction is often possible. The evidence collector may or may not have the ability to perform this vital function. If he does not, his record must be made available to someone who does. For this reason it is essential that his record be complete. Many experienced evidence collectors become very expert in making crime-scene reconstructions quickly, and the ability to do so is one of their most important acquisitions.

In general, physical evidence will be obtained from three main sources: (1) the scene of the crime, (2) the victim, if any, and (3) the suspect and his environment. Crimes against property will usually involve only (1) and (3); crimes against the person will involve all three sources.

THE CRIME SCENE

This will usually be indoors in a room, outdoors, or in an automobile. The treatment of the problem will vary somewhat depending upon the locale.

Indoors

The investigator will first prevent unauthorized persons from entering, or will evict any who are already present. Every person present is contributing to the microscopic residues materials not related to the crime that will confuse the picture and make laboratory work more difficult. Such contamination will rarely prevent the laboratory from arriving at the facts, but it will complicate the study by contributing a mass of irrelevant materials that will require examination.

Photographs of the scene will next be obtained, from a number of angles if possible, to facilitate later determination of such details as exact placement of furniture, the position of the body (if any) and the weapon, and the condition of a broken window or door.

A general survey of the premises, largely accomplished during the photographing, will then be completed, taking precautions against contamination, against disturbing items of importance, and the like. If glass has been broken, the fact should be recorded and the investigator should avoid breaking it further. If the premises have been ransacked, they will need to be searched later for fingerprints, and should not be disturbed more than is absolutely essential. The investigator should note misplaced furniture and other items characteristic of the scene, particularly foreign objects—weapons, tools, or other items that would not normally be there. Sometimes a burglar will leave some item of clothing belonging to him. If present, this may be the most valuable evidence and should be undisturbed until evidence collection proper is started.

The actual collection of evidence should now be started. First, all the larger objects that appear to have material significance will be picked up. These will be handled carefully to avoid disturbing fingerprints or contributing extraneous prints.

Firearms and other weapons require special care because of the probability that they will carry fingerprints. Various techniques are used for handling small firearms—techniques ranging from insertion of a pencil in the barrel to the treacherous practice of threading a string through the trigger guard. To prevent the eradication of fingerprint evidence in transportation, a firearm or a knife could be processed for latent fingerprints at the scene. The object is moved only when it is determined no valuable fingerprints are present in areas the investigator will touch. A pair of cotton gloves on the hands of the investigator will be helpful. A white cotton handkerchief may be wrapped around the hands or the object in order to avoid touching it with the fingers. A pair of forceps is useful for such small objects as can be handled with them. Each object is placed in a proper receptacle. Paper bags of various sizes are suitable for the smaller objects. Cellophane bags are preferable if obtainable. Larger objects may be wrapped in ordinary wrapping paper and tied. It should be borne in mind that given time, moderate temperature, and an enclosed situation, many items of evidence will develop moldy growths. The investigators should take steps to prevent this. The largest objects, which cannot be wrapped, will usually be transported as found, care being taken to disturb them as little as possible. If fingerprints are likely to be found on such an object, it may be necessary to search for them before moving it. Only seldom is there any point in transporting large objects, because the evidence they carry can ordinarily be collected at the scene. If clothing or bedding is involved, it should be rolled and tied in a bundle with wrapping paper. Unless the items of clothing or bedding have already been in contact with each other they should be wrapped separately.

Every article collected for examination must carry an identifying mark, placed on the object itself or on its wrapper. If it is the wrapper that is marked at the crime scene, at a later time, and before any chance mixing of wrappers can occur, a permanent mark should be placed on the object itself. Writing with ink, scratching with an awl or a knife blade, or other similar means may be used. The marks should include the date, the place of origin, and the name or initials of the person who collected the evidence. This information is often placed on the wrapper only, or on a tie-on and the object itself is merely initialed for identification. Record must be kept in a notebook of the objects collected, the time and place, witnesses present, and other pertinent information. Sketches of the position of objects, the relationship of various pieces of evidence to the surroundings and to each other, distances and similar information are often essential and always valuable. Although photographs have already recorded most of the relative positions, the camera tends to distort objects in the foreground as compared with those in the background, and it will not always give a clear indication of distance or even spatial relationships. The dimensioned sketch is more useful for this purpose in many instances. To obtain the dimensions, a pocket steel tape should always be available.

The Collection of Physical Evidence 37

The smaller items of evidence should now be sought. This will entail collection of (1) microscopic evidence and (2) fingerprints. The two will not ordinarily be found in the same places, and the taking of one need not disturb the other, except for the fact that fingerprint powder will be mixed with all the microscopic evidence if the prints are developed first. On the other hand, collecting microscopic evidence need not disturb a single print except those in dust, if the work is carefully done. Care in this instance means largely to avoid leaving new fingerprints. Useful prints are obtained only from rather firm solid surfaces, so such surfaces should not be touched. Carpets, clothing, fabric-covered upholstery, and regions of firm surface which are out of normal reach may be safely handled.

Any obvious items of microscopic evidence such as hairs, fragments of glass, wood, metal, vegetable debris, mud, or other small visible items foreign to the normal environment should be picked up carefully with forceps and placed in small cellophane bags, glass vials, or paper envelopes, each of which should be labeled immediately as to origin, date, name of collector, and other pertinent data. After all such items have been collected, the premises should be swept with an electric vacuum sweeper equipped with a filter attachment (described in Chapter 3). Floors, windowsills, and other likely places for the collection of evidence should be swept. This will not disturb fingerprints, bloodstains, or similar residues, if moderate care is exercised. The contents of the filter compartment should be removed by brushing into cellophane bags or covered glass dishes, each of which is then labeled.

Only at this stage should the search for fingerprints be made. Likely spots such as doorknobs, window ledges, and bureau handles that might have been touched by the criminal should be examined visually, dusted with an appropriate powder, or developed by other suitable means (see Chapter 6). Any prints located are photographed with a fingerprint or other camera. Dusted prints may then be lifted if desired, with Scotch tape or a special lifting tape, and then labeled. Prints should *not* be lifted until the print has been photographed and a record made of its original location.

Miscellaneous evidence and standards should now be collected, as indicated by the nature of the crime and of the scene.

(1) If entry was forced, it is essential that all tool marks be found and recorded, and possibly removed to the laboratory on the object originally marked. Seldom is it necessary to saw out window ledges, pieces of doors, or similar objects, because casts can be made of every mark that shows distinctive shape or characteristics. A properly made cast will reproduce accurately even the microscopic markings made by a tool when such marks are present. Casts should not be made, however, unless it is virtually impossible to transport the intact object to the laboratory. Even in the event that casts must

ultimately be made, it is better to make them in the laboratory rather than in the field. All casts, marks removed in toto, etc., must be packaged and labeled carefully.

(2) If glass was broken, paint scraped or chipped, wooden or metal objects damaged, or any other type of material disturbed, a standard of the material should be taken from the scene for later comparison with similar material found on the person, clothing, or loot of a suspect apprehended later. This simple matter of obtaining adequate standards should never be overlooked. Otherwise the tendency of owners to repair or replace damaged property will result in the loss of the original material necessary for standards of comparison.

(3) In crimes of violence, physiological residues such as blood, semen, urine, and flesh may be present at the scene of the crime. To locate them, the investigator can pass a portable ultraviolet lamp over rugs, carpets, woodwork, bedding, and similar objects. Stains invisible in ordinary light will be revealed, and a preliminary indication of the nature of any stain is often obtainable by this examination, which is described in detail in Chapter 17.

(4) Tests may be made on dried stains found at the scene of the crime to ascertain presence of blood. These tests may be performed by the luminol, benzidine, or other catalytic tests described in Chapter 15. Suspicious stains, or the objects carrying them, must be removed to the laboratory for complete examination. Often enough blood is available so that a significant amount may be scraped off and placed in a glass vial. Cracks in the floor, soil carrying blood, and other spots that may collect and conceal blood and resist efforts to remove it should be examined with special care. It is very common for blood deposits to be scrubbed and largely removed before any investigation is made, but such spots will frequently retain sufficient blood to make possible every type of test normally used.

(5) Fresh blood may occasionally be found at the scene of a crime. When this occurs, a sample must be taken by pipet, transferred to a vial of physiological saline, and taken immediately to the laboratory, where extensive tests should be made. Finding fresh blood is rare; blood is ordinarily dry or at least clotted at the time of the investigation. More commonly greatly diluted blood is found in sink traps, basins, or other vessels in which a criminal may have washed blood from his person or clothing. If this action is suspected, a sample of the water that may contain blood is taken to the laboratory for examination.

(6) Suspected seminal, urinary, or other stains are best transported to the laboratory in the object containing them. Otherwise, a piece of the object carrying the stain may be cut out and transported when possible. As a last resort, scrapings are removed for later examination. Seminal stains should be handled as little as possible to prevent damage to the spermatozoa. Definite

testing for the nature of stains is almost always impossible in the field and should not be attempted except in emergencies.

Special procedures may be needed in unusual, or even in routine phases of evidence collection. The skilled investigator will ordinarily recognize these special cases and act accordingly. Only occasionally is it necessary to carry out more than a fraction of the various operations outlined above. However, *it is better to collect more than is needed, rather than less.* No task is so troublesome, and at times so embarrassing, as to return at a later date to collect something previously missed only to find that it has been destroyed or lost. Stains may be removed, rooms repainted or papered, furniture and rugs replaced. Often, indeed, even the occupants are different. The probability of obtaining missed materials for standards, or for other purposes, is usually slight after the lapse of any appreciable amount of time.

One special case concerns the relation of fingerprint search to the collection of other types of evidence. Though the preferred order was discussed above, these are instances in which it is desirable to alter the order of working. If a good, clear print is seen initially, it is often best to deal with it first. However, this exception does not alter the rule that less damage will be done to fingerprints by the general search of the crime scene than will be done to the other evidence by searching for fingerprints first. Again, the experienced investigator should be capable of altering the order to suit the actual circumstances.

Outdoors

When a crime occurs in the open, the same general principles and order of operations applied to indoor crime scenes are used. However, the difference in the type of locale will shift the emphasis considerably. Fingerprints will usually be absent or undetectable, because they will now be on trees, leaves, fences, and other rough surfaces. Only occasionally is it useful even to look for them except on objects such as tools, guns, knives, etc., that have been found abandoned in the neighborhood. Examination of the object should then be made in the laboratory. Likewise, the vacuum-sweeping of the locale is ordinarily useless except under some very special circumstances. Tool marks will ordinarily, although not necessarily, be absent. For example, twigs were cut in connection with a crime, and it was proved that a knife taken later from a suspect had made the cuts. Ax cuts have also figured in a number of crimes. In such an event the preservation of the cut surfaces is of the greatest importance.

PRELIMINARY EXAMINATION. The scene must be approached with the greatest circumspection, even more so than with an indoor crime. After the scene is thoroughly photographed, the investigator should carefully search for traces of the crime in broken grass, weeds, or bushes; or impressed in the soil. When foot tracks or tire-tread marks are found, they should be photographed, and a cast should be made. Broken vegetation should be examined for the presence of hairs or fibers and for clues to the details of the crime.

The importance of broken vegetation and inspection of minute details of other features of the scene may be illustrated by an actual instance. In a case involving the rape of a young girl the victim was rendered unconscious by a fall in which her head struck a stone. Thorough examination of the area allowed recovery of the stone, and on it were found traces of blood. After falling, she was rolled on her back and shifted in the direction of her head. A piece of stick had penetrated her clothing, and this was found. On it were fibers from both her dress and her slip, and the garments showed rents from which could be obtained the distance her body was shifted. A large weed was broken and bent in a semicircle corresponding to the position and shape of the rapist's knee. All of these very significant items of evidence had been overlooked in a week of investigation by police and other investigators. From these and other observations the crime was reconstructed and later confirmed, though the girl herself knew little about it because she was unconscious.

In another rape, which occurred at night in a vacant lot, the spot at which the act occurred could not be located until an intensive and almost microscopic search was made of all the broken vegetation. When located, this spot yielded so much evidence that the conviction of a particular one of several suspects became a virtual certainty. Without the painstaking work of locating the exact spot, the evidence would not have been found and, in all probability, the culprit would have gone free.

VISIBLE EVIDENCE. The general rules for the collection of visible evidence are followed in outdoor crime-scene investigation. In addition, after search has yielded all the fragments, hair, fibers, and other debris that can be found, the vegetation from the exact spot of the commission of the crime should be removed to cardboard cartons and moved to the laboratory where it may be given an even more thorough examination. It is not the vegetation itself that is of interest, but the material mixed with it and carried on it.

In addition to vegetation, samples of soil should be collected. This is especially important in case footprints are found. Such samples should come directly from the footprint after it has been photographed and reproduced by a cast. Bits of broken bottles or other glass should always be taken from the area; in many instances the perpetrator of the crime has stepped on one or more such fragments, rebreaking it and collecting minute fragments of it in his pants and shoes. If special materials such as coal, builder's sand, plaster, wood, or concrete are present, samples should be taken of each variety. Similar material will often be found in the clothing of anyone who committed a crime in that area. Blood may have been spilled, and if it can be located it should be collected, even if mixed with oil or other debris. Semen, if located, must also be collected.

The general rule for collection of material at outdoor crime scenes is, like that for indoor scenes, to take a little of everything at the time, even if its connection with the crime appears dubious. It is easier to collect everything significant immediately after the commission of a crime. It is not so easy to locate it after children have played in the area, rubbish has been dumped, cultivation started, or a dozen other contingencies have arisen.

Variations of the general procedure will have to be improvised by the investigator to suit the circumstances. If there is any doubt about the utility of any object or material, it should be taken. It is far easier to discard worthless objects and materials that have come to the laboratory than to obtain missing ones that have not come. There should never be any doubt in the mind of the investigator as to what he should take. Absolutely anything that may have been in or close to the sphere of the crime should either be taken or sampled, and the slightest doubt that arises should be resolved by taking the doubtful object.

Vehicles

Crimes are often committed in an automobile or similar vehicle, such as a train, streetcar, or bus. This is a special case, very similar to the crime committed indoors, but with a more restricted area to consider. The general procedure is identical with that for a room, except for those variations related to the limited area. Items such as glass, sweepings of the upholstery and floors, and fingerprints are dealt with as described above. Searches for blood and semen are often necessary. Hairs and fibers are especially important, and are usually more abundant in a vehicle than they would be in a room.

Hit-and-run cases, in which the actual occurrence is outside the car and the nature of the crime is reasonably well defined, call for a considerably curtailed procedure. Glass, paint, and blood are the three most common types of available evidence. *Fibers* and *hairs* are also very important in such cases, since the victim often leaves one or both on the car in considerable quantity. To collect them requires patient and careful scrutiny, with magnification, of the entire questioned surface. It is usually convenient to collect fibers and hairs before any other evidence is collected, because they are more readily lost than any other items of evidence.

Paint and *glass* are often chipped or broken by the impact, and samples of both will persist at the scene of the accident. For purposes of comparison, any broken glass on the car is removed and labeled as to origin; and samples of paint are chipped from the car, preferably where the paint is already broken.

Grease, tar, and *road soil* samples may prove to be significant, and should be taken for later comparison with any found on the clothing of the victim or at the scene of the accident.

After the collection of the above types of evidence, the car should be examined for *bloodstains*. The luminol test (see Chapter 15) is especially valuable in the rapid checking of an entire car front for stains. Positive test results must be interpreted with considerable caution because of the relatively large area of metallic surfaces exposed. Blanks are run on all metal surfaces to confirm any positive test, and the area that shows luminescence is then checked with the benzidine or phenolphthalin test. If enough blood is present, a microcrystalline test, performed in the laboratory with scrapings removed from the car, can be made. Tests for species and blood groups are also possible when the blood sample is sufficient in quantity. When there is little or no visible blood but a strong positive luminol reaction, the preferred technique is to concentrate the blood on filter paper by means of capillary action. Alternatively, simple soaking with wet filter paper will allow chemical blood tests, but rarely species or blood-group tests. Benzidine and other color tests can be readily made in the field.

One other important possibility should not be overlooked. When a body is struck violently by a car, the clothing often impresses its weave pattern on the paint or metal, particularly when the surface of the car is lightly coated with grease and road dirt. Such *cloth impressions* must be photographed in natural size for comparison with the clothing of the victim. It is ordinarily sufficient to place a ruler beside the cloth impression and photograph the two together, after which the picture may be enlarged to exact size, as indicated by the image of the ruler.

A further possibility is that the car may shed some item on impact with the body, e.g., a bolt. If any such object is present at the scene of the accident, a corresponding item from the suspected car must always be taken for comparison.

Occasionally, a vehicle runs over a prone body, either present before impact, or by an unusual circumstance knocked into the prone position by the impact. This is more likely with children than with adults. In such instances the underside of the vehicle should be carefully inspected for grease wipes, adhering hair and similar deposits, torn pieces of clothing, or other unusual material. The car should be raised on a hoist for this inspection so that photographic records can be made and all significant details can be observed and noted. The hoisting equipment available at service stations can normally be utilized for this phase of the investigation. Other unusual circumstances that are encountered will call upon the investigator for the full exercise of all his ingenuity and imagination. These qualities should be cultivated and exercised to the utmost at all times.

THE VICTIM

The obtaining of physical evidence by the examination of a victim is usually an involved process requiring the services of medical and other specialists, rather than those of the police inspector or even the police criminalist. There are, however, numerous functions of the greatest importance to be performed by police personnel whether the victim is living or dead. If the victim is dead, the body should be photographed from several positions before it is disturbed, if that is at all possible. If the body has been moved, it should be restored to the original position as described by the first witness, and photographed there. Close-up pictures should be taken of any wounds or other significant features. In case of hanging or strangulation, such detailed pictures should include any marks on the throat. A ruler should be included in such pictures so that exact dimensions may be obtained in enlarged photographs to be printed later. It is of less importance to photograph drowned bodies, but even here it is well to keep photographic records.

Clothing

All clothing should be taken to the laboratory as soon as it is taken from the body, and it should be collected with as little miscellaneous contamination as possible. This is important whether the victim is alive or dead. Hospital attendants should not be allowed to handle clothing after it has been removed, as they customarily brush it and store it in a wardrobe, thereby destroying or losing much of the evidence it carries.

The collection of clothing from the victim should be a prescribed and invariable portion of the routine of investigation. Clothing should be wrapped carefully, preferably a separate package for each garment, and transported with a minimum of handling to the laboratory. Every effort must be made to prevent its contamination, either by police investigators, morgue or hospital attendants, or ambulance orderlies. Some contamination is inevitable in handling a clothed body. If, however, everyone who handles it is dressed in a white cotton uniform, gown, or similar garment, and contact is kept to a minimum, the amount of contamination will usually be slight. White cotton, being present on all clothing, has itself little or no significance and does not constitute a serious contaminant.

In many instances, clothing of a victim will be wet with water, blood, urine, or other liquids at the time it is removed from the body. It may also be heavily contaminated with decomposition products if the body has putrefied. Such clothing cannot be wrapped in a bundle without transferring the liquids and their patterns, as well as inducing further intrusion and development of molds, bacteria, and other microorganisms that will thrive on the physiological materials present. The best solution to this problem is to remove the clothing with as little disturbance as possible and spread it out in a dry place where there is minimum access by persons other than the necessary officials. It may be left there to dry, after which it can be bundled and dealt with as described for initially dry clothing. Another solution that is sometimes practical is to hang the items on clothes hangers, preferably wooden ones to avoid rust stains, and suspend the hangers from a line, keeping adequate space between the garments. An identification slip should be kept with each garment at all stages of the drying and packaging.

Blood

In most crimes of violence a sample of blood should be taken from the victim, whether the latter is alive or dead. If any blood has been shed, by either the victim or the suspect, enough blood must be taken for testing and typing. If this is all that is required, a few drops will suffice. With a dead body, it is better to take a larger sample because it may be impossible to get more if it is needed at a later time. Even if no blood has been shed in the crime, it is still necessary to take blood samples. The question often arises as to whether the victim or the perpetrator of a crime had been drinking: thus a blood sample for alcohol analysis becomes necessary. Ordinarily about 10 ml is sufficient for this purpose, though the exact amount will depend upon the analytical method employed. The victim of an automobile collision, for example, should have an alcohol analysis and a carbon monoxide analysis of his blood made to assist in determining the blame for the accident. If there is any possibility of poisoning, a blood sample is again necessary. From a dead body it is well to take as much as possible, but not less than 10–20 ml. Many times there is no immediately apparent reason for withdrawing blood samples, and later, when it is too late to obtain them, it is found that they are quite essential to the investigation. In case of doubt, a blood sample should be insisted upon.

Hair

The collection of a sample of hair from any body, living or dead, is a very quick and simple matter, and one that is often neglected. It should never be overlooked, even though there may be no known reason at the time for taking such a sample. The reason may not become apparent until after apprehension of the suspect, at which time the victim's hair may be compared with foreign hair taken from the suspect. If, in the meantime, the body has been buried or cremated it is difficult if not impossible to obtain a specimen for comparison. The best head hair samples are obtained by combing, but if this does not yield sufficient hairs, a considerable number should be clipped from several points on the crown, cutting them close to the skin.

Rape victims should always furnish a sample of pubic hair, because it is often found on the person or clothing of the rapist, most frequently on his handkerchief. Pubic hairs should be clipped close to the skin, and must always be obtained in case of rape and murder, because the body is dead and the opportunity to obtain them will not long remain.

Semen

In all rape cases, the examining physician should make smears of any material taken from the vagina. Several slides should be prepared, stained, and mounted. These slides may well be the most important evidence in determining the guilt or innocence of any suspect later apprehended.

In many crimes in which rape is not committed, there is concomitant perverted sex activity and semen may be found on a body in a location other than the vagina. If found, it should be preserved also, preferably on slides. More commonly, the clothing, or objects present at the time of this type of crime, will carry semen, but the possibility of its being on the body itself should not be ignored.

Poisons

In a suspected poisoning the collection of material for analysis is most critical and must be thorough. Because this is a specialized matter, it is discussed in detail in Chapter 27.

Powder Patterns

In shooting cases the question of the distance of the gun at the time of firing will arise. To determine with some accuracy how great this distance was, it may be essential to develop and analyze the powder pattern. If the bullet penetrated clothing, the pattern should be developed and photographed before the clothing is removed from the body, if possible. If the bullet wound is in the skin only, i.e., it did not pass through clothing, the powder pattern should be developed on the skin before the autopsy is performed. The method for studying powder patterns is discussed in Chapter 31.

Wounds

Whenever practical, the criminalist and the police investigator should be present at the autopsy. The criminalist may determine such matters as the angle at which a bullet, knife, or other missile entered the body, the force exerted as indicated by the penetration of bones or other resistant structures, and similar matters. Although this is usually considered to be the task of the autopsy surgeon, many autopsy surgeons are medical men only, whose duty is considered fulfilled when they have determined the cause of death. They commonly overlook many significant matters, not because of any intention to do so, but because their training, background, and philosophy do not encompass the complex ramifications of modern criminal investigation.

Close liaison and cooperation of the criminalist, the police investigator, and the autopsy surgeon or medical examiner are highly productive. Each can instruct the others and learn from them. Such collaboration can yield a highly productive investigation and result in the solution of the crime. The police background, together with the thorough understanding of evidence by the criminalist and the medical knowledge of the autopsy surgeon give thorough representation of every phase of the matter at hand. Many cases have remained unsolved because each of these agents worked independently, destroyed for each other evidence of great significance, and failed to report adequately to each other on their respective findings. Whether attributable to incompetence, interdepartmental jealousies, personal ambitions, or lack of training, such a situation is highly regrettable.

THE SUSPECT

When a suspect is taken into custody by authorized law-enforcement personnel who have good reason for believing him to be the sought-for criminal, at that moment all the care expended upon the collection and preservation of evidence begins to pay dividends. If the suspect is the actual culprit, all types of evidence will rapidly fall into line, and a clear, definite, and convincing case will usually be obtained.

Clothing

The most important evidence obtainable from a suspect will usually be found on his clothing. The first step is to ascertain if the clothing he is wearing was being worn at the time of the commission of the crime. If so, all of it should be taken as evidence immediately. The best practice is to have the suspect stand on a large piece of wrapping paper, shedding to it each piece of clothing as it is removed. All the clothing may be bundled together on the same paper, or, if there are special reasons for doing so, each piece may be retrieved and wrapped separately. The paper on which the suspect stands should be used in the wrapping to recover any items of evidence that have fallen from the garments during their removal. This is particularly important if the suspect is apprehended immediately after or at the time of the crime. While he is undressing, steps may be taken to obtain other clothing for him. The bundle or bundles are to be tied, labeled, and delivered intact to the laboratory for examination. The evidence they may carry is so diverse as to include most of the categories discussed in this volume. As emphasized elsewhere, there is no collector of microscopic evidence as efficient as clothing.

If there is good reason to believe that other clothing was being worn at the time of the crime, a search of the suspect's premises must be made. Any clothing that may have been used at the time of the crime should be taken to the laboratory in wrapped and labeled bundles. It is occasionally profitable to sweep the room in which the suspect sleeps, using the vacuum sweeper and filter attachment.

Hair

A sample of the suspect's head hair, and in the case of rape or other sex crime, a sample of his pubic hair, should be obtained. It is advisable to include as many as 100 hairs from his head. Sometimes this number can be obtained by vigorous combing. If not, additional hairs may be taken by clipping from the crown. If a police officer obtains this sample, the sample should be properly enclosed in an envelope or similar container and labeled as to source, name of officer, and date.

Blood

If any blood has been shed by either victim or suspect, a sample of blood should be taken from the latter. This will be used for comparison to questioned blood, and will serve to implicate or eliminate the suspect if he claims some specific source other than the victim for blood found on his clothing or possessions. If the criminal has shed blood during commission of the crime, the known sample from a suspect will be useful in identifying the source of those deposits. For most purposes a drop or two from the fingertip is sufficient for all necessary testing and typing. Only if a test is to be made for evidence of intoxication is it necessary to obtain a larger sample from the arm.

Miscellaneous

In cases involving personal assault, such as rape, or murder attended by a struggle, the suspect's fingernails should be scraped and the scrapings placed in a labeled vial or cellophane envelope. At times it may be profitable to take a sample of ear wax for examination. This will often carry pollens and other dusts that may place the suspect in an environment characterized by the particular types of dusts found in the ear wax.

Occasionally the suspect will carry a wound, discoloration, skin poisoning, or similar condition, which may be associated with the crime in question. Thus, a suspect who assaulted a victim in a patch of poison oak might well show the typical symptoms of poisoning from that source. If any such evidence occurs on the suspect, it should be noted, described accurately in a notebook and accompanied by the suspect's explanation. A photograph of the blemish may well be taken, particularly if there is reason to believe that the wound or other effect is connected with the crime. This may be of particular importance if the criminal has shed blood during the commission of a crime.

In connection with the search of the suspect's premises, other matters than clothing will, at times, be significant. In poisoning cases a search should be made for poison containers. A search for weapons is often important, and in fact anything that may have been used as a weapon by the criminal is likely to be found on his premises.

Questions concerning the right of police officers to collect such items as blood and hair from a suspect arise at times. It must be remembered that an innocent man is interested in clearing himself, and if it is explained to him that the laboratory tests are the most effective way of clearing him, ordinarily there will be no difficulty. The laboratory, after all, deals only in facts, not in suspicions, circumstances, or personal factors. The guilty man is likely to stand on his rights and refuse to cooperate. His suspicious actions in so doing may be pointed out to him, and at times this will be effective. When he is incarcerated his clothing can certainly be taken. The prison barber may readily obtain a sample of his hair, and the prison physician a sample of his blood. The obtaining of samples by such means is undesirable, but undeniably effective, and serves the interests of justice to both the guilty and the innocent.

ALTERNATIVE PROCEDURES

In the matter of collecting microscopic and other small items of evidence from clothing, from the suspect, the scene, and the victim, for which the vacuum sweeper with filter has been recommended, some investigators prefer to employ Scotch tape to lift all fibers, dusts, and other small residues. The advantages are as follows:

(1) Because the location is precisely known, it is easier to eliminate irrelevant material.
(2) The location itself may have an importance as great as, or even greater than, that of the material itself; e.g., a pubic hair that is foreign and found on the genitalia of the suspect is very significant.
(3) Because the fibers on the tape are then pressed to a clean sheet, they are protected from loss and contamination.
(4) Control samples are taken from locations not contacted by the suspect.

Although these advantages are recognized, the extra labor involved in attempting to cover any significant area with strips of tape is an obvious disadvantage, and failure to cover the entire area runs the risk of missing important evidence. In addition, the precaution of collecting, in advance of sweeping, such objects as visible hairs, glass fragments, etc., largely offsets the advantage of tape collection, and their locations are even more readily determined. In most instances, the procedure recommended earlier in this chapter is rapid and fully effective. In special instances where the extra time and labor are justified, the tape method may be used as a suitable alternative. However, when tape is used for evidence collection, the laboratory examiner will have one additional problem: recovering the individual items from the adhesive of the tape in order to study them more minutely than is possible by simple microscopic examination through transparent tape. The author has found this to be a serious difficulty.

REFERENCES

Arther, R. O.: *Scientific Investigator.* Springfield: Thomas (1970).

Collins, R. L.: "Improved Crime Scene Investigations," *J. Crim. Law, Criminol. and Police Sci.* 52:469 (1961).

Friedem, K.: "Possible Ways of Improving Investigation at the Scene of a Crime," *Kriminalistik* 13:109 (1969).

Harris, R. I.: *Outline of Death Investigation.* Springfield: Thomas (1962).

Inbau, F. E.: *Scientific Police Investigation.* Philadelphia: Chilton (1972).

Kirk, P. L.: "Microscopic Evidence—Its Use in the Investigation of Crime," *J. Crim. Law and Criminol.* 40:362 (1949).

Nickolls, L. C.: *The Scientific Investigation of Crime.* London: Butterworth (1956).

Osterburg, J. W.: *The Crime Laboratory.* Bloomington: Indiana University Press (1968).

Ostler, R. D.: "A Scientific Scenes of Crime Kit," *Police J.* 36:222 (1963).

Smith, H. W.: *Laboratory Aids for the Investigator.* Toronto: Attorney-General's Laboratory (1964).

Soderman, H., and O'Connell, J.: *Modern Criminal Investigation,* 5th ed. New York: Funk and Wagnalls (1962).

Svensson, A., and Wendel, O.: *Techniques of Crime Scene Investigation,* 2nd American ed. New York: American Elsevier (1965).

5
Casts and Replicas

Frequently it is necessary to record markings or characteristics found on an object of evidence that cannot be removed to the laboratory because of its large size or permanent fixity. The evidence is often a tool mark, a break in machinery (e.g., an automobile), or a fixed object that has been involved in a death or injury. Other objects and traces may not be satisfactorily transported because of their fragility. This is true of footprints, tire tracks and the like. Still other objects may not be susceptible to easy direct study because of their physical or optical nature. This is often true of hair scales, for example. It is a valid activity of the police investigator to make casts or replicas of such objects so that the three-dimensional reproduction that results may be used for examination and comparison. The laboratory worker, also, may make such casts and replicas. If an object must be destroyed or defaced in order to examine it, a cast may be made first for purposes of record. The general methods of casting are given here with the assumption that the investigator will purchase ready-made materials.

PLASTER CASTS

Casting with plaster is suitable for larger objects that do not require microscopically accurate reproduction. Commonly, shoe impressions and the tracks of vehicles in mud may be satisfactorily reproduced in this way. *Tool marks, however, and other structures having important microscopic features cannot be satisfactorily cast with plaster.* Ordinary commercial plaster of paris (partially dehydrated calcium sulfate: $(CaSO_4)_2 \cdot H_2O$) may be used for most purposes. The appropriate amount of powder is placed in a basin or similar vessel and water is added with constant stirring until a rather thick, but pourable slurry results. This mixture is poured into the shoeprint or other mark to be reproduced and is allowed to harden. Care is taken that the fluid mixture flows smoothly without trapping air bubbles at the critical surface, and with as little disturbance of that surface as possible. For a large casting a wire screen or similar reinforcing material must be inserted into the soft plaster before it hardens, to prevent breakage on removing the cast from the mold. Alternate layers of plaster and woven fabric are sometimes employed for both lightness and strength.

A good grade of plaster of paris such as is used by dental technicians is suitable for the reproduction of small visible details.

When the material forming the objects being cast is very easily disturbed, it is good practice to spray it lightly with a little lacquer or collodion before making the reproduction, to prevent distortion and damage. The lacquer must be allowed to dry completely before the plaster is applied.

In the presence of water the rehydration of plaster of paris begins at once and the mixture sets to a solid mass in a few minutes. The setting time may be prolonged to an hour or more by the addition of a small amount of colloidal material. Usually the label on the carton will give an indication of the setting time of the brand being used. As soon as the casting is hard it may be lifted. Soil, vegetable material, and other loose objects may be found adhering to its surface. Such objects can be stripped from the cast by means of a brush soft enough not to damage the plaster surface. Scraping with a knife blade or other hard object must be avoided. After the cast is completely hard it may, if necessary, be washed with water, but it must not be soaked or kept in water any longer than necessary.

The casting method described above gives a *positive* reproduction of the *original* object. The cast of a shoeprint will correspond to the shoe sole that made it. A negative die may be made from the positive cast after the latter has been carefully coated with a thin layer of lacquer, wax, or grease to prevent the sticking of the second plaster application to the first—or positive—casting.

Applications

The two most commonly cast impressions are those of tire treads and shoe soles. However, *not all* such marks are suitable for casting. Also, the detail they may show can be destroyed in the effort to make a cast. If the impression was made in a soft material such as mud, so that the impression has definite depth, plaster casting is proper. Similar markings in dust on a solid surface cannot be reproduced in the same manner. Here, photography may be the only method that will work, although some dust prints can be preserved by a method to be described later.

A further caution is in order: unless there is reason to believe that the print is in some manner attached to the crime, there is little if any value in making a cast of it. In one instance, the body of a murdered girl was found in a muddy vacant lot. The public, press photographers, and numerous police officers trampled the lot thoroughly, so that there was a multitude of shoe impressions. At that stage, the police technician and his commanding officer arrived with plaster, and made casts of some impressions selected either at random or because they were fresh-looking impressions. Naturally, no use was ever made of these casts. The lesson is clear: the technician must be there early enough to preserve valuable evidence, or the scene must be guarded against contamination. Both are good operating rules that are not always applied.

Tire treads sometimes present another problem. Impressions may be very short or quite long, depending upon the amount of soft material through which the tire rolled. Usually one portion of the tread impression will be of very poor quality, while a shorter portion of it may be very well recorded. The decision as to how much of such an impression should be reproduced by casting is often quite difficult. Careful inspection of the impression should be made, and all portions that show good detail should be reproduced, regardless of their length. The ideal cast would show fine detail throughout a length corresponding to the entire circumference of the tire—a matter of 6–8 ft. with most tires. Although the type of tread and the amount of wear that can be determined from a short section are very useful, no absolute identification of a tire is possible from these factors alone. Specific points of damage and individuality will be very difficult to locate in less than an entire-circumference print.

Fortunately, although only a short section of a tire impression may be available for casting, a suspect tire may be available for comparison. In such a situation, the entire circumference of the tire may be utilized in making a cast, and the problem is then to determine whether the short section from the scene can be matched with a corresponding short section of the total cast derived from the tire in question. The factors of importance are not just the general matters of tread pattern and wear, but the presence or absence of specific points of damage, which may appear as cuts, gouges, punctures, and prominent abrasions. If these features are present, they must also be in corresponding locations on the two casts, and they must have the proper dimensional interrelationships.

DETAIL CASTS

When microscopic detail is required, as in the study of tool marks or striations on solid objects, and the object is too large to be removed to the laboratory, a special type of cast must be made. Plaster of paris is not satisfactory for detail work, so other materials are used. Traditionally, the best material for this purpose had been moulage, which is still commonly employed by dentists for the highly fidelity of reproduction. Moulage has many advantages, but it is difficult to employ properly. Moulage casts must always be positives, because the negative is not stable. Because of this and other difficulties, moulage has largely been replaced by silicone rubbers, which are commercially available from most police suppliers. Silicone rubbers are commonly used to provide permanent negative casts, but satisfactory positive casts may be made from them if desired. This can be done by covering the negative with a thin coating of grease or wax and making another silicone cast from it. In practice, silicone positives are rarely made.

Silicone Casts

The silicones employed for casting are actually plastic-like in that they undergo polymerization in the presence of a catalyst. The base materials are viscous liquids. The material comes in two containers, in one of which is the unpolymerized base material. In the other is the catalyst that induces polymerization. The contents of the two containers are well mixed according to the manufacturer's instructions, and the material is applied to the surface to be cast. The silicone material is left in place for the length of time required for polymerization to be completed, and is then removed. Ordinarily the cast is gray in color and rather like rubber. It is permanent, and it may be surface-treated to simulate the color or reflectivity desired. Fine aluminum powder will give it a metallic sheen. Dyes will color it, and if it is exposed to the smoke from burning magnesium ribbon it will be coated with a fine layer of magnesium oxide and nitride. Some investigators use the latter method regularly to render the surface somewhat dull and uniform, allowing the major characteristics of the cast to appear and diminishing the minor irregularities. This improves the photographic reproduction of the markings. This technique is *not* recommended when the very finest detail must be seen.

Moulage Casts

Although, as indicated above, moulage has largely been replaced by silicone for the casting of tool marks and similar items of evidence, not even silicone is superior to moulage for fine detail and fidelity. It is also uniquely useful for making casts of body parts, wounds, faces for masks, and the like. It is more difficult to use than either plaster or silicone, in part because the negative material is not stable and must be used immediately as a mold for a positive cast. Varieties of dental moulage are available at dental supply houses. Negative moulage does not tightly adhere to any surface, and may be used to cast objects of all types except those damaged by moisture. Various formulas based upon agar, casein, and a filler are generally available. An advantageous form is obtained by freeze-drying and powdering. The resulting powder, is easily reconstituted in any desired amount by stirring it into suitable quantities of boiling water. The positive material contains carnauba wax and rosin as its main constituents.

MOULAGE NEGATIVE CASTING. Dry powder or strips of negative moulage are heated in a double boiler with enough water to produce a mixture having the consistency of boiled oatmeal. The mixture is poured directly on the object to be cast and is restrained with a dam of clay or wax if necessary. Metal or rubber rings are suitable to restrain the flow when flat surfaces are being cast. For casts of body parts, the molten material is allowed to cool until just ready to solidify, at which temperature it is too cool to produce scalding. On cooling, the material sets to a consistency similar to that of hard gelatin gel.

MOULAGE POSITIVE CASTING. The positive material, which is hard and somewhat brittle, must be melted promptly after the making of the negative cast, and must be poured before the negative has time to dry and shrink. (If stored in a tightly closed container, the negative can be retained without shrinkage for a few hours.) When a large object is being cast, the positive should be reinforced by embedding some wire mesh within it. The temperature of the positive moulage should be as low as possible to avoid melting the negative cast, so the melted positive is allowed to cool until it begins to solidify around the edges of the container. At this point it may be poured.

MODELING BODY PARTS WITH MOULAGE. The technique of use in modeling body parts is similar to that described above, except that minimum working temperatures must be used throughout. Making face masks of living subjects requires that tubes be inserted in the nostrils, and the negative cast must be removed with great care to avoid pulling hairs and the resulting damage to the cast. Often it is simpler to brush on the melted negative material rather than to pour it. Application of the method to the reproduction of *wounds* and *scars* is sometimes especially helpful in providing a permanent and lifelike record. The positive may be tinted to reproduce the color of the original with considerable fidelity to the natural appearance. A major advantage of such casting, as compared with color photography (also useful for recording details of body parts) is that all three dimensions of a wound, for example, are recorded permanently.

WAX IMPRESSIONS

The use of wax for reproduction of surfaces and objects has not been widely favored in criminal investigation for a number of reasons. Most waxes, like moulage negative, are not very rigid in large pieces. Positive replicas may be made from most wax negatives only with plaster, which, unlike moulage, fails to give good microscopic detail. Waxes also adhere to some surfaces, which is not the case with moulage negative.

There are some uses for which wax is better than most other casting materials, and there are a good many waxes available from the dental-supply trade. The large number of waxes offering a variety of special properties is one of the strongest points in favor of this material. If it is desired to carry a minimum of equipment and make a cast rapidly at the scene of a crime, a supply of dental wax may be very valuable. Breaks in portions of large objects, for example, may often be modeled advantageously with wax.

The method of applying wax depends upon the type and softness of the particular wax. With a soft wax a satisfactory impression may be obtained by merely forcing the wax against the marked surface, and then working the wax loose. The harder waxes require softening by a little heat. In exceptional cases the wax is melted and poured or applied with a brush.

Oil-clay mixtures such as Plasticine are analogous to soft wax in properties, uses, and method of application. Inexpensive and readily available, they have a number of other uses and should be kept among the supplies of the criminal investigator. A case involving the loss of a bolt from an automobile fender will illustrate. The sheet metal of the fender had corroded and allowed the nut to pull through, carrying with it a piece of metal approximately the same size and shape as the nut. The shape of the remaining hole in the fender could not be easily recorded by moulage, plaster, or any of the other usual casting materials. It was readily molded by forcing through the hole a lump of Plasticine, which extruded in the shape of the hole and retained the form. It was thus possible to prove that the bolt with its adhering piece of metal had come from this particular car. The impression can be made more permanent by reproducing it in moulage from the Plasticine negative.

THERMOPLASTIC CASTING

A number of plastics, when heated to moderate temperatures, become sufficiently soft to take a microscopically accurate imprint under applied pressure. Little use has been made of these materials, except in the field of hair casting to reproduce the minutiae of scale structure. So accurate are thermoplastic impressions of hair scales that they are susceptible to examination under the highest powers of the microscope.

Similar application to tool marks, erased paper surfaces, and other objects bearing important microscopic detail has been shown to be practical under some circumstances. Even bullet and tool marks may be reproduced in this manner. Because the plastic is usually in the form of a solid sheet, it is not easily adaptable to highly irregular and irregularly curved surfaces. On flat surfaces it presents a minimum of difficulty.

A sheet of suitable plastic, e.g., Vinylite (or Lucite), is placed on the surface or small object to be reproduced. A heavy glass plate is laid on the plastic sheet and is weighted to apply pressure. An infrared heat lamp is placed close to the assembly so that the heat rays, which are little absorbed by the glass but strongly absorbed by the plastic, will soften the latter. In a few minutes the softened plastic will be firmly and accurately forced into all the existing irregularities in the object being recorded. The assembly is left undisturbed to cool to room temperature, the imprinted plastic to regain its original firmness.

Electric hot plates and furnaces have been used advantageously as heat sources for the casting of irregular and curved surfaces where extensive general softening is required. These heat sources are more difficult to control than the heat lamp, and are therefore less suitable for the casting of flat surfaces.

MISCELLANEOUS CASTS

Any material that can be softened by warming may be used for certain types of casting. If the temperature necessary for softening is too high, the object being reproduced will be damaged. Metals would be excellent casting materials but for this circumstance. The single exception is Wood's metal, which melts below 70°C. It has been recommended for the casting of dusty fingerprints. The melting properties of the material are excellent, but on solidifying it tends to form coarse crystals that cause the formation of pits in the cast. It does not ordinarily yield good results for this reason. The quality of the cast is improved if the object can be warmed to about the melting temperature of the casting alloy, and if pressure is applied with a cold surface so solidification begins at the top while the metal is still molten at the contact surface. The liquid metal is forced against the surface being copied, thus minimizing pit formation.

A technique developed at the Wisconsin State Crime Laboratory (private communication) consists of spraying molten Wood's metal (70°C) by means of compressed gas onto the surface to be reproduced while keeping that surface quite warm on a hot plate. Casts made in this manner have exceptionally good detail and fidelity. The technique should find many applications. A major advantage of this procedure is its applicability to highly irregular and oddly shaped surafces. The method requires special equipment, and may therefore be delayed in general application.

Many other materials find occasional use in casting. Certain adhesives, e.g.,

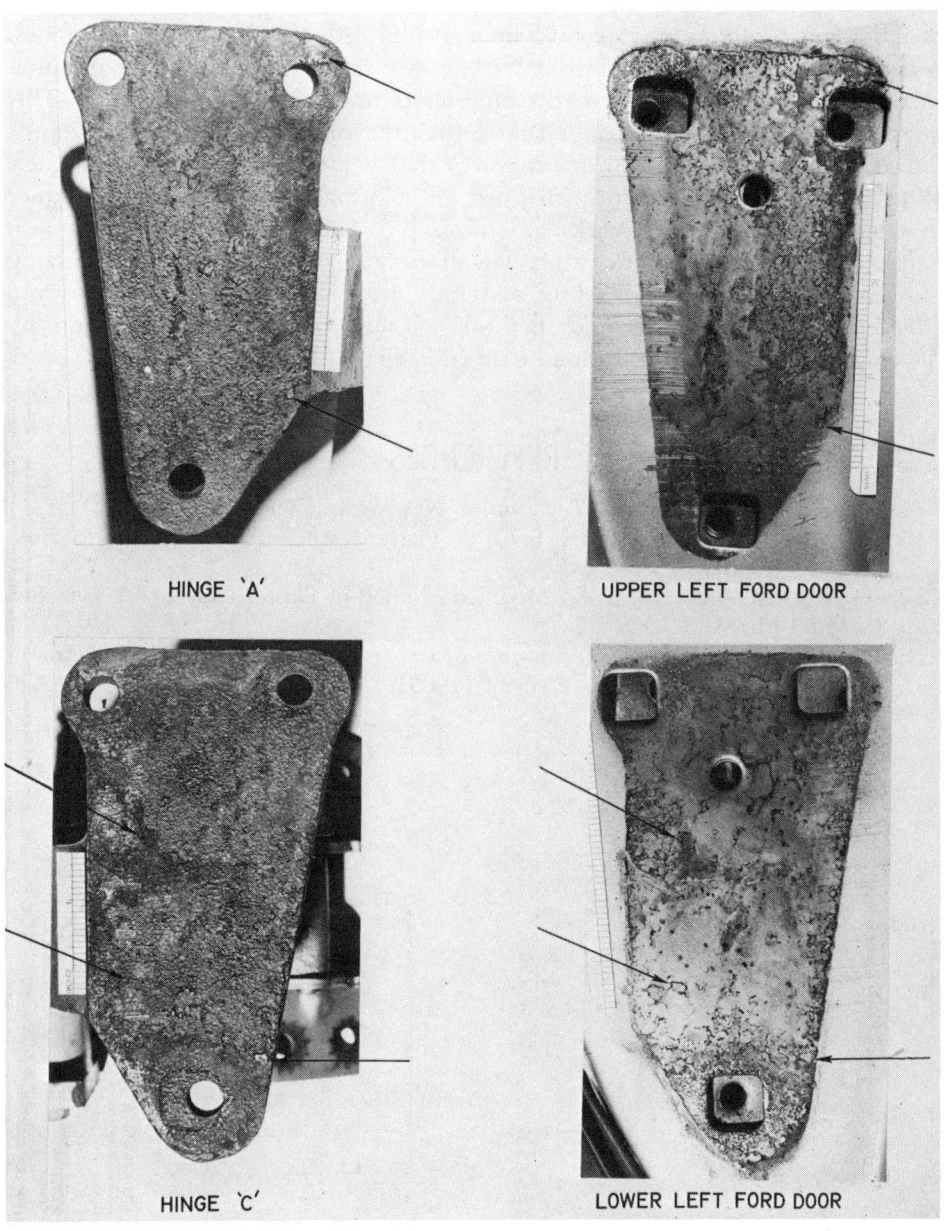

FIGURE 5-1. A "natural" replica in paint was obtained when a door was stripped from a stolen auto. (Courtesy of Duayne J. Dillon.)

bookbinder's flexible glue, give excellent results with metallic or glass surfaces. A commercial material, Faxfilm, has come into rather limited use for molding small marks such as rifling marks on bullets and marks left by tools. This material is essentially a lacquer that is painted on the surface to be reproduced, combined with a transparent strip that is attached to the wet lacquer. When the strip is subsequently stripped off, it brings with it the dried lacquer in which the questioned marks are imprinted. Gelatin and rubber are also employed for some types of casting. The investigator will profit by familiarizing himself with the common casting materials, by giving attention to new and effective casting materials and methods as they become available, and by developing skill in the utilization of several reliable techniques.

REFERENCES

Beadle, J. A.: *Castings: Current Techniques.* New York: Gleichenhaus (1972).
Bulbulian, A. H.: "A Professional Look at Plaster Casts," *FBI Law Enfor. Bull.* 34(9):2 (1965).
Chee, H. W., and Wilson, S. J.: "A Modified Method of Plaster Casting," *J. For. Sci. Soc.* 4:83 (1963).
Svensson, A., and Wendel, O.: *Techniques of Crime Scene Investigation*, 2nd American ed. New York: American Elsevier (1965).

6
Fingerprints

It has long been recognized that the patterns of the friction ridges of a person's fingertips are, for practical purposes, individual, and constitute positive means of identifying the person. The achievement of this degree of recognition and the development of practical methods for utilizing this unequivocal form of physical evidence were the result of a long and interesting process that called forth the efforts of many persons and evoked strong controversy. The fascinating, detailed history of the early phase of this identification technique may be found in *The Century of the Detective* by Jurgen Thorwald.*

Even today, much remains to be accomplished both technically and interpretatively in dealing with fingerprint evidence. The determination of an identity by this means rests on a probability just as truly as does any other form of identification. The actual probability is determined by the number of points of identity that are available, so a fingerprint identification may be very certain, or it may merely be an indication of possible origin. The actual individuality of the fingerprint is probably absolute, but the points that are used in its evaluation constitute only a very small part of the identifying characteristics present on the finger. Thus, when circumstances are favorable, the probability can readily be raised so high as to constitute virtual certainty and be accepted as such by courts of law.

For identification purposes, the ridge patterns of the palms of the hands, the toes, and the soles of the feet may be used as effectively as may fingerprints.

---

* J. Thorwald, *The Century of the Detective*. New York: Harcourt, Brace and World (1964).

At times this is a most important fact to remember because palmprints are sometimes found when fingerprints are absent or unrecognizable; occasionally even prints of the bare foot are encountered. Lip prints, although not often seen, can be used in a similar manner for a reasonably positive identification, and may be treated in much the same manner as are fingerprints.

Fingerprints and fingerprinting, summarized under the general term "dactyloscopy," have been treated quite thoroughly in the literature and are well understood in police circles. In this volume will be developed certain considerations that extend or clarify the general knowledge of this subject without reconsidering the extensive details of the field.

The use of fingerprints in law enforcement takes two main directions: (1) general identification by means of recorded prints of large numbers of individuals, and (2) specific identification by means of latent prints left at the scene of a crime, on a weapon, or in another incriminating location. The *first function* is met by recording all the prints of individuals who pass through police departments as suspects, applicants for certain types of position in public and private service, military personnel, and, through voluntary cooperation, the general public. The usefulness of large files of fingerprints, such as those maintained by the Federal Bureau of Investigation and by many state identification bureaus, is obvious in the identification of dead bodies, for persons suspected of operating under aliases, of amnesia victims, and for similar needs. The *second function* has been generally less useful for two reasons: (1) criminals attempt to avoid leaving latent prints in incriminating locations, and (2) police are often less than thorough in their search for the prints that are left. Latent prints should always be sought, and the more carefully the police make this search, the more frequent will be their identification of culprits. The process can be laborious because the latent prints that may be found cannot readily be located in a ten-finger print file. Much progress in the direction of locating recorded fingerprints by computerized methods appears to be in the offing. An effective single-print file would also simplify the search, but a workable system is very difficult to set up.

Even if the investigator does not locate fingerprints, it does not signify that the crime cannot be solved. Actually, the more careful the criminal is not to leave prints, the less likely it is that he will be equally careful about other forms of physical evidence.

THE BASIS OF FINGERPRINTS. Those portions of the body that are subjected to the friction of vigorous usage, i.e. the fingers, the palms of the hands, the toes, and the soles of the feet, carry small ridges that are more or less parallel to each other and are termed *friction ridges*. Along each ridge is located a row of pores that appear as small pits along the ridge top. Similar skin structures are found in some animals, particularly those whose life-habit is arboreal, such as the

Fingerprints

anthropoids. In no other species have friction ridges developed in such detail and profusion as on the human hand and finger. This distinction may have resulted from the more extensive and varied use of the human hand, and from the utility of the ridged structure in providing a firm grip to the hand and a sensitive touch to the finger. The latter characteristic results from the sweat of the sensory nerve endings in the friction ridges. The relation of the sweat glands to the ridges is interesting. In an evolutionary sense it was probably the fusion of the sweat-gland orifices that formed the friction ridges.

THE BASIS OF CLASSIFICATION. The inherent complexity of large numbers of friction ridges located with a high degree of randomness results in an almost infinite diversity of patterns no two of which have ever been found to be identical. This very complexity has led to great difficulties in developing a proper classification scheme, since every major feature will be found so greatly diversified as to merge gradually into another major feature, without any abrupt transition. The resulting ambiguity in the definition of a feature has given rise to most of the difficulties in the classification of fingerprints. Largely as a result, there are more than fifty classification systems (including modifications) in use, of which the Galton-Henry (often called the Henry) system is the most widely known in the United States and in a number of other countries. It is also the basis of many of the other systems. Variations of this system are common, and the fingerprint expert will need to know at least some of the rudiments of these variations. He must be completely familiar with at least the Henry system and one single-print classification method. The additional basic system, used particularly in South America, is the Vucetich system. It also has a number of variations.

The common ten-finger classifications are based upon the recognition of certain fundamental structures such as the "loop," the "arch," and the "whorl," and variants of these basic structures, along with their distribution on the fingers. Secondary factors include the direction of slope on the ridges, the distance (in terms of ridges) between the right or left delta and the core. Arbitrary conventions are used throughout so as to divide any given set of prints into one of two (or more) categories. Throughout the systems of classification, errors and difficulties occur only in the interpretation and definition of the various features, as these features merge into each other gradually.

Single-print classifications, having fewer features on which to base the identification, must take into account more details of the print than are necessary with the ten-finger classifications. The best-known single-print classification is the Battley system, which employs a glass plate ruled with a series of seven concentric circles that serve as a frame of reference. Here also, the basic pattern of arches, loops, and whorls, and their variants, serves for primary classification of each individual finger, after which the core pattern, position in the glass of the left delta, ridge counts from delta to core, and other similar details are recorded as part of the classification. Variations are necessary with certain basic patterns such as the twinned loop.:

Learning the basic fingerprint-classification systems is a relatively simple matter, but learning to recognize accurately the variants so as to attain consistency of classification requires long experience and the greatest care.

ROUTINE FINGERPRINTING

Recording of the prints of a living individual is relatively simple and is familiar to identification officers. Ordinary printer's ink is used because maximum contrast and permanence may be achieved with it. There are, however, numerous other systems that avoid the aesthetically objectionable printer's ink on the hands. Perhaps the most useful manual for routine police purposes is the one published by the Federal Bureau of Investigation in 1963, entitled *The Science of Fingerprints*. Some of the other methods are discussed by Cummins and Midlo.

The recording of fingerprints is laborious even under ordinary circumstances, and in this age of excellent duplicating equipment it should be possible for a single recording to be very carefully made, and the required number of reprints to be obtained by copying. However, this happens only occasionally. With dead bodies, the difficulty of making satisfactory fingerprints is greatly increased because of possible rigor mortis, decomposition of the tissue, and other disturbing factors. Special knowledge is often required to make good impressions of fingerprints under these circumstances. This also is discussed at length in the F.B.I. bulletin previously mentioned. It has been observed that even though the flesh is so far decomposed that none of the standard fingerprinting methods gives satisfactory results, the ridge structure of the fingers can still be seen. Under these circumstances, the hands themselves may be placed under a low-power stereoscopic microscope so that a classification may be made. The examiner must keep in mind that what he is observing is a mirror image of the desired fingerprint. This method may also be used with the detached skin of the finger or palm, for comparison with other prints.

In actual crime investigation one rarely obtains latent prints from ten fingers; usually prints from one or two fingers only are found. If the prints of a suspect are at hand, a comparison is not difficult, but when he is unknown and must be located by searching a ten-print file, the labor and time involved can be overwhelming. Single-print files are sometimes available, but they need to be much more generally established. Much effort is now being devoted to the computer treatment of fingerprints to develop practical means for recording and filing the prints of single fingers as a direct aid to investigation. Such developments are greatly needed.

Despite the general acceptance of printer's ink as the recording medium of choice, in nearly every instance the prints made by police department personnel fail to show a great deal of the detail present—detail that could be very useful in making comparisons with small, fragmentary latent prints. Although it has long been known that the pore arrangement along the ridges is highly individual, and that the ridges themselves often show minor deviations that are permanent, the subject of *poroscopy*, dealing with the pore characteristics, has been grossly neglected. Its neglect has largely been due to the generally poor pore registration achieved by conventional printing methods. It is certainly possible in this technological age to develop a method that reproduces even the fine detail of the skin surface without smearing the skin with printer's ink, which is both disagreeable and difficult to remove. Many years ago it was shown that exposed photographic paper could be used to reveal fine pore detail by moistening the fingertip with developing solution and lightly touching it to the paper. This is admittedly an impractical procedure for routine application, but it could be a starting point for the development of better and faster methods of recording fingerprints.

The methods of classifying fingerprints and filing them, as well as the details of print structure, are discussed extensively in the references listed at the end of this chapter.

LATENT PRINTS

A fingerprint card in a file is nothing more than excess baggage unless the person whose prints were recorded on that card must be identified because he has become an unidentified body, or because he has left latent prints at the scene of a crime or accident. Contact of any part of the body with a surface results in the transfer of certain materials from the skin to that surface. If this skin is ridged, as is that of fingertips, palms, and feet, a pattern that makes an identification possible is left in the transferred material. Such prints are termed *latent prints* because their visibility is low unless they are developed. Many special types of print, other than the ordinary latent type, are encountered and will be discussed in later sections.

Development of Latent Prints (General)

It has been pointed out that much more detail exists in every print than is ordinarily developed. The reason for this is obvious. Nearly all latent prints (except those on paper) are developed by the use of powders, and the powder adhering on top of the print actually covers and obscures fine detail while it develops only the grosser features. This matter has been well discussed by MacDonell (private communication), who emphasizes the superiority of any kind of gas or vapor that will produce the desired effect over any solid material such as powder. One inherent defect of powders is their tendency to "paint," or fill in spaces between the ridges. This is only in part a function of the powder used; it is also related to the effect of the bristles of the brush with which the powder is applied and to the skill of the person handling the brush. MacDonell's "MAGNA Brush" (Laboratory of Forensic Science, Box 1111, Corning, N.Y. 14830), which has no bristles, is often effective in avoiding this problem. It is less satisfactory than the conventional brush on some old prints, which require that the powder be "worked in" before it will adhere satisfactorily. An ideal procedure for general development of latent prints is not yet available, and when it is devised it is likely to be some kind of fuming or spraying method, rather than one employing powder.

Photographing the latent print is always recommended when the undeveloped print is quite visible. No developed print can reveal the fine detail that is present in the undeveloped latent, and these fine details can often be captured by good photography. There are few latent prints that are not actually visible unless properly illuminated; and if proper illumination makes them visible, it also makes them subject to photographic recording. Although more time and effort are probably expended in a very careful search with flashlight, or other easily controlled light, to locate a print, and to photograph it with proper illumination, the improved results will in many instances justify the trouble. After the print has been photographed, it can be developed with powder, or by any other satisfactory procedure, an insurance against the possibility that the photography may not have been satisfactory.

Visible Prints

Very frequently prints found at a crime scene are quite easily visible, and thus cannot properly be termed "latent." These include actual negative *replica prints* in soft material such as wax, soft paint, cheese, and similar materials that form three-dimensional replicas; prints recorded with *blood*; and prints made by *grease* or other dark contamination on the fingertip. Such prints do not usually require any development and, in fact, few of them are even subject to satisfactory development. They must be carefully photographed, either at exact size (fingerprint camera), or with a ruler included in the picture so that the photographic reproduction may be accurately dimensioned. Such prints will rarely be overlooked because they are generally seen without difficulty. However, because of their special nature they often lead to difficulty either in recording them or interpreting them. If such a print is found on material that can be removed to the laboratory, this should be done. Otherwise, they must be photographically recorded before any alteration whatever is permitted in the environment containing them. Indented replica prints in soft materials may be reproduced by casting, but this procedure should invariably *follow* photography, rather than substitute for it.

Prints in blood are sometimes misinterpreted because of the viscous nature of the blood. As blood clots, its viscosity changes. The blood on the finger that made the print may have been on the ridges if older and tacky; or, if fresh, in the valleys between the ridges. In the latter instance, it is the valleys rather than the ridges that are recorded, and the print must be tone reversed photographically. Although this occurrence is to be expected, instances are known in which it has baffled otherwise skilled fingerprint specialists. Some bloody deposits that showed both effects in the same print have been noted. Such cases require the greatest care in their study and interpretation.

Latent Palm Prints

Despite the concentration of attention upon fingerprints, it is not uncommon for an investigator to locate a print made by some portion of the palm, often not accompanied by a usable fingerprint. Such prints are just as valuable as fingerprints, and may be even more so, provided that standard prints can be obtained. They will not be found in available fingerprint files; so a suspect must be located and his palm prints recorded. The possibility of identification in such an instance may be even better than with a fingerprint because of the greater complexity of the palm markings combined with just as high a degree of individuality.

In the examination of palm prints, the major problem is the orientation of the latent print with the proper portion of the standard palm print. In addition to friction ridges the standard palm print contains a large number of characteristic major flexure creases (folds) some of which may be present in the print and will assist greatly in this phase of the comparison. Unfortunately, total palm prints are rarely encountered. Were they as common as fingerprints, it is likely that they would have been utilized instead of the latter for record files and for general identification of individuals. The fragmentary palm prints that are available from time to time are usually treated in exactly the same way as are fingerprints, i.e. by examination for individual points of identity such as bifurcations, ending ridges, and similar features. In the event that the print is relatively complete, fold lines may also be used, along with scars and other individual characteristics.

Development by Powders

The method most commonly employed for the development of latent prints depends upon powders that, when brushed on the print, adhere to the oil deposited upon areas contacted by the friction ridges. Although many powdered materials will adhere, not all are suitable for use. In selecting a powder, the following should be considered: *First*, the powder should show a strong contrast to the background so that the powdered print may be effectively photographed. On a dark surface a gray or white powder is used, whereas on a light surface a black powder is to be preferred. *Second*, but more important, is the adhesive character of the powder. This property varies greatly among the many powders commercially available. Other things being equal, the best powder is one that adheres firmly to the grease of the print and is readily brushed from the interstices between the imprints of the ridges. Some powders show good adhesion but little differential effect, sticking not only to the ridge marks but also to the intermediate spaces. Aluminum powder, which is the base most commonly used for gray powders, is one of the materials that sticks indiscriminately to surfaces of nearly all kinds, to produce the effect known as *painting*. Thus aluminum powder must be mixed with some material that possesses a high adhesion differential. One of the common gray powders, called "chalk and mercury" though it sometimes contains neither chalk nor mercury, is among the more satisfactory types of powder, but it often exhibits some painting also. Mercury poisoning has been caused by this powder and as a result its use is diminishing.

Black powders, usually based upon carbon black as their main constituent, show considerable variations in adhesion properties. Here also the adhesion is governed by materials other than the carbon itself. With both the gray and the black powders the components and formulas are often trade secrets, and few if any of the commercial powders are uniformly useful and reliable. For this reason the experienced fingerprint expert may, according to the conditions of the investigation and his own experience, use a variety of powders, and may frequently disagree with others as to the best powder to use.

Fingerprints are occasionally developed by means of colored, luminescent, or fluorescent powders. So many formulas are available that the experience and personal preference of the investigator will be the determining factors in his choice. For example, the so-called "dragon's blood," a resinous powder of vegetable origin, was for a time popular, particularly for use on papers. It appears to be used little at present. Its advantage was supposed to reside in the fact that after dusting the print with this powder one could melt it with a little heat and achieve an effect similar to printing. The material works well with fresh prints, but not with older ones.

It is possible by means of a luminescent powder to make the powder its own illuminator in recording the print on photographic paper. The powder contains luminescent salts mixed with conditioning agents. After dusting a print with the powder it is exposed to strong light that will cause it to glow spontaneously. A piece of enlarging paper pressed tightly against the print will record a very fair negative picture without the use of a camera.

Development by Fuming

Any material whose fumes are preferentially absorbed by either oils or by the uncoated portion of the supporting surface might be employed to develop a latent fingerprint. Iodine fumes are differentially retained by the oils of the finger; hence the use of an iodine fuming device is one of the very best methods of locating reasonably fresh latent prints. It is less suitable for their recording because the evanescence of the fumes results in rapid fading. Use of iodine fuming for the discovery of fingerprints does not, however, generally interfere with their subsequent development by other methods. A print developed by iodine vapor is of a yellow-brown color, so this fuming method will not work equally well on all surfaces. Dark backgrounds, and especially brown surfaces, tend to obscure such a print. White paper in particular, and light surfaces in general are most effectively explored by this method. If the print is to be recorded, a camera must be ready to photograph it immediately. Breathing on iodine-fumed prints on paper will usually cause them to darken from a reaction between the iodine and the starch sizing in the paper. Such prints are quite permanent compared to those not so treated. Old prints are not readily developed by iodine fuming.

Development with Silver Nitrate

After a fingerprint has been placed, the grease and moisture will dissipate with the passage of time, but the salt from the perspiration persists indefinitely and will be as concentrated in an old as in a fresh print. If the chloride of the salt is reacted with a soluble sliver salt to form insoluble silver chloride, one of the light-sensitive components of photographic film and paper, the print can be developed just as a picture is, and will give a permanent black-and-white record. Alternatively, some investigators prefer to allow the print to blacken under the influence of light only. Several techniques are available for this process. Old prints on paper may often be developed by means of silver only, because everything has been lost from the print except the salt. It is not simple to apply the silver nitrate method to many types of surfaces, and it should ordinarily be employed only after other methods have been tried without success.

Development with Ninhydrin

The ninhydrin method of developing fingerprints has been used almost exclusively for prints on paper, for which it is well adapted. The reagent is sprayed in a fine mist on the marked surface. After a lapse of several hours the developed print will become a clearly visible red-violet. The reaction is very sensitive, gives good detail, and may be hastened by the application of heat. This is a method for laboratory application; it is not adaptable for use in the field. The prints developed by this technique are permanent.

Development with Osmic Acid

The osmic acid method is also a laboratory procedure totally unsuited to field use. The material to be tested, usually paper, is placed in a sealed container in which fumes of osmic acid (very poisonous) are present, and allowed to stand. After some hours, depending upon the concentration of the vapor, the fingerprint will develop as a strong black print that is permanent. In addition to the good quality of the print obtained, the method affords a marked advantage when a number of papers must be searched for invisible fingerprints. All papers can be placed in one container, and any prints that are present will be developed simultaneously.

Lifting of Prints

By lifting a print is meant the transfer of a reproduction or facsimile of the print from the surface on which it is found to a medium suitable for comparison and study. Photographing a fingerprint is one form of lifting it: the photographed print exists in reproduction as a picture. The more common usage of the term refers to the physical removal of fingerprint powder dusted on the print. This is a relatively simple matter of procuring a broad adhesive tape similar to Scotch tape, touching one end of it to the surface not covered by the dusted print, and lowering the tape from this anchorage so that it covers the print smoothly. The tape is then stroked down uniformly on the dusted print, after which it is carefully pulled loose from one end. The dust will be retained on the sticky surface of the tape without distortion or damage. The tape can then be placed on a paper or glass surface (preferably the latter) so that it is available for photography or for direct examination. Sometimes the end of the tape is folded over the lifted print to enclose the powder between two layers of tape. This procedure may lead to difficulty in the form of folds or smears, and is generally not recommended except as an emergency measure. Even if the original print has been photographed prior to dusting, it is well to photograph it after dusting and before lifting. A valuable (and often omitted) precaution at this stage is the securing of a second photograph, one taken from a distance to show the location of the print in the environment and its relation to other objects. Without this photograph, the fingerprint technician may be unable to give the original position of the print when he ultimately testifies regarding it. Such a photograph is also of great utility to a jury whose members wish to know not only the identity of the print, but also exactly where the print was found.

Although lifting tape is ordinarily used for lifting the developed fingerprint, other methods have been recommended. Perhaps the most valuable of these is the use of a nylon aerosol spray, identified as Arcote.* This material may be sprayed on irregular and curved surfaces; it is quickly applied, and it presents none of the difficulties encountered with tape, such as folding or adhering accidentally to undesired objects. Because the dried aerosol film is very thin and may be difficult to remove otherwise, the print is outlined with masking tape placed as close to the margins of the print as possible. The aerosol is sprayed on uniformly to form a reasonably thick coat that first appears white, but changes to a bluish or gray tint on drying, which requires about ten minutes. The print is lifted by means of the masking tape, which frames and reinforces it, and is transferred, with careful flattening, to a stiff white card.

COMPARISON OF PRINTS

The most critical portion of the fingerprint study is the comparison of a latent print, located at a point of interest, with standard prints from a file or elsewhere. This task is usually the responsibility of an identification officer, but in difficult cases the comparisons will frequently be made by laboratory personnel. In addition to locating a similar known print of a reasonable suspect, which may in some instances be an almost insurmountable problem, the sources of difficulty are as follows:

(1) Distortion of the latent print (sometimes of the standard as well) due to the manner of its being placed on the surface. The flesh of the fingertip or palm is very pliable, and can be forced into irregular forms, especially under the conditions of physical activity characteristic of burglary operations, for example. Curved and irregular surfaces may cause quite irregular distortion also.

(2) The fragmental character of the latent print, which may vary from a mere speck up to a virtually complete impression. The smaller the fragment, the more difficult will be the task of finding its counterpart on a standard. Even more critical sometimes is the fact that the latent fragmental print may have come from an unfavorable portion of the finger, so that it does not show a delta or a core, or any other readily identified point of reference.

(3) The almost invariably present smearing or smudging of at least a portion of the available latent. The smudges often cover important features of the print, and in extreme instances the entire print is smeared and is therefore useless for purposes of comparison.

(4) Orientation of the latent with respect to the standard. To a degree, this problem is similar to (1) in that an undistorted print will be far more easily

---

* Arcote is a product of Atlantic Research Co., Alexandria, Virginia.

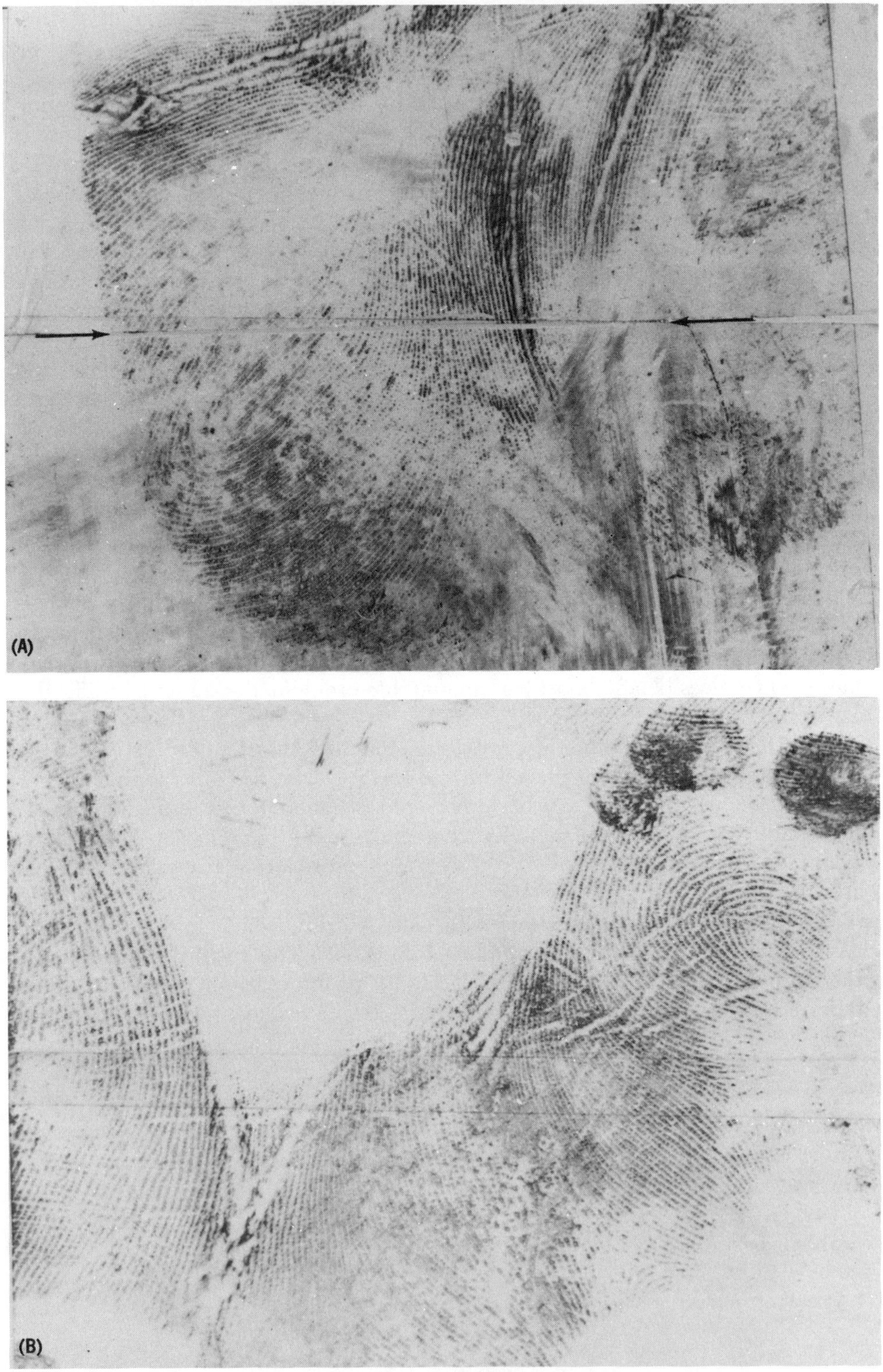

FIGURE 6-1. A common error that is made when lifting palmprints is that the overlapping edges of the tape are not firmly pressed onto the dusted print, creating a discontinuity in the lift (A). Correctly lifted print (B).

Fingerprints

oriented than a distorted one. Orientation is generally much more difficult with palm prints than with fingerprints because of the larger area and greater variation in direction of the friction ridges.

(5) Magnification, which is always necessary for a fine comparison. Some workers prefer to use a pair of fingerprint magnifiers with the original lifts or photographs printed at a one-to-one scale; others prefer to magnify photographically to equal enlargement and study the enlargements visually. The latter method may be limited by the quality of the photography, but should present no problems when the photography is properly done.

The *points of comparison* are features that are subject to easy recognition. Naturally, the first of these would be the general pattern and its configuration. Distortion and other factors may make this the poorest of the various features. Actually, the overall pattern is more useful for orientation than for identification. The best features are (1) ridge endings; (2) forks, or bifurcations; (3) short ridges; (4) enclosures; and (5) islands, and these are related to cores or deltas when the latter features are present. A number of accidental characteristics are also useful when present, e.g. scars, folds, or other irregularities that are not a part of the ridge pattern itself. In dusted prints it is not always simple to recognize a feature, e.g. a ridge ending, but tracing the edges on both sides of a doubtful area will generally guide the judgment. Even a bifurcation may be mistaken as a double ridge ending if the connection was not properly developed. Skilled and experienced fingerprint personnel will not often be disturbed by such difficulties, but the beginner may find them quite baffling.

Each verifiable feature that agrees in location on two prints being compared is referred to as a point. Each such point contributes some probability to an identity of origin. Clearly one point, or a few, falls far short of indicating identical origin. In this country it is customary to require more than seven or eight points of identity before an identical source can be claimed. In some other countries, more points of identity are demanded. The important issue here is that if two good prints are being compared, the number of points will generally be much greater than the minimum, but with a small latent, the total number of conventional points present may be less. The smaller number of points will limit the value of the identification of sources by making it a little less probable than can be accepted as virtual certainty. If only six points were present in the latent, and all agreed, it would still be valuable evidence, but if only six points out of a possible twelve or more that could be seen were in agreement, it would be very dubious evidence. Also, although no two prints have thus far been found to be identical except when they came from the same source, this does not mean that no second person with an identical print could be found on earth. Statistical calculations indicate a finite probability that, with twelve points, there could be a number of such individuals. On the other hand, it must be realized that we are speaking of conventional points of comparison,

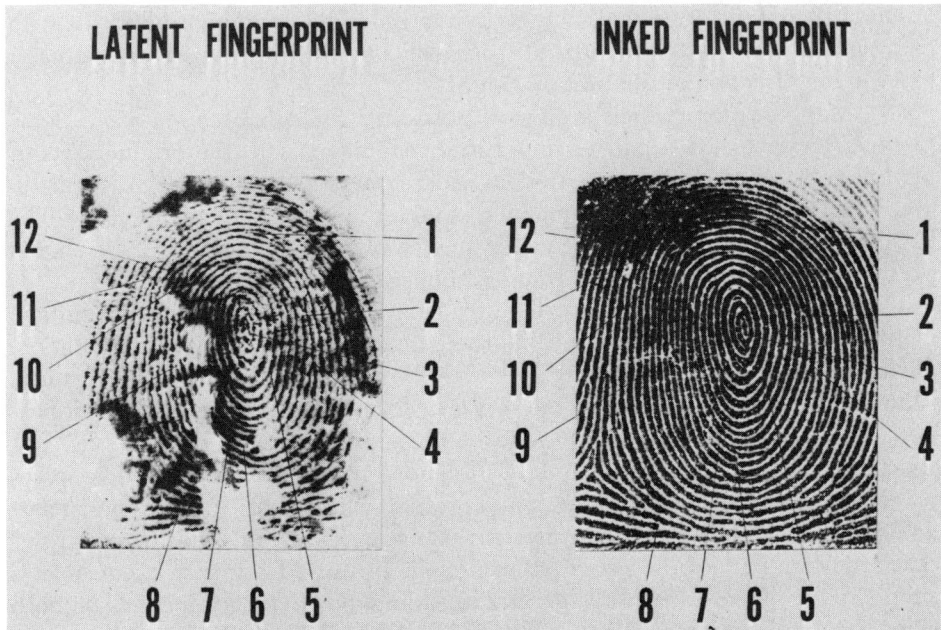

FIGURE 6-2. Fingerprint Comparison. (Courtesy of the Contra Costa County Criminalistics Laboratory.)

not of all of the much finer detail of pores, etc., that would undoubtedly individualize the print. Such detail is not likely to be present in the practical situation because of the less-than-perfect methods which must be used at this time.

COMPUTERIZATION OF PRINTS

Because fingerprints are patterns that are subject to treatment by the computer, and also because dealing with prints by visual and manual methods is very laborious, there has been in recent years a very considerable effort to place the whole subject on a basis that can be handled by the computer. Portions of this program have been highly successful, and other portions have achieved enough success to indicate that ultimately, and perhaps soon, the entire scheme of filing, searching, and comparison operations may be carried out by the computer, with a vast saving of manpower and a corresponding achievement in rapidly available results. There are few if any general operations of the crime investigator in which this result is more desirable.

The computer can store almost unlimited numbers of facsimile prints, and relate them to the personal biographies and characteristics of their makers. It can very rapidly search such a file and bring forth the information stored, and then transmit it to the interested person, even at a great distance. It can read a print, and perhaps classify it in a computer system, rather than in the Henry system. In theory at least, and perhaps in practice, it can compare such a print with a questioned print for purposes of identification. This last step is highly doubtful at this writing, but it is to be expected as a practical matter in time. The computer's difficulties with fragmental latent prints will be similar to those of the fingerprint examiner, and for largely the same basic reasons. The computer can even be designed to read and record the print directly from the finger, although it is not known to this author that this development has yet been made. For economic and other reasons it is not likely that the computer will make the fingerprint technician obsolete in the near future. The expensive facilities required for all of the functions listed will necessarily be limited to main centers, and will not be available to the small police department that must fingerprint an occasional suspect.

REFERENCES

Cummins, H., and Midlo, C.: *Finger Prints, Palms and Soles.* New York: Dover (1961).
Federal Bureau of Investigation: *The Science of Fingerprints,* U.S. Government Printing Office, Washington, D.C.: (1963).
Field, A. T.: *Fingerprint Handbook.* Springfield: Thomas (1971).
Galton, F.: *Fingerprints* (reprod. of 1892 ed.). New York: Da Capo (1966).
Moenssens, A.: *Fingerprints and the Law.* Philadelphia: Chilton (1969).
Moenssens, A.: *Fingerprint Techniques.* Philadelphia: Chilton (1971).
Scott, W. R.: *Fingerprint Mechanics: Fingerprints from Crime Scene to Courtroom.* Springfield: Thomas (1951).
Svensson, A., and Wendel, O.: *Techniques of Crime Scene Investigation,* 2nd American ed. New York: American Elsevier (1965).

7
Tracks and Trails

Included among the important varieties of physical evidence are miscellaneous characteristic markings such as shoeprints, footprints, tire-tread impressions, and traces left by dragged or dropped objects and retained in soil or some other medium. Probably shoeprints and tire tracks are most frequently encountered, and the techniques employed in their study are usually applicable to other similar types of marking.

SHOEPRINTS

Shoeprints are found in two forms: *impression prints* in mud, sand, mortar, or other soft material, and *residue prints* made on solid surfaces by dust, mud, flour, blood, or similar media.

Impression Prints

Impression prints, such as a shoeprint in soft earth, wet sand, or a similar material that can record the shape and dimensions of the object that made the print, should first be photographed, if this is possible and practical. A ruler should be placed beside the print so that the exact scale will be recorded in the photograph, and the camera should be aimed directly down on the print to avoid distortion of perspective. Although the photograph of an impression is of value for purposes of record, and even for comparison of detail, it is less useful than is a good cast of the impression.

Casting of shoeprints is ordinarily done with fine plaster of paris mixed to the proper consistency with water and poured carefully into the print so as to disturb it as little as possible yet fill it completely. It is good practice to embed in the wet plaster a piece of medium-mesh wire, such as rabbit or chicken fencing. The wire mesh gives mechanical strength to the cast and minimizes the danger of breakage. After the plaster has solidified, the entire piece is carefully removed from the impression print, and any adhering soil particles are gently removed with a soft brush. A portion of the resulting cast will represent, with a considerable degree of fidelity, the object that made the impression. Though the fine detail of a print may not be completely reproduced by a plaster cast, this defect in the method is rarely serious because the soil itself does not reproduce fine detail even as well as does the plaster.

If, as rarely happens, the detail of the impression is so good as to make possible a cast bearing greater refinement of detail than can be obtained with plaster, *moulage positive material* may be employed. The material is liquefied by heating, then poured into the impression, and a wire screen is inserted immediately to impart strength. The resulting hard cast bears a very detailed reproduction of the impression and represents the object that made it. Moulage *negative* may be used similarly to capture the details of the object that made the impression, and from this the impression itself may be duplicated with moulage positive. Such an impression represents the original print rather than the object that made it. The advantage of using moulage negative rather than the positive lies in the fact that the negative adheres less to the print than does the positive. This advantage is largely offset by the greater amount of labor and time required.

Some experience and judgment on the part of the investigator are necessary to decide manner of treating an impression. If the impression has been satisfactorily photographed before casting, the failure of the cast is less serious. Photographing the impression is an important precaution, because casts do sometimes fail, either because of unfavorable conditions or because of the operator's inexperience. Properly performed casting is almost always successful. For the amateur or the inexperienced investigator plaster casting is recommended because of its comparative simplicity, even though it offers only limited reproduction of fine detail.

EXAMINATION OF CASTS. The cast of a shoe impression is normally compared with the shoe suspected of having made the original impression. If there is an identity, all dimensions, patterns, flaws, irregularities, and other observable features should be in essential agreement between the cast and the shoe. Allowance must be made for abnormalities in the mode of making the track, such as struggling, the carrying of a heavy weight, or the maintenance of balance on a slippery surface. When a considerable amount of time has elapsed before the suspected shoe is obtained, the wear that may have occurred in

FIGURE 7-1. Shoe impressions at the scene of a burglary. The location of impressions on the stairs indicated that at least two individuals were responsible. (Courtesy of John E. Murdock.)

the meantime must be taken into account. It is important to remember that there may be a relatively large number of shoes of the same or similar size and shape that have in common the same type of rubber heels, or other similarities. Thus, a general similarity, although useful in the sense of probability, is insufficient for the establishment of identity. The nature of class characteristics of the sole must also be understood.

The probability is low that two similar shoes will be worn in exactly the same pattern, or damaged at the same points to the same extent and in the same way. Thus, the comparison of such irregular features is much more significant than the comparison of size, shape, and pattern alone, though these also must correspond. Naturally, all observable features must show the degree of similarity that would be expected under the circumstances before an identity can be claimed. In some cases it will be impossible to state positively that a certain shoe made the questioned print, but it may still be said that the particular shoe could have made it, i.e., it cannot be excluded. Such evidence may be quite helpful when properly supported by other facts that point in the

IMPRESSIONS IN SOIL

FROM FLOOR OF SUSPECTS' VEHICLE

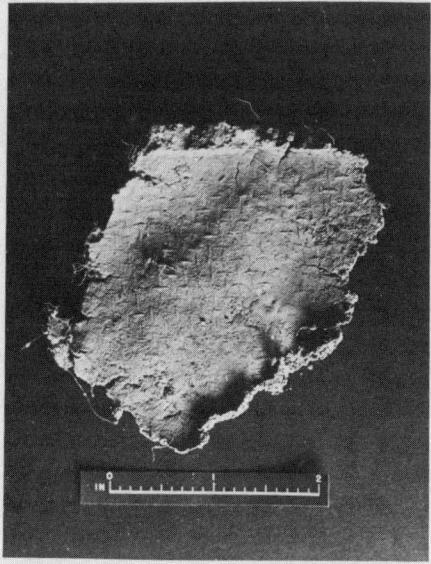

FOUND IN PATIO OF MODEL HOME NO. 240

FIGURE 7-2. Shoe casts in mud. A muddy shoe may leave a trail of mud cast fragments, at times allowing a suspect to be associated with a crime scene. (Courtesy of Stephen P. McJunkins.)

same direction. Unsupported, it is valueless. This conclusion will usually follow when the print itself is not clear.

Comparison of the features of the cast with those of the original object is usually facilitated by means of enlarged photographs. These must be made to the same magnification, as can readily be accomplished by photographing a ruler with each of the objects to be compared.

Residue Prints

Prints made in dust, or deposited by a shoe or other object in the form of blood, grease, or other residue on the shoe, can be well reproduced by photography alone. Before the print is photographed, a ruler should be placed beside it and the lighting adjusted to intensify the print's details. To avoid distortion, the camera should be aligned perpendicularly to the plane of the printed surface. Here it is the print itself that is subjected to comparison, rather than a duplicate of the object that made it. For this reason the direct comparison with a suspected object is made with some difficulty because one is the mirror image of the other. If feasible, a comparison print should be made from the suspected shoe or other object in a manner that repeats, as nearly as possible, the action that was accompanied by the depositing of the questioned print. This may necessitate the exercise of ingenuity, as it is not always practical to use the same material or the same method of application that gave rise to the questioned print.

If possible, the standard print should be made with the same material as the questioned print and on the same type of surface. When this is done, the resulting photographs exhibit the greatest similarity of appearance. A piece of plate glass is useful as a surface on which to deposit the standard print, because it is smooth and firm, and it contributes no distracting background to the photographs.

Residue footprints are often found at the scene of a safe burglary. If, in gaining entry to the safe, the burglar penetrates its insulation, he can scarcely avoid walking in the insulation and leaving dust prints wherever he walks. *Investigators must be very careful not to destroy such prints* by walking on them when entering the premises. The prints are not always conspicuous, and a special search for them should precede any activity that may disturb the scene. When good prints are present, they may well be the most important evidence located, because it is often possible to make very reliable identification of the shoes that made the prints.

Lifting has been highly successful in developing and preserving dust prints. A flexible black plastic sheet, which is commercially available, is carefully placed on the dust print. When the plastic is lifted, the dust will adhere to it, leaving an excellent, finely detailed print that may be photographed. A second

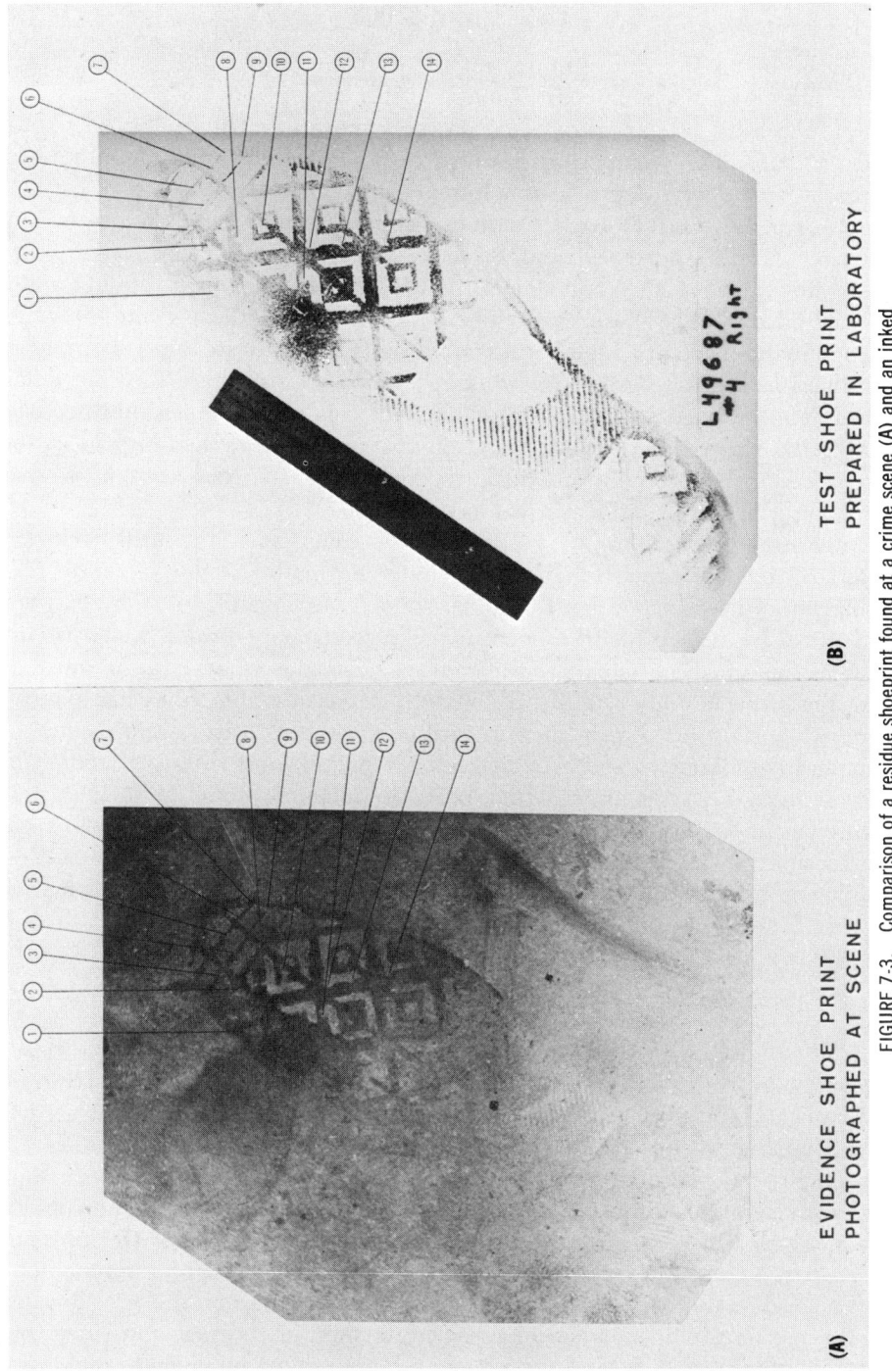

FIGURE 7-3. Comparison of a residue shoeprint found at a crime scene (A) and an inked impression of the suspect's shoe (B). (Courtesy of Stephen M. Ojena.)

lift may be taken from the same print for even better detail, because it will pick up finer dust after the coarser material has been removed by the first lift. Several successive lifts are possible from the same print. The quality of photographs of such lifts is superior, because dust adhering to the smooth black surface provides good contrast for photography.

Casts of residue prints are sometimes possible to make and to use advantageously. For this purpose moulage negative is preferable to plaster. Some investigators have used Wood's metal, which may be melted in boiling water and applied directly. These casts, when successfully made, are probably the best obtainable. Wood's metal is extraordinarily difficult to apply because it crystallizes in a coarse granular structure, which may obscure the fine detail desired. The most successful casts made with this material are produced by spraying the superheated liquid metal on the surface after heating the latter. This procedure is often impractical, especially for an item such as a shoe impression. With rigid surfaces it works very well.

Comparison of photographs of prints, lifts, casts, and standards is implemented by enlargements, all of which must be made to the same ratio of magnification. Dimensions must be in reasonable agreement, but they may not be identical by reason of difference in the placement of prints. Patterns produced in manufacture must naturally agree, and the wear pattern must be either the same or only slightly different if a considerable time has elapsed during which the shoe has been worn. All cuts, gouges, and abrasions must be noted and compared as to their character, location, and distance from each other. It must be remembered that positive indications are most important because the shoe may receive additional damage in wear after the crime has been committed. Some markings that do not agree are of less significance than a similar number that do agree, and a conservative and thorough examination will very frequently yield a definite decision as to the identity.

TIRE TREADS

The common use of the automobile in the commission of crime, in the disposal of dead bodies, and in similar activities, makes very important the study of tire treads and their tracks. From a technical standpoint, the treatment of such marks is analogous to that of footprints, involving either photography alone, or photography in combination with casting, usually with plaster. *Fine detail is usually not as important with a tire tread as it is with footprints.* The traction surface of the tire is so large by comparison that the portion of the tire that made a particular mark cannot usually be determined. The circumference of a tire is a good many feet, and damage may occur anywhere on the tire. Because damage markings wil be useful in the identification of the tire, and since they cannot be predicted as to position, special attention must be given to making as complete a cast as possible.

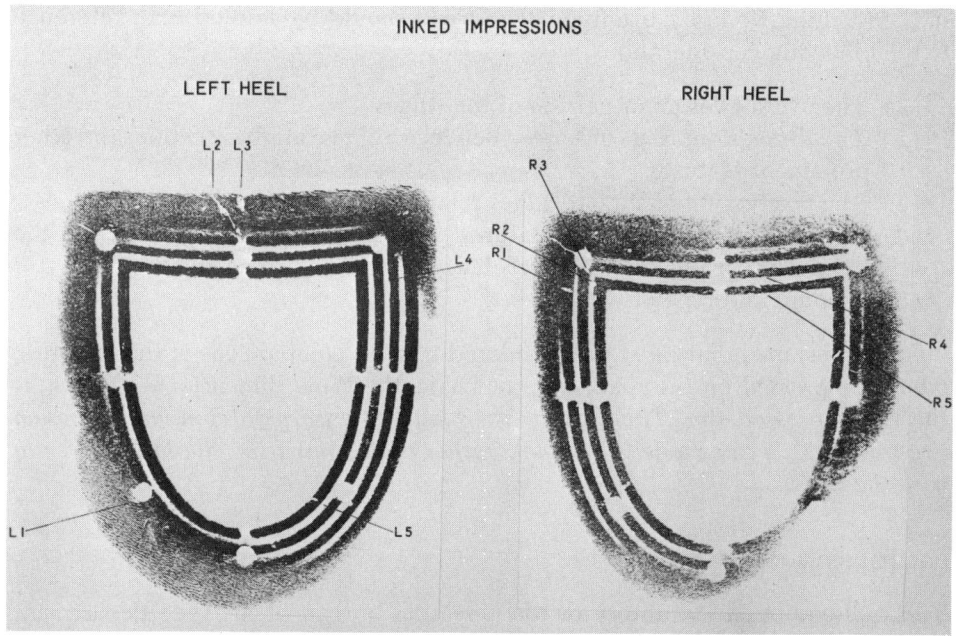

FIGURE 7-4. Inked impressions of a pair of shoes showing irregularities due to wear and damage. (Courtesy of Stephen P. McJunkins.)

In unusual circumstances, a characteristic of a tire, such as an inserted section or patch, or a peculiar injury to the tire, may be noted. When this occurs, the identification of the tire may often be made with a very high degree of certainty. In the ordinary case no such feature will be present, and only the general nature of the tire will be determinable. Because there are four tires on an automobile, there may be as many as four different tread patterns present, arranged in an observable pattern. It is sometimes possible to identify a particular car with considerable certainty from this factor alone.

Tread Characteristics

The characteristics of tire treads are altered frequently, and over a period of time they may be changed radically. At the present time, most tires have a series of parallel zigzag ridges, the zigzag pattern itself not being very characteristic of the make. However, the widths of the ridges and the trenches between the ridges differ among the various brands. The ratio of the length of a section of the pattern to its width may vary, and the degree of parallelism of the ridges may differ markedly. Moreover, in some tires the ridges are wholly or partially cut transversely in order to improve the grip on a smooth roadway, and others have holes designed to create a partial vacuum effect when compressed against the surface of the street. All these features are useful in the identification of a tire tread. The tread should be studied with reference to the following considerations:

(1) The overall design or pattern of the ridges
(2) The dimensions, e.g. distances between ridges, angles, sections, or other prominent features
(3) The positioning of similar ridges relative to each other
(4) Unusual and distinctive features, whether originally present in the tread itself or put there as a result of repair, wear, or accident
(5) Amount and type of wear

A circumstance that must be considered in such comparisons is that the tire, when compressed on the road, does not have the same dimensional pattern as the uncompressed tire. *Therefore it is usually necessary to compare a known tire track with a questioned tire track, rather than comparing the latter directly with the tire.*

COMPARISON STANDARDS

The well-equipped laboratory or identification bureau of a police department should have on hand a collection of common tire treads representative of tires in current use. This collection must be continuously revised to eliminate obsolete treads and to include new designs as they are produced.

The same considerations apply to other materials, such as rubber heels,

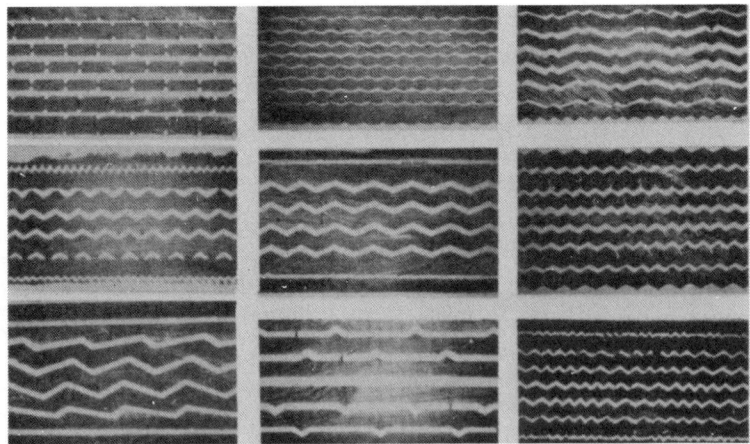

FIGURE 7-5. Some tire treads, illustrating marked individuality of similar patterns: left to right, (upper) U. S. Royal, Dunlop, Pacific Cushion; (middle) Goodyear, Savoy Master, Firestone; (lower) General, Firestone, Pacific.

which may readily be collected and are very useful when footprints are discovered in criminal investigation. The problem of dealing with tracks of the common types is relatively simple when its principles and limitations are understood. The competent identification officer may readily train himself to become expert in this field, and only rarely will the more highly skilled laboratory investigator be required.

MISCELLANEOUS TRACKS

Tire treads of bicycles, wagons, and other vehicles may occasionally require investigation. They are studied in essentially the same manner as other tracks. Animal tracks are encountered infrequently in all but exceptional investigations. Considerable specialized knowledge of such tracks would be necessary in order to attain the status of an expert. Cattle and horse tracks are the most common animal tracks encountered in criminal investigation, and both are readily identified from their character and size. The relatively large cloven hoof of the cow leaves a track that is easily distinguished from the tracks of the smaller cloven hooves of sheep or swine. The horse, with a rather large solid hoof, usually shod, leaves a track that is also readily distinguished. Much can be deduced by examination of the shoe marks, and such variables as limping of the horse, speed, and even the load can be estimated by those experienced in the field.

TRAILS

A trail is distinguished from a track by its continuity: it is made up of a series of tracks. Interpretation and following of trails can be of the greatest importance in open country and in regions of very sparse population. It is of little importance where the police problems are most critical, viz., in more or less urban districts where the greatest percentage of crimes occur. For this reason, it is of limited interest to law-enforcement officers in this country.

Experienced trailers can tell a great deal of the stature, the load carried, and unusual features of the person who has left a particular trail. Although the field is specialized and somewhat unusual, the keen but untrained observer with good judgment may obtain considerable information from examining a trail. For example, a man carrying a heavy load will sink into the earth to more than the usual depth; his steps will be shorter than normal, and he may stagger, or stop for rest. A large man will ordinarily have a larger foot than a smaller man, and he may or may not make a deeper impression because of this fact. The length of the walking stride will tell much about the length of leg, and consequently the height, of the author of the tracks. A walking man normally applies the impact of the stride to his heels, thus making their marks noticeably prominent. A running man, on the contrary, makes a different kind of trail in which the toe trends are more pronounced. The heel impression of the runner is likely to be at an angle because his feet strike the ground differently. The toes push the soil backward in running much more than in walking. The tread of a man struggling either with another individual or in the effort to move a heavy or obstinate object, such as a heavy load or a stuck window, will show shoe-scrapes in the soil, double prints, and other distortions of ordinary tracks. Careful study may reveal an indefinite number of conclusions when a trail is properly analyzed.

Unusual but significant circumstances arise at times in the examination of trails and tracks. In one instance a burglar, operating barefooted, walked through wet grass and then on a sidewalk. The humidity being high, the wet tracks and the trail they made on the sidewalk were still clearly visible when the police arrived. By photographing the trail, measuring the length of stride, size of foot, and similar factors, a reasonably good determination of the stature of the man, as well as his walking habit, was derived. In this instance speed was of the essence, because the wet foot tracks were far from permanent, and they were not subject to casting, lifting, or other conventional methods, except photography.

Properly interpreted, both tracks and trails can yield a great deal of information other than the identity of the person who made them. The latter point, however, is usually most critical in criminal investigation. For this reason, mastery of photography and of casting is essential in dealing with all kinds of tracks, traces, and trails.

REFERENCES

Abbott, J. R., and Germann, A. C.: *Footwear Evidence*. Springfield: Thomas (1964).
Chavigny, M.: "Tracks of Vehicles," *Am. J. Police Sci.* 1:156 (1930).
Gross, H.: *Criminal Investigation,* 5th ed. Edited by R. L. Jackson. Toronto: Carswell (1962).
Gupta, S. R.: "Footprint and Shoeprint Identification," *Intern. Crim. Pol. Rev.* 205:55 (1967).
Joling, R. J.: "Shoeprints: Quantum of Proof," *J. For. Sci.* 13:223 (1968).
Puri, D. K. S.: "Footprints," *Intern. Crim. Pol. Rev.* 187:106 (1965).
Tiller, C. D.: "Examination of Footprints at Crime Scenes," *RCMP Gazette* 24:12 (1962).

8
Photography

No technique is more valuable to the police officer or the laboratory criminalist than photography, and in an ideal system, every investigator would possess considerable photographic facility. There are many extensive and complete texts dealing with the subject, some of which are listed at the end of this chapter. Some deal with theory and advanced technique; others with routine operation and especially with darkroom procedures. Texts of both types should be consulted by the student of photography, because neither aspect will receive extensive treatment here. This chapter is designed to be of use to the investigator who needs to learn the fundamentals of the field and how to apply them to the highly specialized areas of crime-scene investigation and, to some extent, evidence photography. Both areas have features that demand special techniques not ordinarily used in conventional photography, and these features are not always understood, even by experienced photographers.

PHOTOGRAPHY AND THE POLICE

Police photography consists largely of the recording of crime and accident scenes and is customarily carried out by a police photographer who is specialized in such work. Because he is rarely with the first officer on the scene, he may miss recording the original appearance of the scene. It will not long remain as it was at the time of the crime, because of the invasion by the curious, the press, and various official personnel who have little interest in the photographic record. Ambulance attendants, for example, often effectively destroy a crime scene. In order to preserve evidence, then, the first officer on the scene should photograph it, and the investigating officer should use his authority to control or restrict both the intrusion of unauthorized persons and the movement of authorized persons within the scene. Likewise, when fires occur, the earliest official personnel present are in the best position to see and record the fire in its early and most critical stages.

In response to this obvious need, great interest has developed in immediate photography at the crime or fire scene, and there has been a tendency to utilize inexpensive, automatic cameras, e.g. the Instamatic and its imitators. Unfortunately, this has sometimes been done in lieu of giving limited basic instruction in photography to the officers concerned. It may be stated as a valid generalization that *almost any photograph taken before a scene is disturbed is better than no photograph at this stage.* Thus, there is some logic to this growing practice. On the other hand, even the Instamatic type of camera will generally fail in the hands of a person who has no grasp of the fundamentals of photography; and if the least expensive cameras (for example, those equipped with plastic lenses and automatic in only a few features) are employed, the best that can be hoped for is an inferior result. Despite all claims to the contrary, every camera has limitations, and some compromise must be made between those with unacceptable limitations and the high-priced instruments with fewer drawbacks. The police administration will profit by the upgrading of equipment, and even more by improvement in photographic skills on the part of its officers. Small departments lacking a photographic unit may have among their personnel an individual for whom photography has special interest, or who is already an amateur photographer. Official support of the skill, knowledge, or interest of this person is an excellent investment.

It is to be hoped that ultimately every police unit will have photographic equipment available at all times, in addition to at least minimal skill in its utilization. Of course, under operating conditions, not every crime or accident scene can be photographed immediately on discovery, because of other more pressing duties of the police. But many opportunities are missed because the police are not conscious of the possibilities and the advantages of early photographic recording. The California Highway Patrol, for instance, photographs a high percentage of its accident cases under quite adverse conditions and with generally excellent results. Highway accident scenes certainly present as great a challenge to the officers as would any other type of crime scene. Hence, this accomplishment of the California Highway Patrol demonstrates the results that may be achieved when the officers are conscious of the service they can contribute.

THE CAMERA

Essentially, the camera is merely a light-tight box containing a lens for producing an image, and a holder for film or plate on which the image is focused. All the other accessories are for adjustment to produce sharp focus, to control the amount of light admitted, to change the depth of focus, and to increase the speed and convenience of operation. It is these accessories that increase the cost of the camera, which in its simple form is inherently inexpensive (with the exception of the lens, which will vary greatly in price and performance).

Automatic Cameras

The seasoned photographer generally prefers to adjust his camera to the optimum setting for the subject and the conditions. This takes both time and skill. If these are not available, an automatic camera will substitute. The word "automatic" is often a misnomer; many such cameras require matching of needles or other manual adjustment, and others require that one parameter be determined by the operator, e.g. a shutter speed. Most also require a setting of the ASA number to match the film speed. At least one camera on the market accomplishes all of these things automatically, will use flash if required, not firing it when the light is adequate. This camera is also quite inexpensive and could relieve the officer of many small preliminary tasks while making useful photographs fairly certain.

Polaroid Land Cameras

The remarkable picture-in-a-minute Polaroid camera cannot be neglected in this discussion. Its value is enhanced by the fact that it operates both in color and black-and-white. In many respects the Polaroid camera is almost ideal for some types of investigation, where a reasonably good record is essential, and when it is not convenient to wait for darkroom processing. Insurance adjusters, for example, make excellent use of it. For crime-scene and evidence photography it is definitely inferior to conventional cameras, primarily because its format is neither as convenient as the smaller 35mm nor large enough for easy inspection of the resulting photographs. In addition, Polaroid prints are not simple to enlarge or duplicate, except in the 4 × 5-inch format. The extremely high speeds available in black-and-white film recommend the Polaroid camera for poor lighting conditions. Its use with color film, while also very convenient, only occasionally gives color values as true as are obtained by conventional color photography, in part because field conditions are not so susceptible to reliable control as are darkroom conditions. The Land process is relatively expensive although this expense is far outweighed by the cost of establishing a darkroom where there is none initially available. However, a darkroom is a virtual necessity to the criminalist, for other uses as well as for making routine photographs, so its avoidance by using Polaroid is not an actual economy. Laboratory use of Polaroid is probably much more advantageous than field utilization, because of the many more-specialized needs of laboratory photography. It is certain, however, that Polaroid has made significant contributions to field photography, and has a definite future in that area.

The Lens

Although often taken for granted, the lens not only is the most important unit of the camera, but also it influences the quality of the photograph more than do all other components combined. The reason that lenses are often taken for granted is that, in this age, excellent lenses are the rule rather than the exception. This was not generally true until the German lens makers achieved excellent lens combinations; and now the Japanese have produced glass even better adapted to fine lenses than had been available previously. Other countries, including France and the United States, also produce fine lenses. Unfortunately, the effort to produce low-priced cameras has caused a cheapening in lens quality in some quarters; the best lenses are usually found in the more expensive cameras, although even the cheaper ones are quite capable of producing acceptable photographs.

The simple lens consists only of a biconvex piece of glass or plastic that bends light rays and converges them into a plane of focus, thus producing an image of the object viewed by the lens. This lens suffers from both spherical and chromatic aberration, and its converging power is limited. To eliminate these inherent errors, a number of additional elements must also be included. These are often biconcave elements of glass differing from the main elements in refractive index and dispersion. Lens formulation today is a highly complex technology, which has made possible the general excellence of lenses on most cameras.

The investigator needs to know that no lens equally suited to all uses and conditions can ever be constructed. Because of this fact, innumerable specialized lenses have been designed for specific uses, and the competent photographer will not depend on a single lens for all situations. Some of the variations in lenses, with their specific applications, are as follows:

(1) *Normal lenses*, defined as general-purpose lenses for ordinary photography, are standard equipment on most cameras. Although more technical definitions of normal lenses are available, such lenses may be thought of as having focal lengths so chosen that the photograph approximates the field of clear normal vision of the unmoving eye. In all instances, the image will be greatly reduced as compared with the object photographed, and will be in accord with the rule relating to focal length mentioned below.

(2) *Process and macro lenses* are corrected for close-up photography in which the image size on the negative is approximately the same as the object photographed. This is referred to as one-to-one copy and is utilized largely for document copying and for some other specialized evidence photography.

(3) *Wide-angle lenses* are designed to encompass a very wide field of view. These lenses are expensive because of their complexity and the high cost of their manufacture and, depending on the type of focusing system, they may be difficult to focus because of their inherent shallow depth of field. However, they are extremely valuable to the photographer who must work in close quarters as, for example, photographing a murder scene in a small basement. Under these circumstances, a normal lens includes only a portion of the scene, and multiple photographs must be overlapped, at the risk of possible confusion.

(4) *Telephoto lenses*, of widely varying focal lengths, are used in taking photographs of relatively distant objects without corresponding reduction in size. The shortest lenses in this category are probably the short-form 80mm to 100mm lenses available for 35mm cameras. The 135mm lens is quite popular because it is not so difficult to hold steady as are lenses with longer focal lengths, and it will photograph most distant objects satisfactorily. The 400mm lens is very large, being effectively a telescope. Both binocular arrangements and telescopes are used for distance photography as well.

(5) *Enlarging lenses* are used for projecting images of negatives to a sheet of enlarging paper in making enlargements. Although any normal lens may be used for this purpose, the method by which they are corrected renders them incapable of transmitting an equivalent amount of light in both directions. Turning a normal lens backward in the mount generally improves its quality if it is to be used as an enlarging lens. The enlarging lens is designed for projecting images at relatively close distances.

(6) *Zoom lenses* are a relatively recent development. The individual lens units are so chosen and mounted that the effective focal length of the lens can be widely altered. Such a lens might cover the range from wide angle to telephoto, although most are better adapted to the telephoto application than to wide-angle use. Thus, the subject may cover all of the negative, or a very small part of it, the magnification being chosen at will. Zoom lenses are especially useful for television. They are also widely employed in movie cameras, and in microscopes of certain types. Despite their enormous versatility, their resolution is generally inferior to that of a good fixed-focal-length lens.

Lenses are also classified in other frames of reference. An *achromatic* lens is one that is corrected for chromatic aberration. An *anastigmat* lens, the most common type of camera lens, being free of astigmatism, is a generally well-corrected lens. A *coated lens* is one in which the lens elements have been coated to suppress internal reflections that reduce contrast and impair the quality of the image. This coating accounts for the yellow-purple tinge noted when the lens is examined by reflected light. Nearly all modern lenses are coated. The lensmaker's art is an impressive one and has made possible the very high quality of most modern cameras.

The most important specific designation of a lens is its *focal length*. This is the distance from the lens to the image when the light entering the lens is parallel, i.e., when the object is at "infinite" distance. The focal length is the basis for classification of a lens as normal, wide angle, or telephoto, when related to the format, or size of film. A lens classified as telephoto for a 35mm camera would be normal, or even wide angle for a larger film size. The general rule for considering a lens as "normal" is that the focal length should be approximately equal to the diagonal of the film to be covered by the image. Thus, a 35mm film would correspond to a normal lens of about 50mm focal length. An 8 × 10-inch film would require a lens 12–14 inches focal length. This does not mean that other than normal-focal-length lenses cannot be used, but different arrangements of mounting will be required, and special purposes will be served.

For optimum results, combined with the type of flexibility that is desirable, the investigator should not rely on a single lens. With such a limitation, his general crime- and accident-scene photography will be excellent until he has to take photographs in an extremely limited space where a wide-angle lens is essential, or until his significant evidence is distant and inaccessible. This situation occurs frequently in both fire and accident photography, for example. With three lenses (a wide angle, a normal, and a telephoto) nearly every situation can be adequately covered. Numerous manufacturers of cameras provide for a rapid change of lenses on the same camera. Many commercial cameras do not provide for this type of change in the field, and these cannot be recommended for the types of specialized photography often encountered by the investigator. On the other hand, the simpler matter of obtaining pictures quickly, encountered by the ordinary police photographer, may not require the flexibility that is built into the better-designed all-purpose camera.

The Diaphragm

Except for some very fine special-purpose lenses, every good lens assembly includes an iris diaphragm, so called because its action simulates that of the iris of the eye. It may be opened and closed so as to give any desired aperture, progressively blocking out the outer portions of the lens and employing only the central portion as it is closed. This has two effects: it diminishes the amount of light admitted in unit time; and it expands the field that is in sharp focus, as mentioned above, while diminishing the effects of aberrations in the lens. The resolution of the lens is reduced, however, by stopping it down excessively with the diaphragm.

The lever that controls the diaphragm is graduated in f/numbers, defined as the ratio of focal length to the effective diameter of the lens. The numbers increase as the diaphragm is closed. They represent relative aperture, or proportion of the lens that is used. The smallest number on the scale is the maximum aperture of the lens, and the smaller it is, the faster the lens, i.e., the more light it is capable of gathering. In practice, apertures larger than $f/4.5$ are rarely used except for photographing moving objects, or in situations having a low level of available light. Very fast lenses with apertures corresponding to numbers even less than 1 are obtainable, and f/numbers between 1 and 2 are relatively common. In the 35mm format $f/1.4$ and $f/1.8$ are common. Because of the increased difficulty of correction, the cost of such lenses is high, and their use by investigators, except for surveillance work, is so infrequent that their purchase is not recommended.

The series of f/stops on a lens is related to the size of the lens opening relative to the focal length. The diaphragm diameter is decreased by a factor equal to the square root of two. The result is that the area of each successive marked f/stop decreases by a factor of two. The conventional series of f/stops starts at 0.5 and results in the following sequence: 0.5, 0.7, 1.0, 1.4, 2.0, 2.8, 4, 5.6, 8, 11, 16, 22, 32, and so on. Each of the numbers of this series represents a relative aperture that will pass twice as much light as the next larger number and one-half as much as the next smaller.

The proper control of the diaphragm is one of the most important lessons to be learned by the beginning photographer. The correct diaphragm opening is directly related to the sensitivity of the film used and the amount of light being reflected from the subject. Indirectly, diaphragm opening is determined by the shutter speed, because the combination of shutter speed and f/stop determine the total amount of light that strikes the film. These two factors will be balanced between the need to prevent significant movement of the cameras during exposure and the need to provide sufficient depth of field to cover the depth of the subject field. It should be remembered that the diaphragm must be closed as much as is practical to increase the depth of focus, but in photographing perfectly flat objects it may be left open, provided the focus is sharp. When the opening is reduced, the exposure time must be increased correspondingly. As a matter of convenience, the diaphragm will not be closed more than is necessary for the particular conditions encountered.

The Shutter

Most cameras are equipped with a shutter that controls the length of time light is admitted into the camera box. A proper shutter will allow the following: time exposures in which the shutter opens on one movement of the control device and closes on a second similar movement; bulb exposures in which the shutter stays open as long as the control device is actuated; and a series of exposures in which actuation of the control automatically opens the shutter for periods of fractions of a second. The better shutters give speeds in the latter series ranging from perhaps one second to 1/500 second, and some shutters extend this range. Again it is ordinarily unnecessary to expend the extra funds to obtain very fast shutter speeds because their primary use is for photographing rapidly moving objects, a purpose rarely encountered by the investigator or criminalist. Nearly all laboratory photography is carried out with time exposures or the longer fractional speeds. Crime scenes are also normally static and allow longer exposures unless the camera is hand-held.

Shutters are of various types. Most common is a shutter mounted between the lens elements, and composed of flat vanes that overlap and are snapped out of the way when the shutter is opened. Several types of mechanism actuate the vanes; of these the Compur type is perhaps best known. Another excellent type is the focal-plane shutter, which is not a part of the lens assembly but is placed directly in front of and close to the film. It consists of curtains mounted on rollers that are so controlled as to allow all of the exposure speeds possible with other types of shutter. One advantage of the focal-plane shutter is that the lens can be removed while the camera is loaded. A disadvantage is the fact that short exposures are made by drawing a narrow slit in the curtains over the film at a predetermined speed so that different portions of the film are actually exposed at different times. If the subject is moving rapidly, the effect can be grotesque. For still objects, the focal-plane shutter is unexcelled.

Reflex cameras are ordinarily equipped with focal-plane shutters. Ahead of the shutter is placed a mirror at a 45° angle to the film. The mirror reflects the focused image to a ground glass. When the shutter is released, the mirror swings aside and the film is exposed by the ordinary action of the focal-plane shutter. Barrel-type reflex shutters are also available. In these the mirror and an auxiliary vane serve as shutter, but the action is in other respects similar to the ordinary type. Reflex cameras are exceptionally useful to the investigator, particularly for close-up and photomicrographic work. They should not be confused with a number of double-lens "reflex" cameras in which the focus is achieved with one lens and the picture exposed through the other. These are of limited value for criminalistic work and are rarely used.

The chief task of the beginning photographer is to learn the relations between shutter speed and diaphragm opening as related to the illumination, the depth of object, the distortions due to imperfect corrections of the lens, and the resolution of the lens.

The Filmholder

This is a device that allows the removal of one frame of film or one plate from the camera and the insertion of another. For roll film, it consists of two rollers on which the film is wound. Cut film is individually loaded into the holder and protected during handling by a slide that must be removed before exposing the film. Film pack is similar to cut film except that each film is individually attached to a strip of paper by which it may be drawn downward, around a guide, and up in the rear of a metal holder in which the film is packed. Such holders contain twelve films and require only one loading. They are less used than cut film or roll film, but are very convenient. Plates are sensitized surfaces placed on glass sheets instead of on cellulose acetate or polyester sheets. The holder is similar to that for cut film but larger to accommodate the extra thickness of the plate as compared with film.

The size of *filmholder* is generally determined by the format of the camera, except in the case of large-format cameras, which may be fitted with various size film backs. The choice of format for different purposes is discussed elsewhere. Some cameras, e.g., press-type cameras, require interchangeability of the holder with a ground glass for focusing. Reflex cameras have the advantage of focusing on ground glass without any interchange being necessary.

Exposure Meters

The total exposure of the film is the result of the diaphragm setting and the shutter speed. If for various reasons limitations are placed on one, a corresponding alteration of the other is necessary. With much experience, a photographer will learn to set the exposure correctly most of the time, but even the most experienced prefer to use an exposure meter, and the beginner must expect many ruined photographs unless he uses a meter.

Automatic cameras contain an exposure meter built into the camera, and no supplemental meter is required. For all other cameras, the meter is virtually essential. Meters work on two different principles. Less-expensive meters are nearly always equipped with an ordinary photocell (selenium), which is suitable for almost every requirement. The more expensive contain photoconductive elements (sulfides of certain metals) whose resistance is altered by the amount of light striking them. They contain a battery to generate a potential; this is not needed with the photocell. The advantage of photoconductive meters lies in their greater sensitivity. This allows, for example, monitoring of light from a small region inside a camera, for which the photocell type is not sensitive enough. Many automatic cameras utilize photocells, but for overall light intensity rather than through-the-lens measurement of illumination. The photoconductive meter will also measure the minute amount of light that exists in an almost totally dark room. It is the more versatile meter, but is not required under ordinary conditions.

Tripods

With every camera, time and bulb exposures require the use of a tripod or an equivalent steadying support. Snapshot exposures can be made with a hand-held camera, provided the operator has a reasonably steady hand. The shorter the exposure, the less will small camera movements influence it. Heavy cameras are much more difficult to hand-hold than are small cameras, and anything larger than a press camera should be mounted on a tripod.

Camera movement is one of two major causes of fuzzy or blurred negatives. The other is failure to focus the camera properly. Both camera movement and improper focusing are exaggerated with cameras using long focal length lenses, and minimized with short focal length lenses, such as are used on 35mm and smaller cameras. The tripod prevents camera movement and makes it easier to adjust for sharp focus.

FILMS

As indicated above, films are obtainable as rolls, cut (or sheet) film, film pack, and plates. The types of film obtainable in these categories are not the same, the number being least in roll films other than 35mm. In the latter size, an exceptional range of film types may be obtained. Sheet film may also be purchased in most types. Film pack is relatively little used and is available in limited types of film; plates are essentially obsolete at this time.

Black-and-White Film

With black-and-white film, the most important factors in the choice of film are: (1) color sensitivity, (2) contrast, (3) speed, and (4) graininess. The color sensitivity must be taken into account in photography of all colored objects, even though the picture is black and white. For many purposes, the ideal film is one that renders the intensity of all the colors approximately as they are evaluated by the eye. At times, it is desired to emphasize differences in color intensity; and for black-and-white objects, e.g. documents, the question of color is unimportant. The speed of the film is ordinarily unimportant in criminal investigation, because rapidly moving objects are photographed only rarely, and illumination can be adjusted to give good results with slow films. Graininess of the film is of great importance when extreme enlargement must be achieved.

With respect to color sensitivity, the following three types of film are recognized: (1) Non-color-sensitized, or color-blind film, having no special treatment to alter the ordinary sensitivity of a silver halide emulsion. This film is primarily sensitive in the blue-violet and ultraviolet and blue regions of the spectrum, and is comparatively little used. (2) Orthochromatic film is sensitive in the ultraviolet, blue, and green regions of the spectrum. Many of the films that find important application in general and criminalistic photography are in this category. Being insensitive in the red spectral region, such film may be handled in red light, though some care must be used to filter out any other stray light and to keep the intensity low. (3) Panchromatic film is sensitive in the regions mentioned and in the red region as well. It is subclassified as Type B, which approximates rather closely the sensitivity of the human eye in the visible spectrum, and Type C, which is extremely sensitive in the yellow and red regions. Panchromatic film is generally developed and handled in total darkness.

In addition to these common types of film, there is a large variety of special films, including infrared-sensitive film, which is valuable to the criminalist, spectrographic plates, X-ray film, and others necessary for special purposes. All films are to some extent altered in their characteristics by the use of filters that remove by subtractive absorption some of the colors in the incident light. Most such special effects are produced with panchromatic film, which can be prevented from registering any desired portion of the spectrum. This often allows the production of marked contrast between dissimilar colors of equal photographic intensity.

The contrast desired in a picture is largely regulated by the choice of film. Process film, which may be either orthochromatic or panchromatic, has little latitude and great contrast. (By latitude is meant the ability of the film to respond linearly to regions of dark and light in the field photographed. A film of wide latitude gives a nearly linear response to light intensity in both the bright and shadowed areas.) The faster films, which are ordinarily panchromatic, have a wide latitude, produce fine detail, and are deficient in contrast as compared with the slow process film.

Grain size is a factor, particularly when a high degree of enlargement is desired. By grain size is meant the size of the small particles of metallic silver that give the blackness to both film and paper after development. Different varieties of film vary considerably in this regard. As a rule, the faster the film, the greater is the graininess. If the particles are relatively coarse, enlargement of the negative will produce a speckled effect on the print, with corresponding loss of fine detail. If only low degree of enlargement is necessary, the grain size is of less importance. This factor is influenced by the type of developer and development conditions used, as well as by the type of film.

Table 8-1 lists films available for various purposes.

Color Film

Two basic types of color film materials are available for general as well as police photography. If *transparencies* are desired for projection, two classes of film are available, one for amateur development and one processed only by commercial facilities. Kodak produces Ektachrome for the former use and Kodachrome for the latter. Ektachrome X and High Speed Ektachrome are the fastest, Ektachrome X giving a little better quality and slower speed. Kodachrome X is similar to Ektachrome X, except for the difference in processing. Several other brands of color film of excellent quality are available.

TABLE 8-1 Suggested Kodak Black-and-White Films for Various Purposes*

Subject	Sheet film	Roll film	35mm film
indoor crime scenes (supplemental lighting)	Plus X, Tri-X, Royal Pan	Plus X, Panatomic X	Plus X, Tri-X, Panatomic X
outdoor crime scenes	Plus X, Tri-X Royal Pan	Plus X, Panatomic X	Panatomic X
indoor—laboratory specimens (supplemental lighting)	Panatomic X	Panatomic X	Panatomic X
copies—black and white	contrast process, orthochromatic		high contrast copy
copies—color	contrast process, panchromatic		high contrast copy
copies—continuous tone, black and white	commercial orthochromatic	Plus X	Panatomic X
photomicrography	Super Panchromatic Press Type B	Plus X	Panatomic X, Plus X

* The above table is limited to Kodak film primarily because of its general availability. Equivalent films obtainable from other manufacturers, both foreign and domestic, will be preferred by many photographers. Polaroid film is characterized by a very great speed in black and white. Among Adox products is a very slow thin-emulsion film that produces superior enlargements. Others could be mentioned.

If *color prints* are to be made, color-negative film, rather than reversal positive film (as in transparencies) should be employed. Both Ektacolor and Kodacolor films are in this category, and both may be processed by the amateur. Color prints can be made from the negatives in the noncommercial darkroom, using Kodak's Rapid Color Processor with an appropriate color head enlarger. Although the process is somewhat demanding, it is well worthwhile if the volume of color printing is sufficient. Color-negative materials can also be used to make black-and-white prints and color slides where needed.

ILLUMINATION

The most difficult phase of photography is probably the arrangement of illumination. When the photographer has mastered this point, he is likely to be little troubled with the other technical problems of making photographs. This is true for the photography of scenes, persons, and microscopic objects. The camera cannot interpret the interplay of light and shadow as does the eye. If the picture is to represent the object as it would be interpreted by the eye, the illumination must be such as to produce all the necessary variations in light and shadow in their precise locations. This is particularly true in the matter of depth, which is often represented in the picture merely as the difference in intensity of light. By contrast, the eye perceives depth by virtue of binocular vision, and it may also change focus slightly in perceiving portions that lie at different distances.

Illuminating Devices

TUNGSTEN FILAMENT. No type of illumination has surpassed the ordinary tungsten filament lamp for general utility and effectiveness. Daylight is excellent but its intensity cannot be readily controlled, and it is not suitable for indoor photography, which is what the investigator is primarily concerned with. The spectral characteristics of the tungsten lamp are sufficiently constant for black-and-white photography without any special control. For color photography, the lamp used may require more consideration because the colors are altered if the current fluctuates owing to a change in filament temperature.

PHOTOFLOOD. The photoflood lamp is a simple tungsten filament lamp similar to standard tungsten lamps in all respects except that it is designed with lower resistance in the filament. This allows more current to pass, with the production of higher temperature and a greater amount of illumination. The life of the lamp is correspondingly reduced. A photoflood should not be allowed to burn continuously or for longer periods than absolutely necessary. Its use is analogous to that of the simple tungsten lamp except for color photography. Here the spectral characteristics are different and must be allowed for.

PHOTOFLASH. Because of the inconvenience of utilizing lighting based on incandescent bulbs, various types of flash units are now routinely employed by virtually everyone who take photographs. The equipment requires less arrangement, it is faster to use, and when properly arranged, it is approximately as satisfactory in its results. Early photoflash units depended on the rapid burning of foil enclosed in a glass envelope, although an even earlier technique was to combust a tray of magnesium powder in air. The first photoflash bulbs were quite large, as they were made to screw into ordinary light sockets.

At this time, far more efficient flashbulbs are available, much smaller, with bayonet bases, and with high light output. They remain popular because of their smallness and efficiency, despite the fact that they are expendable.

The *electronic flash*, actually a glass tube of xenon through which an electric discharge is created by charged condensers, has to some extent displaced the flashbulb. These units, like photoflash, are not large or cumbersome, and they may be used repeatedly, with occasional replacement or recharging of batteries. The investigator who utilizes a camera is well advised to have an electronic flash available, or lacking that, a flash unit for use with bulbs.

Proper *employment of photoflash* of either type involves the following considerations:

(1) In essentially dark conditions, photoflash units are good substitutes for photoflood lamps or other incandescent sources of light. For interior photography of small or moderate areas, they provide sufficient illumination without unusual arrangement. In exterior areas, or in very large enclosures, this may be true, as discussed below.

(2) They are not effective at great distances, interior or exterior, without supplementation. The distance covered with a flashbulb or electronic flash will be determined by the film speed, the output of the light source, and the maximum aperture of the lens used. The distance will be modified by prevailing conditions, primarily due to the reflectivity surfaces between the light source and the object photographed. It is common to see persons ineffectually using their flash units at parades, in large theaters, and the like because they do not realize the distance limitation of any type of illumination at the camera position.

(3) In order to correlate the camera setting with the use of flash, a guide number must be used. This is determined both by the intensity of the light emitted and the speed of the film. The *guide number* is obtained by multiplying the distance to the object by the f/stop setting. Therefore, a guide number of 100 would mean that if the distance is 10 feet, the f/stop should be close to 10, generally 11. The greater the light output of the unit, and the faster the film used, the larger the guide numbers will be. All films provide tables of guide numbers on the accompanying data sheet, and on all packages of flashbulbs are tables relating the bulbs to films of varying speeds. Every photographer should test his own equipment to establish the exact guide number before doing critical photography, because of other variations not covered by tables.

(4) The light output of the unit is determined by more than one factor. A flashbulb is predictable, as is a single flash from an electronic flash. However, both operate with reflectors, and the nature of the reflector is a very important factor in determining the light reaching the object photographed. Because there are large differences in the size and efficiency of reflectors, there will also be corresponding differences in the guide number. This fact argues strongly for determination of the guide number by the photographer for his own equipment and conditions.

(5) In using electronic flash illumination, shutter speed is not involved because the flash is essentially instantaneous, and all that is critical is that the shutter be open at the time of the flash. It is also important to consider that

the time-lag period varies with different types of flash, and the camera will ordinarily have an M synchronization applying to bulbs, and an X synchronization applying to electronic flash. The X and M settings should not be confused. *Leaf type* shutters can be used at any speed with electronic flash but with focal-plane shutters there is a maximum permissible shutter speed, generally 1/60 second or less. This requirement is based on the fact that at higher shutter speeds a slit of varying width travels across the film plane and at no time is the film frame fully exposed. Unlike electronic flash, flashbulbs have a total burning time that is considerable compared to the shorter shutter speeds. For this reason, the guide numbers for flashbulbs will be greater for the slower shutter speeds, up to the point where all the illumination is produced during the period that the shutter is open.

The most common result of not understanding these basic principles is seen at scenes of accidents and fires, where distances of significant objects may be considerable. If night photographs are taken of the accident, or any photographs are taken in an unlighted burned warehouse, only those objects close to the camera will show and the other related objects will be lost in darkness. Some solutions to this situation follow.

Comparatively *distant objects* will be properly photographed only if illuminated, and this will require a source of light close to them. One effective method, little used now, is to string a long cord with multiple sockets throughout the area of interest, place the requisite number of flashbulbs in the sockets, and fire them simultaneously with the camera shutter open. At present, *slave lights* provide a more acceptable method. A photocell triggers a second flash unit (the slave) by means of the light emitted by the flash on the camera. Such units may be distributed to all parts requiring secondary illumination without the necessity of stringing wire. When using slave lights, it is important to remember that the exposure to be used is the same with or without slave supplement to the flash on the camera, and it remains the same regardless of the number of slave units. The reason for this is that the area illuminated is increased, but the intensity of any point is no greater than the best illuminated portion with a single flash. The film responds only to intensity, not to total illuminated area. Slave units have not been widely used in police investigation, largely because of a lack of familiarity with the equipment. Numerous commercial units are available, and they can be constructed without great difficulty. They may use either flashbulbs or electronic light source.

Daylight use of flash is recommended when areas that contain significant information are in shadow, as is often the case. The presence of bright sunshine increases contrast in the photograph, so that light areas may be white and shadows black. The flash will diminish the contrast, making detail much clearer in both highlights and shadows, as long as the diaphragm opening is reduced below meter reading. The appropriate camera setting is generally between that indicated by a meter reading and that indicated by the guide number system that applies to darkness. Cameras equipped with focal-plane shutters are not suitable for outdoor daylight flash, unless a very slow film is used, since the fastest desirable shutter speed for flash is about 1/30 second.

Outdoor Illumination

Although outdoor daylight photography must be done without direct control of the illumination, some points of choosing and evaluating conditions are important.

(1) As a general rule, scenes are best taken with the sun behind the photographer, and the objects of interest directly illuminated. The photograph taken in direct sunlight will be unusually contrasty and harsh, and the effect will be greatest with nearby objects. Here, a fill-in flash is recommended.

(2) Cloudy or overcast days permit more even and generally more satisfactory photographs. This is especially true with color.

(3) When photographs must be taken into the sun, the lens should be shaded. This situation often occurs in investigations.

(4) Detail may be obtained in situations where there is too little contrast by choosing an angle of the camera which allows the "glare" from the sun to reflect directly from the object to the lens. This technique can be applied to skid-mark photography in accident investigation, where the angle of the light is critical in revealing tire markings. The effect desired will be visible to the eye, and if it is not, do not expect the camera to see it. The technique effectively rules out photography of such marks with the sun directly overhead. In general, midmorning and midafternoon illumination is better than noon.

(5) Except for special situations where glare can be utilized, as in (4) above, the photographer should position his camera so that glare from the sun is eliminated. This also holds for reflections from glass, chromium plate, and similar reflective surfaces. In photographing markings on glass, reflection can sometimes be avoided by placing paper on the opposite side of the glass. The same technique may be used with mirrors, by placing the paper so that its reflection covers the area of interest.

Arrangement of Lights

Many objects, notably documents, are illuminated best by flat lighting, i.e., lighting in which there is no direct reflection into the camera lens, giving a smooth, uniform illumination without highlights. This is achieved by placing lights on at least two sides of the object, on a level with the camera lens. A complete circle of lights is sometimes used effectively. A number of lightbulbs uniformly spaced gives more even illumination than a single bulb of equivalent light output. Individual lights must be placed farther from the object than they are from each other.

When three-dimensional portrayal is necessary, this type of lighting should not be employed. Here it is desirable to create highlights and shadows, so an unsymmetrical arrangement of the lights is used. Often this is achieved by directing a light from the front at medium intensity, and a stronger light from the side, bottom, or top so as to cast shadows and highlights on the features to be emphasized. Here, the photographer will have to experiment until the desired result is obtained. It should be noted that the average individual is accustomed to seeing pictures that have been illuminated from the upper right-hand corner. If this is done, the picture will have a familiarity to it that may well be lacking with major illumination from other angles.

When extreme three-dimensional effects are desired, as in studying small indentations in a paper or other surfaces, all the lights are directed from the side, top, or bottom, with no general illumination. This has the effect of creating highlights and shadows even from minute irregularities in the surface. The nearer the light is to the plane of the surface, the greater will be the effect. If such irregularities are significant in the two-dimensional consideration of the surface, a useful technique is to arrange the light at an angle to both directions, e.g. from a corner, in which case shadows may be cast in both directions. Experimentation with light will be necessary to produce the desired effect.

To photograph opaque portions of an otherwise transparent system, as with gradient tubes containing soil or hair fragments, an evenly illuminated field behind the object may be used. This is readily obtained with a fluorescent light covered by a ground glass or thin paper to diffuse the incident light.

COLOR VS. BLACK–AND–WHITE PHOTOGRAPHS

The quality of color photographs has been so improved in recent years, and their popularity as an amateur medium has so increased, that there is a strong trend toward color on the part of many photographers. On the other hand, the ease of making black-and-white photographs, and their relatively low cost recommend them whenever they adequately serve a purpose. The investigator needs both, and he also needs to know when it is appropriate to use one or the other. Some general rules may be formulated.

(1) Black and white discriminates only light-intensity differences; so two completely different colors side by side may reflect the same light intensity and be indistinguishable.

(2) Color photographs tend to minimize or obscure very fine detail.

(3) Color film must be quite accurately exposed in order to obtain a useful photograph, whereas black-and-white film gives more latitude. Under conditions of doubtful light intensity, color should be avoided.

(4) Objects in shadow will appear dark on both types of film, but sometimes color will reveal them as shadows rather than as significant features. Rendition of shadow detail will be improved by supplemental lighting.

(5) Color is required when the object of major interest is distinguished by its color, e.g. a red traffic light. Delicate colors in flames may be seen in color but not in black and white.

(6) The greater latitude of black-and-white film will make it more suitable for rapid photography, in which there is no time for careful preparation.

(7) Reflectivity of some surfaces is greatly influenced by the angle of illumination. Charred surfaces are a good illustration, since the same black char can photograph as both white and black, depending only on the angle of the reflected light. Color is generally more satisfactory for this type of situation.

(8) When no obvious reason exists for choosing color, the inherent advantages of black-and-white photography recommend it as preferable.

MOTION PICTURES VS. STILL PHOTOGRAPHS

The sole advantage of moving pictures over still pictures is that they delineate movement or time sequence of events, rather than freezing some part of the movement at an instant in time. For a few purposes there can be no substitute for the motion picture, and these almost invariably involve a continuum of movement, either of the subject or of the camera. Such situations are uncommon in investigation, because most evidence, crime scenes and accident scenes, are not in movement, and camera position can be altered by a succession of exposures with still photographs. The motion picture is costly as compared with still photographs, and it is not easily processed in the facilities commonly available. To have it processed elsewhere involves both loss of time and the risk of loss or damage to the film.

DEVELOPING NEGATIVES AND PRINTS

The development of negatives is a critical operation because an error here can destroy valuable photographs, which at the very least must be retaken and at worst are permanently lost. Print development (including enlarging) is less critical, because a failure is readily rectified. Detailed discussion of darkroom procedure is out of place here. Innumerable routines are available from manufacturers; these are found in general books and pamphlets. Chemicals should be purchased in ready-to-use form, and manufacturer's instructions should be followed precisely.

Developers are mildly alkaline reducing agents that convert silver salts, such as the chloride and bromide, previously sensitized by exposure to light, into elemental silver. It is this very finely dispersed metal in a film or paper that makes up the image constituting a picture. Silver salts that have not been exposed to light are more difficult to reduce to the free metal, so the reducing agent must exert a preferential action, reducing the sensitized portion of the silver salt without affecting that which has not been so sensitized.

Film developers are generally stronger in their action than are paper developers. Also, developers suitable for silver chloride papers (used for contact prints) must be diluted before use with silver bromide papers (suitable for enlargements). Rapid-acting developers ordinarily build higher contrast than slow developers, whereas the latter yield a finer grain size. Detailed enlargements should therefore be made from negatives developed in a slow-acting developer, and for a very contrasty picture a more rapid acting developer should be used. These generalizations are subject to modification depending on the use of a variety of chemicals and conditions that give somewhat different effects.

The image captured on film or paper is "fixed" (made permanent) by dissolving from the sensitive coating any remaining unexposed and unreduced silver salt. The fixing bath is a solution of sodium thiosulfate (called "hypo" because of an early misunderstanding of its composition), or the more rapidly acting ammonium thiosulfate. This is an essential and frequently underrated portion of the routine of the darkroom. In complete fixing gives a picture that becomes yellow or brown with age, and the rate of its discoloration is partially dependent on the degree of incompleteness of the fixing. In addition, fixing baths almost always contain certain acidic agents, such as sodium bisulfite, that harden the gelatin in which the silver salts are dispersed on the film or paper. For more vigorous effects, more complex mixtures are used containing stronger hardening agents, such as alum. Fixing chemicals should also be purchased in ready-mixed form and used as instructed.

SMALL-OBJECT PHOTOGRAPHY

Most photography of small and microscopic objects is performed in the laboratory rather than by the police. However, it is often necessary in the field to photograph a knife, hand gun, wounds of a victim, or an item of clothing, not to mention fingerprints, blood spots, and similar evidence. The principles outlined earlier were all relevant, but some special precautions are desirable.

(1) Small objects should always be photographed with a ruler or scale, so that their size is indicated throughout all subsequent photographic operations. This ruler must be placed in the principal plane of focus.

(2) Special care in focusing of the camera must be the rule. At short distances, the plane of sharp focus is relatively thin, and it is essential that if any portion of the object is not in sharp focus, it be a part of no special interest.

(3) A small diaphragm aperture will give much greater depth to the photograph. With cameras having an adjustable diaphragm, focusing will be done so

as to be sure that the regions of interest are in good focus, after which the diaphragm is stopped down to a practical high $f/$value.

(4) The object should be placed at a distance from the camera that allows it to reasonably fill the field of the camera, when this is possible. It may not be possible when the object is very small, if the camera lens cannot operate closely enough.

(5) Special attention must be given to illumination. The principles outlined above apply; the areas of major interest must be properly lighted. Blood spots on the uppers of a shoe, for example, will be difficult to show unless the lighting is very carefully adjusted. Portable lights are useful.

(6) Consideration must be given to whether color or black and white can best record significant portions of the object. In many instances, color will be superior.

INTERPRETING PHOTOGRAPHS

Many of the photographs taken by the police or other investigators will be admitted as evidence in a future court trial, and will require careful interpretation and scrutiny of detail. The photographer should keep this in mind when he takes his photographs; it is essential that he understand the problems encountered by the attorneys and witnesses. The two major problems, aside from low quality pictures, are related to *perspective* and *detail*.

Distortion and Perspective

The term "distortion" is often erroneously used to denote the misrepresentation of perspective in a photograph. *True distortion* occurs only because of lens or focusing errors, as when a poorly corrected lens produces a variation in magnification over the field of view. A lens that is actually defective in its grinding may also produce true distortion. In perspective distortion, the relative sizes of objects do not appear normal. Objects close to the camera are proportionately much too large as compared with objects farther from the camera. A "distorted" picture (contact print) will look perfectly normal if viewed from a distance equal to the focal length of the lens. Enlargement will require a greater viewing distance. By the proper combination of viewing distance, enlargement, and focal length, the actual field of view from the camera position can be duplicated. In this way, perspective distortion can be overcome.

Perspective is related to the problem of obtaining distances and dimensions from photographs. Such values may be obtained from photographs only in favorable circumstances. The two dimensions defining a plane at right angles to the direction in which the camera is aimed may be estimated with good accuracy if there are objects shown with known dimensions. The direction parallel to that which the camera is aimed cannot be estimated more than very roughly under any circumstances, and not at all in most situations. If objects of known dimensions in the plane at right angles are different distances from the camera than the object of interest, it likewise cannot be used because it is proportionately smaller by being farther from the camera, or the reverse. This important principle must always be remembered in interpreting photographs.

Enlargement and Detail

A recurrent question arises as to whether enlarging a photograph will increase the visible detail. The question is compounded by the fact that *no detail can ever be obtained on a print or enlargement if it is not present on the negative.* A fuzzy or blurred negative should not be greatly enlarged, because its imperfections will only be accentuated. However, the resolving power of a negative is much greater than that of the eye, and any sharp, well-focused negative will contain a large amount of detail not visible to the eye. Ideally, enlargement should be increased until all the relevant details are clearly shown. In practice this question can be resolved on the basis of the quality of the negative, and in a specific case, there is an optimal degree of enlargement for each particular negative. Recopying a small print and enlarging it in the hope of obtaining more detail is generally useless; because detail has been lost in the original printing, and still more will be lost in the extra operations.

GENERAL CONSIDERATIONS

Achieving a good picture calls for more than just mechanically going through the various operations, even though failure in any one such operation may prevent a satisfactory result. What is required is a trained eye, experience, perhaps natural ability, and certainly a desire to do a good job. Additionally, the observer who is to see the photograph at a later date must be kept in mind, so that the picture will be relevant to the problem under consideration. The photographer will profit by taking sufficient time to perform each operation carefully, giving consideration to all the consequences.

Few of the occupations of the investigator can contribute so much to his conclusions, his presentations, and to his general satisfaction as the production of adequate photographs. The acquisition of good photographic judgment and effective manipulative expertise should also enable the criminalist to present his findings with convincing clarity.

REFERENCES

Arnold, C. R., ed.: *Applied Photography.* New York: Amphoto (1972).
Engel, C. E., ed.: *Photography for the Scientist.* New York: Academic Press (1968).

Fritsche, K.: *Faults in Photography.* New York: Amphoto (1968).
Horder, A., ed.: *Manual of Photography.* Philadelphia: Chilton (1971).
Katz, J., and Fogel, S. J.: *Photographic Analysis: A Textbook of Photographic Science.* Hastings-on-Hudson, New York: Morgan (1971).
Loveland, R. P.: *Photomicrography.* New York: Wiley (1970). 2 vols.
Mannheim, L. A.: *Filter Practice,* 2nd ed. Philadelphia: Chilton (1969).
Spencer, D. A., ed.: *L. P. Clerc's Photography: Theory and Practice.* New York: Amphoto (1970). 6 vols.

9
Preliminary Examination of Microscopic Evidence

Microscopic or trace evidence is largely obtained from the filter of the vacuum sweeper used for the collection of debris from the scene of a crime, from clothing, and the like. Under some circumstances it is necessary to collect such evidence with forceps under magnification or by other tedious methods. Microscopic evidence generally constitutes an extremely heterogeneous mixture that is often of no value until it has been searched and its contents segregated.

SWEEPINGS

Regardless of the number of items or particles present in sweepings, each has an individual history that may or may not be intertwined with that of the crime being investigated. The sweepings collected should be given a preliminary examination to determine the general nature of the particles and to consider which constituents may have more than casual significance. The material should be transferred to a broad shallow vessel in which it can be spread out for examination. For this the sorting dish described below or a petri dish of the type used by bacteriologists is suitable. Both types are low and flat-bottomed with vertical sidewalls, and both have flat lids that facilitate stacking for storage.

The uncovered dish is placed under the stereoscopic binocular microscope. With a low-power optical combination the sweepings may be readily scanned or minutely examined by teasing the mass with dissecting needles. The bulk of the material will be the usual soil and dust mixed with a very large number of fibers, most of which are fragmented vegetable fibers of miscellaneous origin, many of them cotton. Usually these will have little or no significance because they are of wide occurrence and are found, to a greater or less extent, in every sample.

Included in the mass will be a smaller number of dyed wool fibers, dyed cotton, linen, rayon, nylon, and a large variety of other synthetic fibers that are relatively conspicuous. Sometimes there are metal fragments, wood fragments, glass, paint chips, and other material of somewhat unusual nature. Often there are hairs, sometimes human and sometimes animal. Almost anything may be found in a mass of clothing sweepings, but certain things will be noted rather quickly as having a better-than-average probable significance.

SORTING OF MICROSCOPIC EVIDENCE

Direct preliminary examination of all the available microscopic evidence involved in a case should indicate the types of evidence that must be separated, either because they may connect a suspect with the scene or the victim, or because they will be useful in describing the criminal or in reconstructing the crime. It is then time to separate all such items and segregate them for detailed study and comparison. Vacuum tweezers are now available to transfer evidence with little danger of loss. In this operation the superiority of the plastic sorting dish illustrated* will become evident. Under a flat plastic cover is a main central chamber in which all the sweepings are placed. Around it are a number of smaller chambers or wells covered with a clear plastic ring that has only one opening. Thus, only one side chamber can be open at a time. A particular type of evidence is picked up with fine-tipped forceps or vacuum tweezers (under the low-power stereoscopic binocular microscope) and placed in one of the side wells. The annular lid is turned to open a second well, and evidence of another type is transferred. This process is continued until the evidence is completely sorted and segregated. Thus, all evidence having a common origin is kept in a single vessel and under a single label, but subsequent examinations will be greatly facilitated by having it divided into its significant separate categories.

As an alternative, the sweepings may be sorted in a petri dish, or other flat dish, and the various kinds of evidence placed into separate containers such as glass dishes or vials. This is often less convenient, requiring more space,

* Obtainable from the Microchemical Specialties Co., Berkeley, California 94710.

multiple labels, and more time, but it may be necessary when the accumulation of an electrostatic charge by the evidence material in the plastic sorting dish results in manipulative difficulties. Occasionally, it is possible to save time by mounting the sorted materials directly onto microscope slides for immediate examination. However, this sometimes results in loss of the evidence, and it is recommended only when a single item or a very few similar items are to be placed on a slide. In either of the alternative methods each container or slide must be labeled immediately, because it is very easy to confuse the sources of large numbers of microscopic objects while sorting and mounting them.

It is especially important to isolate all fibers having a distinguishable color or morphology. Any glass fragments, which will usually be recognized by their irregular shapes, conchoidal fractures, transparency, and (sometimes) color, should be separated from the mass. Soil constituents will only occasionally be of value when mixed in sweepings because soil cannot be readily reconstituted for study, and it will have had a variable origin. Mineral fragments may, however, be useful evidence and may be segregated. Paint fragments should also be carefully removed to a separate container. Occasionally an unusual type of fragment may be noted, and it should be removed for special study provided (1) it occurs in evidence obtained from the suspect and also from the victim or the crime scene; or (2) it may indicate the occupation or the customary environment of the suspect.

It is virtually impossible to define all the possible types of evidence found in sweepings. In the future, more of the items found in such materials will be studied and made to yield techniques that will render them of value in the solution of crime. But for the present, it is better to chance some waste of time, and to segregate and label anything which may be useful, rather than to restrict the operation to only those few things that are already known to be connected with the crime.

The preliminary examination and sorting of physical evidence is one of the most tedious operations confronting the criminalist. It is also one of the most profitable, for it is here that the evidence is most likely to be productive. Larger items can be—and often are—discarded, hidden, or destroyed. The microscopic evidence will persist, despite the criminal's efforts to dispose of all traces. This is true because the criminal will not be aware of it in sufficient detail even though he may realize its importance and because he will be unable to prevent its presence or to destroy it all by any reasonable means. In numerous criminal investigations, when there were no useful witnesses and no large items of evidence, there was still ample microscopic evidence to prove conclusively the guilt of the suspected person. Likewise a considerable number of former suspects owe their liberty to the fact that significant microscopic evidence, by its absence, indicated their innocence, even though circumstances tended to link them with the crime.

RELATION TO LARGE ITEMS OF EVIDENCE

A special aspect of the preliminary examination of microscopic evidence is its use to connect macroscopic evidence with the crime. For example, a particular knife is used to stab an individual, cut a telephone wire, or pry up a window. Perhaps it has been abandoned at the scene of the crime and its owner is unknown. Subsequently, a suspect is taken into custody. If that suspect had carried the knife in his pocket, it is possible that a comparison of the microscopic evidence from the pocket with that from the knife will prove possession. In this case the knife (gun, or other item in question) is opened up or disassembled on clean paper, and, with a needle, all cracks, crevices, and recesses in it are carefully cleaned. The residue obtained will be quite similar in composition to typical sweepings, and its significant individual constituents may be segregated and studied. It is often possible to state that the object was carried in one specific pocket and not in another one of the same garment.

In this type of examination also, such material as white cotton fibers and fragmentary vegetable fibers have little or no significance because they will be found to some extent in every pocket. Other clothing fibers that are significant will, as a rule, be found in quantity, as will also nonfibrous materials of considerable individuality. Quite often, for example, such a tool or object will carry hairs from its owners, which can be demonstrated as being consistent with the hair of that individual. Here too, the occupation of the owner may be shown, and in this sense the tool itself can be used as an aid in identifying an uncaptured criminal.

Very frequently an item or items found in the pocket may check with the materials at the crime scene that have been in contact with the tool. If, for instance, the knife was used to cut a wire, not only the knife but also the pocket in which it was carried may show bits of copper, insulation, and the like. When this occurs there is a double degree of probability that the owner, the knife, and the crime are connected. The possibilities of this type of evidence are usually limited much more by the patience or ingenuity of the investigator than by any deficiency of the evidence itself.

A new type of tape with a special water-soluble adhesive has recently become available. The tape is applied to any surface and removed. The adhesive can then be dissolved and any trace evidence recovered. This technique holds much promise for the recovery of fiber evidence, gunpowder fragments, and other types of microscopic evidence.

VALUE OF MICROSCOPIC EVIDENCE

The meticulous and thorough nature of the work required in the segregation and examination of microscopic evidence is a deterrent to its general use. At times it is trying on the examiner's patience, and it requires a significant amount of time. Moreover, it is not so glamorous as the psychological and deductive investigations pursued by the fictional detective and at times attempted by real detectives. The investigator must remember that the proof of a single fact is more important than any number of theories, leads, or hunches. Microscopic evidence is capable of proving facts of great significance. No defense attorney, however clever or dramatic, can ever obliterate the effect on a jury of one proven and significant fact that has been clearly demonstrated to and understood by its members. For this reason all the time and patience expended in examining, sorting, comparing, and testing microscopic bits of evidence is time well invested and never entirely wasted. Pursuing the solution of a crime is, like genius, much more perspiration than inspiration. It requires an infinite capacity for taking pains, and patience and perseverance blended with skill and experience. In no field of criminal investigation are the opportunities so great and the reward more satisfying than in the study and use of microscopic evidence.

REFERENCES

Benedetti-Pichler, A. A.: *Identification of Materials.* New York: Academic Press (1964).

Nickolls, L. C.: *The Scientific Investigation of Crime.* London: Butterworth (1956).

O'Hara, C. E., and Osterburg, J. W.: *Introduction to Criminalistics.* Bloomington: Indiana University Press (1972).

Svensson, A., and Wendell, O.: *Techniques of Crime Scene Investigation,* 2nd American ed. New York: American Elsevier (1965).

10
Clothing and Cloth

Clothing is so important to the laboratory examiner that it merits consideration apart from all other forms of evidence. It is important not so much for itself as for what it may carry, although it is, in itself, evidence of a very useful type. Often the criminal's clothes will be much better remembered than his face or figure, and they are also much more easily described by witnesses. Clothing is more readily noted at a distance than are physiognomy, posture, or other characteristics of the criminal, with the possible exception of stature, hair, or skin color.

In times past, virtually all clothing was constructed of cloth made from natural fibers, either animal hair such as wool, or vegetable fibers such as linen and cotton, silk being common in some parts of the world and a rarity elsewhere. Today, the development of regenerated fibers (rayon) and synthetic fibers has altered greatly the incidence of cloth types and their significance as evidence. The synthetic fibers especially have undergone so rapid a development that any statement made about them today may be obsolete tomorrow. Since the use in textiles of the traditional natural fibers persists, the combination of natural and man-made fibers has greatly increased the possibility of utilizing clothing and fibers from it as definitive physical evidence.

Equal in importance to the variety of fibers is the variety of dyes and cloth treatments that are encountered. Modern dyeing techniques permit the use of innumerable colors and shades of color in fabrics. Many different dyeing techniques are used, so that differences may be noted between fabrics of nearly identical color.

Aside from the cloth itself, which will be dealt with in greater detail in a later section in this chapter, clothing is particularly significant as evidence because most clothes pick up and carry other items of evidence. It is often possible to discover in pockets, pants cuffs, and on cloth surfaces enough microscopic evidence to determine the wearer's occupation, his habits, the nature of his environment, where he has been, and—most important—whether he was associated with a particular crime. Pockets especially yield significant information because individuals habitually carry a specific type of thing in a particular pocket. The comb, carried in the pocket, gives to it standard hair samples. In another pocket will be the wallet; in still another, loose change, etc. If the person has carried a knife or a gun, the weapon will often be contaminated with the specific types of materials found in the particular pocket in which it has been carried. Not only is it possible that clothing will pick up and carry minute fragments of glass when the wearer breaks a window or a bottle, but in fact it is almost impossible for him to do so without retaining such fragments in his shoes and clothing. He contacts mud or dust, and he carries the soil. He works in a machine shop, and carries metal fragments. He is a mechanic and carries grease, or he is a miller or baker and carries flour. If he works in construction, he carries cement, brick dust, sawdust, and soil, or perhaps plaster and paint. If he is neat and brushes his clothes frequently, he still almost invariably overlooks the pants cuffs, or attempts with little success to clean them. His pockets are veritable storehouses of information regarding him. Even the free cloth surfaces show stains from food, urine, semen, blood, grease, and many other substances. Moreover, most clothes carry on their surfaces not only deposits from materials that were liquid but solid particles as well. The latter always include considerable numbers of loose fibers, some of which came from the clothing itself and many of which originated in other clothing with which the suspect's clothing has been in contact. It also includes hair from the wearer and from other individuals who have been in close contact; tiny fragments of glass, metal, soil, skin scales—in fact, almost anything small enough to penetrate partially the weave of the cloth and light enough to stick. The amount of material carried on the exposed surfaces will ordinarily be less than that in the cuffs and pockets, but not always: many of the clothes that arrive at the laboratory are dirty indeed. Perhaps this is because a large proportion of criminals come from social strata in which cleanliness is not considered an essential virtue. The victim's clothing also is often dirty. Frequently this is the result of the rough treatment it has received during the commission of the crime, plus the addition of blood, semen, or other materials.

From the laboratory viewpoint, it is usually advantageous to receive dirty clothing because then there is a greater amount of evidence to be studied and a better chance of solving the crime. Jailers, hospital and morgue attendants, and even deputy sheriffs often have an irresistible urge to clean the clothing of the deceased, the suspect, or the living victim, and they must be vigorously restrained from yielding to that urge.

Clothing will ordinarily be wrapped and tied before being sent to the laboratory. There may be instances in which it is not possible or desirable to deprive the suspect of his clothing, in which case extraction of evidence from it by the vacuum sweeper may be carried out while the clothing is still on the wearer. It is, however, much simpler to perform this operation on shed clothing.

SPECIAL ITEMS OF CLOTHING

Shoes

Among the very prolific sources of evidence are shoes. Markings on the bottoms of the soles are significant because they vary greatly between the shoes of a person who merely walks in the shoes on conventional surfaces and those of one who climbs fences, prowls backyards, and so forth. The climbing of fences or other barriers is often indicated by marks ahead of the heels and behind the soles. The shoes of bicyclists sometimes show similar markings at these locations; hence, caution is necessary in the interpretation of such traces. The shoes of welders will often have small spheres of metal embedded in the leather. Persons who have fallen will usually have a rotary scratch on the sole of one shoe only; however, such markings are not limited to the shoes of persons who have fallen.

The preliminary examination of shoes differs in some respects from that of cloth garments such as suits, shirts, or underwear because of their different nature and the types of evidence they may carry. One shoe at a time is placed on clean wrapping paper and its general condition is observed. Stains possibly caused by blood, grease, or other materials are noted. The presence of mud or soil is particularly significant. If present, such incrustations are removed partially or wholly and placed in clean vials with notations as to the exact source and the region of the shoe from which the sample has been removed. Different mud flakes may have different origins, and should be removed separately and stored separately. Most commonly such mud samples will be found around the edges of the soles, at the rear of the sole on the bottom of the shoe, and on the bottom surface of the heel. Mud present in nail holes in the heels is ordinarily of little value because mud once impressed into these cavities may be carried for long periods, and so may have had an origin in almost any location where the shoes have been worn. Mud recently acquired will be more restricted in its possible origin, and if the shoes are secured shortly after the commission of the crime there is an excellent chance that part of it at least may have a connection with the crime.

Minute examination, with magnification, must be made of the soles and heels of the shoes. Fragments of glass, gravel stones, and similar solid objects are frequently found embedded in the leather or rubber surface. These fragments must be teased out with a needle and saved for further examination. Glass obtained in this way has been used to prove the guilt of burglars who stepped on the glass at the scene of the crime and carried the fragments with them. It must be remembered that merely walking on such objects is not usually sufficient to embed them in solid leather or rubber. Examination of many shoes after walking over gravel has seldom shown any embedding of the material, through loose pieces may be carried in cracks or may adhere to tar, chewing gum, etc. A pair of burglars tearing up a tar-and-gravel roof to gain entrance pulled upward on boards and tar paper, thus exerting unusual force on their shoes. The force caused many little stones to be embedded, every one of which was later matched by similar gravel taken from the same roof. Glass fragments become embedded more easily because they commonly have sharp edges that cut into the shoe surface. Since such glass can be matched with very great precision by comparison with samples of standard glass, it is highly important that no piece of glass in a shoe sole be overlooked or lost.

The inside of the shoe should also be examined carefully. It is less likely to yield significant evidence because it is constantly being swept by the sock on inserting and removing the foot, and any object larger than dust or fibers will be felt and deliberately removed. In the instance mentioned above, one fairly large gravel stone was found inside one of the shoes. Since this burglar was arrested on the morning following the crime, he probably had not put the shoe on again after returning from the burglary.

Also frequently found on shoes are smears of tar, paint, chewing gum, or other liquid or semiliquid materials that may be stepped on. In tearing up the tar-and-gravel mentioned, the burglars had stepped on tar and a considerable amount was smeared on the bottoms of their shoes. Another burglar who climbed a fire escape to the third story of a recently painted house had four different kinds of paint on his shoes. Each of these corresponded exactly with one of the four types of paint used on the house. Such evidence is necessarily convincing when it is established that the suspect is not a painter, and in fact had no other paint on his shoes except the four types from the house in question. Stains of any kind on the shoes should always be examined with the greatest care because many materials that are spilled are stepped on by people in the vicinity. If this occurs at the scene of a crime, the stain may be highly significant. Bloodstains are particularly important in the investigation of assaults and murders. Although blood on leather is usually difficult to study, it may be more than normally significant when found. Other possibilities of this kind will occur to the mind of the alert investigator.

Underwear

Underpants are of special interest, particular in the investigation of rape. Almost invariably they will carry seminal stains, whether the garment is taken from the suspect or from the victim. Although such stains will be found in the garments of innocent persons, the absence of such a stain in a suspect's underpants is tentative evidence of innocence. He may have changed underpants, or some other circumstance may have prevented staining, but these explanations are unlikely in view of the haste that usually accompanies such a crime. If there are no facts that point strongly to the guilt of a suspect accused of rape, and his underpants show no seminal stains, he should be released. If other circumstances point strongly to his guilt, it is well to search further for another pair of underpants that may have been removed and placed with dirty laundry or otherwise concealed. Blood on the underpants of a suspect is highly significant, and when accompanied by seminal stains it may on examination provide almost conclusive evidence of guilt.

Hats

A hat is occasionally lost from a criminal's head during flight and may be recovered by the police. Aside from the usual dust and miscellaneous debris, the hat is also a common carrier of hair, and in fact is nearly unique in that any hairs found in a hat are almost certainly from the wearer. This is not necessarily the case with hairs found on other garments.

Rather frequently hairs are found under the sweatband of a hat, even when the hat is new and almost devoid of perspiration stains and microscopic debris. In one instance, two hold-up men were caught as a result of finding one such hair in a hat one of them lost while being pursued by the police. The hair itself did not provide proof of guilt, but it was the one necessary clue to their identity and led to their capture in another city some days later.

Gloves

Gloves, when recovered, are often excellent sources of evidence. They have the same tendency to accumulate debris that characterizes pockets and pants cuffs. In addition, because they are worn on the hands, they are closest to the points at which contact with the environment of the actual crime is established. Their common use to prevent leaving fingerprints gives them a high incidence in criminal evidence. To illustrate their value: a criminal forced his way into a locked car by breaking the window with a pistol butt. He was wearing kid gloves. Inside one such glove, found later in his possession, was embedded a sharp fragment of glass, and the area around this point was stained with blood. Evidently the glass had cut his hand, and both blood that could be matched

Clothing and Cloth

to his blood group and the glass fragment that could be matched with the broken window were available.

Fur Coats

Fur coats do not often prove significant as evidence or sources of evidence in crimes in a warmer locale. They are expected to have more forensic value in colder climates. The high incidence of women as victims of crime, and the fact that a considerable proportion of women wear furs at times, gives the fur coat a significant value when it is involved in a crime. Furs do not pick up miscellaneous debris proportionately as well as does woven fabric because the parallel fur hair does not trap microscopic fragments as well as does a weave. However, some such material will inevitably adhere to fur and should be examined in much the same manner as debris found on woven material. In addition, there is a fair probability that fur hairs, most of them dyed, and easily distinguished and identified, will be found on the clothing of the criminal. The presence of any dyed animal hair is often uniquely valuable whether it traces to a fur coat or to a toy made of animal fur, or to any other similar source.

CLOTH AS EVIDENCE

Cloth, as distinct from clothing, is often important evidence in its own right. Fragments of intact cloth may be torn from garments during the commission of a crime or, more commonly, cloth fragments are intentionally removed from larger pieces for use in the commission of a crime. Cloth adhesive tape has been used in this manner in the construction of a mechanism for exploding a bomb. Fragments of cloth have been unintentionally left at the scene of a crime where they were used for constructing a gag or bindings. In a number of crimes fragments of cloth have been torn from the intruder's clothing by protruding nails, or by wires, as he climbed through windows, and over fences and other barriers.

In one additional respect cloth itself can become important as evidence. It may leave impressions in dust, paint, grease, or similar materials. This is especially common in automobile accidents in which pedestrians are struck violently and their clothing leaves a distinct impression of the cloth weave on the car surface.

Cloth Comparisons

When a sizable fragment of cloth occurs in evidence, a thorough search for the larger piece from which it was cut or torn is essential. When this has been located, the two pieces must be compared. The process of comparison is relatively simple and it may give conclusive proof of the origin of the fragment. The factors that must be compared are: (1) dimensions, (2) shape, (3) color, (4) cloth type, (5) pattern of dyeing, (6) weave, (7) thread count and comparison, and (8) direction of twist of the threads.

Ordinarily the method of comparing the above features is rather obvious, with the possible exception of the last feature mentioned. The difficulty will vary with the conditions and it may at times be considerable. In the bomb case mentioned above, a wire was fastened to the winding knob of an alarm clock by means of cloth adhesive tape. Many adhesive tapes are similar in general appearance, being made of white cotton, produced in quantity, not dyed, and of a simple and common type of weave. However, it is as difficult to duplicate a piece of adhesive tape exactly as it is to duplicate exactly any other manufactured article, which means that it is nearly impossible. The adhesive tape from which the piece had been taken was found. A rectangular piece of the same dimensions as the piece from the bomb had been cut from it. A thread count showed the same number of threads in both directions on both pieces. Not all of the threads were of the same size, as is almost invariably true of cloth made from natural fibers. A comparison of the thread sizes along the lines of cutting revealed that they corresponded thread-for-thread between the cut surfaces of the original and of the fragment, thus providing almost conclusive proof of the origin of the fragment. Even when there are

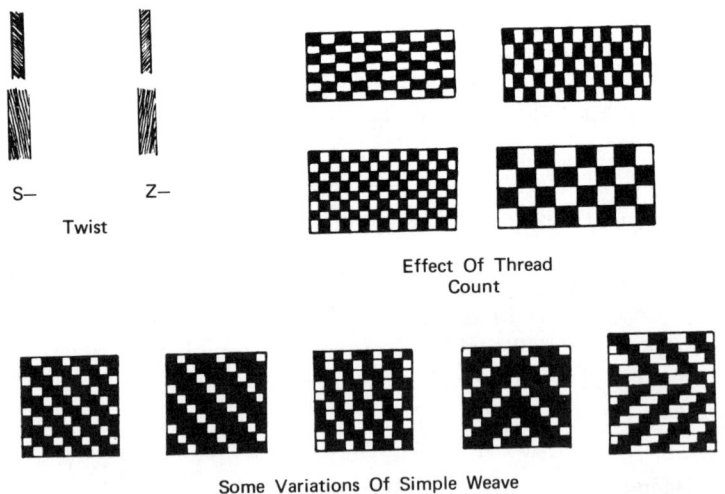

FIGURE 10-1. Diagrammatic representation of factors that influence cloth patterns: (upper left) direction of twist, and effect of degree of twist, which is related to hardness of cloth; (upper right) simple variation of thread count; (lower) effect of altering the weave arrangement.

other important features for comparison, such as the pattern of dyeing, it is essential that thread counts and comparisons be made before identity is claimed unless the other features are in themselves so definite as not to leave any doubt.

THREAD COMPARISONS. In many instances thread comparisons may be made by direct photography of the two samples of cloth. The corresponding edges are placed as closely together as possible without obscuring the details of the cut or tear, and a photograph is taken. The photograph is enlarged enough to reveal the similarity of corresponding threads. When the pieces have been separated by tearing, rather than by cutting, the problem is often more difficult. If there are good reference features such as the pattern of dyeing, the presence of atypical threads—either larger or smaller than normal—may be observed and their positions relative to the dye pattern determined. Also, thread counts between reference points in a pattern may be made. With a reasonable degree of ingenuity a solution for most of the problems of this kind can be found, but the solution is not always as easy as would be supposed from the basic simplicity of the problem.

SMALL FRAGMENTS. When the fragment consists of a single thread or of only a few, as may occur if a piece of cloth has been snagged on a nail, the comparison will be difficult and the examination less conclusive than if some of the intact cloth is found. However, it is not impossible to trace a very small fragment to the original cloth. If a suspected original is found, it will first be examined carefully for any rents or tears that could have given rise to the fragment in question. Having located such a tear, one may determine whether its dimensions agree with those of the fragment. The color and general appearance of the threads must be consistent with those of the cloth. Then other similar threads are removed from the fabric, preferably by tearing from a location other than that suspected of being the original tear. The comparison threads and the questioned threads are examined carefully as to size, approximate number of fibers per thread, degree and type of twist, appearance and arrangement of kinks due to weaving, and any other similar factors observable in the particular threads.

Failure to obtain exact correspondence of all factors does not necessarily mean that the tentative supposition of origin is incorrect. If most of the factors are in agreement and the discrepancies are minor, the probability of common origin is high. Because some variations exist among threads, the observed differences may have been caused merely by the circumstance that the comparison threads do not include the particular thread from which the fragment was torn. If, to prove the identity, it is necessary to locate the exact thread, careful photographs are taken of the spot and a detailed record is made of the dimensions, the number of threads broken, and all other pertinent details before extracting the thread in question and altering the appearance of the rent.

Further information can be obtained by direct comparison of the fibers themselves. The general problem of fiber comparison is dealt with in Chapter 11. In isolated cases the thread may consist of mixtures of fibers or fiber types, all of which can be subjected to comparative study. More commonly a given thread contains one kind of fiber only, and only one color, so that the comparison of fibers is of only limited utility.

Cloth Impressions

Cloth impressions may occur under two sets of conditions. First, they are made when cloth is pressed into material of sufficient plasticity to receive and retain the imprint. This includes mud, wet paint, chewing gum, and similar materials. When located, such impressions should always be photographed immediately, care being taken to avoid distortion from oblique camera angles and to include in the picture a ruler or a piece of engineer's paper to establish the exact dimensions of the imprint for later study. If possible, the original impression should be preserved intact. In many instances it may not be possible, so comparison by means of photographs may be necessary. At times a cast of the impression can be made with moulage, molten Wood's metal, or some other suitable casting material. Casting must always follow rather than precede photographing the impression.

Standards for comparison should be made from the suspected cloth in a manner as close as possible to the manner in which the questioned impression was made. Thus, a dust impression is best compared with a dust impression, and a paint impression with a paint impression. If making a standard in this way is impractical, some other means will be used. The cloth may be pressed into Plasticine or modeling clay, for example. The standard impression should be photographed, and the photographs compared at exactly the same magnification. This is usually more practical than the comparison of the original impressions. Often the two photographs may be cut through the middle and the edges placed together for comparison. If the agreement is convincing, even though not exact, the variation may be attributable to the inevitable change in the dimensions of photographic printing paper during drying. In this situation, if the negatives were made to the same magnification, they may be cut, placed side by side, and printed together to provide a comparison photograph. In the laboratory it is simple enough to take both negatives with exactly the same magnification. In the field it is not simple. When the magnifications on the negatives are not identical, and difficulty is encountered because of the change in size of print paper, another useful expedient is to enlarge the picture on film instead of on paper, since film size does not alter as does paper size. Glass plates such as are used for printing lantern slides may be used advantageously except that they cannot be cut to edge-to-edge comparison.

Cloth impressions on hard surfaces, such as the fenders or bumpers of automobiles, differ from those discussed above only in one important manner, that

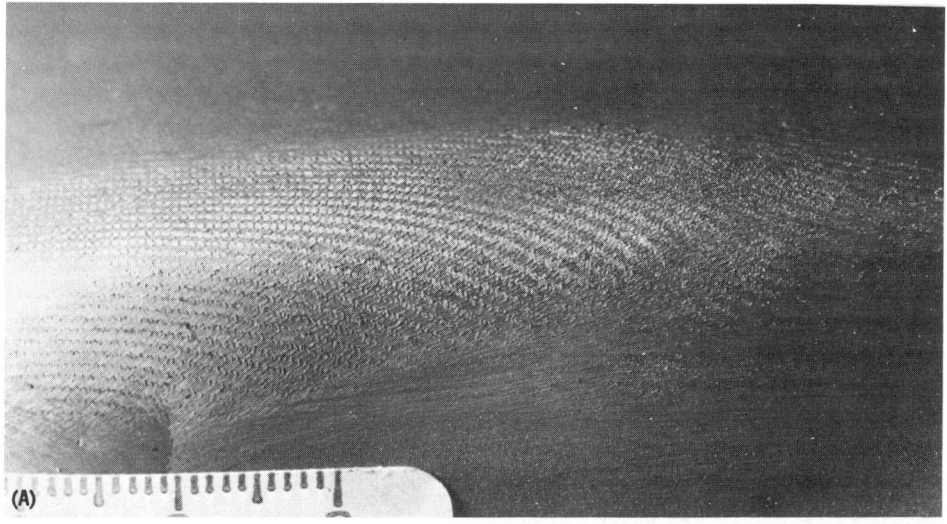

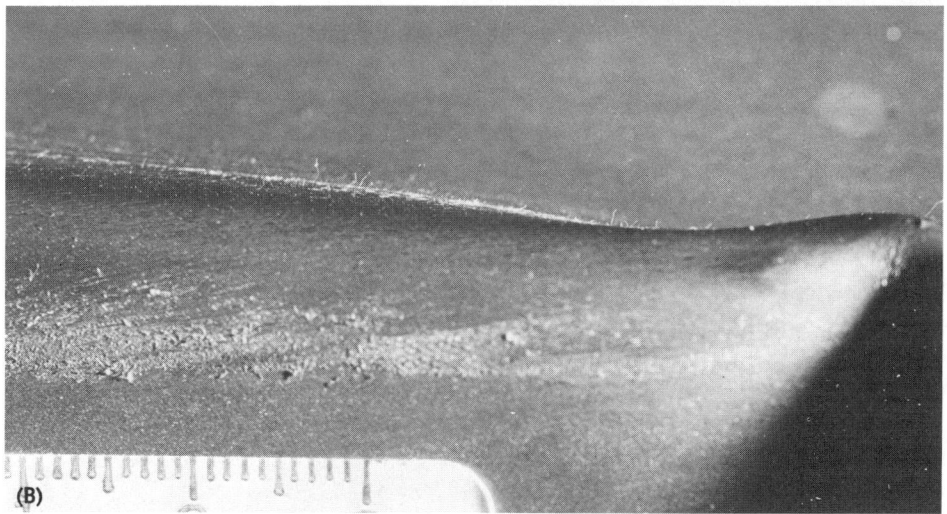

FIGURE 10-2. (A) In a vehicular homicide the fabric pattern of the victim's trousers was impressed into the painted surface of the fender. (B) The same area of the fender, photographed from an oblique angle, showed that fibers from the trousers were also imbedded in the paint. (Courtesy of John E. Murdock.)

is, they were made with considerable force on a nonplastic surface. The force may have distorted the weave marks somewhat, and the impression will not have sufficient depth for reproduction by casting. Because of the surface characteristics, reliance must be placed almost entirely on photography for the comparisons that are to be made.

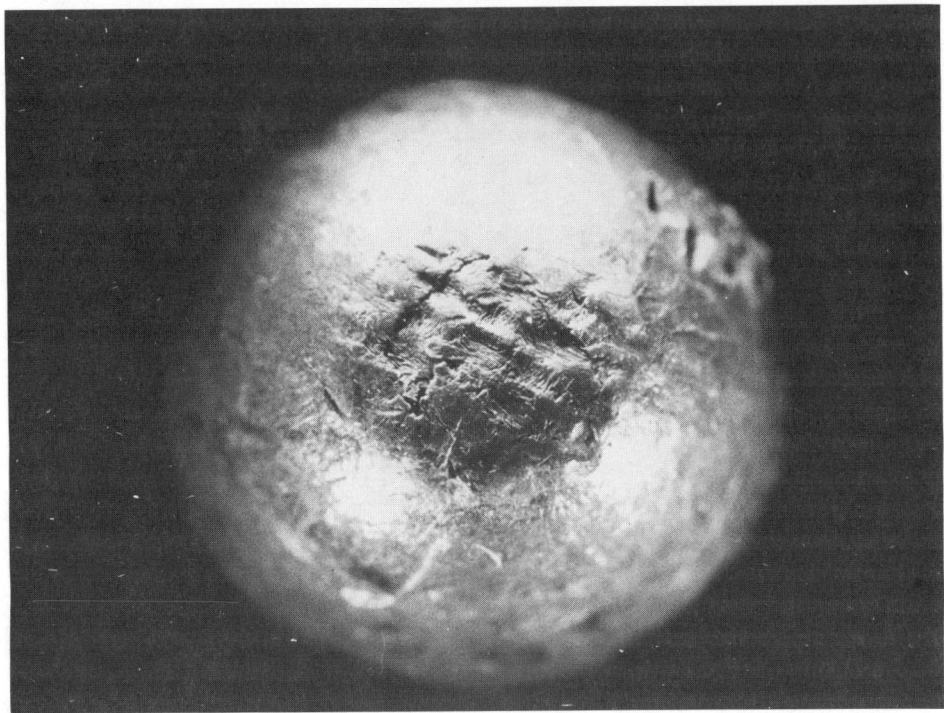

FIGURE 10-3. A police officer wash shot with the .38 cal. bullet shown above. As the bullet passed through the stiff fabric of his uniform, the pattern of the cloth was impressed into the head of the bullet; in addition, fibers from the cloth were found adhering to the bullet nose. (Courtesy of John E. Murdock.)

Standards will present more difficulty with this type of impression. Plasticine or clay may be used satisfactorily at times. If this does not give satisfactory standards, a suitable method is to procure a surface like the one struck, lay the cloth sample on it, and give it a hard blow with a sandbag or mallet. Alternatively, a block of wood may be laid on the cloth and the block struck a hard blow. Intelligent adaptation to existing conditions and a little experimentation will usually solve such difficulties.

It must always be remembered in comparing cloth and cloth impressions that there are many standard types of weave, and that the duplication of a cloth impression is in itself not proof that the standard cloth was that which made the impression, since many cloths have the same weave. When an impression matches the clothing of the victim, the evidence is highly valuable even though it alone may not be conclusive. Most important, the presence of such a cloth impression on the hard paint of an automobile is almost conclusive proof that the car has struck such cloth forcibly, and has therefore been in an accident. However, the impression may have been made in dust or grease rather than by forcible impact. This possibility must be checked. A dirty surface on a fender might well receive an impression from the clothing of someone who was leaning on it. If by remote chance this impression were identical with that obtained from a hit-and-run victim's suit, a serious error could result. Such possible confusion can be avoided by careful examination of the surface carrying the impression, noting the location on the car to determine whether it could have struck the victim, and searching for confirmatory evidence in the form of blood, hairs, fibers, broken glass, and similar residues. A simple check may be made by the investigator by pressing his own clothing to another, similar portion of the car and noting whether the hardest pressure he can exert will leave an impression. If not, it is almost certain that the questioned impression was placed with force.

REFERENCES

Garner, W.: *Textile Laboratory Manual.* New York: American Elsevier (1967).

Grover, E. B., and Hamby, D. S.: *Handbook of Textile Testing and Quality Control.* New York: Textile Book Publishers (1960).

Hearle, J. W.: *Structural Mechanics of Fibers, Yarns and Fabrics.* Plainfield, New Jersey: Textile Book Service (1969).

Martin, O.: "Criminalistic Investigation of Textiles," *Kriminalistik* 9:457 (1955).

Robinson, A. T. C., and Marks, R.: *Woven Cloth Construction.* New York: Plenum Press (1967).

11
Fibers

Small items of evidence, i.e., microscopic materials, are often fibrous in nature. Most of the vegetable kingdom is built up of fibers of one sort or another, and animals contribute multitudes of fiber-like hairs. Even some mineral materials are fibrous: e.g., asbestos. It is therefore not surprising that the most conspicuous fractions of any set of sweepings are likely to be masses of fibers. Those of random vegetable origin are not likely to have great value as evidence except in a very unusual situation.

Two classes of fibers are almost always of significance and must always receive attention. These are (1) hairs, which will be discussed in Chapter 13, and (2) textile fibers.

The construction of cloth from fibrous materials is one of the oldest arts of mankind and is today the basis of one of the largest developments of the industrial age. Originally, the only fibers available for cloth construction were of natural origin: certain animal fibers such as wool, and a few vegetable fibers such as linen and cotton. Although the natural fibers are still major components of modern fabrics, they have been supplemented and partially replaced by a very large assortment of regenerated fibers, and especially by synthetic fibers. This increase in the raw materials of textile manufacture has greatly enriched the possibilities of fibers as evidence, expanding still further their already great significance.

The natural fibers generally have less strength than the synthetic, so tend to break more easily. For this reason, their potential as evidence, when they are present, is greater than that of the greater probability of transfer.

Fibers

Crimes involving bodily contact between the criminal and his victim are usually accompanied by extensive contact of their respective clothing. These cases include most crimes against the person, such as homicide during a struggle, sex offenses, and assaults. In car thefts the criminal contacts the upholstery of the automobile. In burglary, he contacts the objects in the region broken into or searched. In all such contacts clothing fibers will be transferred from the criminal to his victim or to the environment, and from the victim or the environment to the culprit. This is true because clothing always carries loose fibers, most of which have broken from the cloth itself, and many of which have been accumulated from contacts with other clothing in a wardrobe or elsewhere. It is these loose fibers that are collected by another cloth when contact is established, so that all such fibers may be shared between any two cloths that touch or rub each other. Because of the very general occurrence of this effect, fibers will ordinarily be among the most prominent features of the evidence, and may be found where there is no other significant evidence.

COLLECTION OF FIBERS

As indicated earlier, the use of the vacuum sweeper with a special filter is always effective in collecting fibers as well as other fine debris from a surface. Its major limitation is its lack of selectivity, both as to the type of material collected and, to a lesser extent, the region from which it is collected. It is not a valid assumption that a fiber transfer will be totally haphazard. For example, the presence of a specific type of fiber on the right sleeve may have an entirely different significance than would the same fiber on the lapel, or on the middle of the back. A similar consideration will apply to fibers on bedding or furniture. If the fiber in question were underneath the covers of a bed it would have a different significance than it would have if found on the top surface of the bedcover. For these reasons the astute collector of evidence may in many instances inspect a garment or other cloth object very carefully and extract characteristic fibers from selected areas with fine forceps, package them individually and note the exact locations from which they were obtained. Some investigators prefer the use of wide strips of Scotch tape, or other transparent adhesive tape, which collects very efficiently, and from precisely defined areas. It has been shown in a number of instances that the location of the fiber is more valuable as evidence than is the mere presence or transfer of the fiber. The tape method is nearly ideal for this purpose, but it very often causes complications in later laboratory examinations. The adhesive is difficult to remove from fibrous materials, and without its removal some examinations are not practical.

FIBERS IN SWEEPINGS

As has been remarked, the most impressive characteristic of the majority of sweepings is the multitude of fibers present. Only certain types of fiber are likely to be of value as evidence, and these may be mixed with very large quantities of irrelevant fibers. The task of separating significant fibers from the mass, and segregating the various useful types, is a time-consuming one that is sometimes neglected because of the labor involved. Since this is a laboratory operation it will not be discussed in detail here. It may be noted that various methods other than selection of individual fibers under low-power microscope and separation with fine forceps have been developed, but it is doubtful if any of them is superior for fiber separation. In general, *the fibers that are of interest are those that have sufficient individuality so that their probable origin may be traced.* These are ordinarily dyed textile fibers of all types, as well as white fibers of certain less common types. White cotton is found in all sweepings, and cannot be considered to have any evidential significance. White wool is a little less common and may possibly be significant, whereas certain white synthetics may be sufficiently uncommon to have general value. Such fibers must be positively identified as to chemical composition if they are to be of any value; unlike dyed fibers they cannot be reliably distinguished by color. Though white is customarily regarded as an absence of color, the eye distinguishes many gradations within the spectrum of so-called "white" fabrics. For example, white woolen fabric resembles a white cotton sheet more in name than in visual impression.

TYPES OF TEXTILE FIBERS

The fibers used in the construction of textile fabrics may be classified as follows:

(1) Natural fibers
    (a) Animal: wool, silk, mohair, and other animal hairs
    (b) Vegetable: cotton, linen, hemp
(2) Regenerated fibers: rayons
(3) Synthetic fibers: nylon, dacron, and many others
(4) Miscellaneous and unusual fibers, as fiber glass, metals, asbestos

The fiber expert must be able to recognize most of the fibers he encounters in evidence, but some of them will appear so infrequently that they do not warrant extended treatment here. Those that will be seen frequently are wool, cotton, mercerized cotton, rayon, silk, linen, and possibly a dozen classes of synthetic fibers. In the last category, not only are there many types in use at present, but the number is increasing steadily, so that it is necessary for the student of fibers to keep abreast of new developments if he is to deal with all the synthetics he may encounter. Numerous books and journal references are available as guides in the identification of synthetic fibers, but such publications may rapidly become obsolete.

Animal fibers require particular attention because specialty fabrics may incorporate a rather wide variety of animal hairs. The hairs of the alpaca (Peruvian llama), of various goats (including mohair from the Angora goat), of camels, rabbits, and of several other fur-bearers such as mink, will occasionally be encountered. Hairs will be discussed in Chapter 13. Many excellent references are available.

Natural Fibers

WOOL. Fibers of wool, because they are animal hairs, are normally covered by scales. Under magnification, the scales give an appearance similar to that of very irregular shingles on a roof. Wool varies greatly in its fiber-diameter, or coarseness. Coarse wool particularly will often show a very indistinct scale structure. The scale edges may be abraded by wear, so that some coarse wool fibers actually appear denuded of scales. In contrast, very fine wool fibers usually show a pronounced scale structure. This may represent, in part, the difference between the fur and the down hairs of the sheep, or differences in the coats of various breeds of sheep. Wool from different portions of the body of the sheep is also known to differ.

A medulla, or core, is not frequently observed in wool, but in some wools it is quite pronounced. The presence or absence of a medulla probably depends upon the breed of sheep. For the purpose of the crime investigator, these differences are important only insofar as they affect his judgment in the matching of fibers. In all cases, wool-fiber samples should be identical as to type and visible characteristics of fiber, as well as in color, before they can be considered to match. At first sight it might appear that since a cloth will contain both coarse and fine wool fibers of similar color, the match could be made on the basis of color alone. That this is not the case follows from the fact that the same dye will not necessarily show an identical microscopic appearance with coarse and fine fibers of wool. The amount of dye viewed in the two cases may be different and the contribution of the fiber itself to the appearance is different. Thus, unless the fibers are of the same size and type, the color match cannot be definitely established.

SILK. Though usually the product of the common silkworm, *Bombyx mori*, silk may be seen in several modifications obtained from other related species. It is a long, continuous fiber, and will be found as fragments only after breaks have been caused by mechanical damage or by wear. Raw silk is made up of double fibers, each fibril of which is roughly triangular in cross-section. Each double fiber is embedded in a roughly elliptical structure of a gelatinous protein called *sericin*. In the longitudinal view the fiber shows an irregular surface structure with transverse fissures, creases, folds, and uneven lumps, most of which have resulted from the reeling operation. In many longitudinal views the two fibrils will be seen separately, and at intervals there will be visible separations between them, sometimes for a considerable distance.

Degummed silk is silk from which the sericin has been removed. It is very smooth, translucent, and structureless, with occasional constrictions, lumps or swellings. Wild silk is distinctly different in appearance, being broad, composed of numerous fibrils, and having longitudinal striations. At intervals there are flat places in which the striations are obliterated. This is the effect of the crossing of fibers before the material has hardened completely.

Raw degummed silk is one of the lightest of all textile fibers. The silk of commerce is usually weighed with tin oxide, which is precipitated within the fibers. After immersion in saturated stannic chloride solution the silk is subjected to prolonged washing to encourage the formation of stannic oxide by hydrolysis. Reversal of this reaction is prevented by subsequent immersion in sodium phosphate solution.

COTTON. A vegetable textile fiber, cotton is quite distinctive in appearance and will rarely be difficult to identify by microscopic examination. Each cotton fiber is a single cell in the form of a flattened elongated tube that resembles a twisted ribbon. The twisted appearance is a characteristic feature of this fiber, and it is evident in all but the very shortest fragments. Occasionally the twist will be obscured by mashing of the fiber, but careful microscopic examination will almost invariably reveal it.

Another distinguishing characteristic of cotton fiber is that the central area of a dry-mounted cotton fiber always appears darkened because of air inclusions in the hollow canal and possibly also in the fibrillar structure of the fiber itself. In transmitted light this appearance hinders the accurate observation of the color of the fiber if it has been dyed a light shade. White cotton examined with transmitted light in a dry mount never appears white, but gray. And if the fiber is placed in a mounting fluid, the light colors may be more accurately evaluated, but the fiber is then difficult to recover for any subsequent study. Reflected illumination is usually to be preferred because it allows better evaluation of the color and does not alter or damage the fiber.

Mercerized cotton is cotton treated with relatively strong caustic solutions that produce a marked swelling of the fiber. Mercerizing is accompanied by some loss in length, though manufacturers attempt to minimize such loss by carrying out the mercerizing process on either the spun thread or the woven fabric while it is held under tension. The swelling causes virtual closing of the internal canal and smoothing of the surface appearance of the fiber, so that the twisted appearance of the original fiber is obscured. It is, however, nearly always possible to observe the twist by careful examination even after mercerization, but the characteristic twisted-ribbon effect is largely lost. The sheen of the fiber is greatly increased, giving mercerized cotton fabric a silky appearance.

Mercerization is most extensively used in the manufacture of thread, partly because the process imparts increased tensile strength to the cotton. Because of its limited use mercerized cotton is not found as commonly in evidence materials as is ordinary cotton. Socks and stockings are sometimes made from mercerized cotton, as are also various items of women's apparel. Though variations in the degree of mercerization alter considerably the visible characteristics of fabrics, with the help of the microscope they are not difficult to identify. Certain chemical tests are available for identifying mercerized cotton, but their results are not appreciably more definite than microscopic appearance alone. To a large extent mercerized cotton has been replaced by fabrics woven of synthetic fibers.

LINEN. The linen fiber is typically vegetable in appearance. It is free of the scales that cover animal fibers, nonuniform in diameter, and irregular in surface structure. Different linen fibers vary greatly in diameter and in surface appearance. Linen does not resemble cotton (from which it is very easily distinguished), but it also possesses a clearly visible fibrillar structure. The most characteristic feature of use in the identification of linen is the appearance of nodes that, under magnification, resemble the nodes of bamboo. These may be emphasized by application of chemical stains employed for distinguishing fibers.

Linen is uncommon in criminal evidence. It is used particularly in manufacture of high-grade tablecloths and napkins and fine handkerchiefs: items not often involved in crime. It is scarce in men's clothing, having been replaced by cotton, rayon, nylon, or silk. Linen is sometimes used for women's clothing, but even here it is relatively scarce.

Regenerated Fibers

RAYON. The term "rayon" originally covered fibers of regenerated cellulose and of cellulose derivatives. An early derivative, cellulose nitrate, has become obsolete because of its flammability. Acetylated cellulose fiber, once classified among the rayons, is now referred to as "acetate." All the cellulosic fibers are readily identified and separated by means of chemical and morphological differences, one or the other of which is always applicable.

Rayon is usually manufactured by some modification of either the viscose process or the cuprammonium (Bemberg) process, the former being much more common. In both processes cellulose from cotton, wood, or other suitable plant material is dissolved, the differences in the method of solution being the basis for their various designations. The solution is forced through a very small orifice in a device called a "spinneret" into a bath that causes the cellulose to precipitate—regenerate—as rayon fiber. In addition, tension is applied to stretch the fiber, inducing an orientation of the molecules and greatly increasing fiber strength. It is then washed, dried, and stored on spindles or reels. Thus, rayon is essentially the same material as cotton, but its configuration has been determined by chemical and mechanical processes rather than by natural growth of the plant that formed the cellulose.

From the standpoint of the criminal investigator or the laboratory criminalist, the essential facts regarding rayons are those which may be used to identify such fibers, determine their type, and assess the degree of similarity between two or more such fibers by means of comparison studies.

Viscose rayon and cuprammonium rayon are both composed of cellulose, the chief constituent of cotton. They therefore have a chemistry similar to that of cotton and are chemically similar to each other. Morphologically they are quite distinct. In the viscose process the stretching of the fiber is accompanied by lateral shrinkage, which gives rise to a very uneven cross section. On the surface this unevenness has the appearance of parallel striations, which are not found in this exaggerated form in any natural fiber. The cuprammonium fiber, on the other hand, is almost cylindrical and smooth, not characteristic of any natural *plant* fiber, though a similar appearance is frequent in silk. Acetate, like viscose, shrinks greatly and irregularly, imparting a similar but somewhat less uneven appearance to the cross section. Acetate, being chemically different, is readily distinguishable by its great solubility in acetone, in which both viscose and cuprammonium rayons are quite insoluble. There are also marked differences in staining reactions, specific gravity, refractive index, appearance under polarized light, and other properties. The physical properties of greatest importance to the textile manufacturer, such as tensile strength, sheen, and absorption of moisture, are of little interest to the criminal investigator and will not be discussed.

Rayon fibers have historically been made as continuous filaments as long as the reel capacity, and such fiber is used to a considerable extent in undergarments, stockings, and similar articles in which great smoothness is desired. In recent years, nearly all rayons have also been manufactured in shorter fiber lengths that can be spun and woven as are the natural fibers and made to give a similar appearance. Aside from the matter of length, spun rayon is identical with the continuous types. They show other marked differences in diameter of fiber, and in the presence or absence of fillers added to suppress the glossy appearance of the fiber. The filler will appear throughout the fiber as granular inclusions, and is seen more commonly in spun rayon than in the continuous filament.

It is of interest also that the materials from which rayon is made may be equally well fabricated in forms other than fibers. Thus, the same viscose process is used to manufacture cellophane; and the acetate process is used in the manufacture of safety film, which is employed almost universally in photography. It is found also in many manufactured plastic articles.

Synthetic Fibers

Not many years ago garments made from synthetic fibers were rare, and acceptance of them came only slowly, with the exception of nylon stockings and a few types of undergarments. Today, all this has changed, and a very high proportion of all garments either contains such fibers as admixtures or is totally composed of synthetic material. A survey made in 1964 indicated a total production of man-made fibers approaching 3 billion lb/year. Unquestionably it is much higher at this writing. Thus, the problem of the criminalist has been correspondingly altered for a number of reasons. Not only must he know how to identify the various new fibers almost as soon as they are produced, but the frequency of stray fibers in his evidence has shifted sharply. Synthetics tend to shed fibers less than do fabrics made of natural fibers, but the great diversity of the synthetics adds new dimensions to the possibilities of practical evidential value when they are found. Now not only color is involved; the wide range of different basic fibers provides the basis for increased discrimination.

Synthetic fibers fall into several chemical categories, most of which are occupied by competing products of different manufacturers, each with his own trademark name. Variations among different manufactured varieties of the same basic products unquestionably exist, but each category is characterized in common as to general properties. For example, nylon is employed widely in uses that require high tensile strength, and polyester fibers are highly wrinkle resistant. The various categories or chemical types of fibers will be presented separately.

ACETATE. All acetate fibers are made by acetylating cellulose. Celanese, Du Pont, Eastman, and FMC are prominent manufacturers of acetate fibers. The starting material is usually wood pulp, which is converted into cellulose acetate. When at least 92% of the hydroxyl groups of the cellulose are acetylated, the fiber may be termed *triacetate*. Trademarks for such products include Arnel, Celanese acetate, Celaperm, Acele, Estron, Chromspun, and Avisco acetate. Compared with other acetate fibers, triacetate withstands somewhat higher temperatures in ironing, is more crease resistant, and dyes better. It has poor abrasion resistance, however, is weaker than acetate, and may be damaged by light.

NYLON. Among the very common types of synthetic fibers are the nylons. They

are polyamides linked in long chains in which recurrent groups ($-\text{C}-\text{NH}-$)
$\overset{\parallel}{\text{O}}$
are integral. The two common types of nylon are Nylon 66 and Nylon 6. The latter is distinguishable from the former by its slightly lower melting point. The processes employed in making the several types of nylon differ somewhat and result in some chemical variations. Starting materials in their manufacture, often stated as "coal, water, and air," are derivatives of coal tar such as benzene or phenol, hydrogen and ammonia and sodium hydroxide. The monomer molecules are linked under high temperature to form long chains. The cooled polymerized material is heated to melt it, and then passed through a spinneret to form rather coarse fibers, which, at this stage, lacking orientation of the chains, are weak. The coarse fibers are cold drawn into a very long fiber that has great tensile strength. Nylon finds widely varied uses in the manufacture of several types of garments, ropes, and cordage for use where lightness and great strength are required. In the massive form, nylon finds many uses in the manufacture of common articles.

ACRYLICS. The acrylic fibers include all long-chain synthetic polymers that are composed of at least 85% by weight of acrylonitrile units: ($-\text{CH}_2-\overset{|}{\underset{\text{CN}}{\text{CH}}}-$).
In practice the acrylonitrile is copolymerized with 5–15% of a second monomer, which may differ in the products of various manufacturers. Variations in the copolymer result in different physical properties and dyeing characteristics. Fibers in this group are quite widely used in the manufacture of fabrics. Among their trade names are Acrilan, Creslan, Orlon and Zefran.

POLYESTERS. Polyesters are fibers composed of any long-chain polymer in which at least 85% by weight are esters of dihydric alcohols and terephthalic acid (p-$\text{HOOC}-\text{C}_6\text{H}_4-\text{COOH}$). They include such trade names as Kodel, Dacron, Vycron, and Fortrel. While they share most of the advantages and disadvantages of other synthetics, they have been used increasingly in recent years because of their high resistance to wrinkling. Wash-and-wear and noniron clothing will almost invariably be composed wholly or in part of polyester fibers.

SARAN. Saran is a manufactured fiber in which the fiber-forming substance may be any long-chain synthetic polymer containing at least 80% by weight vinylidine chloride units: ($-\text{CH}_2-\text{CCl}_2-$). This material is water-repellent and has little chemical activity. Thus, it does not spot or alter readily, and finds its main uses in rugs, lawn and patio furniture, and industrial fabrics. It is little used in garments. A variation is a copolymer containing 15% polyvinyl chloride and marketed under the names Vectra and Dow Badische's Saran. Rovana is a flat monofilament fiber of Saran.

OLEFINS. These fibers include any long-chain synthetic polymer containing at least 85% by weight ethylene, propylene, or other olefin unit. The fibers are related chemically to polyethylene and polypropylene, which are commonly used for containers and similar items. The fibers melt rather easily and are difficult to dye. They find considerable use in automobile seat covers and outdoor furniture. They will also be encountered in hosiery, sweaters, carpets, and cordage. Trade names include DLP and Herculon.

MODACRYLICS. Fibers in this category are similar to the acrylic fibers except that they contain 35% or more by weight acrylonitrile ($-CH_2-CH-$) and up to
$$\underset{CN}{|}$$
85% other long-chain polymers. Their greatest use is in deep-pile fabrics such as floor coverings, draperies, blankets, and heavy coats. Dynel and Verel are trade names.

VINYON. Fibers in this category are based on vinyl chloride polymers and include any long-chain synthetic polymer containing at least 85% by weight of that monomer ($-CH_2-CHCl-$). This type of fiber melts rather than burns, but melts at quite a low temperature. It is strong and very elastic, and is easily heat-bonded to other fibers. *Vinal*, based similarly on vinyl alcohol, has been manufactured, but is very uncommon.

SPANDEX. This term applies to long-chain synthetic polymers in which at least 85% by weight of the material consists of segmented polyurethane. Spandex is light, soft, and has good holding power, which makes it suitable for foundation garments, swimwear, and special elastic products such as surgical hose. It is used generally in certain stretch garments. Trademarks include Vyrene, Glospan, Lycra, and Blue C.

Miscellaneous Fibers

Other vegetable fibers that are occasionally utilized in fabrics (sacks, etc.) but rarely in clothing are jute, and less commonly hemp, sisal, and ramie fibers. Because of their common use in cordage, they will be treated in some detail in the section on that subject. (See Chapter 12.)

Animal fibers other than wool that are sometimes present in evidence are goat hair, which includes mohair, cashmere, and common goat hair; camel hair, from both the dromedary and the bactrian camel; llama hair, from which are obtained vicuna, alpaca, guanaco, and the common llama; cow hair, used in coarse carpet yarns, stuffing, blankets, and felts; horse hair, used chiefly in upholstery and stuffing; rabbit hair, found ordinarily in felt hats; and a variety of hair from other fur-bearing animals such as the muskrat. Because animal hairs are of more general interest in other connections than in ordinary clothing and miscellaneous fabrics, these and other animal hairs will be considered separately. (See Chapter 13.)

In addition to the miscellaneous natural and synthetic fibers, there are also a variety of manufactured fibers that are not related to the plastics, or classified in another group of synthetics. These include rubber and synthetic elastomers which find use in garments that must be stretched; glass fibers manufactured by a number of companies and used largely for drapery material; and metallic fibers, which may consist of metal, plastic coated with metal, metal coated with plastic, or a core completely covered with metal. These fibers are often incorporated as decorative supplements to the more conventional fibers in specialty cloth.

USES AND LIMITATIONS OF FIBER EVIDENCE

Fibers that may have been transferred during the commission of a crime are of the greatest utility as physical evidence because of the ease with which loose fibers are transferred from one cloth to another or to a noncloth surface. Before any claim can be made regarding the likelihood that two fibers have a common origin, it is essential that the fibers be proved to be of the same kind of material, have the same color, and agree in any other morphological characteristics that are visible under the microscope. Such examination is strictly a criminalistics function rather than a police function. However, the value of fibrous evidence may in some instances be so obvious that the police officer will observe similarities of color or an unusual type of fiber. He must be highly conscious of fibers at all times so that this type of evidence will be carefully collected, protected from contamination, and well preserved for later laboratory study.

The proper interpretation of fiber matches remains difficult because of the absence of careful statistical studies to determine the degree of dependence of fiber characteristics upon each other. For example, is it more likely that a light blue wool fiber will be found in a garment composed primarily of dark blue wool than in a gray suit? Such matters have not been determined, although considerable incidence data are available, and empirical study has established a very great value associated with fiber evidence. Some additional interesting illustrations of uncommon fiber evidence are given in the following section.

UNUSUAL AND NONTEXTILE FIBERS

Fibers of unusual types may be found on both the clothing of a victim and that of a suspect. Because the fibers are uncommon, the probative value of finding such a match tends to be far greater than is the case with common textile fibers. For example, a small child who was raped in her bed had on her nightgown some dyed cat hairs that were matched by similar hairs found on the clothing of a suspect. The source of the hairs was found to be a toy dog belonging to the child. It is virtually certain that the presence of a particular type and color of dyed cat hairs on a man's clothing would be much less common than, for instance, a specific shade of blue wool fiber.

In another rape case whose locale was a public park, natural squirrel hairs were found both on the victim's clothing and on that of the suspect. Because natural squirrel hairs are now almost never used in fur coats or other articles of clothing, it was probable that the hairs originated in the park. Investigation revealed that squirrels lived in this park. Again, the value of this particular fiber match was probably greater than that of any common textile fiber, and its interpretation involved not only contact of two sets of clothing but probable contact of both of them with the park environment.

Textile fibers from sources other than clothing itself must never be overlooked or minimized. Bedding is one of the best possible sources of loose fibers and will always occur in evidence from crimes in which bed clothing is involved. Fibers from a sack in which burglar tools or loot are transported by criminals are often useful items of evidence. For example, a fence is scaled and the bag of tools is placed on top while the owner climbs. Many times, fibers from the bag will be left behind. Fertilizer bags are often used for carrying burglary tools, and may be marked with stenciled advertising matter. Fibers carrying paint from the stenciling may be identified exceptionally well, and will never be confused with dyed fibers.

REFERENCES

Berg, S.: "Evidentiary Value of Textile Fibers," *Arch. f. Kriminol.* 127:97 (1961).
Bergh, A. K.: "Some Aspects Relative to the Identification of Synthetic Fibers," *Intern. Crim. Pol. Rev.* 10:246 (1955).
Burd, D. Q., and Kirk, P. L.: "Clothing Fibers as Evidence," *J. Crim. Law and Criminol.* 32:353 (1941).
Carter, M. E.: *Essential Fiber Chemistry.* New York: Dekker (1971).
Kornreich, E.: *Introduction to Fibers and Fabrics.* New York: American Elsevier (1966).
Longhetti, A., and Roche, G.: "Microscopic Identification of Man-made Fibers from the Criminalistics Point of View," *J. For. Sci.* 3:303 (1958).
Martin, O.: "Criminalistic Investigation of Textiles," *Kriminalistik* 9:457 (1955).
Mauersberger, H. R.: *Matthews' Textile Fibers,* 6th ed. New York: Wiley (1954).
Press, J. J. (ed.): *Man-made Textile Encyclopedia.* New York: Textile Book Publishers (1959).
Sweating, O. J., ed.: *The Science and Technology of Polymer Fibers.* New York: Textile Book Publishers (1970). 2 vols.

12
Ropes, Cordage, and Packaging Material

Materials such as rope, cord, feed and fertilizer bags, and paper bags and cartons may often be encountered as evidence in criminal investigation. Explosive and incendiary materials are sometimes tied with a cord. Ropes are used in the binding, garroting, and hanging of a victim, in burglaries, and in various other types of crime. Feed and fertilizer bags are used to transport burglary tools, loot, and contraband.

In recent years, many new packaging materials have been added to the standard materials. Adhesive tapes are now widely used for sealing packages, and sheet plastic materials have partially superseded paper for use in special situations. Perhaps most significant of all, plastic foams in a wide variety of forms are used for filling voids in packages. Especially in preparing heavy or fragile objects for shipment, foam plastic (styrene or urethane foam) is formed to fit around objects to be packed. In other instances, smaller pieces of similar foam, molded in a variety of shapes, are simply poured into the package. Some special types of material, such as chemicals in glass containers, are surrounded within the package by vermiculite particles that have been treated to loosen them and render them resilient and soft. Because a very wide variety of materials may be utilized in packaging, the investigating officer must be keenly aware of the possibilities of such materials as potential evidence, and must make sure that they are preserved and ultimately examined.

MATERIALS OF CONSTRUCTION

String, cord, twine, and rope are made chiefly from cotton and the vascular fibers (flax, jute, sisal, and hemp). Rope is usually constructed of hemp or sisal fibers, and the preferred material is hemp, a well-known variety of which is termed *manila*. Cotton is commonly used for smaller cords and strings, light rope such as that employed for clothesline, and intermediate-strength wrapping cords. It is simple to distinguish between cotton and the vascular fibers, but difficult to distinguish between different types of the coarse vascular fibers. Staining and chemical tests may be required.

All common cordage materials are of vegetable origin; however, cords made of silk or nylon are used for special purposes. Fishing line may be made of nylon, silk, or linen; parachute cords are commonly made from nylon because of its great strength and its availability in single continuous lengths. A few miscellaneous fibers are encountered. These include insulating and padding materials such as kapok, milkweed, asbestos, and glass fibers. The latter two are woven into cords or fabric for such special applications as electrical insulation. They are sometimes found on knife blades used to cut telephone wires or other special objects. Some very inexpensive types of cord are constructed of twisted paper. The almost universal use of paper as a wrapping and packaging material makes it of frequent occurrence in physical evidence.

ROPE

As distinguished from cord or string, rope is made by twisting strands together. Each strand has been made by the twisting of threads, and each thread has been made by the twisting of fibers. Variations exist, as in ornamental ropes that are sometimes braided. Also, in a small rope the distinction between a thread and a strand may disappear. In all instances, rope is made by a multiple spinning procedure, whereas simple spinning results in a thread or cord.

Rope is always examined with respect to the following features:

(1) Its diameter, obtained by means of numerous measurements with a caliper.
(2) The direction of twist: "S" (clockwise) or "Z" (counterclockwise).
(3) The number of twists per unit of length. If sufficient rope is available, this should be determined in terms of the number of twists per foot in order to reduce the error of measurement. Very short lengths may require counting the number of twists in one inch or a few inches.
(4) The material from which the rope is constructed, e.g., hemp, sisal, cotton.
(5) The number of strands.
(6) The number of threads per strand.

(7) The average number of fibers per thread, which is determined by making cross-sectional cuts in several places, counting the fibers in each cross section, and calculating the average of the fiber counts.

If it is suspected that a piece of rope from one location, e.g., the home of the suspect, has the same origin as another piece found in a different location, e.g., the scene of the crime, all of the above-listed values should agree closely if a common source is to be claimed. Some variation may be accepted in items (1) and (6), but all the other characteristics must be in exact agreement. The finding of such a complete identity does not in itself prove a common origin, because the same type of rope may be found in a number of places. Proof of difference in ropes is more significant because it definitely establishes a difference of origin.

At times the alert investigator will observe other factors that can serve to establish a much greater probability of common origin, such as the presence of contaminating material of an unusual kind on both ropes, and—above all—a similarity in the amount and distribution of such contamination. Grease, paint, manure, grass stain, and many other materials can be accumulated on the surfaces of a rope during use. The alert investigator may find matching stains on two sections of a severed rope, one at the scene of the crime and the other among the suspect's belongings. The value of such stains is greater the more uncommon or characteristic they are.

A special circumstance in one burglary investigation was so unusual as virtually to prove identity in itself. A piece of rope used to drag a stolen safe was broken at the unattached end. Another broken piece of rope, taken from a suspect's car, was similar in all ordinary respects to the first. Routine examination of the ropes for the factors listed yielded the interesting information that the broken ends of both ropes consisted of three strands, two of which had seven threads, and one that had only six threads. Information was elicited that this represented an unusual error in manufacture, because a rope-spinning machine is stopped immediately if a thread is dropped, and the faulty section of rope is removed. No three-strand, twenty-thread rope is ever intentionally manufactured. Further study revealed that some distance from the break in the rope both pieces carried twenty-one threads. Had there been no other evidence, this single important fact might well have been conclusive in establishing identity of source of the two pieces of rope, and therefore the guilt of the defendants.

CORDS AND STRINGS

The wider occurrence of cords and strings gives them a significance somewhat less than that of rope. Ordinary cotton string, for example, is almost invariably used in every household and business. The significance of any item of physical

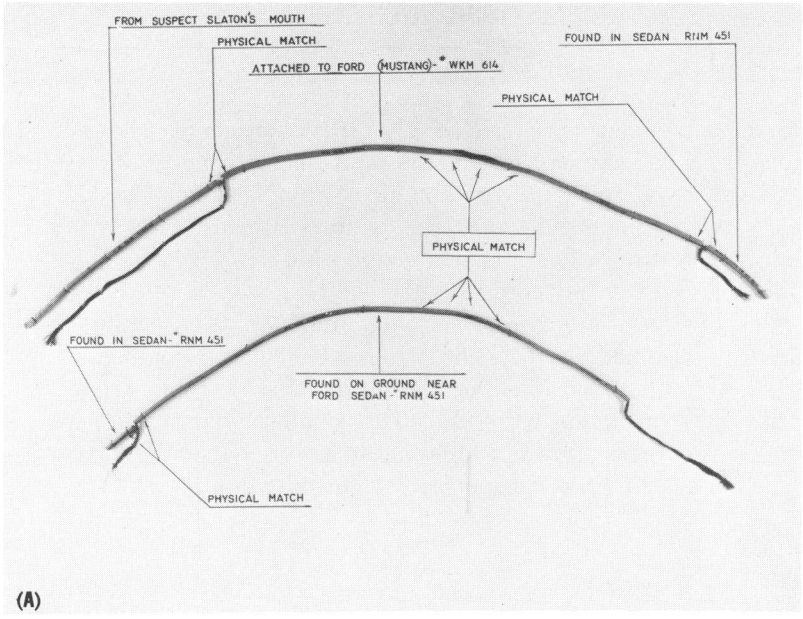

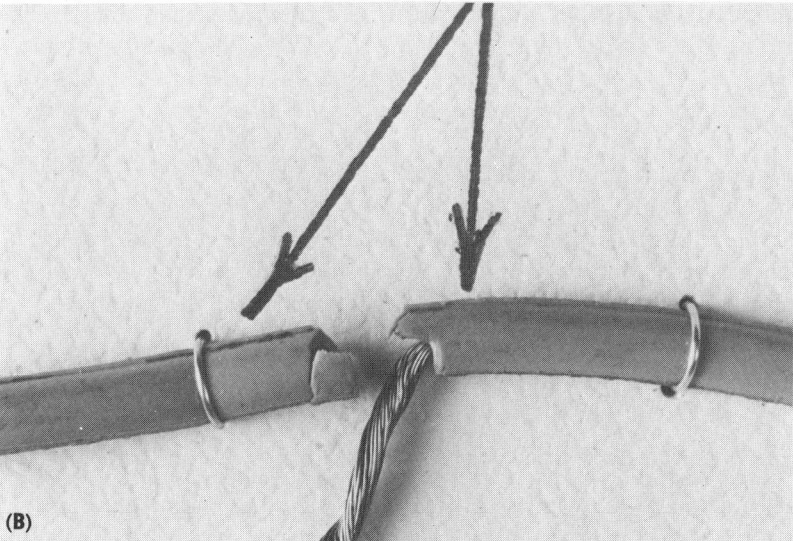

FIGURE 12-1. (A) The two halves of a household electrical cord and fragments of insulation were found in two stolen autos. When the suspect was apprehended, he was chewing on a section of insulation. A physical match was effected between the unchewed end and a section of cord found in one of the vehicles. Other sections of cord from both vehicles could also be matched, linking the suspect to both of them.
(B) Close-up of the unchewed section of insulation and the cord found in one of the stolen autos. (Courtesy of John E. Murdock.)

evidence is directly proportional to its degree of uncommonness, or its deviation from the average item of its type. But strings and cords have an added value because they accumulate relatively great amounts of residues and debris. A cotton string collects particles, fibers, and microscopic residues much more readily for a given surface area than does any but the most loosely woven cloths. For this reason, particularly, the competent investigator will never scorn the lowly cotton string when it is involved in his case.

Variation in string and cord is sufficient to justify careful examination at all times. The size, the tightness of spinning, and the average fiber counts should be determined in the comparison of strings. Ornamental cords and strings, when found, have an added significance because they are more variable than ordinary string and are produced in smaller quantity. If two pieces of cord under examination are not identical, it is proof that they differ in origin; hence the cord is eliminated from further consideration.

DEBRIS

Of primary importance in the study of rope, string, or cord is its cargo of microscopic materials that will often define a previous environment. The study of these residues is detailed under the respective treatments of microscopic evidence. (See Chapter 9.) The value of such evidence may be illustrated by the case of a cord that was used to tie a bundle of dynamite. The cord carried enough debris to identify the place at which the lethal device had been assembled. Round sand grains indicated the existence there of a stream. Pollens identified a certain type of tree whose normal environment is a stream bank. Animal hairs identified the domestic animal population of the spot. This combination of stream, animals, and trees was found at only one of three possible locations, and led to the apprehension of the maker of the bomb.

PACKAGING MATERIAL

Paper

Paper of many types, weights, and colors is found in paper packaging. It may range from tissue paper to heavy corrugated paper and cardboard. Few other materials show such wide variation. On the other hand, paper is mass-produced in tremendous quantities, so that wide distribution of a single type of paper is likely. This fact tends to diminish the value of paper packaging as evidence.

Examination of paper packaging materials should be made with respect to the following factors:

(1) *Thickness*, or weight of the paper, measured with a micrometer. A paper

micrometer is to be preferred, but a good ratchet type of mechanic's micrometer will serve.
(2) *Color*, conditioned by the type of pulp, by bleaching, artificial coloring, impregnation, and imprinting.
(3) *Type of surface*, sized or unsized, glossy or matte, and special finishes.
(4) If corrugated, the *number of corrugations* per unit length, and the thickness of the corrugating material and of the surface paper layers.
(5) *Embossing*, if present.
(6) Presence of *cut* or *torn edges*. If the counterpart can be found, the matching edges of the tear prove identity of origin.
(7) *Nature of the pulp* from which the paper was made. This includes the type of pulp (sulfite, ground, etc.) and the type of fiber used (nature of wood, rag, or other source). This determination is intricate and depends upon staining and microscopic examination.
(8) *Inclusions*, specks and spots. These are almost universally present and may be very distinctive.
(9) *Nature of sizing*. This requires chemical investigation by means of special qualitative tests.
(10) *Superimposed surface materials*, such as writing, markings, stenciling, contamination from spillage of liquids, and any other effect on the surface of the paper that did not result from manufacturing operations.

Of the factors listed above, those which involve simple observation and measurement may be readily determined by the investigating officer. Chemical and microscopic testing should be done in the laboratory by skilled personnel. If the nature of the problem merits very careful examination and there is reason to believe that paper packaging material is critical to the solution, it is proper to carry out all available tests, because the ultimate value of the evidence can, under proper conditions, be very great.

All the above considerations are also applicable to cord made of paper, and to paper tapes used to seal packages. The tape is most readily identified by direct comparison with a series of tapes obtained from a variety of sources until one that matches the questioned sample is located. An additional factor is that when the package is opened the tape is cut or torn. If, by chance, the separated portions are located in different places, they can be reassembled by visual matching of the cut or torn edges. As an alternative, it is sometimes possible to implicate the possessor of a roll of such tape by matching the cut end of a tape used for packaging an illicit item with the remaining cut end of that roll of tape. Although such opportunities may be rare, they do occur, and the possibility should not be overlooked, since it may offer a very simple solution to a difficult problem.

Adhesives used on tapes are of various types, many of them not publicized by the manufacturer. However, proper laboratory tests may serve to identify the type of adhesive, and comparative tests can establish a common type of adhesive on two or more samples in evidence. This possibility has not been well developed, but it is so obvious that the investigator should not overlook it in deciding what questions shall be asked of the laboratory. Several procedures are applicable to the comparison.

Plastics

Plastics are increasingly used as packaging materials. They occur in the form of sheet materials such as cellophane (regenerated cellulose similar to rayon) and polyethylene sheet. Identification of the material is easy with infrared spectrometry, and with other methods. Dimensions, appearance, and cut or torn edges are sometimes available for study and comparison. Such materials are sometimes colored or filled with other substances for decorative effects, as in Christmas wrappings. Although they are generally the product of mass manufacture, individual items may still retain a considerable degree of uniqueness, and should be available for study.

Loose plastic chunks occur in evidence only rarely. However, the methods for their study are known and simple, so that when they are found there is assurance that they can at least be identified as are other plastics. In addition to the value of simple identification of type, the possibility exists that there may be additional factors that would make them of even greater value through study of their condition, contaminations, fractures, and other factors.

REFERENCES

Browning, B. L.: *The Analysis of Paper.* New York: Dekker (1969).
Himmelfarb, D.: *Technology of Cordage Fibers and Rope.* Plainfield, New Jersey: Textile Book Service (1957).
Mauersberger, H. R.: *Matthews' Textile Fibers,* 6th ed. New York: Wiley (1954).
Purtell, D. J., and Casey, M. A.: "Paper Tapes and Labels Encountered in Document Examination," *J. For. Sci.* 11:496 (1966).
Snyder, P., and Snyder, A.: *Knots and Lines Illustrated.* Tuckahoe, New York: De Graff (1970).
Strelis, I., and Kennedy, R. W.: *Identification of North American Commercial Pulpwoods and Pulp Fibers.* University of Toronto Press (1967).

13
Hair

Hair is extremely important as physical evidence. It must be collected in every case in which it occurs, and subjected to thorough study. The laboratory investigator who examines it must have a broad knowledge of the general nature of hair and a reasonable amount of detailed experience in its examination. Except for certain simple preliminary examinations, such as the determination of color, it is dangerous to depend on any but expert study of hair found in evidence.

Hair consists principally of a bundle of fibrils each of which is composed of a chemically inert type of protein known as *keratin*, an albuminoid. Hair also contains pigment granules, and medullary material in the core, or medulla. It carries certain excretory products, notably arsenic, silica, possibly lead and iron, and a variety of known organic compounds. In recent years the development of an ultrasensitive method of analysis, *neutron activation analysis*, has made it possible to demonstrate the presence in hair of numerous trace elements that are largely, though not exclusively, metallic. To date about nineteen trace elements have been found. Some of them, such as sodium and chlorine, are normal constituents of the body with known physiological functions, but a majority of them are relatively uncommon and were not previously known to be present in significant quantity in the living organism. These include gold, molybdenum, tungsten, and even some rare-earth elements. Most of these are present in quantities too small to be detected by chemical methods, which explains why they were not previously demonstrated to be present.

The hair shaft is more or less coated with an oily secretion from the sebaceous glands of the scalp. The main shaft, composed of keratin fibrils, is surrounded by a layer of cuticle that appears as a large number of overlapping scales resembling the scales of a fish or the shingles on a roof. The free end of each scale points away from the hair follicle. Some evidence indicates that the scaly layer is part of a cuticular sheath rather than separate scales, though this seems to be contradicted by the fact that pressure on the hair shaft causes the scales to drop off.

The study of hair embraces three main considerations: (1) *morphology*, or structure, (2) *chemistry*, and (3) physical properties. Of these, morphology and physical properties have been most useful for purposes of examination. The continuing micro-modifications of chemical techniques have brought hair analysis well within the chemist's province.

MORPHOLOGY OF HAIR

Each hair grows from a specialized organ called a hair follicle. In this follicle cells become keratinized (hardened), and assume a definite orientation in the forming shaft, which is extruded as a hair. The various phases of the extrusion are

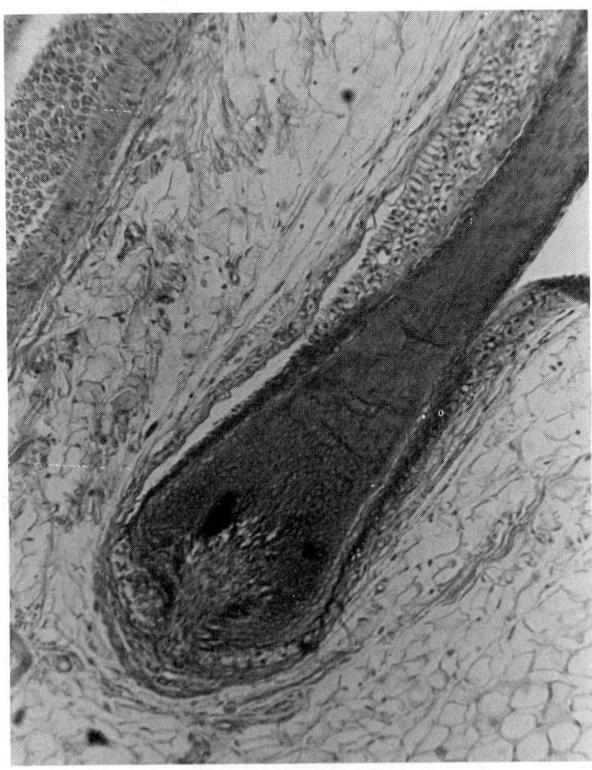

FIGURE 13-1. Human hair follicle, 100X. (Courtesy of Edward T. Blake.)

not usually uniform or equivalent. The first part of the hair that is extruded is pointed, probably in all cases. The size of the shaft increases either gradually or rather abruptly. In some hair, notably in human head hair, the established diameter is maintained thereafter quite uniformly. Human body hair and most animal hair behave differently, the diameter of animal hairs passing through a maximum stage and then diminishing. Hairs of the latter type grow to a more or less uniform length and finally fall out, to be replaced by new hairs. Human hair likewise falls out at times, and may be replaced by completely new hairs, each of which is pointed when first extruded.

The hair that is formed in the follicle is rarely round in cross section, but may be oval, ribbonlike, triangular, or a variety of other shapes. It consists of three main parts: the *cortex* or main part of the shaft, which is the portion made up of keratin fibrils and which may resemble a hollow cylinder; the *medulla* or core of the hair, which in animals is usually very prominent but may be merely indicated by an empty canal in human hair and in the hair of a few animals; and the *cuticle*, the scaly covering of the hair shaft.

In many animals most of the colored material of the hair is in the medulla, though this is not true of all animals. In humans most of the color is normally in the cortex, though grayed hair often shows a "pepper and salt" appearance from residual color in the medulla.

Wide structural variations exist in the hair of animals and, for that matter, in human hair as well. In most animals the coat is double, consisting of a fine inner layer of *down hairs* that provide insulation against low temperatures, and an outer layer of *guard hairs* that are long and prominent, usually coarse in texture, and the most noticeable feature of a fur. The guard hairs apparently serve for decorative purposes and for protection against rain. There are additional variants such as the special hairs of the tail, eyelashes, mane, etc., which differ widely in the same animal as well as between species. Wool, the body hair of sheep, resembles human head hair in that it exhibits approximately uniform properties along the shaft and continues to grow despite repeated clipping. Man, however, has several distinct types of hair that differ with sex and age and location on the body. Many humans show a fine down hair and a coarse guard hair on their bodies and, in fact, some have two distinguishable types of head hair.

Man's body hair is in some respects similar to an animal's fur in that most of it grows to a more or less definite length and drops out; whereas his head hair resembles sheep's wool much more closely. In man differences also exist between the hair of the crown, nape and temple, the eyebrow, the eyelash, the nostril, the ear, the beard, chest, underarm, arm and leg, and the pubic region. These factors of difference are, to some extent, related to the sex. Complete information and understanding regarding all the variations of human hair has never been achieved, even by those who have spent a lifetime of study on the subject.

Fortunately, the hair that becomes important as evidence usually comes from a somewhat restricted source, and can be dealt with much more effectively than would be possible if all types of human hair occurred frequently. Head hair and pubic hair must often be examined as evidence. The other types are encountered only occasionally.

Despite the apparent simplicity of proposed schemes for the classification of all types of human hair, such efforts have met with little success. They have a certain value when used with the cautious reservations imposed by experience and study, but their value even in this sense is limited. Experience in examining hair, and study of its characteristics, will supply far more information than can be obtained by the study of any classification scheme.

The gross morphology of the questioned hair must be studied, as hair comparison can never be made with precision between two hairs with extremely different structures. This is equivalent to saying that head hairs may not be compared with pubic hairs with any expectation of more than a bare possibility of identical origin. Body hairs present the greatest problem in this regard because they are so extremely variable, often to the point where even their bodily origin cannot be determined with certainty. Because of the variability, the rule that must be followed in making hair comparisons is that the questioned hair is to be compared with hairs from a suspect source only when the *length* (of a complete hair), the *diameter*, and the condition of *curl, kink,* or *straightness* are approximately the same, and the *color variation* along the hair is reasonably similar. Without finding this much agreement, no expert can ever be certain that any conclusions are necessarily accurate, since the hairs themselves are not necessarily of the same type. A corollary of this statement is that the investigating officer who hopes for a hair comparison to be made must take extraordinary pains to make certain that the standards provided have a range of gross morphology that may be expected to bracket the questioned hair or hairs. Many errors are made by inexperienced persons who attempt to compare hairs that, judging from their gross morphology, are clearly not comparable. The validity of evidence based upon such comparisons is invariably suspect.

Medulla

The medulla, or core, of a hair varies widely with the species and is one of the more valuable morphological characters available for species identification. In many animals the medulla is very broad, occupying up to two-thirds or more of the shaft diameter. In man and certain anthropoids the medulla is narrow, occupying only about one-third of the shaft width. In several animal species, including the horse and the cow, the *medullary index*, or the ratio of the medulla to the diameter of the hair, is intermediate, being about one-half.

FIGURE 13-2. Scanning electron micrograph of human hair. The ends were sliced off, revealing a central medulla (inner dark circle), cortex, and cuticle, 500X. (Courtesy of Emil Bernstein and Ella Kairinen, Gillette Company Research Institute.)

In most other animals the medulla occupies more than half the width of the hair.

Medullas are classified as *continuous, intermittent,* or *fragmental.* Most animal hairs have continuous or intermittent medullas, though here again sheep's wool resembles human hair more than it does that of most animals. The pattern of intermittent medullas is often very striking and characteristic, and is an excellent factor for species identification. Human hair normally shows fragmental medulla, but many individual hairs show no medullary material at all, and sometimes a single hair may have an almost continuous medulla. In no case does one encounter an intermittent or patterned medulla in human hair, and the lack of any medulla is much more common than is continuous

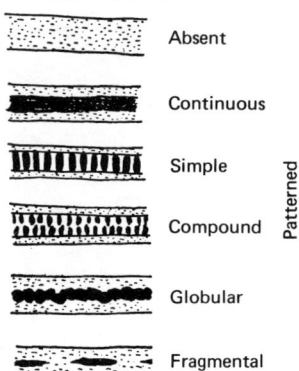

FIGURE 13-3. Schematic representation of types of hair medullas.

medullation. There is evidence to indicate that only hairs above a certain diameter will contain medullation, and the larger the hair the more nearly continuous the medullation will be. *This generalization*, like many others propounded for hair, *is to be considered as a tendency only.*

Cortex

From the structural standpoint, the cortex of the hair is most important. From the standpoint of identification, it is at present least important. Aside from the pigment that it sometimes carries, only its physical properties have been used to any extent for purposes of identification. The keratin of which the cortex is composed has been the subject of the most extensive chemical investigations made on hair, and much is known of its chemical structure. Morphologically the cortex of the hair must be considered merely as a hollow cylinder composed of fine fibrils of pseudocrystalline protein and carrying pigment materials as inclusions.

The *pigment distribution*, as opposed to the main cortical components, is of definite use in the identification and individualization of hair. In the first place, the pigment granules may exhibit a *peripheral* or a *central distribution*, a factor that varies between species and to some extent is variable in human hair. Even more important, the mode of laying down pigment varies considerably among individual people, hence, the study of the pigment distribution is one of the more valuable characteristics for individualization. The *amount of pigment* also varies from practically zero to very high values, thus determining the depth of color in the hair. Some hairs, particularly blond ones, sometimes show air spaces or vacuoles, termed *cortical fusi* by Hausman ["Structural Characteristics of the Hair of Mammals," Am. Naturalist 54:496 (1920)]. Their value in hair identification and individualization is somewhat uncertain, but in the author's experience it appears to be considerable because, though they do not occur in large numbers in most hair specimens, they are occasionally found in profusion. The latter condition is most often observed in "tow-head" children, the milky appearance of whose hair is attributable to the large number of air vacuoles in their hair. A few adults also show extensive presence of the same phenomenon, and most adults have a few such vacuoles in the region close to the roots of some hairs.

Cuticle

The type and appearance of hair scales is a very important consideration in determining species, and is of definite value also in individualizing human head hair. Many systems for the classification of hair scales have been proposed. That of Hausman, which is illustrated in Figure 13-3, is widely accepted. Except for their contribution to the nomenclature of scale types, the value of such classifications is doubtful. To a considerable degree all differentiations of hair scales are subjectively recognized and arbitrarily designated. At present the terms are useful chiefly in designating gross differences of type and pattern.

In terms of the Hausman classification, the scales of most mammalian hairs are imbricate rather than coronal, and the great majority are either crenate or flattened. The distinction between these two subtypes is based on the degree of irregularity of the edge, the crenate being serrated, and the flattened, relatively smooth. Human hair scales are ordinarily placed in the category of flattened, though their edges are far from smooth. They do not, however, pro-

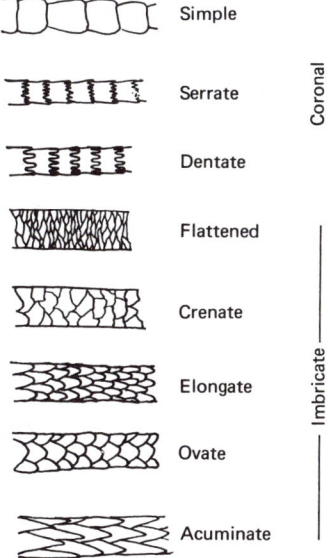

FIGURE 13-4. Schematic representation of types of hair scales. (Modified from classification of Hausman.)

trude outward from the shaft to the extent shown by most animal hair scales; hence the relatively smooth appearance of the surface of a human hair as compared with the typical saw-toothed appearance usually seen on animal hairs. No clean-cut demarcation between the successive subclasses is usually observable, each subclass fading into the next by an almost continuous variation. Between the two main classes the distinction is quite apparent.

The size of the scale has been shown to bear a relationship to the diameter of the hair shaft. Its proximal–distal dimensions are statistically less as the hair shaft diameter is increased. This relationship exists throughout all types of animal hairs as well as human, but the size of scale varies between species, and to a significant extent between human individuals.

In addition, the pattern made by the scale edges is an individualizing factor observable between hairs from different human beings. This pattern is never totally uniform, but it shows characteristics that are readily recognized by persons adept in the examination of hairs. Uniformity of scales versus variability, angularity of edges versus transverse regularity, smoothness versus raggedness of edges, and several other variables all give the experienced investigator an opportunity to distinguish between the hairs of different persons. The examination is highly subjective, and should never be attempted by anyone who has not had a great deal of experience in the study of hair.

Roots

Dropped and pulled hairs will show a root—shrunken in the first instance and full-size in the second. The appearance is that of a bulb, more or less pear-shaped, at the end of the hair.

Any hair appearing in evidence should be checked for the presence or absence of a root. If present, its condition should be noted. A dry, shrunken root indicates a hair that fell spontaneously or at least was easily removed; a fresh, round root would imply that the hair was pulled, as during a struggle. In the latter event, it is probable that a small amount of tissue is adhering to the hair root.

Growth of Hair

The growth of hair is intimately connected with the individual's development and, to a considerable extent, to his genetic makeup. Baldness is inherited as a sex-influenced dominant characteristic. A man need inherit it from only one parent to become bald. Rarely will a woman become totally bald, even if she inherits baldness from both lines of ancestry. Hair color is also an inherited characteristic, and there is reason to believe that other factors in the morphology of hair are inherited in some manner.

In the physical development of a person, body hairs of the armpit and pubic regions and facial hairs (whiskers) appear at puberty. Males also develop at about this time a greater and quite variable amount of hair on the chest, arms, legs, and elsewhere. At all ages, females tend to have lighter or sparser hair than males except on the head, although there is much variability. Both the distribution and the quantity of hair are statistically very different in the two sexes. Because of the quantity and variety of hair, especially on the male, confusion as to the hair type often occurs when isolated hairs are located in evidence, and errors from this source are rather frequent.

The *individual hair*, at least on the head, exhibits also a growth cycle that is independent of the general pattern. A new hair emerges from the follicle as a pointed shaft, this initiation of growth being known as the *anagen phase*. Growth continues for a time, and then ceases (*catagen phase*), after which it remains in a period of rest or nongrowth, known as the *telogen phase*. The hair will then be loosened by the natural shrinkage and detachment of the root, after which the follicle will start a new cycle of hair growth. During growth, the hair elongates on the scalp 0.33–0.5 mm per day. It is evident that two adjacent hairs may be in different phases of growth, so that corresponding distances from the roots do not provide any assurance that the time intervals of growth also correspond.

Each hair follicle operates independently of the others in its cycle and in the type of hair produced. Thus, one follicle that is producing a single gray hair in the midst of dark hairs will continue to produce the gray hair independently. The length of the cycle is also known to differ with different types of hair, the cycle for the scalp being the longest, averaging twenty months or more. The length of cycle of most hair types is at present inadequately known, but it is clear that all of the hairs of the entire body can be expected to be replaced at intervals. This fact accounts for most of the telogen (fallen) hairs that occur in evidence. Hairs taken by cutting or plucking for use as standards will usually be in other phases of growth. For some purposes, especially those concerned with trace element comparison, these differences have important implications. They do not seem to be closely related to morphology, because the hair, once formed in the follicle, changes more from external than from internal factors after it has reached complete keratinization and has become stabilized in structure.

CHEMISTRY OF HAIR

Though much is known of the chemistry of hair, it is only in the last few years that serious attention has been given to the forensic use of such information. The increased interest has arisen, at least in part, from new information regarding trace elements. Conventional chemical methods for the study of hair are destructive of the evidence, and may or may not produce useful information.

Such methods are also relatively insensitive to small differences. Advances in the study of the major—i.e., organic—constituents of the hair are to be expected but current utilization of hair chemistry is centered primarily on the presence and relative quantities of nineteen elements found in hair as trace constituents.

Primary Components

The main chemical components of hair are *proteins*, largely the stable and unreactive keratin of which the greater part of the hair shaft is composed, and the *pigments*, which are of a melanin type believed to be derived chiefly from the amino acid tyrosine. Though much is known of the structure of the keratins, it is not certain that differences of a significant nature exist between the keratin of one species or individual and another. Thus, the chemistry of keratin is, at present, a subject of secondary interest to the criminal investigator.

Hairs vary considerably in the stability of their structure, and such variations may in time become the basis for significant differential studies. It is assumed that such variations are the result of differences in the keratin component of hair, though this also is largely surmise. It is sufficient to state that keratin is a type of protein known to occur in long chains that are interconnected in such a way as to form stable fibrils. One of the chief connecting groups is the disulfide, –S–S–, so situated that one sulfur atom is attached to one chain and its partner is attached to another chain lying parallel to the first. Thus, many protein molecules are tied together through disulfide groups. Reagents that reduce this group, such as inorganic sulfides, or mercaptoacetic acid, destroy the stability of keratin, making it susceptible to the same types of chemical reaction as are many other proteins. These reagents are employed in depilatories and in some permanent wave preparations.

Reagents that oxidize the disulfide group also destroy the stability of the keratin. A reagent such as sodium hypochlorite dissolves hair, wool, and other keratin structures rather rapidly. Variation in the rate of solution of hair in this reagent is considerable and indicates significant variations in the constituent keratins. Many depilatories act on the principle of reducing the stabilizing groups and dissolving the remaining nonresistant protein. Alkaline sulfides have long been used for this purpose, and more recently a number of other alkaline reducing agents have been promoted. These are organic materials such as thioglycolic acid that are used, in greater dilution and with less alkalinity, to produce permanent waving of the hair.

The *pigment* of the hair has received limited study, and complete understanding of it is still lacking. At present it is believed that a brown melanin pigment is responsible for both brown and black color of hair, the amount of the pigment determining the shade. Although most of the pigment is found in granules in the cortex, there are indications of considerable diffuse pigmentation throughout the hair, including the medulla. Diffuse pigmentation is often visible, particularly in blond hair, probably because of the clearer observation through a light-colored cortex.

The pigment of red hair is slightly more controversial in nature. There are good indications that it is more highly oxidized than brown pigment, and also that it may be an iron-containing compound. It is very probable that red pigment differs chemically from brown pigment. The total number of pigments to be found in hair is not certain. Some authors believe that there are as many as four, and others think there is only one. It is probable that all hair pigments are closely related chemically, and that the visible differences may primarily represent different degrees of oxidation, or other small chemical variations.

Minor Constituents

Several organic minor constituents are known to be present in hair. Others have been reported, but without clarification as to whether they were actually a part of the hair or were merely carried on the surface of the hair. The oily secretion of the sebaceous glands is certainly in the latter class, and is expected to be of regular occurrence. Other materials that have been reported include uric acid, cholesterol, and certain vitamins. Recently it has been demonstrated that the blood group antigens of the ABC system are present in hair, and it is now possible to determine the blood group of the donor of a hair. The material that constitutes the visible medulla is still not known with certainty, but is undoubtedly a minor organic constituent. Viewed microscopically, this material appears black in most instances, brown in others, and essentially colorless in some others. If the hair is sectioned longitudinally so as to expose the medullary content, it will—in some instances at least, and possibly always—prove to be white. However, its porous character gives rise to refraction effects that account for the apparent dark color. More investigation of this material should be pursued relative both to its composition and to its optical properties.

There appears to be a difference in chemical stability between hair scales and cortical keratin. It has been generally accepted that the scales also are keratinous, but it is not improbable that factors other than the physical structure of the scale may be found to account for the observed difference. Presumably the attachment of the scales to the shaft could be structurally weak as compared with the shaft itself.

At this time there is little that can be visualized as a suitable technique for individualizing the hair on the basis of minor constituents. One approach that is under investigation is that of pyrolysis–gas chromatography, which has been so successful in dealing with other complex organic mixtures. When pyrolyzed —destroyed by heat—hairs give rise to a large number of products that can be separated and analyzed by the gas chromatograph. The products are, in large measure, clearly attributable to the major constituent of hair, keratin. Minor constituents should produce alterations in the recorder tracing. Such variations have been shown to exist. Whether or not they will prove to be sufficiently definite to provide a positive discrimination between hairs of two different persons in a significant number of instances is not yet certain. Distinct differences have been observed in some instances, but the technique is still subject to some uncontrolled variability that makes a final evaluation difficult. Here there is a very promising field for further investigation.

Trace Elements

Certain toxic elements, such as arsenic and thallium, are preferentially excreted in the hair and in other keratinaceous appendages such as the nails. Hair is therefore often the tissue analyzed in the detection of arsenic poisoning, because the route taken by arsenic to the hair is a direct metabolic one. However, hair will also absorb and hold tightly arsenic that has been externally applied; so that it cannot be assumed that hair analysis is always capable of indicating poisoning from arsenic. Lead, silica, iron, and phosphorus are other elements that have long been known to exist in small quantities in some hair.

Since the introduction of neutron activation analysis many more trace elements have been found in hair samples. Definitive proof that they result from metabolic activity rather than from external contamination is not available, but there are strong indications that most of them are constituents of the hair. It is generally believed that these elements have their origin in nutritional materials, drugs, water, and other sources that contribute to the internal environment of the body, and that they enter the hair during its formation. The distribution of these trace elements in hairs of different persons has been found to be highly individual. This finding raises the hope that the technique of neutron activation analysis will ultimately provide a definite identification of the person from whom the hair or hairs were derived. Approximately nineteen trace elements have been reported as existing in some samples of hair. It would be surprising if a single analysis of a single sample were ever to detect all of these. Both the unlikely chance of their all being in one sample and the technical limitations that are always present would seem to rule out such a result. It is inappropriate to discuss these limitations and possibilities here. It may be mentioned, however, that the analysis of a single hair has not been found adequate for personal identification to date, both because of the difficulty of making a complete analysis of a single hair, and because of the fact that variations may be considerable from hair to hair of the same person. Bundles of hair are usually employed so that the variability of individual hairs is largely eliminated and an informative analysis is achieved. Bundles of hair from a single individual are only occasionally found in evidence; so that this technique must be considered to be of limited applicability in its present state of development. Neutron activation analysis is not a cure-all for the problems of the criminalist who must obtain from minimal source material a maximum of information in a form that facilitates the development of precise and definite opinions for court presentation. Fortunately, this approach to hair identification has been supported for research, and progress has been made and is continuing.

PHYSICAL PROPERTIES OF HAIR

As is the case with all materials that vary in chemical composition or physical structure, hair shows a definite, though limited, variability in its physical properties. This variability provides a statistical basis for the individualization of hair. So far as is known, the examination of hair for purposes of species identification has been focused almost entirely upon morphological differences rather than upon physical properties.

The structural complexity of hair is reflected in the chemical variety observable in its components. Thus the pigment, the medullary material, and the cortical keratin represent chemical differences that are reflected in their properties. The minor constituents of hair also are known to be quite variable. These differences are inevitably reflected, for example, in the *density* of hair. There are distinct indications that properties determined primarily by the keratin are variable, though it is less clear why this should be. The *refractive index* of hair is not absolutely constant, but varies between individual hairs from an individual, between individuals, between sexes, and probably between races. These variations are small but definitely significant, and the manner in which the measurements are made indicates the primary role of keratin in determining this property.

Because certain animal hairs, such as wool, are used extensively in textiles, such properties as tensile strength, elongation under tension, and elasticity have received attention from the textile industry. Some of these properties are markedly affected by variations of humidity, for example, which restricts their usefulness in criminal investigation.

The property *birefringence* is shown by all hairs, and preliminary studies indicate its possible use in criminal investigation. So far, however, nothing decisive has been found. A number of practical difficulties interfere with the use of this property: difficulties attributable to the lack of homogeneity in the hair shaft, the irregular shape and variable diameter of the hair, and similar factors that complicate the measurement.

Although it is difficult to evaluate the ultimate uses of physical properties in the study of hair as evidence, the present status of two of these properties indicates great extension of their use in the future. These two properties are *refractive index* and *density*.

Refractive Index

The refractive index of a pure compound is a constant, under standard conditions, and is an extremely valuable factor in the identification of the compound. When applied to hair, which is not a pure compound and is not even homogeneous, it is apparent that the refractive index is an empirical value and that its determination must be performed in a prescribed and reproducible manner in order to achieve significant results. Employing a standardized procedure, Greenwell, Willner, and Kirk ["Human Hair Studies III. Refractive Index of Crown Hair." *J. Crim. Law and Criminology* 31:746 (1941)] studied the refractive indices of 2,529 hairs taken from 97 individuals. In hair from Caucasian males the mean value of the refractive index was found to be about 0.004 unit lower than that of hair from Caucasian females. Differences in the refractive indices of hair samples from individuals were sufficient to exclude, on the average, two out of three individuals by comparison of such values with those obtained from a questioned hair. Hair from non-Caucasians did not appear to show the same sex-linked difference observed in hairs from Caucasians. However, the number of such hairs examined was small. It is possible that the absolute values of the refractive indices obtained were somewhat low because of maladjustment of the Abbe refractometer with which the liquids used as standards were calibrated. The *relative* significance of the readings is, however, unaffected by this shift in the absolute values recorded.

Density

Studies of the density of hair have been far less extensive than studies of refractive index. The evidence now available indicates that density is a more valuable factor in the individualization of hair than is refractive index, because the

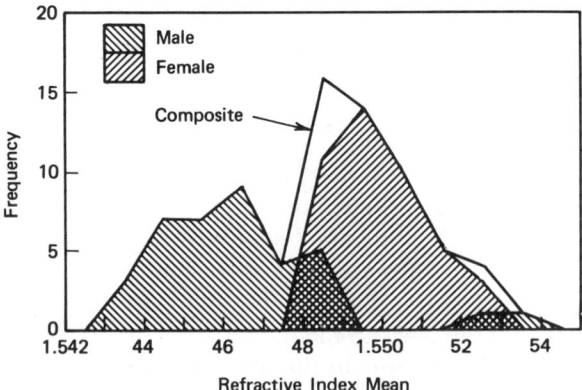

FIGURE 13-5. Frequency distribution of refractive indexes of human hair. (J. Crim. Law & Criminol., 31:746, 1940-41.)

determination and use of density as a comparative factor permits a hair to be picked from among samples taken from perhaps as many as eight or ten persons. The relation of the density of the hair to sex, age, or race is at present almost completely unknown. It is fair to assume that some such relation exists and that further investigation will make it applicable to forensic problems. The investigator should be forewarned that to determine the density range of a person's hair many very short segments of hair must be cut, and these are very difficult to see in a gradient tube. The procedure is therefore difficult and time-consuming, and is usually employed only when other individualizing techniques are not applicable.

COLLECTION OF QUESTIONED HAIRS

Samples of questioned hair will most commonly be found in vacuum sweepings or will be picked from a suspect's clothing. Occasionally hairs will be carried on weapons that have been used in assaults; less frequently they will be found in such instruments as razors or on objects customarily carried in a pocket. Combs frequently provide the investigator with questioned or standard hair. In crimes involving struggle, a victim may have hairs grasped in his hands or caught under his fingernails. The scene of the crime may often contain hairs of the perpetrator. Sometimes they will be mixed with hairs of so many other persons who normally frequent the area of the crime that they will be virtually impossible to locate and identify; but in other instances, no such difficulty will arise. The fact that many people shed hairs to a considerable extent wherever they happen to be is for the criminal investigator a very fortunate circumstance.

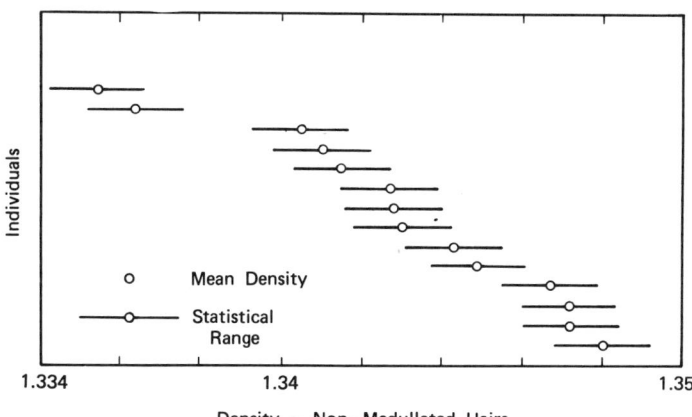

FIGURE 13-6. Density distribution of human hair—mean ±3 times the standard error of the mean of 14 male Caucasians of college age. (Data from L. J. Goin, Thesis, University of California, 1948.)

In one instance, hairs of a victim were found in the room of the perpetrator a number of miles distant from the crime scene. Inasmuch as the victim was a blond female and the perpetrator was a black man, it was not difficult to locate the hairs in question. Careful search for hairs should always be made in the investigation of a crime. If this is done, hairs will be found in a large proportion of all crimes, perhaps in nearly half of them. All questioned hairs that can be located should be placed in clean glass vials, or in paper or cellophane envelopes, and labeled as to source, time of collection, and the name of the collector. They should be preserved until such time as they are to be subjected to laboratory examination.

Hair Standards

Standard hairs, necessary for comparison with questioned hairs, are best collected from the head, pubes, axillae, and other relevant body areas of the individual suspected of being the source of the questioned hairs. A very suitable method of obtaining head hair is to comb the hair vigorously with a clean fine-toothed comb. This will, in most instances, provide a sampling of hair most nearly comparable with the hair that would have been shed by the individual. There is no definite rule as to how much hair is to be taken; that will be determined by the number and extent of the examinations to be made. A sample of 100 hairs is desirable, but a smaller number is usually sufficient, and even a single hair may yield valuable information.

Combings usually provide a more satisfactory sample than does a clipped lock that is taken from a limited region and may not be representative of the entire head of hair. If the sampling must be done by clipping, it is best to take just a few hairs from one region of the head, a few more from another, and so on, until a widely representative sample is obtained. Clipping should be done close to the scalp; and it is helpful if the hairs can be laid parallel and the clipped end marked to allow compensation for any alterations along the hair. Pulled hair is probably preferable to clippings in that it provides complete hair lengths. It is not essential to have the root in a standard sample, and it is almost never worth the extra difficulty encountered in obtaining it.

Barber clippings are the least useful of standard hair samples. In the first place, the barber removes most of the hair from the nape and the temple regions, so that his clippings are not completely representative of the crown hair that is most likely to be found in sweepings and droppings. Even more important is the fact that the clipper or shears used by the barber will almost always be contaminated by the hair of other individuals; so that a standard secured from the barber may represent the hair of two or more people and lead to uncertainty of source. If a prison barber is called upon to take such a sample unknown to the suspect, he should be instructed to clean his tools and comb very carefully before starting, and to attempt to obtain crown hairs by combing rather than to clip the nape and the temples for the sample.

If neutron activation analysis is to be used in the examination of the hair, it is especially important that a large sample of hair be taken, and that the rules given above be followed carefully. For this procedure, bundles of hair are necessary for the most precise analysis, and it is desirable that all the hair be in the same growth phase.

Dead Bodies

Homicide victims, in particular, should always have a sample of hair removed before burial or cremation. Even though no hair is known to exist among the items of microscopic evidence, should some appear later, it would be necessary to disinter the body to obtain a standard. The collection is so simple and takes so little time, that it should never be neglected, and a rather large sample should always be taken.

PRELIMINARY EXAMINATION OF HAIR

It may often be practical for the field investigator to note certain factors regarding a sample of hair before submitting it to the laboratory for thorough study. Such a preliminary examination may aid in determining whether significant results are to be expected from detailed examination. Care must be taken at all times to avoid altering the hair itself or the debris carried on it during such a preliminary observation. Perhaps it is even more important to avoid contaminating the sample as many police investigators do by trying on the suspect's hat, and by similar thoughtlessness.

The *ends of the hair* should be examined under low magnification. If the hair has fallen, a shrunken root will be observed on one end. If the hair was pulled, a complete root may be observed, or the hair may have been broken. Either of these details may indicate that the hair was removed forcibly, as during a struggle. The presence of sharp bends or breaks along the length of the hair may indicate that it was broken by a weapon. Thus, a person who has been beaten on the head will often show many such broken and flattened hairs, and may be expected to shed some of them. If both ends of the hair have been cut, a sharp weapon may have been used.

The *general appearance of the hair shaft* is significant. If the hair is relatively straight, and particularly if it is of uniform diameter, it is likely to be a head hair. If it is curly, kinky, and of variable diameter, it is probably a body hair, and from its length one can deduce the part of the body from which it probably came. This will assist the investigator in deciding what types of hair must be taken for standards, and may save time in seeking such standards after the preliminary laboratory examination

Much has been written about the determination of the portion of the body from which a hair was derived, and tables summarizing such identification have been published.[*] The greatest caution must be exercised in applying such an oversimplified scheme to actual examinations. Not only are the variations actually found in hairs much greater and more numerous than is indicated, but many of the published values of diameter, etc., are incorrect. When caution is properly exercised and experience is available, such schemes are of some value, but experience alone may be even more useful in arriving at a proper identification. It is important that, when possible, only entire hairs be studied to determine the body region of their origin. If only fragments are available, the determination of bodily origin may be very difficult and will require extreme care and conservatism to avoid gross errors.

HUMAN HAIR VS. OTHER ANIMAL HAIR

In most of the above discussion, it has been assumed that human rather than hair from other animals (hereafter called *animal* hair) was under consideration, because of the greater incidence and significance of human hair in criminal investigation. Animal hair is often very important as physical evidence, and its distinction from human hair and its identification as to species are very important matters. Because the experienced laboratory worker will have little difficulty in making the distinction at any time, the police investigator will rarely be required to do so. His chief function is to make sure that any hairs whatever, either human or animal, that may be employed to established facts pertinent to the investigation be collected and examined by an expert. The basis of the distinction between animal and human hairs was discussed earlier in this chapter, in the section entitled "Morphology." For convenience it is summarized here.

The *diameter* of animal hair is often very different from that of human air. Both coarser and finer animal hairs are common. Human hair ranges in diameter from about 50 to 150 microns. The diameter of animal hairs may commonly be less than half that of the finest or more than twice that of the coarsest human hair. Often this fact alone is sufficient to distinguish between human and animal hairs.

The *medulla* of animal hair usually occupies more than one-half the diameter of the hair shaft, whereas in human hair the medullary diameter is rarely

---

[*] H. Söderman and J. J. O'Connell: *Modern Criminal Investigation*, Chap. XII. New York: Funk and Wagnalls (1936).

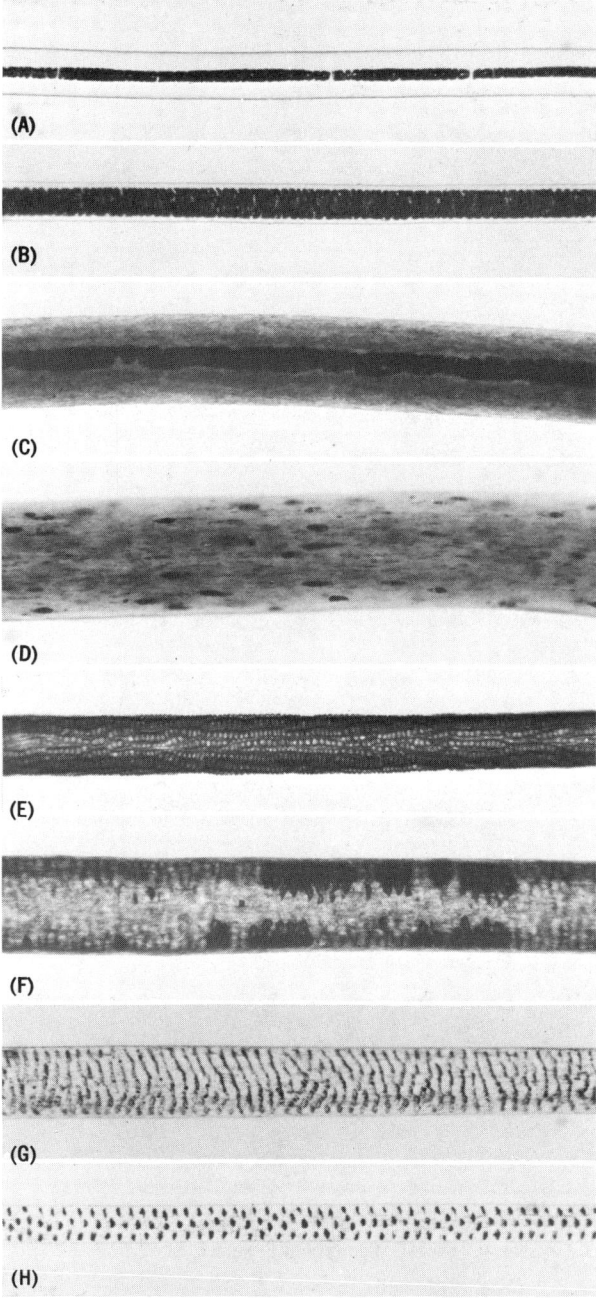

FIGURE 13-7. Photomicrographs of some common animal hairs, 80x. (A) dog, (B) cat, (C) horse, (D) cow, (E) rabbit, (F) squirrel, (G) mouse, (H) rat. (Courtesy of Edward T. Blake.)

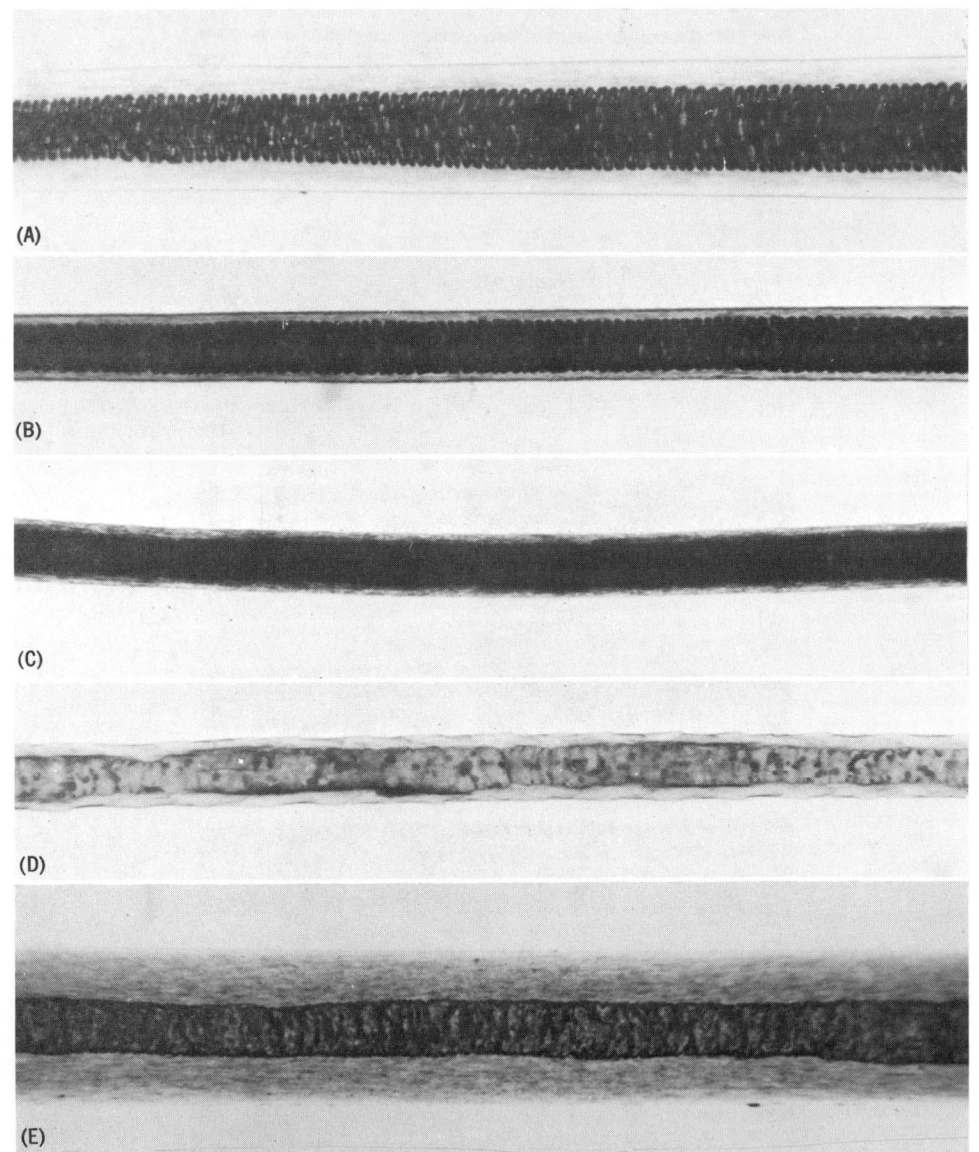

FIGURE 13-8. Photomicrographs of some fur hairs, 80X. (A) mink, (B) sable, (C) fox, (D) seal, (E) beaver. (Courtesy of Edward T. Blake.)

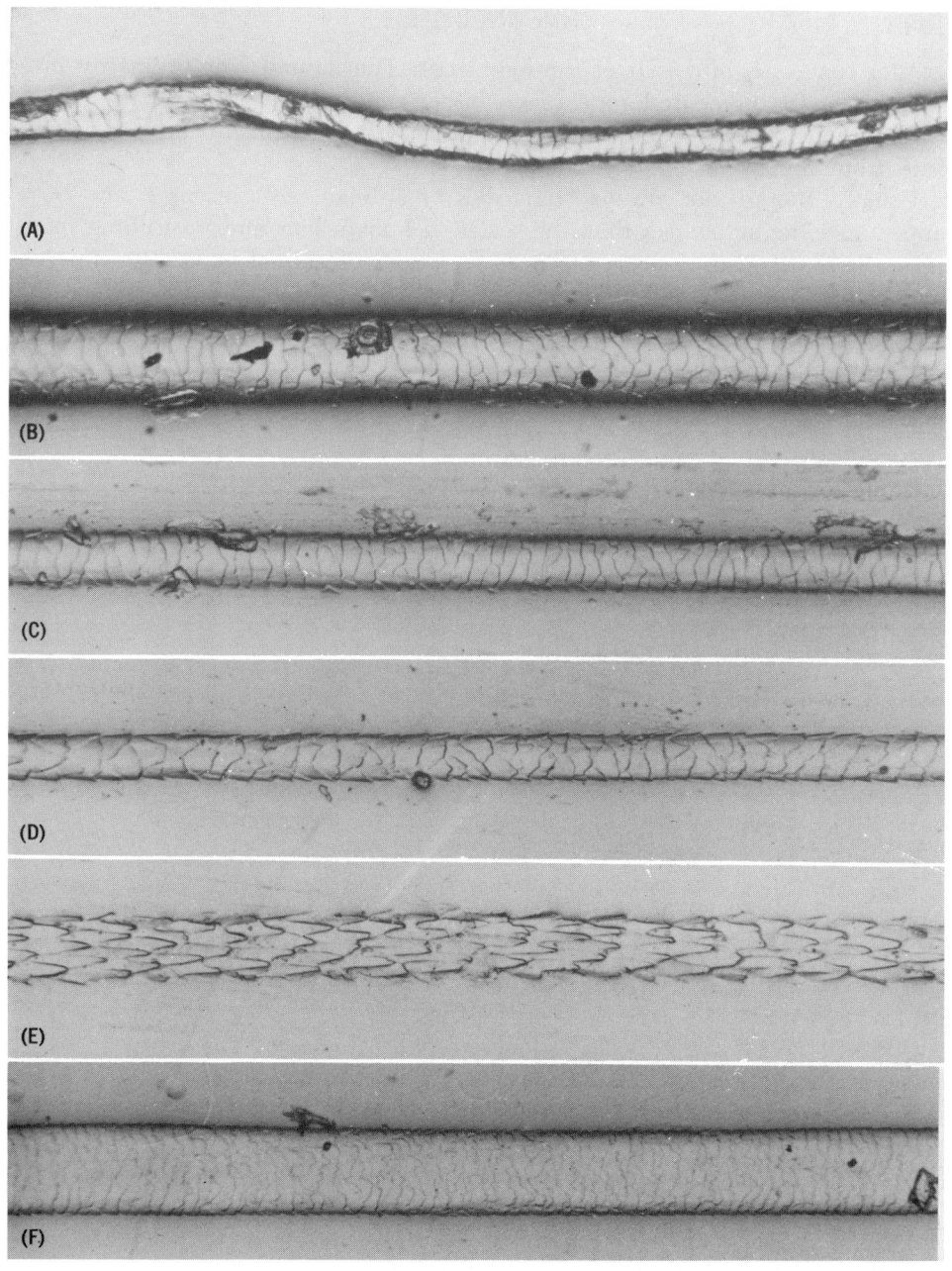

FIGURE 13-9. Scale casts of some animal hairs, 80X. (A) sheep, (B) dog, (C) cat, (D) skunk, (E) fox, (F) squirrel. (Courtesy of Edward T. Blake.)

greater than one-third that of the hair shaft. The animal hair ordinarily presents a heavily pigmented appearance, either continuously or in a pattern that is continuous. The appearance of the medulla will distinguish nearly all animal hairs from human hairs.

Usually, though not always, the scales of animal hair present a saw-tooth appearance, being coarser than the scales of human hair and protruding more from the shaft. Also, in most instances the scales of animal hairs differ in type and pattern from those of human hair. Often it is impossible to observe the scales of an animal hair because of the dense medullary pigmentation. If necessary a plastic cast may be made to reveal all of the fine surface structure. The scales, properly studied, will distinguish nearly all animal hairs from human hair.

Identification of Animal Hair

The identification of the species of animal from which a hair was derived is a matter for the laboratory criminalist, not for the police investigator. Further,

FIGURE 13-10. Human hairs from a single individual, 80X. (A) head hair, (B) chest hair, (C) pubic hair. (Courtesy of Edward T. Blake.)

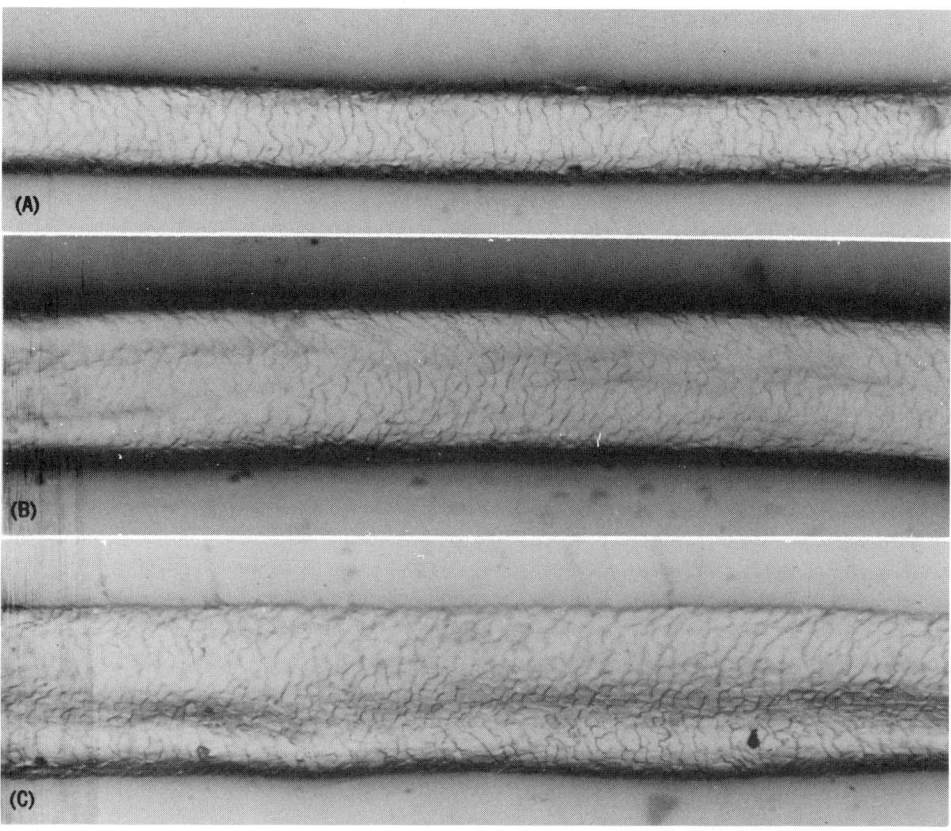

FIGURE 13-11. Scale casts of human hairs from a single individual. (A) head, (B) chest, (C) pubic. (Courtesy of Edward T. Blake.)

it is more important to establish identity between hairs from a questioned and a known source than it is to identify the species origin. Most of the activity of the hair expert is expended in comparing the factors listed above to establish identity of source, and determining a few additional factors such as length, color, and character of tips. The identification of species rests almost entirely on comparison with hairs from known sources. Both the identity and the species origin can be determined with a high degree of reliability by the expert who is properly equipped with standards and experience.

THE FUTURE OF HUMAN HAIR AS EVIDENCE

Of all the common types of evidence that require study, only hair, blood, and semen are common and come directly from the person. If it is assumed that hair is actually unique to the individual, it is then one of three types of material which might be used directly for personal identification by laboratory methods. That hair is actually unique to the individual is very probable since, if it were not, it would be the exception to the general rule of biological individuality. It therefore merits the most careful and extensive investigation aimed at fulfilling the tremendous possibilities it presents. Because hair studies are slow and often difficult, there has been a tendency to minimize the importance of hair as evidence. Simple and rapid methods capable of producing decisive results in this field may be possible, but not without much more extensive and thorough research investigation. The challenge to fill this assignment is presented to the workers in the field, and it is hoped that it will not be disregarded. It seems safe to predict that such efforts might well result in one of the most valuable sets of techniques for establishing personal identity by putting to use evidence that cannot readily be kept from the possession of law-enforcement agents.

REFERENCES

Appleyard, H. M.: *Guide to the Identification of Animal Fibers.* Torridon, Leeds: Wool Industry Research Association (1960).

Borasky, R., ed.: *Ultrastructure of Protein Fibers.* New York: Academic Press (1963).

Eddy, M. W., and Raring, J. C.: "Technique in Hair, Fur and Wool Identification," *Proc. Penn. Acad. Sci.* 15:164 (1941).

Forslev, A. W.: "Nondestructive Neutron Activation Analysis of Hair," *J. For. Sci.* 11:217 (1966).

Jones, D. N.: "The Study of Human Hair as an Aid to the Investigation of Crime," *J. For. Med.* 3:55 (1956).

Montagna, W., and Ellis, R. A., eds.: *The Biology of Hair Growth.* New York: Academic Press (1958).

Niyogi, S. K.: "A Study of Human Hairs in Forensic Work," *Proc. Canad. Soc. For. Sci.* 2:105 (1963).

Perkons, A. K., and Jervis, R. E.: "Trace Elements in Human Head Hair," *J. For. Sci.* 6:50 (1966).

Trotter, M.: "A Review of the Classification of Hair," *Am. J. Phys. Anthropol.* 24:105 (1938).

Wildman, A. B.: *The Microscopy of Animal Textile Fibers.* Torridon, Leeds: Wool Industry Research Association (1954).

14

Blood: Physical Investigation

Blood is one of the most important and most frequently encountered types of evidence in criminal investigation. It can be found in connection with almost every type of criminal activity, and it should not be overlooked even in those cases that would not usually be expected to involve bloodshed. Further, when blood is found at the scene of a crime, it should be carefully studied with respect to its appearance and distribution, for this may provide information of great value to the investigation.

The blood distribution pattern is of special importance. The blood may be in a pool or smeared or splattered; the features of the blood distribution pattern are governed by the events and conditions of the bloodshedding. By a careful consideration of the physical processes involved in the formation of blood distribution patterns, it is possible to reconstruct details of the criminal activity. It can be stated emphatically that *no other type of investigation of blood will yield so much useful information as an analysis of the blood distribution pattern.* This fact has not been widely appreciated, and many investigators have neglected the very obvious information that is available from this source. Thus much information has been lost, and in consequence many crimes have been unsolved or improperly interpreted.

BLOOD FROM THE VICTIM. In murder, assault, rape, mayhem, and similar crimes of violence, blood may occur on: (1) the victim's person; (2) the scene of the crime; (3) the culprit; and (4) the weapon. The distribution and appearance of blood spots and bloody areas on the victim and his clothing may be used to interpret and reconstruct details of the crime or the event that produced the bleeding, such as the victim's position at the time of shedding the blood, and the portion of the body from which the blood was lost.

In one crime in which a female victim was stabbed through the heart, a considerable quantity of blood had flowed between the breasts and below and around the right breast. In addition to this, a much larger quantity of blood serum had flowed around the left side and to the back of her clothing, which was soaked with serum. From these facts it was clear that she was in a sitting or partly reclining position, tilted to the right, at the time the knife was withdrawn. The body was not moved for some time, as indicated by the extensive clotting of the blood shed internally. The body was then moved to a lying position, being tilted somewhat to the left either while being carried or as placed, and during carriage the head was low, allowing serum to flow over the left shoulder and down around the left side of the back. Since the crime was committed in the culprit's automobile, the sequence of events was of importance in reconstructing the actions of the murderer.

The victim's blood at the scene of the crime is useful chiefly in interpreting and reconstructing the course of events. Its distribution and quantity, and the appearance of the spots or areas, will usually give vital information of this type. Blood spots, particularly, can be interpreted in terms of their origin, the distance they traveled, and their velocity. A drop of blood striking most surfaces at right angles gives rise to a symmetrical star-shaped pattern of secondary spatters completely encircling the primary spot. The greater the velocity of the drop of blood, the greater will be the spread of the secondary spatters. If the drop strikes the surface at an angle other than 90°, the spatter will be asymmetrical, and the spot will assume a pear shape. The effect will be heightened by greater velocity of the drop and by smaller angle of incidence. This type of interpretation is often extremely helpful in determining not only the course of events but frequently their cause as well.

The victim's blood on the person or clothing of a suspect is obviously of importance. In a crime of great violence such as a beating with a club, or a knife battle, the blood may be expected to have a wide distribution on the suspect's clothing. In a rape, it is likely to be found in the genital region of the perpetrator and on his pants, and particularly on his underwear. Its distribution is again of the greatest significance in the reconstruction of the crime, and its presence alone is prime evidence of guilt.

The victim's blood on a weapon is usually valuable only in determining that the particular weapon under examination is the one sought. Here also, at times, the distribution and quantity of blood aid in reconstructing the crime or in determining how the weapon was used.

BLOOD FROM THE PERPETRATOR. Although not so common as the blood of the victim, blood from the perpetrator of a crime occurs quite frequently in the same general locations as the victim's blood. When there is a struggle, the

Blood: Physical Investigation 169

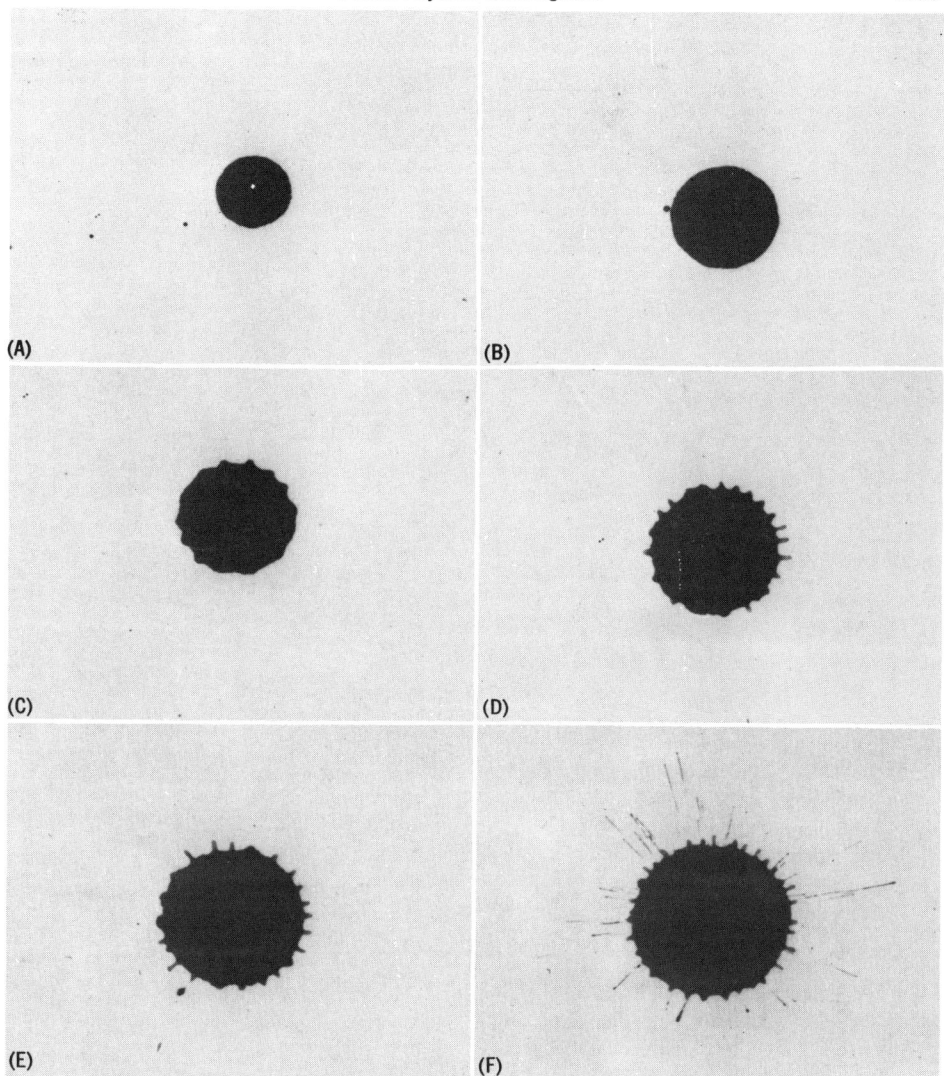

FIGURE 14-1. The effect of velocity on blood spatters. A single drop of blood dropped perpendicularly the distances indicated: (A) 2 in., (B) 4 in., (C) 8 in., (D) 16 in., (E) 32 in., (F) 60 in. (Courtesy of John I. Thornton.)

criminal is occasionally wounded and may shed his blood at the scene, on the victim, or even on the weapon. Mishaps that occur in the commission of a crime often lead to bleeding on the part of the perpetrator. In one case, a protruding nail scratched a burglar entering a building and caused bleeding. Working in the dark, the criminal may easily fall and injure himself; he may be injured by gunfire, or even by the tools he uses in effecting an entry. The

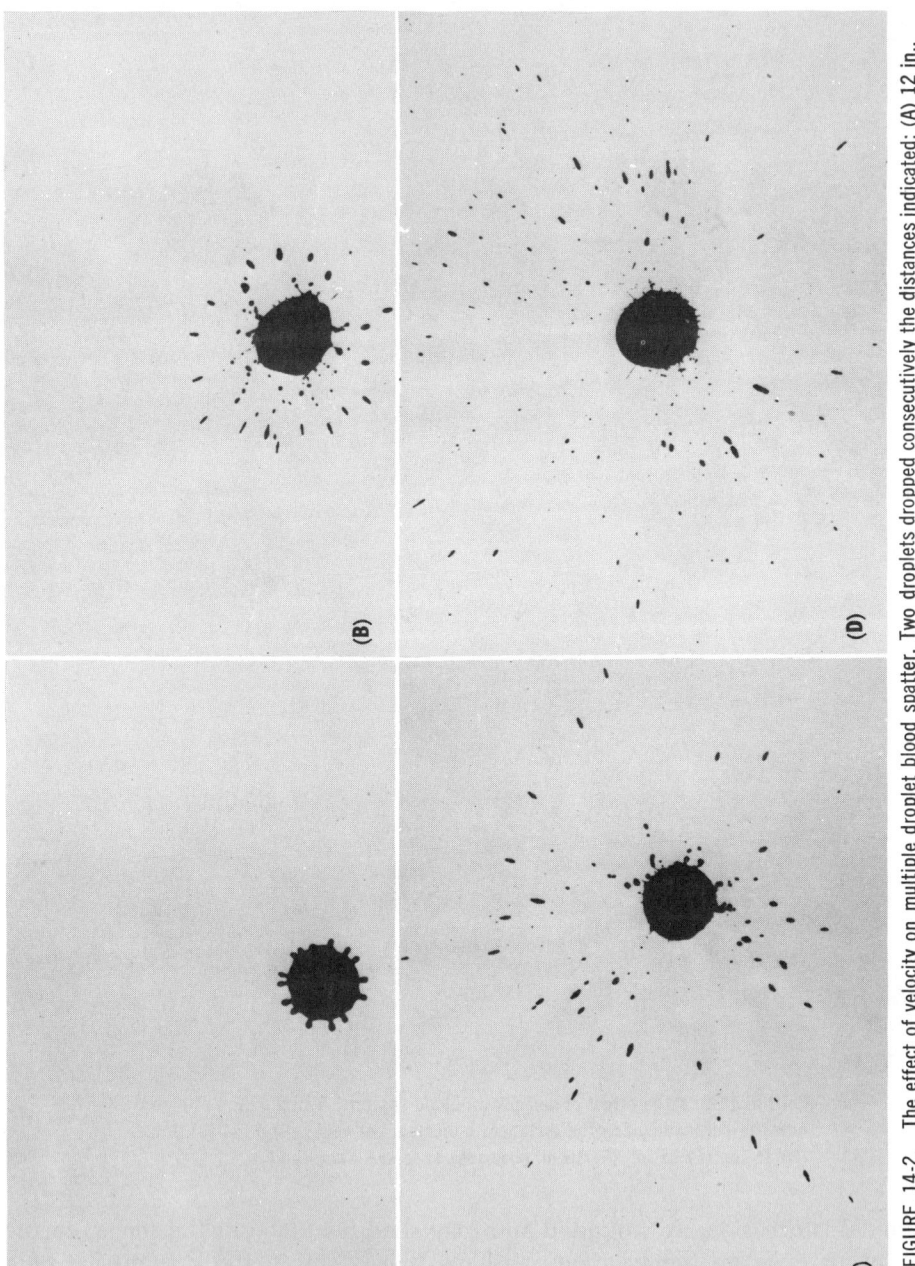

FIGURE 14-2. The effect of velocity on multiple droplet blood spatter. Two droplets dropped consecutively the distances indicated: (A) 12 in., (B) 24 in., (C) 36 in., (D) 48 in. (Courtesy of John I. Thornton.)

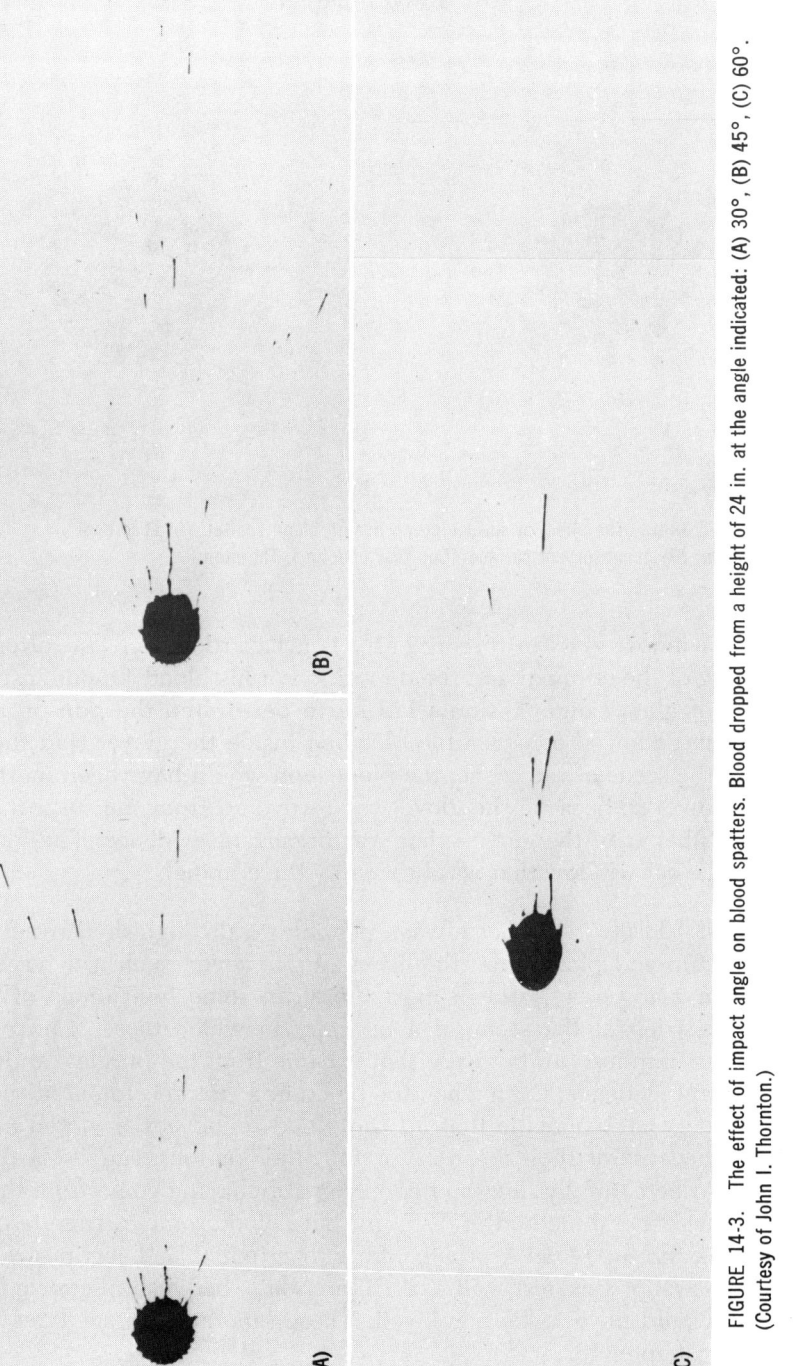

FIGURE 14-3. The effect of impact angle on blood spatters. Blood dropped from a height of 24 in. at the angle indicated: (A) 30°, (B) 45°, (C) 60°. (Courtesy of John I. Thornton.)

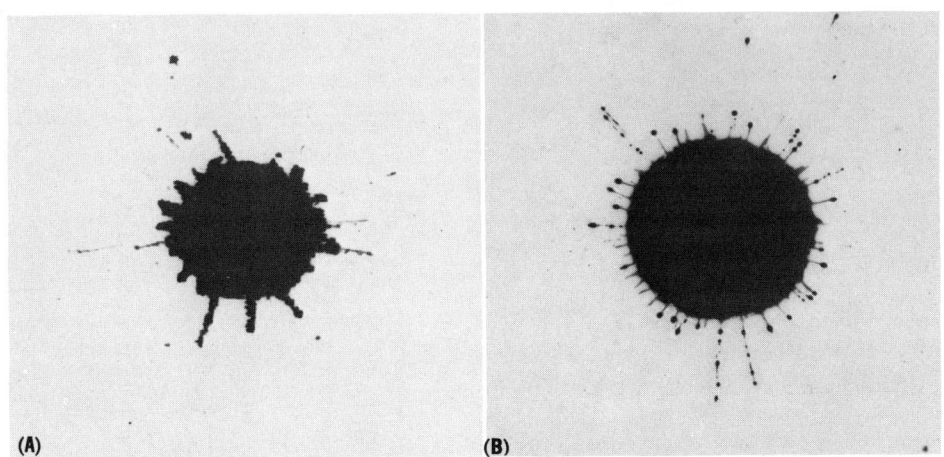

FIGURE 14-4. The effect of surface properties on blood spatter. (A) absorbent surface, (B) nonabsorbent surface. (Courtesy of John I. Thornton.)

breaking of window glass in forcing entry is a hazardous act that often leads to the cutting of the criminal and the deposition of his blood. In one instance, a small piece of glass caught inside a kid glove penetrated the skin on a criminal's hand and allowed considerable bleeding inside the glove. Had the latter been left at the scene of the crime, the bloodstain would have been most useful evidence. However, because the glove was recovered from the suspect, it was the glass—rather than the glove—that was important evidence. The glass had come from the car window that was broken by the criminal.

DISTINCTION OF SOURCE. It is not always possible to distinguish between blood from the victim and blood from the criminal. However, such a determination is possible in many cases, and in most there are some indications of source. When blood is left at the scene of a burglary in which there is no personal victim, the assumption can be made that it came from the burglar, and is thus most important evidence. Even when the blood of a victim is found at the scene of a crime, it is not axiomatic that *all* the blood found is the victim's. Bloodstains that, because of their location, or for other reasons, suggest a different source should be carefully investigated as possibly having come from the criminal. The most general method of distinguishing blood samples from two different people is that of *blood grouping*. If both criminal and victim are of the same blood group, this test will not differentiate between them, and other techniques would have to be employed. These laboratory procedures will be discussed in Chapter 16.

BLOOD DISTRIBUTION PATTERNS

Several types of blood distribution patterns are encountered in the investigation of crime scenes. *Pools* of blood, usually found under a victim, indicate heavy bleeding. Bloody *contact areas*, ranging in size from a small spot to a widespread area, result from contact of a bloody object with a surface. Blood *smears* are the result of contact with movement, as when a bloody head brushes a wall. It is usually possible to determine the direction of the movement. Blood may also appear as *spots* that result from the impact of airborne blood droplets with surfaces.

The analysis of blood-spot patterns has received considerable attention in the author's laboratory. More recently, the subject has been studied in great detail by H. L. MacDonell, and his work marks the current standard of reference. Blood droplets may become airborne by a variety of mechanisms, e.g., sprays, splatters, splashes; it is usually possible to determine from the blood-spot pattern the generating mechanism as well as the point of origin. This determination can be made because projected blood droplets are subject to physical laws and hence behave in a predictable fashion. The following principles apply to the interpretation of blood-spot patterns:

(1) Because of the high viscosity of blood, a considerable amount of force is required to break up a drop into the very small drops whose marks are seen at many crime scenes, each droplet having left a very small spot.

(2) A single force sufficient to produce very tiny drops of blood will also propel them very rapidly across rather long distances.

(3) Large spots left by large drops invariably resulted from forces insufficient to break them into droplets and accelerate them to high velocity.

(4) Every blood drop traveling through the air is under the constant influence of gravity, and will fall freely during its traverse, just as any other thrown or propelled object (a bullet, a baseball, etc.).

(5) Large drops that travel for any significant distance are freed and propelled by centrifugal or similar forces that accelerate them to such an extent that they break loose from the surface holding them, e.g., a swung weapon.

(6) The strong impact of a solid object on a blood-bearing surface compresses the blood violently, causing it to spurt out radically, like the spokes of a wheel. Large drops that are propelled by this compressive force do not travel far. Smaller drops, torn from a larger volume of the blood, have received a disproportionately large amount of total energy, and may be thrown at high velocity for considerable distances.

(7) Falling drops (as distinct from sprayed drops) are always rather large, being limited only by the surface tension and viscosity of the blood. Such drops may flow from wounds, drop from blood-soaked clothing, etc., and gen-

erally leave spots in the neighborhood of ½–¾ inch in diameter. Forcefully discharged drops may leave spots smaller than 1/32 in diameter, depending on the force supplied.

(8) The initial behavior of free-falling drops obeys the usual formula for free-falling objects:

$$d = \tfrac{1}{2} gt^2$$

where g is the gravitation constant approximately equal to 32 ft/sec^2, and d is the distance of fall in time, t. Thus, for a fall of 4 ft, the time is ½ sec. For the velocity of a falling object, the following formula is used:

$$v = gt$$

This formula holds for all objects falling in a vacuum, and it gives a better approximation for high-density objects falling in air than for low-density objects, since the air resistance retards the latter more than the former. Every object will accelerate while falling until the air resistance is equal to the acceleration of gravity, after which its rate of fall becomes constant at the *terminal velocity*. Blood has a relatively low density, and its terminal velocity in air is about 25 ft/sec, according to MacDonell.

(9) Blood drops that are forcibly driven downward at speeds greater than terminal velocity will not follow these formulas, but will travel at progressively slower speeds until they reach the terminal velocity. This may be an important consideration in interpreting drops that have moved downward. If forcibly ejected downward, they will be smaller than normal, just as are drops forcibly ejected in other directions. If free-falling, they will be of normal size, giving spots of approximately ½–¾ inch in diameter.

(10) The size of a blood spot in relation to the volume of the drop forming it will vary with the surface it impacts. A nonabsorbent surface, if wettable, will allow the formation of a larger and thinner spot than will a water-repellent solid surface. An absorbent surface will allow the drop to spread to a still larger area by virtue of its capillary action.

There are a number of methods by which blood is set in motion through the air, and the above principles may be used to determine the manner of its propulsion as a practical matter. Obviously it is not necessary to trace the behavior of every drop at a murder scene, but rather to study several areas for their general features. These will indicate how each area was bloodied, and whether all the blood was propelled by a single act or by multiple acts that may have been similar or different in nature. The methods of propulsion are as follows:

(1) Free fall under gravity alone, characterized by large drops of uniform size.

(2) Propulsion by impact, in which the blood is compressed between two

surfaces; e.g., a bloody head and a weapon beating that head. This produces the radial pattern described above, with larger drops close to the center and smaller ones at a distance.

(3) Propulsion from moving objects, e.g., bloody weapons. Here, the blood drops vary in size, but tend to be rather large, and may travel considerable distances. Massive deposits of blood may break away, in rather large drops and at high velocity, from a swinging object. This resembles the physics of a slingshot or a catapult. The largest blood spot produced will not, however, be larger than a freely formed drop that falls under gravity alone. The blood separates from such a moving object from two causes: (a) centrifugal force acting on blood swung in an arc; and (b) abrupt change of direction of the moving object, as reversal of direction between successive strokes, as in beating.

(4) Lateral mechanical transport, effected when quantities of blood adhere to a surface that is moving laterally, but not in an arc. Such blood will draw into drops, and if free to fall, will fall as stationary blood falls. Because of this effect, blood cannot be carried for any significant distance on ordinary flat surfaces before the excess falls free, leaving on the surface a film that will not form drops. Thus, no bloody weapon will leave a trail from dropping blood for any great distance, even though the weapon itself remains bloody.

The above description applies only to blood drops that move through the air. The interpretation of blood that is transferred from object to object is different, but not necessarily simpler. The form of the transferred bloody area is usually larger, irregular in outline, and clearly not in accord with the analysis of single drops that produce spots. Some types of transfer are highly significant. For example, the mark left by a bloody head that makes contact with a wall or floor will show a very irregular brushing pattern from the hair. This locates the head at this position during the violent activity of the murder. Transfers from bloody clothing may show the weave of the cloth, and blood deposited by flowing against a cloth will quite often show a weave pattern. Bloody fingerprints can serve to identify the hand that placed them, but they can also be confusing. (See Chapter 6.) Washed areas show hemolysis, i.e., the rupturing of the blood corpuscles, which alters the appearance and reduces the intensity of the red color. Chunks of dried blood clot are sometimes encountered. These have usually been flipped off a moving object, and they indicate that the blood was drawn somewhat earlier and was given time to clot before being deposited where it is found. Arterial spurts, resulting from the cutting of an artery, resemble a single spurt from a garden hose in that they tend to produce an oval pattern distinct from the other types of blood pattern described.

The effect of water on blood during washing, or in a situation in which a wet garment contacts deposited blood, is especially interesting. The water not only hemolyzes the blood, as mentioned above, but it often brings about movement through the cloth, thus carrying the blood to regions not originally bloody.

FIGURE 14-5. (A) Blood splatter at a homicide scene. The axe was used to murder a man. (B) The angle and distribution of blood splatter on the wall was found to be due to blood thrown from the axe during its backward swing indicating repeated blows to the victim's body. (Courtesy of Robert R. Ogle and John I. Thornton.)

These situations are usually easy to recognize. They may show a boundary of the travel of liquid as a visible, irregular line; and the sharp edges of any blood spot which were originally present may have been lost by diffusion. Such effects will sometimes be seen when blood has been lost by the water movement, as when blood has been sponged from a garment. Even though the amount of blood remaining is likely to be minimal, no sponging operation will prevent the detection of the blood.

INVESTIGATION OF BLOOD IN THE FIELD

The Victim

Blood found on the person or clothing of a victim of murder, rape, assault, or other crime of physical violence is usually the victim's own blood. It is not for this reason insignificant. *The clothing of the victim should be removed and carefully preserved.* This general instruction applies also to all forms of evidence *on* clothing, and makes necessary this definite and careful routine:

(1) Avoid contaminating the clothing during removal and storage.
(2) If it is necessary to cut the clothes off the victim, avoid cutting through breaks caused by bullets, knives, or other weapons. Avoid cutting through bloody areas as much as possible.
(3) Do not place the clothing on a dirty floor or other dirty surface, but use clean wrapping paper or a similar clean surface.
(4) Make no effort to clean the clothing.
(5) Do not fold wet garments together, but spread them out on a clean surface and let them dry. Folding would permit wet blood to be transferred to originally uncontaminated regions.
(6) Strive to preserve all garments in (as nearly as possible) the same condition as that in which they were found.
(7) Remove all garments to the laboratory for examination.

Bloody garments may be wrapped in large sheets of wrapping paper or enclosed in paper garment bags. Each garment should be wrapped separately and should not come into contact with other clothing during wrapping or transport. These rules are necessary to protect from contamination not only the blood carried on the clothing, but also all the other evidence that may be present.

The Scene

Because every crime scene in which blood has been shed is somewhat different from every other one, a preliminary assessment of the scene is required. If blood has been thrown through the air, the situation will differ from that of a scene in which all of the shed blood has flowed to the floor. In either situation, the following steps are essential:

(1) If liquid blood is still present, it will be found only in relatively large deposits or pools. The liquid should be promptly sampled with a medicine dropper or pipet and the sample placed in a vial containing an anticoagulant. The vial should then be tightly capped for delivery to the laboratory. Speed is important here because the blood will quickly become coagulated, retracted, and dried. Liquid blood is not usually encountered at crime scenes except when large pools are present.

(2) Photographs showing all portions of the blood pattern should be made for record and for detailed study at a later time.

(3) The blood distribution pattern should be thoroughly studied. This is generally the most important step. If *no spots have been left by drops of blood* thrown through the air, attention should be directed to the significance of pools, smears, and contact areas in their relation to the activity associated with the crime. Often the action sequence of the crime is clarified greatly by such a study. In other instances, e.g., where a single pool of blood is found under a victim, little more information is obtainable than that he was killed instantly, fell, and bled.

If there is blood spotting on the floor, walls, furniture, or other objects, each spotted area should be examined. The major points to seek are these:

(a) Radial patterns and their centers.
(b) A gap (or gaps) in a radial pattern. Such a gap may show the position of the attacker if he has intercepted blood flying toward him.
(c) Areas of heavy spatter that indicate the swinging of a weapon or perhaps spurting from violent impact or from the severing of an artery.
(d) Spots far removed from the center of activity. These would indicate either exceptionally strong forces or variations in movement or position of the persons.
(e) Transfer or contact smears, including bloody fingerprints, cloth patterns, etc.
(f) Interrelation of various portions of the blood-spot pattern. An effort should be made to determine from the size and shape of the pattern the origin of the individual spots, or of a group of spots, bearing in mind that each drop that flew had its own trajectory.
(g) Any abnormal or difficult-to-explain features of the pattern. Such variations may be most critical in their informational content, since the spots may have come from the assailant rather than from the victim, or they may indicate some unexpected type of action that is of great significance.

(4) Finally, samples of the blood stains should be collected for laboratory

analysis. These may be scraped into shell vials or other suitable containers; and, where the blood is reasonably plentiful, a rather large sample should be removed. Blood on portable articles should not be removed in the field; the entire article should be taken to the laboratory. For simple benzidine testing one may use cotton-tipped swabs, either handmade or purchased, e.g., Q-Tips. Moisten the swab with cold water, rub it on a spot, label and preserve it for testing. This procedure will provide ample blood for color tests, and will leave the spot visibly in place. *The exact source of the blood sample in terms of the total blood pattern must be placed on the label, marked on a photograph or otherwise made identifiable as to exact origin.* If, for instance, two samples represent different blood groups, it is of critical importance to know which sample came from which region of the crime scene.

DOUBTFUL BLOOD STAINS. All stains suspected of being blood should be checked chemically, even when their nature is not especially doubtful. Such stains usually appear red or brown, but other colors may be noted at times. Thus, blood on wallpaper may dissolve dye from the paper and produce unusual colors. Fresh stains will be more red than old stains, the latter often appearing like iron rust. On some garments and surfaces the characteristic color of bloodstains will not be visible because of the nature and color of the surface. Here, chemical testing is imperative. Examination under an ultraviolet lamp is often helpful, since the blood appears black under this illumination, whereas the surface carrying the blood may show a fluorescent color. This contrast is useful for locating and delineating the stain, but it is not to be considered as a positive indication of blood. *All stains suspected of being blood should be tested by appropriate chemical methods.*

HIDDEN BLOOD. Frequently there will be no visible blood in a locale that is believed to have been bloody, such as the scene of a suspected interior crime, or in or on an automobile. This situation can result from washing before the discovery of the crime, or from the fact that little blood was deposited, as in the case in numerous hit-and-run accidents. Exterior crime scenes are not likely to be cleaned, but the nature of the terrain may make difficult the location of blood in such a place.

In all such instances it is preferred that a laboratory specialist do the searching, since chemical tests will be required. There are several approaches to this problem, any or all of which may be expected to succeed, because it is virtually impossible to remove blood so completely that remaining traces cannot be detected by chemical methods. Where the area in question is small, e.g., clothing or automobile seats, the preferred method is to cover the area with wet filter paper, which is pressed into contact and allowed to remain for several minutes. The paper is removed and sprayed with benzidine reagent. Very small areas of the questioned surface may be rubbed with wet cotton swabs, which are then tested with benzidine. A positive benzidine test is not absolute proof of the presence of blood, but it is an indication of probable presence. Other more conclusive procedures are available for confirmatory testing.

When blood traces are suspected in large areas, such as a portion of a large room or house, the luminol test is applied. In total darkness, fresh reagent is sprayed with a glass or plastic atomizer over all questioned areas. If blood traces are present they will give rise to a rather strong and persistent glow in the dark. This is an indication, not *absolute proof*, of the presence of blood; it must be borne in mind that false luminescence is regularly encountered on metal surfaces. Luminol is primarily a search reagent for relatively large areas. Often it may reveal a crack into which blood has soaked and from which the blood can be recovered for more extensive testing. Properly used, neither the luminol test nor the benzidine test will prevent further tests from being applied successfully.

A search of the area for hidden blood must be very thorough, and must take into account the circumstances surrounding the crime. Bloody hands will certainly be washed at the first opportunity, and some diluted blood will remain for a considerable time in the trap of a sink used for hand-washing. The water should be removed and tested for the presence of diluted blood. In the absence of immediately available washing facilities, the culprit will probably wipe his hands on something other than his own clothing. Obvious materials such as bloody towels, handkerchiefs, or rags will not ordinarily be overlooked by the investigator, but the underside of a table, the back of a drape, or the bottom of a rug might very well be missed. The careful investigator will certainly search all such places where the culprit might conceal blood wiped from his hands. The luminol test method is particularly advantageous for such a search, though it may often be possible to see such wiped blood and to test it by other methods that do not require darkness.

Cracks in floors call for special consideration. If blood has been shed on a floor, the floor will most certainly be scrubbed in order to conceal the crime. However, scrubbing will not eliminate blood that has seeped into floor cracks, though it will quite effectively prevent visual detection. Here again, the luminol spray is valuable. If a positive luminol test is obtained, it is simple to scrape out the contents of the crack for more detailed examination.

The Suspect

The suspect is not ordinarily taken into custody until ample time has elapsed for him to clean blood from his person and to clean or dispose of his clothing. Accordingly, the investigator's only recourse is to make a careful and thorough search for the clothing, or for any fragments of it that may have survived the cleaning or disposal treatment. When clothing is recovered that is obviously or possibly bloody, it should be wrapped as described for the victim's clothing, and sent to the laboratory with all possible promptness. If this clothing gives evidence of having been washed recently, it is particularly suspect and should be seized immediately. It is extremely difficult to remove blood from clothing so completely that it cannot be detected by the more sensitive chemical testing methods.

REFERENCES

MacDonell, Herbert L.: *Flight Characteristics and Stain Patterns of Human Blood.* Washington, D.C.: U.S. Government Printing Office (1971).

Polson, C. J.: *Essentials of Forensic Medicine,* 2nd ed. Springfield: Thomas (1965). Chap. 9.

Svensson, Arne, and Wendel, Otto: *Techniques of Crime Scene Investigation,* 2nd ed. (Joseph D. Nicol, ed.) New York: American Elsevier (1965).

15
Blood: General Testing

Because the presence of blood at a crime scene is not always apparent, it is sometimes necessary to use chemical tests to detect and visualize the blood evidence. Chemical and immunological tests also play an important part in the laboratory analysis of blood evidence; they are used to test whether presumptive stains are really blood, to determine the species origin of the blood, and to gain information about the identity of the blood donor. The application of these tests is the responsibility of the laboratory personnel, but police investigators will do well to become familiar with the limitations and capabilities of tests commonly used. In this chapter, the tests for blood and the tests for species origin are discussed; in Chapter 16, the topic of blood individuality is considered.

TESTS FOR THE PRESENCE OF BLOOD

The necessity of a test for blood arises in two situations. A sensitive test is needed to detect the presence of blood evidence that is not apparent on direct visual inspection. Examples would include the detection of small blood spots on patterned wallpaper and blood in floorboard cracks. Reliable tests are also needed to verify that a stain presumed to be blood really is blood. Upon occasion, food stains, paint, rust, and other materials may be thought to be blood until chemical testing proves otherwise.

All the chemical tests currently in use for the detection of blood are tests for heme or its derivatives. Heme is noncovalently attached to hemoglobin, the oxygen-transporting protein of blood; it is the chemical moiety that lends the distinctive red color to blood. Although hemoglobin is found only in red blood cells, other heme proteins are present in the blood and tissues of animals and in the tissues of plants and microorganisms. Thus, mashed insects, insect bites, fly specks and the like can be sources of difficulty. The location of such spots and their characteristic small size will ordinarily distinguish them clearly from the rather large areas of blood that are commonly deposited in the commission of a crime. Blood that has been carried by insects may be found mingled with their crushed remains. Careful search with magnification is usually necessary in such a situation, since the remains of the insect may be quite small and inconspicuous.

The tests for blood are of two types: (1) tests for the catalytic peroxidase activity of heme, which include the sensitive but not entirely specific color and luminescence tests; and (2) crystal tests for heme derivatives. The latter tests are quite specific for heme, but are relatively insensitive.

Catalytic Tests

The color and luminescence tests for blood all depend upon the fact that various colorless materials can be oxidized to colored or to luminescent materials. Hydrogen peroxide is the oxidizing agent usually employed, but sodium perborate may also be used. The reaction proceeds at a very slow rate unless a catalyst is present. Heme is a very active catalyst for the reaction, giving rise to rapid oxidation of the colorless compound by the peroxide or perborate.

The catalytic tests are highly sensitive to minute traces of hemoglobin and its derivatives, but they all suffer from interference by some materials other than hemoglobin. Other heme proteins such as catalase and the peroxidases will give a positive reaction. In addition, a positive reaction will be given by some strong oxidizing agents and metallic salts that do not require the presence of a catalyst for the reaction to proceed.

The reagents most commonly employed are benzidine, phenolphthalin, the leuco base of malachite green (a green dye), and luminol (3-aminophthalhydrazide). Guaiac and other materials have been employed at times. The sensitivities of the tests listed are variously reported by different authors. The variances are undoubtedly attributable to differences in reagent concentrations, in methods of preparing the samples, and in the mode of expressing the results. Comparative sensitivity data are given in Table 15–1. All tests were made with varying dilutions of the same blood and as nearly as possible in the same manner. The test data do not necessarily represent the highest sensitivities obtainable, but they provide a relatively correct comparison of the four common reagents.

Because of the great sensitivity of the color and luminescence reactions, tests based upon them are used to locate such deposits as washed blood spots and

TABLE 15–1 Sensitivity of Blood Tests

Test	Dilution of blood	Time for positive reaction, sec.	Duration, min.
benzidine (in glacial acetic acid)	1:300,000	10	10
benzidine	1:100,000	1	
leuco-malachite green	1:100,000	15	7
phenolphthalin (original stock)	1:100,000	3	30+
	1:5,000,000	20	
phenolphthalin (dry reagents)	1:10,000	20	10
luminol	1:5,000,000*	5	15+

* Proescher and Moody give a sensitivity of 1:100,000 for the luminol test for decomposed blood. They recommend preliminary spraying with hydrochloric acid to decompose hemoglobin and increase the sensitivity of the test.

for greatly diluted blood such as may be found in the water in sink traps. These tests serve also for the preliminary identification of visible bloodstains; almost instantaneous reactions will result with all of these reagents. There are a few materials other than blood that will also react to the reagents, but the responses are generally slower, fainter, and more doubtful. With reasonable caution, interference from most sources can be recognized. Under most conditions, catalytic tests properly performed leave little doubt as to the presence or absence of blood. It is, however, dangerous to conclude positively that blood is present when the test is not strong and definite and when only a single test is used. When positive tests are given by the four common reagents, and particularly by the alkaline reagents, little doubt exists that hemoglobin is present.

The blood-test kit described in Chapter 3 allows any or all of the common blood tests by color or luminescence to be performed readily under field conditions. This enables the field investigator to show presence or absence of blood almost positively without any laboratory examination whatever. Although it is less convenient than operation in the laboratory, this alternative is at times of great value because of such factors as limited time, or anticipated willful destruction of blood spots.

Interferences

When no color or luminescence results from the testing of a suspected stain or surface, the absence of response has always been accepted as proof of the absence of blood, and, in fact, this is usually the case. However, it has been found in recent years that this assumption can be false under some conditions.

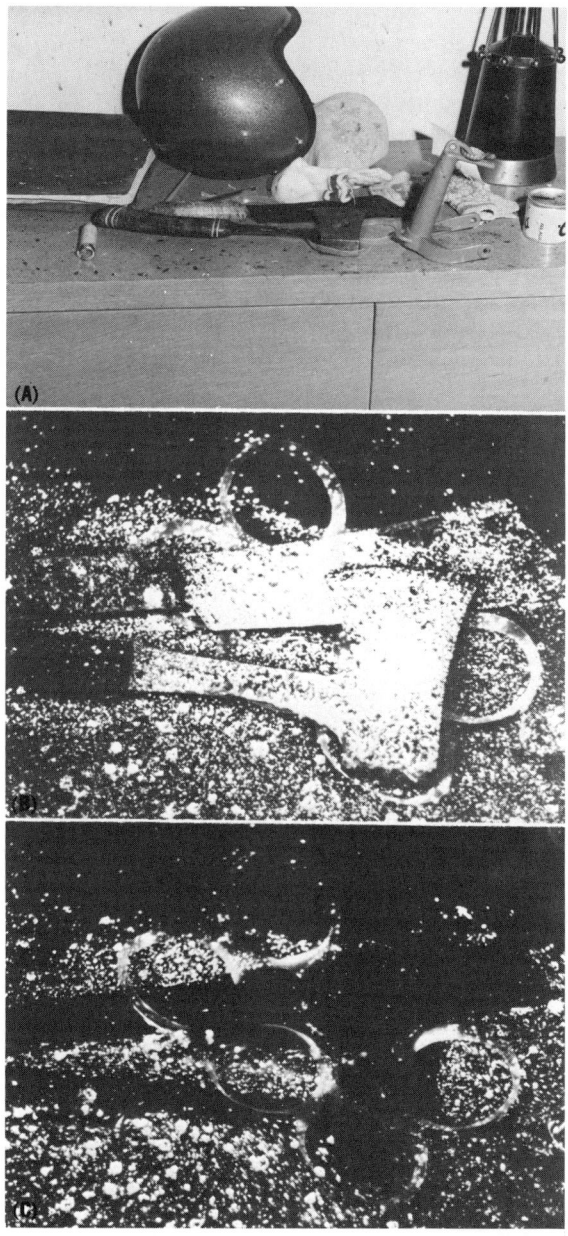

FIGURE 15-1. The luminol reagent used to visualize blood stains. A man was shot in the head spraying blood and tissue on the chest of drawers behind him (A). The suspect claimed that he was being attacked with the hatchet and cleaver at the time the shot was fired. The hatchet and cleaver on the chest top were sprayed with the luminol reagent before (B) and after (C) they were removed. The absence of blood under these weapons indicated that they were lying on the chest top and not in the victim's hands when the shot was fired. (Courtesy of John I. Thornton.)

Strong reducing agents such as ascorbic acid will inhibit the catalytic tests. Thus a little blood mixed with fresh orange juice would, in all probability, not be detectable. Possibly other chemicals also can inhibit these tests, although details on their nature are not available. In one instance, such an inhibitor had definitely been used, and a positive benzidine test was not obtained although it is certain that blood had left a stain in the region tested. On the same surface, in an area where the inhibitor had not been applied, stains of exactly the same appearance and distribution gave very strong benzidine tests. Thus, at this time it is necessary for the criminalist to modify his testimony as to the absence of blood by stating that no *demonstrable* blood was present, if the tests were negative.

The preoccupation has always been with false positive tests: a danger of which every investigator is aware. When a positive test is obtained, it is necessary to consider whether something other than blood may have been responsible for this result. Fortunately, it is rather simple to avoid difficulties from these sources. The types of material that can lead to such false positive tests may be summarized in two groups:

Group 1: Materials other than hemoglobin that contain heme. These include a variety of oxidative enzymes and other heme proteins present in some fresh vegetable materials (see listing below), in animal tissues (red meat), and in several microorganisms.

Group 2: Some chemical oxidants. (Also listed below.) The plant peroxidases of Group 1 are unstable and can be readily destroyed by heating or by complete drying. The catalytic activity of the heme in blood, on the other hand, is not appreciably changed by heating to 100°C. So far as is known, no vegetable peroxidase will do this, and many have been tested.

Materials of Group 2 cannot be so easily eliminated. However, their presence may be detected by dividing the color reagent into two parts, one of which is the oxidant (peroxide or perborate), the second, the other ingredients. The latter solution is applied first. If there are suitable oxidants present, a positive test will be obtained without the test oxidant. In this event, no regular test of this material is possible.

A further point of importance is that alkaline reagents such as phenolphthalin and luminol are much less affected by the enzymic materials than are the acid reagents (benzidine, leuco-malachite green). A combination of two procedures, one acid and the other alkaline, gives considerable certainty that false positives will be avoided. A few vegetable materials, notably the milky exudate of dandelion root or poinsettia root, will give false positive reactions with an alkaline reagent, luminol. No comparable findings have been made with phenolphthalin, but it is possible that some interfering material may yet be found. The luminol test was at one time claimed to be absolutely specific for blood, but it has long been very clear that numerous metal salts give false positives with luminol, and the use of this reagent on metal surfaces is without significance. The reagent would be very satisfactory for the detection of copper ions. With the exception of this source of false positive reactions, the luminol test can be controlled for reliability by the same means as are applicable to the color tests: drying and heating of samples before testing. Another interesting point is that old and partially decomposed blood gives stronger tests with luminol than does fresh blood. The latter may be artificially aged with a spray of dilute hydrochloric acid, but except for searching large areas, the extra trouble is not worthwhile, in comparison with other available tests for blood.

In the author's laboratory, interferences with the *benzidine test*, attributable to the presence of peroxidases, have been encountered in:

horseradishes lemons
radishes grapefruits
oranges grass and other green leaves

In all instances, the tests are slower and weaker than with blood, and in the case of the citrus fruits the test originates in the pulp, not in the juice cells. Boiling the material for a few moments destroys the false positive test, and does not destroy the test with blood, though heating a dry bloodstain much above 100°C does destroy the true positive test also.

Pinker ["The Preliminary Chemical Tests for Blood." *Proc. 20th Annual Convention, Int. Assoc. Identification*, p. 38 (1934).] reports interference with the benzidine test from the peroxidases of:

asparagus banana dandelion root
carrot cauliflower black fig pulp
horse radish lettuce (romaine) green onion bulb
garden peas potato radish
summer squash green beans watermelon

He states further that the peroxidase reaction of the above substances is readily destroyed not only by boiling but by drying and on standing. Thus, the chief

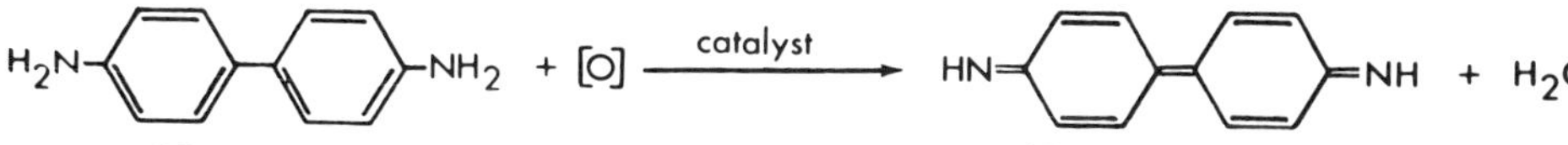

$$H_2N-\bigcirc-\bigcirc-NH_2 + [O] \xrightarrow{catalyst} HN=\bigcirc=\bigcirc=NH + H_2O$$

BENZIDINE BENZIDINE BLUE

FIGURE 15-2. Proposed mechanism of the benzidine reaction. (Adapted from Fritz Feigl, Spot Tests in Organic Analysis, Elsevier Publishing Co., New York, 1956, p. 93, courtesy of Edward T. Blake.)

source of much accidental staining (cooked foods) will not give the test; and dried stains, the common form in which such evidence is found, are not usually susceptible to false positive reactions. Pinker lists also certain chemicals and pharmaceuticals that may give false positive reactions. For the most part these are strong oxidants such as hypochlorites, persulfates, permanganates, chromates, etc., and iodine. Lead oxides give false positives, and this is perhaps one of the most dangerous interferences since lead oxides occur at times in paint and in plumber's "whiting" which, particularly after burning, will yield a strong benzidine test. Whiting was shown to be the source of a positive benzidine test on a burned pipe that was claimed to be a murder weapon in a spectacular trial.

Hundreds of materials likely to produce stains on clothing have been tested in various laboratories and found to produce *no reaction* with the benzidine reagent. These include:

eggs	tomato juice
Coca-Cola	iron rust
saliva	orange juice
semen	wine (numerous varieties)
coffee	urine (normal)
tobacco (and tar from pipe cleanings)	feces (usually)
most chemicals and pharmaceuticals	mayonnaise
milk	inks
whiskey	most food products
perspiration	

Interference with the *phenolphthalin* test is far less in all comparative studies than with the benzidine or other color tests. In fact, some investigators consider that this test can produce almost conclusive proof of the presence of blood. Those materials listed above that were found in the author's laboratory to produce strong interference with the benzidine test in no case gave any interference with the phenolphthalin test, and this was true without heating or aging the sample. This conclusion has been confirmed by the work of Pinker, who found that no vegetable or food material reacted strongly with phenolphthalin, and in only a few cases were there weak or doubtful reactions. Further, he found no definite reactions with pharmaceuticals, and only a few with pure chemical substances. These included cobaltous nitrate, potassium ferricyanide, sodium cobaltinitrite, and some sulfocyanates, all of which are most unlikely to be confused with blood in criminalistic practice.

The phenolphthalin test is considerably more difficult to carry out than is the benzidine test, both in the matter of preparing the reagent and in its application. For this reason it has been less popular than the relatively less sensitive and specific benzidine test. Nickolls [*The Scientific Investigation of*

Crime. London: Butterworth and Co. (1956).] has emphasized the problems encountered in the use of phenolphthalin and considers the benzidine test to be far more practical. Inasmuch as the latter test is simpler to use and is adequate for most practical purposes, his comments must be taken seriously. When properly employed, with a double reagent and with preliminary heating of doubtful samples, it is certainly adequate for practical application, both in the field and in the laboratory.

The *leuco-malachite green* (tetramethyldiaminotriphenlymethane) *test* is to be considered as intermediate between the benzidine test and the phenolphthalin test with respect to interference. It responds to the same types of interfering materials as does benzidine and has about the same sensitivity; however, it is inferior to phenolphthalin in both particulars.

In the use of all three of the color tests, one should doubt the significance of any response that is characterized by (1) slowness of color development, (2) faintness of color, (3) color at a spot only, not over an area, and (4) abnormal appearance of color. The tests are all more reliable when applied to old, dry stains than with fresh material because of the possible presence of peroxidases in material other than blood. As the investigator becomes more experienced in the use of color tests, he will become better qualified to interpret doubtful reactions.

Crystal Tests

There are a number of crystal tests for blood that are far less sensitive than the chemical tests but are considered to be more specific. Of these, the Teichmann and the Takayama tests are the best known and most widely used. The Teichmann test consists of crystallizing from glacial acetic acid the hydrochloride of heme, termed *hematin*, in the form of brown prisms that frequently show enlarged tips. The Teichmann test is applicable to very small amounts of blood, such as may adhere to a single cloth fiber that has been withdrawn from a stained area. If no blood is visible it will ordinarily be impossible to obtain Teichmann crystals. When the Teichmann test is positive, i.e., when characteristic crystals of hematin are formed under the proper testing conditions, there is no doubt of the nature of the stain tested. In general, when the available blood is sufficient in quantity, the Teichmann test, or an equivalent one, should be used as a confirmation of the color tests, which are usually performed first. At times, the Teichmann test fails because of the presence of foreign matter in the blood. This is particularly likely to occur when the blood has been recovered from a wooden or leather surface, presumably because of the tannins in these materials, which precipitate the blood proteins. The failure to obtain a good Teichmann test is *not* proof of the absence of blood.

The so-called Takayama test likewise depends upon the formation of characteristic crystals, those of pyridine hemochromogen. The sensitivity and specificity of this test are essentially the same as those of the Teichmann test. It is superior to the latter in that it can often be used to obtain positive tests with blood taken from wooden or leather surfaces. The failure to obtain a positive Takayama test also does not necessarily indicate the absence of blood.

A more recently developed test, in which crystals of thiocyanhemochromogen are formed, has been found to be superior in that it is less time-consuming, requires only very small quantities of blood, and thus far has shown no interference.

Spectroscopic Tests

As ordinarily performed, blood testing by absorption spectroscopy is a less sensitive method than the chemical tests described above. When properly performed, it is as specific as the crystal tests, but probably not more so. Difficulty arises from the fact that hemoglobin and its derivatives and decomposition products all have characteristic absorption spectra that differ greatly among themselves. Unless the conditions are so adjusted that any hemoglobin or hemoglobin derivatives present are definitely in one known and specific form, the complexities of the resulting spectrum may nullify all attempts to interpret it. Methods are available for converting hemoglobin to a hemochromogen, or even to a porphyrin, and then measuring it. If the blood is reasonably fresh, the hemoglobin can all be converted to methemoglobin or, possibly, to reduced hemoglobin, both of which have characteristic absorption spectra. There are several satisfactory forms into which all of the blood pigment can be converted when the sample is fresh. Because the blood encountered by the criminalist is not always fresh, some of these forms cannot be dependably produced. As a general rule, the use of the spectroscope or the spectrophotometer for identifying a bloodstain is far more trouble than the chemical or crystal tests and gives less satisfactory results.

TESTS FOR SPECIES ORIGIN OF BLOOD

It will commonly be necessary for the criminalist to determine whether a sample of blood is of human origin or, if not, from what species it did come. Questions concerning deer blood are often raised because of possible violations of the game laws. Cattle blood may occasionally be tested in connection with the butchering of stolen cattle. Many similar questions will require investigation.

Immunological Tests

The tests for species determination are almost exclusively immunological in nature. If an animal is injected with a protein molecule from another species, it will recognize this protein as foreign and will produce an antiprotein or *antibody*, which specifically binds to the foreign protein. In this context, the foreign protein is called the *antigen*. The reaction of the antibody with the antigen facilitates the breakdown and removal of the antigen from the host animal's system. This is the same type of reaction that is effective in natural immunity to disease. When the animal is invaded by disease agents, such as measles virus, or the pneumococcus that causes pneumonia, antibodies are formed against these foreign protein agents and confer a degree of immunity to recurrence of the disease. Some immunities are quite permanent, whereas others wear off in a period of time.

In order to apply this principle to the question of species testing, it is necessary to immunize an animal (usually a rabbit) with human blood serum or the blood serum of another species in a prescribed manner until the rabbit has produced a sufficient level of antibodies to give a strong reaction. The antigen-antibody reaction is detected by the formation of a precipitate of the antibody-antigen complex; this is the *precipitin* reaction. Antibodies are relatively specific, but not absolutely specific for the immunizing antigen. For example, antibodies prepared against human blood will give a strong reaction if mixed with human blood, a slightly weaker reaction with the blood of apes, a weaker yet reaction with monkey blood, and a weak or absent reaction with the blood of other, nonprimate species. Thus a negative test (barring interferences) indicates that the blood being tested is not from the same species as the immunizing antigen; but a positive test does not indicate they are from the same species. When testing for human blood, this source of confusion is rarely encountered since the need to distinguish between human and ape blood does not often arise. Cross-reactivity is a problem, however, if the analyst must distinguish closely related species, such as beef and deer. It is possible to use immunological techniques for absolute species determination, but this requires the application of more delicate procedures that involve some special facilities and expertise.

Relatively little blood is required for immunological tests for species origin. In general, there should be enough blood to impart some color to an extract of the stain. This requirement is met by almost any stain that is visible to the eye. There are particular circumstances, however, when it may not be possible to obtain reliable results. Blood on shoes and on unpainted wood, as well as in some other situations, may not give a good test. Leather and wood possess tannins that are protein precipitants, and these tannins may precipitate the blood being tested and also the antibody in the testing serum, thus rendering the test useless. Except in the situations mentioned, protein precipitants are not often encountered.

All immunological species tests for the origin of blood samples should be performed only by individuals who are reasonably skilled in their techniques and interpretation. Even in the precipitin test there are numerous technical

192 CRIME INVESTIGATION

variations, the sensitivity and reliability of which are not identical. In unskilled hands there is a definite danger of error and misinterpretation. Fundamentally, the tests are very simple, but experience with them is essential to their reliability.

Corpuscles in Species Identification

Some authorities in the field of serology emphasize the value of studying the appearance of the corpuscles to determine the species of the blood. It is true that the size, morphology, and appearance of the corpuscles from different species are quite different and are often characteristic. On this basis it is pos-

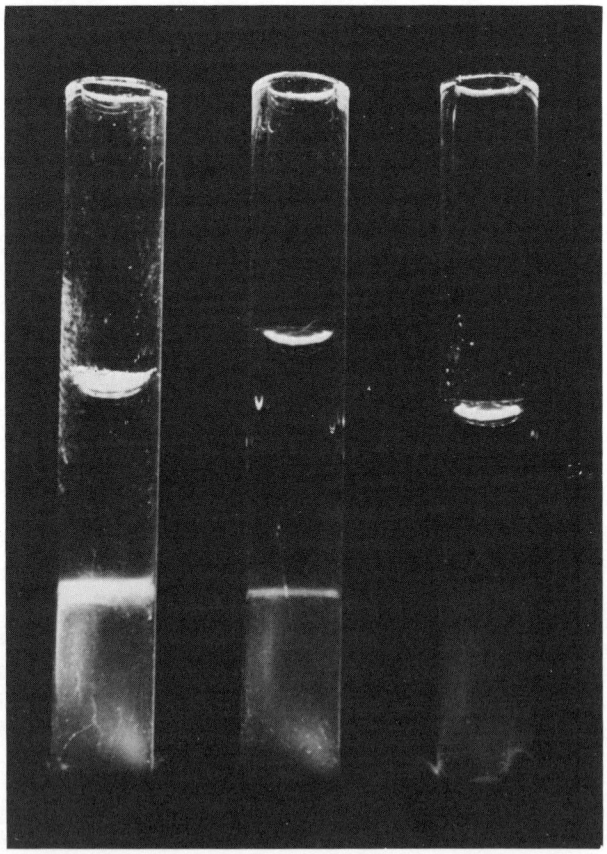

FIGURE 15-3. Precipitin reaction in tubes. The lower portion of all tubes contains anti-human serum. From left to right the upper layer of the tubes contains human serum, Rhesus macaque serum, and rabbit serum. The white precipitation at the interface of the two layers indicates a positive reaction. Rhesus macaque (an old world monkey) cross-reacts with anti-human serum but rabbit serum does not. (Courtesy of Edward T. Blake.)

sible to state that the questioned blood cannot be from any of a large number of species and that it must have come from a particular species, or from one of a few species having similar corpuscles. As an illustration, avian corpuscles are nucleated and may be recognized on this basis. It is difficult or impossible to distinguish from the corpuscular appearance along all the species of birds from each other, but a suspected blood that was nucleated could be stated to have come from a bird rather than from a mammal. As valuable as this approach may be potentially, its use is rare in practical criminalistics for the reason that the condition of the blood received by the criminalist is usually such as to preclude obtaining any corpuscles in a normal state.

Suppose that a bloodstain is found on some clothing, where it has dried. In the drying process the increasing salt concentration of the blood has caused crenation of the corpuscles. Soaking the dry blood in physiological saline solution results in a hypertonic condition (i.e., stronger than blood in salt concentration) and the corpuscles remain shrunken (crenated). The attempt to adjust the salt concentration to normal by dilution is difficult, and will ordinarily fail. Moreover, many bloodstains have been so treated after being deposited that few of the corpuscles are even intact. In the fortunate case where normal corpuscles can be found, close examination of them is of great value in the determination of species. In the usual situation such study is of negligible value.

WASHED BLOODSTAINS

Criminals commonly attempt to destroy blood evidence in homes and automobiles by washing it from clothing, rugs and upholstery, and from other surfaces. Persons who accidentally deposit blood on similar items do the same. Thus, proof that blood has been washed from a garment or another item is not in itself significant evidence. It is, nevertheless, of great interest to know whether blood has been washed from an item associated with a suspect who, if guilty, should probably have been bloodied. The distribution of the blood is highly important, but after washing, blood will not be apparent to the eye. It can be developed in some instances, and it should be when possible.

When bloodstained items are washed, the blood is rarely totally removed. Much of it is washed away, but the remainder is diluted and soaks further into the surface, if the latter is absorbent. This sequence is especially probable in the case of napped textiles such as are used for rugs, but it is true also, to a lesser extent, for almost any cloth item. Even weapons and other articles with solid and nonabsorbent surfaces commonly have enough irregularity of surface to prevent complete removal of blood by sponging, wiping, or other similar operations. As many as four successive washings of bloody clothing by automatic washers, commercial laundries, hand washing in cold or hot water, with and without detergent, have left residual blood, detectable by chemical tests. In virtually no instance was a single washing by any of these means effective, nor was dry cleaning. Knife blades and similar items, even when showing no visible blood, can be tested positively when blood has been present earlier. In one test, a slightly rusty blade was sponged with a wet towel ten consecutive times before the benzidine test for blood become doubtful.

If blood has ever been on an object, it is almost certain that washing or wiping will still leave enough of the blood for catalytic blood tests to reveal its presence. Thus, in any instance in which such a determination is significant, the tests should be made. On the other hand, the value of the tests, when positive, must not be overrated. The tests that will work are responsive to animal blood also, to blood accidentally applied at any time, and to the interfering substances already discussed, if specific precautions are not taken to prevent the interference. Frequently, the amount of blood remaining after reasonable thorough washing is also sufficient to permit the application of tests for species or for blood grouping.

As indicated in Chapter 14, the development of a blood pattern on washed garments can be of great significance. In a murder by beating, blood spatters will be found on the lower portions of the perpetrator's clothing if the victim was on the ground; or on the upper portions if the victim was in a raised position, as on a bed. Also, there will have been many spots initially whose identity will generally not have been entirely lost in washing or sponging. A useful technique for the detection of a blood pattern is to spread the garments on a large sheet of glass, placing on the portions of interest large pieces of filter paper that have been wet with distilled water. On top of the damp paper another sheet of glass is laid, and the garment is left to soak for at least a half hour. The filter paper is then removed, dried, and sprayed with benzidine reagent, or other suitable test solution. Both the presence of blood and any remaining blood pattern will be detected. Such a pattern can then be related to the portion of the garment from which it was soaked. This operation is normally done in the laboratory rather than by police investigators, but it is not difficult and can be carried out with less than complete training in criminalistics.

AGE OF BLOODSTAINS

Much work has been done in the effort to determine the age of shed blood in stains, and considerable pertinent literature is available on the subject. It is well to know that there are many reactions that occur in blood even after drying, because there is still a very significant quantity of water present in what appears to be a totally dry stain. Little is known about many of these reactions, especially pertaining to their rate; and for lack of this knowledge most of them remain unexploited. Thus, it would be most dangerous, at this time, to estimate the age of a bloodstain except in the most general terms.

The most apparent marker of age in dried blood is the change in color from reddish brown through progressively darker shades until it becomes almost black. This sequence of color change is attributable for the most part to alterations in the hemoglobin, although other reactions cannot be excluded. Recent spectrophotometric studies have suggested that the change in color is regular with time for blood samples kept under similar conditions. However the effects of different storage conditions have not been fully investigated. The most that can be said is that the greatest caution must be exercised in making statements about the age of bloodstains. Further research may do much to clarify this important matter.

REFERENCES

Coetzee, M. D.: "Human and Animal Blood Stains, An Absorption Technique for Their Differentiation," *J. For. Med.* 5:163 (1958).

Culliford, B. J., and Nickolls, L. C.: "The Benzidine Test—A Critical Review," *J. For. Sci.* 9:175 (1964).

Fiori, A.: "Detection and Identification of Bloodstains," in F. Lundquist, ed., *Methods of Forensic Science,* Vol. 1. New York: Interscience (1962).

Greaves, A. V.: "The Use of Takayama's Solution in the Identification of Blood Stains," *Brit. Med. J.* 1:932 (1932).

Hunt, A. C., Corby, C., and Dodd, B. E.: "The Identification of Human Blood Stains," *J. For. Med.* 7:112 (1960).

Kind, S. S., Patterson, D., and Owen, G. W.: "Estimation of the Age of Dried Blood Stains by a Spectrophotometric Method," *For. Sci.* 1:27 (1972).

Poulson, C. J.: *Essentials of Forensic Medicine,* 2nd ed. Springfield: Thomas (1965). Chap. 9.

Proescher, F., and Moody, A. M.: "Detection of Blood by Means of Chemiluminescence," *J. Lab. Clin. Med.* 24:1183 (1939).

Schleyer, F.: "Investigation of Biological Stains with Regard to Species Origin," in F. Lundquist, ed. *Methods of Forensic Science,* Vol. 1. New York: Interscience (1962).

16
Blood: Individual Factors

The blood of every human being is unique. That is to say, it is possible in principle to distinguish the blood of any two persons. The individuality of blood stems from both genetic and environmental factors; both sources of variation have received considerable attention over the past two decades with the result that many more individualizing factors are known now than when the first edition of this book was written. Utilization of these individualization factors in crime laboratories has lagged considerably behind the knowledge of their existence, but there is some evidence that this situation is beginning to be corrected.

The genetic variation in blood is a reflection of the great amount of genetic variation that distinguishes each individual in the human population. The biological information that determines genetic variability is present at birth and is constant throughout the life of an individual. The blood groups are the best-known examples of genetic variation in the human population. The blood-group factors are located on the surface of red cells; they are detected by immunological techniques. Genetic markers are also found on the surface of other cell types in blood, i.e. on the white cells and the platelets. In addition, within the last decade, extensive genetic variation of the plasma proteins and the red-cell enzymes has been discovered. These genetic markers are distinguished by electrophoretic techniques. When enough of these factors in a blood sample are known, the blood is well characterized as to its individual origin.

Although genetically controlled factors are most important in assessing the individuality of blood, there are other factors, environmental in origin, that can be significant in particular situations. Obviously, these cannot be factors that change rapidly with nutritional influences, such as fat in the blood, lactic acid generated by exercise, or glucose, which is in balance with a number of varying regulatory factors. Rather, they are relatively long-term effects such as antibodies to disease. An individual who has had measles or mumps will carry in his blood, for life, the antibodies to that disease; the person who has not had measles or mumps will not carry such antibodies. It seems evident that if a total antibody profile were determined for an individual, it would be found to reflect that person's medical history with respect to exposure to various bacterial and viral diseases. Though factors of this type are not as useful as the genetically controlled constant factors, they should not be disregarded (as they generally are at present).

The analysis of blood with respect to its individuality involves special knowledge and experience. There are many pitfalls for the novice and for the unwary. Any person who undertakes studies of this type must master the appropriate knowledge and skills and must keep in practice lest skills become rusty.

BLOOD GROUPS

It is a well-known fact, first emphasized in connection with blood transfusions, that not all human blood is compatible with that of any given individual. This incompatibility arises from the fact that the blood plasma of one individual may contain antibodies that will agglutinate the corpuscles of another person. This is a highly critical matter in transfusion, because if an incompatible blood is injected it may promptly cause the death of the recipient. The common types of blood are well known; they can be conveniently identified, and their distribution in human populations has been the subject of extensive investigation.

About twelve red-cell blood-group systems are known at present. The ABO system was the first to be discovered; it provides the easiest determinations, and is the system most often utilized in both the clinical and the crime laboratory. The next best known is the Rh system, which has marked clinical importance, but receives limited attention in crime laboratories. Limited attention is also given to the MNSs system despite its great potential value to the crime laboratory. The other blood-group systems are virtually unused in the crime laboratory.

The ABO System

The ABO blood-group system was discovered by Landsteiner about the turn of the century. He found that the plasma from some individuals agglutinated the red cells from other individuals. He was able to distinguish four classes of agglutination behavior; these four classes have come to be designated as O, A,

B, and AB blood types. Although several alternative nomenclatures for the ABO types have been employed in the past, the universal nomenclature, i.e., A, B, AB, and O, has gained almost exclusive acceptance. The relationship between the ABO blood types is shown in Table 16-1.

In agglutinating systems, such as the ABO system, the cellular antigens are sometimes called *agglutinogens* and the plasma antibodies are called *agglutinins*. However, this usage appears to be on the wane and the cellular antigens are simply referred to as blood-group antigens or blood-group substances. The ABO blood-group substances have for the most part been chemically characterized; they are polysaccharide in nature and may be attached to lipid or protein in the membrane of the red cell. The A substance differs chemically from the B substance in that the former possesses an N-acetyl galactosamine as its nonreducing terminal sugar whereas the latter has a galactose in that position. The A substance appears to exist in several forms that give rise to subgroups A_1, A_2 and the very rare A_3. The subgroups all react with anti-A antisera but can be distinguished by the use of some adsorbed anti-A sera; they can also be distinguished by the use of certain plant extracts that contain specific agglutinating proteins called lectins. Lectins will be described in a later section in this chapter. The chemical basis of the subgroups is not known. It should be noted that blood-group substances are to be found in a great variety of material; hog gastric mucosa, for example, contains an A substance.

Although the synthesis of the blood-group substances is a complex process, the ABO type is determined by the action of genes at a single genetic locus. The A genes (including the subgroup genes), the B genes, and the O genes are transmitted according to the Mendelian laws of inheritance; the expression of the A and B genes is dominant over the O genes. The dominance of A and B gene expression means that persons with different genotypes may be of the same blood type. The blood group of a person is, in reality, a reference to the phenotype of that person. When we test for group A and find A agglutinogen present in the blood, we have proved merely that one gene of the pair at the ABO locus is an A gene. Actually, as noted above, there are two well-known A factors. An A individual (phenotype) could have paired genes as follows: A_1A_1, A_1A_2, A_1O, A_2A_2, or A_2O. Each of these is a genotype, but all will test as

TABLE 16–1 The ABO Blood-Group System

Blood type	Red-cell antigens present	Antibodies present in plasma
A	A	anti-B
B	B	anti-A
AB	AB	
O		anti-A, anti-B

A group, unless special tests are applied to distinguish A_1 from A_2, as may be done. Only one B factor has been found, but B individuals may be in either BB or BO genotypes. Likewise, AB individuals may be in A_1B or A_2B genotypes. O-group individuals are invariably OO. However, this gives a total of ten genotypes corresponding to four blood groups.

The fact that the ABO system follows the laws of Mendelian inheritance allows its use for the determination of paternity. A particular combination of blood groups in parents can produce only certain groups in their offspring. (See Table 16-2.) If the blood group of the child, of the mother, and of the suspected father are all known, *it is possible to state that the suspected father could have been the actual father or that he could not possibly have been the father.* It is never possible to state that he *is* the father, only that he *could be* the father. If the blood type of the alleged father is consistent with parenthood, it merely means that he is one of the many who could have formed such a possible combination with the genes of the mother. On the other hand, if the type of the putative father is inconsistent with parenthood, he can be definitely excluded from parentage.

Grouping in the ABO system is usually performed by testing the unknown red cells for agglutination reactions with a panel of antisera of known specificity; thus the presence of the blood-group substance is detected. Upon occasion, tests are performed to determine the agglutinating specificity of the plasma antibodies on a panel of cells of known type. Several rare cases have

TABLE 16–2 Inheritance of Blood Groups

Suspected father	Known mother	Possible for child	Impossible for child
O	O	O	A, B, AB*
O	A	O, A	B, AB
O	B	O, B	A, AB
O	AB	A, B	O*, AB
A	O	O, A	B, AB*
A	A	O, A	B, AB
A	B	O, A, B, AB	
A	AB	A, B, AB	O*
B	O	O, B	A, AB*
B	A	O, A, B, AB	
B	B	O, B	A, AB
B	AB	B, A, AB	O*
AB	O	A, B	O, AB*
AB	A	A, B, AB	O
AB	B	A, B, AB	O
AB	AB	A, B, AB	O*

* Impossible from the mother in any mating, and not subject to question.

been noted where the expected reciprocal relationship of blood-group antigen and agglutinating antibody has not been observed, e.g., a type O person with no anti-A or anti-B. In blood-testing practice it is relatively uncommon to test for both agglutinogen and agglutinin, so it is not known how often this might occur.

The grouping of dried bloodstains is somewhat more complex. The *Lattes slide technique* tests for agglutinating antibody; it involves testing an extract of the bloodstain for its agglutinating activity wih red cells of different types. Thus if anti-B activity is found, the stain would be type A (see Table 16-1). The Lattes test is less frequently used than antibody adsorption techniques, which test for the presence of the blood-group substances. Several antibody adsorption techniques are in use; perhaps the most common is the adsorption–elution method. In the adsorption–elution test, agglutinating antibody is incubated with the bloodstain; if the antibody and the stain are of the same type, then antibody will be adsorbed to the stain. The stain is washed free of nonadsorbed material and the adsorbed antibody is eluted off the stain at elevated temperature; the presence of antibody is detected by the agglutination of the appropriate test cells.

The ABO blood-group substances are found not only on red cells but on almost all tissues. Both hair and bone can be and have been typed by adsorption techniques; in every case, the hair, bone, or tissue type corresponds to the red-cell determination as expected. In some individuals, the blood-group substances are secreted into the physiological fluids. These individuals, called *secretors*, make up about 75% of the population. In secretors, it is possible to type semen, perspiration, saliva, etc. In nonsecretors, these fluids cannot be typed even though the blood and tissues are typable.

The distribution of the ABO blood types in various populations has been extensively studied. Table 16-3 indicates the approximate incidence of the four major blood groups in the American population. Considerable variation has been found between populations; for example, Oriental populations are characterized by a higher incidence of the B type than Western European populations. Mourant has compiled the racial variations. It will be noted that the

TABLE 16-3 The Simple Blood Groups

Designation			Content		Occurrence in population, %
Universal	Moss	Jansky	Corpuscles	Plasma	
O	4	1	no agglutinogen	a and b	43
A	2	2	A	b	40
B	3	3	B	a	14
AB	1	4	A and B	no agglutinin	3

value of a blood type in crime investigation varies inversely with its frequency in the population. If we know the criminal is type O, then almost half the human race is included. But if we know the criminal's blood type to be AB, then about 95% of the population is eliminated as suspect and the value of the blood evidence is correspondingly greater.

The MN System

It has long been known that agglutinogens other than A and B exist in the blood corpuscles. Of these, M and N agglutinogens have been recognized the longest and are the most valuable at present for criminalistic purposes. In contrast to the ABO system, in the MN system the corresponding agglutinins are not found in the plasma or serum, and for this reason they have no medical significance. Three blood groups are recognized: M, N, and MN, characterized by the presence in the corpuscle of one or the other or both of the antigens. The frequencies of the three groups are, respectively, about 30%, 22%, and 48% in the white population of the United States.

The detection of the M and N antigens depends upon sera taken from animals immunized against these antigens and freed of other agglutinins, as is also done in the preparation of A and B agglutinins. The MN system is of considerable criminalistic significance because each of the four ABO groups may be subdivided into three MN groups; thus the use of these two systems subdivides the population into twelve. Under modern conditions the operation is possible with dry bloodstains. Both lectins and sera may be used, but the most favorable procedure appears to be the use of anti-M serum and anti-N lectin because of the superiority of each of these over its alternative.

The MN type of a person is determined at a single genetic locus. Three genotypes are possible, MM, MN, and NN, which correspond to the three phenotypes M, MN, and N. Genetically associated with the MN system is the Ss system; it has not found forensic application. In addition to their value in individualizing blood, the MN system is very useful in paternity determinations, as is shown in Table 16-4.

The Rh System

Another blood-grouping system associated with the corpuscles is the Rh system, which is of great importance in medical practice. The Rh factor was discovered in the blood of the rhesus monkey, from which its name is derived. For medical purposes, persons are generally classified only as Rh+ or Rh−, depending upon the presence or absence of one of a number of Rh antigens that alone is medically significant. Although this specific Rh antigen is capable of producing agglutinins in persons who lack the agglutinogen, the agglutinin is not normally present in the blood. When fresh blood is available, it is simple

TABLE 16–4 Inheritance of M and N Factors

Suspected father	Known mother	Possible for child	Impossible for child
M	M	M	MN, N*
M	N	MN	N, M*
M	MN	M, MN	N
N	M	MN	M, N*
N	N	N	MN, N*
N	MN	N, MN	M
MN	M	M, MN	N
MN	N	N, MN	M
MN	MN	M, N, MN	

* Impossible combination with the mother and therefore not encountered.

to test not only for this antigen, but also for the presence or absence of other antigens of the Rh system. Five out of a theoretical six Rh antigens are known; but not all of them are equally simple to detect.

Dried bloodstains are difficult to test for any of the Rh antigens. However, recent work has shown that relatively fresh stains can be reliably Rh typed. Inasmuch as rather special techniques are required to achieve this, it may be some time before it becomes routine. The Rh grouping is most valuable in determining paternity by blood test, in that the possible combinations of factors are relatively numerous. Some thirty-six genotypes (possible gene combinations) exist, ranging in incidence from approximately 0.0001% to over 32% in the white population. Not all of these are readily detected, and a considerably smaller number are likely to be encountered in practice. An additional problem encountered in the use of Rh typing for paternity determinations is the lack of basic knowledge about the nature of the Rh substances. This has given rise to a dispute about nomenclature that may confuse the inexperienced analyst.

Other Cellular Factors

At least six other factors have been described by various investigators, and, in several instances, they have been studied for their forensic importance. Although a few are detectable in dried bloodstains, they are of low incidence and require special sera for their demonstration. They have not been shown to have a value commensurate with the difficulty of identifying them. It has been calculated that if all of the cellular blood groups were available for the separation of the world's population into groups, there would be nearly three million such subpopulations, the rarest of which would not be expected in the population of the world, and the most common being found in less than 0.5% of the world's population.

LECTINS

Lectins deserve a special section for their great value in blood grouping. Lectins are specific agglutinating proteins found in extracts of various plant materials.

The best known of these is an extract of the seeds of ordinary gorse, or furze, *Ulex europaeus*, a spiny evergreen shrub of the bean family. The simple extract is termed *anti-H lectin*, and is used to determine whether or not a person is a secretor. This is especially useful when physiological fluids other than blood are to be grouped. It should be used also with doubtful ABO groupings in which no A or B agglutinogen is found. The absence of both factors would be interpreted as indicating an O-group individual, but if there are other difficulties in the grouping such that neither factor is located, an error will be made. This can be checked by the use of anti-H.

The anti-H lectin can be separated into two fractions, an anti-A_2 and an anti-O, and both fractions are obtainable commercially. The latter serves even more specifically in rechecking a doubtful O blood than does anti-H. The anti-A_2 is useful for detecting this factor as opposed to A_1. It is of interest that the successful use of anti-O lectin demonstrates the presence of an O factor, although, when injected into an animal, the factor will not stimulate the production of anti-O in its blood.

Another plant extract, that of *Dolichos biflorus*, a twining herb known as *horse grain*, is effective in agglutinating the cells of an A_1 individual. Its use in conjunction with anti-A_2 lectin will determine satisfactorily whether the individual belongs to one or the other subgroup. Similar utilization with blood from members of the AB group will distinguish A_1B from A_2B individuals. Distinctions can also be made between persons of the genotype A_1A_2 as compared with A_1A_1 or A_1O. It is likewise possible to determine the blood group of an individual in A_2O or A_2A_2 by adding the lectin for O to the scheme. To date, it has not been possible to discriminate between A_1A_1 and A_1O, which are, unfortunately, the two most frequently met genotypes of the A group.

Lectins have also been found for the identification of M and N factors. That for M has proved to be less satisfactory than anti-M serum, which is readily available. On the other hand, anti-N, prepared from one of the vetches, *Vicia graminae*, is considerably more satisfactory than most batches of anti-N serum.

BLOOD PROTEIN FACTORS

Brief attention has been given to the conventional blood groups, all of which are based upon cellular factors attached to the red cells and are genetically controlled. All of these factors *tend* toward the individualization of blood, but even combined they still have only limited value in the ultimate determination of the person from whom the blood was obtained. They do have very great value in excluding the person from whom the blood was *not* obtained, which is often essential, but is somewhat less than could be hoped for. However, a number of other factors exist in blood which are useful for individualization.

Serum Proteins

A considerable number of genetic markers exist in the serum. Their use can increase greatly the discriminatory value of blood testing. Several of these provide an actual grouping of blood that is based upon types of factors totally different from the ordinary blood groups. Being genetically controlled, they have the same validity in individualization as do the customary and better-understood blood groups. Some of them are more difficult to determine than are the cellular blood groups, and only a few of them have been applied to dried blood or utilized in actual criminal investigation. These include the Gm factor, which has been shown to be applicable to crime investigation, but is difficult to determine; the Gc factor, which is of doubtful significance; the Inv factor, which has been studied to a limited degree; and the haptoglobins. The latter are being used in a few laboratories and can now be studied rather satisfactorily. Each of the above factors will divide blood samples into several groups, usually about four. Being totally independent of all the other grouping systems, each such factor increases markedly the possible discrimination.

Although the ultimate value of serum grouping in the individualization of blood is very great, it is apparent that relatively little is being done in this area in crime laboratories. The major difficulty is that if each type of factor must be determined individually, the requirement for time and facilities is multiplied even faster than is the information potentially obtainable. For this reason, among others, criminalists have shown little interest in developing in their own laboratories the knowledge and facility required to bring to fruition the great possibilities inherent in the serum factors. It is possible to cut down this barrier by developing techniques that will allow the determination of several factors at once. This may be achieved by electrophoretic techniques as will be discussed in a later section of this chapter.

Blood Enzyme Markers

Enzymes are proteins that specifically catalyze chemical reactions; they are the key to the metabolic processes that sustain life. Within the past 15–20 years, it has been shown that enzymes are far more heterogeneous than was previously thought. This heterogeneity is of several sorts; of primary concern to this discussion is that many enzymes are genetically variable and this variability can be detected by electrophoresis. In fact, it has been shown that perhaps 30% of the enzymes in the human population are genetically polymorphic. The list of genetic marker enzymes grows every year and it is impossible to present an up-to-date enumeration; the interested reader is referred to books by Giblett and by Harris and to review articles in the genetics literature.

Using the known genetically polymorphic enzymes, it is possible to subdivide the human population into more than 10 billion subpopulations. It is obvious that these systems can be of great forensic significance. Little effort has been made in this country to develop forensic applications; however, in Europe, and particularly in England, research and development have led to crime laboratory usage. It is to be expected that it will not be too many years before the enzyme markers are commonly used for purposes of blood individualization.

Hemoglobin

Over 100 genetic variants of human hemoglobin are known. Most of these are rare but several are common enough to warrant mention. The sickle-cell variant, HbS, is found in about 20% of the Negro population. Another variant, HbC, is found in lower frequency, also in the Negro population.

Another type of hemoglobin variation is observed in humans; this variation is observed in all normal individuals. Before birth, the dominant form of hemoglobin is HbF, fetal hemoglobin. At the time of birth, HbF synthesis ceases and normal adult hemoglobin, HbA, becomes the dominant form. However, a small amount of HbA_2 may be observed at birth. HbF can be used as a marker for fetal blood, which may be significant in investigation involving abortion.

Almost without exception, the various forms and variants of hemoglobin can be detected and differentiated by electrophoresis techniques, which are neither difficult nor time-consuming, as well-standardized methods are available. However, few criminalistics laboratories have begun to use the hemoglobin-related techniques. To be sure, at the outset the investigator will have no reason to suspect that he may have some rare combination of hemoglobins in the sample before him. He therefore does not look for it, and nobody will ever know how many crimes have remained unsolved because he, and others like him, did not look. Lack of basic training, combined with a common tendency to do only that which everyone does routinely, has crippled the effectiveness of the crime laboratory to an indefensible degree.

Electrophoresis and Immunoelectrophoresis

The best method for distinguishing variant forms of blood proteins and enzymes is electrophoresis. Every protein possesses a characteristic electric charge. In electrophoresis the proteins are placed in an electric field; their movement in the field is a function of their characteristic charge. Thus a mixture of proteins wil be resolved into many fractions; serum contains some twenty identifiable fractions after electrophoresis. Normally, protein is detected with a protein stain. However, with some proteins and with the enzymes, it is possible to stain for a specific protein. Experimentation with the use of specific staining has been greatly responsible for the current knowledge regarding the genetic variation of enzymes. Another specific method for localizing proteins is to use antibodies; if proteins are separated by electrophoresis and then diffused against antisera, the constituent proteins will individually precipitate as separate bands. *Immunoelectrophoresis* has proven particularly valuable for the demonstration of genetic variation in serum proteins. Studies with immunoelectrophoresis have in addition suggested that the immunoelectric profile of each individual is unique; research has not yet been sufficient to determine the full potential of this method.

These procedures do not substitute for blood grouping; rather, they provide added information. Other supplemental tests are available for determining antibodies of disease and other antigens. Taken together, the available techniques for the examination of blood constitute a very powerful tool for establishing the individual origin of a blood sample.

REFERENCES

Culliford, B. J.: *The Examination and Typing of Bloodstains in the Crime Laboratory.* Washington, D.C.: U.S. Government Printing Office (1971).
Giblett, E. R.: *Genetic Markers in Human Blood.* Philadelphia: F. A. Davis (1969).
Grabar, P., and Burtin, P.: *Immuno-electrophoretic Analysis.* New York: Elsevier (1964).
Harris, H.: *The Principles of Human Biochemical Genetics.* New York: Elsevier (1970).
Jonxis, J. H. P., and Huisman, T. H. J.: *A Laboratory Manual on Abnormal Haemoglobins,* 2nd ed. Oxford: Blackwell (1968).
Mourant, A. E.: *The ABO Blood Groups.* Springfield: Thomas (1958).
Moureau, P.: "Determination of Blood Groups in Blood Stains," in F. Lundquist, ed., *Methods of Forensic Science,* Vol. 2. New York: Interscience (1963).
Outteridge, R. A.: "Recent Advances in the Grouping of Dried Blood and Secretion Stains," in A. S. Curry, ed., *Methods of Forensic Science,* Vol. 4. New York: Interscience (1965).
Prokop, O., and Uhlenbruck, G.: *Human Blood and Serum Groups.* New York: Interscience (1969).
Race, R. R., and Sanger, R.: *Blood Groups in Man,* 5th ed. Philadelphia: Davis (1968).
Watkins, W. M.: "Blood Group Substances," *Science* 152:172 (1966).
Wiener, A. S.: *An Rh-Hr Syllabus,* 2nd ed. New York: Grune and Stratton (1963).
Yunis, J. J.: *Biochemical Methods in Red Cell Genetics.* New York: Academic Press (1969).

17
Physiological Fluids Other than Blood

Although blood is the most common physiological fluid that requires investigation, semen runs a close second because of the high incidence of sex crimes and crimes associated with sex irregularities. Occasionally other fluids, such as saliva, urine, perspiration, pus, milk, and lymph may be encountered, and it is not uncommon to find stains of nasal mucus, tears, and the like. Apart from blood and semen, both of which have been studied extensively, there are few physiological fluids for which universally recognized tests are available. Some fluids may be distinguished without much difficulty. For example, pus is full of white corpuscles and bacterial residues. The common occurrence of perspiration under the arms and over diffuse areas, and of saliva on cigarette butts, suggests strongly the nature of stains found in these locations. In addition to indications from location or from special and obvious constituents, there are known methods by which at least a portion of the stains from these fluids can be distinguished and identified. It is particularly important, however, that the primary attention be devoted to semen because of its special significance as evidence.

SEMEN

Semen, or seminal fluid, consists of a highly proteinaceous serum which normally contains a very large number of spermatozoa, or male germ cells. In sterility, as from venereal disease, the spermatozoa may be lacking in the seminal fluid. In these instances, positive proof of the nature of the stain is difficult. Semen is relatively rich in choline, which is virtually absent in most other physiological fluids, and in citric acid, fructose, and acid phosphatase, which also are found in much smaller or negligible quantities in other body fluids. Semen gives none of the presumptive tests for blood but it is subject to grouping in a certain percentage of individuals.

Seminal stains should be expected in any case involving sexual activity, and may be present in crimes in which there is no special reason to suspect such acts. In the murder of a girl by stabbing, no sexual assault had occurred; yet semen was found on the handle of the knife. That the deposit was there as a result of activity during the commission of the crime, or at about that time, was evident from the fact that the knife was purchased the day before the crime and was recovered by the police the following day. In another instance, where multiple rape was charged, massive quantities of semen were found on the ring of the victim. She had been a willing participant, but brought charges because she thought that her ring had been stolen. Actually it had slipped from her finger because of the massive contamination, and was found between the cushions of the car in which the acts had occurred. In conjunction with other evidence, the presence of the semen on the ring was effective in establishing that no crime had been committed.

Semen stains will usually occur on the clothing of the victim or of the perpetrator, or both, particularly on the underclothing. The presence of stains on bedding, on mattresses, automobile robes, and similar materials is occasionally of great significance. In addition to external stains, there may be a considerable deposit of semen in the vagina of the victim of an assault. In this case, the attending physician should swab the vagina and make a number of slides from the smears. These should be stained and mounted so as to make available a large number of spermatozoa for later study.

Investigation

The preliminary search for semen stains may be one of the most frustrating aspects of the investigation of a sex crime. Formerly the ultraviolet lamp was used to detect the presence of semen, because of the strong bluish-white fluorescence of such stains. This method of search is still very useful for the examination of materials that have not been subjected to laundering. However, it is now rarely useful with sheets, shirts, underwear, and similar articles that almost invariably carry highly fluorescent "brighteners" derived from detergents. Fluorescence of a stain, even when it is of the correct color, is *not proof* of the presence of semen, but only an indication of the possible nature of the stain. Also, the color of a semen stain may not be true because of the admixture of other fluorescent materials that yield a different composite color.

Extensive seminal stains may have a stiff, "starched" feel, and can often be located by testing with the fingers for spots or areas that give a tactile impression different from that of the surrounding fabric. Examination under the stereoscopic binocular microscope may also reveal a crusted appearance of the fibers. Neither of these methods is so convenient or so instructive as is examination under ultraviolet light when this method is applicable. Another advantage of the latter examination is that it may at the same time reveal stains of other origin. When detected, such stained areas may be marked with a wax pencil for later examination by other means. The absence of fluorescence may be interpreted as indicating at least the absence of semen, except that even the absence of semen may not usually be detected when the article being examined has been subjected to modern laundering methods.

If suspicious stains are located, or if a garment is suspected of having stains that cannot be located, the entire garment should be submitted to the laboratory. If this is not feasible, the area of interest may be removed for laboratory examination. Here the suspected area will be subjected to detailed examination for spermatozoa, and chemical tests will be performed.

In addition to the time-tested microscopic search for spermatozoa, there are a variety of chemical tests for identifying seminal stains. Some investigators refuse to make a positive identification of such a stain without finding spermatozoa; but it must be pointed out that the semen of sterile males does not contain spermatozoa. Also, mechanical friction, sunlight, bacterial action, and other factors sometimes damage the cells to such an extent that their detection and recognition is all but impossible. In all such instances the chemical tests will still serve well, and they are always useful for preliminary testing.

The single chemical test that has proved most serviceable is the test for the presence of the acid phosphatase enzyme. Many body fluids other than semen also contain this enzyme; however, the quantity of acid phosphatase activity in semen is some 400 times greater than in any other body fluid. Hence in the analysis of stained material, a relatively insensitive test will give a strong positive acid phosphatase indication with semen, but the same test will fail with other body fluids. Alternatively, some investigators prefer to make a quantitative determination, rather than depending upon an inconclusive test. Seminal stains that have aged over ten years have yielded strong positive tests; and many investigators consider such a test, when properly performed and with proper controls, as being nearly conclusive evidence of the presence or absence of semen. In view of the possibility of misidentification of spermatozoa, which are sometimes simulated by artifacts, and their absence in the semen of sterile men, a positive acid phosphatase test is probably not inferior to a direct identification of spermatazoa in the analysis of suspected seminal stains. Good practice indicates the desirability of conducting both tests and of expecting both to give positive results before making an unequivocal identification.

The analysis of vaginal swabs or smears poses a somewhat different problem, as acid phosphatase is normally present in vaginal secretions. Although the level of acid phosphatase in the vagina is higher after sexual intercourse, owing to the contribution of the semen, a strong acid phosphatase test is not a reliable indication of recent sexual activity. At present, the identification of spermatozoa in a vaginal smear is the only reliable test of recent intercourse.

Additional chemical tests involve the detection of choline. Two procedures for the identification of choline depend upon crystal formation: the Florence test, which employs potassium tri-iodide, and the Barberios test in which picric acid is the reagent. Thin-layer chromatography may also be employed in the analysis of choline. There seems to be little doubt that choline occurs in significant amounts only in semen, but no conclusive proof of this is yet available. Furthermore, neither of the crystal tests is specific for the identification of choline except to the degree that the crystals formed are subject to direct visual identification. It seems clear that the tests for choline are valuable only as confirmatory evidence, and cannot be accepted alone when spermatozoa are not present.

A number of newer procedures for the identification of semen have become available, although their application in operating laboratories has lagged behind their development. Several are immunological in nature and depend upon precipitin testing on a variety of support media. These procedures are highly specific, capable of distinguishing the human origin of the semen as well as making the identification. Origin in species other than man can be determined by gel electrophoresis, which, along with immunoelectrophoresis, has provided detailed knowledge of many components of semen. Semen is unique in the rather large number of its constituents found only in very small traces in other body fluids, if at all. These include fructose, salts of citric acid, spermine, neuraminic acid, and zinc. Possibilities for additional types of testing are excellent, but research is needed to determine what value these tests might have.

Morphology of Spermatozoa

There are certain indications that the morphology of spermatozoa may be characteristic in some individuals. Not all of the spermatozoa in the semen of an individual are normal in appearance or uniform in dimensions, and the variations from normal take several directions. The distribution of the various abnormalities and deviations appears to be quite constant and a statistical summary of these details may serve to identify the individual in whom the spermatozoa originated. Study of the detailed morphology is a task for the highly skilled investigator; it requires well-prepared slides made preferably of liquid semen, well-stained, and examined under the oil-immersion microscope at high magnification. It is expected that, within a reasonable time, the accumulated results of research efforts will determine whether or not an individual can be positively identified by a study of his spermatozoa. Even if positive identification through spermatozoa proves to be impossible, a suspect may still be shown from such studies to be innocent by virtue of great deviations from spermatozoa obtained from the victim.

Determination of the species from which spermatozoa have come is possible to a considerable extent in the hands of the skilled investigator. Although, as a rule, the cells from different species appear quite different, their size and appearance bear no recognizable relation to the size and appearance of the animal. The question of species will be raised very rarely, however, except in cases of suspected bestiality.

Spermatozoa are amazingly resistant to chemical reagents. They do not change form or disintegrate in the presence of dilute alkalies or acids, and will withstand even concentrated sulfuric acid for considerable periods of time. They are, however, quite fragile when dry and, for this reason, a dry stain suspected of being seminal in origin must be handled with great care to avoid friction and breaking of the crust. Special care should be exercised in packing and handling garments suspected of carrying seminal stains to avoid any unnecessary mechanical action on the dried stains.

URINE

A search with ultraviolet illumination will occasionally reveal dried urine stains on a garment or other surface, although the considerations of optical brighteners discussed in relation to semen apply equally to urine stains. The fluorescence of urine is less intense than that of semen, and is ordinarily yellowish in color rather than white. The garment carrying it will not have the typical "starched" appearance and feel, or the incrustation visible under the microscope that are characteristic of most seminal stains. The best way to determine whether or not a stain that fluoresces is urine is to remove a small piece of the fabric and brush it over a small flame until fumes appear. These will have the very characteristic odor of urine, which is different from that of any other physiological fluid. The presence of sulfate in urine, which distinguishes it from all other physiological fluids, can be easily determined by chemical testing, as can the phosphate content, which is very much greater in urine than in other body fluids. Urine also contains large amounts of urea, creatine and creatinine as compared with the other fluids of the body. Qualitative chemical testing methods alone are insufficient for absolute identification of a fluid sample such as urine because of the presence of the same constituents in smaller quantities in the perspiration, the blood, and possibly in other body fluids.

PERSPIRATION

Perspiration also fluoresces under ultraviolet illumination, but with such low intensity as to represent a very poor diagnostic test. The appearance of perspiration stains is ordinarily very different from those of semen, being found as rather large areas of more or less uniform density. Their position is often quite clearly indicative of their origin. The best test for perspiration, and one of the few that can distinguish it clearly from urine, is to remove a small sample of the cloth, heat it to fuming and smell the fumes. The odor is strong, but distinctly different from that of urine.

SALIVA

Saliva rarely requires identification because its occurrence is normally restricted to spittle or to coatings on items that have been in the mouth. With some difficulty saliva can be distinguished from the other physiological fluids by the fact that it contains thiocyanate ion in detectable quantities, and if the sample is reasonably fresh, it will contain a significant amount of the enzyme amylase. Amylase can be detected by its catalysis of the hydrolysis of starch. Amylases and other starch-splitting enzymes exist in some vegetable materials, but these show maximum activity under conditions different from those required by the saliva amylase, so that a reliable differentiation may be achieved. Amylase is also found in blood and in some other body fluids, but at very low levels compared to saliva. If properly run with the appropriate controls, the test for amylase is a quite reliable test for saliva. It should be noted that salivary amylase is genetically polymorphic; this enzyme may eventually prove useful in distinguishing between individuals.

SERUM

The presence of serum on the clothing of the victim of a crime is not at all rare, but it is often overlooked; it is often found on victims who have died from internal hemorrhage. If, after the blood has clotted internally, the body is moved, it is serum rather than blood that exudes from the wound. Serum is highly proteinaceous, yellow in color, and viscous. Stains from it will be stiff, and will usually show a little reddish tinge from incompletely separated and hemolysed cells. Because of the presence of hemoglobin from this source, serum gives the same chemical tests as does blood, but lacks the strong color of the latter. The presence of serum is more useful in the reconstruction of the crime than in any other aspect of the investigation, and it should never be disregarded.

STAINS OF MIXED AND MISCELLANEOUS ORIGIN

On occasion, fluids of various origin may be mixed together in a stain. For example, in a case of forced oral copulation, stains containing a mixture of saliva and semen were found on the clothing of both the assailant and the victim. The detection of both fluids might have been missed had not the investigator conducted a careful analysis of the stained material.

Also, from time to time the investigator will need to know the origin of stains that may not be due to the fluids discussed above. Examples are stains of vomitus, or of milk spilled at a prior meal. A conclusive identification of milk would require an immunological test; the appropriate antisera would have to be obtained from a milk research laboratory, since commercial antisera are not available. Vomitus, on the other hand, can usually be identified by examination under the microscope; it will generally carry partially digested food residues. In addition, it is usually quite acidic, as may be shown by acid test papers. It contains also quite a number of enzymes, especially pepsin, for which identifying methods are available. An innovative laboratory has an excellent chance of making the necessary identification in such a case.

TYPING OF FLUIDS

Physiological fluids may, in many instances, be used to determine the ABO blood group of the individual from whom they originated. About 75% of the human population secrete soluble ABO substances into their body fluids; such individuals are called secretors. Both saliva and semen are rich sources of these secreted substances; urine is not susceptible to reliable typing.

The typing of stains is not as useful a technique as might be initially supposed. The secreted blood-group substances correspond to the normal blood group of an individual. All secretors secrete an H substance; type O individuals secrete only this H substance. Type A individuals secrete also an A substance, type B individuals secrete a B substance, and type AB individuals secrete both A and B substances in addition to the H substance. Failure to obtain a positive test with any typing reagent indicates: (1) the stain was from a nonsecretor, or (2) an insufficient amount of stain was present for typing purposes. If only anti-A and anti-B sera are used for typing and no reaction is obtained, there is a third possibility: the stain is from a type O secretor.

Additional complications exist in any instance in which a stain is contaminated with blood or fluids from another individual.

The methods by which fluids other than blood are grouped are analogous to those decribed for blood. However, the technical difficulties are somewhat greater, and for this reason the typing of fluids other than blood should be attempted only by persons experienced in serological techniques.

REFERENCES

Baccetti, B., ed.: *Comparative Spermatology.* New York: Academic Press (1970).

Coombs, R. R. A., Richards, C. B., and Dodd, B.: "Immunological Identification of Human Seminal Stains," *J. Crim. Law, Criminol., and Pol. Sci.* 57:107 (1966).

Cosgrave, M. St. J.: "Medical Examination in Alleged Sexual Offenses," *J. For. Sci. Soc.* 3:88 (1963).

Giertsen, J. C.: "Faecal Matter in Stains, Their Identification," *J. For. Med.* 8:99 (1961).

Jones, D. N.: "The Task of the Forensic Science Laboratory in the Investigation of Sexual Offences," *J. For. Sci. Soc.* 3:88 (1963).

Kind, S. S.: "The Acid Phosphatase Test," in A. S. Curry, ed., *Methods of Forensic Science*, Vol. 3. New York: Interscience (1964).

Mann, T.: *Biochemistry of Semen and of the Male Reproductive Tract.* New York: Wiley (1964).

Nelson, D. F., and Kirk, P. L.: "The Identification of Saliva," *J. For. Med.* 10:14 (1963).

Rupp, J. C.: "Sperm Survival and Prostatic Acid Phosphatase Activity in Victims of Sexual Assault," *J. For. Sci.* 14:177 (1969).

18
Cosmetics

Cosmetics are among the types of evidence that must receive attention in the criminalistics laboratory. Their neglect hitherto has been partly attributable to their infrequent occurrence, but chiefly to the facts that they are found in small quantities and that the routine methods for evaluation have not been widely publicized. In crimes against women, especially, the transfer of lipstick and other facial makeup is relatively common; and nail polish has appeared as physical evidence in numerous cases. Hair preparations may be involved in an investigation, and in some crimes it has proved to be of great significance. Eye makeup and mascara are now widely used and may be expected to appear in physical evidence from time to time. Quite often the cosmetic preparation is of more interest in the reconstruction of the crime than in the identification of the criminal, but the cosmetic evidence can contribute to both of these important criminalistic functions.

COSMETICS AS EVIDENCE

Nearly all cosmetics are designed to modify the personal appearance in some particular, or to restore a pre-existent appearance. In the first category are such items as makeup, lipstick, nail polish, mascara, and rouge, along with hair tint, dye, and bleach. Hair sprays are perhaps the best illustration of the latter category. Cosmetics of the first class are primarily important because they may be transferred on contact, leaving stains or smears on clothing, automobiles, cigarettes, and bedding. Such smears are proof of contact with a surface carrying the cosmetic, and, to the extent that the cosmetic can be identified, they aid in identifying the source. The proof of contact is most important in the interpretation of a crime. In one murder, the victim was grasped around the neck by the arms of the assailant and shot through the pinioned head. Transferred makeup on the clothes of the suspect showed where the victim's face had been held. The makeup smears, combined with powder burns and blood in an appropriate arrangement on the clothing of the suspect, elucidated the details of the shooting. Similar transfers will often be observed in abnormal sex activity in which lipstick or makeup may be present on the underpants of a suspect.

Cosmetics of the second category enter the evidence picture in a somewhat different manner. Most of these are hair preparations such as grooming aids, sprays, and tonics, and they will alter effectively the surface condition of the hair. Most hair identification is performed with well-washed hairs; but in washing the hair one of its important identifying characteristics is removed. Hair normally carries certain lipids—fatty materials—as a natural secretion. The usefulness of these materials in the individualization of hair is uncertain at present. However, when the surface material is altered by the application of any cosmetic substance, a new factor is added that may be useful in the individualization of the hair. In one case the suspect was in the habit of applying olive oil liberally to his hair. He dropped a comb at the scene of a burglary, and the teeth of the comb were literally filled with the oil. Identification of the material on the comb as olive oil was almost as significant as the finding that hairs carried by the same comb matched morphologically the hairs on his head.

TYPES OF COSMETICS

Although there is a continuing increase in the uses and compositions of cosmetics, most modern cosmetics are based upon relatively ancient formulas and crafts. The most important types will be discussed here.

LIPSTICKS. The following types of ingredients are used in lipsticks:

(1) *Coloring.* Insoluble colors blended with titanium dioxide. The solid colors in lipsticks, which constitute 6–15%, are mainly pigments, pigment toners, and lakes of soluble dyes. White lipsticks are pigmented with titanium dioxide only.

(2) *Stainers.* These are halogenated derivatives of fluorescein, also called eosins or bromo-acids. Staining dyes, which constitute 1–3% of the lipstick, also contribute to its color.

(3) *Stain solvents.* In lipsticks, high solubility is desirable. Only esters (diethyl sebacate), glycols, and glycol esters are used. A good dye solvent is mono-isopropanolamine.

(4) *Lipstick bases.* These consist of suitable blends of oils, fats, and waxes of vegetable, animal, mineral, and synthetic origin. Castor oil–beeswax is a standard blend used in conjunction with other waxes such as carnauba, ozokerite, candelilla, lanolin, and even petroleum jelly in small quantity. Sometimes stearates and oleates are used.

(5) *Perfume and Flavoring.* These are variable.

ROUGE. Most of the materials used for lipsticks, such as oils, fats, and waxes, are also used for rouge. The colors employed are the nonstaining pigments. Ten to fifteen percent of dry color may be contained in the finished product. Bromo-acids are not used. Originally rouge was red iron oxide, the familiar polishing rouge that is used today.

EYE MAKEUP. Many of the oils, fats, and waxes found in lipstick are used also for eye make-up. In addition to these, certain hydrophilic materials such as glycerine and propylene glycol are employed. No perfume is added, as may be true of other cosmetics also. The coal-tar colors, often used in other cosmetics, are not used near the eyes, the permitted colors being inorganic in nature. Iridescent effects are achieved by the addition of fish scale or a little aluminum powder.

MASCARA. Because mascara must wet the surface to which it is applied, it is made with a maximum wax and water content and a minimum of oils and fats. The color is milled in glycerine and propylene glycol, both of which are good wetting agents.

NAIL LACQUER. Nail lacquer, also called nail polish, is one of the most important cosmetics from the standpoint of evidence. It is relatively complex in composition, and contains the following types of material.:

(1) A film-forming material, usually nitrocellulose.
(2) An adhesive material; in former times resin-shellac, this has now been replaced by polyester resin, especially aryl sulfonamide formaldehyde resin.
(3) A plasticizer, usually dibutylphthalate, 15–18%.
(4) A solvent mixture composed of volatile materials, including esters, acetates, ketones such as methyl ethyl ketone, and glycol ethers.
(5) Color and/or pigment. Organic dyes are used, but most lake pigments are unsatisfactory. In recent years more inorganic pigments have been incorporated in fingernail preparations; e.g., synthetic iron oxides, titanium oxide, ultramarine blue and green, chrome oxide greens, iron black, and carbon black. Conventional red polishes have contained a number of red dyes. The present trend is toward greater mineral content and unusual—sometimes bizarre—effects including iridescence created by

incorporating small amounts of natural pearl substance obtained from the scales of various fishes, especially herring.

HAIR PREPARATIONS. Among the many materials used on the hair, some, such as shampoos, are quickly removed. Some, for example, hair tonics, are relatively evanescent, and some, such as bleaches and dyes, leave relatively permanent effects, although they themselves may or may not be retained. Still other hair preparations, such as sprays, tend to remain though they do not produce permanent effects. Little study has been given to most of these materials as evidence, because emphasis has been placed upon the individualization of the hair itself rather than the material carried on it. Clearly, overlooking this type of evidence when it is applicable does not differ from the neglect of any other type of evidence of comparable basic value. More attention has been given to hair dyes than to other preparations for the hair, presumably because their effects are visible. As will be developed later, this emphasis may not be more valuable than would be a similar emphasis placed upon hair sprays, for example.

Although the distinctions are not absolute, cosmetic hair preparations may be grouped as (1) cleansing agents, (2) grooming agents, and (3) color-altering agents. In practice, the only components of these preparations that are of criminalistic interest are those that either remain on the hair to some extent or alter the hair in some determinable fashion. Most of a cleansing agent will be washed out in rinsing the hair, but some constituent material may remain in detectable quantity. *Detergents* commonly used include soaps, alcohol sulfates, alcohol, polyethylene glycol, ether sulfates, and phenol polyethylene glycol sulfates. Little appears to have been done in testing the retention of these materials, although some of them, notably ordinary soaps, tend to leave a film in hard water, and the glycols serve as moistening agents in some tonic and setting formulations. Many *modified oils* (fatty acid derivatives) and *ethanolamine derivatives* are blended with the detergent in shampoos. Because these serve as conditioning as well as cleansing agents, they will be expected to persist on the hair to a greater extent than do simple cleansers.

Hairdressings intended primarily for men are expected to remain on the hair for an appreciable time, with the exception of certain volatile constituents. These preparations typically contain such materials as fatty acid esters, mineral oil, petroleum jelly, lanolin, aluminum stearate, and beeswax. Nonoily hair dressings, also used predominantly by men, will usually have much of the oil replaced by gums such as gum tragacanth, by alcohols including ethyl alcohol and the higher alcohols, and esters such as propylene glycol laurate and polypropylene glycol laurate. Similar constituents will be found also in hairdressings for women, and at present these are largely dispensed in pressure-spray cans. Formulations intended for women are likely to differ from those designed for men, but the properties desired in both will be similar, and there will be considerable similarity in the constituents.

Hair colorants are of several classes. The simplest is merely the bleach, which is based on a rather strong hydrogen peroxide solution. Darkening of the hair, either bleached or unbleached, or altering its basic color (usually after bleaching) requires the use of actual colorants or dyes, which may be either preformed or generated in the hair. Dye molecules are generally too large to penetrate the hair shaft and are therefore applied as surface tint. Depending upon various factors of their application, the permanence of such dyeing is quite variable. However, at least traces of the dye will be present on the hair, and the opportunity to demonstrate its presence exists, though this opportunity has been largely unfulfilled in the practice of criminalistics. *Oxidation dyes* that cover gray or intensify the color of black or dark-brown hair have long been used and are still common. These are usually based upon the application of diamines such as *p-phenylenediamine,* or its derivatives, whose molecules are small enough to penetrate the hair shaft. They are oxidized in place by hydrogen peroxide to form conjugated molecules with black and brown colors. Hair dyed in this manner is rather easily seen under the microscope to be dyed. The dye is relatively permanent.

Because of the wide variety of dyes used on hair and the prevalence of hair dyeing, especially among women, the development and application of laboratory procedures for detecting and identifying such dyes should add a new dimension to the individualization of hair. It is unfortunate that so little research has been done in this direction.

COLLECTION OF COSMETIC EVIDENCE

Because of the small amounts of cosmetic preparations that are likely to be located in evidence, the police officer is well advised to remove to the laboratory the entire object that bears such evidence, without attempting to separate such a sample. Ordinarily it is not difficult to do this, because such stains are most prevalent on garments, which may acquire almost any type of cosmetic stain, except perhaps hair preparations. Lipstick is often carried on cigarette butts. When cosmetic stains are noticed on any item of evidence, it is important to collect from the scene all cosmetic preparations that could have given rise to such stains. Since lipstick is most common, a careful search for all tubes of this material should be made, in handbags, drawers, bathroom cupboards, on dresser tops, and in similar places where lipsticks might be laid down, carried or stored.

If the stain is apparently derived from makeup, all items of this type should be collected for use as reference standards. The stain itself will be useless without the availability of all possible sources of the staining material, if indeed the stain can be shown to be associated with the crime. Similar considerations will be applicable to mascara and other types of eye makeup.

Nail polish is in a slightly different category. Evidence of this sort will most commonly occur in the form of chips broken from the nails, during a struggle, for example, with an attacker. Such chips may become attached to the clothing of the attacker, or they may merely be found at the scene and, therefore, be of less value as evidence. The chips should be carefully removed from their location with fine forceps and placed in small evidence containers. As with the other cosmetics, it is important that all bottles of nail polish be collected and sent to the laboratory. Nail polish has figured in murder cases quite frequently, and even fatal poisoning has been attributed to the drinking of the material.

Hair preparations will rarely be available except as they exist on hairs of concern in the study of the crime. Thus, the questioned hair preparation is automatically collected if the hairs are collected, as they should always be. As with other cosmetic preparations, it is necessary that a possible source be found. This may be in the premises of a suspect, if the hair is indicated as possibly being from him. It may also be in the premises of a victim, if this is a probable source of the hair. In any event, without comparison standards the crime laboratory may not be able to utilize such evidence at all, and it is the business of the field investigator to provide such standards when possible. Hair brushes and combs should not be overlooked in this regard.

EXAMINATION OF EVIDENCE

The examination of evidence is in the province of the crime laboratory rather than in that of the police investigator. However, some indications of the nature of such an examination are in order here. Lipsticks may generally be compared and often identified by means of chromatography, or even by careful color comparison, because their most important identifying constituents are the dyes that give them their characteristic colors. Although other components may be useful in the comparison, little or nothing has been done with them up to this time.

Nail lacquers have received some study and may be identified with a reasonable degree of success. Comparisons are definitely possible, but are generally limited to direct color comparison, because their most important identifying constitutents are the dyes used in giving them their characteristic colors. Although other components may be useful in the comparison, little use has been made of them up to the present.

Aside from some claims for the methods of determining evidence of bleaching from a hair sample, and the often very obvious presence of hair dye, there are few techniques available for the comparison of hair preparations. A number of laboratory approaches are possible, especially in the analysis of materials used in hair sprays. The fact that standardized techniques have not been developed for the study and identification of these materials indicates a lack of concern rather than a lack of ability on the part of laboratory workers. In general, hairs that may contain and carry material in abundance are carefully washed to remove as much as possible of such evidence before anything is done to study the hair. The examination of the material so removed could, at times, be approximately as important as the hair itself.

REFERENCES

Balsam, M. S., and Sagarin, E., eds.: *Cosmetics: Science and Technology.* New York: Wiley (1972). 2 vols.

DeNavarre, M. G.: *The Chemistry and Manufacture of Cosmetics.* Cincinnati: Van Nostrand Reinhold (1962). 2 vols.

Hibbott, H. W.: *Handbook of Cosmetic Science.* Elmsford, New York: Pergamon (1963).

Lucas, D., and Eijgelaar, G.: "An Evaluation of a Technique for the Examination of Lipstick Stains," *J. For. Sci.* 6:354 (1961).

19
Crystalline Evidence

In the debris collected by the vacuum sweeper will be innumerable small, solid objects, many crystalline in nature. Crystalline materials are also frequently recovered in pure form from sources other than the vacuum sweeper. In testing unknown materials in the laboratory, the chemist often forms crystals that sometimes require special procedures for identification because they are not recognizable from the nature of the test and the testing conditions. It is also not uncommon for two or more crystalline materials to be found in a mixture when the mixing is itself evidence of criminal activity. In one case bichloride of mercury was mixed with the sugar in the sugar bowls in a restaurant and a number of persons were violently sickened from eating the sugar. The application of elementary crystallographic methods made the segregation and testing of the evidence very simple.

The same principles are frequently used to distinguish between quartz (sand) and glass. Though quartz is crystalline and glass is not, they appear similar under the microscope. This mixture will often be found in the debris collected in pants cuffs. In an unusual case, a pistol butt was found to contain a minute fragment of clear material. The prosecution claimed that the fragment was glass, whereas the defense claimed that it was sand. It became necessary to determine whether the pistol had been used to break a window or, as claimed by the defense, to break up a piece of sandstone.

Crystalline materials warrant separate consideration because the unique character of crystals makes them susceptible to a number of very special types of study that are highly effective in revealing their distinguishing characteristics. This fact results from the completely orderly arrangement and orientation of the constituent molecules or ions in what is termed the *crystal lattice*. Only crystalline (or pseudocrystalline) materials are characterized by such definite and reproducible structural arrangement and exhibit so high a degree of symmetry and such marked effects upon transmitted light.

It is not the purpose of this chapter to give detailed consideration to ordinary optical *crystallography*, which deals with the optical properties of crystals. Rather, the criminalistic possibilities inherent in such study will be outlined with the intent of stimulating the criminalist to explore this field thoroughly and to employ petrographic method freely as the most positive approach to the identification of crystalline materials with the single exception of the X-ray diffraction technique.

THE NATURE AND PROPERTIES OF CRYSTALS

Crystals are commonly recognized by their characteristic and reproducible symmetrical shapes. The symmetry of a crystal results from the ordered arrangement of its constituent atoms or ions in the crystal lattice. The classification of crystals into *systems* is based upon the various types of symmetry that they exhibit, the simplest crystalline forms corresponding to the simplest crystal lattices. For example, the cube is one of the simplest three-dimensional forms. Cubic crystals (isometric system) owe their form to a simple cubic lattice in which the different components occupy alternate positions. Sodium chloride crystals are illustrative of the isometric system, the sodium ions and chloride ions being arranged alternately at the eight "corners" of the cubic lattice. The more complex the lattice, the less simple is the crystalline form and the less obvious is the symmetry.

Five out of the six main crystal systems show the property of *birefringence*, or *anisotropism*, or *double refraction*, i.e., the property of exhibiting different refractive indexes for light passing through the crystal in different directions. Anisotropic crystals also polarize light passing through them in certain directions, and exhibit a number of other quite characteristic optical properties. Isometric crystals, the only class that shows no such effects, consists of only a few materials, notably the uni-univalent salts such as sodium chloride (table salt) and the other halide salts of sodium, potassium, ammonium, and the other alkali metals, which are comparatively rare. Most of the crystals in this class are cubic in habit and are therefore readily recognized by their crystalline shape. With these few exceptions, all crystals are readily distinguished from noncrystalline materials by means of the polarizing microscope, which is known as the petrographic microscope when it is specifically designed for mineralogical examinations or for petrology. The polarizing microscope, in which ordinary illumination is replaced with polarized light, brings into the field of observation all of the common optical properties of anisotropic materials including several crystal constants such as the *type of extinction and its angle*, the *birefringence*, the *sign of elongation* (or *optic sign*), the *pleochroism*, and the two or three characteristic *refractive indexes* characteristic of the various primary orientations. Most of the crystals found in evidence are too small to have their characteristic facet angles measured by means of a goniometer, so it is often necessary to use, instead, the profile angles as observed under the microscope.

The examination of crystals under polarized light requires the expertise of the specialist. In the hands of the trained petrologist or chemical microscopist every crystalline material is clearly distinguishable from every other crystalline material. The value of such identification is potentially very great as compared with data obtainable by any other technique. It is definite and unambiguous in nearly instance, and it is comparatively rapid. It is regrettable that this technique has not been more widely exploited in systematic criminalistics. Crystalline evidence is not unusual, and it is almost unique in the ease of positive identification when properly studied by means of the polarizing microscope.

Recognizing Crystals

Even the untrained laboratory worker can use the polarizing microscope to advantage in many cases, merely by knowing how to distinguish between the appearance of crystalline and noncrystalline materials when they are illuminated by polarized light. Assume the simple problem mentioned above, the differentiation between fragments of quartz and of glass. When placed between crossed Nicol prisms (or Polaroid discs) on the stage of the microscope and rotated horizontally through a circle, while the background field of the microscope will appear uniformly black, the glass particles will be all but invisible, or if badly strained will show a trace of gray. Quartz, which is strongly anisotropic, will alternately appear black and a succession of colors as the stage is rotated. The orientations in which quartz appears black will recur at every 90° of rotation, with the succession of bright colors appearing between, reaching maximum brightness at 45° of rotation from the position of blackness (called *extinction*). This set of observations should occupy one or two minutes of time, and when the test is properly performed it is conclusive. Some judgment and experience with the technique are necessary because of the fact that a large piece of material will show a greater color effect than will a small piece of the same material. Also, glass that is badly strained will show more color than will be shown by one that is less strained: the more color, the greater the strain. By running a set of control tests with quartz and glass fragments of appropriate sizes, the distinction can be made quite definite because it is extremely unlikely that any piece of glass, however badly strained, will be as birefringent as quartz is normally. Also, the quartz particle shows four points of extinction, whereas glass will often show no definite extinction. There is further differentiation in that the quartz particle shows a constant birefringence that can be measured by determining the thickness of the particle and calculating the constant, whereas similar treatment of a piece of strained glass would not yield a constant value of birefringence.

Using the Polarizing Microscope to Segregate Evidence

One of the simplest and most useful general applications of the polarizing microscope is its employment for the sorting and isolation of various kinds of evidence. Assume that a number of small particles, some of them crystalline and others amorphous, are mixed. Under polarized light the crystalline particles are readily revealed by their color between crossed Nicol prisms, whereas the amorphous materials commonly appear black in all orientations. Thus the various types of evidence are clearly distinguished and may be segregated for detailed identification.

Pseudocrystalline Material

The property of birefringence is applicable to some types of evidence not usually considered to be crystalline. Actually, all that is required to produce polarization effects is a degree of orientation of the particles, molecules, micelles, or ions of which the material is composed. Both hairs and fibers, which are among the commonest types of evidence, have in their structures sufficient orientation to exhibit birefringence, though somewhat more weakly than do most crystals. Moreover, the degree of birefringence will vary considerably among different types of fiber and different hair samples. Because it is comparatively simple to measure the birefringence of a material with the polarizing microscope, this is a useful method of differentiating fibers of various types and origins, particularly the synthetic fibers such as rayons, and nylon. Applicability to the individualization of hair awaits further study and evaluation.

Many materials exhibit a measurable degree of birefringence that is closely related to small differences of chemical composition that cause slight variations in the crystal structure or in the orientation of the molecules. For example, the degree of nitration of nitrocellulose used in smokeless powder and in lacquer is indicated by the birefringence of each product. Thus, an attractive field exists for further application of polarized light to criminalistic examination of noncrystalline materials.

Crystal Form and Habit

Quite apart from the crystal system, which, like the optical properties, is a function of the crystal lattice, is the *crystal habit*. This term refers to the way in which crystals grow, e.g., as needles, plates, dendritic forms, or twinned. Observable with or without magnification, crystal habit is the most obvious crystalline property though it is not a direct function of the lattice or the system. The understanding of crystal habit is primarily applicable to methods of chemical microscopy as described in detail by Chamot and Mason. This follows from the fact that the habit of crystal growth is best observed with freshly grown crystals and will rarely be seen in the preexistent crystals found in evidence. These will have been broken, worn, and contaminated to such a degree that the habit is not adequately revealed. The crystal habit bears no necessary relationship to the optical properties upon which are based identifications of unaltered original crystals as distinct from newly formed crystals that have resulted from the application of specific reagents.

X-RAY DIFFRACTION

The study of crystalline materials by X-ray diffraction is a specialized technique that is relatively new in the field of criminalistics and offers promise for much future development. When X rays are passed through crystals, the rays are diffracted in a pattern determined by the position, the arrangement, and the size of the crystal's constituent units, these features being repeated throughout the crystalline structure. Every substance has its own characteristic spatial arrangement, likewise, each crystalline substance has its own characteristic crystal lattice that, in turn, produces its own distinctive effect upon the X-ray beam. Thus, two compounds that crystallize in the same system, or type of lattice, will produce similar X-ray diffraction lines, but the lines will be spaced differently because of differences in the sizes of the constituent units. Materials belonging to different crystal systems produce different types of diffraction pattern. Thus, a study of the diffraction pattern can identify the material composing the crystal by establishing its structure and dimensions. The diffraction pattern can also serve for the comparison of two crystalline materials suspected of being identical. Mixtures of crystals may be studied by this technique, and their approximate quantitative composition determined. Many important applications of this technique have been found, and increased utilization of X-ray diffraction methods is to be expected.

The drawbacks of the X-ray diffraction techniques are the relatively high cost of X-ray sources and diffraction cameras and the necessity of having someone reasonably familiar with the theory and practice of the technique. The same may be said of other advanced instrumental methods, such as spectrography. It is probable that X-ray diffraction will ultimately prove at least as useful as spectrography, or even more useful, despite the fact that the spectrograph has long been used in this field. The employment of the Geiger-Mueller counter instead of the camera to evaluate the diffraction lines is a comparatively recent development that simplifies the general use of X-ray identification but introduces some new complications, attributable to a comparatively complex electronic circuit in the counter tube.

MISCELLANEOUS TECHNIQUES

Hot Stage Techniques

Another set of approaches to the indentification and evaluation of crystalline materials as evidence involve hot stage methods. These include not only the simple determination of physical constants, but embrace also eutectic melts that divide crystals into separate phases, and complex formations that may increase the phases still more. These are laboratory procedures, but they have frequently been neglected in the laboratories. Not only are these techniques very useful, but their speed and economy should be recognized by all law-enforcement personnel.

Small Particulate Evidence

In discussions of crystalline evidence it is generally assumed that the particle size permits study by ordinary microscopic methods. Very little crystalline evidence smaller than this has been utilized in crime investigation, but not because it bears no useful information. Particles close to the lower limits of resolution by the microscope are small enough to be airborne and, hence, constitute much of the particulate pollution of the atmosphere. Because of their importance as air pollutants, small particles have been subjected to increased investigative effort in recent years. It seems apparent that the study of particles of this size in connection with environmental identification could be most valuable. Effective methods are now available, and all investigators who are concerned with the development of advanced technology for crime investigation should be actively aware of the possibilities. They are, of course, not limited to crystalline particles, although most small particles are found to be crystalline or pseudocrystalline.

Dispersion Staining

Dispersion staining is a relatively recent and a most valuable addition to the technique of the microscopist. It is based upon the dispersion of the sample, and it requires a minimum of equipment, little time, and a small amount of skill. Although it is not a procedure recommended for direct application by the police, it should be immediately available to them in the laboratory for the examination of a wide variety of particulate evidence, both crystalline and noncrystalline.

REFERENCES

Chamot, E. M., and Mason, C. W.: *Handbook of Chemical Microscopy*, 3rd ed., Vol. 1. New York: Wiley (1958).

Chamot, E. M., and Mason, C. W.: *Handbook of Chemical Microscopy*, 2nd ed., Vol. 2. New York: Wiley (1940).

Cocks, F. B.: "Trace Evidence in the Form of Dust," *Australian Pol. J.* 22:153 (1968).

Correns, C. W.: *Introduction to Mineralogy*. New York: Springer-Verlag (1969).

Cox, K. G.: *Introduction to the Practical Study of Crystals, Minerals and Rocks*. New York: McGraw-Hill (1969).

Forlini, L.: "Expanded and Revised Tables for the Determination of Unknowns by Dispersion Staining," *The Microscope* 17:29 (1969).

Gracias, C. E., and O'Dell, J. H.: "Applications of Microscopy to the Analysis of Composite Materials," *The Microscope* 17:161 (1969).

Hartshorne, N. H.: *Crystals and the Polarizing Microscope*. New York: American Elsevier (1970).

McCrone, W., and Delly, J.: *The Particle Atlas*, 2nd ed. Ann Arbor, Mich.: Ann Arbor Press (1972). 4 vols.

Martin, E. P.: "The Importance of Microscopic Traces Found at the Scene," *Inter. Crim. Pol. Rev.* 204:15 (1967).

20
Special Chemical Evidence

Occasionally the investigator will encounter evidence that, for want of a better designation, can be termed *chemical evidence*. In its broad sense this term would encompass all evidence requiring chemical testing. For simplicity it may be taken to include those miscellaneous chemical substances that cannot be placed in a restricted category of evidence (such as poisons or physiological fluids). Some illustrations of this type of material will clarify the definition.

A family was startled by the sound of breaking glass and the thudding of a solid object as it passed into the house. Investigation showed a black aromatic liquid on the front of the house, a whiskey bottle containing some of the liquid that had been thrown through the window and had spread some of its contents on the drapes, furniture, rugs, and floor. Chemical examination showed the liquid to be creosote of coal-tar origin, a fluid difficult to remove from an object it wets because of its thorough penetration and low solubility.

Furniture in another house was badly damaged by chemical action. During the absence of the family the upholstery was eaten through and intensely stained by the act of a marauder. Chemical examination was required and showed that nitric acid was the causative agent.

A sample of coffee was submitted for examination because it possessed an unusual flavor that suggested poisoning had been attempted. Chemical examination proved that the coffee contained nothing in toxic amount but that bismuth and cadmium salts were present in small quantity.

A lady who had discharged her chauffeur was confronted with frozen bearings in the motor of her automobile. Despite the efforts of the garage mechanic to clean the gasoline feed lines, the tank, and the carburetor so thoroughly as to effectively destroy all the evidence, it could be proved by chemical means that the gasoline had contained ordinary sugar, which was responsible for the damage to the motor. Cases similar to this were not infrequent in military aviation during World War II. Naphthalene has also been used in this manner, as have other organic substances that are partially decomposed by the heat of the motor and altered into a sticky carbonaceous mass that immobilizes the moving parts of the motor.

Qualitative analysis will be required in many instances to determine the presence of undesirable chemical agents in food, drinking water, fuel, and a number of other materials. This possibility can arise in almost any type of investigation, but it is most common in the various forms of *sabotage*.

Asphalt is a type of chemical evidence frequently encountered in ordinary criminal investigations. It is commonly found on the shoes of burglars as a result of their walking over fresh paving, and, more important, from stepping on the debris formed by cutting holes through tar-and-gravel roofs to gain entry into stores below. Obviously, the better the discrimination between various samples of asphalt, the more useful will be such asphalt traces as evidence. Ordinary chemical testing of asphalt is relatively ineffective, but with highly sophisticated chromatographic methods even minute traces of asphalt of different origin can be distinguished. Hence the mere fact that asphalt is a very widespread and common material in the environment does not disqualify it as evidence. Such evidence is rarely conclusive, but few types of evidence in and of themselves *are c*onclusive. When accompanied by other corroborative evidence, asphalt identification is valuable, and should be neither overlooked nor discredited.

Similar considerations are applicable to a number of materials primarily of petroleum or coal-tar origin. Among the commonest are *lubricating oils* and *greases*. Grease stains are admittedly very common in ordinary life, but because they are unsightly they will not be allowed to persist except on clothing worn in pursuit of a mechanical trade or hobby, or under conditions that may involve a crime where there is no opportunity to eliminate them from ordinary clothing. Thus, the presence of oil or grease stains on clothing requires an explanation. This will be simple if the wearer engages in legitimate mechanical operations that expose him to grease or oil. Otherwise, the explanation itself becomes important. Greases and lubricating oils show very significant variations in chemical composition, and are for this reason even more useful as evidence than is asphalt. By proper utilization of a variety of instrumental procedures, such greases and oils can often be reliably identified as to probable source. Even when the source is common and widely used, such a determination, coupled with the fact of the presence of the material in a location where it would not ordinarily be found, can have a very significant influence in the decision of a case.

Waxes, both natural and refined or derived, are such common constituents of industrial and household materials that their existence in evidence is virtually guaranteed. However, methods for wax identification are not numerous or well known. The difficulties of identification are compounded by the common blending of waxes with other components of industrial and household products. The laboratory personnel must acquire a reasonable familiarity with waxes, an understanding of their properties, and expertise in methods for their identification. A general appreciation by police officers and investigators of the many varied uses of wax will often be helpful in ensuring recognition of its importance as evidence and in making certain its proper collection.

Shoes, because of their extensive contact with the environment, are likely carriers of traces of materials requiring chemical as well as microscopic study. On the soles, and especially on the heels, shoes collect an assortment of such items as chewing gum, spilled food, asphalt, oils and greases, floor wax, paint, beverages, candy, solid fragments of all kinds—in short, a very wide sampling of portable evidence. If any of these are somewhat unusual, and if chemical study indicates that their counterparts are found in the immediate crime scene, the value of the finding is very great indeed. Thus, the shoes of a suspect should always be examined for the presence of any such materials, so laboratory tests may be performed.

INVESTIGATION

The identification of such miscellaneous substances as those discussed above, especially when they are present in only the most minute amounts, is a task for the qualitative microchemist, i.e., the expert who has been trained in the use of the microscope as an analytical tool and who is experienced in spot testing. *Chemical microscopy* is concerned with the microscopic study of chemical reactions, and particularly with crystal formation that results from the addition of suitable reagents. *Spot tests* are refinements of standard color tests adapted for the detection of minute quantities, usually by means of the formation of indicative colors. Not infrequently tests are required that employ biochemical techniques of a specialized nature, or tests of other kinds that are not usually included as spot tests or chemical microscopy. In such instances, a detailed knowledge of chemical testing methods in general is required, along with a knowledge of microchemical techniques. The solution of such problems is not a matter for the ordinary police investigator or the ordinary chemist. It demands the services of the specialized chemist-criminalist whose training is both broad and thorough. Newer techniques, such as the various types of chromatography, are very valuable, if not virtually indispensable, in dealing with miscellaneous types of chemical evidence.

Chromatography has become such an integral part of crime laboratory investigation that the laboratory criminalist is usually in a position to deal with special chemical evidence.

From the standpoint of the police investigator, the essential problem is that of obtaining and preserving the evidence, and making sure that it is placed in competent hands for laboratory testing. When possible, the criminalist should take his own samples, since there is often a need for employing a special sampling technique. It is usually not desirable to deliver special chemical evidence to the ordinary chemical analyst, or to the clinical laboratory technician, no matter how skillful they may be. Analytical technicians and analysts are usually familiar with large scale testing methods only, and are no more capable of performing a proper identification test on a minute sample than is a person almost untrained in chemistry. The police investigator should not assume that a chemist or analyst is capable of assisting with this kind of evidence merely because he has been trained in some form of chemistry. Microchemical criminalistic training is as far from that of the chemist as is criminalistics itself. Failure to understand this results in one of the most frequent errors made by police investigators seeking laboratory help.

COLLECTION OF EVIDENCE

The police investigator who must himself collect materials for analysis should follow the rule of taking as much evidence as possible and guarding it from contamination or loss. For example, a chemical substance has soaked into upholstery. If possible, all of the damaged portion of the upholstery should be removed to the laboratory for examination. Despite the greatest effort it may be extraordinarily difficult for the criminalist to remove from the cloth and padding an appreciable amount of the material to be tested. Even though much was originally present, it has largely reacted with the material upon which it was deposited, and the most minute quantities may be all that can be made available for testing.

Material on a floor poses a difficult problem in sampling. If the substance is liquid it may have collected in a low place on the floor. A medicine dropper carefully applied may retrieve a few drops of the original material. If no such puddles remain, the stained surface of the floor should be carefully scraped with a sharp knife, cutting down as far as necessary to retrieve a maximum of the material absorbed into the floor.

Special Chemical Evidence

Occasionally, *a practically empty bottle* will be recovered. If as much as a drop of the original contents remains, the bottle should be tightly stoppered and removed to the laboratory. If there is no visible liquid content but the inner surfaces of the bottle are wet, the same procedure is to be followed, because the material on the sides can be washed out and analyzed by microchemical techniques. Contaminated liquids, food, water, and the like, are removed to the laboratory in toto. Collection of this type of evidence should be made at the earliest possible moment to minimize the effect of evaporation, air oxidation, and soaking into the supporting surface.

Frequently the material of interest is available only in the form of a smear or stain on an object such as a garment or a shoe, a vehicle, or a piece of furniture. In such an instance the entire object that bears the stain should be removed to the laboratory. There it will be possible to apply special methods for removing the stain or smear, methods that would not be practical in the field. Pieces of wall or floor may be physically cut out and removed if the situation demands such drastic action. Efforts on the part of the officer to remove such stains by other less extreme measures will often result in failure and disappointment, and should therefore be avoided if possible.

PRELIMINARY EXAMINATION

When chemical evidence arrives in the laboratory, the criminalist will be confronted by an almost infinite number of possibilities as to its nature, and in most instances will need to possess not ony microchemical training, but good chemical judgment as well. Careful observation of the appearance and the odor of the material will often provide useful indications of its fundamental nature. For example, many strong acids produce rather characteristic effects. Sulfuric acid dehydrates organic material, thus producing a black char. Yellow or brown residues result from the action of nitric acid on many organic materials. Hydrochloric acid, on the other hand, does not cause conspicuous discoloration of organic substances, but it may cause a slow deterioration and decomposition of cloth and other materials. Many organic materials are dissolved by sodium hydroxide solution and other caustics, which often leave a white ring of solid at the edges of the damaged area. The wet material will feel soapy and may attack the skin. Many organic materials, such as creosote and tar, are recognizable to a considerable extent by their consistency, color, and odor. Frequently a small sample of such material will, when heated rather strongly, give off fumes of very characteristic odor even though the original material has little or no odor. This is particularly valuable for preliminary testing.

If *strong acid* is suspected, it is useful to apply a piece of *Congo red paper* to the moist material. If the paper turns blue, a fairly strong acid condition is demonstrated. This alone is insufficient proof of the presence of strong acid, because some weak acids will turn this paper blue. Sometimes the material upon which strong acid has been thrown may itself neutralize the acid sufficiently to inhibit this simple test. The chemist is likely to recognize such an effect on the basis of his knowledge of the properties of the stained material.

If *caustic* is suspected, a similar test may be run with *phenolphthalein paper* to serve as a preliminary indication of the alkaline nature of the stain. This test is more readily interpreted than those listed above because few natural objects or surfaces are sufficiently acidic either to neutralize the caustic completely or to interfere with the test. *Litmus paper,* which is frequently used by the inexperienced in testing for acidity or alkalinity, is virtually useless for either test because it changes color so close to the neutral point that faint traces of almost any acidic or basic substance will alter its color.

Organic and inorganic substances may usually be distinguished from each other by heating a minute quantity of the material on a small piece of platinum foil and observing continuously the effects of heat. If the substance undergoes a series of changes that result in a carbonaceous residue, it is organic or contains organic matter. If it is not charred, burned, or volatilized by the heat, it is inorganic. The remaining material, ashed or otherwise, will resemble the original sample in quantity. This test will fail occasionally. Some inorganic materials, such as ammonium salts, are completely volatile when heated and leave no residue; and some highly hydrated inorganic compounds pass through a whole series of changes during heating. The latter materials usually leave an ash, which still indicates their inorganic nature. Some essentially organic materials may contain as impurities inorganic constituents that leave a characteristic ash. This is true of all unaltered biological materials. With these, heat produces both charring and ash, but the quantity of ash is far less than the amount of original material.

SOLUBILITY

It is important to determine the solubility of the material in question. For this purpose the microscope is very useful. A small sample of the substance is placed under the microscope and a drop of solvent is applied. By careful observation the chemist can usually determine whether it dissolves, and to what extent. If there is doubt, the solvent should be evaporated without heat and the slide then examined for any residue that may have been deposited on drying. If a slight residue remains, an equal volume of the solvent should be evaporated as a control. If there is dissolved material in the solvent, it will then be ascertained whether this is the cause of the observed residue.

Most substances tested will show an appreciable solubility either in water or in one or more fat-dissolving organic solvents such as acetone, benzene, carbon tetrachloride, toluene, or an alcohol. By determining which type of solvent dissolves the questioned substance one gains some idea of its origin as well as good indications for further investigation. This is most useful in dealing with organic compounds, because few inorganic compounds are very soluble in the organic solvents. Caution is necessary because some corrosive or injurious materials, such as strong acids and alkalies, are soluble in alcohol or acetone to an appreciable extent. They are rarely soluble in benzene, however.

Many materials used in sabotage are completely harmless except under very special conditions. Thus, sugar or naphthalene, both of which are normally harmless, virtually ruin an automobile motor if they are added to the gasoline. Tests for such substances assume criminalistic importance only in terms of their criminal misuse. Sand or emery placed in a bearing fall into the same category. There are many other normally innocuous materials that come under the scrutiny of the laboratory because of their vicious misapplication.

INORGANIC SUBSTANCES

When small quantities of inorganic materials are recovered as evidence, the method of choice for their examination is *chemical microscopy*, as exemplified by the system of Chamot and Mason. This technique employs appropriate reagents to form crystals of characteristic habit and appearance, which are then identified under the microscope. These tests are not only sensitive, but they are far more specific than most of the alternative procedures, and are much simpler and cheaper to carry out than are other specific methods.

Under some circumstances the *spot test* technique, which was largely developed by Feigl, may be more effective, though this happens rarely. As compared with chemical microscopy, spot tests are nearly as rapid, sometimes a little more sensitive, and somewhat less specific. Failures may occur with either technique, and some familiarity with both is desirable on the part of laboratory criminalists.

Other possible means of applying final tests include the spectrograph, the polarograph, and the X-ray diffraction camera, all of which are expensive and complex as compared with either spot testing or crystal identification. A more serious limitation is that only the well-trained specialist is likely to achieve, with the complex instruments, results that are generally useful and completely reliable. The investigator who can qualify in one of these fields is very often too specialized to be capable of effective general investigation.

In recent years new and sophisticated instrumental approaches to the analysis of inorganic materials have been developed. Among the most valuable of these are neutron activation analysis, atomic absorption spectroscopy, and X-ray emission spectroscopy. All three of these techniques are highly sensitive and specific, and are capable of yielding results considerably more complete and useful than those obtainable by the simpler methods mentioned above. All require very expensive equipment not generally available in the crime laboratory. However, when the need for such refined and extensive results is very great, access to the equipment can usually be obtained. Many organic materials, such as oils and greases, may contain inorganic impurities, and the above-mentioned techniques are capable of identifying both.

ORGANIC SUBSTANCES

When a material in evidence is found to be organic in nature, identifying it is difficult unless there are special conditions that give a clue to the nature of the material. It is uncommon to find a pure organic compound used in sabotage, although this does happen at times. Ordinarily the substance used is a commercial product of great complexity. This is true of all greases, tars, creosotes, and similar materials. Accurate analysis of this type of mixture is virtually impossible when the quantity is minimal, but it can sometimes be identified on the basis of its properties compared with standards from a suspected source. A most useful set of properties consists of the solubilities of the questioned material in a series of solvents. If the unknown and a standard are uniformly similar in their solubilities, it is at least likely that they are the same mixture of materials, because different mixtures will rarely show identical solubilities throughout a complete series of solvents of different properties. Such a series would include water, alcohol, acetone, dioxane, benzene, ether, dilute hydrochloric acid, dilute sodium hydroxide, ammonium hydroxide, and concentrated sulfuric acid. Other solvents may be added to this list, and in special cases they will be very important.

When a small quantity of a questioned organic material can be obtained in pure form and it is believed to be a *single organic compound* rather than a complex mixture, its identification will follow one of the standard procedures such as those of Pasto and Johnson, Mullikan, Shriner, Fuson, and Curtin, or Schneider. The determination of physical properties is particularly important, and limiting the investigation to these properties may be very economical of time. The melting point and boiling point, both of which can be determined with minute quantities of material, are useful. Even more valuable are the refractive index and the optical crystallographic properties that are discussed briefly in Chapter 19. This is a task for the expert chemical microscopist, not one for the ordinary chemist, and still less for the ordinary police laboratory technician who has not received special training.

Some *complex organic materials* may be identified by testing for their components and studying their over-all properties. For example, creosote contains phenolic compounds detectable by chemical methods. Some materials may contain proteinaceous compounds for which specific tests are available,

Special Chemical Evidence 237

and not infrequently they may contain sulfhydryl compounds (mercaptans, noted for their foul odor) used in stench bombs. Specific tests exist for the sulfhydryl group, thus facilitating identification. Greases and oils will sometimes have only their physical properties and, particularly, their insolubility in concentrated sulfuric acid to identify them. However, some greases contain metallic soaps that can be identified through the metal and by means of hydrolysis in strong caustic solutions. The thoroughly trained chemical microscopist will be able to apply his understanding of these chemical facts and his ability to carry out a large number of distinguishing tests with minimum quantities of material.

As is true for inorganic materials, newer methods of an instrumental nature are available for the analysis of both simple and complex organic material. Perhaps the most generally useful of these instruments is the infrared spectrometer, which is now rather common in crime laboratories and is virtually indispensable if many organic compounds must be examined. Chromatography of several types now permits rapid separation of mixtures into their individual components, and pyrolysis–gas chromatography offers a very sensitive procedure for the analysis and comparison of both simple and complex organic mixtures, whether or not they contain inorganic constituents also.

DYES AND PIGMENTS

Soluble colored materials, both organic and inorganic, may be identified most accurately by means of their absorption spectra. This examination is usually performed by means of the spectroscope equipped with an absorption cell, or by means of the hand spectroscope applied to the microscope. If the concentration of the colored constituent in solution is sufficient, this method is effective. The observation consists in identifying the absorption bands by comparison with standard absorption bands of known substances. However, if the sample concentration is low, the dispersion and sensitivity of the hand spectroscope is inadequate for positive, conclusive results. Use of a photoelectric spectrophotometer is recommended in such identifications, particularly if dyes are involved. The finer characteristics of the absorption spectrum will then be revealed, and the strength of absorption in all regions will be accurately evaluated. Most identifications of colored materials, when made by means of a spectrophotometer having a dispersion wave band (effective slit width) not wider than 5 millimicrons can be considered positive. When this technique is combined with proper use of capillary absorption cells, the amount of material that can be accurately studied is roughly 1/1000 of the minimum sample size required by any conventional microchemical method. Infrared spectrophotometry is extremely valuable for the identification of dyes and pigments, as well as other organic and inorganic materials. Combined with thin-layer

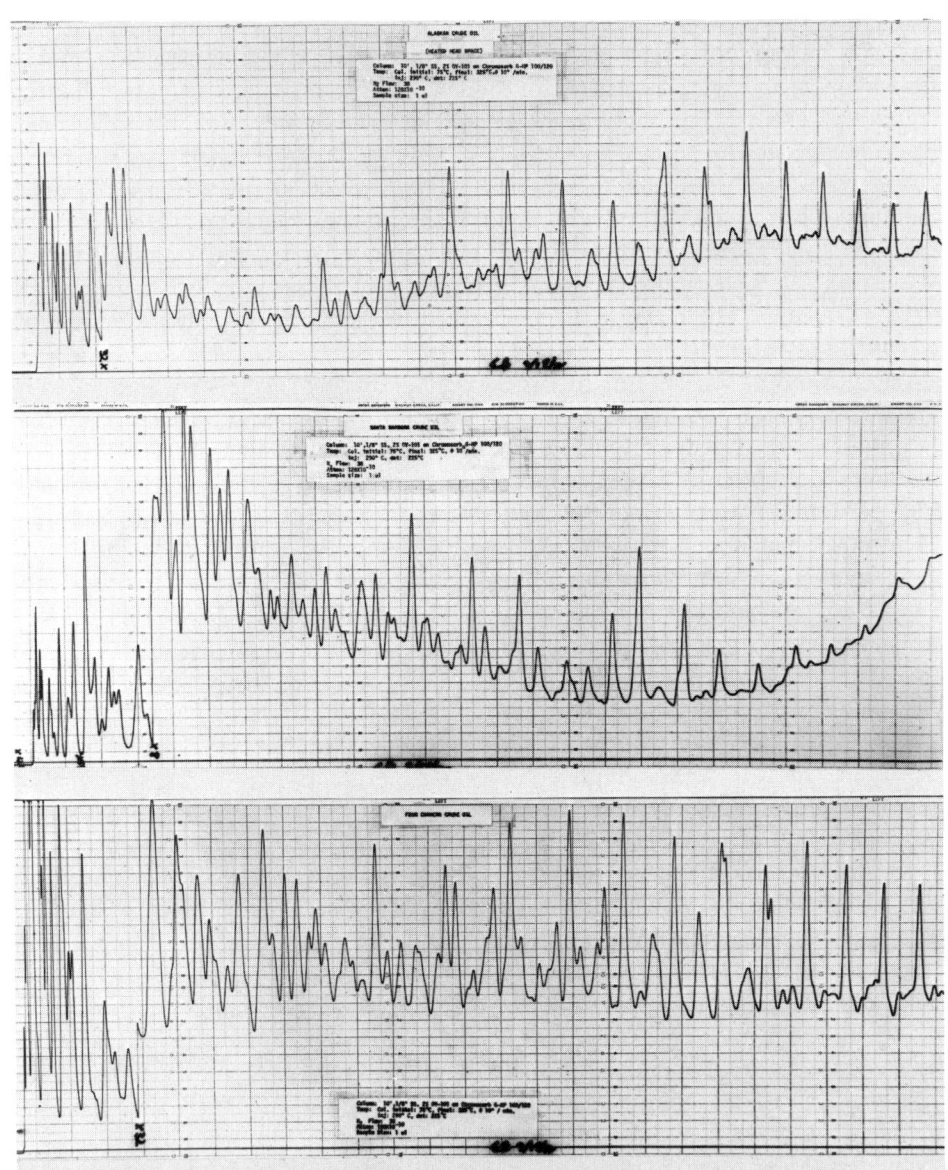

FIGURE 20-1. Gas chromatograms of crude oils. Gas chromatographic analysis can aid in determining the source of oil spills in pollution cases. From top to bottom: Alaskan crude, Santa Barbara crude, Four Corners crude. (Courtesy of Edward T. Blake.)

chromatography, or even with paper chromatography, which permits the separation of individual colored components, these methods render the identification of colored materials virtually infallible when they are properly applied.

Insoluble pigments present a more difficult problem than do the soluble colors. Because they are inorganic materials, their identity is often indicated by their color and insolubility. The methods of the chemical microscopist are ordinarily the best choice for their identification, as is the case with most colorless inorganic compounds. The spectrograph is often useful, as is the X-ray diffraction camera. In some instances optical crystallographic methods may also be employed successfully.

REFERENCES

Alimarin, I. P., and Petrikova, M. N., eds.: *Inorganic Ultramicroanalysis.* Elmsford, New York: Pergamon (1964).

Benedetti-Pichler, A. A.: *Identification of Materials.* New York: Springer-Verlag (1964).

Cheronis, N. D., and Entrikin, J. B.: *Identification of Organic Compounds.* New York: Wiley–Interscience (1963).

Ewing, G.: *Instrumental Methods of Chemical Analysis,* 3rd ed. New York: McGraw-Hill (1969).

Feigl, F.: *Spot Tests in Inorganic Analysis,* 5th ed. New York: American Elsevier (1958).

Feigl, F.: *Spot Tests in Organic Analysis,* 7th ed. New York: American Elsevier (1966).

Heftmann, E.: *Chromatography.* New York: Reinhold (1967).

Mulliken, S.: *The Identification of Pure Organic Compounds.* Vol. 1–4. New York: Wiley (1941–1948).

Pasto, D. J., and Johnson, C. R.: *Organic Structure Determination.* Englewood Cliffs, N.J.: Prentice-Hall (1969).

Schneider, F.: *Qualitative Organic Microanalysis.* New York: Wiley (1946).

Shriner, R. L., Fuson, R. C., and Curtin, D. Y.: *The Systematic Identification of Organic Compounds.* 4th ed., New York: Wiley (1956).

21
Paint

There are three different forms in which the criminal investigator may find paint in physical evidence: (1) *chips* from old paint; (2) *smears* of either fresh paint or dry paint that has become "chalked"; and (3) *intact* paint on objects.

Old paint often becomes detached as chips or flakes that may be found adhering to the surface of clothing, and lodged in pants cuffs, pockets, or other recesses. At times it is found in the neighborhood of the crime. For example, a safe that was being loaded into an automobile by burglars lost paint in the form of chips, which were found on the ground along with other paint chips that had been knocked from the vehicle. In such a crime careful search for paint chips is always essential. Paint chips have been found in the sweepings from housebreakers' clothing, sometimes in surprisingly large pieces. Frequently they may also be found at the scene of an automobile collision, either with another vehicle or with pedestrians. It is important to realize that when *paint chips* are found in evidence, the surface from which they were removed may have been damaged. This surface may show indentation, abrasion, or some other type of deformation. The implication is perhaps most important in the analysis of vehicular impacts.

Paint *smears* are most valuable as evidence when the criminal acquires them on his shoes or clothing from recently painted buildings or objects at the scene of the crime. The amount of undried paint transferred is likely to be considerable and, therefore, susceptible to effective examination. A pair of shoes belonging to a suspected burglar carried smears of four distinguishably different paints, corresponding to those applied to the house entered.

Smears of dry paint are often transferred as a result of the "chalking" effect that permits some old paints to be rubbed off easily. Normal dry paint may also be smeared in significant quantity when considerable force is used. A burglar, in striking the knob of a safe, transferred useful quantities of paint from the hammer to the safe dial, thus providing the investigators with significant physical evidence.

Much more frequently, smears of dry paint not in a chalked condition will constitute evidence. This type of smear occurs only when sufficient force is applied to break and fragment the paint film and is most characteristic of vehicular impacts. Such transferred paint smears are used to determine which car struck another, especially when several vehicles have collided. Impacts of vehicles with stationary painted objects are in the same category.

Intact paint is often found on large items of physical evidence, and occasionally there will be significant quantities present on small objects. Painted concrete fragments figured in a safe-cracking case, painted wood in a manslaughter case in which a car had collided with a painted wooden curb, a painted feed sack in a burglary, and a painted trademark on a woman's stocking in a kidnapping and rape case. Innumerable instances of this kind have been encountered and can be expected.

THE PHYSICAL NATURE OF PAINT

Nearly everyone is familiar with the fact that paint is a viscous, opaque, white or colored liquid that, when spread on a surface, will harden into a more or less opaque and durable coating. What is not always so clear is that paints are either suspensions or emulsions of various solids in a liquid (oil, or sometimes water) that upon drying retains the suspended solids as inclusions in the dry film. Such suspended materials are generally inorganic (mineral) in nature, whereas the film proper is organic in nature. The emulsion paints differ from the oil-base paints in that *both* the organic material and any suspended inorganic material are in the organic phase of the emulsion. The organic film-forming material is termed the *vehicle,* and the inorganic suspended material is termed the *pigment.* In respect to its physical properties, the quality of a paint is largely determined by the organic vehicle, but its color and hiding power are determined by the pigment. Because the pigment and the vehicle are usually of different chemical types, and many different vehicle–pigment combinations may be found, all paint identifications must rest upon the study of *both types of material.* With varnishes and lacquers the general situation may differ in that they do not always carry inorganic pigments. In addition, there is an increasing use of organic coloring matter, which usually is not suspended, but is dissolved in the vehicle. This is more frequently the case with varnishes and lacquers than with ordinary paints.

As paint ages and weathers it often undergoes several changes. Sun fading is common, as is the darkening of interior enamels. The paint may also crack, blister, or peel. Such deterioration implies either a poor quality of paint or inexpert application. Some paints often show the "chalking" effect that results from the disintegration of the film of oxidized oil in which the pigment was dispersed. Chalking does not necessarily indicate that the paint is of poor quality, but rather that it was made according to a recipe that is intended to make the paint self-cleaning by the gradual washing away of the outer surface.

THE CHEMICAL NATURE OF PAINT

Paints and related surface coatings are of almost infinite variety, and new types of paint are introduced rather frequently. Resins alone are available in many types, each of which has numerous variations, as indicated in Table 21-1.

TABLE 21-1 Types of Solvents Used with Various Resins

Resin family	Solvents	Will tolerate
butadiene–styrene	ketones acetates glycol–ethers aromatics aliphatics	alcohols
modified butadiene–styrene	ketones acetates glycol–ethers aromatics	alcohols aliphatics
nitrocellulose	ketones acetates glycol–ethers	alcohols aromatics aliphatics
acrylics	ketones acetates glycol–ethers aromatics	alcohols aliphatics
epoxies	ketones acetates glycol-ethers	mixed solvents alcohols/aromatics
vinyl chloride–acetate copolymers	ketones selected acetates	aromatics nitroparaffins
polyvinyl butyral	alcohols ketones	

Solvents must be selected for their compatibility with the resin and the other constituents of the paint. When it is considered that this table is limited to only a portion of the main groupings of paints, it becomes clear why so much variation is to be expected in paints obtained from different sources.

AUTOMOTIVE FINISHES. Two types are used: (1) enamel, and (2) lacquer. Most lacquers have been replaced by solvent-type plastic paint, currently of acrylic derivation, which is used on General Motors products. Other manufacturers adhere to the use of enamels, which fact simplifies the discrimination between two large classes of vehicles from which a paint sample may have come. Of course, the refinishing of the car may nullify this simple discrimination.

STRUCTURAL PAINTS. Generally, structural paints are classified as (1) drying-oil paints, (2) solvent paints, and (3) emulsion-type water-base paints. This last type of coating, which is rapidly increasing in general use, consists most

TABLE 21–1 (Continued)

Resin family	Solvents	Will tolerate

alkyds	alcohols
	glycol–ethers
	aromatics
	    (short oil types)
	aliphatics
	    (long oil types)	

phenolics, alcohol-soluble	alcohols glycol–ethers	aromatics
ureas and melamines	alcohols/aromatics	aliphatics
cellulose acetate	acetone methyl acetate ethyl acetate	mixed solvents acetone methanol toluene
cellulose acetate butyrate	ketones acetates aromatics	toluene/ethanol
urethanes (not oil modified)	ketones acetates	aromatics
silicones	aromatics alcohols	glycol–ethers
ethyl cellulose	lower acetates lower alcohols	toluene

commonly of a polyvinyl acetate or an acrylic emulsion of a synthetic body material suspended in water. Emulsion paints were originally limited to interior use, but they have now been accepted for exterior painting of buildings as well. The traditional exterior paint is a mixture of pigment suspended in boiled linseed oil (or other drying oil), which has been suitably modified by additives and thinner. Enamels, more generally used for interior trim and for water-resistant surfaces in kitchens and bathrooms, contain various natural or synthetic additives. The many developments in paint technology, and in the number and variety of materials added to paint, make it impractical to discuss the subject in depth here.

DRYING-OIL PAINT. The oldest of all *modern* paints is based upon the fact that certain vegetable oils that possess a high degree of chemical unsaturation will, on exposure to air, undergo a process of oxidation and polymerization that produces tough films, which give to the paint its strength and durability. This oxidation process is *autocatalytic*: the products of the early oxidation catalyze (accelerate) the rate of subsequent oxidation, so that, once started, the process increases in rate until the unsaturated material has become scarce and the reaction slows. Linseed oil was formerly the most extensively used drying oil, but it has been partly superseded by other unsaturated oils, among which tung oil is one of the most important. Others include castor oil and soybean oil. Early paints of this type consisted of little else than a drying oil, a thinner, and a suspended pigment. Today, the situation is greatly complicated by the addition of a host of other materials to most paints, especially to enamels and to corrosion-resistant paints formulated for marine application. Drying oils are now combined with other constituents, such as phthalic anhydride, which condense with the oils to form the characteristic tough, resinous enamel coatings.

SOLVENT-TYPE PAINTS. Paints in this category are formed by dissolving a suitable vehicle, in dry form, in a compatible volatile solvent. After the solution has been applied to the desired surface, the solvent evaporates, leaving behind the dry vehicle and any pigments that were suspended in it. Paints in this category are commonly used for automobile finishing, for which a very hard, adherent coating is required. They include the lacquers, some enamels, varnishes, and acrylic coatings. The acrylics have also been adapted for floor coverings and other uses.

EMULSION PAINTS. When a suitable plastic material is emulsified in water it may be applied to a surface as a paint, and the water will evaporate leaving behind a tough, durable coating. The two kinds of plastic currently most used for such paint are polyvinyl acetate (PVA) and the acrylic resins, the latter having the same base as the common acrylic plastics such as Plexiglas and Lucite. The main application of these materials has been for interior walls, but they are suited to exterior painting as well and are sometimes so used. Their main advantages are ease of application, lack of odor, and washability. They also provide a flat rather than a glossy finish, which makes them attractive for interiors.

EXAMINATION OF PAINTS

In field examination, little is possible beyond noting the color of a paint transfer or a chip. Care must be taken in describing the color of a paint, as the appearance of a paint chip or smear may deviate considerably from that of the original paint. If there is doubt, a laboratory examination is indicated.

There are a considerable number of approaches to the laboratory examination of paint evidence; the approach chosen will vary in accordance with the type of coating in question, i.e., paint, varnish, lacquer, etc. The nature of the vehicle of the paint will generally be impossible to ascertain without recourse to chemical and instrumental methods. Identification of the pigment may be simpler because of its perceptible color. However, it would be unwise to speculate on the nature of the pigment without subjecting it also to laboratory examination.

Differentiation between drying-oil paints and solvent paints is usually fairly simple. Acetone or Cellosolve and some other solvents will dissolve lacquer rapidly. Alcohol dissolves shellac. No simple solvent attacks drying-oil paint rapidly, though some surface effect can be obtained with solvents. Ordinarily this consists of a swelling and softening of the paint rather than a true solution. Fairly strong alkali solution will destroy most drying-oil paints on prolonged contact. The distinctions obtained by observing the effects of solvents and chemical reagents on the vehicle are of value only when it is observed that two paint samples suspected of being identical show the same behavior. Without this preliminary agreement no identity of source could be claimed. However, identity *cannot* be based merely upon similar chemical behavior of the vehicle.

PAINT SECTIONS

When a paint sample is intact, even in small pieces such as flakes or on the surface of an object, it should be sectioned across the layer. This is accomplished by cutting straight through the layer with a razor blade. The flake itself shows the cross section, but the broken surface is usually very irregular. Small, brittle pieces may be embedded in paraffin and the paraffin block cut through with a sharp blade or sectioned with a simple microtome. Mounting in thermoplastic is rather widely employed. The cut or broken edge of the paint chip should be examined very carefully under the microscope. Usually the higher powers of the stereoscopic binocular microscope are adequate, e.g., 50×. At times the Ultropak or a similar vertical illuminator is required for the study of fine detail. This cross-section examination will reveal: (1) the number of layers of paint, (2) the color of each layer and the order of the colors, (3) the viscosity of the paint at the time of application, estimated from the thickness of the layer, which will be greater with a thick than with a thin paint, and (4) inclusions of soil and other debris on the surfaces of the various layers.

When two paint samples are from different sources it is highly probable that marked differences will be observed in one or more of the above factors. If they are from the same source, they will usually agree closely. It is to be expected that some variation may be noted in factor (3), as this is not necessarily constant, the thickness of a layer varying to some extent with conditions and with properties other than viscosity alone. Viscosity *is*, however, a major factor, as will be observed in comparing a priming coat with a finish coat. The first is made thin with a high oil and thinner content, whereas the finish coat is usually applied rather heavily to produce good covering and a smooth appearance. In many instances three, four, or more layers will be observed, each of which corresponds to a repainting. Sometimes much debris will be found in the interface between a particular pair of adjoining layers, and little if any in others. Such factors should be consistent between samples from the same source, and notable differences will cast doubt on the identity of their source. The presence of debris between layers is most characteristic of house paints, and especially of applications made by amateur painters. Debris is not expected to occur between the layers of automobile paint unless a careless amateur has repainted the car.

Occasionally the persistent investigator will prove absolute identity of source of paint flakes without any cross-sectional examination or instrumental analysis. If a flake of reasonable size is broken from an automobile, for example, the matching broken surface will sometimes be found on the vehicle. Thus, if such a flake is found beside the victim of a collision, or on his person, it should be compared with broken edges of paint on any vehicle suspected of having lost the chip. It is possible to find an exact fit of the broken edge and thereby obtain virtually absolute proof of origin.

Similarly, the matching of striations on paint flakes with like markings on the surface from which the flakes were broken has also served to establish identity of source. By far the most common source of such marking is paint that has been applied over metal, as in the finishing of automobiles. Abrasion markings on the metal surface that have resulted from the method of preparing the metal for painting will leave a perfect impression on the paint. These marks

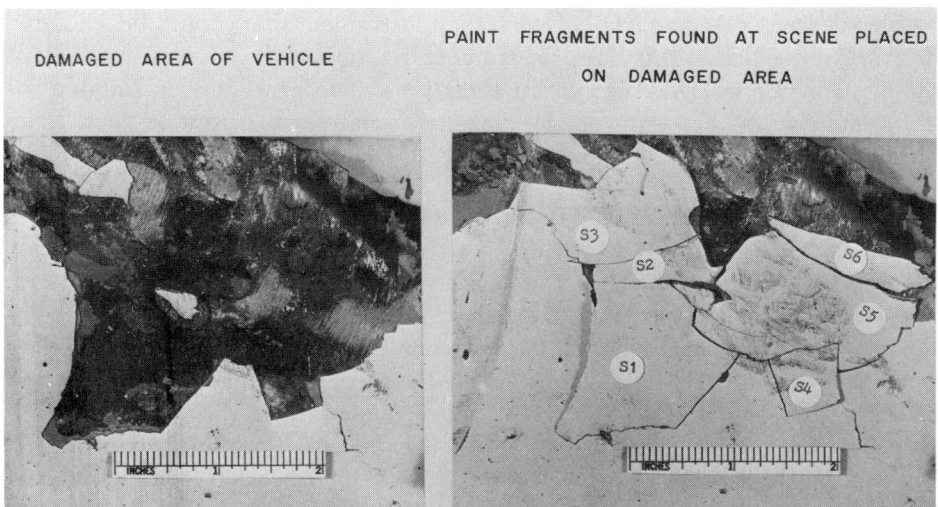

FIGURE 21-1. In a hit and run accident paint fragments from the fender of the vehicle were left at the scene. The responsible vehicle was identified by piecing these fragments into the damaged area of a suspected auto. (Courtesy of Duayne J. Dillon.)

will generally be found on the primer coat rather than on the top coat, although they may occur there also, from other causes. Such markings are treated quite similarly to tool marks. Wood and other materials occasionally have surface markings that have been reproduced by a coating of paint, but this is less common.

The matching of broken edges and of surface marks on paint chips with their counterparts on the surfaces from which the chips have been broken occurs only rarely in practice, but both are so conclusive in establishing identity of source that any reasonable time spent in searching for such identities is well spent.

IDENTIFICATION OF PAINT VEHICLE

Several excellent laboratory methods are now available for the identification of the type of vehicle present in a paint sample and for the comparison of vehicles contained in two or more paint samples to detect small differences. The methods require special equipment and knowledge proper to the laboratory criminalist and should not be attempted by police officers.

INFRARED SPECTROSCOPY. Each organic compound exhibits a selective absorption of the invisible infrared wavelengths (heat rays) that serves to identify the chemical structure almost unequivocally. This selective absorption is measured by the infrared (IR) spectrophotometer, an instrument that should be available to every crime laboratory. The instrument requires only a very small paint sample, and the analysis occupies a short time. The procedure is suitable for the identification of paint vehicle, and such analyses are routine in a large proportion of effective crime laboratories.

PYROLYSIS-GAS CHROMATOGRAPHY. If a minute bit of paint is heated in a pyrolyzer until it is decomposed, and the vapors are analyzed by a gas chromatograph, the decomposition products of the sample will yield a characteristic pattern. This will serve to identify unequivocally the nature of the vehicle in the paint sample. This technique is usually somewhat more sensitive than infrared to small differences between samples and is therefore considered as the method of choice in some laboratories. The sample is destroyed in the pyrolysis, but it may be considerably smaller than even that required for infrared analysis. The equipment is somewhat less expensive, but the operation is not simpler to perform and the time requirement is generally not less than that for infrared spectroscopy.

Each of the above procedures has added a dimension to paint analysis that was not available when only the pigment was routinely studied. Now the entire chemical composition of the paint is involved in the comparison, and no two paint samples can be considered identical until both vehicle and pigment have been shown to give identical responses to the methods now available for their examination. In actuality, much can be done by employing multiple solvents to test the vehicle and microscopic methods to compare pigment distributions. The choice of these methods is justifiable only in the absence of modern instruments from which much more reliable information may be obtained.

PIGMENT COMPOSITION

Paint pigments, like paint vehicles, can be reliably identified and compared by several methods. In practice only the constituent chemical elements of the pigment are usually identified, the comparison being made between different paint samples on the basis of their gross elemental composition. When the necessary instruments are available, the examination may be extended beyond simple elementary inventory. All such procedures are strictly limited to laboratory application. Wet chemical analytical methods are too slow, too unreliable, and require too much sample to be of value in pigment comparison.

A large number of mineral pigments are routinely used in paint, and organic colors are also being employed. The latter are more difficult to identify than are mineral pigments. A limited list of common pigments is given in Table 21-2. For an extended list that includes the properties of the pigments the work of Crown may be consulted. The following methods for the evaluation of paint samples in terms of pigment comparison embrace both the relatively new instrumental procedures and the less sophisticated older techniques.

TABLE 21-2 Common Paint Pigments*

Common name	Chemical nature	Color	Remarks
white lead	$Pb(OH)_2 \cdot 2\,PbCO_3$	white	formerly the most common white pigment
titanium white	titanium dioxide, TiO_2	white	great opacity and durability; outside paint; the most common white pigment
zinc white	zinc oxide, ZnO	white	white enamels and art paint
antimony white	antimonous oxide, Sb_2O_3	white	paint and linoleum
lithopone	zinc sulfide, ZnS, and barium sulfate, $BaSO_4$	white	precipitated in molecular proportions and calcined
barytes	barium sulfate, $BaSO_4$	white	extender and adulterant
white lake	hydrated alumina, $Al_2O_3 \cdot 3\,H_2O$	white	extender and adulterant
whiting	calcium carbonate, $CaCO_3$	white	extender and adulterant
terra alba	calcium sulfate, $CaSO_4$	white	extender and adulterant
carbon black	carbon (amorphous)	black	variable color and strength depending upon source
vine black	carbon (amorphous)	bluish-black	artist's color
graphite	carbon (crystalline)	black	special purposes
black iron oxide	magnetic iron oxide, Fe_3O_4	black	oil and size color; also in ceramic coloring

(Continued)

TABLE 21–2 (Continued)

Common name	Chemical nature	Color	Remarks
lead chromes	lead chromates of variable composition: PbCrO$_4$, and PbCrO$_4 \cdot$ PbO	yellow red	color depends upon composition and method of preparation
zinc yellow	zinc chromate, K$_2$O $\cdot$ 4 ZnCrO$_4$		low covering power, but quite permanent; used in mixed colors
cadmium yellow	cadmium sulfide, CdS	yellow to orange	oil and water color
aureolin (cobalt yellow)	potassium cobaltinitrite, K$_3$Co(NO$_2$)$_6$	yellow	artist's color
ochre	Fe$_2$O$_3$ in clay	yellow-brown	
chrome oxide green	Cr$_2$O$_3$	green	very permanent; wide industrial use
Guignet's green (viridian)	hydrated chromium sesquioxide	green	permanent; soluble in boiling HCl
cobalt greens	solid solutions of Zn and Co oxides	green	artist's oil and watercolor

chrome or Brunswick green	composite of chrome yellow and Chinese blue	green	most common green pigment
zinc greens	composite of zinc chrome and Chinese blue	green	artist's color, enamel, printing ink
prussian blues	complex alkaline ferric ferrocyanides	blue	variable composition and coloring
Turnbull's blue	complex ferrous ferricyanides	blue	special purpose coloring
cobalt blues (1) smalts	potassium cobaltous silicates	blue	very permanent; includes King's blue and azure blue
(2) cobalt blue or cobalt ultramarine	cobaltous aluminate of variable composition	blue	many shades under different common names
red oxides of iron	impure Fe_2O_3	bluish-red to pale red-brown	color variable; includes several common pigments
red lead	lead tetroxide	red	extensively used as priming coat
cadmium scarlet	modification of cadmium yellow	red	

* Many variations of basic pigment materials are used to produce specific colors under special names. These are sometimes mixtures of basic pigments. Other modifications may result from raw materials that contribute specific adulterants, from adulteration during manufacture, from variations in the degree of grinding, or from calcining.

EMISSION SPECTROGRAPHY. The oldest procedure for the identification of most mineral elements—and still a reliable one—employs the emission spectrograph. It is best applied to individual layers of paint that have been separated mechanically or by empirical application of various solvents. The sample may be quite small (a milligram or so); it is destroyed in the analysis, and it yields spectral lines indicative of mineral composition. Nearly all of the mineral elements may be detected by this technique. It cannot be assumed that the pigments in the successive layers on a painted object will be alike, so it is essential that the samples being compared represent the same layer. An additional difficulty occasionally encountered is that the spectrograph, like other instruments, cannot distinguish between paint constituents and dirt or other foreign matter that may be included in the sample.

NEUTRON ACTIVATION ANALYSIS. This is a radiochemical procedure that yields information similar to that obtained from the emission spectrograph. The method is more sensitive in the detection of most of the elements, so that some additional information should be obtainable relative to minor elements present in trace amounts. Actually, the main advantage to date of the greater sensitivity of this method has been its applicability to samples of considerably smaller size. The sample is not destroyed in the process. The equipment is very expensive and it is generally available for use only through agencies external to the crime laboratory. It has been used successfully in a number of crime investigations.

X-RAY DIFFRACTION. This procedure utilizes instrumentation available in a number of the better-equipped laboratories. Instead of indicating the constituent elements of the pigment, it reveals the crystal characteristics, which are absolutely individual to the compounds. Thus, the type of information obtainable is somewhat more complete. The sample may be minute if a diffraction camera is available. Scanning will require a larger sample. Sensitivity to trace components is not good, but the main constituents are well resolved. This technique is routinely employed in some laboratories.

A number of additional instrumental approaches are available for pigment analysis and comparison, e.g., X-ray fluorescence, and the electron probe. These techniques still await general application to the problem of paint identification.

Several of the older procedures, now generally displaced by the newer instrumental methods, may still be very serviceable in the laboratory that lacks access to modern instrumentation. They may also be applicable to the occasional special problem.

PIGMENT DISTRIBUTION

The pigment distribution of a paint is a numerical statement of the relative abundance of the recognizable pigments and fillers that can be differentiated in a pulverized sample of the paint. Its usefulness and statistical validity are based upon the fact that few paints contain only one or two solid materials. Finish coats usually contain several pigments that have been mixed to achieve a particular color effect. Even white paints often contain small amounts of colored pigments, which have been added to modify the whiteness. Because professional painters customarily mix their paints on the job, dry samples derived from their work show many variations.

Preparation of a paint sample for the determination of its pigment distribution consists of breaking the vehicle as completely as possible with solvents and by grinding. The various distinguishable pigment particles are then counted comparatively by using a ruled ocular grid micrometer under rather high powers of the microscope. The results are somewhat empirical, because a complete disruption of the paint vehicle is rarely possible, and some judgment must be exercised in distinguishing the various particles. However, this procedure enables an individual to distinguish between samples of apparently similar paint that have been subjected to identical preparatory treatment. The complete determination of pigment distribution is very effective in testing for identity of source and has been applied successfully to several criminal cases.

MISCELLANEOUS TECHNIQUES

EMPIRICAL MICROCHEMICAL TESTING. It is not always necessary to determine identity of two paint samples with the greatest certainty, and for lack of available facilities it is often not possible to do so. It may suffice to determine by simple means a marked similarity of properties and behavior in the paint samples. The characteristics of paint vehicles may be rather easily tested by the application of a number of solvents in which the samples will behave alike or differently. Suitable reagents may be applied to the samples under low-power magnification to gain some idea of the chemical character of the pigments. A scheme such as that of Klug, Schumert, and Vagnina may be applicable. In fact, any reagent that will produce different results on two paint samples will suffice to distinguish between them. On the other hand, similarity of behavior does *not* prove identity of composition; and in general these methods should be avoided except in very special instances. As indicated above, the various classes of paints may often be sharply differentiated by the solubility of their vehicles.

PAINT DENSITY. Some studies of the density of paint fragments as determined by the density gradient tube have shown great variability in this property. Paints from different sources but similar in appearance differed in density. Multiple samples from the same source showed the same density. The difficulty of determining the density of multilayer samples is considerable, whether done by means of the gradient tube or by other methods. Whatever the method, paint density determinations must be made one layer at a time. Another source of difficulty is that the liquids in the gradient tube tend to alter the vehicles of some paints, so that the readings must be made without delay. If the paint samples being compared are identical, this vehicle alteration should occur equally in the two samples if they are of the same size and shape. Otherwise, there will be some difference in the rate of penetration of the paint chips by the liquid.

ORGANIC COLORS. Some paints, and especially lacquers, contain color in the form of organic dyes. These cannot be compared by the techniques applicable to the mineral pigments. When they are present in lacquers or paints that can be dissolved with solvents, the liberated dyes may be identified and compared by means of the spectrophotometer. Ordinarily, comparison in the visible range is all that is required. There are also chromatographic methods that can be applied in suitable instances, and the dyes as well as the vehicle are susceptible to infrared examination.

REFERENCES

Banov, A.: *Paints and Coating Handbook*. Farmington, Mich.: Structures Pub. Co. (1972).

Brewer, J. G., and Burd, D. Q.: "Paint Comparison. A Method for the Preparation of Cross Sections of Paint Chips," *J. Crim. Law and Criminol.* 40:230 (1949).

Bryan, D., and Guinn, V. P.: "Forensic Activation Analysis—Trace Level Elements in Commercial Paints," *Trans. Amer. Nuclear Soc.* 9:589 (1966).

Crown, D. A.: *The Forensic Examination of Paints and Pigments*. Springfield: Thomas (1968).

Gaynes, N. I.: *Formulation of Organic Coatings*. Cincinnati: Van Nostrand Reinhold (1967).

Heilman, W. R.: "Nondestructive Infrared and X-Ray Diffraction Analyses of Paints and Plastics," *J. For. Sci.* 5:338 (1960).

Jain, N. C., Fontan, C. R., and Kirk, P. L.: Identification of Paints by Pyrolysis–Gas Chromatography," *J. For. Sci. Soc.* 5:102 (1965).

Klug, F., Schumert, O., and Vagnina, L. L.: "A Microchemical Procedure for Paint-Chip Comparisons," *J. For. Sci.* 4:91 (1959).

O'Neill, L. A.: "Analysis of Paints by Infrared Spectroscopy," *Med., Sci., and Law* 7:145 (1967).

Schlesinger, H. L., Lukens, H. R., Bryan, D. E., Guinn, V. P., and Hackleman, R. P.: *Forensic Neutron Activation Analysis of Paint*. Springfield, Virginia: National Technical Information Service Publication #GA-10142 (1970).

Turner, G. P.: *Introduction to Paint Chemistry*. Scranton, Pa.: Barnes and Noble (1967).

22
Glass

Despite the popular application of the word "crystal" to elegant glass goblets, glass is a *noncrystalline* material of widely varied composition. Common glass is a colloidal mixture of silica (SiO_2) with the oxides of two or more metals. Glass is sometimes described as a "solid solution" whose components are prevented from crystallizing out by mutual interference with each other's crystalline patterns. This idea is supported by the fact that glass occasionally becomes turbid from the partial crystallization of its components. This alteration is known as *devitrification*.

Glassmaking is among the most ancient of man's technical achievements, so the glassmaker's vocabulary is rich in deeply entrenched nonscientific terms. Among these are, for example, "crown glass" and "flint glass," the former denoting glass of low refractive dispersion which is suitable for ordinary optical use and for windowpanes, and the latter referring to a glass of high density and high refractive dispersion such as is used for ornamental cut glass. Table 22-1 provides a sampling of glass types in terms of percentage composition, and is indicative of the wide variations, both qualitative and quantitative, to be expected among glass samples found in evidence. If, with patience and some skill, the criminalist can demonstrate an agreement of physical properties between glass fragments collected at the scene of a crime and other bits of glass retrieved from the cuffs of a suspect's trousers, he is in a position to ask some penetrating questions and perhaps to answer a few.

The wide range in the percentage of silica contained in the fifteen varieties of glass listed in the table (96.3%–46.6%) is indicative of the variations to be expected in glass samples. However, the most immediate applicable basis of

TABLE 22-1 Composition of Some Typical Glasses, %

Type	SiO$_2$	Na$_2$O	K$_2$O	MgO	CaO	PbO	B$_2$O$_3$	Al$_2$O$_3$	Fe$_2$O$_3$	ZnO	BaO
machine-made container	74.00	17.00		3.50	5.00			0.5	0.5		
flat-drawn window	72.14	12.60		2.62	11.24			1.06	0.15		
lead bottle	63.00	7.60	6.00	0.20	0.30	21.0		0.6	0.6		
bottle, light-green	64.30	5.87	2.56	5.61	14.73			4.89	1.18		
silex	77.90	4.10	2.30		0.80			0.80			
pyrex apparatus	80.50	3.80	0.40				14.10	2.20			
borosilicate crown	69.58	8.44	8.37	0.07	0.07		12.90	0.04	0.01		2.54
light barium crown	48.10	1.00	7.50				9.91			10.1	28.30
light barium flint	49.10	1.00	8.50			19.3	4.50			8.5	13.00
ordinary silicate flint	46.60	1.50	7.80			43.8					
silica glass (fused silica)	99.5+										
96% silica glass	96.3	<.02	<0.2				2.9	0.4			
soda lime plate glass	71–73	12–14		1–4	10–12			0.5–1.5			
soda lime containers	70–73	13–16		10–13	10–13			1.5–2.5			
soda lime electric lightbulbs	73.6	16.0	0.6	3.6	5.2			1.0			

comparison is *color*. Table 22-2, although not free of subjective evaluations, may serve as a starting point. Iridescent glassware is made by spraying the hot glass surface with $SnCl_4$ or $FeCl_3$. This effect is also seen in old glass that has been exposed to air and light for a long period of time.

VARIATIONS IN GLASS

In the classical manufacture of glass it is customary to mix sand, metallic oxides or carbonates, and the secondary ingredients in a melting crucible that is lined with a special resistant refractory, and to melt the whole mass at very high temperatures. The resulting molten mass is very viscous and, because of its high temperature and correspondingly high solvent properties on any mixing device that is introduced, it is not simple to agitate. For this reason it is very difficult to mix the batch sufficiently to ensure that the entire charge will be of uniform composition. Also, because the refractory lining of the crucible is somewhat soluble in the glass, some of its soluble constituents will be added to the molten mass. At the surface of the liquid there is a continuous loss of some of the more volatile constituents of the melt. When this inhomogeneous molten mass is poured into a mold, or removed and blown into a shape, it would be surprising indeed if there was no variation in the composition of the glass forming various objects, or even in different portions of the same object, though all of them have been made from the same batch of glass.

Variations are also to be expected among glass samples derived from different charges of the crucible, as the measurements of the raw materials are only approximately reproduced. Glass sands from different localities, or even from the same quarry or dune, vary in composition and contribute their variations to the product. A given amount of sand will not necessarily contribute the same composition to the glass in successive batches. In view of the differences that

TABLE 22–2 Some Varieties of Colored Glass

Colors	Additives	Color	Additives
milk glass	SnO_2 or CaF_2	olive green	CuO and charcoal
white	CaF_2 + Al compound	canary yellow	U_2O_5 (fluorescent)
amethyst	CoO and MnO	golden yellow	CdS
violet	MnO	reddish yellow (amber)	S and charcoal
dark blue	CoO	orange	CdS and Se
aquamarine blue	CuO and charcoal	red	CuO
pale green	FeO	ruby red	colloidal Au
green	Na_2CrO_4 or CuO	traffic-light red	Cds, ZnO, Se, charcoal

exist between glass factories and between the various types of glass produced by a single factory, it becomes apparent that glass is an extremely diverse material. Practical evidence of this fact may be seen in the extraordinary precautions necessary in the manufacture of optical glass for lenses and prisms, in which uniform optical properties are dependent upon uniform composition. Optical glass of good quality is much more expensive to make than common glass, and the cost increases very rapidly with the size of the uniform glass blank which is required. It is much simpler to make a small piece of glass of uniform composition and properties than to make a large piece of like uniformity.

In response to the enormously expanded market for glass, attendant upon the vast requirements for automobiles, buildings, beverage bottles, and other items, the technology of glass manufacture has advanced at a rapid rate. Today, glass items for which there is a mass market are usually produced by continuous tank methods supplemented by mechanized feed of the raw materials. The result has been a greatly increased uniformity of composition in the product. Formerly, headlight lenses, for example, could be rather readily distinguished from each other on the basis of compositional variations; but sealed beam units, now universally used, are remarkably uniform. Automobile windowglass has fallen into a similar pattern of uniformity. At this writing it is not safe to depend upon discrimination among such mass-produced items by the employment of conventional methods without making a considerable study to determine how much variation is to be expected among samples of a particular type of glass object.

At the same time, many objects are still made by small batch methods and, in addition, there is some unavoidable variation in raw material specifications, so that the methods that have long been so valuable in the crime laboratory have not suddenly been rendered obsolete. Rather, they must be used with far more caution than formerly. Also, discrimination between fragments from different types of glass is still very simple, and the criminalist and police investigator will encounter a great many glass samples broken from objects that were made before the era of high compositional control.

STRENGTH OF GLASS

An understanding of the behavior of glass under stress is of particular importance to the criminalist in the investigation of accidents, and may occasionally be serviceable in the reconstruction of a crime. *The strength of glass resides largely in the surface.* For this reason a submicroscopic crack in the surface layer will spread under stress and ultimately break the entire glass object. A bundle of fine glass threads is much stronger than a solid piece of the same cross-sectional area. Tensile strengths of glass are variously reported as about

8,000–12,000 psi (pounds per square inch), with wide deviations from this value range under special circumstances. This very high value is not in obvious accord with the common phenomenon of the bursting of glass bottles under relatively slight pressures, and the apparently spontaneous breaking that is occasionally observed in old glass. Strengths up to 100,000 psi may be achieved in glass that is free of surface cracks.

The surface condition of a glass object is most critical in determining the strength of the object. Every glass break is a failure under tension; the break always follows a bending away from the applied force, and the opposite side of the glass, being under tension, is the point at which the break starts. The lever action that accompanies the bending thrust applies a tremendous force to a very small part of the cross-sectional area.

Freshly made glass objects possess much greater tensile strength than do old glass objects. Erosion and alteration of the surface are undoubtedly responsible for this difference. Alkaline solutions are especially destructive to glass because they dissolve the surface layers and react differentially upon the various constituents of the glass, removing chiefly the silica. Acids have little effect on most glasses, though some types of glass are much more rapidly affected by them than are others. The strength of some glass is actually increased by treatment with acid. When glass breaks without any strong or sudden force being applied, it is almost certain that the surface of the glass has been damaged, slightly cracked, or eroded. Heat strains may also produce this effect. Thorough discussions of these effects are to be found in publications on glass technology.

Safety Glass

Virtually all automobile glass is *safety glass*. So also is glass used for a number of other purposes, chiefly in construction. Safety glasses are of two general types, each of which has several modifications. The first is *laminated* glass, in which two relatively thin sheets of glass are sandwiched together with an intermediate sheet of plastic, usually polyvinyl chloride. Such glass has long been used for windshields, and remains preeminent for this purpose. Laminated glass is somewhat stronger than other glass of the same thickness, being more flexible because of its layered structure. More important, when laminated glass is broken, the fragments, which would otherwise constitute a very serious hazard, tend to remain attached to the plastic layer, thus reducing the likelihood of serious injury to the occupants of the car. The principles that apply to the breakage of single sheets of glass are applicable to laminated glass also.

Tempered glass is a second type of safety glass that is now rapidly increasing in use. This safety glass is made in single sheets, but the surfaces are chilled rapidly at a particular point in the cooling so that heavy compressive stresses are produced in each surface of the sheet. A sheet of glass made in this manner is much stronger than a comparable sheet of untempered glass. In addition, when tempered glass is broken it either forms small squares or "dicing," without the sharp tapered edges that characterize ordinary glass, or it may be reduced almost to a powder. The increased strength of this glass will prevent many fractures that would otherwise occur, and when it is broken and pieces of glass are thrown, they are not likely to inflict serious cuts. It is obvious that the principles that govern the mode of fracturing ordinary glass do not apply to tempered glass. It should be added that other manufacturing methods, including ion-exchange treatment, are sometimes used instead of temperature control to produce similar tempering effects in safety glass.

Glass Fiber

As has been noted above, glass has a high tensile strength that resides primarily in its surfaces. When glass is drawn into the form of fine fibers, the strength per unit of cross-sectional area is greatly increased. Because it is relatively cheap and a poor conductor of heat and electricity, glass fiber is used as an insulator. It is employed in chemical laboratories for various purposes, and it is woven into fabrics that are durable, fireproof, and sunproof. Because of its lightness and great strength it is embedded in plastics as a reinforcing material. Fiberglass sheets are used extensively in building construction, for automobile bodies, for tires, and even for bulletproof armor. At present glass fiber is an unlikely type of physical evidence, but it may be encountered occasionally, and when it is relevant the investigator should collect it as he would any other kind of evidence.

INVESTIGATION INVOLVING GLASS

The investigator will encounter ordinary glass as evidence very frequently. Windows, automobile glass, broken bottles, and other glass objects figure in burglaries, murders, assaults, and in many other types of crime.

When a criminal breaks a window, he will invariably collect minute pieces of glass in his clothing, particularly in his pants cuffs, breast pockets, and, to a lesser extent, on the surface of the cloth. The reason for this is discussed in the section of this chapter on glass fracture. Such fragments are ordinarily quite minute and may be removed with the vacuum sweeper. The occasional larger fragments should be collected carefully.

The remainder of any broken glass object found at the scene a of a crime should be collected in its entirety if it is not too large. At least the portions adjacent to the actual break are of critical importance in the examination, and must not be overlooked or lost. The examination of properly collected glass may be expected to determine the validity of the following possibilities:

(1) A large fragment may sometimes be stated to have come from a particular glass object that has been broken.
(2) A fragment may be stated to have come from a particular region or spot in the original broken object.
(3) A fragment may be stated to have come from a particular kind of broken glass object, e.g., a spectacle lens, or a windowpane.
(4) The origin of a fracture, its direction, and the direction of the force that produced it may be traced from the larger glass fragments.
(5) The order of occurrence of multiple fractures may sometimes be determined.
(6) A minute fragment may often be stated with a high degree of probability to have come from a particular broken glass object, or it may be definitely determined that it did not come from that object.

There are few types of evidence that can be subjected to such numerous and accurate studies as are applicable to glass fractures and glass fragments. Furthermore, the techniques used in studying glass are relatively rapid and simple. For these reasons the alert investigator will never overlook the glass that occurs in evidence; and it will rate very high in his priority list of items to be examined.

GLASS FRACTURES

When a force is applied to a sheet of glass, the latter bends in the direction of the force, so that the side to which the force is applied is subjected to com-

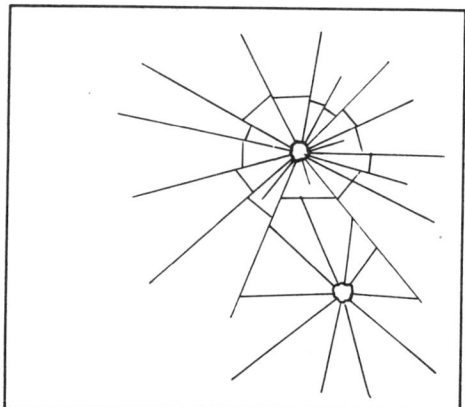

FIGURE 22-1. Multiple glass fractures, showing radial and cross fractures, illustrating effect of first fracture in stopping cracks of second fracture.

pression and the opposite side is put under tension. The fracture starts when this tension is sufficient to pull the glass apart and start a crack. When this occurs, shearing forces are set up along the crack; they cause spreading in a series of conchoidal (shell-shaped) fractures that leave the broken surfaces marked with typical curved striations. Often a hemispherical piece of glass is broken out of the sheet on the side opposite the blow, even when the missile, or other instrument, does not penetrate the glass. When a bullet strikes a glass sheet at high velocity, a more or less circular piece is removed, the exit side of the hole being larger than the entrance. Careful examination may also show that a piece smaller in diameter than the bullet was expelled first, the entering bullet effecting a secondary reaming of the hole.

When a missile breaks a piece of ordinary glass, the resulting cracks radiate in a more or less star-shaped pattern from the point at which the break started. If larger pieces of glass fall out, they will have broken across the sectors between the radiating cracks, forming triangular pieces, two sides of which are the original cracks, the third a secondary cross break. At times two or more bullets have penetrated a single window or windshield. In such instances it is possible to determine the angle of approach of each bullet and the order of their penetration. Where the star-shaped radiating cracks of the second break meet those of the first, the second break terminates.

A sheet of glass rarely breaks squarely across at right angles to its surfaces. If a piece of glass is broken from a larger piece, the sharp edge remaining on the larger piece will normally be on the side to which the force was applied. The reverse will be true of the fragment broken off. In addition to this edge effect, the conchoidal striations along the broken edge indicate the lines of strain. *The direction of the break will be in the line approximately perpendicular to these striations, progressing from the concave to the convex side.* Study of these striations will usually indicate both the side on which the break advanced first and the direction of the advance. This also indicates the direction of the breaking force, as the break starts on the side opposite to the place at which the force was applied, and advances on that side also. If a considerable number of the fragments broken from a piece of glass are available, a very detailed and accurate analysis of the fracture may be made.

Backward Fragmentation

When a sheet of glass is broken, not only is tension produced opposite to the point of application of the force, but a corresponding compression is produced at the point of application. This compression follows all the cracks produced on the concave side of the bent glass. As the crack forms, the contact surface is diminished to a thin line along the side of the broken edge upon which all of the compression is exerted. This commonly causes chipping of the edges on

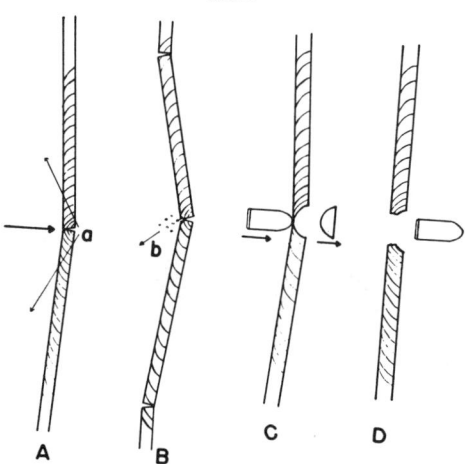

FIGURE 22-2. Principle of glass fracture: (A) method of fracture caused by force applied at a point showing conchoidal striae on radial edges; (B) later stage showing back-scattering of fragments from the near edge under compression; (C) action of bullet on thick glass; (D) final reaming of the bullet hole.

that side. When chips break loose, they fly with considerable force because of the relatively great compression. Thus, while most of the broken glass travels in the direction of the applied force, many fine chips are thrown in the opposite direction. It is these chips that bombard the clothing of the burglar who has broken the window. Their small size prevents notice of their impact. Unless they strike an eye or cut the skin, the person who has broken the glass is unaware of their presence. Often they are forced into the fabric of the person's clothing and adhere for a considerable time. This is the source of most of the glass fragments available to the criminal investigator from the clothing of the suspect.

Large-Fragment Matches

The most conclusive evidence of the source of a piece of broken glass is an exact fit with a broken edge of the original glass. If a piece of glass retrieved from the scene of an automobile accident is to be compared with the remains of a broken headlight, it is first necessary to search carefully for any broken edges that match exactly some part of the edges of the questioned fragment. No two broken edges will match perfectly over any extended length. If an edge match that extends over a reasonable length, e.g., a quarter inch or more, can be found, it is virtual proof that the questioned fragment was broken from

FIGURE 22-3. (A) Typical conchoidal fracture markings on a broken glass surface. (B) Hackle marks perpendicular to the curved conchoidal markings. (Courtesy of Stephen P. McJunkins.)

that exact spot in the original, intact glass. The validity of an edge match is dependent upon probability. The factors contributing to the probability will be (1) the thickness of the glass and variations in thickness; (2) the color and general appearance of the glass; (3) the shape of the break, e.g., straight or curved; and (4) all irregularities and striations on the broken surfaces. Because there are usually a great many irregularities and striations, there will be a comparatively high probability associated even with shortest edge matches. Naturally, the probability becomes greater as the length of the edge match is increased.

Determination of the presence of an exact match is not always simple. Usually when the pieces match exactly, it is not possible to *see* that they do, and more reliance must be placed on the sense of touch. With gentle manipulation the feel of the fit is very convincing. If the pieces fit accurately, all of the small irregularities of the broken surfaces intermesh and hold the pieces together when lateral pressure is applied. Somewhat imperfect matching of pointed corners is of less significance; in fact they are often so chipped as to

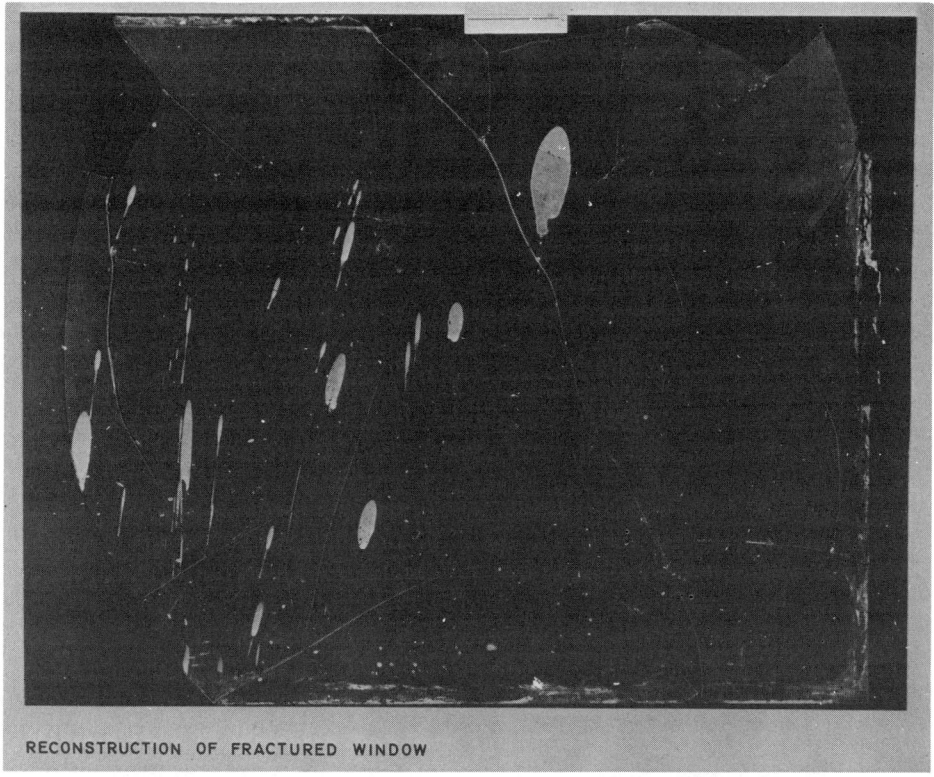

FIGURE 22-4. The reconstruction of a fractured window can aid in determining the location of the breaking force as well as from which side of the glass the force was applied. (Courtesy of Duayne J. Dillon.)

give no appearance of matching at all. Unfortunately, it is only occasionally possible to use the matched-break method because the glass fragments recovered are often much too small. In such cases the comparison must rest upon the properties of the glass itself, rather than upon the broken edges.

Glass which has been formed into special shapes, such as headlight lenses, often permits comparisons not possible with flat glass or smooth glass bottles. If there is a pattern cast into the glass, it may be possible to match the broken edges of the pattern independently of the edge matches. This will not provide proof of identity of origin, but it may establish identity of type, which is very valuable information. The probability that identity of type will be indicative of identity of origin will be equal to the number of such glass articles in use divided by the number of similar glass articles having a different pattern or no pattern at all.

Dimensions of Glass Fragments

In establishing the probable source of a glass fragment it is often helpful to examine it for dimensions and shape such as thickness and curvature. For example, a fragment from a broken windowpane will have flat sides, which are roughly parallel. On the larger fragments of such a glass both sides of the original pane will be represented. A mechanical micrometer may be used to obtain very accurate measurements of the thickness of the fragment and that of the suspected original pane. It must be borne in mind that windowglass is often not of uniform thickness. Measurements must be made all around the broken region of the pane to determine whether or not the questioned fragment matches any portion of the broken standard. Sometimes it is possible, by this means, to determine the exact portion of the broken pane of glass that contributed a specific fragment. However, there must be additional proof that the fragment came from that pane of glass before so precise a claim can be made.

Frequently a glass fragment that shows both original faces is not flat, but curved. The origin of such a fragment is probably a watch crystal or an eyeglass or other lens. The watch crystal will usually be of uniform thickness; that is, the two curved surfaces are parallel to each other. A lens, on the other hand, will be variable in thickness. This difference will ordinarily serve to distinguish the two. If the fragment has come from the outside edge of a lens or crystal, the curvature of the ground edge should also be measured and compared with the curvature of standard similar crystals or lenses.

A hit-and-run victim had his eyeglasses knocked off and one lens broken. A fragment of glass retrieved from the street could easily be shown to be part of the broken lens, by means of comparison. The position of the fragment on the street served to determine the victim's approximate location at the time of being struck, which was the point at issue in court. Thus, the identification of the lens fragment was secondary but essential to the determination of a related question.

Glass Bottle Failures

Glass bottles, and other glass objects such as ovenware, sometimes fail in service and injure the user. Such matters are rarely of criminal concern, but they are a frequent source of litigation in the civil courts. The criminalist who studies glass fracture should also be knowledgeable about this somewhat more complex matter.

A common cause of the failure of a bottle—a beverage bottle, for example, in which the content is under excess gas pressure from carbonation—is a blow to the outside of the bottle due to careless handling or accident. Another not infrequent cause of such failure is weakness of the glass attributable to blemishes or to corrosion from overuse, either of which lowers the strength of the glass to a point at which it is unable to contain the pressurized liquid. The choice between these two alternatives becomes the basis for the determination of liability.

Tests of many beverage bottles show that the bursting strength of most bottles picked up at random ranges from less than 100 psi to over 600 psi. The pressures existing in most bottled carbonated beverages is of the order of 40 psi, but varies considerably from this value. Champagne tends to record higher pressures than are characteristic of most carbonated beverages, commonly running as high as 90–100 psi. Correspondingly, champagne bottles are usually heavier than bottles in which the carbonated beverages are marketed, although they are not always of better quality. Hence it is only the grossly defective bottle that will fail under the usual rather low pressure unless there are external factors, such as overheating, which may raise the pressure considerably. It is known from experience that numerous undisturbed bottles suddenly "explode," and it is also a fact that pre-pressuring bottles on the bottling line in the plant causes many failures before any liquid is added. Thus, either type of failure is reasonably common, and to be expected.

Most such breaks are readily interpreted, though an occasional one is quite difficult. The fracture pattern of an overpressured bottle is likely to include a vertical split along the wall with cracks spreading in a fan shape at both top and bottom. The bottom of the bottle will usually become detached by the extension of the lower cracks. When the bottle has been struck a blow sufficient to cause failure, the characteristic star-shaped pattern will usually be present, but it will be modified by the more-or-less cylindrical shape of the bottle. Conchoidal markings at the point of the application of force will show that the force was exerted from the exterior, but they will usually reverse their direction within a short distance because the force that produced the cracking is rapidly shifted to the pressure within the bottle. Many complications are encountered, and a very careful study of both the total pattern and the fracture surfaces is necessary in all cases. It is also essential that a reasonably large portion of the total bottle be recovered for examination.

GLASS IDENTITY FROM PHYSICAL PROPERTIES

It was shown earlier that glass is actually far from a uniform material, even when the samples under examination have come from a single charge of a glass crucible. The chemical variations observable in different pieces of glass, and even in different portions of the same piece of glass, are reflected as differences in their physical properties. In fact, the physical properties are much more sensitive indicators of such differences than is chemical analysis. This stems from the fact that chemical analysis of glass is subject to small and variable but ever-present errors that obscure small differences in composition. The physical properties, on the other hand, are vastly simpler to measure; the techniques are much more precise and do not destroy the glass.

The properties most useful in glass comparisons are *density* (or specific gravity), *refractive index,* and *dispersion.* Fluorescence, color, hardness, melting range, and other properties may be useful at times. Morris distinguished each of sixty-five glass samples from each other by specific gravity, refractive index, and fluorescence measurements. Gamble, Burd, and Kirk, using more refined techniques of measurement, were able to distinguish each of 100 samples of glass from each other by the use of specific gravity and refractive index alone. The two properties are roughly proportional to each other, but so much individual variation exists that no two points fall in exactly the same position. This permitted each of the 100 samples to be distinguished from the others. Roche and Kirk simplified the technique and studied fifty samples of similar brown bottles, mostly beer bottles, which might be expected to be very much more alike than would, for instance, a windowpane and/or eyeglass lens. Most of the samples could be quickly distinguished by a comparative density method, and all but two of the samples that could not be distinguished in this

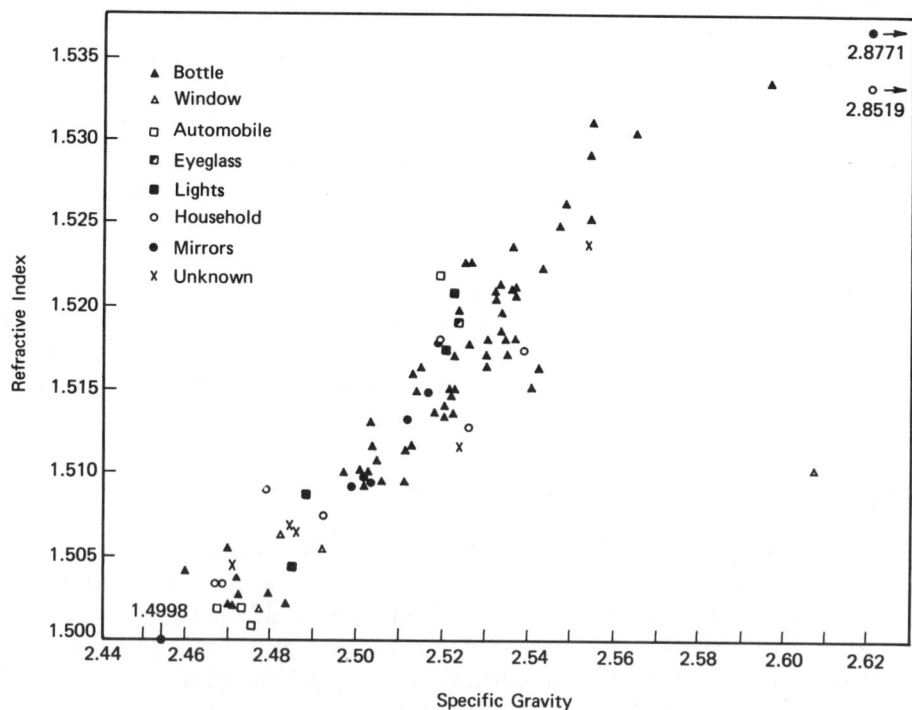

FIGURE 22-5. Refractive index and specific gravity of one hundred miscellaneous glass samples. (J. Crim. Law & Criminol., 33:416, 1943.)

way were separated on the basis of differences in their refractive indexes. Thus it appears that the probability of the two beer bottles being identical with respect to the composition of the glass is about 1 in 25. Burd and Green obtained identical results in the study of fifty headlight lenses. In a study of fifty samples of Lucas 700 Headlamp glass fragments, Nelson was able to distinguish all of the fragments from each other. He compared other physical properties in addition to those employed in either of the prior studies. It is evident that physical properties are of the greatest value in distinguishing glass fragments derived from different sources. However, sufficient study has not yet been devoted to the complete evaluation of the credibility of fragment matching. Changes in manufacturing processes inevitably alter the possibilities of glass comparisons. This effect is of particular importance in the study of automobile glass. There is a pressing need for an extensive and continuing study of glass-fragment-identification methods.

Simple techniques have been effective in the solution of a number of crimes. In the leather soles of a pair of shoes belonging to a burglary suspect were embedded four minute fragments of brown glass. On a ladder used to gain access to the premises were located two brown glass fragments embedded in the wood. One large brown-glass fragment was found beside the safe that had been rifled. By use of the density method alone, the four fragments from the shoes were shown to have four separate origins. The two pieces on the ladder were also different, but one of them was identical with one from the shoes. The glass by the safe was different from all the other samples. The two samples that matched in density were also identical in refractive index. This identity was one link in the chain of physical evidence that led to the conviction of the burglars.

A glass fragment in a glove was shown to be identical with the glass of a broken automobile window that had been fractured by a pistol in the initial act of a kidnapping, rape, and robbery. The glove was taken from one of two suspects who were subsequently sentenced to life imprisonment for the crime. In many instances glass on clothing, glass on shoes, in pants cuffs, and elsewhere has presented strong evidence of the guilt of suspected individuals. Usually, such glass is examined with some idea of a specific crime in mind and a comparison is made between the evidence, or suspect, fragments and the known glass remaining at the scene of the crime or within the headlamp housing of a motor vehicle. It is possible, however, to predict the probable usage of any glass fragment if it is properly characterized. This was demonstrated by MacDonell in his study of the relationship between properties and application of glass.

OTHER PHYSICAL PROPERTIES. It has been shown that *fluorescence* under ultraviolet illumination is useful in determining identity of composition in glass fragments, or the lack of such identity. This discrimination results from the presence of certain constituents that impart a particular type and degree of fluorescence to the glass. Although on occasion fluorescence may be found very useful in distinguishing between two glasses, it is neither so sensitive nor so reliable as the density or the refractive index for this purpose.

In the examination of glass under ultraviolet illumination to confirm an identity, fragments of similar size should be used. Any variation in composition that would alter the fluorescence of glass would be expected to alter the refractive index also, and probably the density as well. If definite differences that are not attributable to difference in sample size are observed in fluorescence, a different source is indicated. Before this conclusion is reached, the glass fragments must be thoroughly washed in acetone, or other proper solvents, to make sure that grease or other foreign material on one of the pieces is not causing the difference in the response. Washing with water may also be necessary for the removal of contaminants insoluble in organic solvents. In any case, the glass samples must be very clean before any conclusions may be based upon their fluorescence.

Another property that has gained increasing importance in recent years is *dispersion*. Glasses that have the same refractive index at some specific wavelength often show a difference in their refractive indices toward other wavelengths of light. Thus, a glass with a high dispersion separates the indices of different wavelengths of light more than does one of lower dispersion. Since the advent of the technique of *dispersion staining* this property has been available for use on a routine basis. Dispersion, like the other physical properties of glass, is directly related to the chemical composition. Any method that will discriminate between glasses of slightly different composition is useful. Dispersion of lenses and prisms is readily measured. Lens systems are designed on the basis of both dispersion and refractive index. Such measurements were not applicable to small fragments of glass until a suitable technique was developed.

Other physical properties that can add to the decisiveness of a claimed identity or difference between glass fragments are *color* and *hardness*. Although color is employed routinely in the preliminary sorting of a mixture of glass fragments, color and hardness are useful in definitive examination of glass in only a limited number of specific instances.

CHEMICAL AND SPECTROGRAPHIC ANALYSIS

CHEMICAL ANALYSIS. As a means of proving identity of glass samples, chemical analysis is virtually worthless. The error in an analysis, though small, may be considerably greater than the small random deviations that occur in glass manufacture. Relatively large differences, such as those that result from different formulas and possibly from different batches, can, of course, be detected. However, the processes involved in the chemical analysis of glass are so complex and difficult that no well-informed investigator would be expected to consider them. The relatively simple comparison of the physical properties of glass samples yields more information of considerably greater discriminatory value.

SPECTROGRAPHIC ANALYSIS. This technique may be used to advantage in determining the identity or nonidentity of glass samples. When made under the same conditions, the spectra of two glass fragments from the same original source are identical. The spectral identity is readily demonstrated to a jury. It is the quantity of the *minor* constituents and contaminants of the glass that are the most significant. Glass ordinarily contains so much sodium, potassium, calcium, and silicon that any difference in the spectral lines for these major constituents is difficult to detect. Trace constituents such as iron, zinc, aluminum, manganese, arsenic, copper, and other elements may be present or absent, and will vary considerably in concentration. Ordinarily the trace constituents will have only a small effect on the physical properties of the glass. Differences in the trace constituents will result from exactly the same factors that affect the composition of the glass with respect to the major constituents. Thus, the spectrographic and physical methods are about equally valuable. In such tests as have been made, no exceptions have been found to the generalization that glasses found to be identical or different by one method have given the same results with the other.

NEUTRON ACTIVATION ANALYSIS. Only partially investigated as a means of comparing glass fragments, this method detects numerous trace elements with more sensitivity than does the spectrograph, and may prove to be of considerable utility in specific instances. The investigations that have been made to date are somewhat less than complete, and there is still some doubt as to the ultimate usefulness of the results.

A complete examination to prove that two glass samples are of identical chemical composition might include comparison of both the physical properties and of the trace elements as determined either by emission spectrography or by neutron activation analysis. However, the cost for equipment and time are so disproportionate between the sophisticated instrumental methods and the simple comparison of physical properties that the omission of the instrumental procedures is usually logical and often necessary. The fact that emission spectroscopy is destructive of the sample is also a deterrent to its general use in crime investigation.

REFERENCES

Cobb, P. G. W.: "A Survey of the Variations of the Physical Properties of Glass," *J. For. Sci. Soc.* 8:71 (1968).

Dabbs, M. D. G.: "Density Distribution of Two Glass Populations," *J. For. Sci Soc.* 8:71 (1968).

Davis, J. E.: "Refractive Index Determinations of Glass Fragments—A Simplified Procedure," *J. Crim. Law and Criminol.* 47:380 (1956).

Gamble, L. H., Burd, D. Q., and Kirk, P. L.: "Glass Fragments as Evidence: A Comparative Study of Physical Properties," *J. Crim. Law and Criminol.* 33:416 (1943).

Grabar, D. G., and Principe, A. H.: "Identification of Glass Fragments by Measurement of Refractive Index and Dispersion," *J. For. Sci.* 8:54 (1963).

Kind, S. S., and Summerscales, L.: "Determination of Specific Gravity of Glass Particles by a Density Gradient Method," *Analyst* 91(1087):669 (1966).

Kirk, P. L.: *Density and Refractive Index: Their Application in Criminal Identification.* Springfield: Thomas (1951).

MacDonell, H. L.: "Identification of Glass Fragments," *J. For. Sci.* 9:244 (1964).

McJunkins, S. P., and Thornton, J. I.: "Glass Fracture Analysis—A Review," *For. Sci.* 2:1 (1973).

Nelson, D. F.: "Illustrating the Fit of Glass Fragments," *J. Crim. Law and Criminol.* 50:312 (1959).

Nelson, D. F.: "The Identification of Lucas 700 Headlamp-Glass Fragments by Their Physical Properties," *Analyst* 84:388 (1959).

Ojena, S. M., and DeForest, P. R.: "A Study of the Refractive Index Variations Within and Between Sealed Beam Headlights Using a Precise Method," *J. For. Sci.* 17:409 (1972).

Ojena, S. M., and DeForest, P. R.: "Precise Refractive-Index Determination by the Immersion Method, Using Phase-Contrast Microscopy and the Mettler Hot Stage," *J. For. Sci. Soc.* 12:315 (1972).

Pearson, E. F., May, R. W., and Dabbs, M. D. G.: "Glass and Paint Fragments Found in Men's Outer Clothing—Report of a Survey," *J. For. Sci.* 16:283 (1971).

Pye, L. D., ed.: *Introduction to Glass Science.* New York: Plenum (1972).

Roche, G. W., and Kirk, P. L.: "Applications of Microchemical Techniques—Differentiation of Similar Glass Fragments by Physical Properties," *J. Crim. Law and Criminol.* 38:168 (1947).

Tryhorn, F. G.: "The Examination of Glass," *J. Crim. Law and Criminol.* 30:404 (1939–1940).

23
Soil

It is not unusual to find on shoes or in pants cuffs small adherent particles of soil that were originally deposited as mud. In this form, soil may be one of the most useful of all types of physical evidence. People avoid stepping in mud when possible, but under certain circumstances the muddying of shoes and clothing is a normal occurrence. A gardener, a farmer, or a construction laborer would be expected to carry mud on his shoes more or less habitually. The ordinary criminal is not likely to step in mud except when his depredations take him off the pavements that are his customary habitat.

Soil is usually found on the bottoms of shoes, to a lesser extent on the sides of the soles and heels, and occasionally on the uppers as well. When a person is thrown to the ground during a struggle, mud may be collected on the stockings or socks, the pants legs, and even on the upper garments. When such deposits of soil are found, they are to be removed carefully to clean, individual containers. Special care must be exercised to ensure that each sample contains soil deposited at one time only, and that the label indicates the part of the clothing from which the sample was obtained. Completely different origins have been proved for soil masses found adhering to two places on the same shoe sole. Had the samples been mixed, both of them would have been rendered useless as evidence.

Soil is useful as evidence precisely to the extent that it can be employed to determine whether or not a person has been at a certain place. This will be possible only to the extent that the soils at different locations differ in some detectable way. It might be expected that the soil at two different locations would differ to some degree, but only careful experiment will determine whether the existing differences are sufficient for detection. Present indications are that it will be a rare phenomenon when soils from two different places are indistinguishable. In fact, differences of composition are often perceived in soil samples obtained from locations separated by only a few feet, or even inches. Among the limited number of soils studied to date, no two have been found to be identical except those taken from within a very few feet of one another. Whether or not this is universally true has not been proved, but the probability of nonidentity in soil samples is certainly very high.

The great variability of soil gives rise to some serious problems of sampling, and because of these difficulties there are two schools of thought as to the utilization of soil as evidence. One point of view is that there are a great many different classes of soil, and that in a particular locality these are often multiple. Persons with this point of view limit their work to the determination of the soil class and its use in conjunction with detailed soil maps and mineralogical study. Even though this approach is solid and conservative, the results have only an eliminative value, which may be quite low. The other point of view involves the effort to obtain, for purposes of comparison, a sample of the soil from the exact spot, if possible, from which it is believed the questioned soil may have come. This sampling problem can be very difficult, and is sometimes insurmountable. On the other hand, in a large number of instances it is quite feasible. For example, the spot at which a girl is raped or a person is murdered may be known, and there may be mud there or close by. Footprints can be seen in mud, and if a shoe that is suspected of having made such prints is located, it is simple to obtain soil from the prints for comparison. Although the sampling is critical in this instance, it is basically the same as with most other types of physical evidence in which the collection of materials of known source for comparison is often the most critical single operation.

Very frequently the point of origin of a soil sample that is significant as evidence cannot be precisely determined. Under these circumstances, the more general approach is uniquely valuable. An unusual soil type may sometimes be characteristic of a rather restricted area. The finding of such soil on the shoes of a suspect may be highly significant if the bearer had no legitimate purpose in visiting in the locality in question.

SOIL FORMATION

In order to appreciate the wide variations observable in the composition of soil it is necessary to understand something of the soil-forming processes. Soil results from the disintegration and decay of rock. The diurnal and seasonal temperature variations cause alternate expansion and contraction of the surface layers of the rock. The resulting minute cracks in the rocky surface form channels that are widened by falling rain and further widened and deepened by the expansion of trapped water during freezing weather, a process known as "frost wedging." Winds carry small sand particles, which etch the rock, and the spores of minute plants lodge in the crevices, expand with absorbed water, grow and multiply, etching the rock still further with the weak acids characteristic of their kind. In due season the original crop of plants will die, and the decay of their structures will begin the process of humus formation. Even if the original rock was granite, given enough time the work of wind, water, and primitive plants will reduce its constituents to sand, clay, and silt. These, along with the humus derived from the plants that have contributed to the slow disintegration, form soil.

Loose soil is moved by wind, water, gravity, animals, and man, so that one can very seldom trace the history of a particular soil backward to a specific kind of rock. Around human habitations the mixing of soil is greatly accelerated by man's activities. Excavations are made, the soil is cultivated and fertilized, refuse is dumped, and earth is moved from place to place.

The rocks from which soils are formed are of many kinds, as may be seen by the examination of exposed rock strata. Some kinds of rock decay much more rapidly than others. For example, under some climatic conditions rocks containing significant quantities of calcium carbonate are disintegrated by the alteration of this constituent to calcium bicarbonate, which is soluble. This reaction accounts for the formation of limestone caves, and its reverse accounts for the refilling of such caves with limestone columns. Conglomerate rocks that contain rapidly decaying constituents give rise to rocky or gravelly soil. Uniform, rapidly decaying rocks yield rather fine soil, usually with a high clay content.

The common mineral constituents of soil are silica, calcite or limestone, numerous silicoaluminates, and smaller amounts of mica, hornblende, various oxides of iron, and hundreds of other possible insolubles. Soil cannot be considered as an entirely inorganic, inert, dead material. In addition to the mineral components that have originated from rock disintegration, there will often be a considerable amount of decomposed organic material known collectively as *humus*. This is one of the most variable constituents of soil, and is therefore of unique value in the fine differentiation of similar soil samples. Soil can be considered as possessing, in an inorganic matrix, a complex biochemical system involving microorganisms, enzymes, porphyrins, and other materials, all of which constitute a very highly stylized ecosystem. The full potential of the biochemical aspects of soil comparison has not yet been recognized.

VARIABILITY OF SOIL

In Table 23–1 the most common components of soil are listed with their densities. The densities of soil constituents furnish the basis for accurate com-

TABLE 23–1 Chief Constituents of Soil*

Substance	Formula	Density
quartz		
opal	$SiO_2 \cdot n\ H_2O$	1.9–2.3
tripolite	$SiO_2 \cdot n\ H_2O$	2.1–2.3
jasper	SiO_2	2.6
quartz	SiO_2	2.6
feldspars		
orthoclase	$KAlSi_3O_8$	2.4–2.6
microcline	$KAlSi_3O_8$	2.5
albite	$NaAlSi_3O_8$	2.6
oligoclase	$NaAlSi_3O_8 + CaAl_2Si_2O_8$	2.6
labradorite	$NaAlSi_3O_8 + CaAl_2Si_2O_8$	2.7
anorthite	$CaAl_2Si_2O_8$	2.7
micas		
muscovite	$H_2KAl_3(SiO_4)_3$	2.7–3.0
lepidolite	$K_2Li_3Al_3(Si_3AlO_{10})_2(OH,F)_4$	2.9
biotite	$K(Mg,Fe)_3Si_3AlO_{10}(OH)_2$	2.7–3.1
hornblende	$Ca_2Na_{0-1}(Mg,Fe)_4(Al,Fe)(Si,Al)_8O_{22}(OH)_2$	2.9–3.4
augite	$Ca(Mg,Fe,Al)(Si,Al)_2O_6$	3.3
gypsum	$CaSO_4 \cdot 2\ H_2O$	2.3
talc	$H_2Mg_2(SiO_3)_4$	2.8
kaolinite (clay)	$H_4Al_2Si_2O_9$	2.6
limonite	$Fe_2O_3 \cdot n\ H_2O$	3.6
serpentine	$H_4Mg_3Si_2O_9$	2.6
magnetite	Fe_3O_4	5.2
calcite	$CaCO_3$	2.7
dolomite	$CaMg(CO_3)_2$	2.9
hematite	Fe_2O_3	5.0

* Reproduced from Goin and Kirk: *J. Crim. Law and Criminol.* 38:267 (1947).

parison of soil samples. Besides the considerable complexity of the mineral constituents, which is partially apparent in the table, the miscellaneous organic constituents contribute a great deal more variation. Because the accumulation of plant and animal residues is often quite highly localized, the organic materials vary greatly in samples taken from points located quite close together. Agricultural cultivation, with its demand for high yield, accounts for additional variation.

Soil samples taken from underneath five windows of the same city residence were studied, and each sample was found to be distinguishable from every other. Two of the samples were very similar to each other, and the other three were also quite similar to each other but were markedly different from the first two. Six samples of soil taken from a shallow grave, which was roughly 2 × 4 ft in area, were also studied. All six samples were distinguishable, although five of the samples were similar. One sample was markedly different from the other five. An unknown soil sample suspected of having come from the same grave was less different from the five similar soil samples than they were from each other. It was markedly different from eight comparison soil samples taken at distances varying from a few feet up to 10 miles away from the site of the grave. In another comparison that was made, soil from a victim's stocking was shown to be identical with soil from a suspect's shoe, and closely similar to soil from the scene of the crime. These samples were markedly different from all but one of several other samples taken in the neighborhood of the crime scene.

COLLECTION OF SOIL SAMPLES

The method employed in studying soil variations is so sensitive that the limiting factor in its application seems to be the reliability of the sampling. Thus, if mud on a suspect's shoe were compared with that from the footprint, they would be found identical; but if the comparison sample were taken at a distance of a foot or more from the footprint, the variation might be too great to permit the establishment of identity. In collecting soil for comparison it is essential that the samples be taken with the greatest care, or else that a considerable number of samples be taken, so that the variability of the soil in the immediate neighborhood of the crime may be established. The samples taken need not be large, though the larger the soil sample the more representative it will be. The questioned soil will usually be very small in amount, and this will limit the amount of comparison soil that is applicable. It may, in turn, be only a small part of a larger representative sample. A handful is an appropriate size sample to take. Shell vials, properly labeled, are suitable containers for collecting and preserving soil samples.

Color, besides being one of the most obvious characteristics of soil, is one of the best factors by which soils may be distinguished from each other, and one of the most rapidly applied. The gross color of coarse soil can be reliably compared by crushing the material and sifting it through a 100-mesh sieve and comparing the powder so obtained. This operation may be omitted when color differences are distinct.

DENSITY DISTRIBUTION OF SOIL

Density distribution is the preferred method for the comparison of soils. It is suitable for the study of very small amounts of soil such as may be collected from mud adhering to shoes or clothing. The method is comparatively rapid and highly sensitive.

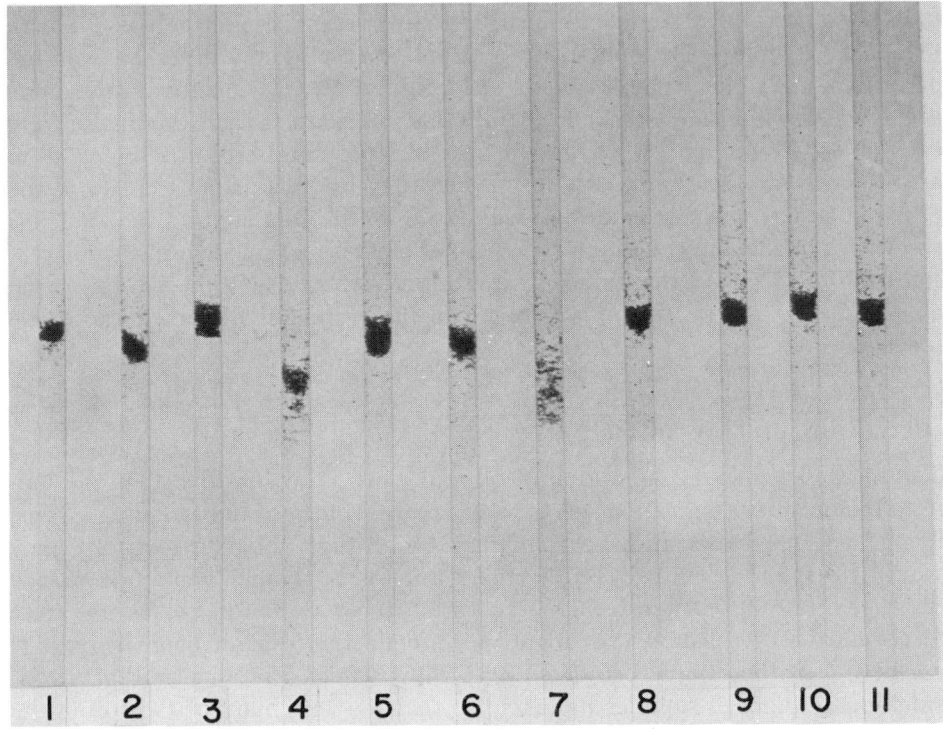

FIGURE 23-1. Soil comparisons by the density gradient tube method reveal similarities in soil samples based upon the differences in the density of the particulate material within the sample. The method is interpreted by comparing the patterns established by the soils in the gradients. The origins of the soil samples are listed below. Marked agreement is noted in the patterns developed by samples 8, 9, 10, and 11.

1. South side of victim's home.
2. Other yard in victim's neighborhood.
3. Victim's yard 50 ft. east of house.
4. Driveway of victim's home.
5. East side of victim's home.
6. Other yard in victim's neighborhood.
7. Area adjacent to front door of victim's home.
8. Same location as No. 1.
9. Blanket in victim's bedroom.
10. Bedspread in victim's bedroom.
11. Suspect's trousers.

(Courtesy of Duayne J. Dillon.)

A narrow glass tube of suitable size is sealed at the bottom and supported firmly in a vertical position. To it are added, by careful pipette technique, several successive layers of different liquids arranged in order of decreasing density. The soil sample is placed on the meniscus at the top of the liquid column. Each soil particle will descend through the liquid until it reaches the portion of the gradient in which it is exactly balanced. Specially prepared weighed samples of soil must be used, for otherwise the observed differences would not represent actual variations in soil composition.

On standing, a continuous density gradient slowly forms, and the soil becomes redistributed in a sort of density spectrum that is even more characteristic than are the bands that are first formed. Identical soil samples in two tubes give identical appearances both as bands and as final distributions. It is unlikely that soils taken from different locations have ever given completely identical patterns. Even a difference of source amounting to a few inches may result in detectable variations, and distances of feet, yards, or miles are almost certain to produce very marked differences in the density distribution.

CHEMICAL AND SPECTROGRAPHIC ANALYSIS

With soil, as with glass and some other types of refractory materials, it is important that the investigator realize the entire inadequacy of so-called "chemical analysis" as a means of determining identity or difference of soil samples. An adequate wet chemical analysis of a soil requires a large sample, e.g., a quart, and is a very involved and time-consuming operation. Because of the inherent difficulties of chemical operations with the highly insoluble silicates and silicoaluminates in soil, the accuracy of such analyses is not high, and the errors will completely obscure small but significant differences. Even the soil chemist relies largely on physical rather than chemical analysis in his evaluation of soils for agricultural purposes. It is probable that chemical analysis as such will never be of great significance in the examination of soil for criminalistic purposes.

Spectrographic analysis is more effective than chemical analysis in the examination of soil. At times it may be of considerable significance. Clearly, the main elementary constituents of soil that emit specific wavelengths of light (spectral lines), namely silicon, calcium, aluminum, magnesium, iron, sodium, and potassium, may all be present in such large amounts as to contribute little value to the interpretation of the spectrogram. The trace elements, on the other hand, would be of the greatest significance, and could be expected to vary to a considerable extent from one soil sample to another. Several of the elements mentioned in the above list might, in the examination of a specific soil, prove to be present in only trace amounts, notably sodium and potassium, and possibly calcium, magnesium, or iron. The use of trace elements as a means of soil identification is comparable to their use in the identification of paint or metal, in both of which it is the minor constituents that are of the greatest significance in establishing an identity. The most serious limitation of the spectrographic method is the difficulty of obtaining a sufficiently uniform sample and an arc in which representative emission lines are formed. The common technique of dissolving the sample and impregnating a carbon electrode is impractical, and the inhomogeneity of soil would make difficult the cup electrode method. Furthermore, the spectrographic analysis is far more difficult and expensive than the simpler and more decisive density-gradient analysis.

As indicated above, some soil experts depend to a large extent on a complete *mineralogical analysis* of soil. This approach is fundamentally very sound, and if performed by an experienced analyst, it may lend itself to a precise comparison of two samples. Often, however, it is more relevant to the determination of *soil type* than to the individualizing of soil samples.

A newer technique that has been utilized to a limited extent in soil comparison is *neutron activation analysis*. This is comparable to spectrographic analysis except for its greater sensitivity to many of the trace elements and its lower sensitivity to some of the common elements such as iron. This technique holds considerable promise, and it will undoubtedly find increasing use. It is slower and more expensive than spectrography, and the sampling problem is no less acute than it is for all the methods previously mentioned.

Differential thermal analysis offers a completely different approach that is gaining support in some laboratories. This technique is unique in that it is concerned with the transitions of the chemical forms of sample constituents—transitions that tend toward uniqueness in any sample by reason of the very great, if not almost unlimited, variations of which soil is capable.

Much progress has recently been made by space scientists in characterizing soils by instrumental analysis. The interest in extraterrestrial soils has resulted in the development of a soil analysis technology that may prove to be of value to the criminalist in the comparison of evidence soils. The techniques of Mossbauer spectroscopy, photometric and polarimetric phase function, thermoluminescence, pyrolysis–gas chromatography, and the ion microprobe mass analyzer have not yet been applied to the forensic comparison of soils, but show considerable promise.

REFERENCES

Bridges, E. M.: *World Soils.* Cambridge University Press (1970).
Buckman, H., and Brady, N. C.: *The Nature and Properties of Soils,* 7th ed. New York: Macmillan (1969).

Fong, W., and Kirk, P. L.: "Identification of Mineral Materials Other Than Soil by the Density-Gradient Tube," *J. Crim. Law and Criminol.* 42:682 (1952).

Frenkel, O. J.: "A Program for Research into the Value of Evidence from Southern Ontario Soils," *Proc. Can. Soc. For. Sci.* 4:23 (1965).

Goin, L. J., and Kirk, P. L.: "Application of Microchemical Techniques: Identity of Soil Samples," *J. Crim. Law and Criminol.* 38:267 (1947).

Heinrich, E. W.: *Microscopic Identification of Minerals.* New York: McGraw-Hill (1966).

Kirk, P. L.: *Density and Refractive Index: Their Application in Criminal Identification.* Springfield: Thomas (1951).

Neil, M. W., and Warren, F. L., eds.: *Soil.* London: Sweet and Maxwell (1962).

Schatz, W., Saale, A., and Halle, D.: "Dirt Scraped from Shoes as a Means of Identification," *Am. J. Police Sci.* 1:55 (1930).

24
Metals

Most metallic evidence consists of tools and weapons, for which well-standardized techniques of investigation are presented in Chapter 31. It is not unusual, however, to find fine metal chips, filings, drillings, or fragments that have been collected in sweepings or carried on larger items of evidence. These metallic fragments result from both the general use of metal tools and from operations involved in breaking through metallic barriers. Burglars are often confronted with sheet metal linings on the doors of business establishments, or with metal fasteners on windows and doors. Although tool marks left on such metallic surfaces are often susceptible to study, sometimes neither tool marks nor other characteristic markings are found. However, the study of metallic fragments recovered from clothing, automobiles, and other sources, may yield valuable information. Likewise, fragments of bullets too extensively damaged for typical mark comparison may yet provide useful details under close examination of the metal.

BROKEN METAL OBJECTS

The simplest kind of metal examination is not really dependent upon the metallic characteristics of the evidence but is based upon the nature of the rupture of a solid material. The examination involves the matching of broken parts, exactly as has been described for broken glass and other broken solid materials. If one fragment, which has been retrieved from a suspect, can be shown to provide a complete physical match with another broken part found at the scene of a crime, the evidence is conclusive. The fit is established, as described in

Chapter 22, by searching for a region in which the shapes of the broken objects appear similar, and then testing by holding them together in different positions. When a fit is found, the pieces go together completely, and when they are firmly pressed together a lateral pressure will not move them. A proper match, once located, leaves no doubt of its significance in the mind of the observer. Cast iron, which is used in many lock parts, is particularly susceptible to clean breakage and thus provides opportunities for direct matching. Soft metals, such as copper and aluminum, will not usually break cleanly but will pull apart with distortion, so that matched edges will be difficult or impossible to establish. Steels vary in their breaking characteristics, but ordinarily they break cleanly enough to allow matching. Brasses and bronze are intermediate between cast iron and copper as regards cleanness of breakage. One of the most common occurrences is the breakage of knife blades used to pry open windows or other barriers. Many cases have been solved by the finding of such a broken blade tip at the scene of the crime and the knife with a broken blade stub on the person of a suspect. A direct match of the parts is conclusive proof of origin. A situation similar to this, and bearing the same implications, is occasionally encountered in stabbings in which the tip of the knife becomes embedded in a bone and breaks off. If the knife with the broken tip is found with the suspect, little else is needed as proof.

Cut Screens

In breaking-and-entering offenses, usually burglary, it is very common for a screen to be cut to effect the entry. Screens made from aluminum or iron wires are usually involved, and when this is the case, much can be determined about the cutting. Such cut wires are invariably bent in the direction of the force applied to the cutting instrument. It is necessary to determine the direction of the movement of the blade along the cut, and also whether the cut was made from inside or outside the screen. Both the bending of the individual wires and the angles of the cut surfaces will often reveal these simple but essential facts. A stereoscopic binocular microscope will give all the necessary information, and in some instances direct visual observation is sufficient. Though this type of information may seem unimportant, the contrary is the fact, for reasons which turn largely upon problems that arise in court. For example: Is the opening cut in the screen sufficiently large to permit entry of the suspect? Was the cut made by a homeowner who wished to simulate burglary in order to collect insurance? Was it possible for a person to make the cut in question in the manner that is claimed? A burglar working from a ladder to gain entry to an upper floor will have to deal with several problems additional to those that exist when access is easy.

Plastic screens, which are also widely used, will give less information than

284 CRIME INVESTIGATION

do cut metal screens. The plastic strands tend to *break* under the pressure of the blade, rather than to allow actual cutting. In addition, the plastic strands will not maintain permanently the bend given them by the cutting blade, as will metal wires.

Metal Fragments

Chips or fragments of metals are often found among sweepings and mixed with debris. Determination of the origin of such metallic evidence may be critical in the solution of the crime. Certain rather superficial examination techniques may be sufficient, in a particular instance, to identify the material. In other cases very thorough examination may be indicated. The investigator will first explore the possibilities from the standpoint of easy identification. If the metal sample came from a sheet metal barrier, the thickness and the surface appearance—e.g. galvanized surface—may be sufficient to establish a good probability of origin, and may mean almost as much as a complete metallographic examination. If the fragment was removed by a tool and the tool is available, it may be possible to duplicate the effect as to dimensions and appearance. The more obvious characteristics, such as these, must never be neglected, and

FIGURE 24-1. In a burglary a drill was used to open a lock. Brass drill turnings were found in the suspect's pants cuff (left) and compared to the drill turnings remaining in the lock (right). (Courtesy of A. Biasotti.)

they are of such a nature that the reasonably well-trained investigator may be competent to make the necessary examinations and comparisons. No useful detail should be overlooked. For example, the chip of metal may bear markings characteristic of the tool that cut the chip. Such identifying marks are sometimes left by lathes, by some drills, by pliers, and by scraping tools in general such as chisels, bars, and screwdrivers, if they are applied with enough force to break out chips of metal. All of the simple possibilities suggested here should be explored before resorting to the more complex and difficult types of examination.

METALLOGRAPHIC EXAMINATION

Metallography is concerned with the crystalline structure of metals and alloys. The techniques employed in determining metallographic structure are, on occasion, of great importance to the criminalist, although they are not always familiar to him. The metal being studied is mounted in a block of plastic, e.g., Bakelite or Lucite, and the block is cut away until the metal is barely exposed. The block and metal are then ground down with a series of abrasive papers of increasing fineness, each of which effectively removes the scratches left by its predecessor and applies a set of finer scratches. When the metal has been ground down with the very finest abrasive paper, its surface is relatively smooth and appears mirrorlike to the eye, but not under the microscope. The specimen is then further smoothed on a polishing wheel containing levigated alumina or a similar fine abrasive, which polishes it to a true mirror surface. In order to reveal the crystal structure of the metal the surface is then usually treated with one of a number of etching solutions, the choice of solution being determined by the kind of metal being studied and the effect desired. Ordinarily the etching solution attacks the metal at the grain boundaries and thus reveals the crystal structure of the metal. The polished and etched specimen is examined with a metallographic microscope, or with any microscope fitted with a good vertical illuminator. The crystal structure observed will be dependent upon the composition of the metal and, to a very great extent, upon the treatment to which it has been subjected in manufacture, i.e., whether it has been cast, cold-rolled, forged, etc. Inclusions and visible phases of the different components of the metal may also be observed. From this examination the metallographer will obtain information as to the type and composition of the metal, and will usually be able to say whether it is probable that two specimens had a common origin, depending on whether the effects of identical composition and treatment are visible in both.

Many variations of the polishing and etching procedures have been described and used. Manual polishing works well for steels and ferrous alloys in general, and well enough for many other alloys, such as brass and bronze, which are comparatively hard. Soft and ductile metals such as copper and platinum are extraordinarily difficult to prepare by mechanical means, and are polished and etched by electrolytic methods in many metallographic laboratories. The proper technique, and particularly the interpretation of metallographic examination, although sometimes most critical to the criminalist, is a matter for the experienced metallographer, or at least for the criminalist trained in metallographic technique and equipped to perform the necessary operations and examination.

It should be understood that the metallurgist and metallographer often perform a number of additional analytical operations in the examination of metals, and that most of these concern studies other than those of regular interest to the criminalist. Failures of machinery are studied with respect to the structure and composition of the metals that failed, and such examinations frequently contribute to court testimony, but only occasionally in the criminal courts. One of the most important tests is that of hardness, which is determined by pressing a diamond point into the surface of the metal and relating the resulting indentation to the force applied. Hardness is expressed in terms of an established scale, such as the Brinell scale, and may be determined by more than one method. Standard procedures are available for application to samples of both macro and micro dimensions. Another phase of the metallurgist's examinations includes chemical analysis to ascertain the composition of the metal, which is strongly correlated in terms of some of the elements present with the properties and physical constants of the metal. Such analysis is discussed later in this chapter, in connection with ordinary criminalistic operations.

RESTORING SERIAL NUMBERS

A frequent task of the criminalist is the restoration of serial numbers that have been ground or filed off a metal object, such as a gun or a stolen piece of machinery, such as a sewing machine or an automobile engine.

When a number is stamped into a metal surface with a die, as is customarily done with the serial numbers identifying many kinds of equipment, the crystalline structure of the metal is compressed, deformed, and partially fractured, not only in the indentations themselves, but for a considerable distance in the apparently unaltered metal below the bottom of the indentations. In the grinding away or filing off of the number, the removal seldom extends through this layer of slightly altered metal, and the patterned alteration produced by the stamping can in most instances be restored so the number is again visible.

The methods for achieving this result are basically the same as those of the metallographer, except that the sample is not preliminarily mounted in plastic and the degree of polish is considerably less than is required for metallographic examination. The sample region is carefully polished down until it is quite smooth, is etched by a suitable procedure or solution, and the number is then read under suitably adjusted illumination. Etching may be done by special solutions only, or it may be done electrolytically. Although it is the more difficult method, the electrolytic etch is favored for general operations, since different metals sometimes require different etching solutions. Other procedures, such as the electrolytic and the Magnaflux method, have been successfully employed.

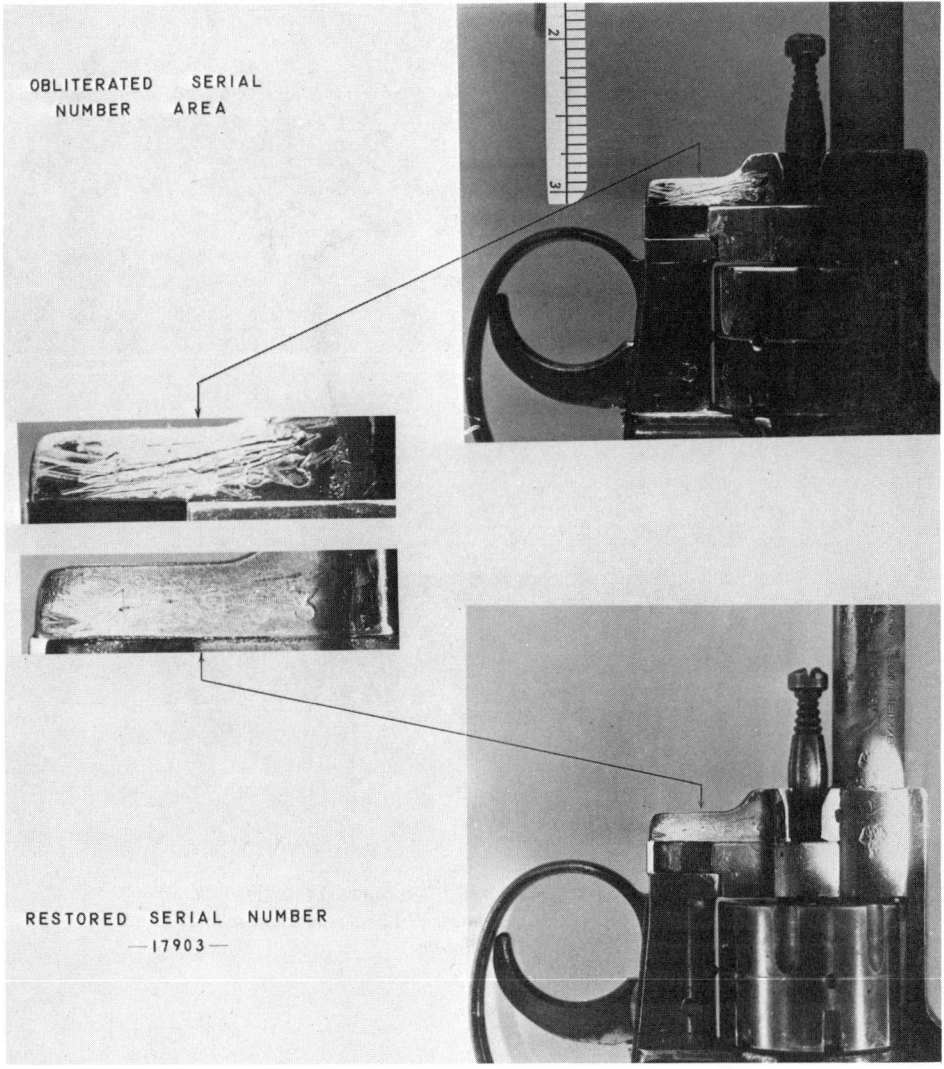

FIGURE 24-2. Serial number restoration on a revolver with Fry's reagent. (Courtesy of John E. Murdock.)

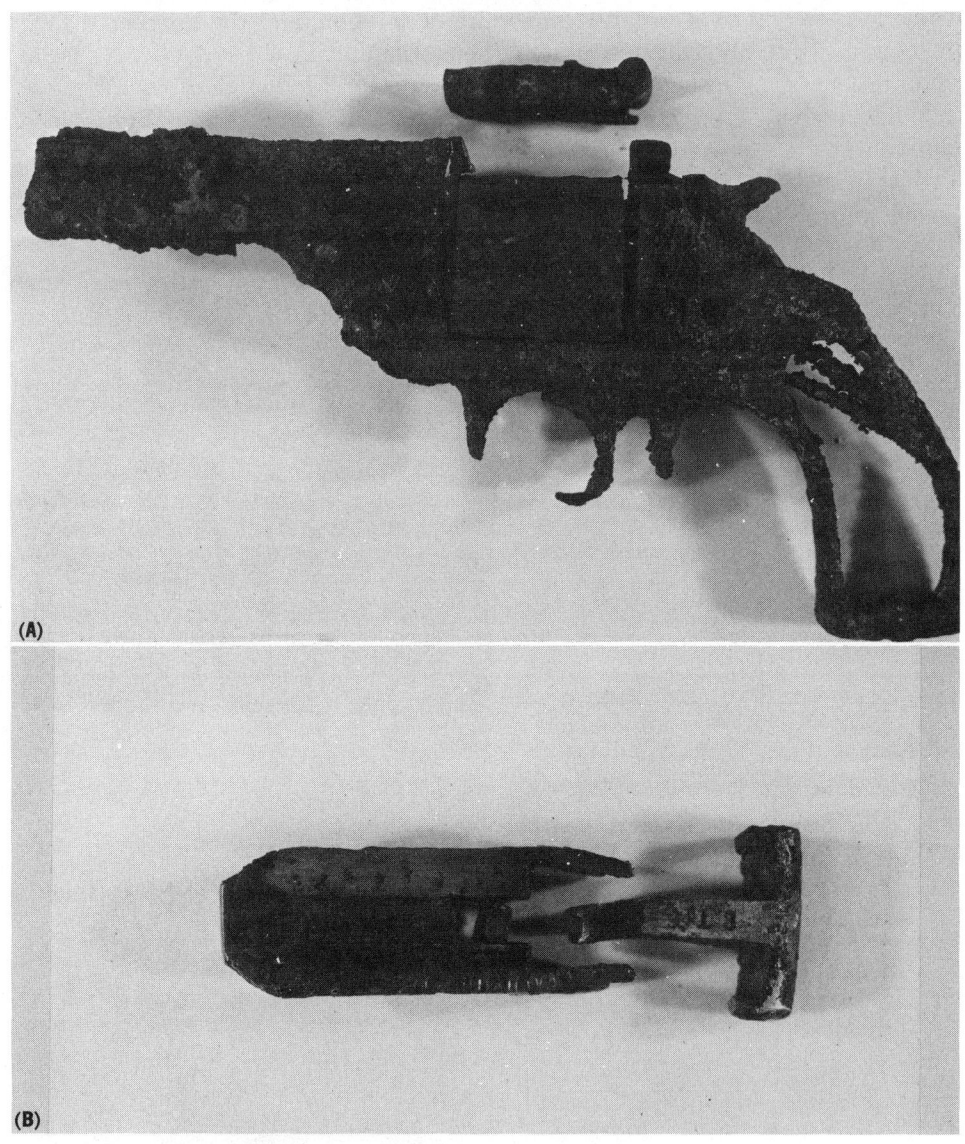

FIGURE 24-3. A revolver was recovered in a corroded condition from San Francisco Bay (A). The serial number (9 1 3) was restored with Fry's reagent (B). (Courtesy of Edward F. Rhodes.)

FIGURE 24-4. It is becoming increasingly more frequent that individuals will inscribe their name and drivers license number on valuable items such as the radio shown in (A). Even though a burglar may attempt to obliterate this inscription (B), it can often be restored (Z 7 8 6 2 5 2) as shown in (C). (Courtesy of Edward F. Rhodes.)

METAL FAILURE

As a separate aspect of metal study, metal failures are most rewarding in the investigation of accidents. They are also of concern from time to time in crimes, and a knowledge of the types of failure, and of their mechanisms, is valuable to field and laboratory investigator alike.

Nearly all metal failures appear to be instantaneous, inasmuch as they are usually discovered at the last stage of the failure. Except for highly energetic events such as automobile collisions, the majority of metal failures are not instantaneous, but *progressive*. This type of failure, more commnly known as "fatigue" failure, normally spans a very considerable time, starting as a microscopic crack in the metal that enlarges until the intact portion becomes overstressed and breaks instantaneously. When the entire break in the metal occurs within a very short time span, the break always results from the application of stresses that are of high magnitude compared with the strength of the metal. These stresses may be tensile (straight pull), *bending* (always involving a tensile component on the outside of the bend), *torsional, shearing*, or *compressive*. These designations actually define the type of force applied as well as the type of fracture produced. The designation of the type of force is equally applicable to both instantaneous and progressive fractures. No fracture is expected to occure without the application of some force.

The basic differences in the two types of fracture lie in the magnitude of the force and the manner of its application. If the force is greater than can be withstood by the metal, an instantaneous fracture results. If it is less, but repetitive in character, and especially when stress becomes concentrated at some point, a progressive "fatigue" fracture is likely to result. Stress concentration may result from a large number of factors, all of which involve discontinuities of the surface or of the internal structure. Most such fractures develop where threads terminate, where there is a change in section of a shaft or similar component, or where there are sharp changes in surface direction, as in fins or gear teeth. Damage to a surface, including stamped numbers, drill holes, imperfections in casting, and a host of other predisposing causes are recognized as contributory to local weakness. At these places stress lines that were originally uniform are pinched together and concentrated. Such lines may result from tensile, torsional, or bending stresses, and may lie in various positions depending upon the shape of the metal object and the nature of the applied forces. Compressive stresses do not ordinarily produce fatigue, and will rarely result in any other type of failure except when they are modified by the buckling of the structure and partly converted into bending and tensile stresses.

In consequence of the almost infinite number of possible combinations of stress and metal configurations there is virtually no limit to the variety of types and appearances observed in metal fractures. However, it is possible to recognize a fatigue fracture, as distinct from an instantaneous one, and often to reconstruct the situation leading to it. A large proportion of such fractures carry on the fracture surface so-called *beach marks*, a series of more or less parallel markings, usually curved, but sometimes relatively straight and quite variable. Their resemblance to beach sand that has been washed by the water gives these fracture markings their name. Because of their frequently concentric formation they are sometimes termed *fish-eyes*, or given a number of other popular designations. It is certain that if such marks are definitely visible on a fractured surface, that part failed over a period of time. The final portion of such a fracture is usually fresh looking and has a rough, crystalline appearance. This is the appearance most characteristic of tensile fractures.

The ductility or brittleness of a metal is made apparent in the mode of its fracture. Both ductile and brittle metals may suffer any type of failure, but their behavior under stress is likely to differ. Copper, and some of its alloys, are particularly ductile, and when fractured show much deformation in the direction of the causative force. Thus, copper wire that is pulled apart is "necked" down very noticeably at the break. Cast iron, on the other hand, if fractured in a similar manner, will not usually show such a distortion but will break off short. In addition to the type of metal, the speed with which a fracture is generated will affect the appearance of the broken surfaces.

Most machinery failures that do not occur as a result of a violent accident are of the progressive, or fatigue, type, originating in design defects, such as improper specifications for a key way, sharp fillets, conjunction of nut edges with thread endings, and many others. Production errors and defects contribute many more causes, while only about 10% are attributable to errors in metallurgy or heat treatment.

QUANTITATIVE ANALYSIS

Occasionally it will be necessary or desirable to determine the chemical composition of metal fragments, particularly when the fragments are too small for metallographic mounting, or in the case of ammunition traces where metallic constituents may be of great importance in determining the make of the ammunition. Chemical analysis is rarely of value in this type of investigation because small differences which may be the means of distinguishing between metals of similar composition will often be lost in the analytical error. Even worse, the trace constituents that are often of the greatest importance will not usually be determined. The spectrograph is only moderately useful for evaluating the major constituents, but it can determine an identity based upon minor elements and, for this reason, is probably the most valuable instrument for metal analysis. In a similar way the polarograph and X-ray diffraction may be of value in certain instances. Neutron activation analysis has recently been shown to have valuable application to the analysis of lead bullets. The method is quite insensitive to lead, which, for this reason, does not interfere with the very sensitive analysis of other metals present in small or trace quantities. Although more sensitive to trace elements than is the spectrograph, neutron activation analysis is a more expensive technique not usually immediately available within the crime laboratory. Quantitative chemical analysis, because of its limitations, is rarely used, but it can identify the general nature of the metal, if this is in doubt. For example, it will distinguish between brass and bronze, or differentiate the various types of steel on the basis of their content of carbon, phosphorus, chromium, nickel, vanadium, and various other elements. These elements are also readily distinguished by the spectrograph.

SPECTROGRAPHIC ANALYSIS

The spectrograph is nearly ideal for the determination of the identities of metals; and metals, in turn, come near to being the ideal evidence for spectrographic analysis. Although the spectrograph may be employed with numerous types of evidence, spectrographic analysis is superior to other techniques in rare instances only, the most outstanding dealing with metal analysis. This follows from the the fact that, when properly excited, all metals yield spectra. Also, metal samples contain a minimum of extraneous material that may cause interference or yield no spectrum. In addition, the form of the metallic sample is optimal for the generation of spectra. There is no other technique of equal simplicity that is clearly superior to spectrographic analysis for the study of metals and alloys.

Fortunately it is not usually necessary to provide a complete quantitative analysis of a metal or an alloy. Even with excellent equipment and meticulous care such an analysis can be performed spectrographically only within an error of about 5%. Under ordinary circumstances all that is required is the comparison of the composition of an unknown metallic sample with that of a known sample. Such a comparison may be made with simple equipment in minimum time, and with great effectiveness. The method involves the registration on a single photographic plate, under conditions as nearly identical as possible, of the spectra of the known and unknown samples, as well as all blank and calibration spectra. When the plate is developed, all the spectra receive the same development and will be strictly comparable, regardless of other conditions. If two samples yield spectra identical in all observable particulars, it is highly suggestive that they are identical in composition, regardless of what that composition may be. It is then relatively simple to describe the qualitative composition of the questioned sample by listing the metals represented by characteristic spectral lines on the identical spectra, and to estimate the relative quantitative composition by noting the relative intensities of the lines. This procedure does not yield a good estimate of the composition of the alloy in terms of actual figures for specific metals, but it does allow the investigator to state whether one sample contains a proportion of a specific metal closely similar to that contained in another sample, or a greater or smaller proportion thereof. Such a statement can be only approximate because small differences in the intensities of corresponding lines will not be perceptible to the eye. However, if the samples actually have different origins, there will almost invariably be differences in some of the constituents of such magnitude as to be readily discernible.

Metal objects of appreciable size may be used directly as electrodes. This is the ideal situation for the spectrographer. By employment of microelectrodes, is even possible to study differences in composition from point to point on a large metallic object. In the examination of very small metal fragments, the preferred technique is to dissolve them in an appropriate metalfree acid and analyze the resulting solution by impregnating or coating a carbon electrode with the solution and using the dried coating as the sample. Numerous techniques for these operations have been described in the literature.

ELECTROPHORETIC ANALYSIS

When it is necessary to determine the identity of a metal, or to detect differences in one or more of the constituents of an alloy, the very simple procedure of paper electrophoresis with electrolytic sampling is applicable. The sample required is so small that it may be removed from any surface by electrolysis without the spot of the removal being subsequently observable. The operation requires only a few minutes, and it will detect all of the common metals present as major constituents. Differences in the intensity of the spots produced by the same metal in different electrophoretograms are indicative of corresponding differences in composition, although not with quantitative accuracy. In an instance involving a broken bronze valve plug, this rapid nondestructive method showed that the tin content at the break differed noticeably from that of the remainder of the metal piece. This was confirmed by much more laborious processes subsequently applied.

PHYSICAL PROPERTIES

Many of the newer alloys are made from the light metals: aluminum, magnesium, and to a lesser extent, beryllium. All alloys exhibit density effects similar in principle to the differences observed in samples of glass, soil, paint, and other materials for which density studies have proved very successful in identification. If the metal piece is large enough, the density may be determined by the Mohr–Westphal balance. Small pieces, on the other hand, will have to be studied by flotation, and the metals that can be floated on the heaviest available liquids are limited to certain of the light metal alloys. In at least one instance, metals of various kinds were found in sweepings. These could be readily grouped into categories by virtue of the fact that some of them floated on heavy liquids such as methylene iodine, whereas others did not. No careful studies are available of the general applicability of density determination to the identification of metals. However, their separation can be accomplished, and there is no reason to assume that density comparisons would not be at least as useful with light metals and alloys as they are with glass and paint.

CHEMICAL PROPERTIES

Comparison between samples of metals may be conveniently made on the basis of their different responses to strong reagents such as mineral acids and, in some instances, alkalies. Metals above hydrogen in the replacement series will dissolve in hydrochloric acid solution, whereas the noble metals, silver, gold, and platinum, are unaffected by this reagent. It is necessary to guard against tempting generalizations in dealing with apparently simple response of acids to metals, because the acids as well as the metals differ in chemical activity, and the degree of dilution of the acid markedly affects the vigor of its reaction upon the metal. There is a distinction to be made between binary acids like hydrochloric acid (HCl) and ternary acids like sulfuric acid (H_2SO_4) and nitric acid (HNO_3). A binary acid has only one pattern of reaction with a metal, and that is a simple substitution of the metal for the hydrogen of the acid, thus:

$$Zn + 2\, HCl \rightarrow ZnCl_2 + H_2 \uparrow$$

On the other hand, a ternary acid like sulfuric acid or nitric acid has an additional mode of reaction that involves the disorganization of the negative ion (SO_4^{2-}) or (NO_3^-). The disorganization of the sulfate ion makes oxygen available for the oxidation of the hydrogen of the acid, forming water and leaving sulfur dioxide, SO_2, as the gaseous product:

$$Cu + 2\, H_2SO_4 \rightarrow CuSO_4 + SO_2 \uparrow + 2\, H_2O$$

Nitric acid is considerably less stable than sulfuric acid, its negative ion having more than one mode of disorganization and hence offering more than one possibility in the formation of the gaseous by-product. Temperature and dilution both affect the result. At ordinary temperatures and moderate dilutions one may expect a reaction like this:

$$3\, Cu + 8\, HNO_3 \rightarrow 3\, Cu(NO_3)_2 + 4\, H_2O + 2\, NO \uparrow$$

The resulting nitric oxide, NO, combines with oxygen in the air to form a brown gas, nitrogen dioxide, NO_2:

$$2\,NO + O_2 \rightarrow 2\,NO_2 \uparrow$$

It should be noted that copper, which comes below hydrogen in the activity series, was not used in the first equation above. Copper does not replace hydrogen and so cannot react with hydrochloric acid. However, if there is a coating of copper oxide on the surface of the metal, the following reaction will occur:

$$CuO + 2\,HCl \rightarrow CuCl_2 + H_2O$$

The liquid will show the characteristic blue color of cupric ion in solution.

Nitric acid, being a strong oxidizing agent, as well as a strong acid, reacts with all the metals except gold and platinum. In such a reaction the metal is in most cases converted to the nitrate, thereby being rendered soluble, and the gaseous by-product is nitric oxide, NO, which is colorless. Tin, antimony, molybdenum, and tungsten are converted to their *oxides*, and the gaseous product of the reaction is NO_2, nitrogen dioxide, which is brown:

$$2\,Sb + 10\,HNO_3\,(conc.) \rightarrow Sb_2O_5 + 10\,NO_2 + 5\,H_2O$$

Very dilute nitric acid will react with zinc thus:

$$4Zn + 10\,HNO_3 \rightarrow 4\,Zn(NO_3)_2 + NH_4NO_3 + 3\,H_2O$$

Aluminum dissolves readily in hydrochloric acid, slowly in sulfuric acid, and is inert to nitric acid. On the other hand, aluminum is soluble in concentrated alkaline solutions, the reaction producing hydrogen and an aluminate:

$$2\,NaOH + Al \rightarrow Na_2AlO_2 + H_2 \uparrow$$

Galvanized iron, in which a film of zinc oxide protects from corrosion a thin layer of zinc that in turn protects the underlying sheet iron, is a familiar early application of protective coating. A more sophisticated modern application of the same idea involves the treatment of alloys of magnesium with chromic acid or selenious acid to coat the metal with corrosion-resistant films.

There are so many differences observable among the numerous metals and their alloys that if two pieces of metal are suspected of having a common origin, careful testing with suitable reagents and close observation of their reactions will often be of value. The technique of chemical microscopy may then be applied to the dissolved metal for qualitative evaluation, and confirmation may be sought in comparisons of solubility. Some of the evidence will be destroyed in the process, as is the case with many other effective methods of examination.

As is true with any other form of evidence, it is essential in the examination of metals that the investigator possess a good fundamental understanding of the material in question, and that his experience be sufficient to give precision and validity to his interpretation of the findings. If there is any doubt concerning the competence of the investigator in this field, a fully qualified metallurgist, spectrographer, or chemist should be consulted.

METALS IN FIRES

Metals frequently constitute exceptionally valuable evidence in the investigation of fires. At virtually every fire scene metallic objects will be found in various states of damage, distortion, and oxidation. Usually they may be readily recognized: electrical wiring and conduit, ducting, nails, flashing, and many more forms. Such objects as are familiar and recognizable in a burned structure, or at an outdoor fire scene, generally contribute little to the study of the fire except an indication of the temperatures reached in the blaze. If metal has been fused by the fire, the temperature climbed at least a little higher than the melting point of that metal. *Aluminum,* for example, melts at 660°C (1220°F). This temperature is exceeded in portions of nearly every structural fire. Hence, it is commonplace to observe misshapen blobs of aluminum that have been melted, then flowed and resolidified. *Brass,* in contrast, melts between about 900°C (1652°F) and 1310°C (1886°F). This temperature will be exceeded only in quite intense combustion such as is more characteristic of fires in some commercial structures than of residence fires. If melted and resolidified brass is located in the remains of a house fire, it is proof of an extraordinarily hot fire. One exception to this rule is to be noted in the case of copper wiring encased in galvanized iron conduit. *Zinc,* used in galvanizing, melts at less than 400°C (750°F), and if the molten zinc comes into contact with copper from which the insulation has been burned off, it will form brass in the molten state, which will rapidly solidify. Copper melts at well over 1000°C (1832°F) and is not expected to be melted by any but the most intense fires. Its presence in a condition that has resulted from melting is often encountered, however, the fusion having taken place as a result of electrical short-circuiting, rather than from the fire.

In one other connection, metals may have a most important role in the investigation of a fire. This occurs when a metal object, or more than one, is found in the ruins but is totally foreign to the original environment. Such an object or metallic residue must be carefully considered as possibly being the remains of an ignition mechanism or of some part of such a device. These often involve wires that are not a part of the electrical service wiring of the original structure, or they may include clockwork mechanisms. They are sometimes tubular in form, but have been corroded through by acids originally contained in them. The investigator must be fully alert to any such object.

REFERENCES

Arai, S.: "The Application of Electrolytic-Polishing to Restore Obliterated Letters on Metal," *J. Crim. Law and Criminol.* 43:809 (1953).

Black, G., and Sinner, J.: "Identification of Plated Coatings," *Metal Finishing* 44:529 (1946).

Daubney, C. G.: "Forensic Chemistry and Criminal Investigation," *Metallurgia* 33:41 (1945).

Lingane, J. I.: *Analytical Chemistry of Selected Metallic Elements.* Cincinnati: Van Nostrand Reinhold (1966).

Mathews, J. H.: "Metallographic Analysis in Crime Detection," *Am. J. Police Sci.* 1:439 (1930).

Maynard, A. W.: *Chemical Spot Tests for Aluminum Alloys.* Springfield, Va.: National Technical Information Service #PB-203655, U.S. Dept. of Commerce (1971).

Miller, H. W.: "Spot Identification of Stainless Steels," *Metals and Alloys* 21:1364 (1946).

Nickolls, L. C.: *The Scientific Investigation of Crime.* London: Butterworth (1956).

Wilson, M. L.: *Nondestructive Rapid Identification of Metals and Alloys by Spot Test.* Tech Brief 70-10520. Hampton, Va.: NASA Langley Research Center (1970).

25
Plastics and Related Materials

The term "plastic" is popularly applied to a group of solid synthetic polymers and copolymers that only a few years ago were of no real concern as evidence. Man is moving progressively into a plastic world, and, corresponding to this fact, plastics are being encountered as evidence with increasing frequency. They are quite amenable to study by a number of methods, and can be most valuable evidence in many instances.

THE NATURE OF PLASTICS

Before the invention of plastics, there were a number of materials that were used in the making of toilet articles such as combs and other small household items, materials having properties very similar to those of present-day plastics. Notable among these was celluloid, made from nitrocellulose and camphor. Cellulose acetate was also used, and it is still employed for photographic film base and for many small objects such as toothbrush handles. Cellulose esters such as these are not totally synthesized, but are similar in physical properties to the plastics that are entirely man-made.

The first true totally synthetic plastic (polymer) was Bakelite, invented by Baekeland in 1909. It is a true polymer, or chain-coupled material, synthesized from phenol and formaldehyde. Its impact on manufacturing was considerable because it had some unique mechanical and electrical properties that were suited to the then-new electronics industry. The trade name Bakelite, originally applied only to phenol-formaldehyde plastic, was later extended to include plastic materials of other types, so that it no longer designates a single kind of polymer.

Within a few years many other types of polymerized materials became available, among the first being the polystyrenes. Today there are a great number of different types of polymers that have useful commercial properties, and a multitude of uses. There are also many copolymers in which the basic units of two types of polymer are merged and coupled with each other, giving new and useful properties to the finished products. In addition it has been found that the properties of plastics are subject to modification by the introduction of other constituents such as plasticizers, coloring materials, fillers, and other desirable additives.

Automobile parts, appliance parts, and a host of other widely used items are manufactured from plastic. In addition, plastics have been gradually usurping the market for textile fibers, properly modified plastics having been found very useful for the manufacture of both clothing and nonclothing fabrics. (See Chapter 11.) The familiarity of such trade names as Nylon, Dacron, and Acrilan is testimony to the wide application and general acceptance of the synthetic fibers used in the construction of clothing. Many types of foot covering are now manufactured from plastics, despite the fact that a plastic substitute for leather was difficult to find. Modifications of plastic formulations appear frequently, some of them having very unusual properties. Plastics have been made into conductors of electricity. Some have been developed that are extremely resistant to heat or chemicals, or both, e.g., Teflon, and others have strengths comparable with or exceeding that of steel.

A very common and strong material consists of fiber glass embedded in a plastic matrix. Although flexible, it is very tough and resilient. It is used for many structural purposes and occasionally for automobile bodies.

One of the largest markets for certain types of plastic, i.e., polyvinyl acetate and acrylic materials, is in paint formulation. Emulsion paints of these materials have been used for interior painting for a considerable number of years, and acrylic enamels are now widely used in painting automobile bodies and other objects. Because of the continuing increase in the substitution of polymers and copolymers for many of the conventional materials of construction, such materials, already of widespread interest as items of physical evidence, will become progressively more important in the crime laboratory.

PLASTICS AS PHYSICAL EVIDENCE

The mere fact that an item of evidence is manufactured of plastic does not ordinarily increase its significance, as compared with a similar item made from some other material, such as wood or metal on the one hand, or wool or cotton on the other. Massive plastic objects may be broken, and the edge fit of such broken pieces may be proof of common origin, as may be the case with glass, paint chips, or metal castings. (See Chapters 21, 22, and 24.) Plastic objects will receive tool marks that can be identified by comparison with standards from the tool. (See Chapter 30.) Textile fibers of synthetic polymers will be transferred during the commission of crimes, and must be identified and compared with known standards of clothing or with stray fibers from the suspected source. (See Chapter 11.) Items constructed of plastics are sometimes used aggressively in the commission of crimes. Plastic replicas of firearms are not uncommon, and their origin and nature may be of significance. Plastic shoehorns have been used to slip the bolts of locked rooms from the outside for purposes of burglary. Nylon stockings are often used as masks, or for strangulation of a victim. Nylon ropes may be employed as are other ropes, and plastic foams, e.g., styrene, are commonly used as packing material. Explosives are often encased in plastic in the construction of bombs. Portions of many weapons of various types may be made of plastic, and in the event that some of the plastic is broken off in the use of such a weapon, the piece becomes important evidence. Paint chips, so very important as physical evidence, will rather frequently have come from plastic emulsion paints, or from plastic spray paints such as are used on automobiles. In fact, there are few situations in which polymers and copolymers, normal or modified, may not be found among the other physical evidence.

EXAMINATION OF PLASTICS

Because of the wide variation in types of plastic and in the materials constructed from them, the examination must likewise be of a variety of types. Distinction may be made immediately between relatively massive objects constructed from plastic and fibers made from polymers. For example, most plastic items in the automobile would be classed as massive. When a piece has been broken from the structure, physical matching by fitting that piece to the remainder is the most useful type of examination that can be made, because virtually absolute proof of origin is possible.

When circumstances preclude a physical match, the next most valuable type of examination is to prove *identity of properties*. Color and appearance must agree as between the questioned sample and the standard thought to have a common origin. This is established visually and microscopically. Next, it is necessary to establish that the chemical constitution and composition are similar or identical. The methods are general and equally applicable to both massive and fibrous materials constructed of polymers or containing them. In addition, plastic materials show various optical effects that are of great value, especially when the material is in a thin sheet or in the form of fibers.

Two good general instrumental methods for establishing the nature of the material and common source are infrared spectrophotometry and pyrolysis–gas chromatography. Both will accurately identify the type of plastic material, and the latter especially will distinguish very small variations between different samples. It is also somewhat more applicable to very small samples—which is often a major advantage.

It must be emphasized in this connection that if two samples of a plastic material, one from a known source, but both suspected of having a common origin, are found to have identical chemical composition as determined by any of the above listed methods, and have in addition a color that is visually indistinguishable under higher powers of the microscope, it is *not proof* of a common origin, but a strong indication that they *may* have a common origin. Evidence of this type must be supplemented by finding the various types or colors of fibers or fragments to achieve a probability of common origin approaching proof. This is not the case when the fragments show a physical fit of a fractured surface, such evidence being so strong as to constitute almost absolute proof.

Anyone collecting evidence at the scene of a crime or in connection with a crime or accident should be very alert to the presence of plastic, either in whole items, or, more commonly, as fragments of a fractured object. This may be a tail-light cover or other part of an automotive vehicle; it may be a portion of a weapon, or it may be an object fractured during a struggle. Whatever the possible origin, the investigating officer should collect it according to the general procedure for collection of evidence. Equally important, he should look for a possible origin of the plastic object. If any such object is located, it also must be recovered for use as a comparison standard. Plastics are so variable in physical properties and chemical structure that direct comparison with a possible source item is the only sure way of determining the significance of the plastic evidence item. Otherwise, only a description of the object can be given, along with a statement of the general type of plastic as determined from chemical or instrumental examinations. As evidence, such information is far less valuable than the establishment of an identity of properties; and best of all is a physical match between the fragment of evidence and a source object of like plastic.

MISCELLANEOUS SIMILAR MATERIALS

Other natural and synthetic materials that are similar in several respects to the group of plastics or polymers, and are likely to be found in physical evidence, are the following:

Elastomers, which include natural and synthetic rubbers, are hydrocarbon compounds. These are characterized by stretchability or elasticity and will be found in garments, automobile tires, belting materials, machinery, and elsewhere. Because they are widely distributed, and often massive, both fragments and smears of such materials are common. In automobile collisions, tires frequently leave deposits on solid surfaces, such as an impacted vehicle; and skid marks invariably contain rubber smears. Industrial accidents very often involve elastomers; and they will also be found as evidence in a considerable number of crimes. Such materials are subject to several of the same considerations as to identification as are plastics, though, unfortunately, less can now be done with them than with the plastics. However, pyrolysis–gas chromatography, for example, is often successful in obtaining useful information as to the source and nature of elastomers.

Silicones are another group of synthetic materials that are often polymeric, although they are not ordinarily regarded as plastics. All of them are based on silicon, which resembles carbon in its fundamental chemical properties and forms some compounds analogous to organic compounds of carbon. Many silicones are utilized in the formation of very thin coatings on other materials to impart to the surface special properties such as nonwettability, or altered optical characteristics. They are also used in an increasing number of industrial applications, and may be found in massive form as silicone rubber. The addition of silicones to waxes, such as floor and automotive wax, is becoming common. One of the interesting members of this group of compounds is polydimethylsiloxane, popularly recognized as "bouncing putty" or "silly putty." This material exhibits an almost unique property. At rest it is very pliable, and will flow into an exact shape of its container in a short time. If struck, it behaves like an elastomer by bouncing or developing a temporary elastic hardening. It may be used for very exact casting, but unfortunately the cast is only temporary because of its easy flowing property. It is unlikely to be found in evidence, but the possibility exists, as it does for less exotic silicon compounds.

TYPES OF PLASTICS COMMONLY FOUND AS EVIDENCE

Any brief listing or discussion of plastics is certain to be incomplete, especially because of the rate at which new materials, and new formulations and combinations of the older materials, are developed. However, the majority of plastic items include in their structure polymerized material from a relatively few monomers. For convenience, the more important types of plastics used for massive objects will be listed here. Many of the same polymers are discussed in Chapter 11, "Fibers," because they are also suitable for fabric manufacture.

ACRYLICS. The most common of the acrylics is the thermoplastic called polymethyl methacrylate, best known in clear sheet form under such trade names as Lucite and Plexiglas. The monomer that is polymerized is methyl methacrylate. Related monomers used for other varieties of plastics in this group include acrylonitrile, which, when polymerized with butadiene and styrene, produces a plastic with high impact strength and resistance to surface abrasion. The ABS (acrylonitrile–butadiene–styrene) combination is widely used in automobiles and household appliances, and is likely to be encountered in evidence. Several closely-related monomers are utilized for special types of plastic.

STYRENES. Unmodified polystyrene is used very extensively because it is inexpensive, is light in weight, possesses a good surface gloss and has other favorable properties. It is manufactured in several grades, which differ in solvent resistance, static, and heat-and-light stability. Because of its utility in containers, refrigerators, electrical equipment, advertising displays, and many other applications, it has become popular with manufacturers and is sold under approximately thirty trade names.

Toughened polystyrene is a class of copolymers with butadiene or a related monomer or copolymer. It is marketed under some twelve trade names. Other important copolymers are styrene-acrylonitrile and ABS (discussed above).

VINYLS. Several forms of vinyl plastics, based on various vinyl compounds as monomers, are manufactured, and each of these is modified further to produce materials of a bewildering variety of properties and corresponding types of utilization. Polyvinyl chloride (PVC) and its copolymers with polyvinyl acetate (PVA) and with vinylidene chloride are the most important plastics containing PVC. When unplasticized, PVC is a hard material similar to horn, and is used for pipes and has certain chemical uses. To give it more flexibility it is often plasticized with a wide variety of substances including dibutyl and dioctyl phthalate, tricresyl phosphate, and various special plasticizers. PVA is best known for its extensive use in emulsion paints.

Other important vinyl plastics are based on polyvinyl alcohol, vinylidene chloride (Saran is a copolymer), a number of polyvinyl acetals (polyvinyl butyral is used as safety-glass interliner), polyvinyl pyrrolidone, polyvinyl propionate, polyvinyl dichloride, polyvinyl pyridine, and others, along with their copolymers. Probably no other plastic base provides so many variations as does polyvinyl alcohol, nor such a variety of products as are included in this group of thermoplastics.

POLYAMIDE. The chief form of the polyamides is nylon, which is produced in a variety of common types, distinguished as Nylon 6, 66, 610, and 11, and several less common types. The chief properties that make nylon unique are its extreme toughness and tensile strength combined with resistance to abrasion

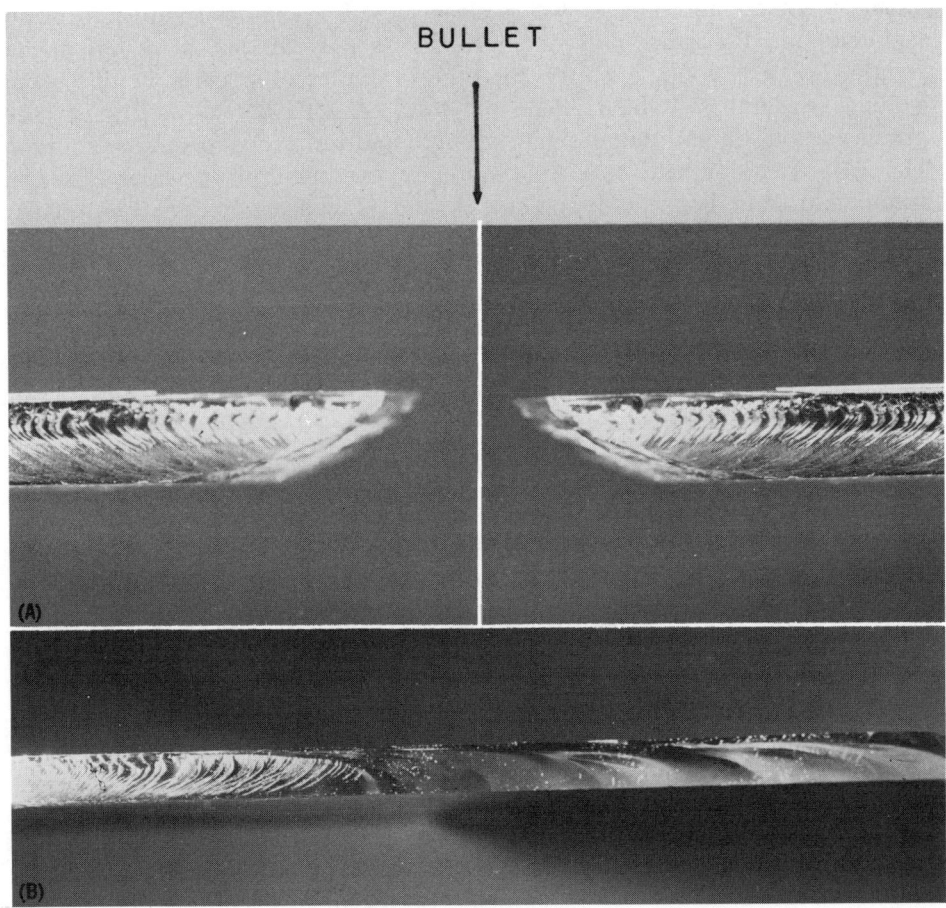

FIGURE 25-1. Plastics are sometimes used as glass substitutes in windows. A bullet was fired through the acrylic plastic shown above. The curved marks in (A) resemble the conchoidal marks found on the surface of glass fractures. In glass conchoidal marks are perpendicular to the opposite surface from which the force was applied. This could lead to confusion in the analysis of plastic fractures. In reality the marks in (A) are hackle marks which are perpendicular to the true conchoidal fracture marks. These conchoidal marks appear further away from the point at which the force was applied as can be seen in (B). This phenomenon is caused by the greater flexibility of the acrylic. (Courtesy of Edward F. Rhodes.)

and heat. Machinery parts are routinely constructed from nylon because of these properties and of the added fact that it is self-lubricating. The various forms of nylon differ in their melting points and in other measurable properties, which can be used to distinguish among them. Various copolymers are available, but far fewer than is the case with other plastic types. Nylon is marketed under a considerable number of trade names.

POLYETHYLENE. Polyethylene is well known because of its wide use in the flexible-container field. Not only is it one of the most flexible plastics, but it is also one of the most resistant to chemical action—a fact that lends it to wide application in chemical-laboratory ware and household utensils. The most significant varieties are distinguished as *low density* and *high density*, the density being related to the degree of crystallinity and to the presence of side chains in the polymer. It does not fracture in the way that many plastics do, and fragments are less likely to be present in evidence.

POLYPROPYLENE. Polypropylene is very similar to polyethylene, both chemically and in terms of its fundamental physical properties. It also is highly resistant chemically, but has a higher stiffness and heat resistance than does polyethylene and retains strength better at elevated temperatures. As compared with most other plastics, few copolymers of polypropylene are available, but it has a wide variety of uses. It is marketed under fewer trade names than is polyethylene: fewer than twenty.

CELLULOSE PLASTICS. Cellulose itself and several of its derivatives form materials that are classified with the plastics, although they are not totally synthetic. Cellulose (regenerated) is best known as rayon, but it also appears as thin sheets (cellophane) and in other forms.

Cellulose acetate is perhaps the most widely distributed of the cellulose-derived plastics. It appears in numerous molded forms—in toilet articles for example—but is most conspicuous as film base and wrapping material. The triacetate is primarily used for magnetic tape, but it is used for several other purposes as well. Cellulose acetate butyrate is another modification with wide application to fountain pens, steering wheels, tool handles, oil pipe, and other items of commerce.

Cellulose nitrate is considered to be the oldest of the thermoplastics, and it is one of the toughest. It has long been known in the form of celluloid. Its extreme flammability limits considerably its desirable applications to such items as spectacle frames, knife handles, and toilet articles.

Cellulose propionate is similar in properties and uses to cellulose acetate butyrate. *Ethyl cellulose* also has a considerable similarity of properties and uses. Vacuum cleaner nozzles and telephone handsets are typical products.

POLYCARBONATE. This is a hard, tough, resilient plastic suitable for various special uses. It is employed in the fabrication of lenses, office machinery, pumps, and parts for electronic equipment. Though it is less common than many plastics, its favorable properties indicate widespread uses and therefore significance as possible evidence.

FLUOROCARBONS. This group of plastic materials is unusual in that they are incombustible and very resistant to heat. They have extreme stability to chemical attack and excellent electrical properties. The first of this series of

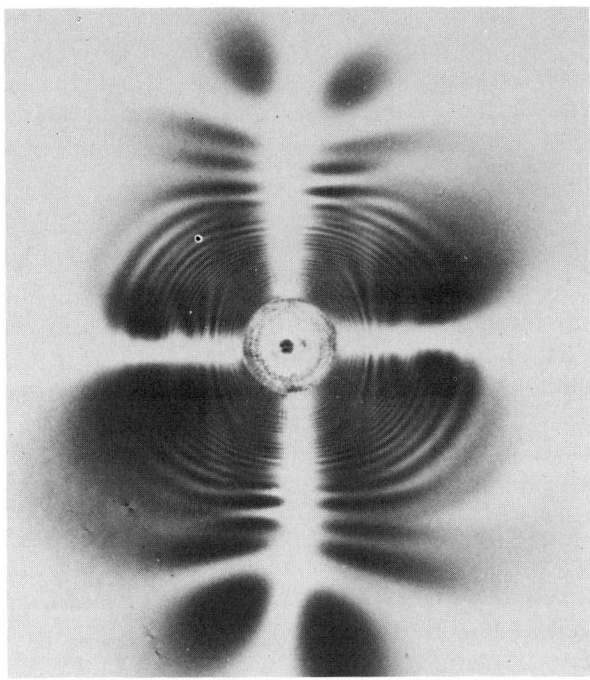

FIGURE 25-2. Polycarbonate is a tough and resilient material. A .38 cal. bullet was fired at a sheet of this material at close range. The plastic did not fracture; but, the impact of the bullet caused severe stress lines in the plastic sheet around the point of impact. The stress lines were visualized with polarizing filters. (Courtesy of Edward F. Rhodes.)

compounds, polytetrafluoroethylene (Teflon), was developed to solve special gasketing problems associated with extreme chemical attack, but its stability to heat and good insulating properties led to its adaptation for special insulation in extreme-high-temperature environments. It has now reached the general public as a lining for cooking utensils. Because it is difficult to process, it is expensive. Substitution of a chlorine atom for one of the fluorines to form *polytrifluorochloroethylene* (PTFCE) improves the required mechanical working conditions while lowering the desirable qualities only a little. A clear form of this plastic is available. Other kinds of fluorinated plastics are manufactured, and their properties are modified by various additives.

POLYURETHANES. Most familiar in the form of foams, the polyurethanes are also made in massive form and are used in coatings as well. Molded polyurethanes are found in bearings and gears, combs, handles, and electrical and radio parts. In the form of film they are found as rainwear, packaging, pressure tape, and insulation. The foam is used in upholstery, mats, insulation, and structural laminations. These and other forms of the polyurethanes have additional applications.

PHENOLICS. The phenolic plastics (phenol–formaldehyde) are thermosetting resins, although in the initial stages of manufacture thermoplastic forms are produced. These are hardened by further heating during processing. They find much use as binders in brake linings, plywood, laminates, and abrasive wheels. They have long been used in radio cabinets, electrical fittings, telephones, cameras, and a host of miscellaneous products. Bakelite, the trade name of one of the phenolic resins, was in general use before most of the plastics were discovered. Many other trade names for phenolic resins are now in use.

AMINO RESINS. The amino resins (urea formaldehyde; melamine formaldehyde) are transparent, odorless and tasteless, hard and abrasion-resistant. They are made in a wide range of colors and are usually filled to make them translucent or opaque. They find much use as industrial moldings and for certain plastic crockery. They are also valuable where resistance to electricity or high temperatures is required. *Melamine-phenolic* resins, more easily molded, represent a useful variation of the amino resins. Amino resins appear widely in coatings, laminates, and finishes for paper and textiles. A large number of amino resins are available: they are marketed under more than forty trade names.

ALKYD RESINS. These resins are manufactured by reacting a dibasic acid or anhydride with a polybasic alcohol. They are thermosetting under the influence of a catalyst. Their widest application is in radio and electrical components in which resistance to moisture and heat must be coupled with good dimensional stability. They are also used as bonding agents in paints and lacquers.

ALLYL RESINS. Somewhat similar to the alkyds in that polyvalent acid and alcohol are used for their manufacture, these resins are even more resistant to moisture and heat. They are important in electrical component moldings, and when laminated with glass cloth they find uses in aircraft and rocket components, as well as in a number of other applications.

POLYESTERS. These materials are formed in two general types: saturated and unsaturated. The former type cannot be cross-linked and is widely used for films, fibers (e.g., Dacron), plasticizers, and as an additive to polyurethane foams. They are formed by reacting a saturated dihydric alcohol, such as ethylene glycol, with a saturated dibasic acid or ester, such as the dimethyl ester of terephthalic acid.

The unsaturated materials utilize dibasic acids, such as fumaric or maleic acids, reacted with a dihydric alcohol, e.g., glycol. Either the acid or the alcohol may be unsaturated, and cross-linking is achieved by the addition of an unsaturated vinyl polymer, such as styrene, followed by curing with a catalyst. The unsaturated material is useful for encapsulation of electrical components, for the mounting of specimens, for colded reinforced plastics (e.g., pipes), and in laminates. Although the polyesters are marketed under about forty trade names, the familiar Mylar (magnetic tape) and the fiber Dacron are perhaps the best known.

EPOXY. The epoxy resins (epoxide) of this group are perhaps better known for their outstanding usefulness as adhesives than for other applications. However, they are also superior for their resistance to electrical, chemical, and environmental conditions. Thus they are the materials of choice for protecting delicate electrical parts in hot, wet climates, being superior to other plastics for these high-duty applications. They are essentially polyhydric alcohols with terminal epoxy groupings. Although they are cross-linked by other procedures, that which is most familiar is ambient-temperature curing with bi- or tri-functional amines.

FOAM PLASTICS. The base materials of plastic foams are not different from those of massive forms of the same plastic. However, they are formed into light material having large open air-cells that reduce the density greatly while maintaining much of the strength and/or rigidity of the substance. Some foams are made to be dimensionally stable, whereas others are formed to be soft and resilient. The first type is useful for such functions as packaging, insulation, and for situations where space needs to be filled while maintaining reasonable rigidity. The second type is more valuable for upholstery filling and in situations where resilience is desired.

Foams are made by several processes. Commonly there is introduced into the basic plastic material a compound that releases a gas when heated, or which vaporizes when heated. When the foam is formed, the heat used causes the release and expansion of gas, which renders the structure porous. Another procedure for cellular foams is to expand the material with steam, forming hollow beads. These are equilibrated with air, and when formed can be fused to each other by proper application of raised temperatures.

Polystyrene foam is the least expensive and the lightest, and therefore finds its chief application as molded packaging and in thermal insulation board. Vinyl (PVC) foams may be made either flexible or rigid. The former variety is useful in shoe pads, upholstery cushioning, and clothing padding. Rigid foam is used for life belts, buoys, and similar applications. *Polyurethane* foams can also be produced in flexible or rigid forms. The former find use in clothing, mattresses, upholstery padding, carpet underlays, and similar applications. The latter is used in insulation, building panels, and interlayers. *Polyethylene* foam is relatively costly and is limited to rather special applications. High-density foam is used in coaxial cables, whereas low-density material is applied to gasketing, bottle caps, and sealers. A number of other synthetic materials of plastic type are used as foams to a lesser extent, including *silicones*, *epoxy*, and *cellulose acetate*.

ELASTOMERS. These materials, like the conventional plastics, are formed by polymerization, but they are distinguished on the basis of their *elasticity* or capacity for stretching. They are rubberlike to a greater or less degree. The group includes not only *natural rubber*, but also the various types of synthetic materials that resemble rubber and are sometimes called synthetic rubber. These polymers are used to a great extent in tires, belting, flexible tubing, and other similar applications formerly reserved to natural rubber or to gutta-percha. Some common synthetic elastomers are the following:

    isobutylene-diolefin copolymer (butyl rubber)
    polychloroprene (neoprene)
    butadiene-styrene copolymer
    butadiene-acrylonitrile copolymer
    alkylene polysulfide
    dimethylsiloxane polymer (silicone)

REFERENCES

Arnold, L. K.: *Introduction to Plastics.* Ames: Iowa State University Press (1968).
Brydson, J. A.: *Plastics Materials,* 2nd ed. Cincinnati: Van Nostrand Reinhold (1970).
Gait, A. J., and Hancock, E. G.: *Plastic and Synthetic Rubbers.* Elmsford, New York: Pergamon (1970).
Gruben, A., and Leiner, H. H.: "What Plastic Is It?" *Modern Plastics,* July 1960, p. 88.
Haslam, J., and Willis, H. A.: *Identification and Analysis of Plastics,* 4th ed. Cincinnati: Von Nostrand Reinhold (1965).
Heilman, W. R.: "Nondestructive Infrared and X-Ray Diffraction Analyses of Paints and Plastics," *J. For. Sci.* 5:338 (1960).
Nelson, D. F., Yee, J. L., and Kirk, P. L.: "The Identification of Plastics by Pyrolysis and Gas Chromatography," *Microchem. J.* 6:225 (1962).
Saunders, K. J.: *Identification of Plastics and Rubbers.* Scranton, Pa.: Barnes and Noble (1966).

26
Vegetable Materials

Materials of plant origin, unlike the soil in which they grow, are seldom continuously variable. They are correspondingly less valuable as evidence than are soils and other materials that exhibit great local variation. The identity of vegetable materials must usually refer to identity of species, or of variety, rather than to individual identity. Lawn grass on the suspect's shoes would be useful in establishing their contact with a lawn, but only in a rare instance could the particular lawn be identified. There are, however, so many plant species and so great a variety of possible plant residues that their study can be extremely valuable in the investigation of crime. Wood, in particular, is very often significant as evidence, particularly in crimes involving burglary. The solution of many crimes has depended to some extent upon pollens, seeds, or leaf fragments.

Species identification of plant materials is a task for the taxonomic botanist, and extends over too large and complex a field for detailed treatment in this volume. The intention here is to indicate the possibilities, so that the police investigator in particular will not overlook botanical evidence merely because its identification calls for specialized expertise.

TYPES OF BOTANICAL EVIDENCE

Any portion of a plant or any material of plant origin may be regarded as botanical evidence. Bacteria and fungi are classified as plants, even though they lack the familiar chlorophyll green, and they should be included along with the more obvious varieties of plant life. They are less frequently significant as evidence, but may be important and valuable in an occasional investigation.

Wood

By far the most important plant evidence is wood. Its wide use as an article of commerce, particularly in building construction and in the manufacture of items of merchandise, brings it within the sphere of almost every crime. It is, therefore, not surprising that criminals carry away from their crimes bits of wood chipped off by a burglar tool, a bullet, or an edged weapon. The finding that such a fragment is Western white fir, when the damaged board is also Western white fir, is pertinent information. In one instance, two species of wood used as timber had been assaulted by tools used to effect an entry. The fragments of both species were present on the tools taken from the suspects, and fragments of no other species of wood were found. Numerous similar situations have been encountered. In these cases it is usual to find only minute fragments adhering to clothing, so that nothing can be said of their exact origin except that they could have come from the damaged door or window-frame. Larger pieces of wood may be more accurately identified as to source by comparing broken surfaces, growth-ring variations, or other pertinent features.

GENERAL STRUCTURE. The cells that make up wood are elongated, for the most part, in the direction of the tree's axis, and thus determine the *grain* of the wood. A smaller number of cells are elongated radially, across the grain. These latter cells compose the wood *rays* that appear as flecks on a quarter-sawn section. Some cells in both the longitudinal and radial elements of the wood are filled with darker material, which is stored food. These cells comprise the *parenchyma,* and are sometimes differentiated as *longitudinal parenchyma* and *ray parenchyma.*

Growth rings constitute the most conspicuous feature of the cross section of wood. These comprise the tree's annual increments of growth. The tree grows only at the cambium layer, i.e., the interface of bark and wood, and at the tips of branches and roots. The growth rate of a tree reflects the seasonal variations in the availability of water, being most rapid in early spring, diminishing with the onset of dry weather, and coming to a virtual stop in the winter. The cells that are formed during the period of rapid growth are con-

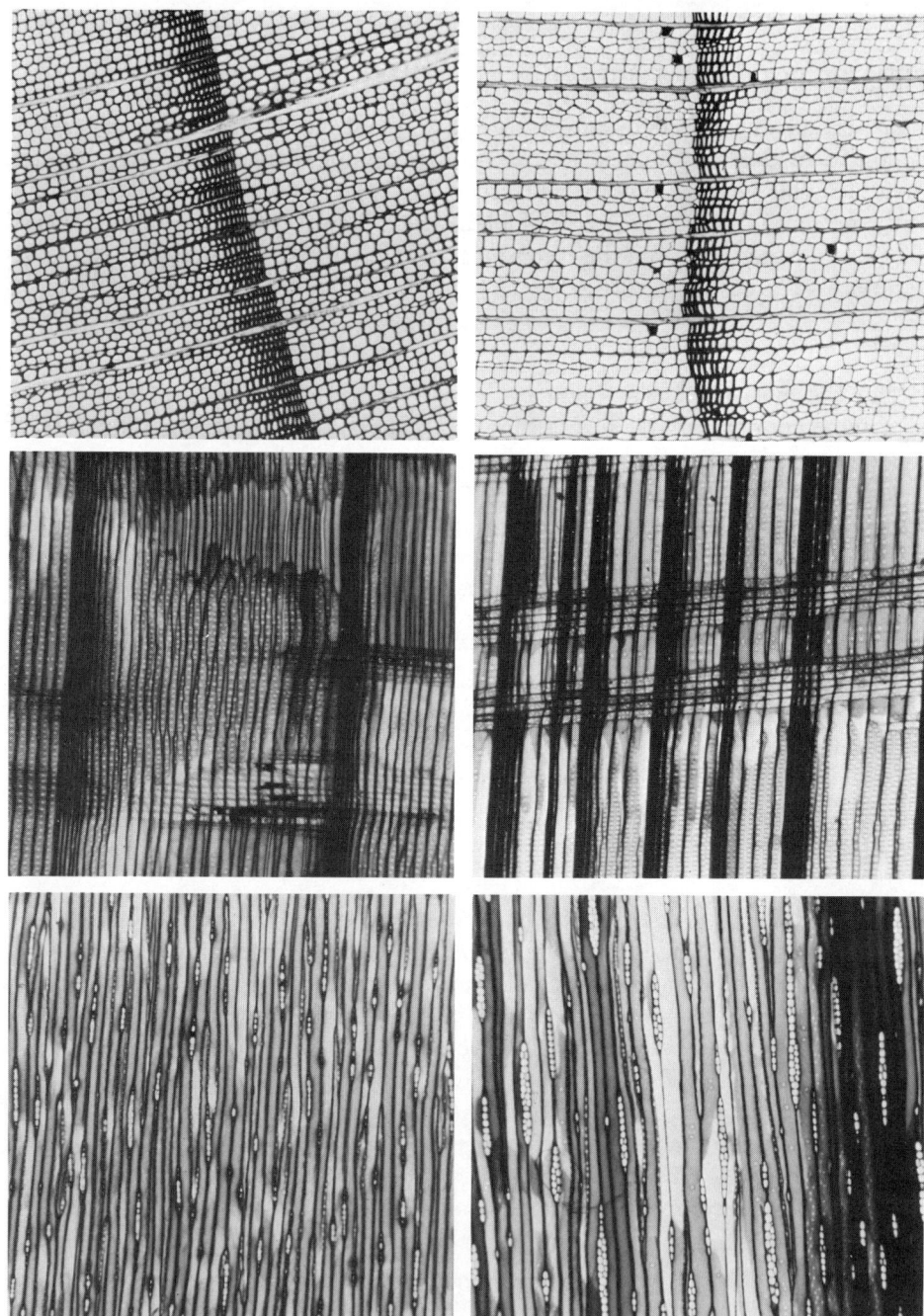

FIGURE 26-1. Soft woods. Left, Pinus ponderosa (ponderosa pine); right, Sequoia sempervirens (redwood). From top to bottom, transverse section, radial section, tangential section, (25X). (Coutesy of Edward T. Blake.)

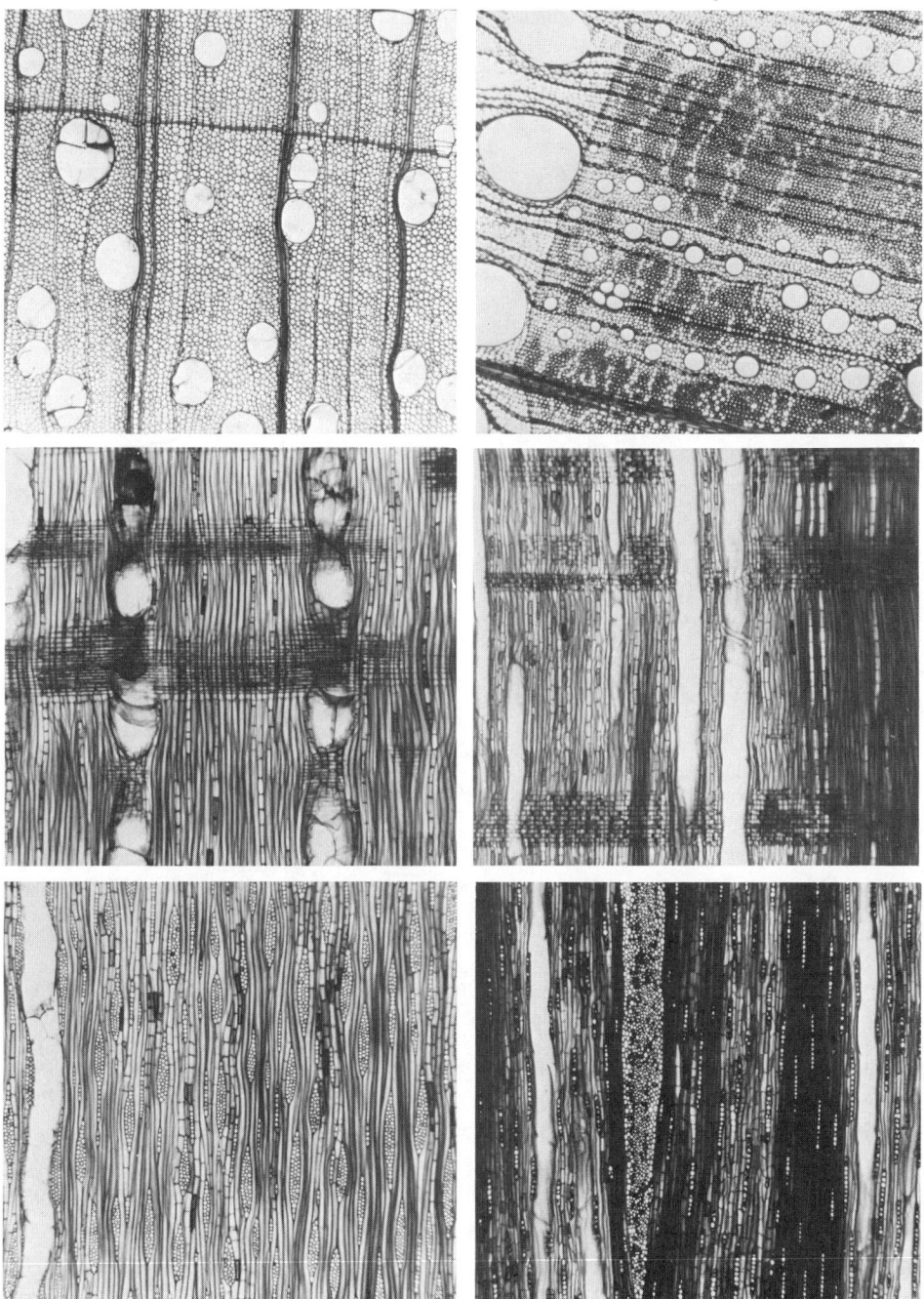

FIGURE 26-2. Hard woods. Left, Juglans nigra, (walnut); right, Quercus borealis, (red oak). From top to bottom, transverse section, radial section, tangential section. (Courtesy of Edward T. Blake.)

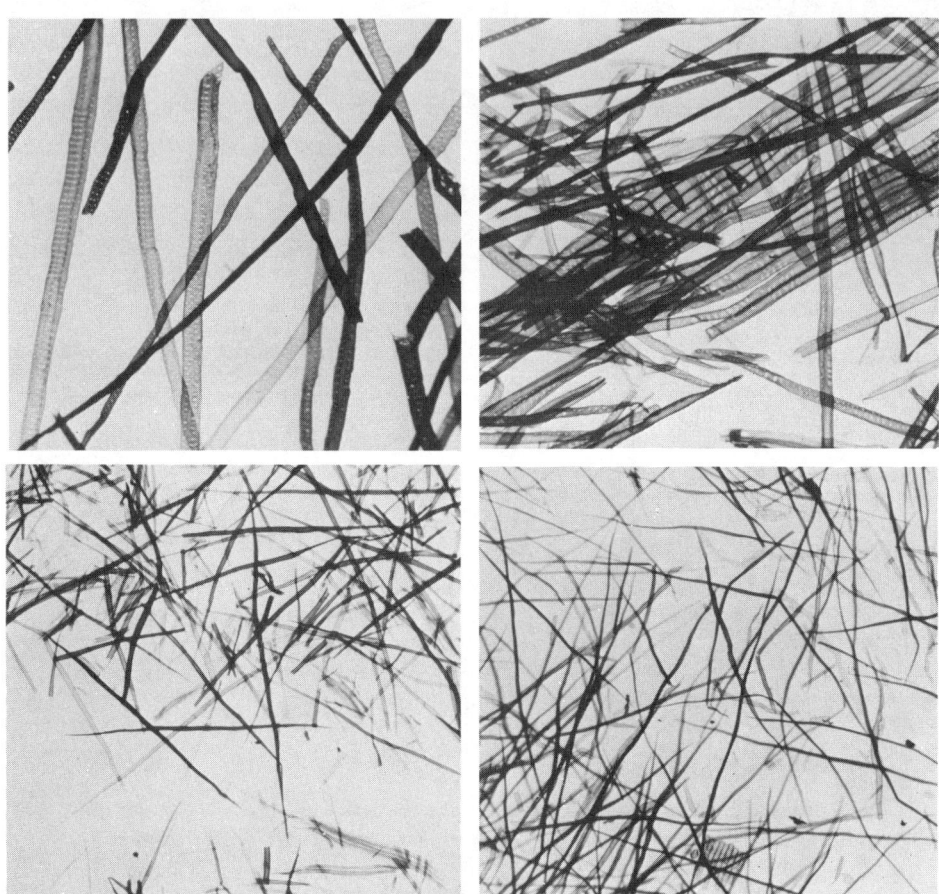

FIGURE 26-3. Wood fibers. Top, soft woods; left, Sequoia sempervirens, (redwood), right, Pinus ponderosa, (ponderosa pine). Bottom, Hard woods, left, Juglans nigra, (walnut), right, Quercus alba, (white oak), 25X. (Courtesy of Edward T. Blake.)

spicuously large, and the gradual diminution of cell diameter produces the visible pattern called "annual rings." In many woods the distribution of other structural details is related to the growth rings. This is particularly true of the *pores*, which may be used to classify woods into two groups, the *ring-porous* and the *diffuse-porous*. Growth rings also affect the color of wood and other physical features.

IDENTIFICATION. Wood is divided into two main categories, *porous* (hard woods) and *nonporous* (soft woods). The distinction lies in the presence of channels, or pores, in the hard woods, which are readily visible under low magnification. The soft woods, which include the wood of the conifers, do not have such channels. Some of them do, however, contain *resin ducts* that distinguish a main subgroup of the nonporous woods. The resin duct differs in appearance from the channels of the hard woods, and it serves a completely different function.

The *grain* and *texture* of wood are important gross features for identification. The color also is useful, particularly when considered in relation to the growth rings and to the sapwood and the heartwood. *Density, taste, odor*, and other gross characteristics are occasionally useful. Final identification of the species of a wood sample ordinarily rests upon a detailed study of the anatomy under microscopic observation. The character and appearance of the *parenchyma* (longitudinal and radial), the *rays*, the *spiral thickenings*, the *pits*, and other minute features, make possible very accurate identifications of species. Because these are microscopic characteristics, they may be observed on minute fragments almost as easily as on large pieces, which are rarely available for investigation.

Exact and detailed methods for the identification of the species of wood samples are given in several standard books on the subject. It is most important that the investigator realize that this is a well-understood and systematically organized field. The determination of the species of minute fragments of wood recovered from clothing, tools, and similar sources is very possible. However, as a rule the police investigator should not attempt wood identification, as it would not be difficult for him to locate competent individuals to perform the identification.

Pollens

With the exception of wood, pollens are more significant than any other plant residues that occur in evidence. Pollen grains are so tiny that they adhere to almost anything, and will invariably be found on clothing, in ear wax, in sweepings, and in other locations. Because their presence is not suspected by the person carrying them, no special effort is made to eliminate them, and if it were, more than likely it would be unsuccessful.

Pollens, like other plant structures, are highly individual as to species, although it is difficult to distinguish between pollens of some species. The identification of the species of plant that has contributed pollen grains to the clothing of a suspect is of value in direct ratio to the uncommonness of the species and its proximity to the environment in question. Evidence based upon pollen identification is more likely to aid in defining the individual's normal habitat than in establishing his brief presence at the scene of the crime. However, this would not be the case if, on entering or leaving a particular locale, he brushed against pollinating flowers. If this happened, he might carry away so much pollen of a certain type as virtually to prove direct contact with the specific type of flower. The ordinary distribution of pollens located on an

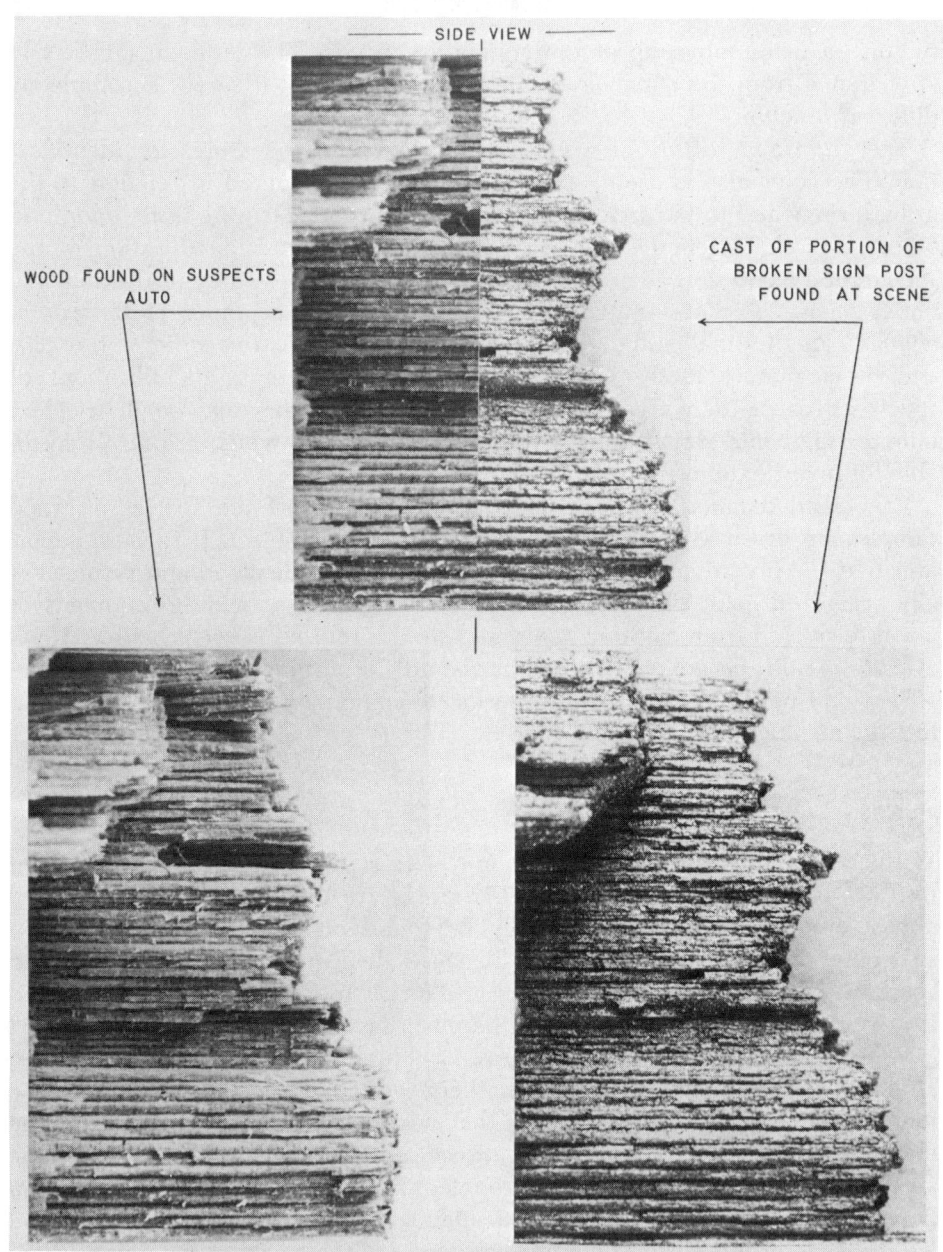

FIGURE 26-4. Physical match of broken sections of wood. (Courtesy of John E. Murdock and Charles H. Smith.)

individual's clothing or in his ear wax is the distribution to which he is customarily exposed; namely, that of his normal environment.

The chief source of pollen in physical evidence is sweepings from clothing. Pollens will be recognized in the fine dust that remains after the removal of hairs, fibers, and the other conspicuous forms of debris.

A homemade bomb containing several sticks of dynamite tied with a cord carried several items of microscopic evidence adhering to the cord. Among these were numerous pollen granules from a kind of tree that grows along streams. The bomb carried worn sand grains also, which would suggest a fast-flowing stream. Other evidence on the cord pointed to a remote habitation and indicated what would be found there. One such dwelling was connected to a recent dynamite sale, and the pollen grains provided investigative leads to the site of the manufacture of the bomb.

Pollen generally contributes information that is supplemental to that available from other evidence, but it is valuable in confirming such indications and in narrowing the possibilities, even when the pollen alone is of only limited value. The value of pollen as evidence is not limited to rural areas, because urban environments, having fewer sources of pollen, give to any pollens that are present in evidence a greater value than they would have in a locale where pollen is plentiful and diverse.

Tobacco

Tobacco is not often discussed under the classification of vegetable remains, but it actually is made up almost entirely of leaf and stem of several varieties of *Nicotiana*. That tobacco can be an important type of physical evidence follows from the fact that criminals smoke it and discard cigarette butts and other tobacco residues at the scenes of their depredations. These residues may often be identified as to brand by printing or other markings on the wrappers, and they demand no special degree of training or astuteness on the part of the investigator. It is also common for such evidence to be overlooked or disregarded. What does it profit to know that a criminal left a Camel cigarette butt at the scene of a crime? Certainly it is of value in eliminating a suspect who habitually smokes Chesterfields. If, by chance, the butt is of an unusual brand, it is highly valuable when a suspect is apprehended and found to use that brand. If no indication of the brand is present on the cigarette butt, the brand may still not be impossible to determine. Investigation shows that the general appearance of individual tobacco fragments in different brands of cigarettes shows variations, some of which are probably significant in brand identification.

If the tobacco found at the scene is the "heel" of a pipe charge or the butt of a cigar, this is even more useful, for several reasons. Fewer people smoke cigars and pipes, as a routine matter, than smoke cigarettes. Also, the identification of pipe tobacco especially, and perhaps that of cigars, is more decisive than that of cigarettes because of its greater variability.

No systematic treatment of tobacco identification appears to be practical at this time. Insofar as the criminalist is concerned, the field is almost totally neglected. A few standard books refer briefly to tobacco, but no systematic research on the identification of various brands of cigarettes, cigars, or pipe tobaccos appears to have been made on the basis of laboratory examination. This field calls urgently for research. For want of such study, tobacco residues found at the crime scene will remain of very limited value.

Tobacco identification rests upon the wide variety of tobaccos that are grown and used for smoking. Tobacconists distinguish regional differences in types of tobacco. Thus, there are Kentucky Burley and North Carolina Burley. At least three Virginia tobaccos are recognized: dark, medium, and light Virginia. Latakia and perique, both black tobaccos, are commonly included in pipe mixtures to impart flavor. Turkish tobacco and some other foreign-grown varieties are well known and widely used. Considerable tobacco is grown in northern latitudes, as, for example, in Minnesota, and it is probable that differences between these crops and the more familiar southern varieties could be readily distinguished. Botanical examination of unburned tobacco should offer real rewards to the investigator.

In addition to the tobacco itself, most mixtures that have been smoked contain other ingredients that may be identifiable by nonbotanical techniques. The extensive use of menthol as a cooling agent for the smoke, of licorice, nitrates, and aromatics, bears an important relation to the identification of tobaccos. Other admixtures of plant origin may occasionally yield important information in the investigation of unsmoked tobacco. Marihuana (marijuana), which is dealt with in connection with narcotics, is an important plant admixture to tobacco. Lavender flowers, pine sawdust, eucalyptus leaves, and other plant materials have been found in cigarettes. Such smoking materials as these are individual, and, in the infrequent instances in which they are encountered, may be decisive in the identification.

Miscellaneous Plant Residues

Seeds, leaf fragments, bark, and twigs are very often found adhering to clothing and to weapons or other objects connected with crime. These usually include fragments of the common weeds that, because of their wide distribution and frequent occurrence, have only a limited value in identification. It is a serious error, however, to assume that this is necessarily the case. It is almost certain that such residues will occasionally have great significance, as in the presence of an unusual species, an unusual combination of species, or a species that cannot be accounted for on any other basis than the one suspected. For this reason it is very ill-advised for the investigator to overlook plant remains of this type merely because they are often of little or no value. The thoroughness of the competent investigator will not permit such a lapse.

The identification of these miscellaneous plant residues is often difficult, and it nearly always requires the expertise of the taxonomic botanist. The value of such a botanical identification is illustrated by a murder in which the head of the victim was found some two years after the murder-and-dismemberment had occurred. Adhering to the cheek was a leaf attached to the flesh by dried blood. It must have become attached at the time of the dismemberment, and was therefore indicative of the site of the crime. Because the leaf was thoroughly dried and largely crumbled by the time it reached the botanist, he was able to determine only the general kind of plant from which it had come, rather than the exact species. It was, however, a leaf from a kind of plant grown only in restricted areas. Furthermore, it could be stated to be an early spring leaf, which fact checked with the date of the murder. It is obvious that under some circumstances such information as this can be of the greatest value.

Many celebrated cases, in both Europe and America, have been solved with the aid of botanical identifications. Sometimes these have been the key elements in investigations that determined the residence of a criminal, the location of a hidden dead body, and other kinds of critical information. In addition to the investigative leads that botanical evidence often provides, it may contribute markedly to final proof in court.

Microorganisms

The taxonomic classification of organisms of low order, many of them microscopic, places a large majority of them among vegetable materials. These include bacteria, yeasts, fungi, algae, and molds. Inasmuch as these materials are almost universally present in the environment, and will grow and multiply wherever conditions are favorable, they will very often be found associated with the evidence from a crime. Some species are highly selective of the conditions for their growth. For example, some molds will develop best in dark locations, such as caves, which are more or less uniformly damp. All of the algae, from the tiny green cell in the fish bowl to the giant seaweed floating in coastal waters, require sunlight to maintain the photosynthetic reaction by which they are fed. Many fungus varieties require specific types of food medium on which to grow.

Because of the wide variety of such organisms and the quantity of available information on their growth habits, life cycles, and requirements, the investigator who is teamed with a good mycologist may have access to many sorts of useful information bearing on a crime in which such organisms can be used as evidence. Although these rich possibilities have been generally overlooked, they have also figured in a good many crime investigations, some of which have been described by Thorwald.* The investigator who realizes the possibilities inherent in microscopic examination will not overlook this type of evidence.

Vegetable Ash

The ash of vegetable material that has been burned bears little relation to the original material. Studies of ash identification have been few and incomplete, and merit little discussion here in view of the fact that the problems are presented elsewhere in this volume (see Chapters 34 and 36).

Several important facts must be understood by the investigator concerning vegetable ash. In the combustion of vegetable materials, much of the structure of the burned material may be retained in the residue, particularly if the combustion has not proceeded far past the charring point. It will often be possible to arrive at useful conclusions regarding the nature of the original material by a careful examination of the remains. For example, although species identification of burned wood will not ordinarily be possible, it may be possible to go even farther than this and determine the specific object that has been burned. The collection of the evidence may pose a difficult problem because of the fragility of vegetable ash, and the person who collects it should have acquired special expertise in this technique before attempting it. A preliminary maneuver for preserving such evidence is the application of a gentle spray of lacquer or shellac, which will permeate the ash and bind it together.

When combustion has been complete and only clean ash remains, only tentative conclusions as to origin may be drawn by direct examination, in most instances. Coherent ash may retain characteristic features that may make identification possible, but if the ash crumbles, as would be the case with cigarette ash, chemical and spectrographic analyses are most valuable. Woven fabrics, papers, tobaccos, and many other materials of vegetable origin show widely variable composition in their ash constituents, both between materials of different types and between different samples of the same kind of evidence. For example, tobaccos from different sources do not have the same amounts of the various metallic ions. This variability is generally observable to a greater or less extent throughout the entire vegetable kingdom. The density-gradient-tube technique is often effective in the identification of the nature of an ash or in establishing identity or nonidentity between two samples of ash. Unfortunately, so few studies have been made of the variations to be expected in ash

---

* J. Thorwald: *The Century of the Detective.* New York: Harcourt, Brace and World (1964).

samples, and the means of demonstrating them, that ash density comparisons cannot yet be utilized to prove or disprove identity of source. Here also lies a fertile field for research.

REFERENCES

Barton, L. V.: *Bibliography of Seeds.* New York: Columbia University Press (1967).
Benson, L.: *Plant Taxonomy: Methods and Principles.* New York: Ronald (1962).
Cronquist, A.: *Evolution and Classification of Flowering Plants.* Boston: Houghton Mifflin (1968).
Esau, K.: *Anatomy of Seed Plants.* New York: Wiley (1960).
Esau, K.: *Plant Anatomy,* 2nd ed. New York: Wiley (1965).
Hyde, H. A.: *An Atlas of Airborne Pollen Analysis.* New York: St. Martin's Press (1958).
Jane, F. W.: *The Structure of Wood.* New York: Fernhill (1970).
Joyce, C. R. B., and Curry, S. H.: *The Botany and Chemistry of Cannabis.* London: Churchill (1970).
Kukachka, B. F.: "Wood Identification: Limitations and Potentialities," *J. For. Sci.* 6:98 (1961).
Stahl, E., ed.: *Drug Analysis by Chromatography and Microscopy.* Michigan: Ann Arbor Press (1973).
Thornton, J. I., and Nakamura, G. R.: "The Identification of Marijuana," *J. For. Sci. Soc.* 6:461 (1972).
Turkel, S.: "Pollen Analysts," *Arch. f. Kdiminol.* 88:69 (1931).

27
Poisons

Homicides by poisoning must often be investigated by the police. In the United States, murders committed by poisoning are less common than are suicides and accidental deaths from this cause. There are, however, a very significant number of poison murders in this country, although the relative proportion of such crimes is smaller than is characteristic of parts of Europe, for example. The poisoning of animals is fairly common in some parts of this country and may demand much of the toxicologist's attention by reason of the considerable economic value of the animals. Forensic problems involving narcotics, although they are closely related to poisonings, will be considered in Chapter 28.

The investigation of poison deaths is often made difficult by the resemblance of the symptoms of some kinds of poisoning to those of various diseases. If the autopsy surgeon finds no obvious cause of death, the suspicion of poisoning arises immediately and must be investigated by laboratory search for actual poison in the remains. Often this is an extremely difficult and time-consuming task, and it should never be undertaken lightly. Testing for poison that is indicated by the *symptoms* of the victim is ordinarily much simpler in that the evidence is often immediately apparent.

The amount of poison available for examination is usually small, whereas the number and variety of possible toxic agents is almost unlimited. These facts demand the greatest care and thoroughness in the work of identification, and they underline the importance of microchemical techniques that require little sample and are both sensitive and rapid. Common poisons may present little difficulty; but unusual poisons are sometimes very difficult to isolate and identify, at times requiring an investment of labor disproportionate to the value of the obtainable evidence. Sensitive modern instruments have greatly improved the ease and reliability of specific identification and require only very small samples. However, where such instrumentation is not available, the microchemical tests are still of great value.

TYPES OF POISONS

It is not generally realized that the word "poison" is a relative term. Thousands of ordinarily innocuous materials may, under special circumstances, be toxic, i.e., detrimental to life or destructive of it. So essential a material as water can, under certain circumstances, be toxic; as when taken to excess in a hot climate without a proper amount of salt. Oxalic acid, a constituent of vegetables such as rhubarb and spinach, has been used as a murder poison many times in Great Britain and elsewhere, and is responsible for the death of many range animals that have eaten certain desert weeds. Taken internally, gasoline and other organic solvents have also caused many deaths, most of them accidental. Even certain hormones and vitamins may be very toxic when taken in excess. Numerous metallic ions, such as those of copper, zinc, and manganese, are essential in small amounts in the diet, but are quite toxic when taken in larger quantities. Many poisonous materials are used in small amounts as narcotics and in drugs, with mild or even beneficial effect.

The most commonly encountered toxic agents in cases of murder, suicide, or accidental death may be grouped in the following classification.

Inorganic Poisons

METALLIC

(1) *Arsenic.* An amphoteric or transition element generally considered as a metal by toxicologists, arsenic in its common forms is generally ingested as an oxide or as an arsenite or arsenate. Arsenic trioxide, As_2O_3, is the best known of these compounds, but many insecticides and sprays contain the arsenates of lead or copper; other toxic forms of arsenic are occasionally encountered. Small amounts of some arsenic compounds are well tolerated and may even have some normal function in the human body, as is known to be the case in some lower forms of life. Numerous compounds of arsenic, some of which are common in seafood, are apparently completely nontoxic. Traces of arsenic are always present in biological materials, and considerable amounts of it are given in the form of drugs or medicinals.

(2) *Mercury.* This is encountered usually in the form of mercury bichloride, but it is poisonous in virtually all of its organic compounds.

(3) *Lead.* Most lead compounds are toxic, but the poisoning effect is com-

monly slow. Chronic lead poisoning from industrial and accidental causes is the most common type.

(4) *Copper.* Mildly toxic copper compounds must be taken in considerable amounts to result in death. Minute amounts of copper are essential to normal nutrition.

(5) *Thallium.* The salts of this metal are intensely poisonous, but until recent years were rarely encountered as poisons. Thallium, now being used as a rodent poison, is among the metals that are brought to the criminalist for assay.

(6) *Beryllium.* One of the lightest of the metals, beryllium has gained commercial importance in relatively recent times as a lining for fluorescent light tubes. However, the recognized high toxicity of beryllium compounds has stimulated research effort toward the substitution of other fluorescent materials for this use. This should result in a reduction of accidental cases of beryllium poisoning.

(7) *Antimony.* The compounds of antimony have long been used as poisons, particularly in the Orient, but they are seldom encountered in this country except as medicinal preparations, of which *tartar emetic* (potassium antimony tartrate) is probably the commonest. Antimony resembles arsenic in its occurrence and properties, except that there are no available indications of any normal physiological functions.

(8) *Radioisotopes.* Radioactive materials need not be metallic, but most of those giving rise to systemic poisoning are, in fact, metallic isotopes. Except for the case some decades ago where workers who painted luminous watch dials were poisoned by the radium isotopes used in the paint, poisoning from radioisotopes is a relatively recent phenomenon. It has resulted from the presence in some environments of a considerable number of possible contaminants. Although Sr^{90} is one of the best known of these, there are many others, including plutonium and uranium isotopes, which may be plentiful in some environments. Several hundred radioisotopes are known, and the radiation hazard is present with virtually all of them.

(9) *Miscellaneous.* Included here are a number of metals whose compounds, when ingested in some quantity, will produce typical toxic reactions, but whose occurrence in actual poisonings is relatively rare. These include bismuth, zinc, cadmium, chromium, barium, nickel, silver, manganese, and others. It will be recalled that most of the metals may be toxic if taken in large quantity.

NONMETALLIC

(1) *Cyanides.* The cyanides of sodium and potassium are most common, and are extremely toxic, even in very small quantities. The detection of the cyanides may be difficult because only small quantities are often present

and because the cyanide salts are readily decomposed even by very weak acids, and the resulting hydrocyanic (prussic) acid may be lost. The action of metallic cyanides is largely dependent upon the release of hydrocyanic acid (HCN) in the stomach upon contact with the acidic gastric juice. HCN is among the most poisonous materials known, producing paralysis of the respiratory center of the brain and destruction of the oxyhemoglobin of the blood, as well as poisoning some of the respiratory enzymes.

(2) *Yellow Phosphorus*. This material is infrequently encountered by the toxicologist because its once common use in rat poisons has diminished in recent years. It is rather readily detected by its phosphorescence when steam-distilled from the sample into a darkened receptacle.

(3) *Fluoride*. This is most commonly encountered in the form of sodium fluoride, which is often used in ant poisons. It is not readily detected in small quantity, but it is not highly toxic, and if enough of it is present to produce fatal or near-fatal results, it is likely to be detectable without unusual difficulty. Recent increases in industrial applications of fluorine and in the form of new compounds may lead to increased significance of fluorides in the field of toxicology.

(4) *Iodine*. Partly because of its ready availability in the form of a tincture, iodine is occasionally involved in accidental or intentional poisoning. Iodine is of forensic significance only in the elementary state because the iodides are not very toxic and will rarely be taken in quantities sufficient to produce serious ill effects.

(5) *Strong Acids and Alkalies*. Strong reagents and caustics, such as sulfuric and nitric acids and sodium, potassium, and ammonium hydroxides, are destructive because of their corrosive action rather than because of any specific toxicity. Their effects are seldom seen except in accidental poisonings, particularly among children. They are unsuitable as means of committing murder, and are most unlikely as means of suicide.

(6) *Strong Oxidants*. A number of strong oxidixing agents are destructive of tissue and are therefore poisonous. Among these are the hypochlorites and related compounds. They are most dangerous by reason of their rapid attack upon living tissue and their general availability in household bleaches and cleansers. Any such product is to be treated as potentially dangerous when ingested, and should be kept out of the reach of children.

(7) *Gases*. In addition to the hydrocyanic acid mentioned above, there are a number of inorganic gases that frequently cause death or severe injury. These include *carbon monoxide, hydrogen sulfide, arsine, phosgene* and others of even less frequent occurrence. Carbon monoxide is of the greatest significance because it is present in automobile exhaust gases and in the fumes of some gas-heating appliances, and is responsible for many suicides and accidental deaths from these sources. Carbon monoxide is also a constituent of manufac-

tured illuminating gas and has long been noted as a major cause of death from this source. It is not present in dangerous amounts in natural gas.

Organic Poisons

VOLATILE SUBSTANCES

(1) *Ethyl Alcohol*. This compound belongs in a category by itself because of its outstanding importance in the general field of criminalistics. It is almost certainly the direct cause of more deaths than is any other poison, and possibly of more than all other poisons combined. Consideration of it as the cause of drunkenness is given in Chapter 29. Discussion of the investigation of alcohol as a poison is almost identical with that given for drunkenness in that quantitative determination is required as proof of death from alcohol just as it is for proof of drunkenness.

(2) *Other Alcohols*. Alcohols other than ethanol are of considerable importance to the criminalist because they are used as solvents and diluents in lacquers and varnishes. For example, *wood alcohol*, known to the chemist as *methanol* or *methyl alcohol*, has long been used as an industrial solvent, despite the fact that it is poisonous and can cause blindness. In recent years it has been largely replaced by *isopropyl alcohol*. *Fusel oil* is a mixture, consisting largely of amyl alcohols, that results from the fermentation of organic materials. Because it dissolves nitrocellulose, it is used as a solvent for enamels and lacquers. It occurs in unaged liquors. In general, the toxicity of the alcohols increases as the hydrocarbon chain lengthens; hence the higher alcohols are progressively more toxic than is ethyl alcohol. Methyl alcohol is an exception to this rule in its destructive effect upon sight, though the quantity of it necessary to produce death differs little from that of ethyl alcohol.

(3) *Aniline* and some of its derivatives are poisonous and occasionally require toxicological identification. The importance of this material is industrial rather than criminalistic, as aniline is used in the dye industry and in related chemical enterprises based upon coal-tar derivatives. Deaths and injuries from it result from industrial hazards and accidents.

(4) *Phenol* is a coal-tar derivative that is still sometimes called by its original name, "carbolic acid." It is found in several widely distributed disinfectants. Because of its common availability it may be the cause of accidental or deliberate poisonings. It acts as a corrosive in the stomach, producing painful and violent symptoms, and is therefore seldom used as a means of suicide. In pure form it is a white or pinkish crystalline solid. It is classed with the volatile organic poisons because it is commonly separated from other materials by steam distillation, the procedure usually employed for the isolation of all of the volatile poisons.

(5) *Miscellaneous Organic Liquids*. Many organic liquids frequently used as solvents, as fuel, or for industrial purposes are toxic when ingested or in-

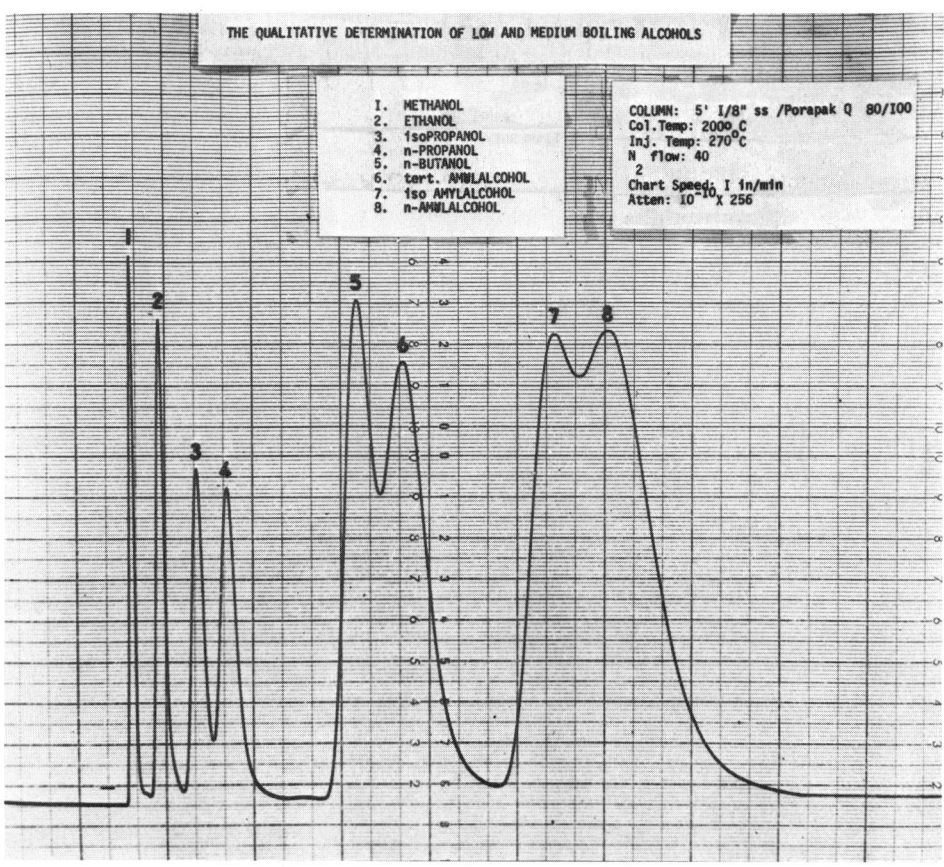

FIGURE 27-1. Alcohols can be identified and quantitatively determined by means of gas chromatography. (Courtesy of Edward T. Blake.)

haled to excess. These include benzene; volatile petroleum products such as gasoline, acetone, and other ketones; various aldehydes; carbon disulfide; carbon tetrachloride; ether; chloroform; and numerous similar materials ordinarily of industrial rather than criminalistic interest. The toxicity of organic liquids is increased by halogenation, and the chlorinated hydrocarbons, especially, have become highly significant as poisons. Aromatic compounds (based on benzene) are regularly more toxic than aliphatic (straight-chain) hydrocarbons. Although systematic treatment of all of these materials by the toxicologist is difficult, identification by means of the gas chromatograph, supplemented by other appropriate techniques, is very simple and positive.

(6) *Miscellaneous.* A large number of volatile organic compounds may be toxic and occasionally require identification. *Chloral hydrate* is one of the more common of these. Like some others, it is a solid and is only volatile in a steam

distillation. Because it is the material commonly employed in "knock-out drops," it may be encountered with significant frequency. *Paraldehyde*, which has a similar physiological effect, is also of relatively common occurrence. Chlorinated compounds, such as DDT, which are intended for use as insecticides, may be diverted to criminal purposes. It should be remembered that many halogenated compounds are more or less toxic to the human organism, and that the volatility of an organic compound is nearly always increased by including one or more halogen atoms in its molecule. Pesticides of the organic phosphate type are even more toxic than the halogenated compounds. For economic reasons both types of pesticide are being used in increasing amounts, and the hazard from them has enlarged correspondingly. Fortunately, deficiencies of methods of their detection and identification have been largely corrected by means of sensitive instrumental analysis. With greater public appreciation of the potential dangers inherent in pest control, the problem should be at least susceptible to solution.

NONVOLATILE MATERIALS

(1) *Alkaloids*. Included in this large and important group are both toxic and relatively nontoxic nitrogen-containing compounds of plant origin. The number of alkaloids that have been described is very great, but those that figure in homicide cases are few. These include strychnine, morphine, cocaine, heroin, brucine, atropine, coniine, and a number of less common alkaloids, as well as some like codeine which, though common, are relatively nontoxic. Many alkaloids are classified as narcotics and are subject to laboratory identification for this reason rather than for toxicity.

(2) *Barbiturates*. In this group are included a number of synthetic sleep-producing drugs much favored by suicides but less commonly used by murderers because of the large dosage required to produced death. Some of the better known of this group are Phenobarbital, Amytal, Veronal, Allonal, and Seconal.

(3) *Glycosides*. This group includes a variety of compounds related chemically to the sugars, intensely toxic when ingested. The most common of the glycosides is *digitalis*, which is widely used in the treatment of heart disease, and is therefore most likely to be encountered in case of death from glycoside poisoning. Chemical tests as such have been of little value in the identification of these materials, but newer instrumental methods have made the isolation and identification of the glycosides relatively simple.

(4) *Drugs and Synthetics*. This very large group of compounds is of more immediate interest in their use context than in their toxicity. (See Chapter 28.) However, virtually all of them show a significant toxicity, and a few, such as heroin, cause numerous deaths. It should be noted that the barbiturates, discussed above, also belong in this category but are isolated because of the high incidence of their lethal use. Many drugs that are not used by addicts or thrill

seekers have occasional importance in toxicology. Most of them have a significant degree of toxicity, and they are taken in excess or by accident from time to time. This includes even common pain-relieving drugs such as aspirin, as well as virtually any of the therapeutic drugs. When one of these has been the effective poison, it may be difficult for a lack of any indication of its possible use and by reason of its not having been included in the usual toxicological routines of the laboratory.

(5) *Miscellaneous.* Here are included a few special poisons of organic nature that may be highly toxic, but are not included in the groups above. Among them are ricin (from castor beans), which is possibly the most toxic of known poisons, botulinus toxin, which is of about the same toxicity, snake and toad venoms, curare, and other little-known and infrequently encountered toxic materials.

To the field investigator the actual toxic agent that has been employed is of less importance than is the form in which it has been used, whether the poisoning has been accidental or intentional, and whether suicide or murder. Few laymen possess the information that would enable them to obtain any but the well-known poisons in pure form. However, many poisonous preparations are made for common uses. It is these materials that are easily accessible to the poisoner or the suicide; yet it is these that the investigator may overlook, being unaware of the nature and the constituents of such materials. In this category are included many antiseptics, some cosmetics, douches, prescription drugs, household and agricultural sprays, rodent and ant poisons, paint and paint solvents, liquid and gaseous fuels, exhaust gases, and industrial chemicals. So diverse are the poisonous constituents of such materials that it is not practicable or desirable to attempt a complete listing here. However, it is of critical importance that the investigator understand that *any* such material is a potential poison, though not always an actual one. Many such materials not commonly considered to be poisonous are actually dangerous if taken in sufficient quantities. The determined suicide can usually find plenty of low-grade poisons that he may have the fortitude to take in sufficient quantity to induce death. This type of poison is of much less value to the murderer, for obvious reasons. These principles were illustrated by a death caused by drinking nail polish. The necessary quantity was so large that it is difficult to believe that such an act could be imposed by another individual, either by force or by stealth.

INVESTIGATION OF SUSPECTED POISONINGS

At the Scene

The field investigator of a case that involves possible poisoning must be particularly alert to the necessity of obtaining certain specific kinds of physical evidence. If the poison was administered by the victim, almost certainly an empty or partly filled container will be found near the body, in the bathroom, or somewhere close by. Any bottle, envelope, container, or other receptacle that might have carried the poison, even though it is unlikely that its original contents were poisonous, should be immediately collected, sealed tightly, adequately labeled, and taken promptly to the laboratory for examination. It is often advisable to take the entire contents of the medicine chest so as to permit a search for materials that are poisonous if taken in sufficient quantity. Only a complete collection of such possible poison containers as tumblers or liquid glasses that have been recently used, empty or nearly empty beverage bottles and pill boxes, and all similar items, will make certain that the significant container is located.

If the poison was not self-administered, it is probable that the poisoner will have made an effort to dispose of the poison container. For this reason, all rubbish, garbage, and disposal vessels should be searched with the greatest care. If the poisoning has occurred out of doors, the entire vicinity should be searched carefully. The poisoner's natural impulse would be to rid himself of the poison container as quickly as possible by hiding it in garbage, throwing it among weeds or underbrush, or disposing of it in any place where it is not likely to be found without deliberate search.

The finding of the poison container will usually make possible the identification of the traces of poison left in it, and will thus greatly simplify the search in the victim's autopsy material which, otherwise, is often quite difficult. Such remaining traces of poison will also serve as a guide to the type of autopsy material that should be taken for examination, thus aiding the autopsy surgeon.

If no poison container is found, it is probable that the poisoner has taken it with him for later disposal. In such a situation, if a likely suspect is known, his person, his premises, clothing, automobile, and customary haunts should be searched as quickly as possible in order to recover the container, if it can be found. Although it is unlikely that the murderer will have been so careless as to keep the container on his person, he may have concealed it in some place associated with his customary movements. If it is found, and the toxicologist can state that the same kind of poison was found in the body of the victim and in the container, it becomes very valuable evidence. The point is so important that no effort should be spared in the pursuit of the container in which the poison was carried.

If the victim is shown to have died from a particular poison, and if no container can be found and no suspect can be connected with the poisoning, it becomes necessary to consider the availability of this poison and the class of people to whom it is available. Assume that cyanide has been shown to be the cause of death. It then seems likely that the administrator of the poison may be either a metallurgist, or other metal worker, as cyanide is used routinely as a flux in metal work; or an electroplater who also uses cyanide in quantity; a chemist or pharmacist who has access to it; or a person who is employed in one of a few other occupations in which cyanide is used. Any such individual found among the victim's acquaintances becomes a possible suspect and should be investigated. Yellow phosphorus would point to someone who had been poisoning rats. Strychnine might indicate a person who was poisoning gophers or other rodents; and lead arsenate would suggest possibly an orchardist or an individual who is employed spraying fruit trees. Bearing in mind that the poisoner will normally employ the poison with which he is familiar and that his familiarity with it will depend upon his past experience, one can often establish indications of possible perpetrators on this basis alone. The investigator will check druggists' poison registers as a routine matter. Although this may sometimes be helpful, usually it will not uncover the clever poisoner who would be unlikely to leave so open a trail. He would use a poison that he could obtain surreptitiously, or one to which he had normal access. So many poisons can be obtained without signing a poison register that there is little need to take this particular chance, and to do so would indicate that the poisoner is less than normally intelligent.

In the field investigation of a poisoning the usual factors of physical evidence are in every respect as important as they are in other crimes. If a person poisons another, the crime will usually involve the presence of the criminal and his victim in the same neighborhood and will result in the usual cross-contamination of the criminal and the environment. Here, again, the clothing, fingerprints, hairs, fibers, and all of the microscopic debris should be collected and examined. In many instances the poisoner and his victim are closely associated, e.g., members of the same family, husband and wife, business associates. In such a situation, little can be determined from the cross-examination, because it is normal to the relationship. This situation may be checked and evaluated on the basis of other information, the implication being either strengthened or eliminated as a possibility.

The Victim

When illness or death is suspected to have been caused by poison, it is of particular importance that the liaison between the police and the medical investigators be extremely close. This cooperation should begin at the first examination of the body at the scene. Not only must the usual photographs be taken, but all medical indications should be noted and made available to both the police and the laboratory toxicologist. It is excellent practice for the police investigator and the toxicologist to be present throughout the autopsy in order to consult fully and in detail. The investigator should obtain, either from the autopsy surgeon or from another competent medical man, certain special information including:

(1) *The indications from symptoms and appearance at and after death* as to the type of poison that would produce the effects noted. This information may

save much time on the part of the laboratory investigator by giving him an indication as to which tests are most likely to give useful results, and it will often forestall time-consuming search for poisons that would be incompatible with the indications noted.

(2) *The condition of the body and its parts*, particularly abnormalities in the color or appearance of the blood, the liver, the inside of the stomach, and any irregular appearance or condition of any organs examined.

The investigator should have available a sufficient number of clean containers, e.g., Mason jars with caps, to receive all desirable samples. These should invariably include: (a) the stomach and its contents; (b) a good sample of liver; and (c) blood (at least 25–50 ml). It is often necessary to obtain, in addition, samples of the brain, kidneys, intestines, and sometimes of the bones if a chronic and fatally acute poisoning by lead or mercury is suspected. Any other organs noted by the autopsy surgeon as showing an abnormal appearance or color that might be attributable to poison should be included in the samples taken.

Although the stomach contents will usually reveal the poison ingested, a sample of blood is essential for determination of the presence and amount of alcohol, and it is useful for several other possible constituents, notably the barbiturates. If death was caused by inhalation of solvents, the liver, brain, and spinal cord will be most valuable. In barbiturate poisoning, particularly, a sample of the liver is very desirable, as is also *speed* in its analysis, because the barbiturates are rapidly destroyed in the body and will rarely persist in stomach contents. The liver also reveals, better than do other organs, the presence of arsenic, chronic poisoning by phosphorus, and various other toxic materials.

It will be seen from the foregoing summary that many organs or tissues that are not ordinarily removed and saved for examination may often be required and should be taken as samples. It is always better to take organs or tissues that are not apparently needed than to find, after interment, that no evidence is available because the correct material was not sampled. The autopsy surgeon may be unfamiliar with the needs of the toxicologist, and will then require instruction from other members of the investigation team. The number of poisonings that remain undetected is still relatively large, and the chief cause of this unfortunate state of affairs is the failure of the various investigators to cooperate effectively in the collection and the study of the evidence. Too often only the stomach and its contents are taken, and in many instances this is inadequate for the necessary examinations.

ISOLATION AND IDENTIFICATION OF POISONS

The police investigator will not be required to isolate or identify poisons; this work comes within the province of the toxicologist. However, it is not amiss for the investigator to have a general understanding of the problems of the toxicologist and the processes by which he seeks to solve them. Such understanding serves to promote cooperation with the toxicologist. The student of toxicology also needs to know something of the background of the field as well as the actual techniques employed.

Inorganic Poisons

Inorganic poisons of the first group are isolated by a number of methods from tissues, stomach contents, and other material with which they are mixed. The simple Reinsch test is valuable as a preliminary isolation method. The sample is acidified with dilute hydrochloric acid, a piece of clean copper wire of foil is placed in it, and the liquid is boiled. Any mercury, bismuth, arsenic, antimony, or silver in the sample will be deposited on the copper as a stain. The stain may then be identified by its appearance and by a number of chemical and microscopic methods. Another procedure of rather general applicability employs extraction with chloroform or carbon tetrachloride in the presence of diphenylthiocarbazone, better known as dithizone. This compound forms colored complexes with many of the heavy metals, compounds that are extractable with the above solvents. By control of the acidity or alkalinity, and by proper use of complexing agents, it is possible to separate the metals from each other and from the contaminants, and to identify the material extracted. Of added importance is the fact that the dithizone complex is also susceptible to reasonably accurate quantitative determination. This is a great advantage in dealing with the heavy metals, some of which are normally present in minute amounts and become toxic only when they reach considerable concentrations.

Another general procedure, which has been perhaps more popular than the facts warrant, is spectrography. The applicable range of the spectrograph is not greater than that of the dithizone procedure, and the accuracy of its quantitative determination is far less, unless elaborate arrangements and precautions are employed. The poorest spectrographic equipment that can be used is as expensive as the best instrumentation for spectrophotometric dithizone determination. If the spectrograph is already available for other purposes, it may be used effectively in the determination of many of the inorganic poisons, but not all.

A number of inorganic poisons, e.g., nonmetals, are not readily detected or determined by means of any of the three general methods discussed. Arsenic is normally detected and determined by chemical tests among which the Gutzeit method is perhaps best known and most widely employed. It has long been recognized that this method is defective for quantitative determination, and that better methods are available. It is too much to expect that attorneys —or even toxicologists—will immediately adopt superior methods; it is more consistent with tradition to demand the older inferior method. The intelligent toxicologist will employ both methods in combination in the hope that he can forestall objections from "erudite" attorneys to any method but the Gutzeit, while at the same time he can prove to himself and the court the reliability of the better procedures and thus participate in the education of the legal profession in matters technical. The analytical determination of inorganic poisons is in all respects identical with the general chemical analysis of biological materials for the same elements and compounds, and it is therefore not in any sense a specialized toxicological matter. Even so, there is still lacking a good, consistent scheme by which all of the important toxic elements and their compounds can be readily detected and determined in an orderly and systematic manner. Research directed toward the devising, improvement, and standarization of such schemes is greatly to be desired.

Volatile Poisons

Although there are some volatile inorganic poisons, volatility is much more common among the organic poisons. The only systematic portion of the procedures for the separation, detection, and quantitative determination of poisons involves steam distillation, and it is employed routinely. Yellow phosphorus is revealed by its phosphorescence. Other volatile poisons in the distillate are identified by chemical tests of considerable diversity and by the determination of physical constants. Gas chromatography has become a preferred method for the examination of volatile poisons, because of its rapidity and reliability. Several other instrumental methods have been developed, but are less available in most localities and are more costly.

Nonvolatile Organic Poisons

The isolation of the nonvolatile organic poisons, which includes the alkaloids and the barbiturates, is based almost entirely upon modifications of the basic procedure of Stas and Otto, which was published before 1850. The method is based upon two facts: (1) most members of this group of poisons are either organic bases or organic acids, with the bases predominating, and (2) the free bases or acids are more soluble in organic solvents than are the water-soluble salts of either. Thus, by shifting from acidic to basic solutions and vice versa, and extracting with ether or chloroform, either bases or acids will be preferentially extracted from each other and from the associated physiological material. It is of interest that so close an adherence to principles that were recognized over a century ago should still be popular, in view of the rapidity of scientific development in fields other than toxicology.

Final identification of most solvent-extracted poisons is now performed by combinations of thin-layer chromatography or gas chromatography and an instrumental identification such as ultraviolet or infrared spectrophotometry.

Solvent extractions, which are most useful in separating poisons from large quantities of physiological materials that would otherwise interfere, are in no sense specific, but require further separation, e.g., by chromatography, and final identification of the separated compound. Color and crystal tests have by no means lost their usefulness: they are most serviceable in laboratories that do not have sophisticated instrumentation. With the passage of time laboratories have become supplied with modern instruments, and the color and crystal tests are used less frequently.

REFERENCES

Amelink, F.: *Identification Methods in Pharmacy and Toxicology.* New York: Wiley-Interscience (1962).

Clark, E. G. C.: *Isolation and Identification of Drugs.* London: Pharmaceutical Press (1969).

Finkle, B. S.: "Forensic Toxicology of Drug Abuse: A Status Report," *Anal. Chem.* 44(9):18A (1972).

Gleason, M. N., Gosselin, R. E., Hodge, H. C., and Smith, R. P.: *Clinical Toxicology of Commercial Products.* Baltimore: Williams and Wilkins (1969).

Stewart, C. P., and Stolman, A., eds.: *Toxicology.* New York: Academic Press (1961). 2 vols.

Stolman, A. ed.: *Progress in Chemical Toxicology.* New York: Academic Press. Vol. 1 (1963); Vol. 2 (1965); Vol. 3 (1967).

Sunshine, I.: *Handbook of Analytical Toxicology.* Cleveland: Chemical Rubber Co. (1969).

Von Oettingen, W. F.: *Poisoning.* Philadelphia: W. B. Saunders (1968).

28
Drugs

Although the term "drug" is often applied to those materials that are used illegally by thrill seekers, addicts, and others, it must be acknowledged that the *legal* use of drugs has increased enormously in response to medical advances and to social factors such as emphasis upon health and disease. In the search for illicit drugs the investigator will encounter a large variety of drugs, carried by persons of all sorts. Antihistamines, pain relievers, cough remedies, vitamins, tranquilizers, and many more have complicated the problems of the field and laboratory identification of drugs. The investigator must be well informed not only about illicit drugs, but he must recognize also the prescription drug and the over-the-counter pill and capsule in order to eliminate them as sources of confusion. Thus he may be obliged to acquire an extremely broad range of knowledge and experience.

A minor complication is introduced by unconventional packaging, such as "bindles" of heroin in paper, plastic bags, rubber balloons, and other innocent-appearing substitutes for the customary capsule. The field investigator will soon become adept at recognizing such forms. The counterfeiting of legitimate drugs presents a more serious problem which requires the expertise of experienced laboratory personnel. The presence of a material in a proper and identifiable capsule gives no guarantee of its composition.

In practical drug investigation, a relatively few materials—notably marihuana and certain of the amphetamines and barbiturates—are encountered frequently. These materials take on local or regional nomenclature and packaging, so that the great bulk of such work does not entail a very broad general knowledge of drugs. As a consequence, many investigators tend to limit their work to these readily recognized materials. It is questionable whether this constitutes thorough law enforcement.

Drugs, narcotics, and poisons constitute a group of materials among which there are no sharp lines of demarcation. Virtually any drug, when taken in excessive amounts, will exhibit toxic properties that can justify its classification as a poison, and only a few poisons are so potent that they cannot be tolerated in small amounts. The term *intoxication,* used in its broadest and most literal sense, describes the effects of all kinds of materials that disturb normal physiological reactions. Such materials are described as having toxic or poisonous properties. In the narrower and more familiar usage, intoxication is equated with drunkenness. Although the term "narcotic" has a fairly precise pharmacological significance, legal usage classifies certain drugs as narcotics, even though not all of them exhibit true narcotic properties. Somewhat more recently there has been a legal classification of "dangerous drugs," which are not included among the narcotics but are in some sense illegal without prescription. Certainly some of the narcotics are among the most dangerous drugs. At present, the law-enforcement apparatus in the field of drugs is enforcing laws that control both narcotics and dangerous drugs. When either of these, because of excessive dosage, causes death, enforcement of the law is carried out by somewhat different agencies.

The natural and synthetic materials that must be considered include not only a very large group of drugs of possible pharmacological importance, but all types of pesticides, liquids that are important as solvents and fuels, numerous poisonous gases, many inorganic (often metallic) compounds, and a host of chemicals of industrial importance that do not belong in any of these categories. With the exception of materials that are generally termed either narcotic or psychedelic, most of the above materials are of significance because of their toxic properties only.

To the criminalist, the highly significant fact about drugs is the proliferation of new synthetic chemical substances, first in the ethical and legal market, and often later in clandestine operations. This fact poses enormous problems of control, which threaten to inundate all the laboratories that identify drugs or otherwise serve law enforcement. Laboratory workers in this field tend to become highly specialized, but few of them can actually become familiar with all the drugs that may be brought to the laboratory.

Many such drugs are common and are easily recognized by enforcement agents, but if *complete* coverage is to be achieved, the police officer must have at his disposal an efficient laboratory staffed with knowledgeable personnel. The task of the police officer is to locate the drug and its possessor, salesman, or user, and, when this can be done readily, to make preliminary identification of the drug. The identification should always be subjected to laboratory testing, however, to ensure the degree of certainty necessary for court purposes and to exclude all legally permissible drugs. The task of the field investigator is difficult, but it is entirely different from that of the laboratory investigator. Both are too specialized for extensive discussion in this volume. It is the intention here to provide preliminary technical aid to the field investigator, and also to orient his thought toward the technical portion of the investigation, most of which will be performed by the laboratory staff.

NATURAL MATERIALS

Marihuana

By all odds, marihuana (also spelled marijuana) is the most widely used illegal "drug" at the present time. Actually not a drug, but dried parts of the hemp plant, *Cannabis sativa* (or *Cannabis indica*), it contains a number of individual compounds of partially understood physiological effect. A variation which is very ancient, but has recently come into favor again, is hashish. This is the concentrated resin of marihuana, and is correspondingly more potent in the characteristic effects. *Cannabis* grows well under widely varied environmental conditions, so it can be cultivated in the relatively far north and also in semitropical regions.

The compounds that may have physiological action are all found in the resin, which is distributed primarily in the flowering parts and the leaves. The stems contain little of these compounds, and the seeds have virtually none. Smoking of the dried plant parts is the ordinary method of use. However, the resin may be extracted, and is sometimes used directly to obtain a more immediate effect. *Cannabis* being a dioecious plant, seed formation is dependent upon the transfer of pollen from the male plant to the female. The pharmacological effect is obtained from either the male or female plant.

COMPONENTS AND PHYSIOLOGICAL ACTION. Few pharmacological questions have led to so much divergence of opinion, exaggeration, misstatement, and general lack of precise knowledge as has the problem of marihuana. Undoubtedly this confusion arises from the fact that public reaction against marihuana has been strong, while at the same time its use has been both illegal and widespread. Thus, unfounded opinion has often been substituted for scientifically proved fact, and there has been far less research applied to the problem than its importance would justify. Although there are a very considerable number of interrelated compounds in the marihuana plant, any of which might give rise to physiological reaction, cannabinol, the most plentiful of these, appears to have little or no effect. Tetrahydrocannabinol, whose recent availability in synthetic form has stimulated research on this question, is the major effective component. It may now be predicted that many of the uncertainties and contradictions that have characterized the problem of marihuana will be resolved.

Although it appears that marihuana is a mildly psychedelic material, even this has been difficult to prove, perhaps in part because of the very great differences in quality observable in the materials used for experimental purposes. Many samples of the plant consist almost entirely of stems and seeds, and would be expected to have little effect, if any. Marihuana samples are usually obtained from confiscated material, so there can be little control over their quality and uniformity. Further complications are attributable to the fact that well-controlled experiments might best be performed with an extract and with some method of administering the drug other than smoking. It has been claimed that burning the material has the effect of destroying the known compounds that are characteristic of *Cannabis*. The products that are formed by heat and are present in the smoke are poorly known. This confusion has given rise to attitudes that range from extreme antagonism to marihuana to an honest and well-documented effort to legalize its use. The principal objection to the latter course is that the use of marihuana leads to the later substitution of more dangerous drugs. No verified research supporting this contention has been found. In the meantime, whether ultimately legal or indefinitely illegal, marihuana remains a serious problem to law-enforcement personnel, a problem to be dealt with in an atmosphere of knowledge and capability, rather than under the pressures of prejudice from both directions that exist today.

IDENTIFICATION. As with other materials included in the list of dangerous drugs, it is not sufficient for the officer to make an identification, nor is it always practical, despite the fact that an experienced officer will seldom misidentify marihuana. The plant is reasonably easy to recognize, and its culture is illegal. Small fragments of leaf or flower parts are somewhat more difficult to identify. Generally, the first step in the identification is botanical in nature: the microscopic examination of the fragment for cystolithic hairs that cover some of the leaf surfaces. Although these hairs are quite characteristic of marihuana, it has recently been pointed out that a considerable number of other plants have leaf-hairs similar enough to those of marihuana that the inexpert might well be mistaken in the identification. A chemical method, the Duquenois test, is considered to be specific for marihuana when a chloroform extraction is included in the procedure. Some laboratory workers prefer a combination of microscopic examination with the Duquenois test; others rely entirely upon the microscope. It must be borne in mind that even the combination of the

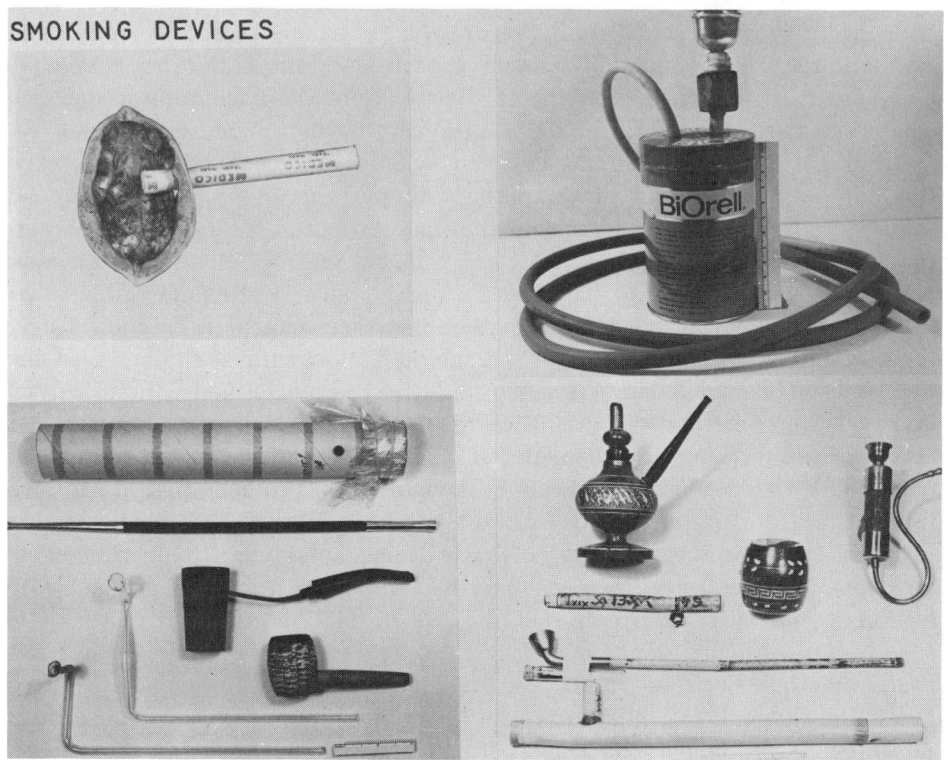

FIGURE 28-1. Various devices used for smoking marihuana, hashish, and/or opium. (Courtesy of the Contra Costa Co. Criminalistics Laboratory.)

two techniques could result in error if both were performed by a careless or inexperienced technician. Positive identification is available by means of either gas chromatography or thin-layer chromatography. Thin-layer chromatography is routinely performed in many laboratories, particularly on residues or extracts. As is always the case, the size of the sample and its condition are major factors in the difficulty or simplicity of making an identification. The experienced investigator will be reasonably sure of identifying marihuana by mere inspection of a good sample. Such an identification is *not* sufficient for court purposes, but it can save time in the application of other tests that are more definitive.

Special samples may require further consideration. *Seeds,* plentiful in low-grade marihuana, may be the only residues recovered, and will therefore require identification, even though they are of no value to the user of marihuana. They are dark—almost black—roughly spherical but generally a little elongated, and range in size from that of small birdshot up to several milli-

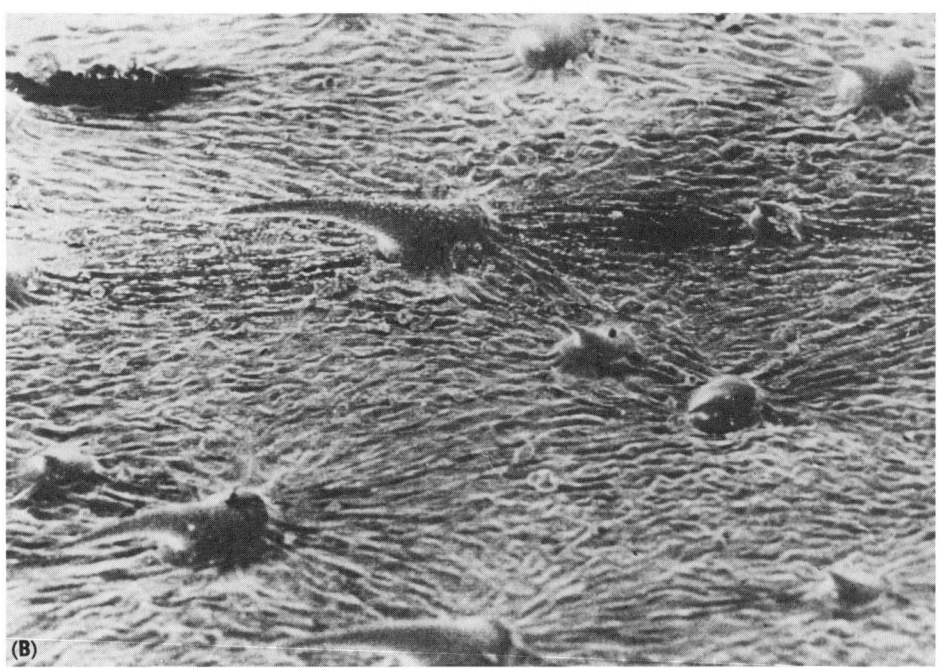

FIGURE 28-2. (A) Growing marihuana plant. (B) Scanning electron micrograph of a marihuana leave fragment. The claw shaped protrusions are cystolithic hairs which are one of the features used in microscopic identification of marihuana leaf fragments, 100X. (Courtesy of Gerald T. Mitosinka.)

meters in diameter. A very characteristic feature of the seed is the presence on its surface of a reticulum, which can ordinarily be recognized without difficulty. There may be seeds of some other species with which those of marihuana might be confused, however. The confusion can be resolved by crushing the questioned seeds and running thin-layer chromatographic comparisons with crushed marihuana seeds. Alternatively, if time permits, the seeds may be sprouted: the marihuana seedling is not difficult to identify. Marihuana *extracts* and *resin concentrates* will yield strong Duquenois tests. They may be even more positively identified by chromatography. Although samples such as these may not often be encountered, marihuana extracts or concentrates are sometimes added to tobacco, to cigarettes, or to other materials. Such evidence requires reextraction and subsequent testing as indicated.

SYNTHETIC MATERIALS

A recent publication on the separation and identification of drugs lists between 6000 and 7000 organic compounds that may be considered as drugs. This compilation certainly is not exhaustive, nor will the total number of existing drugs remain at its present level, but will continue to increase with the addition of new drugs. To expect the field investigator, or even the laboratory investigator, to become immediately familiar with so over-whelming a list of drugs is clearly not realistic. Fortunately, the number of different drugs that are actually encountered is much smaller, and the list can be broken down into a reasonably manageable classification. A few materials that are classified as dangerous drugs are so widely used as to become familiar to the criminalist. These include marihuana, STP (methyldimethoxyamphetamine), LSD (lysergic acid diethylamide), barbiturates, amphetamines including "speed" (methamphetamine), peyote, toluene (glue solvent), and some others that are less common. It cannot be doubted that under different social conditions, tobacco and alcohol would be included in the list of dangerous drugs, as both of them meet the requirements upon which such a list is compiled.

A discussion of the specific tests for the analysis and identification of organic drug materials is beyond the scope of this volume. Generally, an unequivocal identification of a drug is achieved with a combination of chemical and microcrystalline tests, chromatography, and instrumental analysis. The particular tests selected will depend upon the nature of the drug, and the outcome of initial screening test that may suggest a certain family of compounds. Many drugs of abuse, particularly the amphetamines and barbiturates, may be adequately identified by a few simple microcrystalline tests. Other materials, such as LSD, require a more sophisticated approach, which may involve chromatography and spectrophotometry.

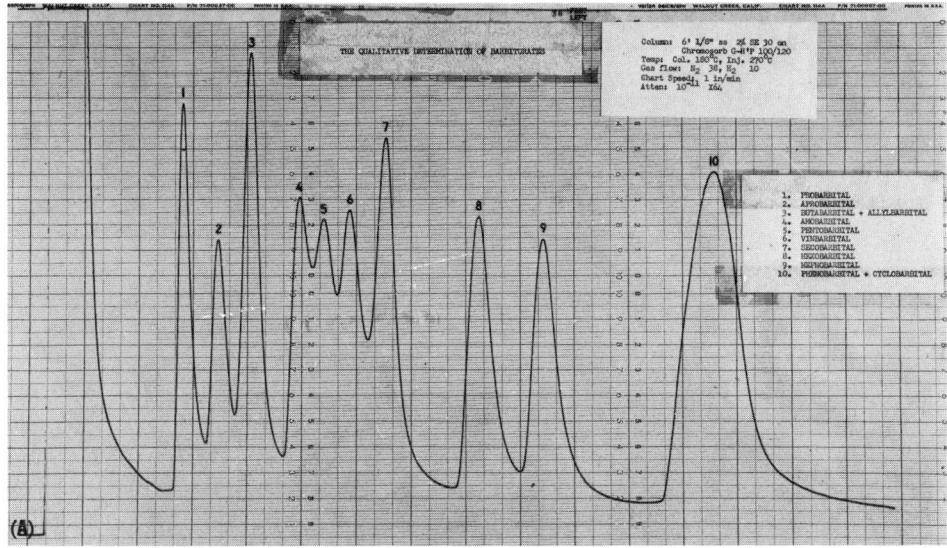

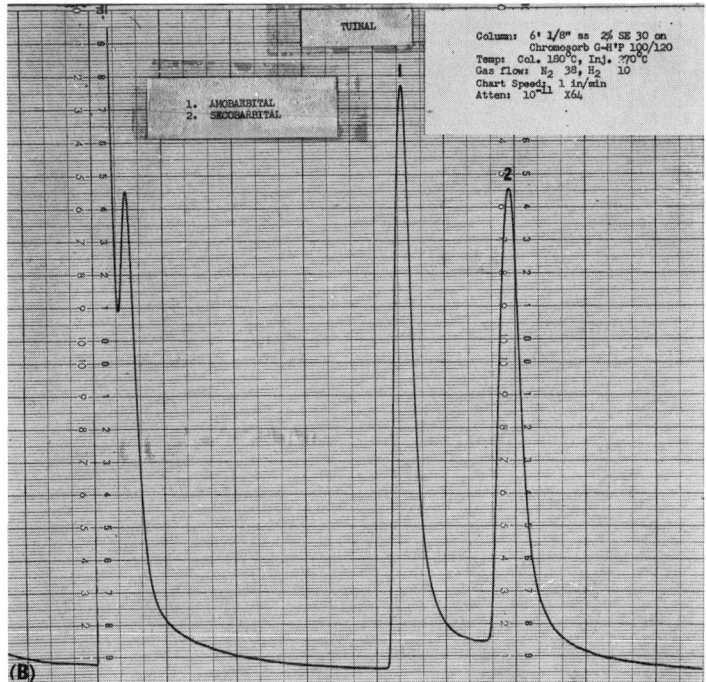

FIGURE 28-3. Many barbiturates can be identified by gas chromatography (A). The barbiturate preparation, Tuinal, is a mixture of amobarbital and secobarbital (B). (Courtesy of Edward T. Blake.)

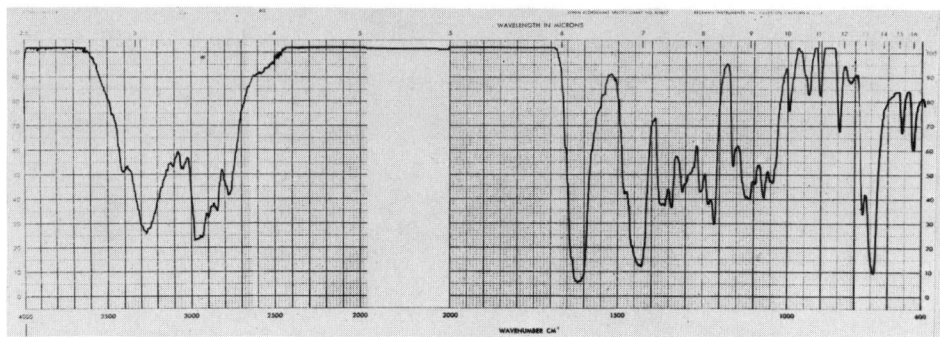

FIGURE 28-4. Infrared spectrum of lysergic acid diethylamide (LSD). Infrared spectroscopy is frequently used for the identification of organic compounds such as drugs. (Courtesy of Dorothy Northey.)

REFERENCES

Clarke, E. G. C.: *Isolation and Identification of Drugs.* London: Pharmaceutical Press (1969).
Davis, J. E.: "Barbiturate Differentiation by Chemical Microscopy," *J. Crim. Law, Criminol. and Pol. Sci.* 52:459 (1961).
Finkle, B. S.: "Forensic Toxicology of Drug Abuse: A Status Report," *Anal. Chem.* 44 (9):18A (1972).
Fulton, C. C.: *Modern Microcrystal Tests for Drugs.* New York: Interscience (1969).
Gupta, R. C., and Kofoed, J.: *Identification Guide—Tablets and Capsules.* Toronto: Canada Law Book (1967).
Hider, C. L.: "The Rapid Identification of Frequently Abused Drugs," *J. For. Sci. Soc.* 11:257 (1971).
Kaistha, K. K., and Jaffe, I. H.: "TLC Techniques for Identification of Narcotics, Barbiturates and CNS Stimulants in a Drug Abuse Screening Program," *J. Pharm. Sci.* 61:679 (1972).
Mule, S. J.: "Methods for the Analysis of Narcotic Analgesics and Amphetamines," *J. Chrom. Sci.* 1972(10):275.
Sunshine, I.: *Handbook of Analytical Toxicology.* Cleveland: Chemical Rubber Co. (1969).
Thornton, J. I., and Nakamura, G. R.: "The Identification of Marijuana," *J. For. Sci. Soc.* 12:461 (1972).
Usdin, E., and Efron, D. A., eds.: *Psychotropic Drugs and Related Compounds.* Washington, D.C.: Public Health Service Publication #1589, U.S. Dept. of HEW (1967).

29
Alcohol*

Alcohol, of all the materials correctly classified as poisons, is probably responsible for more deaths by direct toxic action than any other poison, and possibly for more than are caused by all other poisons together. However, the chief current interest in alcohol is not directly related to its toxicity, and this fact would seem to justify its consideration as a separate forensic science problem.

The growing incidence of traffic accidents, and of other mishaps to which the consumption of alcohol may contribute, has focused the attention of the police laboratory on the problem of alcohol analysis. The literature in the field is voluminous and, in part, confusing and contradictory. Only in recent years have developments in the control of alcohol in connection with traffic safety begun to be scientific and consistent. It has been established, for example, that the majority of persons apprehended on suspicion of driving while under the influence of alcohol are problem drinkers, not occasional moderate drinkers. Both moderate and problem drinkers are social drinkers, therefore the latter term is not an appropriate description. Methods applicable to the analysis of blood, urine, and breath for alcohol content have improved greatly, and are undergoing some degree of standardization and control as to reliability, accuracy, and precision.

Despite this very considerable progress, there remain a large number of laboratory technicians who determine alcohol routinely by questionable

---

* Written in collaboration with Lowell W. Bradford; Director, Laboratory of Criminalistics, County of Santa Clara, San Jose, California.

methods and without any understanding of the pitfalls that exist in such techniques. This has been largely attributable to the misconception that any clinical laboratory will produce satisfactory analyses of alcohol in blood and in similar materials, because the samples are of a type familiar to the technician. It is overlooked that the training of clinical laboratory personnel rarely, if ever, includes quantitative alcohol analysis—a technique that is unrelated to medical technology, the main subject of the laboratory's interest. In fact, some of the least satisfactory methods for this specific purpose are those devised by clinical "laboratory investigators," who are assumed to be competent in all aspects of blood analysis. These methods, unfortunately, have found their way into some of the authorized manuals intended for use in the clinical laboratory, where they will continue to mislead the relatively poorly trained technicians who are routinely employed in such establishments. Sample check programs conducted in some parts of this country have shown that analytical results from clinical laboratories have been far poorer than those from criminalistics laboratories.

Perhaps even more unfortunate is the wide acceptance of quick and easy field methods for breath alcohol samples. Instruments are now available that are capable of accurate analysis of breath for its alcohol content, and their use is becoming widespread. The most prominent of these, at the moment, include the Breathalyzer, Intoxilyzer, and G. C. Intoximeter, which, when properly calibrated, controlled, and serviced, are very reliable. Such devices are still subject to error when used by unskilled or careless operators, or where the supervision involving training, maintenance, and periodic laboratory checks of their operation is not provided.

Many of the other breath-alcohol procedures are not only unreliable, but misleading when used indiscriminately, and without a clear realization of their limitations. Most of them are useful as screening procedures to free persons who have not been drinking significantly, or to indicate the probability that heavier drinking has occurred; thus they can provide the officer with reasonable cause to call for more precise and reliable blood analyses.

Despite all these limitations and uncertainties, it must be emphasized that the determination of alcohol in blood through the analysis of blood, urine, or breath samples has been of the greatest value in the administration of justice, and must be considered an extremely important phase of criminalistics practice. This follows from the fact that the usual case involving alcohol is relatively uncomplicated and may be successfully clarified even when some of the circumstances surrounding the investigation are not satisfactory. Also there are a considerable number of laboratories in which enough care is taken in the assay to allay any serious doubt concerning the validity of their findings. Unfortunately, the number of such laboratories is still too small, proportionately, to encourage the hope that they are leading a general movement toward better chemical test evidence concerning the laws relative to physiological impairment from alcohol.

PHYSIOLOGICAL ASPECTS OF ALCOHOL INGESTION

Any brief discussion of the physiological response to alcohol must be inadequate because of the inherent complexity of the subject and the fact that much remains to be elucidated. The essential facts upon which there seems to be general agreement may be briefly stated as follows:

(1) The rate at which ingested alcohol is absorbed depends upon the dilution in the stomach and the nature of the diluting material. In general, the absorption is slower with greater dilution, but the slowing is not directly proportional to the dilution. In contrast to most food materials, alcohol is mainly absorbed directly from the stomach and duodenum. The rate of absorption may also be influenced by a number of factors including drinking rate and concentration of beverage.

(2) During the period of absorption the concentration of alcohol in the arterial blood is higher than that in the venous blood. Capillary blood is believed to approximate more closely the concentration of alcohol in arterial than in venous blood.

(3) In the postabsorptive phase, the difference in alcohol concentration between arterial and venous blood becomes smaller, and an equilibrium state has been reached.

(4) The concentration of alcohol in the water content of the brain is believed to be similar to that of the water content in the blood, although some evidence is accumulating that may indicate more difference than has been generally assumed. It may vary proportionately with the blood alcohol concentration.

(5) The effects of alcohol on the individual are largely those that result from its effect on the brain and central nervous system.

The effects of alcohol generally manifest themselves in the human adult by passing through several phases.

Phase I, which occurs with 1–3 oz of 100-proof beverage or its equivalent in alcohol content, involves purely subjective effects that involve euphoria. The individual may describe the feeling as a "glow" or a feeling of well being. Depending upon the amount of inhibitions that a person lives with, the release of these inhibitions in Phase I may bring on bizarre behavior to various degrees. Social conduct frequently deviates from normal.

The subject passes into Phase II when blood alcohol levels reach a sufficient level and he begins to show various kinds of impairment in visual acuity. Reaction-time responses are lengthened; manual dexterity is impaired; and, generally speaking, any kind of a test involving decisions complexed with manipulation will show impairment and deterioration from the alcohol-free condition.

A further advance in impairment then brings on the phenomenon denoted by Phase III, which consist of disturbances of balance, walking ability, and speech ability. This is the phase to which the expressions *intoxication* and *drunkenness* are applicable. The subject in Phase III is observed to stagger and to have indistinct or slurred speech.

Phase IV is the description given to a further advanced stage in which subjects become nauseated, regurgitate, or become stuporous. They may go into coma for several hours.

When the nervous system functions controlling heartbeat and breathing mechanisms are sufficiently depressed by the presence of a high concentration of alcohol in the human body, death will occur. The death stage is defined as Phase V.

The impairments that mark these phases are progressive and the onset of each level of nervous-system dysfunction is proportional to two things, alcohol in blood concentration and experience with the consumption of alcohol. The inexperienced drinker may pass into Phase III at a blood alcohol concentration as low as 0.06% and into Phase IV at a blood alcohol concentration as low as 0.15%. However, the experienced drinker may not in all cases appear to have slurred speech or stagger (Phase III) until the blood alcohol concentration is as high as 0.24%.

There is ample research data to show that there is a significant correlation of auto collisions with blood alcohol concentrations of 0.08%. The correlation is progressive with higher blood alcohol concentrations, and the minimum level of 0.08% includes experienced drinkers. Blood alcohol concentrations associated with the beginning of and inclusion of all persons may be summarized as follows:

Phase	Blood alcohol content (includes some people)	Blood alcohol content (includes all people)
I	0.01%	0.05%
II	0.03	0.08
III	0.06	0.24
IV	0.15	0.40
V	no data	0.50

(6) The manifestations of alcoholic influence in different individuals are not uniform. Just as no two people behave exactly alike when equally drunk, the apparent degree of alcoholic influence and the kinds of effects vary in different people at the same blood alcohol concentration. The important point is that in any given person, the phases of impairment occur sequentially. Therefore symptoms of Phase III indicate impairments of Phase II.

(7) Loss of alcohol from the blood and tissues results from its oxidation, which may amount to as much as 10 grams per hour (g/hr). A much smaller

quantity is lost in the breath and the urine. The sum of alcohol elimination processes results in a reduction of blood alcohol levels by 0.02%/hr.

(8) Even comparatively low concentrations of alcohol in blood produce some disturbances in the individual. Often these are not apparent except upon the application of special tests. Reaction time is noticeably affected by alcohol at low concentrations.

(9) Because of the normal behavioral variations that exist from person to person, there is as yet no completely satisfactory method for determining the exact degree of an individual's physiological impairment from alcohol. One person may show a Phase III symptom not shown at all by another.

In the light of the foregoing generalizations it is apparent that any procedure that seeks to establish culpability in cases involving the physiological effects of alcohol must be somewhat arbitrary. It is *not* axiomatic that all individuals who drive motor vehicles when they have been drinking have poorer safety records than do all sober drivers.

Lawmakers who specify speed limits are confronted with a similar anomaly. Although some drivers operate cars more safely at 50 mph than do others at 35 mph, this fact does not prevent the establishment and enforcement of speed laws that apply to the skillful and the unskillful driver alike. In the same sense it is logical that some limits should be set for acceptable alcohol concentration in the blood, even though any such limit is admittedly arbitrary. Prima facie laws in the United States do this.

The original level of 0.15% blood alcohol as prima facie evidence of impairment, which was recommended for legislation by the National Safety Council, is being rapidly lowered to 0.10% in the United States. More rigid concepts exist at considerably lower levels in other countries. This move was sparked by early studies made in Sweden and extended elsewhere. Czechoslovakia specifies a prohibition of no drinking before driving, with an allowable limit of 0.02% blood alcohol concentration. The subject of impairment of the skills involved in driving has now been thoroughly studied, as have also chemical testing methods for alcohol in blood, urine, and breath. Borkenstein's "Grand Rapids Study" is probably the most significant experimental evaluation of the correlation between blood alcohol levels and accident probability available at the present time. It demonstrates a significant correlation of automobile accidents with blood alcohol levels above 0.08%. A review by Harger is the most recent systematic digest of the technical aspects of the physiology and biochemistry of the subject. Bradford has published a series of papers on changing attitudes in enforcement and standards of practice. When it is considered that a drinker must consume 8–10 oz of 100-proof liquor in a short time period to reach a level of 0.14–0.16% blood alcohol concentration, prima facie levels of 0.08% blood alcohol concentration appear to be justified. It seems certain that acceptance of this limit or a similar one will ultimately become quite general. It is not implied that an individual with a little less alcohol than this is necessarily sober, or that one with a little more is definitely drunk. What *is* implied is that *everyone having this much alcohol in his blood is impaired in some significant degree, and more persons are completely unsafe as motor-car operators,* and should not be engaged in any other occupation requiring full use of their senses and skills. This applies to the pedestrian crossing the street who is too slow or erratic in movement to avoid the collision that kills him, and to the operator of any machine or process that can be hazardous when not properly controlled.

It will become ever more necessary for the criminalist to determine the concentration of blood alcohol in suspected drinking drivers and others. For this reason, he must understand the analytical problems involved, the chemical and physiological principles that underlie their solution, and the pitfalls that must be avoided. It is also necessary that a practical system of drinking-driver evidence collection be established, in which the chain of evidence is maintained intact, storage or treatment of evidence prior to analysis cannot invalidate the results, and the arresting officer knows exactly how to proceed with his portion of the investigation.

A metropolitan area of 1 million–1.5 million in population can expect to have 8000–10,000 arrests for operating a motor vehicle while under the influence of alcohol or in combination with drugs in a period of one year. Penalties are becoming more and more severe and enforcement more active as the nation as a whole has come to recognize the severity of this traffic safety problem. The sheer volume of these cases in the court system has caused the development of a specialty in the practice of law. Prosecutors and defense attorneys have had to learn the scientific basis of the problems involved in the analysis and evaluation of test results. It has become a display of forensic science at its best, both operationally and jurisprudentially. Lawyers have more knowledge at their fingertips by virtue of published procedures, data, and dicta in this than in any other kind of a serious misdemeanor. Consequently, it is expected that the documentation of all investigative results will be examined critically for problems that could interfere with admissibility and credibility as evidence in legal proceedings.

CALCULATION OF ALCOHOL LEVELS

If the quantity and the alcoholic concentration of liquor imbibed by an individual are known, together with the time span since the consumption began, it is possible to calculate an approximate peak blood alcohol concentration for him. Conversely, if blood is drawn at some known time interval after an investigated incident, the alcohol concentration found in the blood sample may be extrapolated into past time to obtain a reasonable approximation of the alcohol level at the time of the incident causing investigation, provided that the time of the last drink is known to precede the incident by one hour. Such calculations can be only approximate, by reason of variations in the quantity of alcohol in a drink and, to some extent, because of individual variations among people; however, such extrapolations have evidentiary validity.

Most standard drinks, whether highballs, cocktails, or containers of beer, will contain similar amounts of alcohol. For a 180-lb person, 10 oz of 100-proof liquor (equivalent to 12.5 oz of 80-proof alcohol) consumed in 1–1.5 hr will bring about a maximum level of 0.14–0.16% blood alcohol concentration within an hour of the last drink consumed. Of course, a given amount of alcohol will increase the blood alcohol level of people of different sizes by different amounts. The loss of alcohol, chiefly by oxidation, but also by exhalation and kidney secretion, averages 0.02%/hr. If a suspect is apprehended at 11 P.M., and his blood is sampled at 3 A.M. and found to contain 0.20% alcohol, it follow that, at the time of apprehension, the value was about 0.28%. (The assumption is made that no alcohol was consumed after 10 P.M.)

INVESTIGATION

Two kinds of investigative procedure are applicable, one focused upon perceptible behavioral abnormalities of the suspect and another involving definitive analyses of his breath, urine, and blood for their alcohol content. The observation of an uncertain gait, slurred speech, and the odor of alcohol on the breath is preliminary evidence of Phase III impairment. Numerous indications of impairment, which are sometimes more significant than are the actual test results, may be observed. Some law-enforcement agencies employ the observation-of-performance method exclusively, although others do not agree that it is preferable to chemical testing. Such performance tests are basically physiological and are not properly included within the category of "physical evidence." They are also subject to considerable individual variability, and, in some instances, they may be easily misinterpreted. One of their chief dangers lies in the fact that diabetics in insulin shock and persons with head injuries may appear to be intoxicated whether they have been drinking or not. To guard against such errors, it is advisable to apply the second type of test, which involves the analysis for alcohol content of breath, urine, or blood by appropriate chemical or instrumental methods. These have the great virtue of providing information as to whether the person in question has been, or has not been, drinking, and if he has, the approximate quantity present in the body at the moment can be determined.

At the Scene

Ordinarily the police officer is not in a position to remove blood from a person who is suspected of drunkenness. At the scene, only procedures applicable to

Phase III discovery or breath alcohol analysis should be applied, and these should be of the screening type that ascertain whether there is reasonable cause for further tests. Results of such breath tests should not be used as evidence.

Although operational details differ from one jurisdiction to another, the enforcement procedure encompasses several distinct steps, each of which includes certain fundamental elements. These steps may be outlined as follows:

Step 1. *On-the-scene contact; first impressions of the investigating officers.*
(1) What drew attention to the perpetrator?
(2) Was the subject driving?
(3) Observations and conversation with the subject that caused the officer to think that the subject was suffering an impairment of brain function that might be the effect of ingested alcohol. (The officer's diagnosis of alcoholic intoxication is correct in at least 99% of the cases.)

Step 2. *Further examination at a prepared central facility.*
(1) Planned interrogation (Alcoholic Influence Report Form).
(2) Planned performance tests, for the purpose of detecting only advanced gross impairments (Phase III evidence).
(3) Withdrawal, by a person licensed or authorized, of a physiological specimen to be analyzed for determination of alcohol content. In order of decreasing convenience, the specimen may be blood, breath, or urine. With the last, best results are obtained when the bladder is emptied, and the sample taken 20 minutes later.
(4) Examination by a physician if interrogation indicates a dangerous health condition in the subject, such as epilepsy or other dysfunction of the nervous system, diabetes, use of drugs or medicines, concussion or other possible accidental injuries.

Step 3. *Follow-up by the investigating officer.*
Statements recorded during the planned interrogation should be checked. These particulars should include such details as bars that were visited, times and locations specified, the amount of liquor consumed, the taking of drugs, injuries, etc.

Step 4. *Issuance of complaint, and disposition of the case.*
Police agencies are urged to ask for complaints when the results of blood alcohol tests range from 0.05–0.10% in cases that show clinical symptoms of impairment, and in *all* cases in which blood alcohol levels are greater than 0.10%. In states having different presumptive levels, complaint requests should be governed accordingly.

It is an established fact, experimentally proven and further substantiated by traffic accident data, that *alcoholic influence is perceptible at low blood alcohol levels and can be scientifically determined by blood test alone.* However, it must be recognized that, as a matter of custom, courts and juries may require the police officer to have used *all* the methods enumerated in the four steps of investigation. For this reason the investigation steps presented here will probably continue to constitute the official procedure in most jurisdictions.

The officer at the scene will find that his attention is usually attracted to the perpetrator by his erratic driving, by his violation of a traffic law while in motion, or by a collision. In order that his interrogation may be of maximum value, the investigator should profit by lessons derived from experience. Therefore, a systematic line of questioning must be developed and reduced to a form that can be reproduced for use in any given jurisdiction and distributed among the officers to provide uniformity of practice. The interrogation form should be periodically revised to incorporate any improvements derived from experience. Such a form is not only a questionnaire, but also a guide for limited testing and a checklist for various kinds of useful evidence.

Blood Sampling

If blood samples are taken, a procedure that will fulfill the following requirements must be used:

(1) Provide an intact chain of possession from the person who draws the blood sample to the person who analyzes it.
(2) Ensure proper identification of the sample.
(3) By positive means, prevent all access to the sample to prevent deliberate contamination.
(4) Use a blood container that is secure against accidental contamination.
(5) Use a means of preservation that will keep the alcohol content of the sample from changing and prevent clotting.

These requirements may be easily met by the use of a sealed envelope bearing a format designed to implement the establishment of an identification.

In California standards for drawing and handling blood samples for alcohol analysis have been adopted as a matter of law.* The following is a direct quotation:

---

* Section 13354 (f), California Vehicle Code.

UNIFORM STANDARDS FOR THE DRAWING AND HANDLING OF BLOOD SAMPLES FOR BLOOD ALCOHOL ANALYSES

In accordance with Vehicle Code Section 13354(f), the Department of California Highway Patrol, in cooperation with the Department of Public Health and the Department of Justice, Bureau of Criminal Identification and Investigation, has established uniform standards for the drawing and handling of blood samples for blood alcohol analyses.

Uniform standards for equipment, operating techniques, and the care and preservation of blood samples will tend to assure the reliability of test results and to further their acceptance as evidence.

The Standards are outlined below:

A. EQUIPMENT TO BE USED BY PERSONS DRAWING BLOOD SAMPLES
   1. Disinfectant. Alcohol or other volatile organic disinfectant shall not be used to clean the skin, where a specimen is to be secured.
      a. Use aqueous benzalkonium chloride (zephiran), aqueous merthiolate or other suitable aqueous disinfectant.
   2. Hypodermic Needles and Syringes.
      a. Sterile, disposable hypodermic needles and syringes are recommended. Reusable equipment, if utilized, shall not be cleaned or kept in alcohol or other volatile solvent.
   3. Specially Prepared Tube or Vial.
      a. Only a chemically clean, dry tube or vial with inert stopper should be used. Alcohol or volatile solvents shall not be used to clean the tubes or vials.
      b. Tubes or vials shall contain an anticoagulant and a preservative. Recommended anticoagulants are fluoride, citrate, oxalate, and heparin. Recommended preservatives are fluoride and mercuric chloride.
      c. Tubes or vials shall be of such size as to hold 5 to 10 ml. of blood.
   4. Label for Tube or Vial.
      a. The label of the blood vial or tube shall contain at least the following information:
         (1) Full name of subject.
         (2) Date blood drawn.
         (3) Initials of person drawing blood.
         (4) Initials of witnessing Officer.
   5. Envelope or Other Container Used for Enclosing and Identifying Blood Sample Tube or Vial.
      a. The blood sample envelope or other container label shall include at least the following information:
         (1) Subject's full name.
         (2) Whether subject is alive or dead.
         (3) Submitting agency.
         (4) Geographical location where blood sample was drawn; i.e., name and/or address of hospital, jail, or other facility.
         (5) Name of person drawing blood sample.
         (6) Date blood sample drawn.

Alcohol

(7) Time blood sample drawn.
(8) Signature of witnessing Officer.
(9) A form establishing the chain of possession, such as:

CHAIN OF POSSESSION: (To be filled in by each person having possession of sample.)

Name	Time Received	Date
Name	Time Received	Date
Name	Time Received	Date
Name	Time Received	Date

b. Other information such as agency or laboratory number, offense charged, anatomical location from which blood sample was drawn, or any special instructions may be added.

B. PROCEDURES FOR OBTAINING BLOOD SAMPLES
1. The requesting Officer should witness the withdrawal of the sample. When the Officer witnesses the actual withdrawal of the blood, it may be unnecessary for the person drawing the blood to appear as a witness at the time of the trial.
2. Blood samples may be drawn only by a physician, registered nurse, duly licensed clinical laboratory bioanalyst or clinical laboratory technologist.
   NOTE: Pursuant to Section 13354(d) of the California Vehicle Code, no physician, registered nurse or duly licensed clinical laboratory bioanalyst or clinical laboratory technologist shall incur any civil or criminal liability as a result of the proper drawing of blood sample when requested in writing by a peace officer.
3. Cleanse the skin where the specimen is to be secured with an appropriate nonalcoholic or other nonvolatile disinfectant.
4. Use a sterile hypodermic needle and syringe to draw at least 5 ml. of blood. (It is recommended that disposable type equipment be used.)
5. Transfer the blood sample to the prescribed tube or vial.
6. After transferring blood to the tube or vial, carefully agitate the sample to assure uniform distribution of the preservative and anticoagulant.
7. When withdrawing blood from deceased persons, take sample *only* from femoral vein or other major vein or heart. *Do not use chest cavity.* Take sample before the body is embalmed and guard against use of equipment that has been sterilized in alcohol or contaminated with embalming solutions.

C. IDENTIFICATION AND PRESERVATION OF BLOOD SPECIMENS*
1. The person drawing the blood shall fill out and initial the label and affix it firmly to the tube or vial. The sample shall then be given to the Officer who,

---
* Paragraphs C3 and 4 are superceded by Title 17, California Administration Code, which effectively deletes the refrigeration requirement.

in turn, shall initial the label and place the sample in the prescribed envelope or other container. The Officer shall immediately complete the required information on the envelope or other container label and seal container securely.
2. Appropriate steps to insure security of sample shall be taken.
   a. Once the envelope or other container is sealed, it must not be opened except for analysis in the laboratory.
   b. Each person having possession of the sealed sample shall sign his name in the space provided for recording the "chain of possession."
3. If there is to be an extended period of time before analysis, the sample should be stored under refrigeration.
4. After analysis, a portion of the sample shall be retained under refrigeration until the case has been adjudicated.

Urine as a Sample for Blood Alcohol Determination

The degree of alcoholic influence is based upon the amount of alcohol in the bloodstream. Because there is a direct correlation of alcohol in urine with alcohol in blood at a particular time, urine can be used to determine a blood alcohol level. However, certain precautions must be taken. The following outline summarizes important considerations in the collection and preservation of urine samples to be used for alcohol assay.

(1) In the determination of blood alcohol from urine samples, *caution* is required in order to ensure correct sampling. First, the urinary bladder must be emptied; then 20–30 minutes later a sample can be taken. It is *important to note the time* of voiding in *each* instance. The water content of the urine in this period will contain the same amount of alcohol as the water content of the blood.

(2) When urine is submitted to the laboratory for alcohol analysis, the following specimens should be forwarded to the laboratory:
   (a) Sample of urine taken at the time the subject first voided his bladder. (This may be used for drug analysis.)
   (b) Sample of urine taken after the first voiding. Even if only a small quantity of urine is collected, 5 cc is still sufficient for the determination of alcohol.

(3) A member of the police agency, preferably the arresting officer—or the matron when appropriate—should supervise the collection of the sample so that there will be no question as to its source and no opportunity for the suspect to substitute tap water.

(4) *Chemically clean* wide-mouth jars of about 2-oz capacity, with tight-fitting screw caps, are suitable for the collection of urine samples. They are available through hospital supply and chemical supply companies at nominal cost.

(5) A *dry* preservative should be added to the chemically clean jars. Suitable preservatives are *sodium fluoride* (0.25 g/oz urine) or *mercuric chloride* (3 mg/oz urine). These chemicals are also available through hospital and chemical supply companies at nominal cost. *Caution is urged in their use because both are poisonous substances.*
(6) Urine samples should be collected directly into the prepared jars. The transfer of samples from one receptacle to another should be avoided.
(7) The samples must be clearly and fully labeled as to the *identity of source* and the *time* of obtaining the sample.

Disposition of Evidence Samples

After proper collection of the evidence samples, they are to be made available to a licensed Forensic Alcohol Analysis Laboratory for analysis, usually through the prosecutor's office. The prosecutor will rely heavily upon the results of the analysis and also upon a clear record of proper collection obtained through the police investigation.

Drugs in Impaired-Driver Cases

It is imperative, especially whenever and wherever drug use is widespread, that the possibility of impairment from some drug, or from its combination with alcohol, not be overlooked. When filling out the interrogation sheet, the investigator should inquire as to the use of drugs, and if the reply is affirmative, he should secure a sample of the current dose in possession of the subject. A number of drugs can be identified from a blood sample, but a complete search should include also the analysis of a urine sample. Recent investigations indicate that 21% of all persons arrested for driving under alcoholic influence take some type of drug preparation. In 705 cases in which drug use was acknowledged, 107 different specific drugs were named. Of these, 31% were of a type considered to impair driving skill. They included the following classes: ataractics (tranquilizers), ataxics, sedatives, hypnotics, and analgesic narcotics. In combination with alcohol the effect of both is aggravated.

Blood Alcohol Analysis

It is of critical importance that the analysis of a blood specimen be performed by a dependable method, and particularly by a well-trained analyst. The common assumption that the emergeny hospital laboratory staff are competent to analyze for blood alcohol concentration is often fallacious, and should be avoided. The other assumption, that only a clinical laboratory technologist is capable of performing this analysis, as contrasted with a good analytical chemist, is also fallacious. Blood alcohol analysis is too important a matter to be left to chance, and any laboratory that regularly performs blood analyses for law-enforcement purposes should be checked periodically. This is best accomplished by submitting samples containing precisely known quantities of alcohol for assay to all such laboratories occasionally. Such a checking procedure will not only reveal incompetence where it exists, but will reward excellent performance.

The problem of ensuring competent analyses through correct procedure by qualified analysts will probably never be completely solved. However, California at the present time has taken the lead in requiring licensing of laboratories and analysts who do this work. Title 17 of the California Administrative Code merits study by those who are interested in this subject. The California Association of Criminalists was the first to prescribe standards of performance and discipline of testing for the determination of blood alcohol concentration. The National Safety Council Comittee on Alcohol and Drugs is making studies along this line also. The National Bureau of Standards is studying the matter of reference standards for alcohol analysis and may provide reference standards in the future.

The prosecutor in any given jurisdiction should not be satisfied with his alcohol analysis laboratory unless it is under control by licensing, certification, or supervision by a qualified analytical chemist who engages in check or referee analysis with other laboratories. Experimental evidence indicates that laboratories directly dedicated to traffic enforcement alcohol analyses that handle a large volume of samples are capable of analyzing check samples with precision and accuracy. Medical laboratories and coroner medical examiner laboratories in general do not demonstrate the standard of accuracy required in traffic analyses.

The only recourse for defendants is a thorough cross-examination of evidence presented. To do this, trial attorneys must be knowledgeable in the special body of law on the subject. This, together with an understanding of the technical aspects of the subject and consulting assistance, will enable the attorney to determine whether correct procedure has or has not been employed. If a portion of the sample remains, a referee analysis should be requested in doubtful cases.

The work of the National Safety Council* in developing sources of information, stimulating research, and making recommendations for legislation and standards of practice has been the single most important factor in the development of our current body of knowledge of this subject.

The total scope of the subject of alcohol in traffic investigation is far too broad to be discussed in any detail in one chapter. Indeed, it would be difficult

---

* Reference materials are available on request from the National Safety Council, 425 N. Michigan Avenue, Chicago, Illinois 60611.

to contain the entire subject in one volume. In drinking-driver evidence-collection programs there are many specific subject areas of great depth. A list of references covering most of these areas has been provided at the end of this chapter.

REFERENCES

American Medical Association.: *Alcohol and the Impaired Driver, A Manual on the Medicolegal Aspects of Chemical Tests for Intoxication.* American Medical Association, 535 North Dearborn Street, Chicago, Ill. 60610 (1970).

Borkenstein, R. F.: *The Role of the Drinking Driver in Traffic Accidents,* ed. by A. Dale, Department of Police Administration, Indiana University, Bloomington, Ind. 1964.

Bradford, Lowell W.: "Changing Attitudes in Drinking Driver Enforcement as Reflected by the Actions of Researchers, Courts, Prosecutors and Society," *J. For. Sci. Soc.* 6:204 (1966).

Bradford, Lowell W.: "Drinking Driver Enforcement Problems," *J. Crim. Law, Criminol. and Pol. Sci.* 57:518 (1966).

Bradford, Lowell, W.: "Breathalyzer Experiences under Operational Conditions Recommended by the California Association of Criminalists," *J. For. Sci. Soc.* 9:58 (1969).

Bradford, Lowell W.: "Inquiry into Standards of Practice of Blood Alcohol Analysis," *J. For. Sci. Soc.* 11:127 (1971).

Bradford, Lowell W., Biasotti, A. A., and Finkle, B. S.: "The Occurrence of Some Drugs and Toxic Agents Encountered in Drinking Driver Investigations," *J. For. Sci.* 13:236 (1968).

Donigan, Robert L.: *Chemical Tests and the Law.* Evanston, Ill.: Northwestern University Traffic Institute (1966).

Erwin, Richard E.: *Defense of Drunk Driving Cases,* 2nd ed. New York: Matthew Bender (1964).

Finkle, B. S.: "Drugs in Drinking Drivers: A Study of 2,500 Cases," *J. Safety Research* 1:179 (1969).

Forney, Robert B., and Hughes, Francis W.: *Combined Effects of Alcohol and Other Drugs.* Springfield: Thomas (1968).

30
Tool Marks

Tools of many kinds are used in the perpetration of crimes. Among them, knives and screwdrivers are most common because of their general utility, availability, and ease of concealment. Bits and augurs, bars of several types, saws, pliers, cutters, hammers, sheet-metal strips, drills, and tools specially designed for burglary are frequently encountered by the police investigator. Some of these tools leave very characteristic marks by which the tool may be quite accurately identified. Other tools, such as metal drills, less often leave characteristic signatures behind. Whenever a tool has been used to move an object, to scratch or injure a surface, or otherwise to make any kind of impression on an object, there is at least a good chance that the tool can be identified with reasonable certainty. A thorough search must always be made for the tool. Often it will be found on the suspect, in his automobile, or on his premises. If the tool is not located in any of these places, the search should be extended until all possibilities have been exhausted. Quite often the tool can be traced to its owner by means other than finding it in his possession. A definite knowledge of the tool used in a crime is always important whether or not this information is, in itself, sufficient for a complete solution of the crime.

TYPES OF TOOL MARKS

Virtually infinite variation may be observed among tool marks met in practice, but all tool marks can be grouped into two main types: *compression* marks and *sliding* or scrape marks. Actually, many marks are combinations of the two types. For example, a hammer blow leaves a compression mark, but almost always the hammer glances somewhat at the moment of impact, and leaves a sliding mark also. The edge of a knife used to pry up a window will often leave a perfect impression of its edge as well as excellent sliding marks, which were made by pushing the knife into position. Another type of tool mark sometimes encountered is the *cutting* mark, such as is made by a knife, saw, pointer, or chisel. The cutting mark may be considered as a special case of the sliding mark. If the tool did not move laterally and leave parallel irregularities, its impression would not be characteristic of any particular tool. It is the irregularities in the edge of the blade that is responsible for the detailed features useful in identification.

Compression Marks

Marks made by forcing a tool into a material in such a manner as to leave a negative impression of the tool are termed compression marks. The impression may reproduce the tool rather accurately, or it may be quite unsatisfactory for purposes of identification. Even if the reproduction is excellent, it will be useful only to the extent that the tool is irregular or individual. For example, the impression of a common screwdriver such as is sold in chain stores would ordinarily be of little value unless it bore some characteristic break or abnormality that was imprinted in the mark. The material upon which such a mark is made is critical in determining the quality of the mark. The wood is distorted by the impact of the tool, but springs back partially after the pressure is removed. It often splinters and breaks in a way that destroys the value of the mark.

It is a common practice for the investigator to force the suspected tool into the mark to see if it fits. *This is a very risky practice that must be employed with the greatest discretion.* In the first place, it is very difficult at times to judge whether the tool fits or not because its mere presence in the indentation obscures the surface of contact. In the second place, the impression may be altered in the process unless the tool is applied very carefully.

Frequently the compression mark will show enough individual detail to match the suspected tool with considerable fidelity. This will be observed, for example, in the imprint of a knife blade when the mark shows a distinct edge and when the blade has been nicked or ground in an irregular shape. Wood will sometimes take a clear impression under such conditions, as will paint. Metal, because of its great resistance and rigidity, is not likely to receive a clear impression unless a very heavy tool is used. If a sufficiently deep and definite indentation is made, as may occur with sheet metal, the mark may be of value.

Slide Marks

Marks which are made by a tool during a sliding movement are of much greater general significance than are compression marks. The edge of practically every tool is more or less rough and irregular, and is visibly so at least under magnification. The irregularities record themselves as parallel striations that indicate the direction of the tool's motion. The arrangement of the striations, and their relationships, are highly correlated with the condition and the individuality of the tool edge. When viewed with flat illumination under low powers of the microscope, such marks show a series of highly individual irregular ridges and valleys which offer a reliable proof of their origin.

The value of slide marks varies with the material upon which they have been made. Raw wood rarely takes a definite and useful impression. Such marks on paint are often clear and serviceable. The most valuable sliding marks are usually found on metal surfaces, such as the brass or bronze of door fastenings. Galvanized iron and painted sheet metal take excellent sliding marks, as do safe dials. When a reasonably good specimen of such a mark is found, the identification of the tool that made it is ordinarily both simple and conclusive.

Cutting marks, which are related to sliding marks, are well recorded on raw wood. Green wood is better in this regard than dried wood, but good marks may be recorded on both. A common variation of the cutting mark is made by the jaws of a bolt cutter or a pair of pliers. Normally, bolt cutters do not have sharp edges: they virtually pinch off the bolt. They do, however, leave well-striated marks in many instances, though not in all. The chief use of the bolt cutter in burglary is for cutting the hasps of locks. Pliers, on the other hand, are used for cutting wires, and such cuts are of very common occurrence in many types of crime. Industrial and labor sabotage often involves multiple cutting of wires, and the theft of wire from storage supplies is quite common. Pliers are among the more difficult tools to identify because, although their jaws are relatively large, they cut material of small diameter that can receive only a short marking. Also, there are usually four edges to consider in studying any single mark. The identification of pliers is quite possible, but it is generally very laborious, and it requires a great deal of patience. Neither the bolt cutter nor the side-shears on a pair of pliers can be considered as entirely equivalent to a true cutting tool such as a knife, but the markings they leave resemble knife markings enough to make the same kind of treatment applicable.

VARIATIONS IN SLIDING MARKS. There are many ways in which a tool may be applied to an object. The chief difficulty in comparing tool marks arises from the change in the character of the mark on altering the manner of application of the tool. Assume that a pinch bar is being used to pry open a door. It must be forced into the crack sufficiently to obtain the necessary purchase. This may be accomplished by driving the tool forcibly with the hands, perhaps a number of times. After the bar has been inserted far enough, it is then used as a pry, which causes its edge to move in several directions. Sometimes the bar is inserted with lateral or crosswise movements, or both. It then progresses inward in a series of small movements whose traces are complicated by the alterations in the direction of motion. The mark is affected by the vertical and horizontal angles of application, as well as by the rotation of the tool on its own axis.

In order to ascertain the effect of such angular variations on the character of a tool mark, Burd and Kirk made a study of marks of the same tool applied at different angles. A variation of 10° in vertical angle was not found to produce serious changes in the mark, but 20° deviations altered it too much for accurate identification. Differences in the longitudinal angles produced less serious variations. Rotation of the tool longitudinally produced foreshortening of the mark, but the succession of ridges and valleys was not altered, and identification was possible, up to about 20°. Burd and Greene and others have extended and confirmed these studies, and cite many interesting applications to unusual types of tools and sources of marks.

The factor of variable application of the tool can be controlled in making standards. The tool mark being studied must be examined to determine as accurately as possible the manner of applying the tool. As such scrutiny cannot yield all the necessary information, standards of comparison should be prepared in sufficient numbers and variety to ensure that at least one of them will closely approximate the position of the tool at the time of its original application.

Individuality of Tools

The significance of a tool mark is related directly to the degree of individuality of the tool edge that made the mark. Until recently, most manufacturing methods gave to the product a reasonable degree of individuality when new. This has become less true in recent times. It has been noted by Burd that many cheap tools that are manufactured by mass production methods are now almost identical when first sold. Numerous high-grade tools, which are not changed by use, are now being produced by extremely hard cutting-and-broaching equipment that needs to pass the edge only once. Thus it is expected that increasing difficulty may be encountered in establishing individuality among tools that have been made with the same machine tool. Wear will eventually dispose of the problem, but the new tool may not be identifiable by present methods in terms of the mark it leaves.

In connection with tool individuality, one important consideration should not be overlooked: some *actual* tools might not be considered tools at all. Customarily we think of a tool as an object that has been specially constructed for a particular repetitive use. A wrecking bar, so useful to the burglar, is designed to rip and pry structures apart. However, a large stone, a piece of lumber, or some other object may be used for the same purpose, and, to the criminalist, it also is a tool when it is used as one. In this connection, many odd objects will be encountered by the alert investigator.

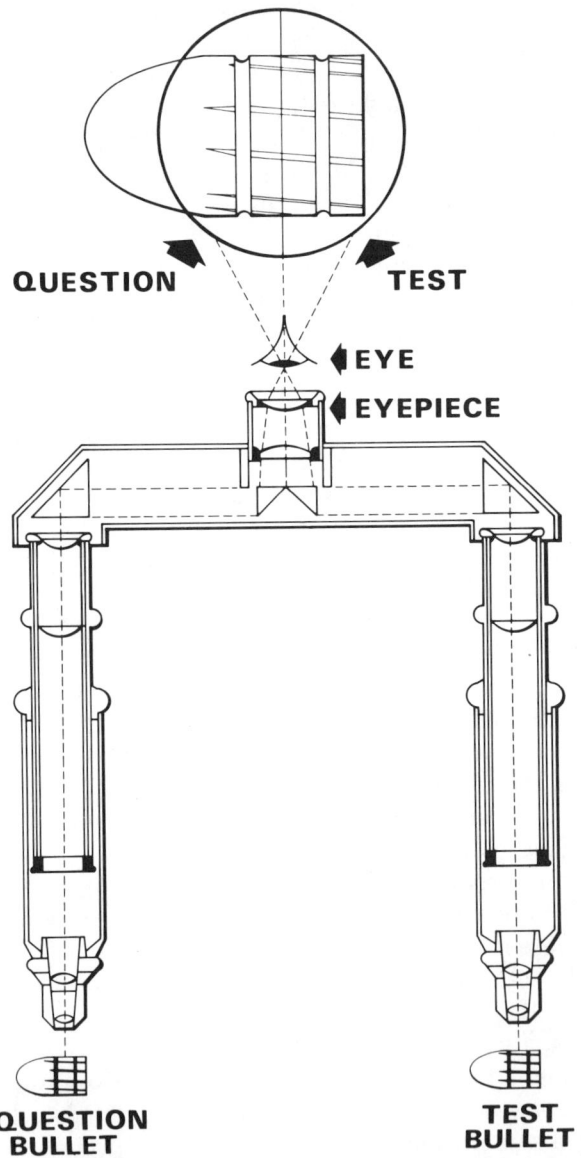

FIGURE 30-1. Schematic diagram of the comparison microscope. This microscope is commonly used for the comparison of tool marks, bullets, and cartridge cases. (Adapted by the Contra Costa Co. Criminalistics Laboratory from a drawing by A. Biasotti.)

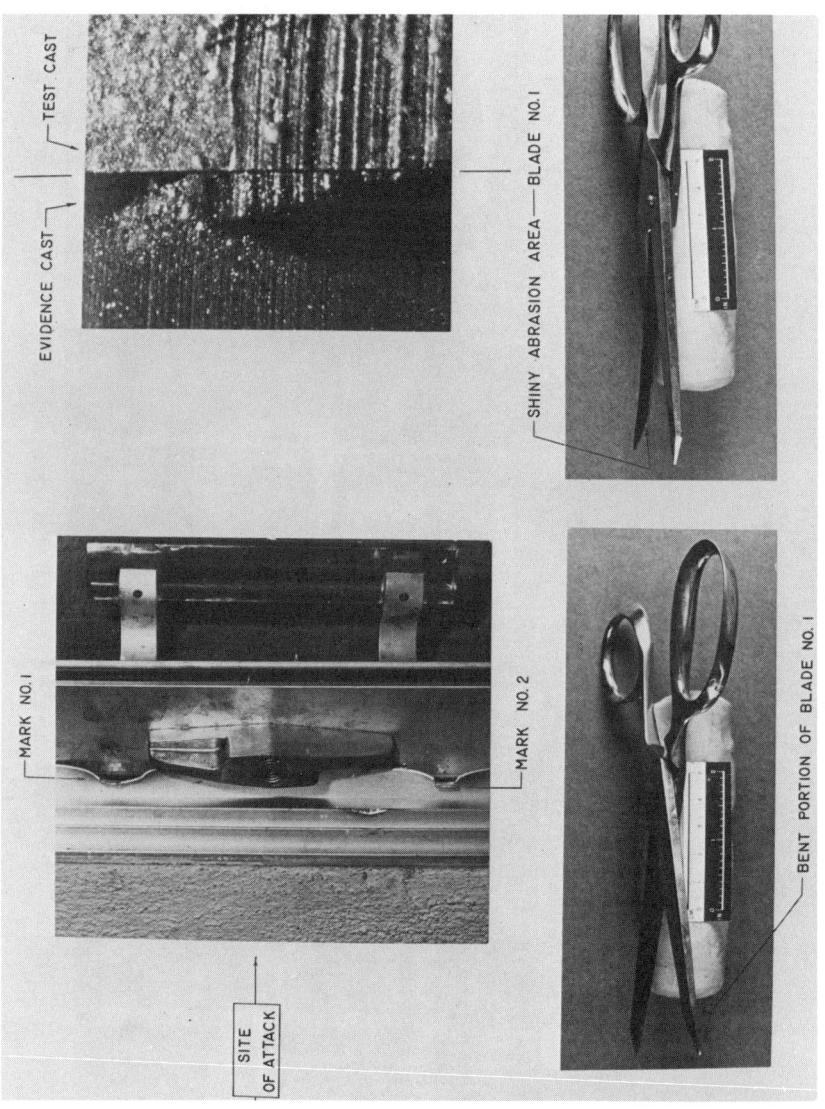

FIGURE 30-2. The lock on a sliding glass door was forced to gain entry to a home. One blade of a pair of scissors found in the suspect's possession was bent indicating the possible use of this portion of the scissors to force the lock. Casts were made of the damaged portion of the lock and test marks made with the scissors. The casts were then compared and an identification effected. (Courtesy of John E. Murdock.)

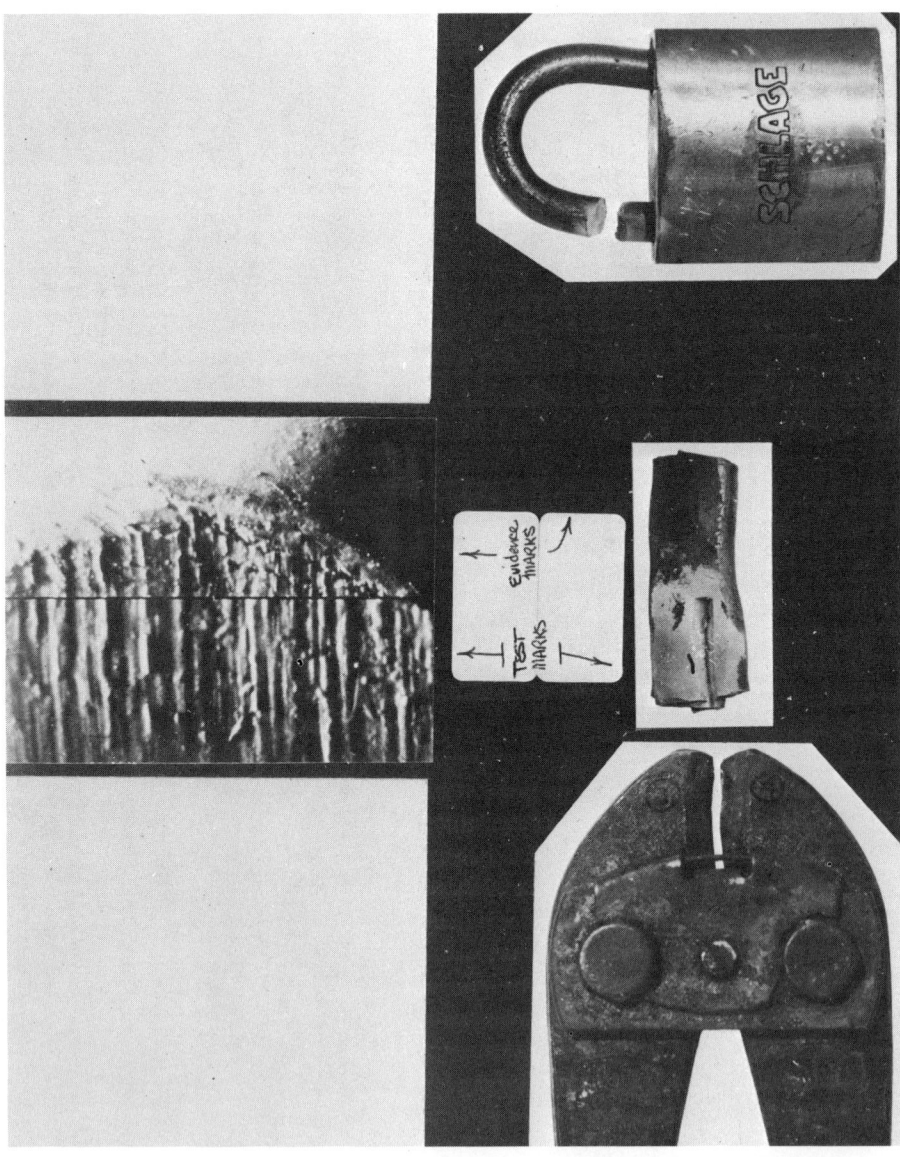

FIGURE 30-3. The boltcutter above was identified as having cut the padlock shackle. (Courtesy of John E. Murdock.)

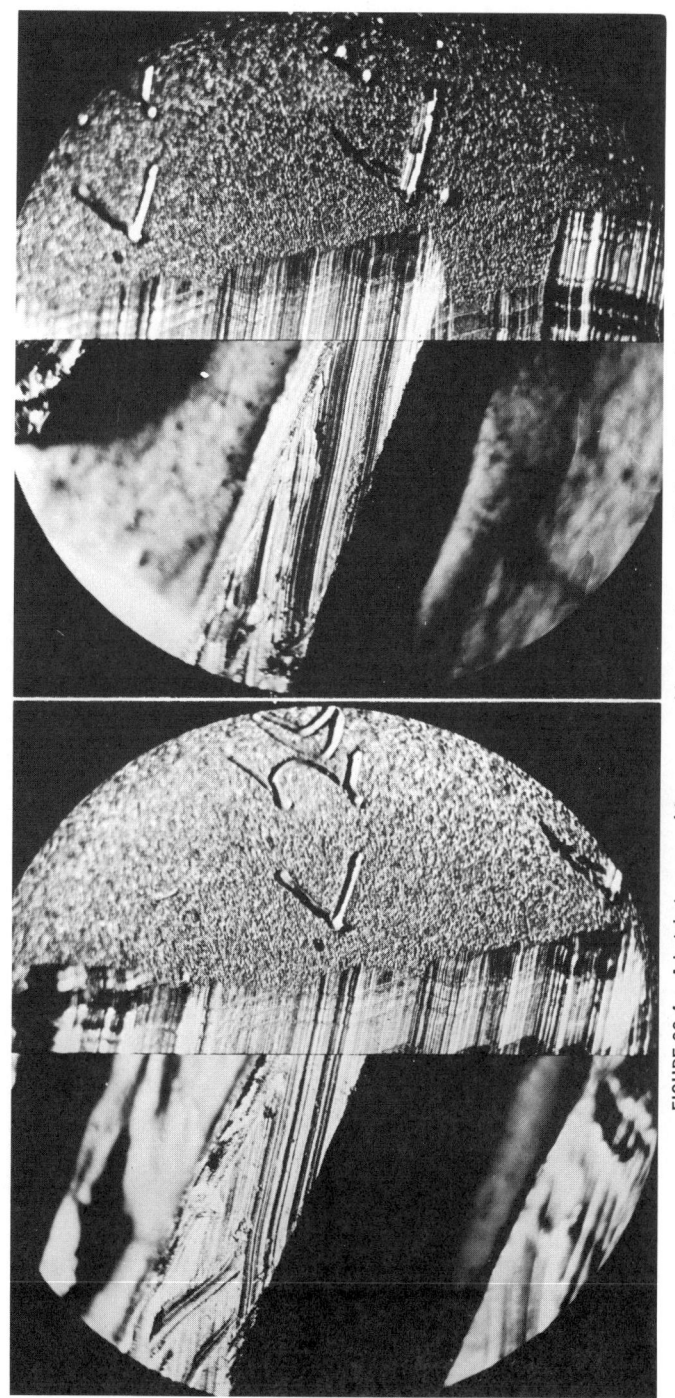

FIGURE 30-4. A hatchet was used to sever a cable at a crime scene. Test marks made with the hatchet (right) were found to match several portions of the cut cable (left). (Courtesy of A. Biasotti.)

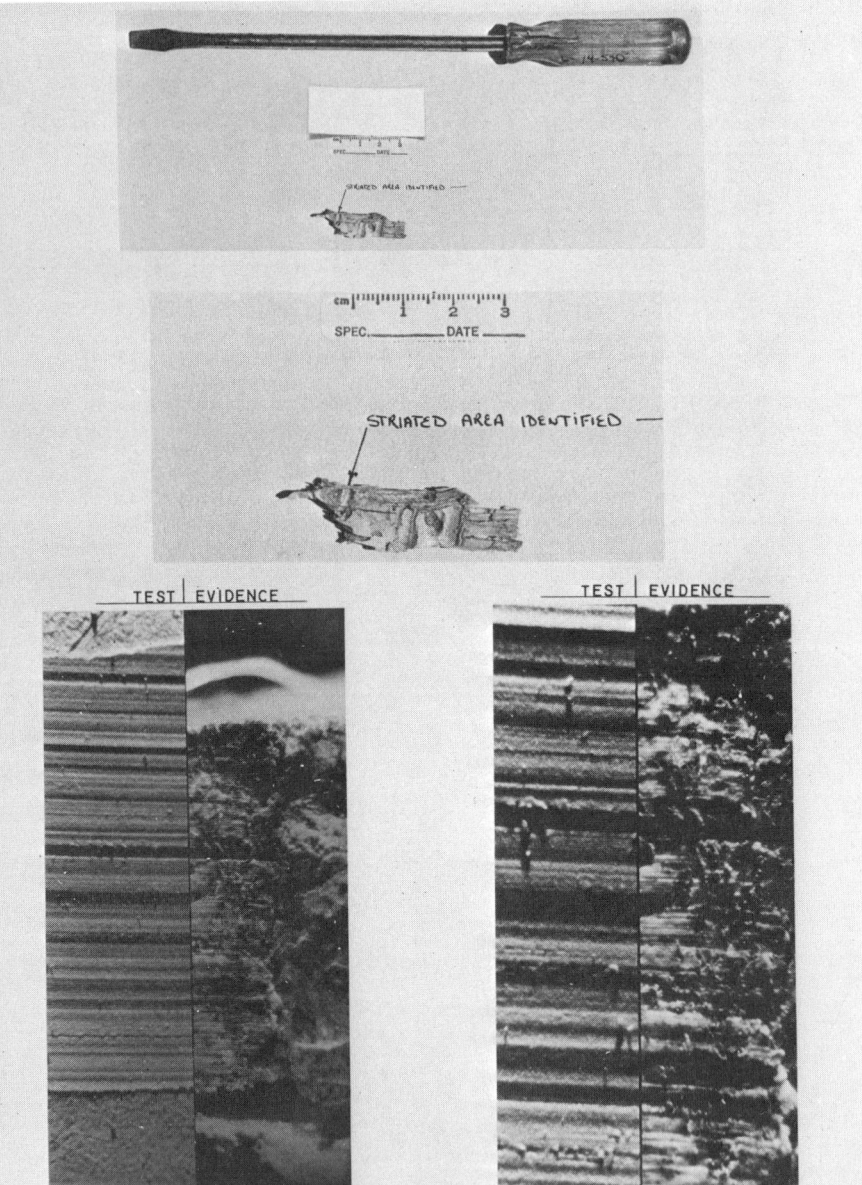

FIGURE 30-5. In the burglary of a home the screwdriver shown above was used to force open a door, leaving pry marks on the painted surface of the door molding. By comparing these marks to test marks made with this tool, the screwdriver was identified as being used to open the door. (Courtesy of John E. Murdock.)

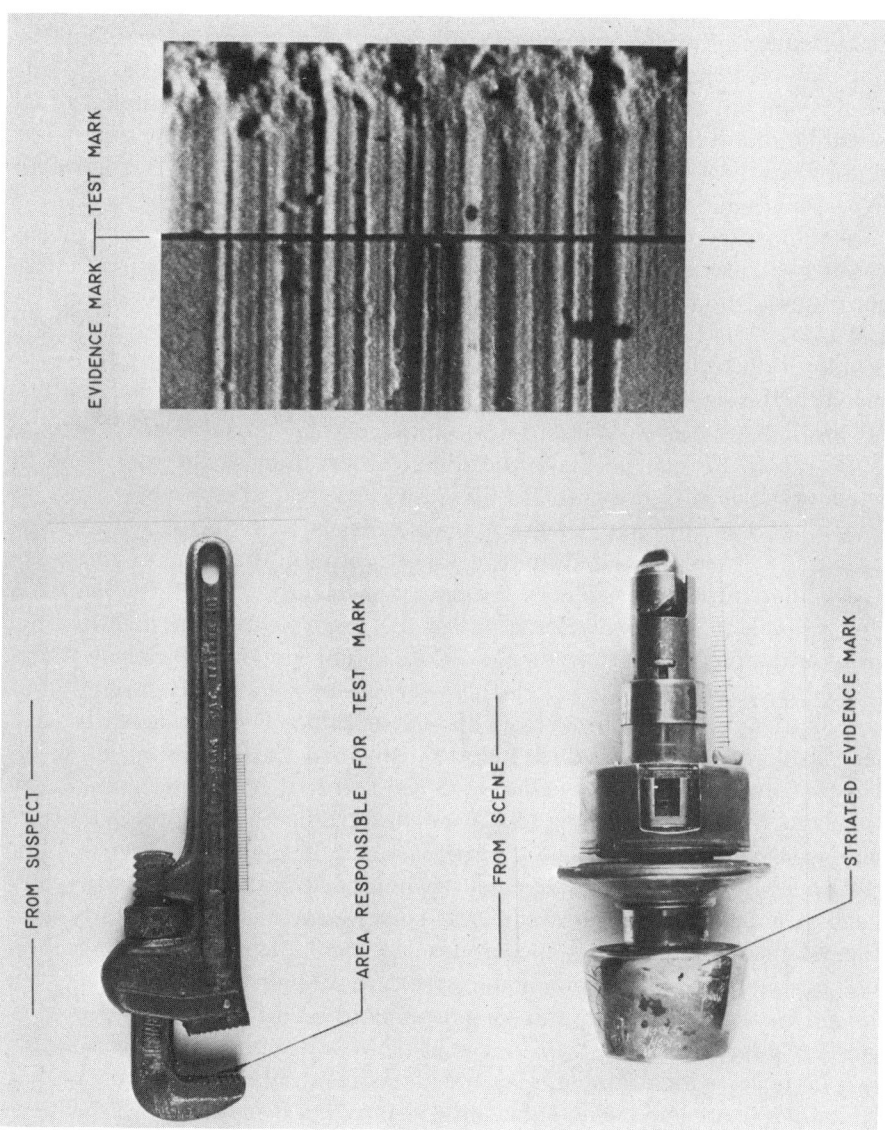

FIGURE 30-6. The pipe wrench was used to break the doorknob in a household burglary. The test mark was made on a lead cylinder. (Courtesy of John E. Murdock.)

INVESTIGATION OF TOOL MARKS

Tool marks must always be expected and sought for in cases involving the breaking and entry into a building, the breaking of slot machines, cash registers, and similar objects, and in all breaking of locks and safes. Occasionally tool marks will be found in other situations. In at least one burglary, the marks left on a tool by nail heads over which the tool was scraped in forcing a hotel door were clear and definite, and led to the conviction of the burglar.

When tool marks are found, it is always well to photograph them as a means of recording their extent, arrangement, and location. Photography of the mark without magnification and special illumination will rarely furnish the means for identification of the tool, and this should not be expected. If it is possible and practicable to do so, the marked object should be removed to the laboratory. Occasionally, the sawing out of a window, door frame, or similar structure, is entirely justified, at least in those instances in which the damage is already quite extensive. When this can be done, the direct observation of the tool mark in the laboratory is usually preferable. When this treatment is impractical, as, for example, when the questioned mark is on a heavy safe or on part of a large permanent structure, a detailed and accurate cast or impression of the mark must be made at the scene. There are several techniques for this operation. The use of moulage has always been one of the best methods for such casting. Its use requires more expertise than do the silicone polymers, such as those manufactured by the Dow Chemical Company. These are applied in semiliquid form and harden in place. Plaster casts do not reproduce detail sufficiently well. Neither Plasticine nor wax has been found satisfactory. Faxfilm has been recommended by Cowles and Dodge, who have claimed that it is more satisfactory than moulage. Methods of casting tool marks are detailed in Chapter 5. Silicone casts are negative only; usually no positive is made. If moulage is used, a positive cast must be made from the negative immediately to avoid drying and shrinkage. A good cast is approximately as suitable for microscopic study as is the original mark, and several techniques are available for improving their microscopic quality. Both impression marks and sliding marks may be well reproduced by skillful casting, and for purposes of record, as well as for comparison, it is advisable to cast all tool marks of each type that show suitable detail. A large safe, for example, may have a large number of tool marks, but it is not known in advance which of them will prove to be subject to clear identification. Judgment of this matter by visual inspection in the field is often an insufficient guide to the selection of one or a few marks for casting.

Under no circumstances may the suspected tool, if present, be inserted into a mark until after good casts have been made, all photographic work at the scene has been done, and comparisons have been made. Some materials, especially, are soft enough to be very easily altered or damaged by such a direct test of fit.

COMPARISON OF TOOL MARKS

In order to determine whether or not a particular suspected tool has made a certain mark, the procedure must be chosen to suit the conditions. In general, it is necessary that the tool be used to make other marks similar in their depth, position, and extent to the marks in question. These standards are then compared with the questioned marks. Almost without exception it is simpler and more decisive to compare two marks with each other than to attempt to compare a mark directly with a tool. An exception to this might be an impression of the irregular edge of a knife blade which could be photographed in close apposition to the blade in order to show corresponding irregularities.

Standards

It is seldom difficult to reach a definite decision about the match of two tool marks if they have been made in a similar manner on similar materials by the impact of corresponding tool surfaces in corresponding position. To implement such a judgment it is necessary that the most careful attention be given to the making of proper standards. It is this phase of the investigation that requires almost all of the time and much of the care expended in comparing tool marks.

Many tool impressions do not immediately reveal the nature of the tool or the manner of its application. Only rarely do such marks show what part of the tool was used, e.g., which side of the screwdriver, or what part of the blade. Only occasionally is it apparent how the tool was held, e.g., at what angles both vertical and horizontal, and how constant was the position of the tool during its movement. This uncertainty may necessitate the making of numerous standards by varying the method of application of the tool. Time will be saved if the investigator makes careful preparation, studying the mark most thoroughly before making the standards.

The *material* upon which the mark is to be made must be chosen carefully. It must be soft enough so that the tool edge will not be altered. It must have a degree of opacity and reflectivity that will correspond closely to those of the material that was originally marked so that it can be photographed satisfactorily. When the original mark is in wood, paint, or soft metal, the standard may be made of the same material. At times this is the only suitable substance, and success will not be achieved with anything except a material closely corresponding to the original. Compression marks in wood provide the best example. Because of the tendency of wood to spring back into position after compression, only the same kind of wood in the same condition can be expected to give identical effects from two applications of the same tool.

When the original mark is on hard metal, such as steel or brass, it is ordinarily not desirable to use the same material for the standard. Sheet lead, tin, or aluminum may be employed as successful substitutes. When it is not possible to apply the tool in the same manner as with the original, e.g., a hard blow with a sledge hammer, it is often satisfactory to use a completely different material. Various hard waxes, properly modified and filled with fine metal powder, lampblack, and other materials to give comparable opacity and reflectivity, can be made to photograph similarly to brass, steel, chrome, or nickel plate, and other metallic surfaces. The softness allows the tool to penetrate easily, thus duplicating approximately the penetration under force in the original hard metal. The material used must not tear, nor should it scratch from the material collected ahead of the tool.

Compression marks may often be duplicated advantageously by means of plasticine, slightly soft plaster, or clay. Waxes of the proper composition may also be used under some circumstances. Attention to the choice of material is vital to the maximum success in obtaining accurate and useful standards.

The *position of the tool* and the *part of it that left the mark* must be approximated accurately in the standards. To achieve this with the least difficulty, the original mark is studied with the greatest care. Often it will be apparent how the tool was applied. For example, if the mark is between the door and the jamb, or between the windowframe and the sill, the tool must have been in a very flat position. The hammer mark on the dial of a safe may show the angle of the blow and the rotational position of the hammer. The shape of the mark may indicate the portion of the hammer that made it. Marks from screwdrivers, bars, and the like will often show the imprint of the edge of the tool, but only rarely will the side of the tool used be apparent.

Having studied the original mark to determine everything possible about the portion of the tool that made it, the direction of the tool's motion, and he position of the tool at the moment of contact, all those regions that might have made the mark are used for making standards. When possible, it is desirable to show the entire edge rather than only a portion of it. This is more easily done with wax combinations than with molten metal. The latter often collects in several separated regions with blank spaces between. The standard impression is applied, as nearly as possible, in the same manner as was used with the original mark. Enough standards are always prepared to duplicate every possible region and position of the tool in question. Until considerable experience has been acquired, this may prove to be a long and tedious undertaking.

Compression Mark Comparison

The questioned mark, or a cast of it, may be photographed side by side with the standard mark or its cast. Sometimes they are advantageously photographed through the comparison microscope so as to show half of each mark in the same picture. More often this procedure is impractical, or fails to demonstrate the identity. By arranging the marks so as to show their obvious points of similarity or difference, and photographing them side by side, it is usually possible to demonstrate the obvious conclusion.

Important dimensions should be accurately measured on corresponding portions of the marks. Often there are, on the tool, angles or curves that are quite characteristic and may be demonstrated on the compression mark. Peculiarities attributable to wear, breakage, or hand shaping should be noted. If they are lacking, the problem is more difficult. Examination of many similar tools to determine the frequency of variations—and therefore the significance of an identity—is then in order. This involves the degree of standardization of manufacture. For example, many screwdrivers have practically indistinguishable shapes, dimensions, and angles, because of this factor. Pinch bars, claw bars, and some other tools are ordinarily hand forged, are almost never closely similar, and may show wide variations.

Variations in Tools

Because one specific edge of a tool is responsible for most tool marks, it is necessary that the investigator consider carefully the condition of that edge with respect to:

(1) Method of manufacture
(2) Wear
(3) Damage

(1) *Manufacture* becomes more important as methods change. Newer mass production methods duplicate edges with considerable fidelity on inexpensive machine-stamped tools. Burd has reported a series of new screwdrivers, of a very inexpensive variety, which are so similar as to prevent definite identification. In dealing with such a tool, the greatest care must be exercised to guard against the danger of misinterpretation. An even more important development is that precision tools are now being equipped with very hard broaches that do not wear as they are used. This probably will give rise to a serious situation, since such broaches can be expected to duplicate tool edges very closely. Studies of this effect are currently lacking, and will have to be made. Meanwhile, the individual investigator is under an obligation to check his results carefully in the evaluation of any tool that may belong in this category. After a new tool has been used for a period of time, the edge will become so altered as to confer a clear individuality. The investigator need only examine the questioned tool carefully to determine whether or not it is new. If so, other, similar new tools must be obtained and tested in relation to the suspect tool.

(2) *Wear* of a tool edge will change its marking slowly but progressively. A worn tool is more individual than a new tool. Hence, more reliable results are obtainable from tools that are worn, provided that the wear pattern has not been altered significantly between the making of a questioned tool mark and

the making of the standard mark to be used for comparison. It is not always possible to obtain matching patterns when a questioned tool has been in regular use between the making of the two marks.

(3) *Damage* to the tool edge will alter it suddenly rather than progressively. If the damage was present before the making of the first mark under comparison it will add to the individuality of the mark. If damage to the tool edge occurred during the interval between the making of the two marks to be compared, the later mark will show alteration, and may not be suitable for comparison. When the alteration is only local, it will usually not prevent a satisfactory match from being obtained.

Unusual Tools

Almost any physical object may, under some circumstances, be used as a tool. A very common tool is a piece of wire, which can be used to open car doors and locks remotely. Even a hairpin is effective in certain circumstances, and a thin metal shim is very effective in opening locks. It is the tool of quite sophisticated design that has been constructed for a specific purpose, such as safe burglary, which is of great importance to the laboratory. In this form of crime the stakes are high, and many safe burglars are accomplished mechanics. Special drilling devices are well known, as are some devices for pulling the safe knob. Ingenuity on the part of safe burglars has produced a considerable number of such special devices. The police and the criminalist alike should be very alert to such contrivances so that they will be recognized when encountered. The finding of such a devise on the person, or in the dwelling or vehicle of a suspect is tantamount to labeling his occupation, but not without identifying the tool and recognizing its specific method of operation. It is appropriate here only to call attention to this very important trend in burglary, rather than to elucidate its details. The persons engaged in the study of such matters should consult with metropolitan laboratories and police for more information, so that the unusual tool will be recognized.

Sliding Mark Comparison

Sliding marks are almost invariably to be compared under the comparison microscope. The original mark and the standard mark are studied when possible; otherwise casts are used. Low-power objectives, e.g., 32 mm or 48 mm, preferably micro-Tessars, must be employed. The marks are placed in corresponding position and direction under the objectives, and a match is sought. The illumination should be sufficiently oblique to shadow the microscopic ridges, and the two marks should be at the same height and position. Having one tilted with respect to the other results in distortion and prevents an accurate match.

SLIDING MARK IDENTITIES. Because the possibilities for variation in tool marks are almost infinite, the presence of a clean-cut correspondence of a reasonable part of the questioned and the standard marks constitutes virtual proof that the same tool made both marks. Usually, if one such identity is found, there will be others as well.

The question as to what constitutes an identity between two sliding-tool marks is a difficult one. As ordinarily viewed, the marks look like a series of parallel light and dark bands of variable width and arrangement. If both marks have the same appearance they are said to be identical. Two marks made with the same tool and under the same conditions may appear to be different because of different lighting or a difference in the tilt of the marks that affects the magnification given by the microscope. The greatest care is therefore necessary to ensure that both marks are horizontal or at least identical in position. The illumination on the two must be as nearly identical as it can be made.

The dark and light lines that are observed are merely shadows or their absence and should not be confused with the more fundamental structures that give rise to them. This is the *profile* of the mark. It represents not only the number and arrangement of lines, but also their relative depth and width as well as their interrelationships. An identity of profile is a true identity. The actual profile of the tool's edge can be seen clearly when the light is correctly adjusted. It is difficult to obtain a clear photograph of the profile directly from the tool except with a stereoscopic camera. However, in evaluating a match the investigator may readily make certain as to whether an identity of profile exists before he commits himself as to the identity of the tool which made the marks.

Inevitably, some matches of markings will be less convincing than others. Some will be unsatisfactory, though suggestive. This situation always raises the question as to what degree of line-matching is necessary before a match can be claimed and a tool identified. It must be admitted that *hitherto there have been no studies which answer this question adequately*. An excellent match will rarely raise questions on the part of anyone, even though some uncertainty may be felt. By making better standards, or by other means, such situations can generally be settled with satisfaction. At present there is no substitute for experience and conservatism in testimony. No witness can truthfully state, "This is the only tool on earth that could have made this mark." Unfortunately, such testimony is not rare. However, a good match accompanied by a good comparison photomicrograph and conservative testimony is nearly always effective. If the match is poor, extra caution is necessary with respect to brash testimony. A few stray lines on one specimen may be justifiably explained as representing sand or grit pushed ahead of the tool or, more often, by intervening wear of the tool. However, the presence of only a few matching lines out of a large number may, in fact, indicate the profile of a different tool, and can be accepted as evidence of a match only with the greatest caution.

Some tool marks contain only a few lines, either because of the narrowness of the tool's edge, an unusual smoothness of the edge, or the lightness of application. If, for example, there are fewer than a half-dozen distinct lines, all of them should match without real discrepancies if an identity of source is to be claimed. Most tool marks will contain twenty such lines, or more, and only two or three of them may be extraneous. An unusually confused mark will require that the investigator have a considerable experience upon which to base any conclusion regarding identity of source.

INVESTIGATION OF SAFE BURGLARIES

The kinds of evidence available at the scene of a safe burglary are both more diverse and more repetitive than is usual in other burglaries. The investigation is not basically specialized in approach, in photography, in the recording of information, or in its general features. However, special attention must be given to some particular types of evidence, as is indicated in the following procedural scheme:

(1) *Without being disturbed significantly*, the scene should be recorded by photographs, sketches, or both, as outlined elsewhere.
(2) The general type of attack should be observed, special note being taken as to whether insulation from the safe has been spilled or spread on the floor.
(3) If there is insulation on the floor, a careful search should be made with the help of a strong light, held in various positions, to locate footprints, Throughout the investigation care must be taken to avoid disturbing any prints that are present or adding any more prints to confuse the situation. The footprints should be carefully photographed in such a way as to record the fine detail. If desired, the footprints may then be lifted by means of a technique that is described elsewhere in this volume. (See Chapter 7.) The quality of a dust foot-impression in safe insulation is likely to be very good, and the skill of the investigator should be such that his record of it is of equal quality.

The dust prints having been dealt with, other items that are less likely to be disturbed or damaged may be investigated. These include the examination of the safe itself.

(4) Tool marks on the safe can be cast if they are not to be made available for examination in the laboratory. This should be done as described elsewhere, and the location of every mark of interest should be recorded carefully, preferably by photographs.

(5) Metal fragments of all types should be carefully collected, packaged, and labeled. These should include any broken fragments of tools, which will be reserved for special attention.

(6) Samples of the safe insulation should be collected, packaged, and labeled.

(7) Any significant residues, such as broken objects, dropped items, the remains of explosives, should be carefully collected, packaged, and labeled. Such residues may include paint chips, which are of special significance.

(8) A careful search for fingerprints should be made, and any that are found should be recorded and lifted. Earlier collection of evidence should not be pursued in such a manner as to alter or obliterate any possible fingerprints. It is simpler to protect fingerprints during most other evidence collection than to protect other evidence from fingerprint dust.

(9) Close attention should be given to the possible presence of hairs and fibers. If, with proper lighting, any such residues can be found, they should be collected. In some situations it may be necessary to use a vacuum sweeper on portions of the scene in order to collect all available materials of this type.

(10) Blood is not expected to be present; but quite commonly it is found because of some injury suffered by the burglar while working. If blood is found, it should be dealt with as described elsewhere in this volume. (See Chapters 14–16.)

(11) In the unlikely event that any tools have been discarded at the scene by the burglar, they should be collected and special attention given to any fingerprints or microscopic debris carried by them.

(12) When examination of the immediate scene has been completed, attention should be given to the means of entrance. As in any other burglary, attention should be centered upon the search for tool marks, fingerprints, either dust impressions or mud prints, and all related significant traces. Broken glass is likely to be present, in which case good standards should be collected. Cut screens or other metal barriers should also be sampled.

If and when a suspect is located, his person and environment should be carefully examined for matching trace evidence: fingerprints, shoeprints, and in fact any and every type of evidence that may be needed for purposes of comparison. The culprit's clothing is often most productive of such evidence; and if he has not disposed of the tools he used in the burglary, his premises, his automobile, or his hangout may well yield them when searched. Few other crimes provide so great a variety of useful evidence as do safe burglaries.

REFERENCES

Biasotti, A. A.: "The Principles of Evidence Evaluation as Applied to Firearms and Tool Mark Identification," *J. For. Sci.* 9:428 (1964).

Brackett, J. W., Jr.: "A Study of Idealized Striated Marks and their Comparison Using Models," *J. For. Sci. Soc.* 10:27 (1970).

Burd, D. Q., and Greene, R. S.: "Tool Mark Comparisons in Criminal Investigations," *J. Crim. Law and Criminol.* 39:379 (1948).

Burd, D. Q., and Kirk, P. L.: "Tool Marks—Factors Involved in Their Comparison and Use as Evidence," *J. Crim. Law and Criminol.* 32:679 (1941–1942).

Cowles, D. L., and Dodge, J. K.: "A Method for Comparison of Tool Marks," *J. Crim. Law and Criminol.* 39:262 (1948).

Freeman, H. G.: *Tool Dictionary*, 2nd ed. New York: Adler (1960).

31
Firearms

Among the commonest types of physical evidence with which the criminalist is concerned are the gun, the bullet, and the cartridge case used in committing a crime. Because of the high incidence of shooting cases in the United States, there are probably more well-qualified firearms examiners in this country than there are specialists of any other kind in the examination of physical evidence, except for fingerprint experts. It is equally true that there are more opportunities for incompetent examiners in this field than there are in most other specialties. The frequent need for such examinations may tempt the unskilled and poorly informed police officer, or the interested layman, to try his hand at it. Although this situation is unfortunate, it should be pointed out that firearms identification is possibly a more suitable and profitable interest for the intelligent police officer than are many other criminalistic specialties. The police officer, the military ordnance man, the skillful amateur shooter, and the gun hobbyist all possess firearms experience that is useful. When this experience is properly supplemented by specialized training, such an individual has a better-than-average chance of becoming a competent firearms examiner.

It might be supposed that the problem of identifying firearms and ammunition should be quite simple because the gun should mark all ammunition fired through it in the same way. This idea is far from correct. There are many other factors to consider in firearms examinations—factors that call for much broader training than is implied by the term "firearms identification," or, as it is sometimes mistermed, "ballistics." Some aspects of firearms study are quite simple; others are highly complex.

The most common question asked of the criminalist is: "Did this gun fire this bullet or this cartridge case?" Often the question can be answered very definitely. This will ordinarily be true when: (1) the bullet is not badly damaged; and (2) the weapon is recovered shortly after the suspected shooting and is still in good condition. This is perhaps the simplest case that confronts the examiner. But the problem is often, if not usually, complicated by the fact that the available bullet has been smashed on striking a bone, the ground, a wall, or some other hard object. The weapon may have been plugged with mud, rusted from contact with water, or deliberately damaged. Some weapons are so badly worn, or mechanically so defective, that they no longer impart a clear signature to the cartridge or bullet. There are many variations due to fouling of the barrel, to unusual or unfavorable characteristics of the ammunition, and to a host of other factors. For these and similar reasons, the competent examiner needs more knowledge than that required in comparing a standard and an unknown bullet or cartridge under the comparison microscope. This chapter will present those aspects of the subject that must be understood at an early date as a prelude to the detailed training of the firearms examiner. The literature of the field is extensive and detailed, although sometimes rather superficial. It should be studied carefully by the student of firearms. He should also be very familiar with weapons: how they operate and how they vary. He must come to understand the behavior of fired bullets—properly called "ballistics"—and many other ramifications of the field. An understanding of at least some of these will be better achieved by long familiarity with the use and handling of guns than by reading about them.

GENERAL INFORMATION. So many makes and models of firearms exist, and they possess such varied characteristics, that many cases inevitably arise in which long experience and a detailed knowledge of the broad field are both required. One may encounter a missile that was fired from an obsolete firearm of a kind of which only a few were ever made, and with which none but the most erudite in the field would ever have a reasonable chance of familiarity. Several such types of weapons are described by Hatcher. The development of the manufacture of firearms has been characterized by such change and variation that much study is necessary to gain familiarity with even the background material. Such information may not have any bearing on the statements of fact offered by a witness, but the absence of reasonably detailed information on these points may seriously affect his standing in court. A simple illustration is the vagary associated with the caliber designations of weapons. Any firearm witness would be expected to understand the meaning of the word "caliber," and to know that it is determined by the diameter of the gun barrel measured between the lands. It is a well-informed witness indeed who can recite accurately all of the designations of caliber that are used and can give their significance. Such information is, actually, more likely to be carried by the gun enthusiast than by the routine police laboratory criminalist.

However irrelevant such detailed information may be in court, it is necessary that the competent witness be more familiar with it than is the cross-examiner who will confront him. He should know, for example, that a .30–'06 caliber refers specifically to a sharp-pointed-nose bullet adopted by the U.S. Army in 1906, and that the caliber refers only to the bullet; not to the rifle. Lack of such knowledge may disqualify him or may discredit accurate testimony given by him as to the weapon that fired the questioned bullet. Nor must it be forgotten that a failure to master much information of a very limited utility may set in him a pattern of failure to master that which is of vital importance. This road leads to the incompetent witness, or even to that more unfortunate being, the dishonest witness.

TYPES OF FIREARMS

The term "firearms" may embrace not only familiar hand weapons including the revolver, the pistol, the rifle, and the shotgun, but also the machine gun and an extensive variety of military artillery. The latter class of weapons, with the exception of the submachine gun, may better be left to the ordnance expert. Crimes committed with firearms other than rifles, pistols, and shotguns are so infrequent as to be statistically negligible. Leading all other weapons in the commission of crimes are the automatic pistol and the revolver, the rifle and the shotgun being less frequently used. An obsolete weapon such as the smoothbore musket, or an unusual firearm disguised as some innocuous object, may sometimes be employed in committing a crime. In such a case the investigator is forced to deviate from standard procedure and to rely heavily on his own resourcefulness.

The evidence presented for examination in a shooting case will usually consist of one weapon or more, one bullet or several, and often cartridge cases or shotgun shells. Ordinarily the bullets or cartridge cases are to be compared with the suspected weapon or with cartridge cases or shells of a shotgun. Less frequently, two evidence bullets are to be compared with each other. If the comparison is to be made between the gun and the bullet, the most effective and convenient method is to fire test bullets through the weapon and compare them with the questioned bullets. Similar methods are applicable to the comparison of cartridge cases or shells, although many more types of marks may be present. The kind of mark left on fired ammunition is a function of the type of firearm and of its individual idiosyncrasies. Most firearm examination is based upon detailed comparisons of such marks. However, other questions regarding the type of gun or the kind of ammunition are occasionally asked;

questions requiring much more investigation and a greater breadth of information.

Pistols

In modern usage the word "pistol" has come to mean a repeating weapon that, following the discharge of one cartridge, will automatically eject the expended cartridge case, load a new cartridge into the chamber, and remain cocked for the next firing. The term "automatic pistol" has found widespread usage, although the action of such a weapon is not truly automatic in the sense that the term is applicable to submachine guns, assault rifles, or other fully automatic weapons.

The pistol consists essentially of a barrel (modern forms being always rifled), a chamber or breech, a lock or firing mechanism, and a magazine housed beneath the grips over the frame. For the examiner the important parts are the *barrel*, because it marks the bullet; the *firing pin*, which indents and marks the primer; the *breech block*, whose face may mark the cartridge case and the primer; the *extractor*, which withdraws the cartridge from the chamber; the *ejector*, which may indent and mark the cartridge case; and possibly the *chamber*, because in rare instances it may mark the cartridge case at the time of the discharge or during insertion or removal of the case.

A pistol may leave additional marks on cartridge cases, some associated with the clip or magazine that holds the extra ammunition, and others derived from the additional mechanisms used in automatic reloading.

Revolvers

As a weapon for criminal use, the revolver may be more widely employed than is the automatic pistol by reason of its lower cost and the enormous numbers of such weapons manufactured. The revolver is so named because it carries a number of cartridges in a revolving multichambered cylinder. The chambers rotate into alignment with the barrel before firing. Thus, the cylinder serves as both magazine and firing chamber.

Some revolvers are of the "top-break" type similar to single-shot pistols; in others the cylinder drops out to the side for loading and unloading. The police model .38-caliber revolver may be considered as a prototype of such weapons. However, revolvers in a multitude of makes, types, and calibers are manufactured.

Revolvers were in use for many years before automatic-loading weapons were developed. Even at the present time, shooting crimes are occasionally committed with the large and often crudely manufactured revolvers of the "frontier" type, or with modern copies of such weapons. It would be uncommon to encounter now a pistol of one of the early types, which were muzzle-

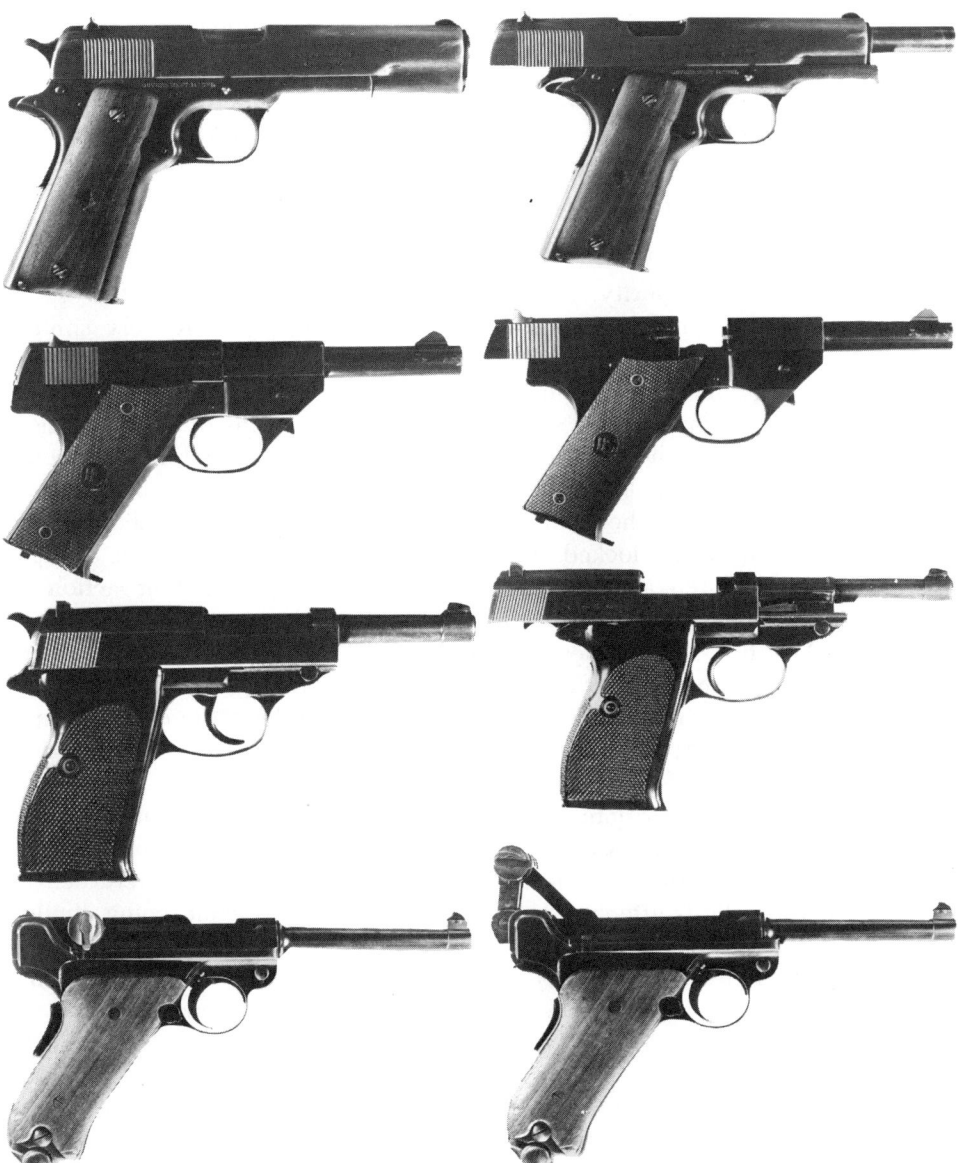

FIGURE 31-1. Pistols. Left, action closed; right, action open. From top to bottom, Colt .45 Automatic model M 1911, Hi-Standard .22, Walthers P-38, Luger 7.65 mm. (Courtesy of John I. Thornton.)

loading and were fired with percussion caps, or one of still earlier date fired with flint and steel. Such weapons are of interest as collectors' items, and some familiarity with them may be of value to the firearms expert. The likelihood of their being encountered as evidence in crime is now too low to warrant complete familiarity with them, except in response to personal interest.

Rifles

Except for greater complexity of loading and firing mechanisms, and the use of much longer barrels and higher-powered ammunition, rifles are very similar to pistols. The single-shot rifle usually is loaded differently from the pistol, but the same kind of mechanical elements leave similar types of marks on the ammunition. The simple rifle is sometimes loaded by means of a lever action that drops and retracts the breech block and operates the extractor. More commonly a bolt action is employed in which the immediate firing mechanism and breech block are made in the form of an elongated steel "bolt" that slides along the axis of the barrel. It is locked into place by means of a lever-handle or lugs, which, on rotation, engage notches in the framework. The bolt action is favored by shooters for accuracy, and it was long the standard in military weapons. Most bolt-action rifles are arranged with a magazine so that the operation of retracting and returning the bolt serves for reloading. A weapon of this type may imprint on cartridge cases marks from both the extractor and the ejector; and often weapons of this type possess two extractors. Lever-action rifles are also adapted for reloading in many models, some of which are very popular for hunting large game. A less widely used design is the so-called "pump" action in which the rifle is reloaded by means of a handle located well forward under the barrel. This is drawn toward the shooter and returned to position. The handle is attached to a sliding bolt, the principle being similar to that of the bolt-action rifle. The reloading operation is performed with the left hand, rather than the right as with both lever- and bolt-action weapons.

Automatic-reloading rifles place still other marks on the cartridge case at times. The magazine mechanism may be more complex, though not necessarily so. Automatic reloading is a rapid and forcible action that ordinarily causes strong marking of the ammunition. Most modern military rifles provide for full automatic operation in which the weapon will fire repeatedly with one depression of the trigger until the supply of ammunition is exhausted, or semiautomatic fire in which the weapon discharges one projectile each time the trigger is depressed.

Regardless of the type of rifle, any marks on the case or bullet will have come from the sources summarized above. Attention must be given to unusual kinds of marks, which often are produced by some special component of a loading mechanism characteristic of a certain make or model of gun. Close

FIGURE 31-2. Revolvers. Left, action closed; right, loading position. From top to bottom, Colt .38 Special, Iver Johnson .38 S&W, Colt .38 Special. (Courtesy of John I. Thornton.)

scrutiny may reveal marks of defects or abnormalities characteristic of the individual gun in question.

Shotguns

Shotguns differ from pistols, revolvers, and rifles in several important respects, but most notably in the type of ammunition used. Because they fire a load consisting of a considerable number of lead pellets (shot), and their barrels are not rifled, there are no markings of significance made by the barrel on the missiles. For this reason it is not ordinarily possible to identify the gun by examining the material fired. A possible exception is the case in which the jagged edge of the muzzle of a "sawed-off" shotgun marks the plastic shot collar in a characteristic manner. If the shell case is recovered, markings on it are almost always effective in identifying the gun from which it was fired. Naturally, the recovery of shell cases occurs less frequently than the recovery of shot.

The action of a shotgun is analogous to that of other firearms. Both single-shot and double-barreled weapons commonly employ a "break" action for reloading. Other reloading mechanisms resemble that of the rifle and operate on the same basic principles. "Pump" action reloading is more common among shotguns than in other firearms. Automatic reloading shotguns are quite commonly used by sportsmen, but their use is rare in the commission of crimes. When they are so employed, the criminalist may experience considerable difficulty in tracing the origin of some of the marks on the shell case that have been caused by the reloading mechanism. However, such marks are likely to be very characteristic and, when found, serve admirably to identify the gun from which the particular shell was fired.

Barrels

It is the barrel of the gun that leaves significant markings on a projectile. Because it is the projectile that is most often recovered after a shooting, the relationship between barrel and bullet must be understood. Virtually all modern firearms other than shotguns contain spiral grooves on the inner surface of the barrel, such grooves being known collectively as the "rifling" of the gun. These grooves impart to the projectile a rotary motion that keeps it stable in flight. The manner in which these grooves are made imparts uniqueness to the barrel, which in turn imparts uniqueness to the fired projectile.

The rifling of a firearm results from one of a number of different manufacturing processes: the use of a hook cutter, a scrape cutter, a button broach, a button swage, or by the hammering of the barrel over a mandrel. In the hook process the grooves are made by a rifling tool—essentially a sharp edge dragged with slight rotation from one end of the barrel to the other, cutting a groove as it moves. Grooves may be cut singly; or, with a multiple cutter, several grooves may be cut simultaneously.

In terms of the individuality of gun barrels, the scrape cutter may be regarded as a minor variant of the hook cutter. In the button broach rifling process a tool consisting of several gangs of exceedingly hard steel is pushed down the barrel. The cutting surfaces of each gang cut progressively deeper grooves, all of the grooves being cut simultaneously. Whereas the hook cutting process may require many passes through the barrel to cut all the grooves, the button broach will cut all of the grooves to the required depth in a single pass through the barrel. The button swage process does not involve cutting at all: it is a metal-forming process. The swage, an extremely hard piece of steel, is machined by diamond-cutting techniques to represent a negative image of the finished barrel interior. A single pass of this swage down the barrel will force the metal of the barrel to conform to the button, and will thus create lands and grooves. The hardness of the button swage may be appreciated in light of the fact that, with guns of some calibers, a single button swage may last through the rifling of 50,000 barrels. In the hammer process, a mandrel bearing a negative image of the finished barrel interior is inserted into the barrel, the barrel then being compressed around the mandrel.

The source of the individuality of a gun barrel is readily apparent in the hook cutter process. The hook, being relatively soft, undergoes continual alteration as it is passed down the barrel. It is not uncommon in this process for the hook to be removed from the tool and resharpened by grinding several times in the course of rifling one weapon. As the hook is continually changed by wear, the barrel of the weapon is being changed also: hence, there is no opportunity for a particular configuration of marks to persist from groove to groove, or from weapon to weapon.

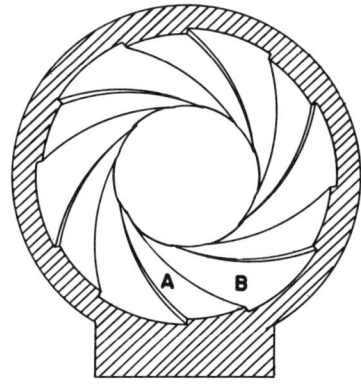

FIGURE 31-3. Interior of gun barrel, six lands, six grooves, right hand twist: **(A)** land; **(B)** groove.

In the button broach process, the broach itself, being quite hard, does not wear appreciably from barrel to barrel. In cutting the grooves, however, the broach pushes along metal chips that it cuts from the barrel. These chips, being "work hardened" by compression, are harder than the steel from which the barrel has originated. The chips and shavings mark the barrel randomly, giving it a useful uniqueness.

The button swage process, being a cold-forming procedure, does not involve the cutting of grooves. It is obvious that a button swage that may serve to rifle 50,000 gun barrels cannot change much between consecutive barrels in the production line. The identification of projectiles fired from weapons rifled by this method should be approached with caution, because consecutively rifled barrels may in fact show some similarity to one another. This is not to suggest, however, that a projectile fired from a button-swaged weapon cannot ordinarily be identified as having been fired from a particular weapon. When a weapon is rifled by a cutting process, the drilling marks around the circumference of the barrel are largely removed, whereas the swaging process merely displaces them with, or without, substantial alteration. Because a striation on a bullet need not arise from a striation along the long axis of the gun barrel, but can originate equally well from a hummock, the drill marks that are at right angles to the long axis of the barrel contribute heavily to the markings on the projectile. These drill marks are often somewhat irregular, and may impart to the barrel a uniqueness equivalent to that of a barrel rifled by a cutting technique.

It might be expected that a gun rifled by the hammering process would be quite similar to others formed around the same mandrel. However, this does not appear to be the case. Variations occur that seem to be attributable to the disruption of microscopic features of the barrel when it is unscrewed from the mandrel. Typically, projectiles fired from barrels consecutively produced by this process can be easily distinguished.

Further irregularities in the barrel occur as results of use, corrosion, or fouling. Pitting of the barrel from rust is not uncommon, and the presence of grit in the barrel may give rise to irregularities produced by scratching. Any irregularity that exists in the barrel of a gun may be expected to leave corresponding marks on the bullet.

It can be argued that, because the same cutter may make numerous grooves in many gun barrels, all such barrels will bear the same tool marks and will thus mark bullets alike. This is certainly possible, and in practice similar markings are occasionally found on bullets fired from different guns. However, as the tool becomes worn and is reground, its pattern is changed at a finite rate. Many of the bullet markings may arise from sources other than rifling-tool marks. It has been claimed that wear and variation in cutting machinery is such that if a rifle barrel is cut to pistol-barrel length and each segment is used to fire similar ammunition, the individual pistol barrels may be distinguished.

Certainly this demonstration would require a high degree of care and expertise on the part of the examiner. If this generalization is correct, it is of the greatest significance to firearms investigation. It is at least improbable that the rifling cutter would reproduce its action so closely and so many times in succession that two successive grooves cut by it would be entirely identical.

Every manufacturer of firearms adopts a standard number of grooves for his gun barrels and, accordingly, the same number of ridges, known as "lands," between grooves. Some gun barrels have five lands and grooves; others have six; still others, eight or ten. The relative widths of lands and grooves and the "pitch" or degree of rotation of the lands and grooves are also standardized. These characteristics of number, dimension, and pitch serve to identify the type of gun that has fired a projectile, provided that the latter is in good enough condition when recovered to allow accurate measurement. A further variable is the direction of the "twist," i.e., the direction of rotation of the lands and grooves, some being rotated to the right and others to the left. Table 31-1 lists some characteristics of common pistols and revolvers.

RELATIONSHIP OF BARREL TO BULLET. The firing of a gun is accompanied by the sudden generation of very high temperature and pressure at the base of the bullet. The rise in temperature serves to soften and expand the bullet significantly, particularly if it is an unjacketed lead missile. The expansion forces the bullet rather tightly into the rifling, tending to make it fill the barrel completely. The degree to which this occurs varies greatly with the type of bullet, the powder charge, and the type and condition of the gun. A revolver may show less expansion than does a pistol because some of the pressure is lost around the end of the revolving cylinder. A considerable portion of the gas will always escape past the bullet, the quantity being greater if the barrel is worn.

Virtually every bullet will be marked by the lands to a considerable extent. Many bullets will record to some extent the marks of the grooves also, although they are not always sufficiently characteristic for purposes of identification. The characteristic marks of both lands and grooves are slowly modified by wear, corrosion, and fouling of the barrel, as well as by alterations of manufacturing methods.

Bullets are made with a diameter slightly greater than that of the barrel of the weapon designed to fire them. If the barrel of the gun is badly worn, or if incorrect ammunition is used, the bullet may fit loosely and receive very irregular markings. If the bullet fails to expand evenly into the barrel, there is certain to be some lateral movement in its passage through the barrel. Even with a perfect barrel and correct ammunition, the bullet does not necessarily advance uniformly along the axis of the barrel, but receives markings more strongly in some places than in others. Sometimes this movement is a sort of spiral in which one side of the bullet is deeply marked and the other is almost

TABLE 31-1 Chief Characteristics of Common Pistols and Revolvers

Make	Caliber	Model	Twist direction*	Amount†	No. of lands	Appr. lands/grooves width
Colt	.22	recent	L	1/14	6	0.5
	all others	recent	L	1/16	6	0.5
Harrington and Richardson	.22, rim fire	old	R	1/12	5	1
	.32, center fire	old	R	1/12	5	1
	.38, center fire	old	R	1/12	5	1
	.22	recent	R	1/16	6	1.0
	all others	recent	R	1/12	6	0.7
Iver Johnson	.22	all	R	1/15.75	5	1
	all others	all	R	1/23.33	5	1
Luger	7.65mm	automatic	R	1/9.84	4	1
	9mm	automatic	R	1/9.84	6	1
Mauser	all	all	R	1/7.875	6	0.4
Remington	.32, .380 A.C.P.	automatic	R	1/16	7	0.3–0.5
Savage	all	all	R	1/12	6	0.4
Smith and Wesson	.22	all	R	1/10,1/15	6	1
	.32	all	R	1/18/75	5	1
	.32–20	military and police	R	1/12	5	1
	.38 and .38/44 special	all	R	1/18.75	5	1
	.44	all	R	1/20	5	1.1
	.45 S and W	.45 Schofield model revolver	R	1/24	5	0.9
	.45 A.C.P.	1917 model	R	1/14.659	6	0.5
	.32 A.C.P.	automatic	R	1/12	6	0.5
	.35 S and W	automatic	R	1/12	6	0.8
Webley and Scott	all	all	R	1/10,15,18,20	6	0.3‡
Thompson	.45 A.C.P.	submachine gun	R	1/16	6	0.5

* L, left. R, right.
† One turn in the indicated number of inches of barrel length.
‡ In most models.

devoid of marking. Revolvers, particularly, produce odd markings at times because the cylinder may not align accurately with the barrel. The nose of the bullet will be marked strongly on one side as it enters the barrel. The misalignment will displace the bullet laterally, causing the base of the bullet to be marked strongly on the opposite side. Many such erratic forms of marking will be observed on bullets that have been fired from various kinds of firearms.

One of the most significant types of firing irregularity is "slippage." As the bullet is thrust forward and engages the lands, it is pushed into them without rotation for a short distance before it begins to turn. This produces a fan-shaped mark at the nose end of each land mark—a detail that in a good barrel is quite short and of little significance. When the lands are badly worn, the bullet may progress down the barrel without rotation, at times producing prominent slippage marks around the entire periphery. If the lands subsequently engage, a second set of normal marks is superimposed. When this occurs, the slippage marks are placed by irregularities in the rear of the barrel, and the normal markings by irregularities toward the muzzle. Every such irregularity places its mark in one form or the other on the bullet, so the character of the marking may be greatly changed by differences in the distance the bullet slips over the rifling before it begins to rotate. Differences in powder charge and condition will produce these differences in distance. For this reason a weapon in this condition will require special precautions in the preparation of known test bullets: the test ammunition must be identical with the evidence ammunition.

Difficuty arises occasionally from the fact that marks impressed by the breech end of the barrel are partially or wholly obliterated by the muzzle end. If this occurs on one bullet but, because of lateral movement, not on another bullet fired from the same weapon, an identification based upon comparison of these bullets may be made very difficult or even impossible. All of the above variations must be recognized by the examiner as handicaps to the investigation, and every precaution must be taken to avoid resulting incorrect conclusions.

Abnormalities in the marking of fired bullets are caused also by deterioration of the ammunition or imperfections in it. Such abnormalities are frequently caused by the presence of soil or other foreign material in the barrel. Fouling of this type would affect the first bullet of a series more strongly than subsequent bullets. The jacketing of ammunition usually reduces the amount of surface marked. Such marks as are made, however, are less readily removed by scouring in the portions of the barrel subsequently traversed, or by down-range impact.

Any bullet fired will be marked only by the barrel and by the object struck. Normally, the marks left by impact with an object are readily distinguished from those left by the barrel. It is, therefore, the sum of the marks left by the barrel that constitutes the signature on the bullet and makes possible the identification of the weapon.

FUNDAMENTALS OF FIREARMS EXAMINATION

The primary concern of the criminalist in firearms investigation is usually focused upon bullets, cartridge cases, and other materials left at the scene of a shooting, rather than upon the weapon itself.

Bullets

When a bullet is submitted for examination, questions of several kinds may be asked by the investigator. Most such questions may be typified by the following examples:

(1) *Did a particular suspected gun fire the bullet?* This, the most common question, can be answered definitely in a large number of cases. The answer is obtained by the detailed comparison of markings on the evidence bullet with corresponding marks on test bullets fired through the suspected gun. Ordinarily a bullet comparison microscope is used for this determination. The suspect bullet and the test bullet are illuminated obliquely in order to create shadows that reveal the ridges and hollows engraved by the gun.

Test bullets are obtained by firing the suspected weapon into a water tank, which stops the bullets with a minimum of damage. The use of a water tank is much more important for the collection of lead bullets than for jacketed ammunition. The surface of a bullet is made quite hot by friction resulting from the action of the gun barrel. The lead, softened thus, is particularly susceptible to having the characteristic striations wiped off by any hard material with which it comes into contact. Boxes filled with cotton waste, once used almost universally for the collection of test bullets, are not entirely suitable for collecting lead projectiles. Although it is, in the aggregate, seemingly soft, raw cotton may wipe off the striations engraved by the barrel and impart other markings to the projectile.

Comparison of bullets under magnification will show not only the primary markings left by the lands and grooves of the gun barrel, which are plainly visible to the unaided eye, but will also reveal the fine striations in all the marks. These are engraved by the small irregularities in the barrel, and are never duplicated exactly by different weapons. The determination of a match is subject to the considerations discussed under tool marks. (See Chapter 30.) In practice, a perfect identity is not to be expected. However, the degree of correspondence is commonly very great between bullets fired through the same barrel, and in most instances the investigator can state: (a) that the bullet was fired from the suspected gun; (b) that the bullet was not fired from the suspected gun; or (c) that the bullet or the barrel through which it was fired is in such poor condition that no determination is possible.

The findings may ordinarily be demonstrated to the jury by means of enlarged photomicrographs that show how the match was obtained. The making of convincing and accurate photomicrographs of bullet matches requires training, equipment, and patience. Skill and careful attention to detail are essential to obtaining good alignment. Bullets that have been made elliptical by lateral flattening will fail to give complete line correspondence.

Abnormalities in the marking of fired bullets are caused by deterioration of the ammunition or imperfections in it, or by wear or damage to the gun barrel or imperfections in its manufacture. Jacketed bullets less frequently expand fully into the entire cross section of the barrel than do unjacketed bullets, and thus receive fewer—but often more reproductive—markings.

(2) *What kind of weapon fired the bullet?* This question may be answered in part if the bullet is not too greatly damaged. A completely mangled bullet, even when it is in more than one piece, may still reveal the caliber of the gun from which it was fired. It is occasionally possible to determine with certainty the exact type and model of weapon from a badly damaged bullet, but more commonly such a specimen serves to exclude only a few makes and models, leaving several possible candidate weapons.

The number and dimensions of the lands and grooves are characteristic of the make and model of a gun, but not exclusively so. This situation results from the fact that certain small manufacturers, often foreign, frequently duplicate the essential characteristics of well-known standard arms. Determination of the caliber of the weapon and the direction and pitch of the rifling may aid in the identification. Though the accurate determination of the pitch of the rifling may be difficult to achieve, it is, when obtainable, a useful factor in the identification. When there is disagreement in these factors between the evidence and the suspected weapon, it can be stated that the bullet in question was not fired from that weapon. It is, however, still possible to name one or more makes and models of gun from which the bullet could have been fired. The more the bullet has been damaged upon impact, the less information may be obtained from it and the more difficult is the determination of the weapon from which it was fired.

Some weapons of a particular caliber exhibit extreme uniformity of rifling with respect to twist and the number and width of lands and grooves. The 9mm Parabellum provides the best example of such uniformity. Even if a well-marked bullet from such a weapon is available, it may not be possible to narrow the list of candidate weapons to fewer than a dozen possible makes or models.

Standard makes of firearms are produced by reasonably uniform methods and details of manufacture. They are also widely distributed. When marks on a questioned bullet agree in all details with those characteristically impressed by such a weapon, it is highly probable that the make and model of the weapon from which the bullet was fired are known. However, if the weapon is a foreign copy, an error is possible. Some firearms are still being handmade by expert gunsmiths. Bullets fired from such guns are very characteristic, but difficult to classify. Crude homemade firearms are also used, and may usually be recognized by such characteristics as a complete lack of rifling.

(3) *What kind of ammunition was used?* Unless a bullet has been badly damaged, it will usually be recognized by the examiner as belonging to a specific type of ammunition. A bullet may be ringed by an indented groove, known as a *cannelure*, which has been impressed by means of a knurling tool against which the bullet has been rolled. Cannelures serve to hold lubricating grease. A jacketed bullet usually has a singe cannelure, which serves as a retainer into which the cartridge case is indented to hold the bullet in place. The number of cannelures, their design, and their dimensions vary widely among bullets produced by different manufacturers, and are correspondingly useful in the identification of the make of ammunition. The caliber of a bullet can usually be determined by measurement or even by weighing the bullet or its fragments. Other features that are useful in the identification of the source of a bullet are its shape and dimensions, and the arrangement of the jacket and core of the bullet; these details vary between different makes.

Another feature that may occasionally be of value is the appearance of the base of the projectile. The lead base of a bullet may show indentations indicative of impinging particles of gunpowder of a particular size and shape. Such marks may be characteristic of powder from a particular manufacture. Some .22-caliber bullets have an initial molded in the base of the bullet; this initial will identify conclusively the manufacturer of the ammunition.

To facilitate the answering of the above primary questions the examiner should keep on hand samples of all types of ammunition in common use so that direct comparisons may be made when necessary. This sample collection must be brought up to date from time to time to take into account alterations in styles and methods of manufacture as they occur. For the same reason, caution must be exercised in applying information obtained from books and other publications, which may have become obsolete.

When the bullet has been greatly deformed, or when only fragments of it have been recovered, comparative chemical analysis of the questioned and the known bullets by instrumental means may yield useful information. The composition of bullets obtained from different manufacturers is to some extent distinctive; so also is the composition of bullets obtained from a given manufacturer at different times. Such analysis requires a considerable amount of labor, so it will be utilized only in the more important and difficult cases. If a damaged bullet appears to contain virtually all the original metal, the weight of the bullet will serve to eliminate all bullets that are lighter and those that are considerably heavier. This information, along with indications obtained from the examination of any remaining features of the original bullet, is useful and is routinely recorded by some bullet examiners.

Occasionally no bullet is found, but a trace from ricochet or other impact may be recovered. Methods are available by which such minute traces may be analyzed with great exactitude through the application of microchemical techniques. The possibilities residing in this approach to bullet examination for type of ammunition have been almost completely neglected.

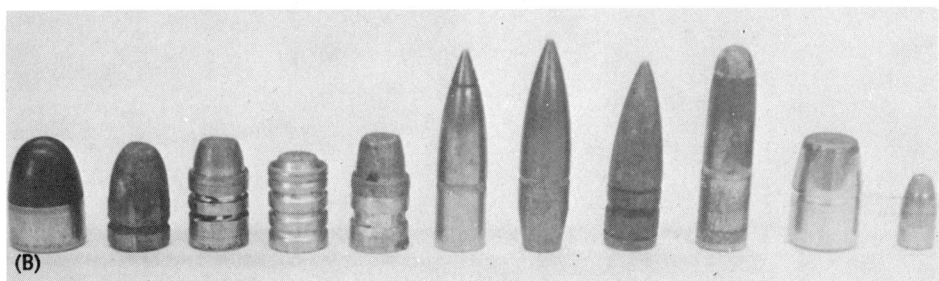

FIGURE 31-4. **(A)** Nominal .38 cal. bullets varying from .357 Magnum on the left to .38 auto on the right. **(B)** Various bullet forms. **(C)** .44 Magnum cartridge showing the gas check to the right of the bullet. (Courtesy of John I. Thornton.)

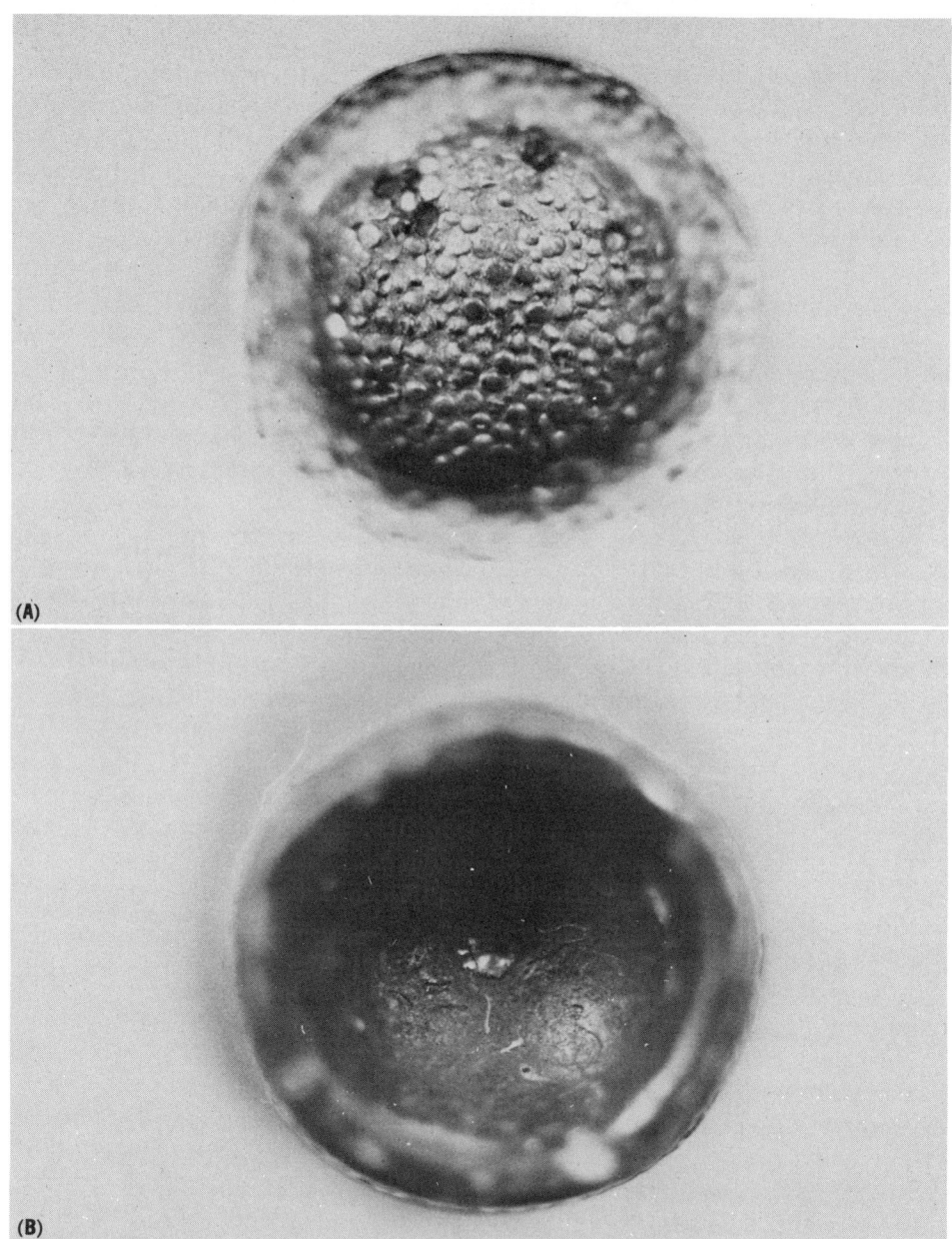

FIGURE 31-5. .38 Special and .357 Magnum bullets have the same size and weight. The powder used in the two cartridges, however, is quite different. When a .357 Magnum cartridge is fired, the powder granules are impressed upon the back of the bullet leaving a characteristic pattern (A). This does not occur with the .38 Special (B). (Courtesy of John I. Thornton.)

Firearms

(5) *From where was the bullet fired?* Ordinarily, bullet examination alone will not answer this question, but the results of such an examination added to other observations may often provide a reasonable answer, and sometimes an accurate one. Careful study must be made of any and all objects that have been struck by the bullet. When the type of gun and the caliber, velocity, and mass of the bullet are known, these facts, combined with information obtained from study of the point of impact, may yield useful deductions.

The angle of the bullet's trajectory at the time of impact may be estimated. The distance of flight may also be estimated by considering the penetration of the bullet in relation to the range and power of the shooting combination. At the end of the normal range the bullet's energy has largely been expended, and gravitational pull has become the major factor in determining the direction of its movement. The early part of a bullet's trajectory will approximate the alignment of the gun barrel. Thus the trajectory is determined by three factors: (a) the bullet's initial velocity, which is gradually decreased by air friction; (b) the constant force of gravity, which produces a continuously accelerating rate of fall; and (c) the spin stability of the projectile, which is related to its

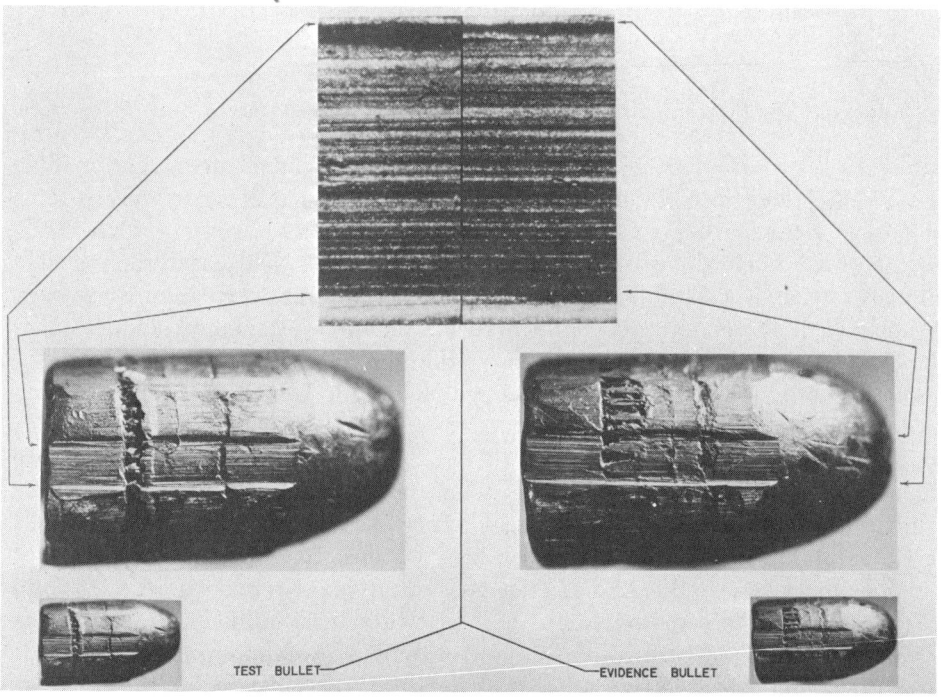

FIGURE 31-6. Comparison of .38 cal. land impression stria. The evidence bullet was removed from the victim; the test bullet was fired from the weapon found in the suspect's possession (Courtesy of John E. Murdock.)

weight, its shape, and the degree of rotation imparted to it by the rifling of the gun barrel. Whenever a projectile strikes an object but continues in its flight, profound divergence occurs from the normal values of its velocity and spin. The interpretation of a bullet's trajectory between the target object and its final resting point should be approached with caution. Some success has been achieved in the determination of such hybrid trapectories through the use of modern computer technology. At the beginning of its flight a bullet's course approximates a straight line that arcs downward at a progressively increasing rate. With a high-power bullet—one ejected at high muzzle velocity —the proof that the bullet's energy was nearly spent when it struck would show that the shot was fired from a considerable distance. The trajectories of bullets shot from small arms, which have comparatively low muzzle-velocities, are calculated on the basis of their correspondingly shorter range. All such considerations of the trajectory of a bullet and its point of impact must be regarded as approximations only. They do, however, serve to show whether the shot was fired from close by or from a more distant point. Angles of impact indicate the direction of the shot. Close observation, appropriate experimentation, and proper interpretation may often lead to valid inferences in answer to the question "From where was the bullet fired?"

Cartridge and Shell Cases

Although fired cases are less often encountered in criminal investigation than are bullets, when found they are usually of significance because they receive at least as clear markings as do bullets, exhibit a greater variety of such markings, and are not ordinarily damaged in firing. When shell cases remain at a crime scene, it is probable that a repeating or automatic weapon was used, because such a weapon ejects the fired cases, and the shooter seldom takes the time necessary to locate and retrieve them. A revolver will carry the cases until they are removed manually, as will a double-barreled shotgun or any type of single-shot weapon.

The questions that are appropriate to the finding of such materials are similar to those that require answers when only bullets are located. Usually, quite definite answers can be given, whether the evidence be shotgun shells or cartridge cases from pistols, revolvers, or rifles. Revolvers and single-shot weapons mark the shell case less than does any type of repeating of automatic weapon and, for that reason, such shell cases are more difficult to identify as having come from a particular weapon or type of weapon. *In general, it is possible to identify a certain firearm as having fired a particular shell or cartridge.* It is often possible to identify the type or make of gun that fired it, though in many instances this must be regarded as tentative identification only. It is nearly always possible to state the type of ammunition used.

FIGURE 31-7. Impression of a .22 cal. cartridge trademark in breechblock grease. The "U" directly below the firing pin port is the trademark of Remington-Peters. (Courtesy of John E. Murdock.)

Identification of the type of ammunition need not depend upon its size, shape, and appearance, being much more simply and positively derived from the markings placed by the manufacturer. Details of these markings are discussed in the more complete works on the investigation of firearms. The thoroughgoing firearms examiner should have available for comparison a considerable number of fired cases of numerous types, and should attempt to keep his collection reasonably up-to-date. Thus, he will recognize quickly most of the shell and cartridge cases presented for examination, and will be able to trace the sources of most of the unusual specimens occasionally encountered.

Identification of the Weapon

The identification of the weapon from which a particular projectile was fired is the most important and the most frequent study of the firearms examiner. It is also very likely to yield results. Such a study is focused upon the characteristic marks left on the case by various portions of the gun's mechanism.

(1) *Breech-Block Marks.* The breech block of a weapon is usually surface-finished by a milling tool or file, either of which leaves on the face of the block

FIGURE 31-8. Comparison of breechblock and firing pin impressions. **(A)** 9 mm Luger. **(B)** .32 cal. Mauser auto. (Courtesy of A. Biasotti.)

tiny scratches that are distinctive, as are the marks of any other kind of tool. At the moment of firing, the base of the shell is forced violently against the breech block and will, in some instances, record and retain an accurate impression of these striations. This is most likely to appear on the primer, which, being made of softer metal, receives an impression more easily than does the main portion of the shell case. Such marks may be found on any fired shell or cartridge and can serve for positive identification, just as other tool marks do.

(2) *Firing-Pin Impressions.* Because the firing pin (or a pointed or edged hammer) must strike the shell (center primer or edge of a rim-fire cartridge) in order to fire the charge, there always will be marks on a fired cartridge from this source. At times they are not distinctly individual, but only rarely are they totally devoid of individuality. Usually they include imperfections, finishing marks, or other completely individual characteristics that are very readily recognized and are rarely or never duplicated by different firing pins. These impressions can be studied by means of the comparison microscope, the questioned evidence being compared with a standard shell or cartridge case that has been fired from the suspected weapon. Evidence obtained from such a comparison is definite when the shape of the firing pin is quite individual. In some cases the comparison is less definite, as not all firing pins are completely characteristic.

(3) *Marks from Extractors and Ejectors.* Virtually all firearms have some form of extractor or ejector. Repeating and automatic arms normally have vigorous ejecting action that will impress definite and recognizable marks on the rim of the cartridge or shell. If these marks are merely indentations on the rim, only their size, location, and shape are useful for comparison. If a sliding action has also been present, as frequently occurs, more positive identifications are possible on the basis of the resulting fine striations. Because of their general occurrence, such marks should always be sought and studied. Frequently they are sufficient in themselves to establish identification.

(4) *Marks Due to Expansion.* At the moment of firing, the entire force of the explosion is exerted on the shell case, tending to expand it. Most firearms contain certain irregularities in the region where the barrel, the breech block, and the extractor meet. For example, the extractor, which is set into the end of the chamber so as to grip the rim of the cartridge or shell, often fits far from perfectly. Hence, it is not at all uncommon to observe a fired case that has been bulged into these irregularities and has received rather characteristic impressions on its surface. This may serve for the identification of the gun, or may even indicate the probable type of gun. Both the occurrence of such marks and their comparison with known cases fired from suspected weapons are helpful in the identification.

(5) *Magazine Marks.* Automatic and repeating weapons always have some type of magazine. The insertion of the unfired cartridge or shell into a maga-

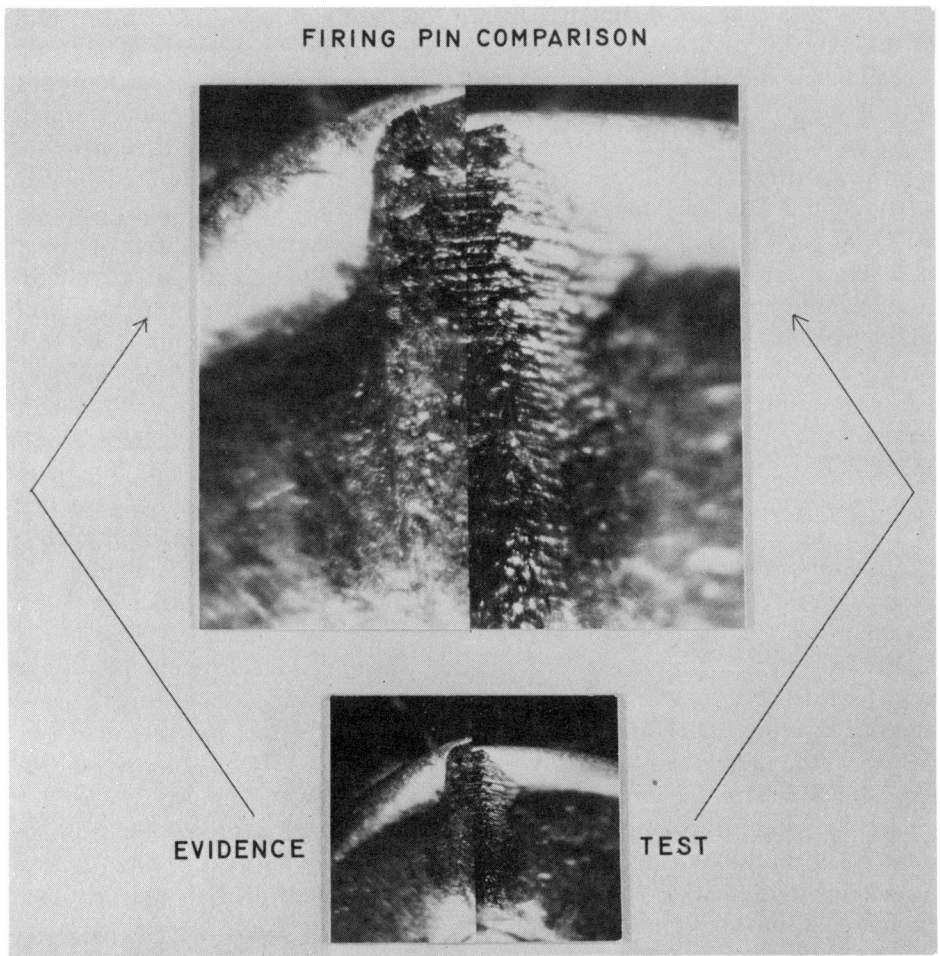

FIGURE 31-9. Comparison of .22 cal. firing pin impressions. The evidence cartridge was found at the scene; the test cartridge was made with the weapon found in the suspect's possession. (Courtesy of Duayne J. Dillon.)

zine involves scraping the sides of the case over metallic portions of the magazine, which are sometimes irregular and thus leave quite characteristic scrape marks on the case. The location of these marks is different from those of most other marks on the shell or cartridge case, and their length is often considerable. Both of these features serve to identify the origin of the marks. When such marks are present and show sufficient line detail, they are very useful for comparison identification.

(6) *Loading Mechanism Marks.* Repeating and automatic weapons are designed to remove a cartridge or shell from the magazine, force it (usually in

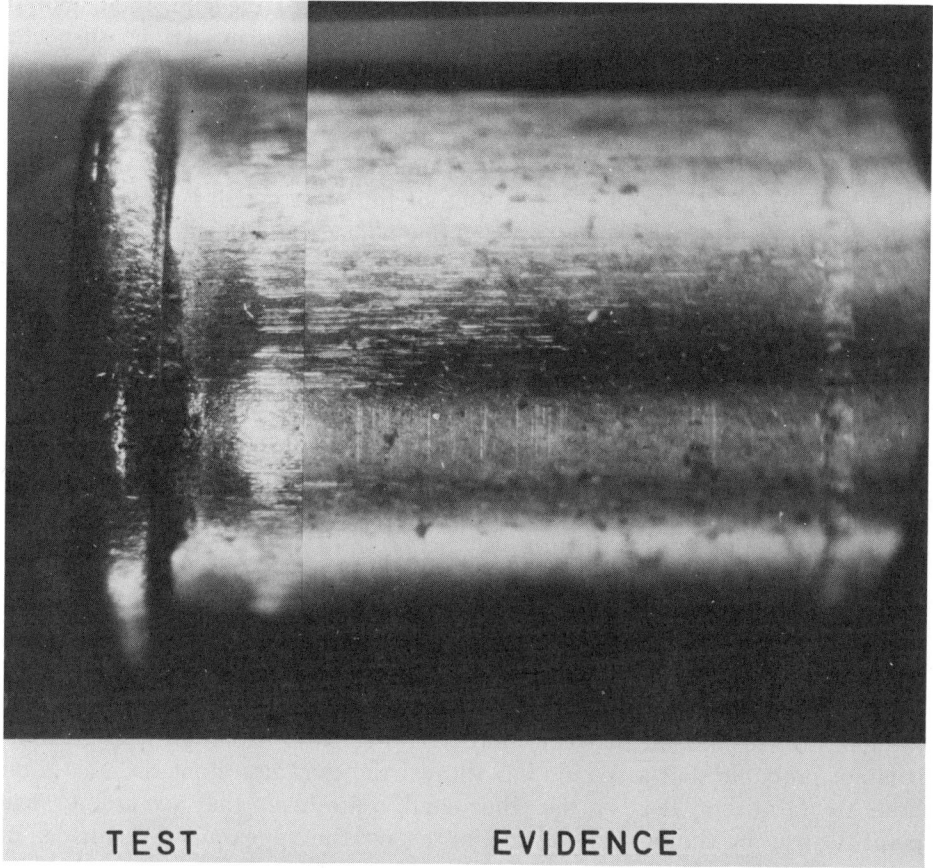

FIGURE 31-10. Comparison of .22 cal. chamber marks caused by cartridge case expansion against the chamber walls and subsequent extraction. (Courtesy of Duayne J. Dillon.)

an upward direction) into line with chamber, and drive it into the latter. While these operations are proceeding, the cartridge or shell is forced over a number of metallic surfaces, some of which may be rough enough to impress scratches or scrape marks on some part of the ammunition. These marks are often somewhat erratic in their recording because of loose and variable contact of the case with marking surface. However, a very distinctive and reproducible form of striated mark occasionally results and, when present, constitutes an excellent basis for comparison identification.

To summarize: the cartridge or shell case usually carries markings that are quite distinctive of the weapon in which it was fired, markings that can be used for positive identification of the weapon. Inasmuch as these marks have arisen from a variety of contacts with several parts of the gun, their analysis is useful in determining the type of weapon sought for in case no suspected weapon is available. The type of ammunition is usually determined very simply from manufacturer's marks, and the size, type, dimensions, and design of the case. This information, added to that derived from analysis of the types and location of the markings will often determine the type of weapon used. Thus, the recovered shell cartridge case is one of the most useful types of physical evidence in shooting cases. The investigating officer should make every possible effort to recover all such evidence and to deliver it to the laboratory, as well as the bullet (if recovered) and any suspected weapons that may be located.

Distance from Which the Shot Was Fired

It is often necessary in the investigation of shooting cases to estimate the distance of a gun from the object struck at the time of firing. This information is particularly important in connection with self-defense pleas. It would be at least improbable that a person shooting in self-defense would be far distant from his target unless he, in turn, was being fired at or threatened by a firearm. Numerous instances arise in which it is apparent from the evidence that the victim was unarmed and it is claimed that he was choking or beating the person who did the shooting. Clearly, a shot fired under these circumstances could not have originated much further away than the length of the gun. Another type of question may also require determination of the distance of the gun: the distinction between murder and suicide. Although it is possible, it is not probable that a suicide has thrown the gun any great distance after firing the fatal shot. It is, on the other hand, quite likely that a murderer will plant the gun by the body of his victim to give the appearance of suicide. In such a situation it is highly probable that the shot came from a gun held at least several feet away, and possibly more distant. At least, if it can be established that such was the case, the possibility of suicide is quite remote.

In addition to determining whether, at impact, the bullet was close to the end of its flight, it is often possible to state with considerable certainty the distance of a gun from the target by a study of patterns and residues left on the latter. These will differ in form and size depending on the circumstances, and will in all cases bear a relationship to the distance. The application of this principle is most obvious in the behavior of charges of shot fired from a shotgun.

SHOT PATTERNS. At close ranges, the shot emerging from the barrel of a shotgun travels with considerable force in a tightly compacted group. Moreover, the wadding is still associated with the shot group up to a few feet from the muzzle. This wadding is soon scattered and lost, and the pellets progressively separate and spread out. As the range increases, the shot may spread to cover several square feet of area but will have little force. Because of this progressive change in the shot and wadding pattern it is possible, if the conditions are favorable, to determine with considerable accuracy the distance of firing. The pattern must be available for study, and the weapon and ammunition must be obtained. Failing this, a simlar weapon and ammunition may be used for comparison, though the results will be somewhat less certain, since it is possible that the degree of wear, damage, and individual variation can be different. The pattern can be affected not only by the type of gun, but by its condition and by the type and condition of the ammunition. For this reason, the results will be most meaningful when the same gun and the same kind of ammunition are used. With them the investigator can make a series of test firings at different measured ranges to determine the pattern that is recorded at any specific distance. A white cloth spread over a board backing makes a suitable target that may be photographed to record the patterns characteristic of all the ranges studied.

POWDER PATTERNS. All firearms, regardless of the type of missile fired, blow burned, unburned, and partially burned powder fragments from the muzzle at the time of firing. These fragments spread behind and around the missile in an approximately conical shape, but because of their low mass they do not travel far. Such material is seldom observed at a distance greater than 6–10 ft ahead of the muzzle of the gun, and at these distances there may be a few detectable fragments, but rarely any perceptible pattern. Closer by, the pattern is usually apparent. Near the muzzle the pattern is relatively confined and dense. The farther from the gun, the wider and thinner grows the pattern. Ordinarily the pattern shows considerable deviation from circular form because of greater leakage past the bullet on one side than on the other. Even using the same gun and the same type of ammunition it is virtually impossible to duplicate closely a powder pattern, the distribution of powder residue being random in nature. However, there will be a certain degree of pattern duplication attributable to the general and specific characteristics of the gun, and this pattern duplication will be manifest on successive firings. Moreover, the spread of the pattern will be similar when the same gun and the same type of ammunition are used. For this reason, a test pattern can make possible a reasonably close estimate of the distance from which a shot has been fired.

Powder patterns are often found on the clothing of the victim, around the area of the bullet hole. For this reason such cloth surfaces should be preserved carefully intact for study, in case it should become necessary to estimate the distance between the gun and the target. Development of the nitrate or nitrite pattern by chemical means is occasionally helpful. In many instances the pattern can be delineated by visual observation of the ash and unburned powder residue. In other cases, particularly when the clothing has been mishandled—as often happens—it is necessary to resort to chemical testing.

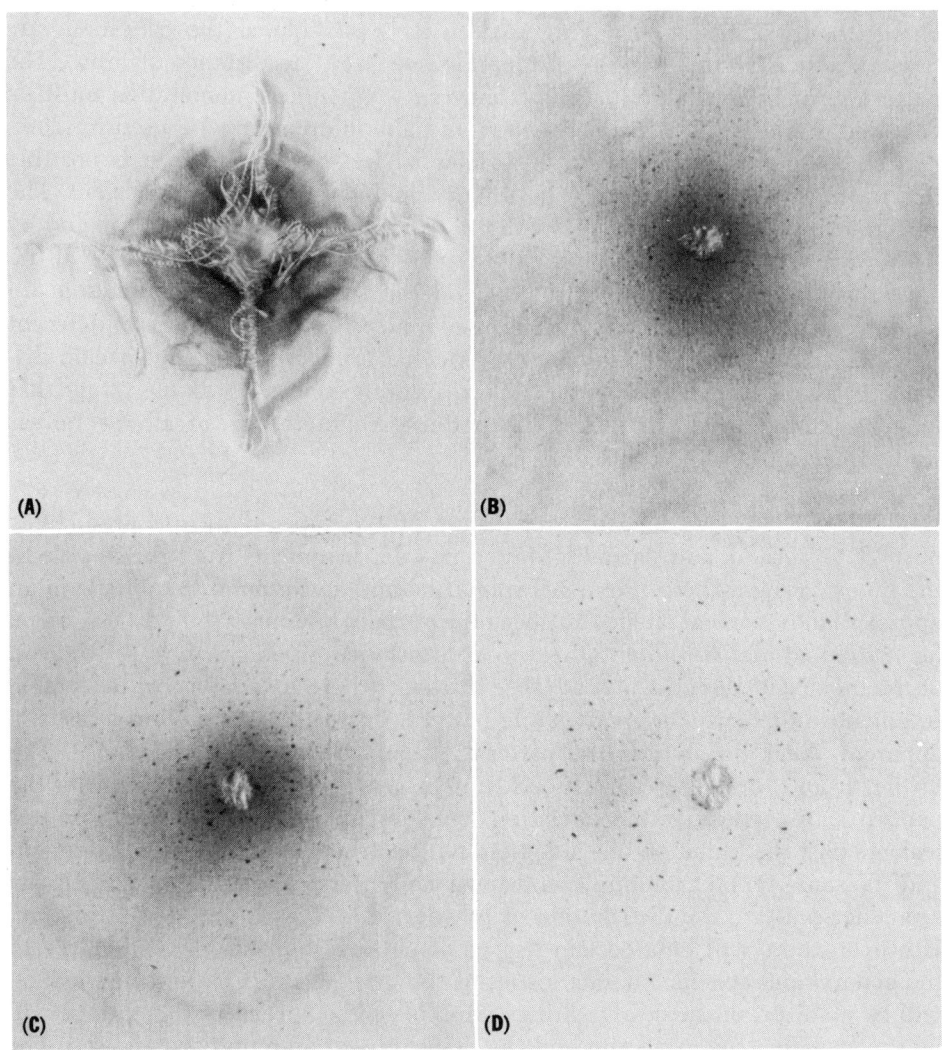

FIGURE 31-11. Powder patterns. The comparison of test powder patterns such as these with evidence patterns (i.e. patterns found on the garment of a gunshot victim) are used to approximate the probable muzzle to target distance. The test patterns were made with a 9mm Smith and Wesson model 39-2 automatic pistol. (A) Contact. (B) Two inches. (C) Four inches. (D) Twelve inches. (Courtesy of Stephen P. McJunkins.)

SMOKE-DARKENING. If a firearm is discharged very close to the target, as happens in suicide and occasionally in murder, scorching of the target, or the deposition of smoke on it, often results. This is caused by the flame that emerges from the muzzle and travels only a short distance from it. This distance will vary with the length of the barrel, the size of the power charge, and possibly with the degree to which the bullet fills the barrel. The presence of a dark smoke deposit is an almost positive proof that the firearm was discharged within a few inches of the object struck. Here, also, a test of the effective distance may be performed. Only rarely does scorching occur as much as 4 inches ahead of the muzzle.

Identifying the Shooter

One of the most important questions to be dealt with in a large proportion of shooting cases is the identity of the person who fired the gun. This question is inevitable when the weapon is not found in the possession of a suspect. The problem is not susceptible to study by any of the standard procedures known to the firearms expert: normally he devotes his attention to the characteristics of firearms, ammunition, and matters directly related thereto. Here the identification must usually rest upon peripheral factors that tie firearms problems tightly to other types of evidence, which are discussed in many of the other chapters of this book.

FINGERPRINTS. The most obvious clue to the identity of the person who fired a gun is provided by the fingerprints left on it. Because this is the first kind of evidence that anyone would suggest, it is likely that the culprit will have considered it and taken measures to ensure that his prints do not remain on the gun. However, when shots are fired in great emotional stress, during serious altercation, or in other distracting circumstances, or by a person too stupid to realize the full import of fingerprints in identification, there may be latent prints left. In every shooting case a search for such prints must be made as a purely routine matter. If the person who finds a firearm has any reason to believe that it may have been used for homicide, he must take precautions to preserve any prints that may remain on the gun. Instances have been known to occur in which a police officer has actually obliterated all useful prints and impressed his own on the weapon. Today, any officer who is found guilty of so negligent an action should, at the very least, be relieved of police duty.

The gun must be retrieved cautiously, particular care being taken to touch only those portions of the weapon unsuitable for the development of latent fingerprints, e.g., checkered grips. To avoid wiping prints off the weapon during transit, an attempt should be made at the scene to develop any latent prints on the exterior of the weapon. The gun may then be safely transported to the laboratory where it may be disassembled and examined for latent prints on interior parts.

RESIDUES. Notably in pocket weapons, and to a lesser extent in rifles and shotguns, hollow portions of a gun will accumulate an assortment of fine debris that is seldom, if ever, cleaned out by the owner. In such an accumulation there will be fibers from clothing, hairs, soil particles, fragments of metals, glass and everything that has collected in the owner's pocket in which the gun has been carried. The weapon may be partly or completely disassembled in the laboratory so that all of the inner recesses may be cleaned out. The collected material can often be matched with corresponding debris taken from the pockets of the suspected person. Although evidence of this type is often overlooked, when it has been fully utilized it has at times been overwhelming in its import or guilt. The methods and considerations that are involved in the study of such evidence are covered elsewhere in this book. (See Chapter 9.)

DERMAL NITRATE TEST. When a gun is fired, powder residue may be blown around the cylinder of a revolver, or between imperfectly fitting parts of other weapons. Traces of such residues are sometimes transferred to the hands of the shooter. The dermal nitrate test was designed to demonstrate the presence of such traces on the hands of a suspect. In many instances, however, the results have been ambiguous, so that proper interpretation has been virtually impossible. The test has been subjected to critical analysis by many workers and, to the satisfaction of most criminalists, has been discredited. In most areas the dermal nitrate test has been totally replaced by neutron activation analysis.

NEUTRON ACTIVATION ANALYSIS. The primer mixtures of all center-fire ammunition and of most .22 rim-fire ammunition contain the elements barium and antimony. Although individuals in some occupations come into contact with barium and antimony, these elements are seldom found on the hands of the general population. An elevated level of barium or antimony on the hands of an individual is, therefore, strongly suggestive of recent handling or firing of a weapon. These residues can be removed by coating the appropriate skin surfaces with molten paraffin and lifting off the coating after it has hardened, or by swabbing the skin with dilute nitric acid. The paraffin casts, or the swabs, can then be subjected to neutron activation analysis to demonstrate the presence or absence of elevated levels of barium or antimony. Neutron activation analysis, by reason of its exceedingly high sensitivity, is one of the few analytical techniques capable of demonstrating the minute traces of primer materials that may be found on the hands of an individual who has fired or handled a weapon.

The casts or the swabs must be sent to an installation that has the necessary neutron generator. After activation in a high neutron flux, the radioactive decay of the elements of interest is determined. The entire process, including radiochemical separation, takes many days; hence neutron activation analysis of gunshot residues does not provide the investigator with a quick answer.

The firearms-discharge residues that may be deposited on the hands of an individual are easily washed off, or wiped off by contact with clothing. The test is, therefore, not applicable if the individual suspected of having fired a weapon has had an opportunity to wash his hands, of if a considerable period of time has elapsed since the shooting incident.

Neutron activation analysis for gunshot residues has been found to be of particular value in differentiating between homicide and suicide. However, if an attempt is to be made to determine gunshot residues by means of neutron activation analysis, the hands of the deceased should be carefully protected until the removal of any possible residues has been performed. Certain of the "inkless" fingerprint inks that are used by mortuary attendants to fingerprint bodies contain considerable amounts of antimony, and if the body is fingerprinted prior to the removal of gunshot residues it may not be possible to place any reliance upon the results of the neutron activation analysis.

REFERENCES

Barnes, F. C.: *Cartridges of the World*, 3rd ed. Chicago: Follett (1972).
Bradford, L. W.: "Firearms and Firearms Wounds," Chap. 20 of F. E. Camps, ed., *Gradwohl's Legal Medicine*. Bristol: John Wrights and Sons (1968).
Burrard, G.: *The Identification of Firearms and Forensic Ballistics*. New York: A. S. Barnes (1962).
Davis, J.: *Tool Marks, Firearms and the Striagraph*. Springfield: Thomas (1958).
Hatcher, J. S., Jury, F. J., and Weller, J.: *Firearms Investigation, Identification, and Evidence*. Harrisburg, Pa.: Stackpole (1957).
Krcma, V.: *Identification and Registration of Firearms*. Springfield: Thomas (1971).
Mathews, J.: *Firearms Identification*. Springfield: Thomas (1972). 3 vols.
Schlesinger, H. L., Lukens, H. R., Guinn, V. P., Hackleman, R. P., and Korts, R. F.: *Special Report on Gunshot Residues Measured by Neutron Activation Analysis*. Springfield, Virginia: National Technical Information Service #GA-9829 (1970).
Smith, W. H. B., and Smith, J. E.: *Small Arms of the World*, 9th ed. Harrisburg, Pa.: Stackpole (1969).
White, H. P., Bearse, R., and Munhall, B. P.: *Centerfire Pistol and Revolver Cartridges*. South Brunswick, New Jersey: A. S. Barnes (1967).

32
Vehicular Accidents

In view of the continuing increase in the number of power-driven vehicles used daily, and in the number of streets, roads, and highways along which they move at ever-increasing speeds, it seems inevitable that there would be a corresponding increase in the number of vehicular accidents and of concomitant injuries and deaths, as well as in the number of consequent lawsuits. These increases have aroused great concern about the need for the reduction of "highway carnage," the usual implication being that the situation is continually worsening. In fairness it must be pointed out that automobile accidents are much less common than ever before in terms of passenger miles, or even in terms of the number of cars on the road. Thus, it must be acknowledged that the programs designed to reduce automobile accidents have had a favorable effect, and it is probable that the proportion of good and careful drivers on the road has never been greater than it is now.

It has also been accepted as axiomatic that automobile accidents are preventable. Unquestionably, they are preventable, but not necessarily by the efforts of any single individual concerned in a specific accident. Mechanical failures are relatively rare, but they constitute a significant portion of accident causes today. As has always been true, the "loose nut behind the wheel" is still more dangerous than the one lower down in the steering gear. Both may cause accidents, and for this reason the pertinent facts of each and every automobile accident should be studied, evaluated, and considered in the elucidation of other accidents. The public has heard more propaganda than facts in its fight against the tragic results of automobile accidents.

The widely publicized slogan "Speed kills" is illustrative. Admittedly a stopped car rarely kills anyone, but neither does it go anywhere. The entire purpose of modern highway construction and automotive engineering is to move people faster to their destinations, with a minimum of risk. A traffic engineer must consider how many vehicles may move over a stretch of freeway at what speed, and then design the freeway to maximize both factors. Otherwise traffic on the road will produce only monumental jams. Although it is true that speed can kill, it is a documented fact that more accidents occur at 35 miles per hour (mph) than at any other speed. The high-velocity accident is more spectacular, but it is correspondingly rarer than the low-speed accident that nobody fears, but which maims and kills a far larger part of the motoring public. These are facts that should always be taken into consideration in litigation concerning automobile accidents.

CAUSES OF VEHICULAR ACCIDENTS

What causes underlie automobile accidents? Careful consideration will demonstrate that there are many, and that emphasis upon one or two causes will not negate the effects of the others. The causes of automobile accidents may be classified as follows:

(1) *The driver's inattention.* When the driver is distracted by conversation, by the sights along the road, or by difficulties within the car, his failure to observe and circumvent potential hazards may result in an accident. This factor has not been made the focus of safety campaigns, though it probably leads to a majority of all accidents, or at least to a large minority of them. Fortunately, many of these accidents are minor.

(2) *The driver's impairment.* Alcohol has led the field in this area. No one can question the fact that drivers whose performance is impaired by alcohol are responsible for many traffic accidents. However, the most sanguinary statistics on this point have never established that drinking is more than a minor cause of accidents. The statistics have nearly always been compiled on the basis that someone involved in the accident had a measurable and potentially dangerous alcoholic content in his blood, rather than being focused on the *exact alcoholic content of the blood of the specific driver who caused the accident.* When statistics are used in a generalized way, they may cloud the issue rather than clarifying it. Driver impairment from sources other than alcohol, such as drugs, is now receiving much attention. Here also lies the source of some automobile accidents, but only a minority of them. Impairments such as these are preventable, and should be prevented. However, one hears

little about the driver whose performance is impaired by fatigue, by loss of sleep, or by psychic disturbance attributable to deep-seated problems in his own life that may turn him, temporarily, into a self-destructive person. It is clear that a normal, careful, and reasonably skillful driver will avoid accidents nearly all of the time.

(3) *Mechanical failure.* Today, machines are built with greater precision than is man. Nevertheless, carelessness on the part of the man who assembles a critical portion of an automobile, and engineering mistakes in the design of brakes, steering gears, even transmissions and differentials, have led to accidents that were not only preventable but *should* have been prevented. Service personnel whose training is incomplete, and who are basically incompetent, have set the stage for many preventable accidents by assembling improperly the complex mechanisms that are characteristic of modern cars. The theory that almost anyone can, in a two-weeks' course at the factory, learn all that is required to follow the detailed instructions of the manufacturer has often been proved fallacious.

(4) *Highway hazards.* Hazards in the environment of the driver, and specifically those of the highway, must not be overlooked. Many defects in the roadways and in the environment surrounding the roadways are serious contributing factors. The design of modern high-speed highways leaves something to be desired, and secondary roads are often potentially dangerous at certain locations. When construction and repair crews block off portions of a highway, they often place their warning signals where the driver coming over the crest of a hill or around a curve will not see them in time to reduce his speed properly. Many highways are inadequately marked with informative directional signs. This deficiency may cause the driver to make dangerous last-minute turns and changes of lane. "Greenbrier Lane" on a freeway sign may be useful to the driver who knows that the lane is an access route to a particular town, but for the great stream of drivers who pass that sign daily it is no more meaningful than are many existing freeway signs.

Environmental hazards are sometimes not preventable. For example, a grade that faces into the setting sun can be extremely hazardous because the driver cannot see well looking toward the sun, and in the attempt to see he may be temporarily blinded to obstructions and to the traffic ahead of him. A sign posted in such a location cannot be read by the drivers whom it was intended to warn or inform. It is debatable whether highway engineers can remedy situations of this kind, but they are dangerous nevertheless. Wet, frosty, or icy streets present hazards that can be partly reduced at the present time, though they account for a considerable number of accidents. Animals that decide to cross highways at inconvenient times cause many accidents. Some control can be exercised in the case of domestic animals; little control is possible with wild animals such as deer. It is generally ineffectual to mark a high-speed thoroughfare with numerous "Deer Crossing" signs. Perhaps high fences could reduce the hazard, but this solution could never be fully satisfactory where a multilane freeway cuts through the natural feeding grounds of wild animals.

Of the four major causes of accidents here listed, the first is probably predominant, the second is a close contender, and the third and fourth are numerically minor but are not to be disregarded. It is small comfort to a widow or to a permanently disabled driver to know that the causative accident was of no commonplace sort.

Investigation of an automobile accident cannot take into account the basic cause, because the real cause is often subjective and will not, therefore, be recognized even by the responsible person. It is perhaps for this reason that attention has been focused upon the driver who is impaired by alcohol or by drugs, mechanical inadequacies being accorded only secondary importance. The latter are things that may, in most instances, be detected and proved. The immediate task of the investigator is to determine, as far as possible, the following aspects of the accident:

(1) *The nature of the occurrence*: that is, who was violating some standard provision of the law by excessive speed, by being on the wrong side of the road, by denying the right of way at an intersection, or by failing to maintain a sufficient distance between vehicles. Answers to these and similar questions can often be determined only after the

(2) *Reconstruction of the occurrence*. Ideally this is a play-by-play breakdown of the several steps immediately preceding, during, and after the impact. It is generally followed by

(3) *Calculations of speed*. Although this aspect of the analysis is properly a portion of the first item above, it must ordinarily be left to the last because it is often necessary to have all of the other facts clearly defined before it is possible to calculate a valid estimate of speed.

TYPES OF VEHICULAR ACCIDENTS

In application, the approach outlined above will require systematic attention to a number of secondary factors that must be under study one by one, the findings being subsequently correlated with each other. Every accident is different from every other one, but it is helpful if the accident being studied is placed in one of several broad categories:

(1) Front-end collisions, including side-swipes that are predominantly front-to-front
(2) Front-to-side impacts, as in intersection accidents
(3) Rear-end collisions

(4) Single-car accidents
(5) Deviant accidents caused by unusual circumstances

Category 5 would be illustrated by a car out of control that spins into another car in an unusual manner; or by one that encounters an unexpected obstruction; or an impact that results as a portion of a roll-over, somersault, or vault.

Accidental impacts of any of the above types may result from any of the basic causes operating in combination with unusual circumstances of terrain, traffic, and accompanying unrelated factors. Such a breakdown of types is primarily useful for preliminary orientation and in describing the accident for purposes of record.

Front-End Collisions

The front-end collision, the frequent and most deadly type of automobile impact, can occur only when one of the vehicles involved, or both of them, occupies space that does not properly belong to it. Usually the most critical question to be answered is *which driver crossed the midline of the highway and invaded the other driver's right of way?* Finding the answer to this question involves the determination of the *point of impact on the roadway*, sometimes also the *direction of impact*, and the *points of contact of the vehicles*. All these matters are treated separately elsewhere in this chapter since they pertain to other types of impact also.

Front-to-Side Impacts

The collision in which the side of a car is impacted by the front of another is common among accidents that occur at street intersections. It occurs also in some complex multivehicular accidents on freeways, and occasionally elsewhere. A car that crosses the road suddenly and unaccountably in front of an approaching car is likely to be struck broadside. Generally such a vehicle is out of control and skidding sidewise, but this is not always the case and cannot be presumed. More often two cars try to cross the same intersection simultaneously at right angles to each other, despite the rules of the road, which are specific on this point. In these instances the question is more often one of physics. An appreciable number of accidents involving this type of impact occur where there is no intersection and under conditions that demand the most careful reconstruction of the collision and the calculation of speeds. It may be pointed out that these accidents are often the most difficult to understand and to reconstruct because they indicate an unusual degree of confusion on the part of the driver who crosses the road, and they involve many factors that are difficult to evaluate.

Rear-End Collisions

Accidents involving rear-end collisions are among the most difficult to evaluate in meaningful terms, although they are among the easiest to understand. Modern traffic inevitably produces lines of cars moving at considerable speeds, one behind the other in close proximity. Whenever any driver in such a line slows suddenly, the driver behind him is placed under an immediate necessity to slow correspondingly. This he often fails to do, and the result is a rear-end collision. Generally, the law is explicit on the point that the responsibility rests on the following driver who does not stop or slow in time, whereas the latter usually feels justified in blaming the driver ahead of him who slowed suddenly or stopped, often without a signal, and thereby blocked the traffic. Because both cars are moving in the same direction, the energy of such impacts is usually small, and resulting personal injuries are likely to be whiplashes rather than more serious trauma. In rear-end collisions the calculations of speed and of the energy of impact are usually more important than they are in other kinds of collision.

Single-Car Accidents

The automobile accident in which only one car is involved occurs with increasing frequency. Such an accident nearly always results from either driver impairment or mechanical failure. For the investigator the important problem is likely to be the determination of which of these two causative factors was operative in a particular accident. In the absence of mechanical failure, factors such as alcohol, drugs, fatigue, and road hypnosis are most frequently significant. However, the possibility of such unpredictables as brake malfunction and steering-gear failure must not be overlooked. In all rear-end collisions it is imperative that a careful mechanical check of the following vehicle be made. It is also mandatory that blood analysis of the driver of the second car be made for the presence of alcohol, carbon monoxide, and—more frequently important —drugs of several kinds. Many such accidents will be solved by one or another of these examinations. Failure of such tests to reveal an adequate probable cause of the accident may require that more complex or subtle causes be sought or postulated. If the driver of the following car has been killed in the accident, or has lost his memory, it may not be possible to determine the exact nature of the accident.

Deviant Accidents

Systematic treatment of deviant accidents is impossible by reason of the wide variation of contributory factors. The principles of the investigation do not differ from those applicable to accidents in the other categories, except that variables are introduced. A few examples will clarify the situation.

(1) Because of excessive speed, loss of control, or some other factor, a light vehicle leaves the roadway and crashes against a metal post, which bends under the impact, forming an inclined plane up which the vehicle slides, and from which it is thrown into a roll-over.

(2) A vehicle leaves the roadway at a relatively high speed and approaches a canal, or large ditch, over which it vaults, and lands on the other side out of control.

(3) A vehicle is thrown into a spin by impact and collides with other vehicles or with fixed objects in an unusual manner.

(4) A vehicle strikes an obstruction, is lifted, and vaults for a distance without contact with the roadway.

(5) A vehicle is impacted heavily on the front end, somersaults over the impacting object and lands upside-down on top of a following vehicle.

Although such accidents are unusual, every investigator encounters a significant number of them. It is important for him to realize the possibilities so that he may evaluate the available evidence.

INVESTIGATION

The principles and procedures of investigation are similar for accidents of all categories. After the general category of the accident has been determined, one of several available orders of procedure will be selected. A preferred procedure is outlined below.

Type of Impact

In order to determine the type of impact, the investigator must know exactly what portions of the involved vehicles were impacted or contacted. Such areas will generally be dented, telescoped, folded, or abraded, and they may show transferred smears or paint chips. Two details of primary importance are the two points—one on each vehicle—at which the initial contact occurred. In the *head-on or rear-end collision*, this will generally be the point of maximum penetration or of maximum movement of the frame elements or, sometimes, of the body sheet steel. This follows from the fact that the vehicles have more kinetic energy at the moment of first contact than they will have subsequently, so that the first contact is the most energetic and does the most damage. In the *sideswipe* the first point of contact may be faint as compared with later penetration, but its location can be found readily by searching for the marking that is nearest to the end from which the impacting vehicle came. The *front-to-side impact* will often be similar to the front-end impact, but it will sometimes resemble the sideswipe, depending chiefly on the relative speed of the two vehicles. This matter is important to observe and utilize also, as is developed later in this chapter.

The point of initial contact having been located, all other contact areas are to be noted, such as those that sometimes result from a secondary spinning collision following the first contact. These secondary contact marks are especially useful in the final reconstruction of the accident. Each type of impact damage exhibits certain identifying characteristics that indicate both the angle and the speed of the local collision. All markings should be classified, at least tentatively, as to the type of causation, because this information will be needed later in the interpretation of the findings.

Angle of Impact

As soon as possible after the locations and types of the various impacts have been determined and tentatively classified, it is especially important to determine the *angle of the initial collision* as it is indicated on each of the vehicles. If the front end of the car is displaced backward, usually one side of the front is displaced more than the other, and often the bumper, the grille structure, or the fenders will give the angle of impact directly. When the side of a car has been directly impacted, the angle of the impact may be readily determined from the imprint of the other car on the impacted surface. By observing all displacements of parts, disregarding any items hanging loosely, the investigator can, in most instances, establish a reliable angle of impact. As soon as the initial impact angle is known for each of the vehicles, they may be positioned exactly as they were at the moment of impact. It is often helpful to cut to scale, from cardboard, "shadow" representations of the areas covered by the two cars, adjust them to the exact angle and position of the initial impact, and tape them together so that the vehicle combination may be compared with a scale drawing of the roadway upon which the accident occurred. This will often make quite clear the distinction between what *could have* and what *could not have* occurred.

Force of Impact

While the other aspects of impact damage are being studied it is possible to observe the amount of force involved as indicated by the character of the damage. In this phase of the investigation it is always important to remember that damage that appears to be extreme may actually be very superficial and vice versa. Body damage, especially, is often very impressive; but car bodies are ordinarily constructed of very light steel sheet suspended on a light framework, and very little force is required to produce extreme deformation in them. By contrast, the main frame members of a car are usually of rather massive construction, and even a slight bending or buckling of such a member will indicate a very energetic impact. The displacement of a motor requires considerable energy, but the displacement of a front wheel is, by comparison, rather minor in its implication. Bumpers are sometimes light and sometimes relatively heavy, but passenger-car bumpers may often be deformed or broken off at the brackets without having sustained a very violent impact. The bumpers of heavy trucks are often exceptions to this generalization, being quite massive and attached to major frame members. Experience and judgment, combined with careful examination, are required to assess properly the force of the impact, but an effort must always be made to estimate it as closely as possible.

Effect of Impact

This seemingly complex matter is determined by simple laws of physics and a few basic interrelationships, which are summarized below.

(1) *The effect of the angle of impact with respect to the centers of gravity.* Newton's first law of motion states that *a body remains in a state of rest or of uniform motion in a straight line unless compelled by some external force acting upon it to change that state.* It is the *center of gravity* of the automobile—or other body—that behaves according to Newton's generalization. Among the external forces that modify the motion of an automobile are included friction of the tires against the roadway and the resistance of the air through which the car moves. These are customarily overlooked because they are very familiar. But the law applies equally to the external force of contact with any obstruction. In practical terms, the law applies roughly as follows: If two vehicles suffer head-on impact centered on both front ends, neither will spin, and the one having the greater energy will drive the other one backward until the "canceled" energy has been transformed into work and heat. If the force of the impact on either vehicle is applied at an angle such that the center of gravity of that vehicle is on one side or the other of the point of application, that vehicle will be thrown into a spin or gyration such as is so commonly observed in head-on collisions. If the direction of the spin is known, the location of the center of gravity is approximately determined, and vice versa. This is one of the reasons for the importance of determining the angle of impact.

Although the location of the center of gravity of any vehicle is somewhat uncertain because of variations in load distribution, it may generally be assumed to be located in the neighborhood of the transmission in front-engine vehicles, and somewhat farther back in rear-engine cars. Naturally, a large load in the rear of a car shifts the center of gravity backward, and an unloaded vehicle will differ somewhat from a loaded one in this respect. Occasionally it may be necessary to determine the location of the center of gravity. (See Chapter 33.)

(2) *The effect of height on the center of gravity.* Not only the longitudinal location of the center of gravity is important: its height may also be of consequence. A force applied to the side of a vehicle and below the center of gravity will tend to produce a roll-over; one applied to the front and below the center of gravity will tend to result in somersaulting. These effects are relatively infrequent as compared with the effect of the angle of impact, but their possibility should not be overlooked.

(3) *The effect of force.* The force with which two vehicles collide has no effect on the inherent tendencies of the vehicles to follow a predictable pattern, but it does have great influence upon the degree to which the pattern is completed. At higher velocities all of the effects are heightened. A car that, impacted at low velocity, may be rotated somewhat and driven to the curb, may under high-velocity impact be spun through more than one complete revolution or sent spinning for a great distance, perhaps in the process producing various secondary impacts. The *force* of the collision is of little consequence in determining the sequence of results, but it is of great *legal* significance because it may be directly related to legal liability, especially as related to speed.

The determination of the force of a collision is based upon the character and extent of the damage, as outlined above, and secondarily, on the behavior of the vehicles before they come to rest. When they are widely separated at rest, it is very probable that the collision was highly energetic. The redistribution of the momentum of the vehicles may be seen in the degree of skidding and spinning that followed the impact. However, this alone may not be a reliable criterion. When two vehicles possessing equal kinetic energy collide head-on at very high velocity, they simply halt at the point of impact and demolish each other, the energy being totally absorbed in the deformation of the metal. Whatever may be the most significant available criterion, an estimate of the relative energy of impact may usually be made by the experienced investigator.

Point of Impact

The point of impact is the *location on the roadway* at which the first contact of the vehicles occurred. Although there are several indications that may be sought, many investigators and police officers place the point of impact quite casually and often incorrectly. In some instances the exact point of impact cannot be determined at all, but must be approximated. In other cases it can be placed with unerring accuracy, and more frequently its location can be approximated with considerable confidence. The indications that will support a judgment are as follows:

BROKEN SKID MARKS. A sharp break in a skid mark is often the very best of all criteria for determining the point of impact. This break represents the exact position of the wheel as it left the skid mark at the moment when impact caused a sharp break or an abrupt alteration in the skid. Unfortunately, this unequivocal mark is seldom found. If two sets of skid marks happen to intersect, they were not made at the same time. However, if the marks tend toward such an intersecting point, breaking off just before reaching it, a very exact determination of the point of impact is probably available.

GOUGE MARKS. Marks made in the pavement by broken metal parts are often considered reliable criteria of the point of impact. However, the metal must be broken before the mark can be made, and the broken piece may be carried some distance before it marks the pavement. It is also possible that the broken metal that made the mark does not represent the point of first contact. Gouges are unquestionably useful, but they must be interpreted with care. In one instance the gouges in the roadway were 40 ft from the point of impact, having been made by a large trailer that overturned, rather than by the tractor that actually impacted the other vehicle. Although gouges in the pavement may provide very useful information about the point of impact, they must be studied thoroughly before they can be considered as reliable indications of the true point of impact, and there must be no doubt of the identity of the object that made the gouge.

DIRT AND DEBRIS. It is very common for mud that collected on the underside of the front fender of a vehicle to be displaced when the fender is impacted. As a rule, this occurs only when the fender itself is folded, distorted, or otherwise violently affected: road accumulations are not so easily jarred loose as is sometimes assumed. When such accumulations are displaced, it is almost always large chunks of dried mud that drop, rather than dust or minor accumulations. When such a chunk drops, it strikes one of the tires and is scattered as dust by the turning tire. Because the dried mud is traveling as fast as the vehicle carrying it, a falling chunk will strike the pavement at a location considerably forward of the point at which it was displaced, unless its fall is deflected by a tire. Thus, the displaced transported debris may serve as a secondary indication of the approximate point of impact. When considered cautiously in the light of these limitations, it may be of value.

DETERMINATION FROM SUBSEQUENT HAPPENINGS. In the impact, some items may be knocked off one or both of the vehicles, and each of these will travel along its own normal trajectory independently of the others. If more than one such object is found, it is sometimes possible to extrapolate their trajectories backward to a point of intersection that may be a valid approximation to the point of impact. Other similar considerations may on occasion be employed to determine the point of impact, if the investigator is astute enough and the circumstances are favorable.

Under the most favorable circumstances, even a single object may give a reasonably good estimate of the point of impact, if that object has clearly been knocked loose by the impact, and if the height of its attachment is known. Here we apply a fundamental law of gravity, which states that

$$h = \tfrac{1}{2}gt^2$$

for objects not moving vertically at the moment they start to fall freely. Knowing the height (h) from which the object fell, the time (t) of the fall can be calculated by applying the equation and using the gravitation constant (g) as 32 ft./sec^2. For example, an object will require ½ second to fall 4 ft. If the speed of the car can be estimated—and thus the speed of the object on the car—the distance between the fallen object and the point of impact may be calculated. Calculations such as this must be used with the greatest caution, and without any extravagant claims for their accuracy, because a falling object that also has a forward momentum is likely to roll or slide, or both, on striking the pavement, and thus inject a factor of uncertainty into the calculations. It is also essential to make certain that the falling object was actually free falling: completely detached from the vehicle throughout its traverse.

Having noted the signs indicative of the point of impact, it is essential to relate them to the *points of contact* of the vehicles. For example, a broken skid mark made by a front wheel indicates the position of the front wheel at the time of impact. This will differ materially from the broken skid mark of a rear wheel. In the same way, fender mud cake will indicate, after allowance for its initial speed, the position of the fender, not the point of impact itself. Thus, appropriate corrections must always be applied to obtain the true point of impact from any of the indications outlined above. The interpretation of gouge marks is an especially treacherous undertaking. Although they usually arise from impacted parts broken off on impact, they may also result from overturning and other events that occurred at some point remote from the actual point of impact. This question can ordinarily be settled by examination of the vehicles themselves to determine what might have caused the gouges. When the situation is favorable, it may be possible to determine the specific object that produced the gouges. In other cases it is possible to determine only their possible origin.

Résumé

At this stage of the investigation the character of the impact has been determined with regard to the vehicles themselves. In addition, the point on the roadway at which the impact occurred has been located. On the basis of this information it should be possible to hypothesize rather accurately the sequence of events that followed the impact. This hypothesis is more valuable as a check upon the reconstruction of the accident than it is for the general understanding of the accident. It is usually possible to determine the directions in which the vehicles were propelled by the impact, whether or not they were thrown into spins, and whether—given sufficient open space—they would be expected to travel long or short distances from the point of impact. *This is an important part of the investigation,* even though it may seem that extrapolating the course of the vehicles after an impact is unnecessary when all that is required to obtain this information is to observe the directions in which they moved and how far. The reason for this seeming anomaly is simple. *In every accident there exists the possibility of an unknown and unsuspected variable*—or more than one—that cannot be taken into account until it is discovered. The most reliable method of discovering such variables is to *compare the predicted events after impact with the actual events* after impact. If they agree within reasonable limits, nothing unusual has been present in the accident, and it can be readily interpreted. If there are large discrepancies between the predicted and the actual movements, a search for the disturbing unknown factors must be initiated immediately. Such discrepancies are not uncommon, and they may lead to very different interpretations than those that appeared to be correct during the early phase of the investigation.

Sequence Following Impact

Only in the unusual accident do both vehicles remain in place at the point of impact. When they do, the interpretation is simple. The two vehicles possessed equal kinetic energies, and they met head-on with their centers of gravity aligned with the direction of movement, and all the energy of impact was absorbed in producing damage—ultimately heat. Far more often in a head-on collision the vehicles travel into ditches, fields, over banks, or to secondary impacts with stationary objects or other moving vehicles. This behavior means that the vehicles' directions of motion were not aligned with their centers of gravity. The distances traveled after impact are indicative of the momenta involved, and under favorable circumstances these are subject to accurate calculation. However, such calculations are often disturbed by such secondary factors as terrain, fixed objects that are impacted, and other unpredictables.

In one instance, a vehicle traveling at about 65 mph impacted another, which was traveling about 70 mph. The latter was the lighter vehicle and had almost exactly the same momentum as the first. The two vehicles telescoped until each was about one-half of its original length. In direct head-on impacts without rotation, it is simple to determine which of the vehicles possessed the greater energy. Because energy is a function of the weight of the vehicle and the square of its velocity, the weights of the two vehicles must be known before any caluculations—or even estimates of speed can be derived.

Assume, now, that the same two vehicles collide head on, but with sidewise displacement, e.g., left front to left front, so that a violent gyratory spin is induced in each one. Energy corresponding to the damage done is absorbed as heat, and the remaining energy is used in propelling the vehicles along their gyratory paths. This latter fraction of energy can be calculated with some degree of certainty in favorable instances. If, for example, all the movement after impact is on paved highway, where a reasonable friction coefficient can be estimated, it can be assumed that this coefficient applies to sliding of tires, whether forward or sidewise. In gyration, about half of the movement is sidewise and half in alignment with the wheels. The over-all friction coefficient is about half of the normal coefficient and (assuming no brake applications) it can be applied to the total distance of gyration. This calculated energy, added to the estimated energy absorbed in producing deformation, will give an approximation of the total energy absorbed and make possible an estimate of the speed of the vehicles.

REFERENCES

Collins, J. C., and Morris, J. L.: *Highway Collision Analysis.* Springfield: Thomas (1967).

Lacy, G. W.: *Scientific Auto Accident Reconstruction.* Albany, New York: Matthew Bender (1964).

O'Hara, C. E., and Osterburg, J. W.: *Introduction to Criminalistics,* 2nd ed. Bloomington: Indiana University Press (1972).

Severy, D. M.: *Automobile Collisions on Purpose.* Institute of Transportation and Traffic Engineering, University of California (November 1960).

Severy, D. M., Mathewson, J. H., and Siegel, A. W.: *Automobile Side Impact Collisions,* Series II, Reprint No. 112. Institute of Transportation and Traffic Engineering, University of California (1962).

33
Vehicular Impact Evidence

Most collisions of vehicles are accidental and are therefore subject to civil codes. There are also many in which criminal actions are filed: hit-and-run misdemeanor cases, felony manslaughters, and others. Whether or not any criminal action is involved, the police are routinely responsible for the investigation of automobile collisions and need to understand at least the general features of such an inquiry. The field is broad, involving many kinds of physical evidence. Some of these, such as paint comparison and the matching of broken parts, are dealt with in other chapters. This chapter is concerned with such matters as speed calculation, angles of impact, and automobile—pedestrian impacts. The general procedure of accident reconstruction will be briefly outlined. The vehicles involved in such accidents are not necessarily passenger automobiles, although these predominate. Trucks, bicycles, motorcycles, and even toys ridden by children are also encountered. Vehicular impacts with pedestrians are not infrequent. Airplanes also may be involved in accidents of criminal concern; however, these encounters are so rare that they will not be discussed here.

RECORDS

The most important single activity of the police in the investigation of vehicular impacts is the keeping of good, clear, and complete records. Even if the officer is later to be accepted as an expert in the case, it is necessary both for the refreshment and corroboration of his memory, and for making the facts available to any other investigator, that all of the *essential* information be available in the record. In most jurisdictions standard forms are provided for the officer to fill out, and these require that the information be relatively complete. However, such forms often fail to provide blanks for some data that can be important. For example, the make and year of the vehicle are requested, but often the model is omitted. For lack of this detail, the weight of the car cannot be known, and an element of uncertainty is injected into subsequent calculations. The designation "1974 Chevrolet 4-door sedan" is a very ambiguous statement.

From the standpoint of the investigating officer, the omission of accurate, essential information occurs primarily in such critical matters as *distances*, which are often estimated or paced, or omitted entirely; *tire marks*, frequently not noticed on wet streets and sometimes not measured carefully; failure to differentiate among radial skids, braking skids, and tire drag marks that have resulted from overacceleration; failure to notice breaks in skid marks; lack of distinction between curved and straight markings; failure to note and record the presence of gouges in the street surface; and failure to observe significant types of damage, paint transfer, and similar useful indications.

The difficulties incident to the investigation of a night-time crash, especially in the rain or snow, sometimes make it virtually impossible for the investigating officer to obtain all the significant information immediately after the accident. He can, and must, make a record of the information called for in his standard form. In addition, it is essential that he take photographs, or have them taken. Before bodies or vehicles are moved, the investigator should make every effort to mark their exact locations, with chalk or crayon if feasible, or with stakes or other devices if crayon cannot be used. He can then return in daylight to take measurements and make further observations, to photograph the markings at the scene, and to scrutinize the road surfaces and the environment. At a later time he may observe the vehicles more closely after they have been removed to a more suitable location. *If possible, all of this should be done during the investigator's initial survey of the accident*, because at that time there will have been no changes in the scene, nor will the vehicles have been altered as sometimes they are in being towed to garages.

Photography at the Scene

If possible, photographic records should be made of the locations and conditions of all vehicles, of road markings and all other relevant details, before anything is moved. Usually, injured persons will have been removed to hospitals immediately, but their absence in the photographs of the scene will be of little consequence to the investigation. The technical details of photography will vary with the local conditions, but *photographs should always be taken*.

At night the use of flash equipment is essential, but often proves inadequate, the background being a dark blur even though objects in the foreground are visible. For such a situation the photographer should use slave flash equipment which will flash in the background when tripped optically by the light from the flash carried on the camera. The slave flash is rarely used, but its use should increase. Regardless of the conditions under which the photographs must be made, care should be taken to include in every exposure suitable points or items of reference. This will make it possible, at a later date, to fit an isolated picture into the total scene. The scene should be photographed from more than one vantage point. There is a tendency to photograph the portion of a vehicle that has sustained the most damage and to overlook less severe damage on the opposite side or end—damage that may be more significant in the final interpretation of the accident. For example, a vehicle that was being towed lost a wheel, impacted another vehicle and overturned, producing much damage. Photographs showed this damage clearly, but omitted the opposite side from which the wheel had come off.

The photographic recording of damage to vehicles may be satisfactorily, even advantageously, postponed, but the locale of an automobile accident and the inter-relation of the affected vehicles cannot be recaptured after the vehicles have been removed. The police photographer must make sure that his photographs depict clearly the relation of the vehicles to each other and to other objects of significance at the scene of the collision. To do this usually requires that exposures be made from a number of different directions.

Except when criminal charges are likely to be placed, the police are seldom required to photograph damaged vehicles after their removal from the scene. At this stage civil authorities and the insurance investigators will generally carry on the examination. Because their purposes are somewhat different, there will be a noticeable difference of emphasis in their analyses. Whereas the police will be interested in marks that may indicate the point of impact with a pedestrian, the insurance investigator will concentrate on damage to the vehicle, which may figure importantly in civil litigation or in claims for damage. The hit-and-run accident will be discussed in a later section in this chapter.

Measurements

Careful measurements must be made of the *lengths* of all *tire marks* and of their *directions* relative to the axis of the road. Walking roller tapes are convenient for such measurements, especially when the markings are long. Such a tape is less precise than a steel tape for straight-line measurement. For curved markings the roller tapes are preferable. A 100-ft steel tape should always be available, and a roller tape is a useful complement.

Sometimes skid marks, or other tire marks, lead directly to the tire that made them. In some departments, it is customary to consider that any tire mark that does not lead to a wheel should be classified as of doubtful origin, even though the mark is fresh and is consistent with the type of accident. It should not be forgotten that at the moment of impact a skidding car may stop skidding because the driver has been violently displaced. If the skid mark leads to the point of impact and appears to be fresh, it is almost certainly related to the accident under investigation, and should be given the same careful study as any other mark.

The *distance of movement* of every vehicle after impact must be measured with reasonable accuracy, because these distances will be important in the reconstruction of the accident. The boundaries of such measurements should be made clear in the record, e.g., front or rear of vehicle, choice of point of impact. Vaguely defined measurements may sometimes be of no more value than a rough pacing of the distance.

POINT OF IMPACT

The point of impact on the roadway must be determined as accurately as possible. There is some disagreement as to the best methods of determining this point. The various indications are as follows:

(1) *Broken, interrupted, or angular skid marks.* A skidding vehicle will leave either straight skid marks or curving marks that follow some sort of regular arc. An abrupt change of direction, a displacement and break in the mark, or a termination of the mark demonstrates absolutely that another force, acting in a different direction, has been superimposed. In nearly every instance this can come only from an impact. The place at which the deviation of the skid mark occurs is the actual position the tire occupied at the time it was displaced by the force of the impact. This provides the best of all indications of the point of impact.

(2) *Gouges* are often—*but not always*—reliable indicators of the point of impact. To teach otherwise, as is sometimes done, is to mislead. In a very large majority of vehicular impacts, the immediate crushing action of the contact between the vehicles breaks and mangles their structures just behind the impact point on each vehicle. To produce a gouge, a metallic object must be broken loose at one end while remaining attached at the other, so that the free end will drop to the street and be pushed into the pavement by the wrecked vehicle to which it is still attached. Such partly detached members may belong to wheel suspensions, body parts, or a broken transmission. It must be noted, however, that if the broken member is part of the transmission, the gouge will occur some feet from the actual point of contact of the vehicles. It is of critical importance to bear in mind that there are, occasionally, special circumstances in which the gouge may be actually far from the point of impact. This was illustrated in the case of a tractor, semitrailer, and full trailer that were overturned in an accident. When the full trailer overturned, it gouged the street 40

ft back of the point of impact. The investigating officer, having been trained to accept gouges as ultimate indications of the point of impact, placed that point 40 ft away from the actual point of impact. Even bearing in mind the routine nature of many investigative officers' training, it is hard to find an excuse for the officer's functioning like an automaton. In this instance there were many additional indications of the point of impact, but the officer's "training" took precedence over everything else.

(3) *Debris* is, by all standards, the least reliable evidence for the determination of the point of impact, although it is often the only indication that exists. Debris is of several types: mud from under fenders, broken glass from headlights, metallic parts broken from the vehicles' own structures, eyeglasses from the victims, and other items. It must be remembered that the debris from a vehicle has been traveling at the same rate as the vehicle that carried it to the point of impact. When broken away or jarred loose from the vehicle, such debris will continue to travel at the same rate while falling to the ground. It takes a half second to fall 4 ft. At 40 mph or about 60 ft/sec, this debris would be expected to move forward 30 ft from the point of impact before striking the ground. In actuality, lateral transfers of such lengths are seldom seen, having been stopped by obstructions. Mud falling from the underside of a fender may strike the rotating tire and be widely scattered. The broken metal object may be propelled ahead, strike the pavement, and roll, slide, or tumble quite an additional distance. Debris, properly interpreted, can be very useful in determining the point of impact; but improperly interpreted, it can also be confusing. In many instances, especially in low-speed impacts, the location of debris does provide a reasonably accurate basis for the determination of the point of impact, but in many other cases it is almost useless. It serves one valuable function in determining the lane in which the impact occurred. When the debris is distributed almost entirely in one lane, it is a very strong indication that the impact occurred in that lane.

To sum up, the investigating officer will need to look for all possible indicators of the point of impact, evaluate them, and arrive at the best estimate possible. He should state clearly on the report the *basis* for his estimate of the point of impact so that this may be taken into account in subsequent investigations.

Movement After Impact

In nearly all instances, the vehicles will continue to move after impact until their residual energy of motion (kinetic energy) has been dissipated. Several variants of this situation occur:

(1) One of the impacting vehicles is essentially stopped by the impact, and transmits its residual energy to the other vehicle, propelling it a comparatively

great distance. Every pool player will see a similarity to the situation in which a square impact of the cue ball will cause the latter to stop rolling as the other ball takes up all of the energy. This reaction can occur only when the direction of force passes through the center of gravity of the impacting vehicle.

(2) Both vehicles change direction and continue to move some distances. In this instance the direction of impact is off center: both vehicles are likely to spin.

(3) The impacting vehicle continues moving for a comparatively great distance, but on an altered course, the impacted vehicle having been brought quickly to a stop.

The reasons for these differences reside in two factors of the impact: (1) the angle of the impact related to the direction of the impacting force and its relation to the angle of the centers of gravity; and (2) the relative kinetic energies or momentums of the impacting vehicles.

Consider two cars whose pathways cross, as in an intersection collision. Each has its own momentum, and the directions of the two momentums are Approximately at right angles. After impact, all of the movement of both vehicles in the direction of car A's path is attributable to the momentum of car A, and all of the movement of both vehicles in the direction of car B's path is attributable to the momentum of car B. Thus, if two vehicles possessing equal momentum meet in a right-front to left-front impact, both will turn 45° and they will proceed together along the resulting oblique line until they are halted by obstructions or frictional effects. The principle that underlies this hypothetical case will be used very frequently by the expert to determine how much of the momentum of each vehicle, after impact, was attributable to its own initial momentum, and how much to that of the other vehicle that was impacted.

Angle of Impact

In the study and interpretation of an accident, the angle of impact is one of the most critical determinations that must be made. It must be related to the orientation of the vehicles relative to each other, which will make possible the determination of the spinning effect upon each of them. The angle of impact is meaningless until it is related to the point of impact on the vehicle and to the center of gravity.

Center of Gravity

The weight of an irregular object such as an automobile may be considered as being concentrated at its center of gravity, which is defined as the point around which the weight of the object is evenly distributed on all sides and in all directions. *Translation* of a vehicle is actually the displacement of its center of gravity; *spin* is largely or totally a rotation around the center of gravity. The position of the center of gravity of a vehicle is not fixed, but shifts in response to changes in the weight distribution of the load. The center of gravity of a typical front-engine car is located about at the transmission, but loading the car heavily will shift the center of gravity backward. A rear-engine car has its center of gravity farther to the rear, whether empty or loaded.

Character of Impact

The additional information that must be observed and reported concerns the manner in which the vehicles struck each other. For example, a *head-on collision* may be centered; it may involve impact of the left front of one car against the left front of the other, or it may involve the right front of one against the right front of the other, although this latter type of impact is relatively rare. A *front-to-side impact* may involve the front of one vehicle striking against the front left side, middle left side, or rear left side. In each instance the effects will differ; hence it is important that the police officer make clear in his records what part of each aspect of each vehicle was involved in the collision. Such specifics are frequently overlooked in reports.

The center of gravity of two colliding vehicles, the angle of impact, and the character of the impact determine the movements of the vehicles after a collision. A total investigation must include the determination of these three factors. They can be derived from a combination of observed directions and distances of travel after impact, plus the indications of angle and direction obtainable from examination of the vehicles themselves. It is the necessity of determining all of these factors that makes it obligatory for the police officer to make accurate observations and measurements and to include them in a record that can be interpreted. Casual, inaccurate, or deficient records will lead to errors of interpretation upon which improper court action is based, often long after the accident has occurred.

ENERGY DISSIPATION IN ACCIDENTS

According to Newton's first law, a body in motion tends to continue in motion in a straight line at uniform velocity. This tendency is expressed in terms of momentum, which is defined as the product of mass (weight) times velocity (speed). Momentum is a vector quantity: that is, it has directional as well as numerical value. Momentum can be either negative or positive, the sign being related to the direction rather than to the quantity. Thus, if two vehicles have identical momentums and strike each other exactly head-on, they can demolish each other. The wreckage of both will remain at the point of impact, their momentums having been of opposite signs.

Vehicular Impact Evidence

In dealing with actual accidents the kinetic energy of the involved vehicles is more useful than their momentums. Kinetic energy is defined as follows:

$$K.E. = \tfrac{1}{2}mv^2 \qquad 1$$

where m is the *mass* and v is the *velocity* in feet per second. Mass is an imaginary quantity that defines the effective weight of a body free of the influence of gravity. Because no weight on earth is free of terrestrial gravity, mass is defined as where W is the weight and g the gravitational acceleration

$$m = \frac{W}{g} \qquad 2$$

constant equal to about 32.2 ft/sec². Thus, weight is approximately equal to mass times 32. For practical purposes, the use of weight instead of mass in equation 1 will lead to a value expressed in foot-poundals rather than in foot-pounds. This substitution is quite acceptable in equations for the calculation of speed.

A vehicle of a specified weight traveling at a specified speed will have a definite and calculable kinetic energy. If the vehicle impacts another body, vehicular or otherwise, and comes ultimately to a stop, its kinetic energy will have been totally dissipated. The manner of the dissipation of this energy is a prime consideration of the investigator. If the driver applied his brakes before the impact, in doing so he dissipated some of the energy. If the braking was hard enough to produce a locked-wheel skid, the amount of energy dissipation may be calculated.

At impact there is dissipated an additional quantity of energy, which may be a very great portion of the total energy or only a small part of it. This energy is utilized in producing deformation, being thereby transformed into heat. This factor may not, at present, be calculated with any accuracy, but it *may be estimated* with reasonable accuracy by those who are experienced in accident investigation.

All energy remaining after the impact is used in producing movement of the vehicles. Sometimes this is a major factor in the total energy dissipation; sometimes it is minor. It is a factor that can be calculated if the record of the accident includes accurate measurements of the movements of the vehicles after impact. As will be seen, the calculation depends also upon the estimate of the friction coefficient—a matter that will be discussed later in this chapter.

In most accidents, there are several ways in which kinetic energy is dissipated. The investigator must know how to take all of them into account. Ordinarily, the police officer is not involved in this relatively complex matter. *His records, however, make possible the calculations of the expert who may follow him,* and are therefore of the greatest significance.

SPEED CALCULATIONS

When a vehicle under full braking slides to a stop, the interpretation is simple and may be calculable on the speed slide rule or the nomograph. This type of calculation may be available for use by the police in automobile-pedestrian accidents, for example, because the human body will produce little or no effect on the speed of the automobile that strikes it. However, such a device is seldom applicable to collisions between two vehicles, because the masses are too great for either one of them to be disregarded, and the energy is absorbed in several ways.

The initial energy of a moving vehicle will have been dissipated when that vehicle stops. If it is *sliding* on its wheels, the vehicle is being brought to a stop by the friction of the tires on the roadway. Under these circumstances the applicable equation is

$$\tfrac{1}{2} mv^2 = m\mu gs$$

where μ is the friction coefficient (drag factor), g the gravitation constant, and s the distance over which the wheels slid. By the time the vehicle has come to a stop, the friction of the tires on the roadway has absorbed energy equivalent to the original kinetic energy of the vehicle. This value is proportional to the weight of the vehicle, the friction coefficient, and the distance of sliding. The presence of m as a first-power function on both sides of the equation allows its cancellation in such a simple calculation. This is equivalent to saying that a Volkswagen and a Cadillac can slide to a stop in the same distance from equal speeds, which is generally true.

A simplified equation derived from the above-stated fact is

$$v^2 = 2\mu\, gs$$

where v is the velocity expressed in feet per second. When the velocity is expressed in miles per hour, the equation assumes the form

$$v = \sqrt{30\mu\, s}$$

This equation is applicable only to *the total braking distance when there is no impact with any object of significant weight,* such as another vehicle. When there is such an impact, the police officer should make no attempt to calculate the speed of the impacting vehicles unless his skill in accident investigation enables him to take into account all the various factors involved in energy absorption.

FRICTION COEFFICIENT (DRAG FACTOR)

The "drag factor" represents the effective friction coefficient—in this instance that between the tires and the road surface. The friction coefficient, μ, is defined as the ratio of the force necessary to slide two objects over each other to the force holding them together, or

$$\mu = \frac{F}{W}$$

where F is the force in pounds necessary to produce sliding and W is the weight, as it is the weight of the vehicle that constitutes the force pressing the surfaces together. The actual determination of this value is an empirical matter, which has been determined by many persons for a large number of conditions. There are many tabulations of friction coefficients in existence.[*]

In order to obtain the precise friction coefficient for a given situation, it is necessary to make a direct determination, using the same vehicle at the same location, and under the same conditions of road surface, wetness, etc. In most accident cases this procedure is not practical, especially when the vehicle has been severely damaged. Thus, it has become customary to choose a coefficient that closely approximates the exact value. Because most accidents occur on traveled macadam or asphalt roads in dry conditions, and there is a reasonable degree of constancy to tire rubber, a value of about 0.7 is generally a conservative and reasonable choice. However, on new pavement a higher value is justified; whereas a lower value would be more realistic if the pavement is in bad repair or very much worn from traffic. Speed is also a factor, the coefficient becoming progressively lower as the speed increases. The type of tread rubber has a small influence on the friction coefficient, as does the degree of its wear. These are all factors over which much dispute is often raised. In actuality, however, changing the coefficient by a considerable amount has only a limited effect upon speed calculations. It becomes a serious factor only when the decision regarding speed must be very close, e.g., when it is of critical importance to know whether an individual was driving just over or just under the speed limit. It is often impossible to settle this type of question conclusively, even though the utmost attention is given to the details of the circumstances. In all calculations based upon estimates of friction coefficient some leeway is allowed, rarely more than ± 5 mph.

Some other factors that are of concern in special cases are the presence of a significant grade, either up or down; wetness of the pavement; the presence of fresh oil; improperly adjusted brakes; and a variety of similar matters. The accident investigator will generally know how to deal with these factors. It is rarely necessary for the police to do so, other than to record accurately the facts, which will have to be considered and evaluated by the investigator.

---

[*] The most suitable is from the book, *Traffic Accident Investigator's Manual for Police* by J. Stannard Baker, Director of Research and Development, The Traffic Institute of Northwestern University, Evanston, Illinois (1957).

BRAKES AND DECELERATION

It is common for the layman, thinking of stopping exclusively in terms of braking, to equate "braking power" and deceleration. Brake failures of various types can and do occur, but with modern hydraulic brakes they are uncommon. Normally such a brake will provide equal pressure to all wheel brakes, and in the end this will cause the wheels to slide. The deceleration is not due directly to the brakes, but to the friction between the sliding tires and the roadway.

Brake condition is usually, although not invariably, indicated by the character of the skid mark. Usually a skid mark is perfectly straight, and its straightness indicates that the brakes were in proper working condition. If one wheel fails to be as well braked as the others, it will drag less and in consequence the vehicle will tend to rotate, and it may go out of control. If a single brake "grabs," the effect is similar. However, some other factors may contribute to such a rotation, or even cause it. The condition of the tire treads may cause unequal gripping of the road; irregularities in the pavement may alter the braking effects of one or more wheels, and some prior lateral force may start the vehicle rotating before the wheels are locked. During a skid, the one factor that is of little consequence is the effort to steer the car. When all four wheels are locked, the car becomes essentially a sled with rubber runners, and steering has virtually no effect upon the direction of its movement.

Deceleration appears to to be almost constant with time under uniform conditions of sliding wheels, but not at all constant with distance. Actually, it is not quite constant with time because the friction coefficient changes with speed. Assume that a vehicle—moving either at high speed or at low speed—is decelerating uniformly at the rate of 16 mph/sec. While losing that 16 mph, the vehicle would travel 90 ft if it were moving at 60 mph before deceleration; but it would travel only 15 ft if it had been moving at 10 mph before deceleration. However, 15 ft is actually greater than the total stopping distance at 10 mph, and the vehicle would be standing still through much of that second.

TIRE MARKS

One of the common and unfortunate deficiencies of police investigators is their failure to study tire markings carefully enough to differentiate among them and to give them proper designations. Tires make marks of several kinds, but not all of them are indicative of sliding. Those that do result from sliding are of several kinds, which may be differentiated as follows:

(1) *Impressions*. In soft ground, or in other material that yields to pressure, the tire will leave a *negative* impression of its tread surface. Such impressions are often left by the tires of a vehicle that has moved from the pavement to a soft shoulder. They are not to be confused with skid marks.

(2) *Tread prints.* These marks are *replicas* of the tread pattern left in thin layers of oil, dust, or similar materials that have been disturbed by the passage of the wheels and have recorded at least some details of the tread pattern. Such marks are related to impression marks as a photograph is related to the photo negative. Tread prints may not indicate any sliding at all; but when they do they will be imperfect. Tread prints will often result when a vehicle that has just been driven in dust or oil proceeds along a hard pavement.

(3) *Skid Marks.* Every skid mark is the result of a sliding tire. It possesses a directional characteristic, and it consists of rubber that has been removed frictionally from a tire tread and smeared on the pavement. Other materials such as soft asphalt may be incorporated in a skid mark. The degree of blackness of the mark is related to the amount of rubber removed from the tire, which in turn is related to the heat generated by the sliding friction.

Two main types of skid marks are differentiated: the *direct* or axial skid, which shows only minimal curvature; and the *rotary* or centrifugal skid, which is made by a tire sliding sidewise or partly sidewise. Skid marks of the latter type are usually curved. However, a car that is sliding *exactly* sidewise will leave straight skid marks. In such an instance designations such as "rotary" or "centrifugal" are scarcely applicable. Sidewise motion of the vehicle and of the tire characterizes both types of skid mark. There are no sharp lines of demarcation between axial skid marks, rotary skid marks, and totally sidewise skid marks, because each type grades smoothly into the next when a vehicle is forced into a spin. However, as this transition occurs, the appearance of the skid mark itself changes. A tire that is sliding ahead under brake will normally leave a mark composed of parallel rib marks, the outside streaks (made by the buttresses) being generally heavier than the inner streaks. As the tire rotates toward a sidewise slippage, the rib marks disappear and the skid mark loses its sharp margins and becomes rather characterless. It is important that the investigating officer note and record the *character* of all skid marks as well as their lengths.

Another matter of great significance that is often overlooked is the distance between skid marks that proceed in the same general direction. If the vehicle slid axially, the width between the skid marks will equal that between the wheels: in the neighborhood of 5 feet for most vehicles. A car sliding sidewise leaves skid marks whose separation is equal to the wheel base: generally 10-11 ft. During a rotary skid, the markings diverge as the car rotates from an axial toward a sidewise orientation. Attention to these critical details will make crystal clear the behavior of the vehicle at the time the skid marks were made. Unfortunately, few investigating officers appear to be aware of the importance of such evidence.

(4) *Drag Marks.* During violent acceleration such as is often practiced in drag racing, and sometimes indulged in by youths even on city streets, the

wheels are spun against the pavement during the acceleration. This sometimes gives rise rise to heavy markings that resemble skid marks very closely. There are two methods by which such marks can be traced to their true source. During the spinning of the wheels, the rubber that is torn off tends to be thrown to the rear; whereas in skidding the rubber is torn off as the tire slides forward. Very close inspection will sometimes, but not always, reveal this distinction. The other method calls for observation of the relation of the marks to the street. Drag marks will usually be in the normal lane of traffic on the right and will continue there, unassociated with any collision, diminishing with distance in the direction of movement. The skid mark associated with an accident may also be wholly in the normal lane of traffic, or it may change into a curving or rotational mark spanning the roadway. It will also give indications of an abrupt halt, rather than merely becoming fainter with distance. None of these criteria is absolute, and in many instances clear-cut distinctions are very difficult. Inasmuch as the drag mark is rarely associated with a collision, the chief importance of distinguishing it is to rule out extraneous drag marks that may be confused with skid marks laid down in connection with an accident.

(5) *Blow-out Marks.* When a tire blows out violently its collapse is so sudden that it sometimes leaves very broad and somewhat rounded markings on the pavement. These markings are easily distinguished from skid marks or other tread marks. They will not be seen when the tire failure has been less violent, but the approximate location of the blow-out is, nevertheless, sometimes deducible from visible change in the characteristics of the tire marking. A wheel with a flat tire will leave marks that are very irregular in shape and orientation, if it leaves marks at all. The presence and character of the markings will depend, for the most part, upon whether the tire folds crosswise of the tread, or merely around the rim. When any positive indication of the point at which a tire blew is available, it should be noted on the diagram or in the record made by the police officer.

(6) *Spinning Vehicles.* Every billiard player knows that he can direct the ball into motion at a predetermined angle by striking it to one side of center. With somewhat greater complication, the same principle is applicable to the impacts of vehicles with each other. First, there must be a clear comprehension of the nature of the *center of gravity.* When a vehicle is impacted in such a manner that a prolongation of the direction of force passes through the center of gravity, the vehicle will tend only to be forced *without rotation* in the direction of the impacting force. If the prolongation of the force direction passes to the *right* of the center of gravity, the vehicle will receive a spinning component in the *counterclockwise* direction. If the prolongation of the force direction passes to the *left* of the center of gravity, the vehicle will receive a spinning component in the *clockwise* direction.

In an energetic collision, one or more of the vehicles involved will nearly always be forced into a spin or some other kind of rotary motion about its center of gravity. In addition, the vehicle's center of gravity may be displaced in either a straight or a curving path. It is always desirable for the investigator to understand the general characteristics of these two types of movement in order to determine which type of movement predominated in the collision under investigation. Tire marks laid down at the scene of a collision will often constitute a detailed record of the movements of the vehicles involved. If such marks are present, they should be meticulously recorded in detail. Sometimes carefully composed photographs provide the best information. Accurate drawings are also helpful. Tire markings laid down on wet streets do not often survive, and in consequence the positions and orientations of the vehicles, plus the locations of primary damage, are all that is available. This information is sometimes sufficient for a good reconstruction, but the investigating officer should provide supplementary detail of markings that *were present* on the road when he made his preliminary examination.

(7) *Vaults, Roll-overs, and Somersaults.* Accidents that occur on irregular ground surfaces, and high-speed impacts especially, often produce vaulting, somersaulting, and roll-over. In a vault, the vehicle leaves the ground completely, flies through the air for some distance, and lands. This occurs over declivities, and it can also be produced by a marked upward incline, which gives the rapidly moving vehicle a significant upward thrust. The investigating officer can often recognize the vault by an interruption in skid marks followed by impact marks made by the vehicle when it struck the ground.

Roll-over is very common. It is recognizable by the presence of scrape marks and indentations high on the sides or on the top of the vehicle, even though the vehicle may have come to rest on its wheels. If the vehicle lands on its side or top, the interpretation is obvious. There is a popular misapprehension that great energy is required to produce roll-over. Such is not the case, it involves a rather small lifting of the center of gravity. If, while sliding sidewise, a vehicle strikes an impediment with its tires, it will commonly roll over. An impact above its center of gravity will also predispose it to a roll-over.

Somersaulting is end-over-end revolution. It is often confused with roll-over. A somersault requires considerably more energy than does a roll-over because of the greater elevation of the center of gravity it involves. Most somersaulting is not directly end-over-end, but proceeds obliquely over a corner. This tends to drop the vehicle on its side from a partially vertical position, which accounts for its frequent misinterpretation. Although it is seldom necessary for the police officer on the scene to differentiate between a somersault and a roll-over, it is essential that the investigator recognize the difference. In one instance, a vehicle struck another head-on, somersaulted completely over top of the impacted vehicle, and landed upside down on the top of a third vehicle, which was following the one initially impacted. From there it rolled off to the side, and was subsequently designated a simple roll-over. The difference between fact and interpretation was considerable.

Vehicles Out of Control

A very common type of accident can result when a vehicle goes out of control and leaves its proper lane of travel. It may go off the road to either the right or the left, impact a stationary object, roll over, or merely slide to a stop. A car out of control often crosses the highway and impacts a vehicle moving in the opposite direction. The indication of a vehicle having been out of control usually consists of long, curving rotary skids, sometimes with indications of braking, and sometimes without. The tire marks are invariably heavier on the outside of the curve because that is the side toward which the weight was being thrown. Sometimes the wheels on the inner side of the curve leave no visible marks, and it appears that only a single right (or left) wheel was skidding. Actually this means that the centrifugal forces were great enough to shift a large fraction of the total weight to the outside wheels: it does not usually indicate braking defects. When the single skid is straight, it justifies the conclusion that the brakes were balanced.

Control of a moving vehicle may be lost in many ways. Excessive speed in rounding a curve is among the common causes of such accidents. On a straight road, speed combined with inattention, sleepiness, boredom, or general fatigue from long hours at the wheel may reduce even the expert driver's efficiency to the danger point. Loss of control may result also from braking or steering defects in the vehicle. It occurs with greater frequency when the road is wet. The analysis of such accidents is one of the most difficult tasks encountered by the investigator. He should be correspondingly knowledgeable, skillful, and thorough. For the investigating officer it is usually sufficient that he recognize that the vehicle went out of control, and to record that fact.

Skid Mark Length

One additional aspect of the police investigation is of the greatest importance —one about which there is much misunderstanding. It is widely assumed, for example, that in a locked-wheel skid all four tires begin promptly to register skid marks. Nothing could be further from the truth. In such a panic stop the body of the car and its contents, which are mounted above the chassis, tend to continue forward while the chassis is being braked. This suddenly shifts a large percentage of the weight to the front wheels. Because they roll free, the front wheels are instantly responsive to the action of the brakes. The rear wheels, on the contrary, being attached indirectly to the motor, possess a much greater total momentum. Thus, for two reasons the rear wheels never start to slide as soon as the front wheels do. It is therefore very common for the first mark registered to be made by the front wheels. In all such instances the argument that the wheel base length should be subtracted from the total skid distance is totally incorrect. Only when there are lighter marks visible ahead of the heavy marks are these latter to be considered as rear wheel skids.

Incipient skid marks are sometimes noted as being present. This means merely that heavy braking short of total sliding has occurred. In such an instance, it is clear that there was partial sliding, because otherwise there would be no mark. It is well known that the most efficient braking is produced just before total sliding occurs, because the tire surface is being slowly renewed against the road, thus diminishing the local heating that softens the rubber and lowers braking efficiency. Thus, all incipient marks should be included in the skid mark length. One precaution must be taken: a light rear-wheel skid may be misinterpreted as incipient for a heavy front-wheel skid, and this error must be guarded against.

ACCIDENTS OF SPECIAL TYPES

Bicycles, motorcycles, skate boards, other small vehicles and their riders, as well as pedestrians, are frequently impacted by automobiles. Such accidents inject variations into the officer's investigative routine.

Pedestrians

The pedestrian is a comparatively soft object of relatively little weight compared with the vehicle that strikes him. Thus, both damage to the vehicle and the effect upon its speed are much less than the corresponding effects of a collision of two automobiles. The effect upon speed can be safely disregarded, but the *damage to the vehicle* is so characteristic of this type of accident as to warrant careful attention. The same is true of *damage* (injury) *to the pedestrian*. The latter effect is strictly related to the dimensions and contours of the front of the vehicle as compared with the size, orientation, and movements of the pedestrian.

The center of gravity of the human is located approximately at the waistline. This places the center of gravity of a child somewhat below the top of the grille or the hood; whereas the center of gravity of an adult is usually above this portion of the vehicle. Thus, on impact a child will be picked up on the front of the car and carried until the deceleration of the car releases the child's body to be carried forward by its own momentum. An adult, on the other hand, will have his feet swept from beneath him, will travel over the hood, usually sliding off to one side or the other. In transit he will almost invariably leave definite dents on the top of the hood, on the fenders, or on both. These indentations commonly result from impacts of limbs. A rounded dent at the rear of the hood will indicate the impact of the head, this kind of indentation being frequently seen when a pedestrian has been struck from the rear.

Dents in the front of the vehicle, around the grille, the hood front, or the headlights are produced only in relatively high-speed impacts: the greater the speed, the deeper the indentation.

Injury to the victim is related to the configuration of the front of the vehicle. Leg fractures in the neighborhood of the knee commonly result from bumper impact. If one leg only is broken, as is generally the case, the indication is that the impact was from that side. An exception to this rule can occur, if, at the moment of impact, the weight of the pedestrian is on the leg opposite to the side of impact and the other foot is off the ground. This variation is rare, however; in such a situation there usually is no leg fracture. Fracture of the pelvis is ordinarily produced by impact with headlights or with the leading edges of fenders. Such fractures are rare when the impact is located to the center of the vehicle front. Skull fractures by vehicle impact is rare because it is not the head that receives the initial high-energy blow. The skull fracture is more likely to result from striking the pavement or the curb when the previously impacted body falls from the car.

The distribution pattern of objects fallen or thrown from an impacted pedestrian may also be of value in the reconstruction of the accident. Pedestrians are frequently knocked out of their shoes. The direction and distance of the shoe's propulsion are related to the position and orientation of the leg at the moment of impact, as well as to the velocity imparted to the foot. Eyeglasses, objects from the pockets, smoking materials dropped from the mouth, and carried objects shaken loose from the hands can also contribute to the total of recoverable information. The interpretation of such evidence is difficult and requires professional expertise. All objects found at the scene of impact must be identified and recorded, and their locations must be measured carefully in relation to some base point which can be established repetitively. This is a proper function of the investigating officer.

Bicycles

Bicycles sometimes run into cars, and cars frequently run into bicycles. Some specific physical considerations are applicable to such accidents. The center of gravity of a bicycle rider is substantially raised both by the height of the vehicle and by the drawn-up leg position required in riding. Thus, the rider–bicycle combination is inherently unstable, even as compared with a pedestrian. The interpretation of an automobile–bicycle impact requires careful study of both the automobile and the bicycle to determine the direction of impact, its severity, and the relative orientations of the vehicles. These considerations, evaluated in terms of the raised center of gravity, will generally make possible a useful and reasonably accurate reconstruction of the accident. From the officer's viewpoint the immediate requirement is the making of complete records and clear photographs of the scene, the vehicles, and the areas of damage. Because both vehicles must be examined later by the expert investigator, it is important that the evidence be preserved, or at least that an adequate record be made of its disposition.

Motorcycles

Motorcycles are usually, though not always, lower than bicycles, so that the elevation of the center of gravity is less significant. On the other hand, the motorcycle is heavier than the bicycle and usually moves considerably faster. Thus, the reconstruction of the automobile–motorcycle accident is intermediate between that of the automobile and bicycle and that of two automobiles. One additional event often occurs: if the motrcycle strikes head-on, it is likely to rear up and toss the rider through the air. This frequently explains the rather great distance that separates the rider's body from the point of impact. This distance is directly related to the speed involved in the impact. As with other accidents, accurate and complete records must be made by the investigating officer, and the evidence should be protected and kept for later examination by the investigating expert.

Hit and Run Accidents

According to most legal codes, the driver who impacts a person, a vehicle, or some other object, and leaves the scene without adequately identifying himself, is subject to rather severe legal penalties. The legal importance attributed to such acts varies from striking animals or fixed objects to striking and killing a pedestrian. In automotive vehicle collisions the damage will usually prevent at least one of the drivers from leaving the scene, but not always. There is, for example, the "phantom car" that lightly sideswipes another and causes a succession of higher-energy collisions.

The officer's investigation of the hit-and-run accident must be especially thorough and imaginative. Because the culpable vehicle is gone, it cannot be observed; but the object struck is subject to detailed study, as is the scene. Especially in high-speed impacts there are often paint chips either on the victim's clothing or on the roadway.

THE SUSPECT VEHICLE. When a vehicle is found that is suspect in a hit-and-run accident, it should be examined by the laboratory with respect not only to the physical evidence already available, but also with respect to all damage observable on the vehicle itself, which, as outlined above, can speak eloquently of the circumstances of the impact. It should also be processed for blood, fibers, hairs, and microscopic materials. Scrapes and wipe marks should be given close scrutiny. These, as well as adhering materials, should be searched for on the bottom of the vehicle after it has been raised on a hoist.

If specific circumstances of the accident are known from study of the victim, his clothing, and the road scene, it is often possible to describe with considerable accuracy the nature of the damage sustained by the missing vehicle. Such a description can be a valuable aid to the investigating officers in their search for the vehicle. For this reason it is wiser to seek the aid of the laboratory immediately after the accident has occurred, rather than to wait until a suspect vehicle has been recovered.

REFERENCES

ASTM Special Tech. Pub. No. 326: *Symposium on Skid Resistance, 1962.* Ann Arbor, Mich.: University Microfilms (1969).

Auten, James H.: *Traffic Crash Investigation.* Springfield: Thomas (1972).

Baker, J. S.: *Traffic Accident Investigator's Manual for Police,* 4th ed. Evanston, Ill.: Northwestern University Traffic Institute (1963).

Bradford, L. W.: "Lamp Filaments," in F. Camps, ed., *Gradwohl's Legal Medicine,* 2nd ed. Baltimore: Williams and Wilkins (1968).

Collins, J. C., and Morris, J. L.: *Highway Collision Analysis.* Springfield: Thomas (1967).

Lacy, G. W.: *Scientific Auto Accident Reconstruction.* Albany, New York: Matthew Render (1964).

34

Physical Evidence from Fires

Many of the techniques that are valuable in the investigation of fires are those of general applicability in the solution of other crimes. When arson is suspected, it should be borne in mind that the arsonist may have broken and entered, in which case a thorough search should be made for any remaining tool marks, broken glass, paint fragments, and similar items of evidence. This simple concept is frequently disregarded by the arson investigator, who, having been trained to think in terms of fire only, may overlook what any alert crime investigator would be expected to recognize, understand, and utilize. The only unique factors in the investigation of a fire are those that result from the fire itself: charring, destruction of combustible evidence, and the alteration of noncombustibles by heat. Obviously, the determination of the origin of a fire requires an intimate knowledge of the behavior of fire, but this knowledge alone is insufficient to solve most arson cases.

The examination of fire residues will vary with the type of fire and the extent of the damage. Three general situations may be distinguished:

(1) *All combustible material has been destroyed.* The remaining noncombustible material may be considerable in quantity and of definite significance. Metal tools and other objects that are foreign to the premises may have been used in entering or in some device for causing ignition. Other objects known to have been present at the locale may have been used by the arsonist and moved or modified by him in the commission of the crime. Such items may aid

in the investigation. Because of the loss of evidence, the investigation of this type of fire is the least productive of results.

(2) *A limited part of the combustible material has been destroyed.* Fires are frequently extinguished at an early stage, so that much combustible material remains. In these cases, not only wood and similar combustible building material, but traces of hydrocarbon solvents used to set the fire and other paraphernalia of the arsonist may be recovered. The investigation of fires of this class often produces conclusive results. The investigator of any such fire should spare no effort in collecting and sifting every shred of evidence.

(3) *An arson attempt has been made unsuccessfully.* At times, the arsonist arranges some device designed to ignite a building during his absence so that he may establish an alibi. Early discovery, or the failure of the device, may prevent the fire from starting. There is usually little excuse for failure to discover the originator of such an abortive attempt, unless he is a person who has no motive other than that of the "fire bug." Even then, the nature of the device and of its parts should, in most instances, yield a solution if all clues are followed conscientiously. Many investigators consider that there is a direct connection between the elaborateness of a fire-setting device and the certainty of solving the crime. Nothing is so hard to trace as a burned match, and few things are so easy to identify as an elaborate timing device, even after it has been damaged or partly destroyed by heat.

Professionals have available to them some ingenious chemical methods for setting fires without leaving much detectable residue. Certain electrical procedures that are extraordinarily difficult to detect have also been developed. Because they are known to only a limited number of persons, it is not appropriate to detail such methods here. However, if there is reason for the investigative agency to suspect a fire of having been the work of such a professional arsonist, a specialized and knowledgeable investigator should be consulted immediately.

THE NATURE OF THE ACTION OF FIRE

Common experience with the behavior and effects of fire is so widespread that it might be assumed that every adult possesses a thorough understanding of it. Experience with fire investigation seems to prove the exact opposite. Statements made repeatedly in the courtroom soon dispel any notion that the man in the street can be assumed to possess an accurate understanding of how fires burn or of the effect they produce. For this reason it seems desirable to outline briefly the important characteristics of combustion and some properties of combustible materials.

Fire has fundamental effects of two kinds: those produced by heat alone, and those that involve the actual consumption of solids, liquids, and gases. *Only gases produce flame.* A flame is visible evidence that a gas is burning.

Whether the gas comes directly from a fuel pipe, or has resulted from the vaporization of a liquid or from the thermal decomposition of a solid is not important. However, it *is* important that the existence of a flame proves the presence in it of combustible gases mixed with air. It is in the flame that most, but not all, combustion actually occurs. A block of charcoal heated to its ignition temperature and maintained in an adequate supply of oxygen will glow and waste away to invisible carbon dioxide gas. Uncombined carbon cannot burn with a flame because the heat liberated in its oxidation is lower than the heat required for its vaporization. Its flameless, glowing combustion is ideal for barbecuing.

With the exception of certain special mixtures that contain their own oxidizing agents, *liquids never burn.* Among these mixtures are special explosives, such as nitroglycerine, which are not comparable with ordinary fuels. A gasoline fire is actually a gasoline *vapor* fire, the liquid only contributing the vapor to the flames.

Most combustible solids such as wood, paper, paint, and plastics undergo pyrolysis when heated strongly. The gaseous products of the pyrolysis feed the flames just as the vapor from a liquid does. Thus, in a wood fire there are usually three types of simultaneous chemical action: (1) gas combustion (flames), (2) pyrolysis caused by the heat of the flames, and (3) glowing surface combustion. As with special liquids, there are also exceptions with special solids. The best illustration is the match head, which contains some oxident along with the fuel. However, the flame of the match is not an exception: it comes from gaseous materials that are pyrolyzed and vaporized from the match head. Thus, *if the heat generated by the flame is effective in producing and igniting a continuing supply of gas by the volatilization of the solid or liquid fuel, the fire is self-propagating.*

Some simple experiments make this principle clear. A considerable bonfire can be built on the upper surface of a tight board floor without burning the floor through. The floor will be charred, but only rarely burned through, and the fire will usually die out when the kindled material has been consumed. Most of the heat of the fire has risen away from the floor, and only that transmitted by conduction or radiation has affected the floor. If, now, the bonfire is replenished until the floor is actually burned through so that heat can travel under the boards, the floor will burn violently. Heat is now being generated below some of the wood and is continuously liberating gases that feed the fire.

If a volatile solvent is poured on a floor and ignited, the heat produced is usually much greater than that of a bonfire, but the effect upon the floor is far less, and sometimes almost undetectable. Because the liquid is not burning, but boiling, the floor is never heated above the boiling temperature of the liquid, which is usually well below the temperature required to produce even visible charring. Normally, such a fire dies when the liquid is exhausted. Claims have been made of fuel oil fires in basements, for example, on concrete floors.

A spontaneous or accidental fire of this character is most improbable. An experiment will demonstrate to kindle a fire with fuel oil spread on concrete is almost impossible. A blow torch will ignite the oil, but when the torch is removed the fire will go out. The mere occurrence of such a fire gives the strongest ground for suspicion of arson. In order to ignite and maintain a fire of this nature, it is almost essential that a more volatile fuel such as gasoline be added to the fuel oil. Addition of the fuel oil is a ruse to stimulate an accidental fire.

The situation is quite different when combustible material is above a fire and close to it, or when a draft blows flames and hot gases directly over the material. In either of these circumstances, the heat of the fire serves to generate more gasous fuel, and the reaction grows. The great vulnerability of window curtains, paper, and the like, to fire is caused partly by this effect. The low ignition temperatures of fibrous and porous materials such as these are closely related to the phenomenon.

Drafts and Air Supply

Several factors contribute to the behavior of a fire. Started in a completely closed space, a fire must shortly become extinguished because of the exhaustion of the available oxygen and the generation of noncombustible gases that smother the flame. If the slightest chimney action develops at any place where the hot gases and flame from the fire come into contact with more combustible material, the rate of combustion is greatly increased. This effect has resulted in catastrophic fires in large buildings where elevator shafts and stairways have functioned as chimneys to direct and conserve the heat of the uprushing flames and gases. Under such conditions the rate of travel of a fire upward is extreme. In the absence of lateral drafts or wine, the relative rate of lateral spread of such a fire is slow, and the rate of progress downward is extremely slow.

Second only to the effect of the draft created by the fire itself, which, unless deflected, tends always to be upward, the influence of a wind or of a lateral drafts due to openings at the side of a fire is of very great importance. Wind is usually a major factor in the spread of forest fires or of fires in buildings that extend over large areas. Lateral drafts that exist inside buildings are important in the analysis of the action of interior fires. If one side of a building is afire and the other is not, the contrast may be attributable to the presence of a main air inlet on the latter side, which may be supplemented by some chimney action on the burning side.

Radiant Heat

Of the three modes by which heat may be transmitted—conduction, convection, and radiation—the last is probably the least generally understood. Heat is transferred directly from one object to another with which it is in contact by *conduction*. Its transfer by the movement of hot gases is known as *convection*. The *radiation* of heat waves from hot objects or flames will heat other objects at a distance. The principle of radiation is utilized in many modern heating appliances such as electric heaters, radiant floor and ceiling heating, and, to a limited extent, in steam or hot water "radiators." It is also the method by which most of an open fire is transmitted horizontally. In the fireplace the heat movement is upward by convection of the hot gases, toward the brick or stone by conduction, and into the room by radiation. All of the heat that is useful for warming the room by such an open fire is that which is transmitted by radiation.

Small fires will not radiate dangerous amounts of heat. Large fires, on the other hand, because of their intensity and their large area, will radiate enormous quantities of heat that can ignite objects at a distance. A burning house may ignite the house next door even when there is no transfer of sparks, flame, or hot gases. Radiant heat is the cause of the phenomenon often described as "bursting into flame." It emphasizes again the fact that the most significant effects of a fire are those of the heat generated, whether that heat travels by conduction, by convection, by radiation, or by contact of glowing solids or hot gases. Any of these can generate combustible gases from organic solids and liquids, and thereby propagate the fire. All of them can char, warp, and destroy objects, both combustible and noncombustible.

The Nature of Combustion

The ordinary fire consists of a self-propagating exothermic (heat-producing) oxidation, the fuel usually being organic material. Fires can be made with strictly inorganic fuel, such as phosphorus or pyrophoric metals, burning in air. Combustion reactions do not necessarily require oxygen. Fluorine gas, for example, will support the combustion of materials that will not burn in air, and with a vigor exceeding that of combustion in oxygen. These exceptions may be of importance in military actions, but are rarely encountered in arson or in ordinary fires.

As an organic material such as wood, paper, gasoline, or oil is consumed, there is formed a large volume of gases that are *products of the combustion* and are not to be confused with the gases produced by heat alone, which are the source of the flame. The gaseous products of the combustion are carbon dioxide and carbon monoxide derived from the carbon of the fuel, water vapor from its hydrogen, and smaller quantities of sulfur dioxide, nitrogen oxides, and other similar materials derived from the minor constituents of the fuel.

For each molecule of carbon dioxide produced, and for each *two* molecules of carbon monoxide or of water vapor produced, one molecule of oxygen from the air is required. Because only one molecule in every five in the atmosphere is oxygen, at any given temperature and pressure five volumes of air are required to produce one volume of carbon dioxide, and half as much for each volume of carbon monoxide or water vapor. Aside from the thermal expansion, there is very little more total gas volume leaving a fire than there is oxygen entering it, the difference being only in the water vapor and carbon monoxide fractions. The nitrogen of the air is increased only by expansion. For every volume of carbon dioxide produced, an equal volume of oxygen has entered into combination, both measurements being made under like temperature and pressure. These volumetric relationships may be summarized thus, using an empirical formula for cellulose:

$$C_6H_{10}O_5 + 6\,O_2 \rightarrow 6\,CO_2 + 5\,H_2O$$

It is evident that the oxygen of the air is a very effective controlling factor in determining the behavior of a fire. Sealing the fire off from its air supply diminishes it immediately, and finally extinguishes it. When the air supply becomes deficient, smoke and soot, and other products of incomplete combustion are formed. The production of smoke is influenced by the temperature of the fire as well as by the supply of oxygen. Many kinds of fuel, when given an adequate air supply and a sufficient ignition, will burn without smoke. Under such conditions soot is never formed. However, green wood and leaves, heavy oils, and some other materials almost invariably produce large quantities of smoke and sometimes soot. This is primarily a matter of the temperature of the fire. Heavy oils have a very high carbon content and a low vapor pressure. Their complete combustion requires a proportionately large oxygen supply, which, in turn, necessitates special means of providing it. When such oils burn without an air injector, atomizer, or a forced draft, they produce a relatively cool and very smoky flame.

Green wood and fresh leaves do not produce a hot fire because their water content is so great that much of the heat is removed in evaporating water, and the resulting temperature is insufficient to induce the complete oxidation of the evolved gases. White smoke is invariable with some dry fuels because of their high inorganic content, the color becoming gray if the combustion is incomplete.

The Nature and Significance of Smoke

Smoke is a suspension in air of solid material the nature of which varies with the type of fuel and with the conditions of combustion. Smoke often contains inorganic materials similar to ash, products distilled from the fuel, carbon particles, and—in industrial smoke—iron rust. Soot, the black component of smoke from a coal or oil fire, has been rather poorly characterized chemically. Often called "carbon," it is certainly composed largely of this material. Usually it contains also a number of complex organic compounds that are sufficiently resistant to oxidation to survive exposure to the heat and flame of the fire. Only rarely will traces of the original fuel be found in the smoke or soot, because even with an inadequate air supply some pyrolysis and oxidation of the fuel almost invariably occurs, unless the fire is very turbulent. A number of specific compounds have been isolated from smoke, among them pyrene and chrysene.

Blackening from smoke can usually be distinguished rather easily from blackening caused by soil or other dark-colored air-borne particles. This is accomplished by microscopic examination of wipings from the blackened surface. Soot, being soft and adhesive, gives a characteristic black smear that is readily recognized under low power magnification. Soil and similar dark materials of other kinds do not give the same smearing effect or appearance, though on a wall or other surface they may look as black as soot.

Burning Characteristics of Combustible Material

In the reconstruction and interpretation of fires it is frequently necessary to calculate the results of some hypothetical combination of fuel and air, or to assess the possibility that the fire may have resulted from some specific cause. If, for example, a gasoline fire were assumed to have originated from fumes reaching a rather distant kindling source, it would be necessary to determine the probable amount of fuel vaporized, the degree of its concomitant dilution in traveling the known distance, and the possibility that the mixture would be in the temperature range, at that point, at which it could be ignited. There is also the related problem of whether a particular possible source of ignition could have been hot enough to kindle the mixture. The necessary assumptions that underlie these considerations should always be chosen with conservatism. On this basis the criminalist may be able to show that a particular hypothetical explanation of the fire could be, or could not be, correct.

Regardless of the nature of these calculations and the competence with which they are applied, it is always necessary to obtain certain fundamental data upon which both the assumptions and the calculations may be based. Although this information is available in the chemical literature, it is scattered and sometimes inaccessible. For this reason, Table 34-1 gives a compilation of fundamental data on the types of fuel that have been most thoroughly studied, and which are often subjects of legal controversy.

To determine the approximate amount of air required for combustion of any fuel, the following formula is useful:

$$A = 11.6 \frac{C + (H - \frac{1}{8} O)}{100}$$

where A = weight of air in pounds (1 lb = about 13.3 ft^3)
C = % of carbon present
H = % hydrogen present
O = % oxygen present

TABLE 34-1 Combustion Properties of Some Common Fuels*

Fuel	Boiling point, °F	Ignition temperature, °F	Air required for combustion
wood			73.4 ft³/lb
coal		>660	
bituminous			144.6 ft³/lb
anthracite			143.4 ft³/lb
methyl alcohol	147*	878	
methane		999*	9.52 ft³/ft³ gas
natural gas		1200–1380*	10–17 ft³/ft³ gas
crude oil	1235–1250*	728–788*	
gasoline	104–390*	495*	15.2 ft³/lb
kerosene	257–347*	810*	

* For data on limiting compositions of combustible mixtures with air, see Chapter 35.

The average compositions of several common fuels are listed below:

gasoline	84% C	16% H	
natural gas	76% C	24% H	
California crude oil	84.4% C	11% H	3.34% O
Texas crude oil	84.6% C	10.9% H	2.87% O

An understanding of the fundamental characteristics of fuels is of primary importance in dealing with an actual fire whose cause must be determined. These characteristics include the *flash point*, the *ignition temperature*, and the *density of the fuel vapor*. Of these the density is easiest to deal with. Virtually all combustible gases are heavier than air, volume for volume. Air is a mixture, so its composition is variable, but for practical purposes a "theoretical mole weight" (MW) of about 29 can be assigned. The most prominent exceptions are hydrogen (MW 2), methane (MW 16), acetylene (MW 26), and carbon monoxide (MW 28). These gases are lighter than air and tend to rise and to mix with the air to form explosive mixtures. Vapors from all ordinary liquids that are flammable are denser than air and will settle under the air, flow along the ground, and settle in low places. This is of importance in dealing with all gases derived from the vaporization of gasoline, common solvents, and other liquids derived from petroleum.

The *flash point* is the lowest temperature at which a liquid gives off sufficient vapor to form a layer of mixed vapor and air that can be ignited. Thus, the flash point of gasoline is the lowest temperature at which a motor can be operated with gasoline. It is not related to the temperature required to produce ignition of the vapor–air mixture: the ignition temperature is always considerably higher.

Ignition temperature refers to the temperature that is just sufficient to ignite a mixture of flammable material and air within the compositional range of flammability. (See Chapter 35.) It varies somewhat with the actual composition of the mixture, and is not applicable unless the mixture is within the rather narrow range of composition that is required. Table 34-2 lists the flash points and ignition temperatures of some common types of fuel and other flammable materials that are involved only in accidental or intentionally set fires.

INVESTIGATION OF FIRES

Tracing the Origin of a Fire

In determining the point at which a fire started, either in a building or in the open, certain almost invariable principles are applicable, principles based upon the general behavior of fires discussed above. Because, in the absence of a down draft, fire travels downward very slowly, it is fairly certain that the origin of a fire will be close to the lowest point of burning or charring. This generalization is inapplicable if a burning roof or floor has collapsed and has physically

TABLE 34-2 Combustion Properties of Some Common Liquid Fuels

Material	Flash point, °F	Ignition temperature, °F
benzene	12	1076
butane (n)	−76	806
carbon disulfide	−22	257
carbon monoxide		1204
denatured alcohol (95%)	60	750
diethyl ether	−20	366
fuel oil #1 (kerosene)	110–165	490
fuel oil #2	110–190	494
fuel oil #6	150+	765
gasoline	−50	495
methane		999
methyl alcohol	54	878
methyl ethyl ketone	30	960
naphtha, coal tar	100–110	900–960
naphtha, Stoddard solvent	100–110	450–500
naphtha, V. M. and P.	20	450–500
octane	56	450
paint liquid	0–80	
propane		874
turpentine	95	488
varnish	<80	
whiskey	82	

carried burning materials downward to kindle a new fire at a level lower than that of the true origin. Due allowance must naturally be made when this has occurred and, in fact, this is to be recognized as a second fire that may have obliterated the origin of the first.

The direction of drafts and wind must next be considered. Often this may be determined from the pattern of the burned area, which may indicate the direction of flame propagation. The point of the fire's origin will be, in general, on the windward side of the burned region, as the fire will have traveled with the wind or draft. A fire in the open may occasionally have its point of origin masked by the shifting of the wind direction.

Another important factor is the tendency of a fire to spread laterally as it progresses. Thus, a fire in the open—in a forest, for example—will then burn in a triangular pattern determined by the prevailing wind, the origin being close to one of the apexes. This pattern is likely to be modified by the terrain. In a building, the general direction of the fire's progress is upward; but this is accompanied by lateral spread so that the lower burned region is narrower than that above. Here also, the origin will be close to the lower apex of the triangular pattern.

Many fires in buildings present complex patterns that result from local variations in the availability of fuel, the arrangement of the structure, localized chimney effects and other factors. Tracing the origin of such a fire may be a complex matter, but in every instance the general rules will hold, being subject only to modifying circumstances, which the investigator will be able to trace.

Locating the point of origin of a fire is essential in most arson investigations because this is the most logical point to search for any accelerant or device used to start the fire. It is likewise important that the point of origin be located even when arson is not involved, because the cause of the fire may then be ascertained in many instances, and measures may be taken to prevent subsequent fires from similar causes. Defective wiring, for example, or overheated appliances, or some other specific cause may become very apparent as soon as the point of origin of a fire has been located. In general, such investigations will be fruitful in the second class of fire listed above. Fires in which all combustible material is destroyed seldom yield to this type of investigation, and the fire of the third class usually requires little investigation.

Kindling Materials

In order for a fire to quickly reach a self-propagating state, kindling material must be within range of the flame, or other igniter. This material must be susceptible to ignition under the existing conditions and capable of maintaining its own combustion while transferring the fire to other more resistant materials. For reasons already presented, an arsonist cannot achieve his objective by dropping a lighted match on an ordinary floor. He can, however, apply the match to curtains, bedding, trash, or other easily combustible materials. The resulting fire will be difficult to trace because of its simplicity. However, most arsonists will be doubtful about the success of their plans when no special arrangements have been made to spread the fire vigorously. The common expedient is to use gasoline, kerosene, or other volatile flammable liquid to ensure a rapid intensification of the fire. Even so, the arsonist's lack of knowledge may cause his plans to fail. If, for instance, he uses a fairly heavy oil, such as fuel oil, it may refuse to burn under the mild conditions of ignition available to him, and damning evidence is left behind. The more volatile liquids such as gasoline, naptha, or benzene may flow through holes in the floor and drop to a lower level of the building, or otherwise find protection from the heat, so that, if the fire is extinguished in time, considerable quantities of liquid may remain. This occurs most often when such combustible fluids are poured over large masses of papers or trash, the solvent soaking into the material, which then acts as an insulator and a wick to protect the underlying solvent from the heat of the fire and to feed it slowly into the base of the flames. *Recovery of such liquid fuels is not unlikely if they are sought immediately after extinguishing a fire that has not reached gross proportions.*

Aside from the volatile and flammable solvents, the most common types of kindling are old papers, cloth, and packing materials. These may or may not be soaked with solvent, and they may have originated in the burned premises or have come from the arsonist's environment. In the latter case, such materials will be of particular significance, because they can serve as sources of fibers, glass, hair, soil, metal, and other kinds of extraneous evidence that might be connected with the arsonist. They may indicate his environment, his occupation, his stature and appearance, and even his identity. Sometimes items of the arsonist's own clothing are used to start the fire and some or all of them remain partly unburned. The investigator will be especially alert for this type of evidence, because it may ultimately be more valuable than anything obtained from the investigation of the fire itself.

Igniters

Probably the match is the means most commonly used in starting a fire. Because the match is usually completely consumed in a fire of any magnitude, it will ordinarily be impossible to trace. However, from force of habit many a person having started a fire will extinguish the match and toss it aside, thus allowing it to remain unconsumed. At times, the partly burned match may become most important and useful evidence, especially if it is of a kind not commonly used in the district, or if it is of an unusual type.

Matches possess a greater degree of individuality than might be expected. Match manufacturers employ different styles, dimensions, and materials. In consequence, many makes of matches are readily identified, even after partial burning. Matches manufactured in one region may be made from one species of wood, such as pine; whereas those from another region may be made of wood of another species, such as Douglas fir. Several different species of wood are used in the manufacture of matches. There is also considerable variety among the so-called "paper matches" in both color and dimensions. Match stems may, or may not, be treated to prevent afterglow; and they may be impregnated with paraffin or other auxiliary fuel to increase the amount of flame they will produce. There are so many variations in the manufacture of matches that it is often possible to obtain vital information from a match, even when it has been largely consumed. The origin of a Pacific Coast forest fire was traced through a partially burned match to a newcomer who had brought with him matches of a type not manufactured on the West Coast. Thus was a baffling crime solved.

The cigarette lighter used by an arsonist will leave no likely clues unless, in the excitement, the lighter is left behind. Lighters lost from pockets are occasionally found at crime scenes.

Sometimes the arsonist constructs and uses a device for setting the fire in his absence. These devices employ many means of ignition, the burning candle being the classic prototype. Other igniters include firearms ammunition, yellow phosphorus, mechanical match strikers, and electrical sparking devices. Even burning glasses, sodium and water, and tracer bullets might be used, though these seem more likely as fictional expedients than as real threats. Elaborate ignition devices, because of their relative complexity, are likely to survive the fire and be recovered, and will usually be traceable to the individuals who constructed them. Ingenuity and persistence on the part of the investigator should clarify most arson cases in which igniters of this type are used.

Collection of Evidence

The investigator of a fire will apply the principles set forth above to the determination of the source of the fire and its starting point. He will provide for all necessary photographs, sketches, and records. The most likely location for finding any physical evidence that may exist is at or near the point of origin of the fire. It is here that there is the greatest likelihood of locating any fire accelerant that may have been used, and search for it should be made as soon after the fire as is practical. The use of a hydrocarbon detector, if available, is strongly recommended for this purpose. If the detector affirms the presence of hydrocarbons, the point where the strongest reading is taken will be the best location in which to collect materials for laboratory investigation.

Certain general rules and methods of procedure should be followed in the collection of both physical objects of interest and materials to be tested for the presence of fire accelerants.

Physical Evidence from Fires   455

(1) Provide a number of containers suitable for collecting various kinds of evidence. Mason jars with caps that may be sealed are excellent for the collection of materials suspected of being saturated with gasoline, oil, or other volatile kindlers. Cartons and wrapping paper may used for burned and damaged items of comparatively large size, such as pieces of scorched timber or partially burned trash.

(2) Collect and store in closed or sealed containers any material suspected of carrying combustible liquids such as gasoline, and transport them to the laboratory with a minimum of delay. This collection will include soil taken from the lowest point of origin; timbers suspected of having been soaked in the kindler; paper, rags, and packing materials that are believed to contain volatile fuel. It should *not* contain material that has been almost completely destroyed by the fire, because any kindler that was once held by such material would have been consumed.

(3) Search the region of origin for any trace of the igniter, preserving any partly burned matches, any wires or other questioned metallic objects, and any burned objects that by their shape and appearance suggest they are foreign to the environment and may have served in some way as igniter.

(4) Make a careful search for containers that might have been used in transporting oil, gasoline, or other combustible liquids. Any that are found are to be sealed and sent to the laboratory.

(5) If the use of combustible liquids is suspected, samples of any gasoline, furnace oil, fly spray, benzene, paint thinner, turpentine, or other similar materials found on the premises will be taken and preserved for future reference and comparison.

(6) A general search will be made for miscellaneous physical evidence that may be connected with the activities or the identity of the arsonist. These include evidence obtained from a point of entry such as a broken window, a forced door, etc., and from any other location that may have had a connection with the movements of anyone setting the fire. The procedure here is that outlined for the investigation of crime scenes in general.

The greatest care is required to avoid the attitude that because the fire has wrought general destruction it has therefore destroyed the evidence that might lead to its solution. This is particularly pertinent with regard to combustible liquids. It is well known that these materials can soak into trash or soil, or even into wood, and will then burn on the surface only. If the fire is extinguished before all of the absorbed liquid is consumed, the remainder, soaked into this fortuitous wick, is still there and may be recovered by prompt and decisive action. *Speed* in the collection of these materials, which may be quite volatile, and *care* in their preservation, are essential. Thorough collection of evidence is necessary as soon as possible after the fire is extinguished. Otherwise, interested parties, workmen, and curious onlookers may nullify much of the value of a complete collection of evidence by probing, mixing, and destroying not only the evidence itself but also the arrangement and relationships between different objects.

Smoke

Smoke is an important product of most fires, one that is usually lost to the investigator. Only rarely will he have firsthand information about this most ephemeral kind of evidence. However, witnesses who have noted the appearance and the odor of the smoke from a fire may provide information of definite value. A chemical analysis of the smoke may be made, in the rare instance in which a suitable sample can be recovered.

Smoke consists largely of carbon, mineral ash, and partially consumed organic materials, along with a variety of invisible gases that impart to the smoke most of its odor. The burning of oil, gasoline, creosote, tar, paint, and similar organic materials is usually accompanied by the formation of a black carbonaceous smoke. The presence of large quantities of black soot in smoke indicates that some such material is being burned. This fact has an important bearing on the problem of arson because of the common use of such materials in starting fires.

Wood smoke is likely to be gray or white, though occasionally it may show considerable black when the air supply is poor. *Green* wood, which yields a lower burning temperature, burns with a very sooty flame. The smoke of a *dry* wood fire will seldom be noticeably black.

The odor of smoke is significant of the material being burned. Burning feathers, wool, and hair produce characteristic acrid odors attributable in part to sulfur dioxide gas derived from the sulfur these materials contain. Burning vegetable materials may produce odors described as pungent, aromatic, etc., which may give the investigator a clue as to the nature of the fuel.

Ash

Although the examination of the ash remaining after a building has burned will rarely be of assistance to the criminalist, such an examination may yield highly significant information about a bonfire, or a fire in an incinerator or fireplace, or about any small fire that may have been used for the destruction of some specific object. The examination of ash has also been of the greatest significance in the interpretation of disasters by tracing the nature of the material burned. Clothing from murdered bodies is sometimes destroyed by burning in a furnace or a bonfire. In all such instances the examination of the ash is essential.

NATURE OF THE MATERIAL BURNED. Often the structure of the ash indicates clearly whether it has resulted from the burning of paper, woven fabric of a specific kind or some other particular kind of material. If this information has possible significance, the fragments are collected very carefully and gently to avoid crumbling, placed in a container of sufficient size so that they will be under no strain or pressure, and taken to the laboratory with a minimum of mechanical disturbance. Such care is essential when writing or printing on charred paper is to be deciphered, or when tests are to made for charred blood. If the ash is extremely fragile, it may be possible to stabilize it somewhat by using an atomizer to spray it gently with a thin lacquer, thus depositing on it a film that will strengthen it enough to permit handling. Burned documents, in particular, should always be treated in this manner when they are to be deciphered.

If the problem under investigation involves burned woven fabric, some information may be obtained from the appearance of the ash itself. However, if it is not possible to determine the nature of the fabric from observation alone, the ash may be subjected to complete chemical or spectrographic analysis in comparison with known burned specimens of the possible types. The mineral composition of cotton, wool, silk, rayon, etc., are all different. Additional mineral materials are used in mordanting dyes in some fabrics. Moreover, cotton from one district is not identical in mineral constitution with cotton from another district. By determining the composition of the ash and using the ratios of Mg/Na/K/Cl, and so on, the type of fabric a burned sample belonged to can often be determined. Ash should not be disregarded because the original material has undergone partial or total destruction by fire.

A useful procedure employs a pair of density gradient tubes to compare the questioned sample of ash with ash from a known similar material. This procedure has been shown to be superior not only in distinguishing different types of paper, cloth, and the like, but in approaching the actual individualization of the material burned. The procedure is applicable only to completely burned samples. If the remains in question are only partly in the form of char, the combustion is completed by heating in a muffle furnace before the application of the test. This technique is applicable only after the complete investigation of any markings that may be on the material in question.

REFERENCES

Battle, B., and Weston, P. B.: *Arson.* New York: Arco (1960).
Bradley, J. N.: *Flame and Combustion Phenomena.* Scranton, Penn.: Barnes and Noble (1969).
Fitch, R. D., and Porter, E. A.: *Accidental or Incendiary?* Springfield: Thomas (1968).
Kirk, P. L.: *Fire Investigation.* New York: Wiley (1969).
Lewis, B., and Von Elbe, G.: *Combustion, Flames, and Explosions of Gases,* 2nd ed. New York: Academic Press (1961).

35
Physical Evidence from Explosions

From the viewpoint of the investigator, explosions may be grouped in categories, the *diffuse* and the *concentrated*, irrespective of the chemical nature of the exploding system. The first group includes explosions of gas mixtures and of dusts, and the second category embraces the detonation of powder, dynamite, and nitroglycerine. A clear differentiation of these two types of explosion is essential to the investigation, because an explosion of the first type is ordinarily accidental, whereas one of the second type is more likely to have been deliberately planned. In the latter case it will often be suggested that the explosion was caused accidentally by leaking gas, dust mixtures, or gasoline fumes, the explanation being offered to cover up the fact that the origin of the explosion was actually incendiary.

The two types of explosion differ markedly in their reaction rates, the diffuse explosion having an explosive rate much slower than that of the concentrated detonation of true explosives. This difference in the duration of the explosive reaction alters markedly the physical effects upon the environment.

DIFFUSE EXPLOSIONS

Gases and Vapors

When illuminating gas or the vapor of gasoline, ether, benzene, or other flammable material is mixed with air in the proper proportions, the mixture is highly explosive and may be detonated by a pilot light, a match, a spark, or any localized high temperature. The explosion can occur wherever the gas-and-air mixture is within the explosive range of the fuel—ordinarily an extended area. The explosion will not extend to regions in which there is an unduly high proportion of either air or gaseous fuel; yet such explosions can wreck buildings and wreak widespread damage.

The range of concentration of the fuel-and-air mixture within which such an explosion can occur is comparatively broad, but not unlimited. Too much dilution with air gives a mixture that cannot be ignited. (This is the obvious reason for handling flammable solvents out of doors.) Too great a concentration of fuel vapor or gas will prevent ignition because there is insufficient oxygen to support the combustion. These considerations are similar to those applicable to fires, the essential difference being inherent in the local conditions. A fire ensues when a small amount of combustible material is ignited and the heat of combustion causes the vaporization of more combustible material. An explosion occurs when a considerable quantity of combustible material is premixed with enough oxygen to constitute an explosive mixture; otherwise a fire, and not an explosion, results.

Consider the explosion or fire resulting from the ignition of vapors from a tank of gasoline. Inside such a tank there is a high concentration of gasoline vapors within the explosive range. Igniting the gas mixture results in an explosion, the heat of which immediately vaporizes more gasoline, thus creating a continuing fire. The force of the initial explosion may also burst the tank, spreading the gasoline and the secondary fire. If the tank is not ruptured, the gasoline explosion may result in the removal of oxygen from the gas space in the tank, and the rush of gases from the opening may blow the burning system away and thus extinguish the fire. Carefully arranged explosions operated on similar principles are used to extinguish oil-well fires.

"Explosions" of another type occur with tanked fuels such as gasoline or oil. These are originated by the heating of the tank from the outside by a fire or another heat source. The fuel in the closed tank is heated and expanded until the internal pressure causes a rupture of the tank. The heated fuel is then sprayed into the exterior fire, is almost instantaneously vaporized, mixed with a large volume of air, and results in a *true* explosion of considerable magnitude. The true explosion results from the pressure effect inside the tank that caused the first "explosion." It is often not appreciated that illuminating gas, gasoline fumes, or similar gases and vapors, are not themselves explosive, or even combustible, unless they are first mixed with sufficient atmospheric oxygen. Table 35–1 indicates the ranges within which such mixtures will explode or burn. With an excess of vapor, fire will follow the explosion; with an excess of air, great force may be generated, but no fuel will remain to burn and no fire will follow unless other materials are kindled by the explosion. At the theoretical mixture, maximum heat and corresponding force will be obtained.

TABLE 35–1 Limits of Explodability*

Vapor or gas	Lower limit, % of gas	Upper limit, % of gas
acetone	2.5	13.0
acetylene	2.5	35–83
ammonia	16.0	27.0
benzene	1.4	8.0
carbon monoxide	12.5	74
ethane	3.2	10.6
ethyl ether	1.85	36.5
ethylene	2.75	28.6
gasoline	1.4	6.0
hydrogen	4.1	74
methane	5.3	14.0
propane	2.4	9.5

* Data taken from Muehlenberger: *Police J.*, 11:101 (1938).

The *flash point* of a liquid fuel has a direct bearing upon its susceptibility to explosive ignition. This is defined as the temperature at which a mixture of air and fuel vapor is sufficient to constitute an explosive mixture. Below this temperature liquid fuels will not burn. The flash point of a gasoline may be as low as $-50°F$, which is the lowest temperature at which a gasoline motor may be started. The flash points of many solvents are not far below ordinary atmospheric temperatures, and those of a considerable number of them are higher. Thus, the choice of a solvent may be important in its bearing upon fire hazard. The flash point of a solvent mixture tends to be close to that of its most volatile major component. Industrial products containing solvents ordinarily have the flash point specified on the container, and disregard of this information has led to many fires and explosions.

Dust and Droplets

Dust explosions resemble explosions of gases and vapors. Minute particles of flammable material, suspended at a favorable concentration in air, need only a source of ignition to initiate explosively violent combustion. The fire in the grain elevator is the prototype, though any kind of dry, colloidally fine carbohydrate suspended in air could serve as the fuel, provided that the air circulation was insufficient to carry away the heat produced by slow oxidation. Fine *droplets* of oil of low vapor pressure, such as fuel oil or lubricating oil, which are not normally explosive or even easily ignited, may become highly explosive when dispersed in the correct quantity of air. Occasionally this results from the faulty behavior of industrial machinery. It resembles a dust explosion more closely than a gas explosion in that it does not involve a uniform mixture of air with gas or vapor, but a homogeneous mixture of droplets in air.

General Characteristics of Diffuse Explosions

One of the characteristics of diffuse explosions, whether resulting from gas, liquid fuel, solvents, or dusts, is the erratic nature of the damage. Objects will be blown in any direction, following no discernible pattern. Interior walls may crumble, throwing fragments in several directions. Exterior walls will be blown outward. A photograph of the explosion scene showing the entire area is very helpful in the interpretation of such an explosion, especially if it can be compared with a similar pre-explosion picture or sketch showing the normal arrangement of walls and furniture. Another characteristic of the diffuse explosion is the absence of local shattering, which is commonly observed after the detonation of faster and more concentrated explosives. Attention to these general features, either at firsthand or by photographs, is often of value in demonstrating the overall pattern of the explosion, which is sometimes obscured by a too-intense concentration upon the details of the scene. The movement of objects will always be away from the greater force, but when an inequality of concentration of the explosive mixture exists in different parts of the space, forces will be exerted in several directions, giving a degree of randomness to the resulting scene. This should never be interpreted as substantiation of the statement of one witness who testified, in a gasoline-vapor explosion case, that he was blown backward into the center of an explosion that had occurred immediately behind him only a few feet distant. The initial force of an explosion is always outward, and its primary effect is usually the most important one, particularly in diffuse explosions.

There is one other important distinction observable between diffuse and concentrated explosions. No crater or area of special damage or special discoloration will ordinarily be observed after a diffuse explosion, whereas such an area of conspicuous damage in the characteristic sign of the concentrated explosion.

CONCENTRATED EXPLOSIONS

Concentrated explosions result only from the detonation of so-called "explosives" such as powder, dynamite, nitroglycerine, and similar materials, each of which constitutes a complete explosive system. They do not require atmospheric oxygen; all ingredients necessary for their functioning are included during their manufacture. Such materials are often termed "fixed" explosives. Fixed explosives that require oxygen contain compounds that are rich in oxygen. Most such explosives depend upon the presence of a high percentage of characteristically unstable nitrogen compounds that on decomposing release large volumes of gaseous products. The decomposition is accompanied by a tremendous outflow of energy, which suddenly expands the several gases produced in the reaction.

In contrast with the diffuse explosion, the forces released in this kind of explosion may be considered as originating at a point and radiating outward from it in all directions. Movable objects within range of such an explosion will usually be blown out radially from this point, and a definite pattern will result. This pattern may also be observed in a photograph of the entire scene, and if a photograph exists of the scene as it was before the explosion, the contrast may be extreme.

Many objections can be raised to the oversimplification of the pattern problem. Small divergences from the pattern will ordinarily be observed, and these will be more numerous in explosions of greater violence in complex environments. For example, in high-explosive military bombing, the effect of the suction following the explosion may be to move objects, break glass, and so on, in the direction opposite to what would be expected. The deflection of forces by objects will also alter the pattern. However, the interpretation of the pattern will still be possible, because displacement of objects by any but a radial force can be related to a visible object whose effct may be evaluated. The suction effect of the explosion is likewise essentially radial, though reversed in direction. Although the explosive material will be completely consumed by the reaction, the study of the pattern may be very important in determining its nature.

Concentrated explosions vary greatly, depending upon the type of explosive used. Nearly all explosives are merely combustible when ignited. Nitroglycerine, though sensitive to shocks, can be burned safely when spread out so that the heat of combustion is not too intense. Dynamite, whose usual essential component is nitroglycerine, is more readily burned without danger of explosion. When detonated by a sharp shock, such as the explosion of a blasting cap, these explosives undergo true explosion whether confined or not. Moreover, nitroglycerine explosives give so rapid a complete combustion that the shock produced is out of proportion to the total energy involved. For example, there may be breakage or damage to a strong structure and proportionately less damage to a weaker structure. Large rocks are broken by "mud capping" with dynamite. This consists of pressing dynamite on the surface of the rock and covering it with a layer of mud. When the dynamite is detonated, the shock is so violent and so localized that the rock is broken, and adherent portions of the mud may often be recovered intact. The same effect is utilized by safecrackers with nitroglycerine. This effect goes beyond a simple study of the forces of explosion and involves dynamic evaluation of very rapidly applied force. Effects such as this have led to the almost superstitious ideas regarding explosions sometimes expressed by the uninformed.

Some other powerful explosives, such as nitrocellulose (gun cotton, smokeless powder), may exert as much total force as nitroglycerine, or more. They will burn at a slower rate, and are much more predictable in their behavior. Even when confined and detonated as in a firearm, these materials explode rather slowly and give powerful propelling force without any danger of bursting the gun barrel. This type of explosive is less commonly used for demolition than are the more rapid-acting explosives. For criminal activity the slower explosives are less suitable because the damage is likely to be less, and the difficulty of exploding any but a confined charge is considerable. Such an explosive used in cracking a safe would be likely to destroy the contents of the safe and possibly might bulge its walls, but fail to break the door.

INVESTIGATION OF EXPLOSIONS

The investigation of explosions, as distinguished from that of explosive devices, will usually follow a course similar to the one outlined below:

(1) *The scene is carefully studied and*, if possible, *photographed in its entirety.* If complete photographic coverage is impossible or impractical, the scene may be sketched. Study of the photographs, as well as the scene itself, will usually determine whether the explosion was of the diffuse or of the concentrated type. This determination is of the greatest importance because a diffuse explosion will normally have resulted from accidental circumstances, whereas a concentrated explosion is more likely to have been the effect of criminal action.

(2) *If a diffuse explosion is indicated*, the investigator will attempt to trace its origin. It is likely to have been followed by a general fire. The random pattern of movement will be apparent. The source of the explosive material may often be inferred from the nature of the premises and of the activities that have normally been carried on there. The presence of stored volatile solvents and similar materials that can lead to explosions is highly significant. The investigator must not overlook the possibility that a saboteur placed a high explosive close to such materials in the expectation that the explosion would be attributed to them. Gas leakage must be carefully checked, especially in an exploded residence or business building. In a grain elevator vegetable dust is the most probable source of ignition, whereas in a coalhandling establishment coal dust is the likely source. When no such obvious source is apparent, the possibility of volatile solvents, deliberately or accidentally placed, must be carefully checked, since the vapors of these materials can lead to diffuse explosions that are sometimes very violent. Containers and detonating mechanisms must be sought in these instances.

(3) *If a concentrated explosion is indicated* the most careful and thorough scrutiny must be given to every square inch of the premises to recover any trace of a detonating mechanism and any item that appears foreign to the

normal environment of the site. Often such a search will give some indication of the nature of the explosive and yield valuable evidence that may lead to the perpetrator. Paper from a stick of dynamite may survive the explosion and be recovered, or fragments of a glass bottle that recently contained nitroglycerine may be found. The latter kind of evidence is most likely to occur in connection with safe burglaries. Because dynamite is normally exploded by a cap, which will often be attached to a fuse, these items are especially likely to be found at the scene of a dynamite explosion. They may also be used with other explosives, of course, but dynamite is the most easily obtainable high explosive, and is therefore frequently employed in the construction of bombs.

(4) An examination of any *remaining structures or materials* that were not too badly damaged by the explosion and probably were not in the immediate neighborhood of the latter, should then be undertaken. For example, a building might have been forcibly entered and the region of entry may have escaped destruction. The evidence produced in forcible entry, such as tool marks, broken glass, shed fibers, and the like might then be sufficient to effect a solution of the case.

All materials collected are wrapped and transported to the laboratory for examination. The greatest danger in this kind of situation is that the destruction appears so extensive and thorough that the investigator may be reluctant to expend the necessary time and efforts to search the premises thoroughly. It must be remembered that all types of detonating mechanisms contain metallic and other more or less indestructible materials. Thus it follows that, if such a mechanism has been used, some traces of it must remain. If this is always kept in mind, the outcome of the investigation of an explosion will be, as it has proved to be in the past, very often successful.

Illustrations and Variants

While a 100-gallon oil drum was being filled with gasoline, an explosion occurred. A large fire ensued during which a second explosion occurred, much larger than the first. Examination of the drum revealed that it had burst. The only witness testified that the drum was actually being filled at the time of the first explosion, but that the explosion did not occur at the drum, but some distance away from it. It could be shown conclusively that the drum was actually stoppered tightly at the time of the initial explosion, for the inside of the steel plug was covered with a layer of soot, as was also all but the bottom of the inside of the drum. The soot could only have come from the burning of gasoline with an insufficient air supply, as would be the case inside an inadequately ventilated drum. The latter burst along its top seams, indicating either a limited explosion inside the drum or, more probably, a great increase of internal pressure exerted by the enclosed gasoline vapor in response to the heat from the fire that was burning around the drum. This explanation was verified by the scorching of paint over the exterior of the drum except along the lower part of its sides where the drum was cooled by vaporizing gasoline within. This vaporization left behind, on the inside of the drum, a series of residual contour-shaped lines of debris. The sequence of events was clear. Some material, probably gasoline spilled on the floor, was ignited and exploded. A considerable fire ensued, and ignited the wood of the building. This fire enveloped the wooden framework supporting the drum; the drum then became hot and finally burst, spraying a large quantity of hot gasoline all over the room and into the air, thus providing fuel for the second violent explosion. Gasoline remaining in the drum continued to burn with an inadequate air supply and deposited soot on the inner surface of the drum and on the screw cap. This sequence of events, which was revealed by the physical remains, pointed unequivocally to the presence of an explosive material in the room initially, and this was denied by the only eyewitness of the fire, a defendant in the case.

Occasionally a very improbable explosion occurs and leads to a quite difficult investigation. In one such episode a hand vacuum sweeper exploded while it was being used in cleaning upholstery and inflicted considerable injury on the operator. The dust bag was almost entirely consumed by heat, and much soot was deposited on the interior surfaces of the fan chamber. Although a dust explosion seemed to be the obvious explanation, this was improbable because the dust was primarily inorganic, being composed mainly of very fine quartz particles. Inside the fan chamber was found a large wall area that had a rippled appearance like that of seashore sand as the tide runs out over it. A film of heavy oil was found to have been given a rippled surface by the current of air blowing over it, and the rippled surface was stabilized by soil particles deposited on it. It was not possible to establish a clean-cut proof that the explosion was caused by atomization of oil in the fan chamber, but no other tenable explanation was suggested. Presumably an excess of rather heavy oil was beaten into fine droplets by the fan, fueling a diffuse explosion on a small scale. The source of ignition remains in doubt. A spark, or some similar phenomenon, must have occurred when there was an explosive mixture inside the fan chamber and dust bag of the cleaner. A possible source of a spark was found in a steel nut holding the fan in place, this nut being in the path of quartz particles entering from the nozzle. The explosion probably did not originate from motor sparks, since there was no evidence of any explosion in the motor chamber, which was separated from the fan chamber by an aluminum partition.

Another fairly common source of small diffuse explosions is the ordinary lead storage battery. During the quick charging of such a battery there is a great deal of hydrogen gas liberated, and probably considerable oxygen as well.

An explosive gas mixture will commonly be present under these conditions. Sparks are also common, due to poor connections or other sources. Acid may be thrown out of the battery by the explosion, injuring persons and damaging property nearby. Investigation by the expert may be necessary.

Clearly the investigation of explosions is not limited to major catastrophes, or even to the destruction of buildings or loss of life. It can include ether explosions in the human lung during surgery under anesthesia, or the detonation of caps or small bombs of the prankster, and numerous other small systems, any of which may cause loss of sight or of life, or other serious physical damage of many kinds.

Spectacular diffuse explosions are not uncommon in connection with various industrial activities. Large storage tanks and railroad tank cars occasionally explode while they are being painted, for example. In such explosions the paint solvents have flash points that are lower than the ambient temperature, and some source of accidental ignition is present. These explosions are rarely of criminal interest, but they quite frequently give rise to civil litigation.

INVESTIGATION OF EXPLOSIVE DEVICES

In addition to the investigation of explosions, it is sometimes necessary to investigate or to dispose of homemade bombs that have been placed with criminal intent but have failed to explode prior to discovery or suspicion regarding them. Such devices are also sent through the mail or by messenger to intended victims. The handling of these devices is extremely hazardous and should, if possible, be done only by a specialist in this field. At times this is not practical, and the police investigator must take the risk of dealing with the device. Some principles may be laid down for such investigations, even though complete coverage is far too lengthy for presentation here.

The suspected bomb will most commonly be of (1) a fuse-and-cap type; (2) a trigger type designed to explode on being opened or moved, through either mechanical or mercury switch action; (3) a time bomb containing some type of clockwork to explode it at a predetermined time; or (4) a bomb triggered by chemical action that will delay its explosion by an uncertain length of time. A bomb of any of these types will be dangerous to disturb during the time that the igniter mechanism is in functioning condition.

The safest procedure, when an unknown package is suspected of being a bomb, is to examine it rapidly *without moving or disturbing it*. If there is a fuse, it is usually best to clear the neighborhood of persons close enough to be injured and wait until the explosion has occurred or until it is certain that no explosion will occur because the fuse is defective or has been wet. Crude dynamite bombs of this type have been extinguished by rain. When no fuse is visible, the ear of a stethoscope should be applied to ascertain if there is a timing mechanism in operation. If a timer is heard, it would be prudent to clear the neighborhood as rapidly as possible. If it seems desirable that the suspected bomb be quenched, it is well to remember that a light oil is preferable to water as a quenching agent, as water can cause explosions with some igniters and is ineffective as a quencher with several explosives. Neither oil nor water can affect a bomb that is sealed in a tight case, and both tend to destroy or obliterate fingerprints and other minute physical evidence by which the origin of the bomb might be traced. Immersion in either oil or water will increase the difficulty of subsequent examination of the explosive.

When the bomb is to be investigated and destroyed, the examination should be made as described above and possibly with even more care. *Care must be taken not to add fingerprints or other physical evidence and to obliterate none. The suspected bomb must not be turned upside down or on its side.* After the preliminary examination, the bomb may then be removed to a safe place to be allowed to age, *the same precautions being followed.* Muehlenberger recommends a concrete shed about 10 ft square with solid, thick walls and a light wooden and tar-paper roof provided with a trap door for entry. In the absence of a prepared bombproof shed of this type, the bomb may be taken to an open space where all persons may be kept away from the bomb until it has reached the time set for its explosion. It should be kept in such a safe place for 48 hours during which time any clockwork mechanism would have run down and any chemical mechanism would have had time to function. If the bomb has not exploded in this span of time, it is reasonably safe to assume that it is likely to explode only as a result of mechanical action, such as opening or upsetting the package. If a bomb shed is available, it should be equipped with a sturdy wooden table about 2 ft square bolted to a thick steel rod that passes through opposite walls of the shed. The suspected bomb is strapped tightly to this table for aging, and at the end of 48 hours the table may be rotated to turn the bomb upside down, which will give it further opportunity to explode harmlessly. If no shed is available, a rotating device may be constructed that can be operated in the open from behind sand bags or some other protection.

If no explosion results from this treatment, the suspected bomb should be carefully photographed. A ruler should be included in the photograph as a reference for size, and the exposures planned so that all markings on the package will be recorded. The package should also be tested for fingerprints, then X-rayed to ascertain the presence and arrangement of metallic objects such as blasting caps, switches, clockwork, batteries, wires, or other devices. When this added information has been carefully evaluated, it is possible to plan the method for opening the package. This is the most hazardous operation remaining. The general rule is to open it by means other than those anticipated even though this may involve much labor and time. All force is to be avoided in opening the device, and the existing closures should be left strictly in place.

Paper and wood are cut through instead of being unfastened. Soldered joints may be dissolved apart with mercury, and closed pipes may be dipped in dilute (10%) sulfuric acid and allowed to stand until the acid has corroded away caps or similar closures. After access to the interior has been gained, wires are cut, batteries are removed, and other steps are taken to neutralize the action of any igniter mechanism revealed by the X-ray. Blasting caps must be removed with great care and with an absolute minimum of force. Any explosive or other material that requires chemical analysis is collected without delay and sent to the laboratory for study and identification.

It is obvious that considerable equipment is required to deal with potentially live bombs, and that such facilities will be available only in locations where there has been—or threatens to be—a succession of bombings. In such circumstances, experts in dealing with bombs have devised procedures that are better than those described here, and they have procured specialized facilities. Workers in this area have designed various remote-handling devices whose operators work behind heavy shielding, which provides protection against premature explosion. With such equipment a man may transport or examine a bomb with reasonable safety. As an added precaution, the foremost authorities recommend that bombs be quenched in liquid nitrogen, which will freeze any known liquid except similar liquefied permanent gases, and will slow down any chemical action to the point at which an otherwise heavy explosion becomes no more than a minor event that is virtually harmless. Liquid nitrogen is not likely to be quickly obtainable unless proper arrangements for its procurement have been made well in advance of need, but its use is practical in regions where bombings are of frequent occurrence.

Evidence from Bombs

In addition to the explosive itself, which may often be traced to its source, all portions of the igniter mechanism must be preserved for study. These will include all wires, tape, clockwork, electrical switches, and similar mechanisms. Such items as these are even more likely to be traceable to the person who constructed the bomb than is the explosive employed. They are commonly homemade and relatively crude, and thus they retain many traces and indications of the maker and his environment. For example, an alarm clock may be used in connection with an electric switch to close a circuit to detonate the bomb. Ordinarily this would involve fastening the wire to the winding handle of the clock; and tape, cord or an odd bit of additional wire is likely to have been used for this purpose. Tape, cord, or wire, and possibly even the alarm clock itself, may be traced to the individual who constructed the bomb.

Bombs have been made by tying sticks of dynamite together in a bundle with cord. The cord may carry many types of microscopic residues that are very significant. These may include human and animal hairs, fibers, pollens, soil residues, paint, and many other materials. All of these have been used successfully in determining the nature of the environment in which the bomb was assembled. Even after a bomb has exploded, some of this evidence may remain and be useful in the solution of the crime.

REFERENCES

Cook, M. A.: *Science of High Explosives*. Cincinnati: Van Nostrand Reinhold (1958).
Davis, T. L.: *Chemistry of Powder and Explosives*. Hollywood, Calif.: Angriff (1972).
Lenz, R. R.: *Explosives and Bomb Disposal Guide*. Springfield: Thomas (1971).
Muehlenberger, C. W.: "The Investigation of Bombs and Explosions," *Police J.* 11:101 (1936).
Ronayne, J. A.: "Investigating Crimes Involving Explosives," *Police* 4:64 (1960).
Stoffel, J.: "Determining the Cause of an Explosion," *Police* 7:64 (1963).
Stoffel, J. F.: *Explosives and Homemade Bombs*, 2nd ed. Springfield: Thomas (1972).
Urbanski, T.: *Chemistry and Technology of Explosives*. Elmsford, New York: Pergamon (1964). 3 vols.

36

Documents

Documents are physical evidence just as are glass, hairs, blood, or fingerprints. The field of specialization known as "document examination" has so developed as to obscure this obvious point, and to place documents in a category quite different from other types of physical evidence. As with other physical evidence, the examination of documents, particularly of handwriting, is based very largely on the determination of identity.

The equipment necessary for document examination is similar to that for other types of evidence. Microscopes, photographic equipment, low-power magnifiers, and chemical reagents are required. In addition, special gauges and reticules are essential to the study of the writing features, widths of lines, thickness of paper, and other physical factors.

TYPES OF EXAMINATION

A variety of examinations may be necessary in the study of a document. These may be outlined as follows:

(1) Physical and chemical examinations, including study and identification of (a) writing materials; (b) erasures, obliterations, and alterations; (c) order and age of writing or typing.

(2) Identification of the authorship of writing.

The physical and chemical examinations of documents may be carried out in a relatively routine and purely objective manner. This phase of document examination is largely mechanical, reproducible, and definite. It may be mastered by the student in a reasonable time and usually produces testimony that is positive, definite, and not easily refuted. It often provides proof of a matter at issue without involving determination of authorship at all, or as a secondary factor only.

Handwriting identification, many authorities to the contrary notwithstanding, has yet to be reduced to the precision and objectivity characteristic of most criminalistics testing. Competent document examiners apply to it a keenness of observation characteristic of the scientist, combined with logical reasoning, and an orderly and thorough examination. In addition, there is a very important factor of experience, and even of intuition, not readily reduced to routine, impossible to teach in a definite manner, and yet highly critical to the end result. A student may be readily trained to compare glass fragments so as to produce definite and correct results. He may learn to type blood almost infallibly within a relatively short time. He cannot rapidly learn to identify handwriting with the same degree of certainty and in a short time. Because the recognition of individual handwriting is a subject more or less familiar to nearly everybody, it is very easy to believe it to be a simple matter. Nothing could be farther from the truth, and probably no field of examination of physical evidence requires more extensive and thorough study. For example, it has been shown conclusively that a large proportion of people fail to identify their own handwriting when it is mixed with similar writing by other people.

For the same basic reasons, testimony on handwriting identification is often the most difficult of all to offer. Most attorneys believe themselves quite expert in identifying handwriting, and indeed many of them do achieve a very considerable proficiency. This very fact gives them a far greater daring in attacking the expert witness, and may at times fortify them with the greatest confidence in their own conclusions, even when the latter are quite incorrect. It cannot be emphasized too strongly that the expert witness must go far beyond the type of proficiency that an intelligent attorney might achieve. He must develop by intensive, purposeful, and well-planned study a large body of knowledge and experience in the field, so that his observations may be interpreted with a breadth and keenness that can never be achieved by the casual student of the subject. Because of the almost infinite ramifications and variations in handwriting, it is never sufficient to attempt a difficult decision of authorship with a superficial and untested background.

The experienced and competent examiner will ordinarily attempt to decide an issue involving documents on the basis of the physical and chemical examination first, as this is the more definite and simple approach. Was an addition or alteration made? Was something added after the document was signed? Was an addition made with a different ink or pen? Was a sheet of a different paper added? Was the paper or ink manufactured prior to the date of the document? If, as sometimes happens, it can be shown that the paper or ink employed in a document was a later manufacture than the date of the document, this alone labels it as fraudulent. If writing or typing has been added above a signature so as to overlap it, the validity of the signature itself may be relatively unimportant, and the overlap allows definite detection of the addition. The document examiner will be constantly aware that such facts as these are more certainly determined than, for example, the authorship of a forgery. In general they will be examined first, and in no case is it permissible to overlook them.

PRELIMINARY EXAMINATION

The investigator who encounters a document that, because of some set of circumstances, may be subject to suspicion of spuriousness will first of all wish to give to it some preliminary examination. This may at times show definite reasons for such suspicion after which the document will then usually be delivered to a qualified document examiner. At other times a preliminary examination may be adequate to eliminate any doubt that exists. Here the greatest care must be used if the investigator has not had sufficient training or experience, because any good grade forgery or skillful alteration may well escape his notice. Factors that should be noted in a written document are as follows:

(1) Presence of obvious erasure, obliteration, or alteration.
(2) Abnormal positioning of a signature with respect to the body of the writing.
(3) Quaver, uncertainty, or distortion in a signature.
(4) Patching, or overwriting, particularly if rather carefully performed.
(5) Use of different inks, different appearance of the lines, crowding, or other unusual appearance.
(6) Noticeable differences in the writing as compared with genuine, or an appearance of genuine letter forms but poor execution of the lines themselves.

The above list does not cover all of the possibilities, but includes most of those that will be readily apparent to the investigator of average skill and experience. There may be other factors not visible in the writing itself, but rather in the known circumstances of the case, which justify expert examination of a document with no direct examination at all by the police investigator. For example, a bad check will always be subject to examination by the expert even though the writing on it appears perfect and there is no other evident reason for suspicion. It is exceedingly important that anything that is done in a preliminary examination of a document should not in any way alter or deface it.

EXEMPLARS

If a sample of handwriting or typewriting must be compared with similar writing of known origin, it is the investigator's duty to collect adequate exemplars on which the determination of the validity of the writing may be based.

Exemplars of typewriters are comparatively simple to obtain if the machine in question is available. Two procedures may be used: (1) copies of the questioned typing may be prepared so that every combination of letters occurring in it are available; and (2) a standard paragraph containing all of the characters of the standard keyboard may be typed. Clearly, the first alternative is to be preferred in an actual case since comparison is then very direct. The second procedure is excellent when samples of a large number of machines are being collected for later comparison purposes, as in assembling museum material. *If the alignment, wear, and imperfections of the machine must be studied, it is essential with either procedure that the exemplar be typed more than once.* If only the letter designs are required for identification of make and model, a single good copy of the standard paragraph may suffice. For a typical standard paragraph, see the section entitled "Dictated Paragraphs."

When the questioned machine is not available, it is necessary to obtain from any available source typed material known or believed to have been typed on that machine. This circumstance arises commonly in civil matters, but is unusual in criminal investigation. The only safe rules to follow here are: Collect as much exemplar material as possible, and be certain to include in the exemplar writing that has been typed in the same time period as the questioned text.

With *handwriting*, it is not the simple task that some have thought to collect proper and adequate exemplars, partly because it is difficult to know when any given number or type of exemplars is actually sufficient. Factors that must be considered in collecting handwritten exemplars are the following:

(1) The age of the questioned writing, as related to the time of writing the exemplars, and to the writer's age and physical condition.

(2) Whether all styles affected by the writer are represented. For example, many people sign important documents in a manner noticeably different from the method used in writing a casual note or keeping an account book or even signing a personal letter or note. Other writers cultivate what they fancy to be entirely different "hands," which indeed do show strong variations from each other. This may be misleading but rarely causes much difficulty to the expert examiner.

(3) The amount of the known writing. No general rule is possible in stating what is enough, but it is always safe to get all possible samples even though the quantity may seem excessive. A desirable amount is one that shows all the ordinary variations made by the writer in question. With some writers this may amount to a considerable number, and of diverse origins, as there is usually

a relationship between the conditions of writing and the variations produced.

(4) At least a portion of the exemplars should have been produced under conditions similar to or comparable with those under which the questioned document was written. This is not always possible, but is one of the most desirable goals at which to aim. For example, if a legal document was signed at a high table, another, similar legal document signed at a high table is the best exemplar.

(5) The writing materials should be as similar as possible to those used in writing the questioned document. This point is obvious but often overlooked. Sometimes a questioned document is written with pencil and a suspected writer is told to write a set of signatures, for example, with a ball-point pen. This should always be avoided.

Frequently, the investigator can do no more than to obtain all the available exemplars and place them in the hands of the examiner, regardless of their adequacy. A reasonable degree of imagination and considerable thought should be expended before this is done. A search of the county clerk's office for deeds, estate settlements, and the like is often productive of exemplars. Voting rosters are a good source of signatures. Relatives and friends often have saved letters, Christmas cards, account books, and memoranda. The bank can sometimes furnish signature cards, and a search of the suspect's premises will reveal canceled checks, records, and memoranda. Signatures on driver's license applications may be available, and stores will have signatures on charge account application forms. Employers will usually have considerable writing of their employees. The investigator with imagination and persistence will rarely fail to locate an impressive list of exemplars. Not all of them are equally valuable and some are often poor standards, but if enough are found the end is served.

Possibly every document examiner has studied documents with inconclusive results, or even committed errors because of the lack of proper exemplars. Many people have been thought to be dishonest because insufficient samples of their handwriting were available for comparison. Furthermore, in disguising his writing the writer often attempts deliberately to vary as much as possible from his normal hand. The measure of his success is certainly the number of features that he can vary outside of his normal limits, and the extent of the variations he can produce. If exemplars are insufficient even to define the normal limits, it is little wonder that a disguise is occasionally encountered that is good enough to prevent a decision on authorship.

Request Exemplars

Frequently, a court official, police officer, or attorney requests or orders an individual to write exemplars for purposes of comparison with a questioned document. Usually this consists of signing his name a given number of times, and perhaps adding his address, or rewriting the words of the questioned document itself. On the face of it, this should be a good procedure because duplication of the material itself is obtained. That such is not the case follows from a little consideration of the circumstances.

As will be developed in greater detail in a succeeding section in this chapter, normal handwriting is an automatic or spontaneous act, requiring no thought on the part of the writer except the words or sentences to be written. The act of writing itself is one of which the writer is essentially unconscious. While writing an ordered or requested exemplar in a courtroom, police station, or attorney's office, under scrutiny, many factors intervene to destroy the automatic nature of the writing. Nervousness is common, and invariably the writer is made acutely aware of the act of writing. Consequently, he takes overconscious direction of it, with production of distortion, errors, and a strained or unnatural result. The product would often serve as a better disguise of his genuine writing than an exemplar of it. When request writing is performed, the following rules should be observed:

(1) Place the writer in a quiet place with a minimum of scrutiny.

(2) Have him write something other than a list of signatures, e.g., his version of the events that led to his present position, or a short history of his life. The purpose of this is to put his mind on what he is writing rather than on how he is writing. It is best to avoid having him copy other written or printed material.

(3) Use a dictated paragraph as a substitute for Rule 2 above. This is an effective procedure because the individual may be made to hurry his writing so he will not have time to disguise it. Also, it can be arranged to contain the critical letters and combinations desired for comparison. Dictation of such a paragraph should be made several times, so that various samples are available, and also to put the writer at ease and develop his normal writing at its normal speed. Each sample should be removed before the next is started so that he cannot copy disguise from one to the other.

(4) Alternatively, an exemplar handwriting form may be used, providing it is well designed and contains all of the letter forms in the questioned text. Requesting the suspect to write all of the capital letters of the alphabet and then all of the small letters is a practice to be avoided; if the exemplar consists of unjointed letters, many valuable characteristics related to the manner in which letters are joined will be lost.

Dictated Paragraphs

When an exemplar is dictated as a paragraph, the content of the latter should be carefully decided in advance. The paragraph is composed to include all the material desired without being so obvious as to arouse in the writer's mind associations that will divert him from free writing. It must be stressed that if the examination is to be truly meaningful, the questioned and exemplar text must contain the same letter combinations.

Consider an illustration of a paragraph design. Suppose that the writer is suspected of forging three signatures, "F. L. Sloan," "John R. James," and "Robt. J. Brown." These contain a number of elements of which the capital letters are particularly important, and the small letter combinations "loan," "ohn," "ames," "obt," and "rown." Another element is the connection of capitals to small letters. These requirements are quite well met by the following paragraph, though others equally good are easily devised:

"While in London, Ralph L. Jones was thrown into the Thames because he would not loan F. J. Brock the Johnny cake he had obtained from Frank R. Slate."

The advantage of such a paragraph is that it has no immediate and apparent connection with the questioned signatures, includes all common letter combinations, and the thought expressed is so foreign to the more serious business at hand that the writer's mind is temporarily diverted in the effort to concentrate on taking down certain foolish dictation. In following the dictation, he forgets the act of writing and does it spontaneously.

The dictated paragraph, when repeated a number of times is one of the best forms of exemplar. If the man's own signature is questioned, it is well to have him sign each copy of the paragraph, thus obtaining this signature also while his mind is still temporarily diverted. The pargarph may be combined advantageously with other forms of exemplar. It remains important that any such additional exemplar material be taken with the above general requirements in mind.

Several standard paragraphs have been widely used because they were designed to include all of the letters, upper and lower case, of the alphabet, and in fact, sometimes all the punctuation marks as well. This system has some obvious advantages, but in most instances it is less satisfactory than the simpler paragraph which is devised to obtain the material desired unconfused with much extraneous material. The unique value of these all-inclusive paragraphs lies in their use with typewriting machines, which may require for their classification a wide variety of characters. Perhaps the most widely used general paragraph is the following one, that given by Osborn:*

"Our London business is good, but Vienna and Berlin are quiet. Mr. D. Lloyd has gone to Switzerland and I hope for good news. He will be there for a week at 1496 Zermott St. and then goes to Turin and Rome and will join Col. Parry and arrive at Athens, Greece, Nov. 27th or Dec. 2nd. Letters there should

---

* *Questioned Documents,* 2nd ed. Albany: Boyd Printing Co. (1929).

be addressed: King James Blvd. 3580. We expect Chas. E. Fuller Tuesday. Dr. L. McQuaid and Robt. Unger, Esq., left on the 'X.Y.' Express tonight."

As has been discussed earlier, other standards are superior for typewriters also, though the above paragraph is as good as any yet devised for obtaining complete registry of all the letters of the English alphabet.

Any dictated or requested exemplar must be witnessed, otherwise the exemplar material may not be admitted as evidence in a court of law.

COPIES AND PHOTOGRAPHS

The document examiner is often requested to examine photostats or photographic copies of questioned documents and of exemplars. Although modern copying techniques are generally rather good from the standpoint of reproducing writing with fidelity, the original copy is invariably to be preferred. This is true especially in the matter of line quality, which is of the greatest significance in examination of disguised writing and of forgeries. A good tracing or even a good drawing of a signature will often be undetectable in a copy. Furthermore, differences in ink, pen, and other writing equipment will ordinarily not be evident at all in the photostat.

LIMITATIONS ON THE INVESTIGATOR

Many of the operations of the expert document examiner make use of equipment not usually available to the police investigator, the detective, or the lawyer. Such items as ultraviolet lamps for fluorescence examination and infrared equipment for photography are often not available, and skill in their use will be lacking.

Adequate document gauges, reticules, special microscopes, light tables, and other illuminators will also usually be unavailable. There may not be proper photographic copying equipment, which cannot be well substituted by common cameras, the lenses of which are not corrected for copying.

More important than these limitations is the fact that few police officers or other investigators of similar background have either the training or experience necessary to qualify as expert document examiners, or the time and incentive to develop that experience. For these and other reasons such individuals are well advised to limit themselves to preliminary examination only, with a view to determining the advisability of submitting the questioned document to a qualified examiner.

PHYSICAL AND CHEMICAL EXAMINATION

The factors that are directly and often simply determined include those concerned with writing material identification and those for which microscopic or chemical examination may be expected to provide a direct answer in favorable instances, e.g., order of writing, study of erasure or obliteration, and similar items.

Writing Material Identification

PENS. The identification of pens is not absolute because of the possibility that a number of pens may have indistinguishable characteristics. The proof of difference between pens is often rather simple except in those unusual instances where a document might have been written with two pens of almost identical characteristics. The study is confined to the lines made by the pens. Ordinarily, it is simplified by the fact that the same writer is involved, and the same writer with the same pen will be expected to duplicate in general the line characteristics as they relate to the pen.

The *general character* of the pen is determined first. *Ballpoint pens* leave a single rounded line showing no nib separation even when pressed heavily. Many ball points accumulate ink on the side of the ball housing, and when the direction of movement is reversed this ink is picked up by the ball and deposited as a smudge on the line. The character of the ball-point ink and the way it goes on the paper will also distinguish these pens. Not being a true liquid, it does not flow into the paper fibers and spread in the same way that fluid inks do. Considerable magnification may be necessary to study this effect.

Fountain pens ordinarily show a more or less round point, but when the pressure is increased there is separation of the nib marks, which is readily detected. A further effect noted with fountain pens is the relative evenness of ink flow as compared with steel pens, which periodically run low on ink and must be replenished.

Steel pens are distinguished by the fact that they usually leave a sharply cut line or indentation at the edge of the line and often give a "scratchy" appearance. The characteristic mentioned above, of running low on ink at intervals, further distinguishes them.

Many variations in pen manufacture prevent absolute distinction even between different pen types. For example, gold pen points sold for use in ordinary holders will show nib characteristics similar to fountain pens and ink flow similar to steel pens. Ball-point pens are not easily distinguished from each other unless there are definite differences in the width of line they draw, or in the ink used in them.

PENCILS. The lead of a common pencil is composed essentially of a mixture of graphite and clay, e.g., kaolin, used as a binder. The soft pencil has a greater proportion of graphite and the hard one contains relatively more clay. Because of the essential simplicity of composition of the pencil lead, pencils have a very limited degree of individuality, and can ordinarily not be identified as individuals. The degree of hardness can be approximated fairly closely and this is an aid to investigation of pencil writing, but a limited one. At times, it is also possible to estimate the quality of the pencil by the fact that the cheaper pencils frequently contain gritty impurities that scratch the paper, whereas a high-grade pencil is expected to be free of such grit.

Copying or indelible pencils contain, in addition to the usual constitutents, aniline dyes that impart a color to the line. Here also, the amount of the colored constituent varies with the hardness, the softer pencils containing more dye (and sometimes graphite) than the harder ones. The presence of dye in the impressions allows easier restoration of erased writing with this type of pencil.

In addition to the main types of pencils used for writing, several varieties of colored pencils and crayons are employed at times in connection with documents that require investigation. This type of writing implement employs various waxes and gums to which are added appropriate dyes. Both clay and graphite are normally absent and the character of the marks is quite different from that of ordinary pencils, both with respect to erasing, and to any chemical tests that may be carried out. The most significant identifying characteristic is the color itself, though the appearance of the line may give an indication as to whether a colored pencil or a crayon was used, and different pencils may at times be distinguished by differences in hardness, pressence of gritty inclusions, and similar factors.

PAPER. The *type and character of paper* are almost infinitely variable, the result of which is the availability of a tremendous number of distinguishable papers. This diversity, which is favorable to identification, is somewhat offset by the fact that paper is almost invariably a mass-produced product, and any given type of paper may be expected to occur in considerable quantity.

The main factors producing differences in paper are as follows:

(1) The type of raw material, which includes a wide variety of fibrous vegetable materials, of which wood is most important, but cotton (rag), esparto, straw, and several other grasses and fibrous plants are employed in some quantity.
(2) The weight (or thickness) of the paper.
(3) The filling and sizing materials, which may include rosin, clay, starch, glue, and various other mineral and organic materials.
(4) The process of manufacturing the pulp, which includes mechanical grinding, the sulfite, soda, and sulfate processes. Papers made by different processes are ordinarily distinguishable either by microscopic or by chemical examination.
(5) The degree of beating of the pulp, which has a marked effect on the strength, absorbency, and physical character of the paper.

(6) Special mechanical processes such as calendering, embossing, and watermarking.

The processes of paper manufacture are not only infinitely variable and of great interest to the document examiner, but so complex as to be clearly in the field of the specialist. The determination of identity of two paper specimens does not necessarily require a knowledge of the process of manufacture, but such understanding is definitely helpful in the interpretation of observations and should be acquired by the expert in the field.

The investigator will necessarily limit himself to a few features only of the paper comparison because complete examination will be beyond the scope of any but the well-equipped expert. The following factors may be readily compared:

(1) *Color.* Under good light, the color of the paper is readily compared. Allowance must be made for dirt, stain, or fading. The blank side of the paper should be used when possible to avoid complications from the writing or printing.

(2) *Surface appearance.* The general nature of the surface finish may be noted at the same time the color is compared. Here, allowance is made for wrinkling and other similar damage.

(3) *Watermarks.* If present, watermarks are the most valuable of identifying characteristics. They are observed by holding the paper to a light source so as to see the light transmitted. Identical watermarks prove identity of manufacturer and type of paper, and usually of weight. Different watermarks are proof of difference even when all other characteristics appear to be identical.

(4) *Weight or thickness.* Papers are designated by weight, which is related to the thickness of the sheet. The thickness should be measured by means of a paper micrometer, which is merely a modified mechanic's micrometer on which the contact surfaces are discs.

(5) *Inclusions.* Sometimes there are visible inclusions in the paper that may be employed very effectively in its identification. They occur mostly in the cheaper grades of paper such as school tablets and in wrapping and some utility papers. A low-power microscope is necessary for their study and it is preferable to have the study made by an experienced examiner. The inclusions are valuable because they are most likely to occur in papers that have no watermarks or other better distinguishing characteristics.

(6) *Other factors.* Very important in paper examination is the study of the paper fibers. This is a matter for the expert because it requires special background and equipment. Pattern or design in the paper is too obvious a characteristic to require comment. Foreign material such as stains and marks may at times be of the greatest importance, but are not paper characteristics and should be readily recognized by the investigator.

Documents

INK. Many types and varieties of writing fluid are used in recording ideas on paper and other materials. In fact, the inkmaker's history and art are so extensive as to have led to a number of complete books on the subject. Some of the elementary essentials of ink chemistry and use will be outlined quite briefly here. The discussion of fluid or fountain pen inks is included for its historical significance, and for application toward those problems involving older documents. The use of the ball-point pen has so eclipsed the use of the fountain pen that it is almost a rarity when a document written with a fluid ink is encountered.

The colored components of writing inks include only a few types of material that give to the ink its class designation. So many variations occur in the formulas used by different manufacturers and in their different products that the commonly published classification of inks is an oversimplification. Of the basic colored ingredients of ink, the most common are:

(1) Iron gallotannate, which has long been and still is the basis of the greatest number of commercial writing inks.
(2) Dyes of organic nature, largely derived from coal tar, which have long been employed to give an initial color to gallotannate inks, but are used today as the entire or chief source of color in a considerable number of inks.
(3) Logwood extract, which is quite black and was used to a considerable extent in the past, and is still employed as a minor constituent of some inks.
(4) Nigrosine, which is one of the earlier black dyes, now little used.
(5) Carbon black, which is the most permanent of all colors when applied as a fine suspension to paper.

Many inks fall in definite classes, depending on the inclusion of one of the types of colored materials listed above. This has long been the accepted basis for the limited type of ink identification commonly made. Under these circumstances, and with proper consideration of the conditions, it is ordinarily possible to determine both brand and type of ink with a high degree of probability. Even in the most unfavorable circumstances it is possible to obtain useful information that excludes most of the possible inks that might have been employed, and to distinguish with considerable precision whether two inks are different or probably the same.

Iron gallotannate inks are the commonly used blue-black inks, but some iron and gallotannic acids are added to inks that are not included in this category. Ferrous sulfate forms with gallotannic acid a compound that is colorless but rapidly undergoes oxidation to form an insoluble and complex ferric salt, the blackness of which increases over some days of oxidation, more slowly over a longer time, and gradually fades over a period of many years. The permanence of the ink is good, because it remains legible for a very long period and is not appreciably affected by water, though it fades more in sunlight than when placed in the dark. These changes on paper provide some indication of the age of the writing, but conclusions of age must be made with the greatest caution because of the numerous possibly unknown factors involved and the fact that all of the changes are slow. No precise determinations of age are at present possible, though considerable differences of age may be distinguished when comparisons are properly controlled with standards and chemical tests to make sure that the same kind of ink is being studied.

Inks of the iron gallotannate type have a further characteristic, often very disturbing to the examiner. They change color and character on standing unused, largely because of oxidation of the dissolved constituents, the formation of insoluble residues, and the change in dispersion of these residues and consequent appearance of the ink. Thus, it can happen that two documents written with exactly the same ink, but at different times in the life of that ink, will vary greatly from this factor alone. All of these points demand that the greatest caution and a high degree of judgment and experience enter in the examination of inks. When proper controls are used, it is nevertheless possible to do much more with inks than is indicated by some authors on the subject.

Dye inks are fundamentally solutions of a single dye or mixture of dyes, usually modified by extraneous constituents to control the fluidity, prevent growth of mold, and alter the penetration or spreading of the ink. Just as a large majority of inks might be classed with the iron gallotannate type because some iron and gallotannic acid are added to them, so also can most inks be classed as dye inks because some dye is added to them. The dyes used are ordinarily synthetic products similar in origin to textile and other dyes, and are usually based on coal tar compounds as raw material. The common designation of "aniline dyes" may often be a misnomer because aniline is only one of several dye bases commonly employed.

Only a limited number of dyes are used alone as the colored constituent of an ink because water-soluble dyes will be subject to "running" and washing out by water. The so-called "washable" inks are likely to be dye inks. Considerable progress has been made in recent years in perfecting dye inks to compete with inks of other types.

Logwood inks are normally made by adding logwood extract to salts of iron, copper, or chromium. The ink has excellent properties except that it is less permanent than iron nutgall ink. The addition of logwood to the latter ink increases the permanence of the writing, and gives it a blacker color as first applied. Logwood ink is readily distinguishable from iron nutgall ink by its reaction with dilute hydrochloric acid.

Nigrosine ink, like logwood ink, is little used at the present time. Nigrosine is also a coal-tar product giving a blue-black or purple-black line that remains the same color throughout the life of the ink. It is never as black as a good iron nutgall ink becomes on oxidation, and it is not stable to application of water, in which it runs like most dye inks to which it is closely akin. Oxalic acid does not affect nigrosine ink, a difference which distinguishes it from both iron nutgall and logwood inks.

Carbon inks are made by suspending fine lampblack in water, with the addition of (1) protective colloids that stabilize the suspension, and (2) materials that on drying give adherence of the ink to the paper and of the particles to each other. The same constituents may serve all of these purposes, and modify the fluidity as well. Vegetable gums are useful, and the blend of these and other similar constituents is the major factor controlling the behavior of the ink. Thus, the India ink used by draftsmen is somewhat more concentrated in carbon and has a higher proportion of stabilizing materials so that it is too viscous to use in fountain pens. A more fluid ink of similar general characteristics may be used successfully with most fountain pens.

Other colored constituents are not normally added to inks of this class. They will contain no iron, dyes, or similar constituents through which they may be confused with other types of ink. No known reagent will cause fading or significant color change of a carbon ink, a point by which these inks are readily identified. Water will cause some of them to smudge, though this tendency can be controlled by proper admixtures of protective materials.

Ball-point inks are quite different in most respects from writing fluids. They are not truly liquid, but a thick solution of dye in a liquid vehicle that is almost invariably a glycol or glycol ether. In spite of certain common tendencies, these inks vary greatly among themselves, and in addition have undergone much improvement since their first introduction. Most ball-point inks write perfectly dry, and will not smear, even immediately after deposition. Thus, some of the generalities that have been published to the effect that "all ball-point inks remain wet," or that "all ball-point inks are oil-base," may miss the point completely because the variations have not been recognized. Some ball-point inks can be differentiated by electrophoresis and chromatography. Inks of this type, however, are often quite uniform, and a successful chemical or instrumental analysis does not ensure that the criminalist will be able to offer an opinion as to source or comment upon the significance of the inks being indistinguishable. There are many manufacturers of ball-point pens, but few manufacturers of the inks. We have, therefore, a situation in which an ink of a particular composition and manufacturer may be encountered in pens of many different makes. This is most apparent in the case of blue ball-point inks, in which inks compounded with two or three of the following four dyes account for virtually all of the blue ink produced: methyl violet, Victoria blue, phthalocyanine, and Rhodamine B.

Examination of inks should be left to the expert, though any investigator may note differences or similarities in appearance, color, or other factors that may carry a significance sufficient to lead him to submit the ink specimens for examination by the expert. Identical appearance always argues identity of the ink, even though many inks will not be distinguished by appearance alone, and similar age must also be assumed. Different appearance is often more deceptive, as writings with the same ink may give a difference in appearance because of blotting, the paper used, dilution or concentration of the ink, contamination by the pen, use of pens with different flow, and similar factors. Age differences alone may produce different appearance. The document examiner receives many ink problems that he cannot solve by any effort no matter how sustained. On the other hand, some ink problems are so simple as to allow effective solution even by the relatively inexpert. To generalize about what can be accomplished in ink examination is impossible without consideration of all the factors in the specific case.

PRINTING INKS.   No extended discussion of printing inks is necessary in this volume because these are only occasionally involved in criminal investigation. A large number of varieties exist, and numerous classes of inks have been developed for specific purposes such as lithography, gravure, and newsprint. Petroleum derivatives and other oils including linseed and tung oils, and various resins and varnish constituents are used in the vehicle. Carbon black is almost the only black pigment used, but a large variety of pigments are employed for colored inks. (See Chapter 21 for a partial listing of pigments.) Because of the employment of mineral pigments, chemical procedures can be developed by which many inks of similar appearance can be differentiated.

Alterations, Obliterations, and Erasures

The methods used for testing and deciphering alterations, obliterations, and erasures are essentially similar though the means of making such alterations are often quite different. Preliminary detection of any such change in a document is made only by careful visual observation. Magnification is often of service, even to the extent of using the stereoscopic binocular microscope. Also helpful is examination with or without magnification under strong illumination that is almost at grazing incidence to the paper surface. Holding the document edgewise to a strong shaded light is the simplest method. Erasures particularly will ordinarily show disturbance of the paper surface. Mechanical erasure produces a greater effect than chemical erasure. Iodine fuming may indicate erasures.

Unusual spacing of words or letters is a suspicious circumstance. Letters or numerals crowded together, or separated at one point considerably more than the average, should be examined with care. Stains may indicate chemical erasure as will the wrinkled effect obtained from wetting the paper and redrying it. Overwriting and patching should be noted if visible, and a search under magnification may be necessary to reveal a careful alteration of this type.

ALTERATIONS. Frequently, an alteration is made merely by overwriting or patching of existing writing. It may also be made after an erasure, but should then be studied as an erasure. The simple alteration ordinarily must be determined under magnification. When the stereoscopic binocular microscope is used with low power, it is almost always apparent what has been altered, because each pen stroke is distinguishable. Both the original and the addition may be deciphered in all but a few instances. Careful photography may aid in the decipherment, but can rarely show anything that cannot be seen with the eye.

The most common alterations are simple overwritings, or the change of numerals, as 1 to 0, or additions. Thus, a check may be "kited" or raised by adding zeros to the end of the numerals and writing the appropriate word (hundred, etc.) after the written figure. An addition of this type may be detected (1) when it is written with a different pen or ink; (2) when it is added in a determinably different hand; (3) when by its crowding or abnormal spacing it is apparent that it was not a part of the original; or (4) when there is a detectable difference in the age of the writing. All of these but (3) are discussed elsewhere in this volume. Ordinarily there are two or more of the above features shown in a given alteration.

OBLITERATIONS. By obliteration is meant the effective destruction of appearance of the writing without actually removing it or rendering it invisible. Scratching over it with a pencil, pen, or wax pencil is the most common method. No effort is then made to hide the alterations, but only the original material. As with alterations, the microscope is most useful for study of obliterations. It will often show the traces of the original writing material used. In one instance, blue wax pencil was used to obliterate red wax pencil writing. The microscope revealed numerous bits of red wax only partially covered by the blue.

Examination with ultraviolet radiation or photography with infrared rays may at times show the material that was obliterated. The mechanical impression made in the original writing or typing may be developed with oblique illumination or by formation of a plastic replica. In some instances, treatment with chemical reagents will remove the overwriting.

ERASURES. Erasure often accompanies alteration or obliteration. It may also be used alone in many instances. Development of erased material is usually critical to the study of any alteration or obliteration. The techniques of restoration are therefore basic, regardless of the type of tampering to which a document has been subjected.

Erasures are produced by (1) chemicals, and (2) mechanical abrasion. Chemicals remove color (of inks) by changing the nature of the colored substance, not by removing it. Abrasion by mechanical erasers actually removes the writing and makes it more difficult to restore. Frequently, the removal is so incomplete that restoration or decipherment is not difficult at all. A thorough mechanical erasure is practically impossible to restore or decipher. Such a removal is relatively simple with pencil writing, more difficult with indelible pencil, and most difficult with ink. Typing is removable in toto, but not without leaving definite indications of the presence of erasure.

The methods of restoring or deciphering erasures may be classified as follows:

(1) Examination with flat lighting, which emphasizes the impressions made by the writing implement.
(2) Fuming with certain vapors. Ammonium sulfide and thiocyanic acid vapors, frequently employed, react with the iron residues left after erasing most inks. Iodine vapor is preferentially adsorbed by the paper fibers. If these have been disturbed differently in different locations, iodine fuming may show the material desired. Alcohol aerosol serves to dissolve slightly the residues of indelible pencil and, by spreading these bits of color, to develop the outline of the writing performed with such a pencil.
(3) Ultraviolet radiation examination. If the material erased was somewhat fluorescent, and was not completely removed, ultraviolet radiation may reveal it.
(4) Infrared photography. Photography by means of infrared rays often reveals material rendered invisible by erasure. This follows from the the differential absorption of infrared rays by materials not removed by the erasure.
(5) Replicas. If there are differences of pressure between the writing implement and the subsequent erasing implement, some impression of the former often remains. This can sometimes be deciphered by oblique lighting, but may be obscured by overwriting or obliteration. It may also fail to be clear because of the characteristics of the paper surface. Formation of a plastic replica will transfer any such impressions to a solid, clear sheet of plastic on which they may be much more readily perceived.

Order and Age of Writing

A frequent request to the document examiner is the determination of the order in which two written or typed specimens were written, or the age or relative age of one or more specimens. Clear decision of some of these questions is possible and sometimes simple. In other instances, no definite decision can be rendered.

The order of writing may ordinarily be determined only when the two portions compared actually overlap so that lines cross at one or more points. Microscopic examination of these points frequently allows a clear demonstration of the order of placing of lines. In cases involving fluid ink, one ink line passing over another allows lateral flow of the second into the paper previously wet by the first. Ink will retract from a greasy first line made, for example, by a wax pencil, and sometimes from a typed character. The ink may coat and cover the typed impression also. The Ultropak illuminator or equivalent device is probably the most useful instrument for this determination. Ink writing over folds in a paper may also be readily perceived by the manner in which the ink runs laterally into the broken paper fibers. No such effect is apparent when the paper is folded after the writing is placed. Magnified pencil lines show the direction of pencil movement because the graphite is dragged from the pencil lead by each of the paper fibers, leaving a little smear of the material ahead of the fiber. When two pencil lines cross, the second line disturbs the graphite arrangement of the first, and superimposes a different distribution. In cases involving ball-point inks, one line passing over another will create a furrow that will disrupt that of the original stroke. The sequence of the strokes may be discerned through a microscopic examination of these crossings. This is generally quite effective, although in particular instances making a replica is found to be more satisfactory. Polydimethylsiloxane, commonly referred to as "Silly Putty" and available in toy stores, is an excellent material for making such replicas, and possesses the additional advantage of delicately removing ink from the writing to make the furrows more apparent. By considering all such factors as these, the experienced examiner will determine successfully the order of writing in a large percentage of the problems submitted to him.

The age of writing may be estimated within rather broad limits by a study of the color of fluid inks, as compared with standards of the same or similar ink. As mentioned earlier, the change of color due to oxidation of ink, followed by fading, is slow and varies with the ink and the conditions of storage. Thus, an old document may ordinarily be distinguished from a recent one with little difficulty, but smaller differences of age in two old documents are ordinarily not possible to determine. Very recent documents may be studied by means of the chloride or sulfate diffusion from the ink line. It has been claimed that this will determine age quite closely within a period of a few weeks after the writing, and give an approximation of age for as much as about 4 years. The method is undoubtedly dependent upon several factors, including the type of ink, and the conditions of storage, particularly the temperature and humidity. When two documents can be compared under truly comparable conditions, e.g., the same ink and storage, it can be of definite but limited service.

With the technology available at the present time, ball-point inks defy an attempt at dating, other than the information supplied by the date of the introduction of this type of pen. For the first wide-scale distribution, the date may be taken as 1943.

Very frequently, there are indirect methods for the approximation of age through extraneous factors. When such fortunate circumstances exist, it is not necessary to depend on the somewhat subjective methods of direct determination. For example, in a case involving some 10 years claimed difference in the age of two property deeds, it was possible to ascertain that they were written at the same time by an examination of the date stamp mark in the record book of the notary who had prepared the deeds. In both stamp marks, the alignment of the continuous rubber date bands was identical, a circumstance that would be highly improbable on any other assumption. This diagnosis was verified through a number of confirmatory factors, and yielded a decision that was far more definite than could in any case have been obtained by means of direct examination of the ink.

Burned and Charred Documents

Deciphering documents that have been burned or partially burned is frequently possible. For this reason, such materials should always be collected most carefully and submitted to the laboratory for examination when any reason for their deciphering exists or is suspected. Without the confirmation of an expert that it is impossible to recover the burned material, such documents should never be neglected even though they appear to be in a badly destroyed condition.

Collection of burned paper fragments must be carried out with the greatest caution and should not be attempted by any but the experienced and qualified investigator. The most common method of collecting such material is to obtain a fine atomizer and charge it with lacquer diluted somewhat with acetone or lacquer solvent. With this, a very fine spray of the lacquer is blown lightly on the charred document in such a manner that the blast of air from the spray does not break or disintegrate the material further. After application of a light spray, and allowing it to dry completely, further application of lacquer may be made until the charred material has developed a definite strength and stiffness. It may then be carefully lifted from the ash, using extra precautions to prevent tearing or further damage in moving it. It should then be placed in a large cardboard box and transported to the laboratory. There, it will be examined under various kinds of illumination, and may be photographed with infrared rays. Chemical fuming methods may also be successful at times. Commonly, the best method of deciphering rests on very careful examination under suitable special illumination. In some cases, the charred document can be made more pliable without the loss of its integrity by soaking in a solution of glycerol and water.

Typewriting

Two main problems in typewriting are ordinarily presented to the investigator or to the document examiner: (1) identification of make and model of a machine from a sample of its typing; and (2) identification of an individual machine from a sample of its typing. To the two questions stated, definite answers can ordinarily be given by the qualified document examiner.

CLASS CHARACTERISTICS OF TYPEWRITERS. Nearly all modern typewriters utilize fixed type characters on swinging bars, suspended in a segment, and having a common center of movement. A modern exception is the IBM Selectric, in which the type is located on a ball that can precess to bring the selected letter into position to strike the ribbon, thereby creating the impression on the paper.

The class characteristics are almost exclusively those embodied in the type design, which is different with every make, and which is periodically substituted or altered by every manufacturer. By close study of the characteristics of the individual letters, it is possible to determine the make of machine used in the preparation of a particular document, and to ascertain the period of manufacture, and the limiting range of serial numbers that must include that of the machine. These periods are sometimes a considerable number of years, sometimes only a few. Frequently, there are differences between portable and office machines of the same manufacture and in the same time period, thus allowing a determination as to whether the machine was of one type or the other.

Identification of make and model of machine has been studied very extensively by document examiners, most of whom have developed keys and codes for the identification. Some utilize formulas similar to fingerprint formulas, and most have a certain regular order of characteristics that are examined. Most of these are difficult to describe, and significant only because the examiner has defined them for himself and recognizes them in terms of his own definition. Such schemes may be readily developed by anyone who cares to employ sufficient time and care. A reasonably complete set of specimens of typing from known machines is a prerequisite to any such study.

The major difficulty attached to the key, code, or formula systems is that they require certain very definite characters to be present in the sample to be examined. This situation is fortuitous, and leads to difficulty with small or specialized specimens that fail to contain the desired letters.

INDIVIDUAL CHARACTERISTICS OF TYPEWRITERS. Every typewriter is individual with respect to certain minor characteristics, the study of which allows identification of that typewriter with a relatively high degree of accuracy. Modern manufacturing methods produce machines with a minimum of deviations from the normal, so that new machines have less by which they can be identified than do old machines, the differences being also accentuated by wear and damage.

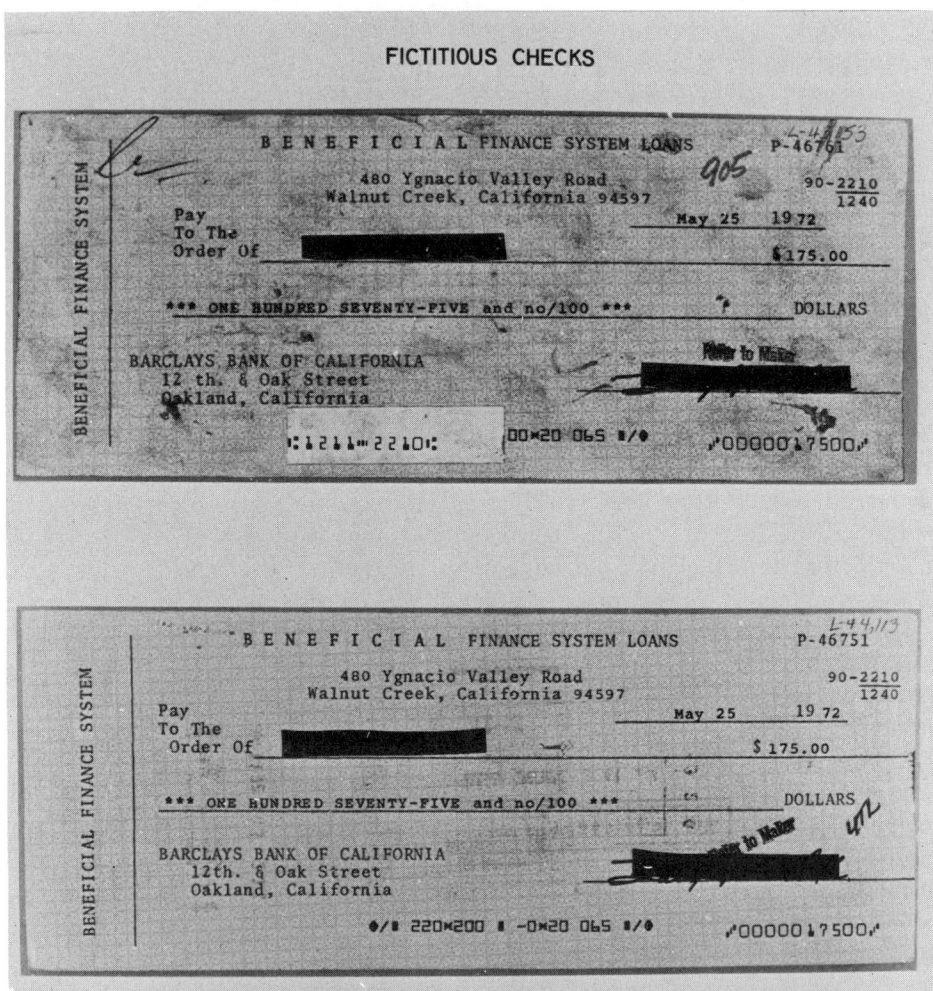

FIGURE 36-1. Fictitious checks. These checks were not printed, but were produced entirely with typewriters. (Courtesy of Duayne J. Dillon.)

The deviations by which typewriters may be identified originate from two sources: (1) slight variations in manufacture, either slight defects in casting the type character or in mounting it; and (2) variations that arise from use and wear of the various mechanical parts, or actual damage inflicted on them. These are of two general classes, deviations in the type characters themselves and in their mounting, and deviations in alignment, spacing, etc., caused by wear in the bearing of the type bars, the carriage, or other mechanical member. It is ordinarily, but not always, possible to ascertain the exact origin of a deviation from perfect performance. Some of these deviations are of constant occurrence and imply a manufacturing defect or an actual and definite damage to the machine. Other deviations are erratic and variable and therefore arise from wear.

Some deviations are major in nature. A piece of a character is sometimes missing through a major defect in casting or from being broken. In very old machines, several such major defects may be found in the same machine. Generally, however, this is not the case, and minor deviations are the only ones available. Careful and detailed comparison of these by means of grids, superimpositions over a strong light, and other means will ordinarily serve to obtain an identification that is relatively certain. In these more difficult cases, only the qualified document examiner should attempt a final determination of identity.

IBM Selectric typewriters are characteristically more difficult to identify, as these instruments do not have type bars which "stack up" and impart damage to other type. A skilled document examiner may nevertheless identify this type of instrument, however. The comparison of documents suspected of having been typed on one of these machines should be entrusted only to a skilled laboratory examiner.

MISCELLANEOUS CHARACTERISTICS. A few features of typed documents other than those mentioned are occasionally significant and require study. Most important is probably the typewriter ribbon. The color of typewriter ribbons varies and is an obvious point which could be important. Ribbons may be compared as to general condition, i.e., the quality of inking done by them, the texture of the cloth as elicited by thread count in the impressed characters, and defects. Typewriter ribbons differ also in basic respects, which are detectable by the expert. The condition of the type characters as to cleaning is often readily determined. Open spaces in the letters characters tend to fill with debris and ink, causing filling-in of letter impressions on paper. Not only may such characteristics be useful in identification, but they may at times be employed to establish the order of two written specimens and similar factors. Most of the other miscellaneous characteristics are accidental in nature and found only on a particular machine. They should not be difficult to recognize when found, and are most useful when present.

If a typewriter ribbon has been recently changed, it may be possible to find the portion on the ribbon where a questioned text was typed by an examination of the impression of the type on the ribbon. The possibility of this occurring is greatly enhanced with office typewriters utilizing a carbon ribbon that makes one passage through the typewriter and is discarded.

HANDWRITING IDENTIFICATION

Primary Factors

The handwriting that is characteristic of an individual is the product of a number of factors, each of which contributes to the final form, style, and characteristics of the writing as it is observed by the reader or the examiner. To fail in understanding the origins of a person's handwriting is to fail at least in part in the ability to examine it effectively. The general and most of the individual characteristics of a specimen of writing are determined basically by:

(1) The system of writing originally learned.
(2) The experience and conditions of use of the hand over a period of time.
(3) The presence or absence of physical abnormalities or defects originating from illness, injury, psychological variations, and other similar conditions.

All of the above factors contribute to the development of the one determining factor—the nerve–muscle reaction pattern, or conditioned reflex pattern of the writer. Writing, like walking, talking, and many other common habitual acts, is a conditioned reflex or set of reflexes; that is, it proceeds more or less spontaneously and without much conscious attention by the writer. Underlying all conditioned reflexes are habitual pathways in the nervous system that tend always to pass nerve impulses according to a predetermined pattern established by training and habit, and modified by mental and emotional factors and particularly by diseases and physical handicaps. Habitual acts can never be completely automatic, being subject to "feedback" control by visual and muscular sensory stimulation. Thus, the eye tells when the writing deviates from the line, and serves to cause a correction to be made. Similarly, the eye gives warning that the end of the line is being approached, thereby altering the writing pattern by stopping it and renewing it on another line, or perhaps crowding it into the remaining space on the same line. This type of control exerts only minor influence on the formation of letters, their proportions, spacing, slant, etc., which are under primary control of the reflex action.

The child, learning to walk, has to experiment with balance, leg and arm movements, and the operation of postural muscles, paying attention to each movement until he masters the pattern that gives him involuntary locomotion. As he practices, the movements gradually become spontaneous because of the establishment in his nervous system of the walking reflexes, and finally he does not voluntarily direct individual movements as he walks.

A similar set of patterns must be developed by the typist. At first, conscious thought must be given to the location of each letter on the typewriter keyboard. Once learned, the finger automatically finds the desired key through operation of the conditioned reflex mechanism. In fact, all learning is largely a matter of developing conditioned reflexes. Handwriting is no exception. Here, also, the child at first must copy laboriously, by drawing, the writing he is attempting to imitate. Even the holding of the pen or pencil is unfamiliar and must be learned, again by establishing conditioned and unconscious reflexes. The type of writing that is first copied will obviously influence the type of writing finally developed, but the influence may be great or small depending on many factors brought to bear later in the writing experience of the penman. All children in a handwriting class tend to write similarly at first, the differences being represented almost entirely as variations in skill of copying. After the writing of each becomes spontaneous, much wider differences and divergencies are rapidly developed, so that by the time a child reaches high-school age every individual of that class is writing a recognizably different and individual hand, even though retaining in general the same fundamental letter styles. Thus, distinguishing different specimens of children's writing may be often quite difficult, simply because the conditioned reflex patterns of each have not yet developed to a point at which the individuality of the writing is apparent. If, at this stage, the amount of writing of the group of children is diminished, as will happen if they leave school at an early age, the writing of the group may be so stereotyped as to be difficult to distinguish.

Many adults adhere very closely through life to the copybook forms they learned as children. In nearly all such instances, these are people who do relatively little writing and that little in a deliberate, unhurried, and sometimes labored manner. The individual who does much writing, particularly under pressure, e.g., the college student taking lecture notes, will show startling changes in his writing over a considerable period of time. These changes are often of a degenerative nature because of the pressure under which the writing is performed, resulting in rapid and careless formation of letters and words. It is, for instance, well known that college students exhibit frequently a writing style more illegible than do many uneducated persons who write very little. Accountants, on the other hand, tend to develop a rather characteristic rapid, but legible, hand.

Speed of writing is one of the most important factors modifying its characteristics and is itself a very significant factor in identification. Some very rapid hands show letter forms that are virtually illegible, but words, phrases, and sentences are readily deciphered. Such hands may be termed highly "developed" even though they may exhibit an unpleasant pictorial effect, lack detailed legibility, and are very faulty from the standpoint of the penman. Other "developed" hands may be aesthetically pleasing and qualify as good penmanship. Developed hands are those in which whole words, phrases, or sentences are written automatically rather than only individual letters or simple letter combinations. Probably the most characteristic feature identifying a well-developed hand is the speed of the writing. This may be estimated from the "t" crosses, "i" dots, terminals, and the general vigor and boldness of the elongated strokes.

The sum total of all of these developmental factors are finally expressed in what we can term the writer's muscular and nervous reactions, i.e., conditioned reflexes, and the facility of the writer in their performance. These are the factors which, after the developmental period, become relatively constant and give to handwriting its reproducibility and individuality, which are the determinants used in the verification of authorship.

Systems

Some authorities emphasize the importance of national and of system characteristics. Thus, the type of handwriting taught at a given period in Italy, or in Great Britain, will differ in significant manner from that taught at the same period in the United States. The habits acquired by the writer in learning any of these national characteristics will often persist through life and be readily recognized by the examiner. However, they may at times be confused with individual characteristics and lead to an incorrect determination of authorship. Similarly, the type of writing taught in a given country, state, city, or school will at times change. Thus, in America, there have been at least two modifications of the Spencerian hand, the angular, the vertical, several modern business hands, and other systems taught at various times and places. The influence of system, like that of national characteristics, is of great importance and should be well understood by the examiner, if for no other reason than to avoid confusion with strictly individual characteristics. For details of national and system differences, the classical work of Osborn and others may be consulted.

Regardless of the undeniable importance of national and system characteristics, it is unfortunate that overemphasis of it has often obscured the real issue in court trials, viz., the authorship of a document or a signature. It must be remembered that there has been little change in system in the teaching of handwriting in America since the general adoption of the modern business hands such as the systems of Palmer, Zaner-Bloser, New Laurel, and others. Except, then, for the occasional document that is older than 40 or 50 years, the question of system will ordinarily arise only with the writing of people who learned to write in the late 1800s or perhaps the early 1900s or among immigrants who learned to write in another country. Such cases may be encountered particularly in connection with wills, because many such documents are written late in life by older people. Aside from the occasional foreign hand, the only systems very frequently observed other than the modern business hands will be the late Spencerian, and an occasional angular or vertical hand. Few specimens of the vertical system remain because of its general slowness and difficulty.

Many middle-aged writers have studied at various times more than one system, another factor that can cause complications in the analysis of system characteristics. It is not infrequent for an individual to have started by learning the late Spencerian system, or even the vertical system, and then changing at a later date to the Palmer or New Laurel system. Several results of such changes may occur. The last system learned may predominate, or the two systems may be largely merged, preserving significant characteristics of each, or in many instances the final writing of such people bears little resemblance to any system. The most ardent advocates of the importance of handwriting systems must admit that nearly all letters in all the ordinary systems are fundamentally similar, else they could not be recognized, and that after a mature style has developed the fact that letter forms are similar to, but not identical with, those of several systems is in no way surprising, or for that matter of great significance. Furthermore, it must be appreciated that, in a polyglot population such as that of America, the fact that a writer shows, for example, Germanic characteristics, is itself an important individual characteristic, in that only a limited fraction of the population does so. The writer is then included in that small percentage, just as a person having type AB blood must belong to the 3% of the population that has this type of blood, and cannot belong to the 97% that are excluded.

Both system and national characteristics are statistically significant in identifying a writing, just as much as is an unusual "t" cross or an abnormal "f" loop. It is to be regretted that the best handwriting authorities have failed to stress this point, and instead have provided unscrupulous and prejudiced advocates with much material that is readily distorted to conceal or discolor the truth of a document problem rather than to clarify it. No witness will easily forget the glee of a cross-examiner who is successful in designating a mentioned class characteristic rather than a personal one. The implication that it is therefore not significant in establishing identity, though erroneous, is usually assumed and accepted. It must be borne in mind also that a large percentage of the writing normally examined will show no outstanding national or system characteristics that will serve either for clarification or confusion of the issue of authorship.

Secondary Factors

Many other factors than those quoted are influential in determining characteristics of a particular sample of writing but not those of a particular writer. Included are the following:

(1) The writing instruments, paper, etc.
(2) The position of the writer and his relation to the writing, e.g., sitting, standing, lying, arms high or low, and similar variations that often affect signatures particularly.
(3) Temporary physical or psychological disturbances such as excitement, fear, pain, exhaustion, injury to the hands or arms, poor eyesight, and similar disabilities or disturbances.
(4) Other temporary variables such as writing without glasses, bad lighting, irregular surface, cramped position, or external interference.

The factors listed above serve primarily to complicate the examination of a document, because most such temporary factors are unknown to the examiner and the changes produced by them are usually not present in the exemplar material with which a writing is compared. They are not the factors that, because they tend toward constancy, are of value in identification. If it is possible to ascertain any such conditions of the writing, it is desirable to attempt to obtain exemplars written under as nearly comparable conditions as possible. In the absence of such exemplars, it must be remembered that the factors that lend to a writing its individuality—those dependent on the muscular pattern of the writer—will still be present throughout the writing, even though the latter may be distorted or altered by temporary circumstances. The examination will be more difficult, and may call for more time and attention than usual. At times, in exaggerated cases, it may even be impossible to arrive at any conclusion that can be upheld. In such an event, the examiner will be wise who refuses to pass an opinion until the question can be resolved with certainty.

Reproducibility of Writing

As was discussed in a preceding chapter (see Chapter 2) in connection with the question of identity, it cannot be too strongly emphasized that absolute identity does not exist in practice with handwriting any more than with other physical evidence. In fact, two specimens of a single letter made by the same writer are rarely completely superimposable. The conditions of writing alone are sufficiently variable to guarantee rare identity, even in the practical sense, between the several specimens of a single letter. This fact is much emphasized by attorneys in cross-examination of expert witnesses, the implication being made that, if a man cannot usually exactly duplicate a letter, then nothing can be determined with regard to his writing. This is an utterly senseless contention, as should be realized by the attorney himself, because if it were true, his own checks could not be honored, nor could those given him by his clients, because the signatures would have no significance. Only the most inept technical witness will permit this absurdity to be imposed on a jury, because it is contrary to all human experience and all careful work done by document examiners.

The *common factor in the handwriting of an individual* that allows its identification is clearly the identity of the muscular and nervous pattern that tends always to reproduce itself, and reflect that reproduction in the writing. It can be broken down into a host of individual factors, listed in many publications on document examination, but basically it is a physiological or *kinetic* rather than a graphic or *static* consistency, and writing examined with this point in mind will yield a clearer conclusion than writing examined alone for its style, system, skill, alignment, terminals, spacing, shading, individual letter characteristics and the rest. Each of these factors alone may be highly variable, but the composite expression of the writer's physiology is not inconsistent. By this it is not meant that an indefinite "feeling" or intuition is to be used. Rather, the examiner must keep in mind while examining the individual characteristics that it is the nerve-muscle reflex pattern that is being examined through the medium of the written record that reveals the pattern.

An almost intuitive approach is utilized by bank clerks and businessmen in identifying signatures, and it is the failure of such individuals to understand the interpretation of the pattern in terms of its details that prevents them from being the actual experts that they may at times assume themselves to be. To establish fully the analysis of an individual reflex pattern requires in practice a careful study of each and every factor of the writing that is its expression, and a virtual statistical analysis of these detailed factors. It is in the latter requirement particularly that most authorities in this field have been deficient. The noted authority, Osborn, in his book, *Questioned Documents*, emphasizes the importance of probability and its application to the study of handwriting. He does not, in the entire book, cite one actual probability of the occurrence of any single factor he discusses. Handwriting analysis, all statements to the contrary, cannot be truly "scientific" until such serious omissions as these are repaired. The qualified examiner, by virtue of long experience and keen observation, can evaluate with reasonable accuracy the importance of a given factor in handwriting. To possess both the experience and careful observation habits may make a thoroughly competent examiner, but it does not make a scientific examiner any more than accurate observation and long study of butterfly's wings makes a scientific entomologist.

Here exists an excellent field for the student of handwriting: to study and classify the characteristics of writing in such a manner that accurate statements instead of mere opinions can be expressed as to the value of given specific features of the writing in question. Great difficulty will attend any such effort, because of that variability present in all normal writing that tends to thwart any effort toward an exact treatment. If it is admitted, as it must be, that handwriting characteristics tend to be reproduced, it follows that the degree of reproducibility and the statistical significance of all specific factors can be evaluated when the investigator is willing to spend the necessary time and effort to do so. The fact that so little progress in this direction has been published is one of the most serious criticisms of those who practice the profession of "document examiner."

Writing Characteristics

Those features of a writing that are determined by the habitual movement characteristics of the writer are necessarily the important ones for study. Many very obvious factors of writing are relatively worthless to the examiner. Size of writing, alone, may mean very little, in spite of the tendency of all writers to adopt a standard size to which they normally adhere. The same writer would automatically vary this factor greatly depending on whether he was writing on a postage stamp or on a blackboard. At the same time, he would vary the movement, because the blackboard would require an arm movement, and the stamp a finger movement. On ruled forms, particularly, wide deviations in size occur with the same writer because of the available space within the lines. *Relative size or proportions*, on the other hand, tend to be more constant and of greater significance. The relationship of individual one-, two-, and three-space letters to each other tends to be rather constant in every hand, and more so in some than in others. Also, the relation of size of individual capitals to small letters tends to be consistent in a given hand. This distinction is often not admitted by attorneys, whether because of ignorance or the desire to confuse the issue. It often happens that proportions are not well retained when the size of the writing changes markedly. If the space is cramped, for example, the tall letters and capitals tend to become smaller as compared with single space letters.

Another feature that has only limited significance is *slant*. Nearly every writer varies the slant to an extreme degree when disguising his hand. Forehand writers write backhand and vice versa. Moreover, slant is often changed through caprice, or because of an unusual writing posture or relation to the paper. Relative slant again is a more useful guide, since it tends to remain constant when the overall slant is changed.

Most significant of all the features studied must be those of which the writer himself is not aware, and therefore does not alter or eliminate. These include a host of minor characteristics, and not not usually include gross letter form, slant, size, or those more obvious factors from which the inexpert are very likely to draw a conclusion. Forms of letters also are readily changed, and in fact many writers habitually vary the forms of one or more letters, notably several capitals, and small "e," "t," "r," and "s." Regardless of such gross variations, any particular letter or letter type will tend to reproduce the *internal proportions, relationships, angles, curves, and idiosyncrasies*. These small factors that often require careful measurement and inspection under magnification are directly determined by the same unconscious nerve–muscle patterns that reproduce themselves with considerable consistency regardless of the gross changes imposed voluntarily on the movement of the writing implement by the writer's will. *Letter (and word) spacing* shows a rather remarkable consistency in both normal and disguised writing of most authors. Many individuals crowd certain letter combinations and spread others, whereas some writers, by avoiding such irregularity in spacing, indicate their authorship to a degree by this very care.

Those somewhat indefinite factors listed as *style, speed, skill,* etc., are very important when properly interpreted, which is possible to a considerable degree by using empirical but definite methods. The rigid definition of these factors is so difficult that only the very expert examiner can utilize them consistently. As ordinarily understood, they often serve to obscure rather than clarify the issue in doubt. These factors are related to another, which we may term *line quality.* A rapidly written line that is smooth and regular is indicative of skill and speed. A wavering, uncertain line indicates slowness in its formation, probable lack of skill, possible presence of tremor of age or illness, and often deliberate disguise or attempt to duplicate another's writing. The conditions must determine which explanation is applicable, and to the skilled examiner there is usually little difficulty in the decision. The character of letter attachments and junctions of strokes falls also in this category and is valuable in the examination.

A skillful writer makes relatively rapid strokes and blends them into a pictorial representation that is legible at least, and pleasing at best. Many rapid writers have a line quality showing speed but an illegibility or a generally displeasing result. The distinction between lack of skill and deliberate falsification is not always easy to make, as both involve voluntary effort that is not automatic as is the normal writing of the experienced penman.

Another factor, which is properly included in the term "line quality," is shading, often defined as the ratio of width of the heavy lines to the light lines. Such a definition is inadequate for pencils, ball-point pens, or stylus-type pens at least, and holds only relatively for ordinary pen nibs that vary in spread with the same pressure. It is the change of pressure and the way it is applied that gives rise to shading, and these differences again tend to be a part of the nerve–muscle habits of the writer. They are expressed at times as a difference in line width, but also as a difference in paper indentation. Since this latter factor also is variable depending on the supporting surface, it is difficult to treat quantitatively except with large amounts of exemplar material. A ball-point pen applied lightly to a piece of paper resting on a blotter can indent considerably as compared with the same pressure used with a solid wood or glass surface or backing. The character of the shading is valuable in determining the pen position in the writer's hand, and should be studied as carefully as the degree of shading. Although shading is an important characteristic to study, the greatest care must be used in its interpretation because of the variability of all the factors by which it may be measured.

Forgery

Forgeries of four main varieties exist. The first was mentioned above: a normal writing of the name or composition of another person with no effort to disguise or to simulate the genuine writing of that person. This type of forgery is readily detected and the writer is easily identified. More common is the second type, the forgery performed with a distinct disguise but with little or no effort to simulate the genuine. These also are readily detected as forgeries but are less suitable for identification of the writer. The difficulty is in direct proportion to the success of the disguise used, which is ordinarily subject to penetration but at times with considerable difficulty. The third type of forgery is the drawn variety, made to simulate the genuine writing by a process of drawing it, rather than writing in the automatic sense. Only the most skillful forgery in this class will approach free writing, and so be difficult to detect. The average forgery of this type is easily detected, but may even be impossible to use for determination of authorship, especially when the amount of writing is very small. This will also be a function of the skill and care of the draftsman. The fourth type of forgery is the traced variety which is most difficult of all to use for determination of authorship. If performed with great skill, and the writing traced is of poor enough quality, it is not always possible to be certain that it is a forgery, though ordinarily there will be sufficient indications for this determination.

Line quality is the most important feature in examining the third and fourth types of forgery, and microscopic examination is essential. The general writing characteristics of the first and second types may be studied with success. The microscope is helpful but not ordinarily essential.

Proper study of line quality in any connection ordinarily requires the microscope. The low-power stereoscopic binocular instrument is most valuable in revealing quaver, uncertainty, pen position, hesitation, pen lifts and stops, and retraces. Perhaps no other portion of the examination of a handwriting specimen is so important as a thorough study of the line quality including observation of all those factors mentioned and others.

General appearance of writing, including letter forms, is usually a deceptive factor when used in the detection of forgery and disguise. In normal writing, is is of course obvious that two specimens of the writing of a single writer will have a similar appearance and form, on which alone most handwriting is identified in the ordinary uses of written documents. This is the general factor that is destroyed first and most effectively in many forged and disguised documents. Moreover, any forgery of quality must by definition have a resemblance to the material forged, though not all forgeries come in this class. When a questioned document has the general appearance and form of the normal writing, it is proof only that no disguise was attempted if genuine, or that the simulation is good if the document is forged. Sometimes the writer is so inept that, even though he attempts disguise, his failure to achieve it prevents even a certainty that such an attempt was made. When the line quality of a suspected forgery is found to be as strong and regular as in the normal writing, and there is no significant difference in the detail of form and appearance of the writing as compared with genuine, it is possible only to conclude that it also is genuine. The alternative conclusion of a perfect forgery cannot be completely eliminated, but perfect forgeries are so rare that it is doubtful if many document examiners have ever seen one.

REFERENCES

Bates, B. P.: *Identification System for Questioned Documents.* Springfield: Thomas (1970).
Bates, B. P.: *Typewriting Identification.* Springfield: Thomas (1971).
Browning, B. L.: *The Analysis of Paper.* New York: Dekker (1969).
Conway, J. V.: *Evidential Documents.* Springfield: Thomas (1959).
Crown, D. A., Conway, J. V. P., and Kirk, P. L.: "Differentiation of Blue Ballpoint Pen Inks," *J. Crim. Law, Criminol, and Pol. Sci.* 52:338 (1961).
Crown, D. A.: "'Landmarks in Typewriting Identification," *J. Crim. Law, Criminol. and Pol. Sci.* 58:105 (1967).
Crown, D. A.: "Class Characteristics of Foreign Typewriters and Typefaces," *J. Crim. Law, Criminol. and Pol. Sci.* 59:298 (1968).
Harrison, W. R.: *Suspect Documents.* New York: Praeger (1958).
Harrison, W. R.: *Forgery Detection.* New York: Praeger (1964).
Hilton, O.: *Scientific Examination of Questioned Documents.* Chicago: Callaghan (1956).
Longhetti, A., and Kirk, P. L.: "Restoration and Decipherment of Erasures and Obliterated or Indented Writing." *J. Crim. Law and Criminol.* 41:518 (1950).
Lukens, H. R., Schlesinger, H. L., Settle, D. M., and Guinn, V. P.: *Forensic Neutron Activation Analysis of Paper.* Springfield: National Technical Information Service #GA-10113 (1970).
Martin, E.: "Identification of Ballpoint Pen Inks," *Intern. Crim. Pol. Rev.* 114:18 (1958).
Osborn, A. S.: *Questioned Documents*, 2nd ed. Albany, New York: Boyd (1929).

Index

ABO bloodgroup system, 197
Absolute identity, 9
Absorption of alcohol, 347
Accidents, vehicular, 410–442
    investigation of, 416
    photography of, 425
Acetate, 131
Acid phosphatase test, 209
Acrylic, fibers, 132
    sheet, 303
Age of writing, 486
Agglutinins, 198
Agglutinogens, 198
Alcohol, analysis of, 357
    intoxication, 348
        investigation of, 348
        levels of, 350
    physiological aspects, 347
    sampling of blood, 353
Alkaloids as poisons, 328
Alterations in documents, 484
Ammunition, identification of type, 394
Aniline as poison, 326
Animal hair, 160
Animal tracks, 83
Anisotropism, 223
Antimony as poison, 324
Arsenic as poison, 323
Arson devices, 444
Ash, importance in fire investigation, 456
    nature of material burned, 457
Automatic rifles, 384
Automotive finishes, 243

Backward scattering of glass, 262

Bacteria, 319
Ballistics (*see* Firearms)
Barberios test, 210
Barbiturates, as drugs, 342
    as poison, 328
Barrels of firearms, 386
    relation to bullet, 389
Benzidine test, interference with, 187
    sensitivity of, 184
Beryllium as poison, 324
Bichloride of mercury as poison, 323
Birefringence, 223
Blood, age of stains, 194
    alcohol, 345–359
    collection, from suspect, 168, 180
        from victim, 167, 177
        for alcohol analysis, 353
    crystal tests for, 189
    distinction of source, 172
    distribution patterns, 173
    enzyme markers, 204
    groups, 197
        inheritance of, 198
    hemoglobin variants, 205
    presence of, 182
    protein factors, 203
    species origin of, 190
    spectroscopic tests for, 190
    testing equipment, 28
    tests, catalytic, 183
        interference with, 184
        sensitivity of, 184
    washed stains of, 193
Bolt action of rifles, 384
Bombs, disposition of, 467

Bombs (*continued*)
  evidence from, 468
  types of, 466
Botanical evidence, types of, 311
Breechblock marks, 399
Bullet, comparison, 392
  deformation of, 393
  from where fired, 397
  holes in glass, 262
  standards, technique of obtaining, 392
  types of, 394

Caliber of firearms, 380
Camera, lens, 88
  shutter, 91
Cameras, 35mm, 19
  fingerprint, 20
  miniature, 20
  Polaroid, 20, 87
  press, 19
  stereoscopic, 20
Cannelures, 394
Cartridge and shell cases, 398
  examination of, 399
Casts and replicas, equipment for, 28
  moulage, 53
  plaster, 51
  silicone, 53
  thermoplastic, 55
  wax, 55
Charred material, collection of, 454
Chemical evidence, 229–239
Chloral hydrate as poison, 327
Class characteristics of firearms, 390
Cloth, as evidence, 117
  factors in, 117
  impressions, 120
  standards of, 122
Clothing, examination of, 112
  fibers, collection of, 125
Collection of blood, 44
Collection of evidence, at crime scene, 35
  in fire investigation, 454
Combustible material, burning characteristics of, 449
Combustion, nature of, 447
Comparison of bullets, 392
Compression marks, 361
Concentrated explosions, 461
  pattern of damage, 462

Conchoidal fracture of glass, 262
Containers for evidence, 26
Cord and string, identification of, 138
Cordage, 136
  debris on, 140
Cortex of hair, 148
Cosmetic evidence, 215–220
  collection of, 219
  examination of, 220
Cotton, 128
Crystalline evidence, 222–228
Crystals, nature and properties, 223
Cuticle of hair, 149
Cyanide as poison, 324

Density, of glass, 268
  of paint, 253
  of soil, 277
Dermal nitrate test, 408
Diffuse explosions, characteristics of, 459
Direction, of break of glass, 261
  of twist of rifling, 389
Dispersion, of glass, 268
  staining, 227
Distance of firing shot, 404
Documents, alterations, obliterations, and erasures, 484
  burned and charred, 488
  handwritten, 491
  physical and chemical examination of, 477
  types of examination, 470
  typewritten, 489
Drugs, 336–344
Dusts as explosives, 460
Dyes and pigments, 237
  in ink, 482
Dynamite, 462

Ejector marks, 401
Energy dissipation in vehicular accidents, 430
Erasure, restoration of, 484
Ethyl alcohol, as poison, 326
  intoxication, 348
Evidence, collection of, 22
  containers, 26
Exemplars, 473
Expansion marks on cartridge cases, 401
Explosions, concentrated, 461
  diffuse, 458

INDEX

Explosions (*continued*)
  investigations of, 463
  of gases and vapors, 458
  of gasoline, 459
  of high explosives, 461
  physical evidence from, 466
Explosive, devices, 466
  limits of gas mixtures, 460
Extractor marks, 401

Fibers, types of, 126
Fiber matches, interpretation of, 134
Film, photographic, black and white, 94
  color, 95
  holder, 92
Fingerprints, as positive identification, 59
  basis of, 60
  classification, 61
  comparison of, 69
  development, with iodine, 67
    with ninhydrin, 67
    with osmic acid, 68
    with powders, 65
    with silver nitrate, 67
  latent, 63
  lifting technique, 68
  on firearms, 407
Fire, determining origin of, 451
  effect of air supply, 446
  investigation of, 451
  kindling materials, 452
  means of igniting, 453
  nature of action, 444
  physical evidence from, collection, 454
  self-propagation of, 445
Firearms, 378–408
  identification from fired bullets, 393
  identification from fired cases, 398
  makes and models, 390
  residues, 407
  types, 381
Firing pin impressions, 401
Florence test, 210
Fluorescence of glass, 269
Fluoride as poison, 325
Fluorocarbon, 305
Forgery, characteristics of, 500
  types of, 499
Fungi, 319

Gases and vapors, 458

Gases and vapors (*continued*)
  as explosives, 459
  as poisons, 325
Glass, backward fragmentation of, 262
  chemical analysis of, 270
  composition of, 256
  density of, 268
  dispersion of, 268
  fluorescence of, 268
  fractures, 261
  identification, by physical properties, 267
    of source, 263
  neutron activation analysis of, 271
  refractive index of, 268
  safety, 259
  spectrographic analysis of, 271
  strength of, 258
  variations in, 257
Glycosides as poisons, 328
Grooves, of rifling, 386
Gunshot residues, 407

Hair, chemistry of, 151
  collection, 157
  cortex, 148
  cuticle, 149
  medulla, 146
  physical properties of, 155
  pigment, 152
  preliminary examination of, 159
  roots, 150
  scales, 149
  species of, 160
  standards, 158
Hair preparations, 218
Handwriting, development of, 492
  exemplars, 473
  identification of, 491
  primary factors in, 492
  reproducibility of, 496
  secondary factors in, 495
  speed of, 493
  systems of, 494
Heavy metals as poisons, 323
Hemoglobin variants, 205
Hit-and-run scenes, 441

Identification, process of, 10
Identity, causal, 12
  of properties, 9
  of source, 12

506 INDEX

Individualization, process of, 10
Igniters, 453
Inflammable liquids, 451
Inks, ball-point pen, 483
    carbon, 483
    dye, 482
    examination of, 484
    iron gallotannate, 481
    logwood, 482
    nigrosine, 482
    nutgall, 481
    printing, 484
    types of, 481
Inorganic poisons, 324
Inorganic substances, 235
Iodine as poison, 324
Iron gallotannate in ink, 481

Lands, of rifling, 389
Latent fingerprints, 63
Lead as poison, 323
Lectins, 203
Lever action rifles, 384
Linen, 129
Lipstick, 216
Loading mechanism marks on cartridge cases, 403
Luminol test, 183

Magazine marks on cartridge cases, 401
Magnifiers, 27
Marihuana, 338
Mascara, 217
Matches, in starting fires, 453
Medulla of hair, 146
Mercury as poison, 323
Metals, 282
    chemical properties of, 294
    failure of, 290
    in fires, 296
    physical properties of, 293
    quantitative analysis of, 291
    serial number restorations in, 286
    spectrographic analysis of, 292
Microorganisms, 319
Microscopic evidence, value of, 6
Miniature camera, 20
MN bloodgroup system, 201
Motion pictures, 102

Nail polish, 217
Neutron activation analysis, of gunshot residues, 408
    of hair, 154
Nitrates in gunshot residues, 408
Nylon in textiles, 131

Obliteration of documents, 485
Optical properties of crystals, 223
Organic substances, 236
Organic poisons, 326
Origin of fires, 451

Packaging materials, 140
Paint, chemical nature of, 242
    examination of, 245
    pigment composition, 245
    pigment distribution, 252
    physical nature of, 241
    sections, 245
    vehicle, 247
Palmprints, 65
Paper identification methods, 479
Perspiration, 212
Phenolphthalin test, 183
Photoflash bulb, 97
Photoflood lamps, 97
Photographs, distortion in, 104
Photostats and photographs of documents, 477
Physical and chemical factors in document examination, 477
Physiological fluids, 207–214
Pigment, in hair, 152
    in paints, 245
Pistols, 382
Pitch of rifling, 389
Plastics, as evidence, 299
    examination of, 300
    nature of, 298
    types of, 302
Poisons, investigation of, 329
    isolation and identification of, 332
    types of, metallic, 323
        nonmetallic, 324
        organic, 326
Polaroid camera, 20
Pollens, 315
Polyamide, 303

INDEX

Polycarbonate, 305
Polyester fibers, 132
Polyethylene, 305
Polypropylene, 305
Powder, as explosive, 461
    charge, effect on bullet slippage, 391
    patterns, 405
Precipitin test, 191
Press camera, 19
Pump action of rifles, 384

Radial cracks in glass, 262
Radiant heat, 446
Rayon, 129
Refractive index of glass, 268
Request exemplars of handwriting, 474
Residue prints, 78
Revolvers, 382
Rh bloodgroup system, 201
Rifles, 384
Rifling of gun barrels, 386
Rope and cordage, 136
Rouge, 217

Safe burglaries, tool marks in, 376
Saliva, 212
Semen, 207–211
    acid phosphatase test for, 209
    crystal tests for, 210
    fluorescence in ultraviolet, 208
    microscopic tests for, 209
Serum, identification of, 212
Shoes, debris in, 114
    prints of, 74
Shotguns, 386
Shot patterns, 404
Silk, 127
Skidding distance, 438
Slant in handwriting, 498
Slide marks, 361
Slippage of bullets, 391
Smoke, around bullet holes, 406
    significance in fire investigation, 456
Soil, chemical analysis of, 279
    collection of, 277
    density distribution of, 277
    differential thermal analysis of, 280
    formation, 274
    mineral constituents of, 276

Soil (*continued*)
    mineralogical examination of, 280
    spectrographic analysis of, 279
    variability of, 275
Solubility, 234
Soot from fires, 456
Spacing in handwriting, 498
Specific gravity of glass, 268
Spectrographic analysis, of glass, 271
    of paint, 252
    of soil, 279
Spermatozoa, 207
    determination of species, 211
    morphology of, 210
Styrenes, 303
Sweat, 212
Sweepings, preliminary examination of, 107
    textile fibers in, 126
Synthetic fibers in textiles, 131

Takayama test, 189
Teichmann test, 189
Test bullets, 392
Textile fibers, types of, 126
Thallium as poison, 324
Thiocyanate ion in saliva, 212
Tire marks, 434
Tire treads, characteristics of, 81
    comparison standards, 82
Tobacco, 317
Tool marks, comparison of, 371, 374
    individuality of, 363
    investigation of, 370
    types of, 360
    variations from tool angle, 362
Tracks, animal, 83
    casts of, 75
    shoe, 74
    tire, 80
Trails, 83
Trajectory of bullet, 397
Twist of rifling, 386
Typing, of bloodstains, 200
    of semen stains, 213
Typewriters, class characteristics of, 489
    identification of make and model, 489
    identity of, 490
    individual characteristics, 489
    ribbons, 491
Typewritten exemplars, 473

Ultraviolet examination, equipment for, 29
Urine, 211

Vacuum sweeper, 23
Vegetable evidence, 310
Vehicular accidents, 410–442
    investigation of, 416
    types of, 413
View camera, 20
Vinyls, 303
Volatile solvent, ignition of, 451

Volatile poisons, 326

Watermarks, 480
Weight and thickness of paper, 480
Wood, identification of, 314
    structure of, 311
Wool fibers, 127
Writing, age of, 486
    order of, 486

X-Ray diffraction, 226